THE CAMBRIDGE HISTORY OF
AMERICAN LITERATURE

Volume 5

1900–1950

THE CAMBRIDGE HISTORY OF AMERICAN LITERATURE

The Cambridge History of American Literature addresses the broad spectrum of new and established directions in all branches of American writing and will include the work of scholars and critics who have shaped, and who continue to shape, what has become a major area of literary scholarship. The authors span three decades of achievement in American literary criticism, thereby speaking for the continuities as well as the disruptions sustained between generations of scholarship. Generously proportioned narratives allow at once for a broader vision and sweep of American literary history than has been possible previously, and while the voice of traditional criticism forms a background for these narratives, it joins forces with the diversity of interests that characterize contemporary literary studies.

The *History* offers wide-ranging, interdisciplinary accounts of American genres and periods. Generated partly by the recent unearthing of previously neglected texts, the expansion of material in American literature coincides with a dramatic increase in the number and variety of approaches to that material. The multifaceted scholarly and critical enterprise embodied in *The Cambridge History of American Literature* addresses these multiplicities – the social, the cultural, the intellectual, and the aesthetic – and demonstrates a richer concept of authority in literary studies than is found in earlier accounts.

This volume is the fullest account to date of American poetry and literary criticism in the modernist period. The history unfolds through three distinct perspectives, which are however connected through a common paradox at the heart of both the poetry and the criticism. Modernist writers sought passionately to escape history even as they passionately engaged it – they championed unfettered creative genius but they believed that the strongest art makes an exacting response to the culture in which it arises. Andrew DuBois and Frank Lentricchia trace this development in the work of Robert Frost, T. S. Eliot, Ezra Pound, and Wallace Stevens. They show how the conditions of literary production in a democratic, market-driven society forced the boldest of the modernists to try to reconcile their need for commercial remuneration with their knowledge that their commitment to high art might never pay. Irene Ramalho Santos broadens the scope of the poetic scene through attention to a wide diversity of writers – with special emphasis on Gertrude Stein, William Carlos Williams, Hart Crane, H. D., Marianne Moore, and Langston Hughes – all of whom, in very different ways, understood the modernist imperative to "make it new" to apply not only the best remnants of Western civilization, but also to hitherto unrepresented constituencies of contemporary society. William Cain describes the literary critical counterpart to that achievement. Combining social and intellectual history with literary biography, he traces both the rise of an internationalist academic aesthetics and the process by which the study of a distinctive national literature was instituted. His narrative ranges from the early progressivists through the major Americanists and the New Criticism, documenting the conflicting forces that shaped the special role of the literary critic in the United States. Considered together, these three narratives convey the astonishing modernist poetic achievement in its full cultural, institutional, and aesthetic complexity.

THE CAMBRIDGE HISTORY OF AMERICAN LITERATURE

Volume 5
Poetry and Criticism
1900–1950

General Editor

SACVAN BERCOVITCH
Harvard University

PUBLISHED BY THE PRESS SYNDICATE OF THE UNIVERSITY OF CAMBRIDGE
The Pitt Building, Trumpington Street, Cambridge CB2 1RP, United Kingdom

CAMBRIDGE UNIVERSITY PRESS
The Edinburgh Building, Cambridge CB2 2RU, UK
40 West 20th Street, New York, NY 10011-4211, USA
477 Williamstown Road, Port Melbourne, VIC 3207, Australia
Ruiz de Alarcón 13, 28014 Madrid, Spain
Dock House, The Waterfront, Cape Town 8001, South Africa

http://www.cambridge.org

© Cambridge University Press 2003

First published 2003

Printed in the United Kingdom at the University Press, Cambridge

Typeface Garamond 3 11/13 pt   *System* LaTeX 2ε [TB]

A catalogue record for this book is available from the British Library

ISBN 0 521 30109 2 hardback

CONTENTS

ACKNOWLEDGMENTS

FROM THE GENERAL EDITOR

My thanks to Harvard University for continuing support of this project. I am thankful for the encouragement and editorial assistance of Ray Ryan of Cambridge University Press. My special thanks to Peter Buttigieg, a superb research assistant, and my gratitude to Jonathan Fortescue, who did the Chronology and helped compile the Bibliography. Jonathan is also the main author of the second half of the Introduction, summarizing the connections between the different parts of this volume. He represents a new generation of Americanists for whom, we hope, this Literary History will provide both inspiration and provocation.

Sacvan Bercovitch

MODERNIST LYRIC IN THE CULTURE OF CAPITAL

For the example he sets as a scholar and critic, and for his strong support, patience, and kindness, I thank Sacvan Bercovitch. An earlier version of this section was published as *Modernist Quartet* (Cambridge University Press, 1994).

Frank Lentricchia

Some of this work was test-driven at the Harvard Humanities Center Graduate Student Conference on "Failure," organized by Anna Henchman and Rebecca Schoff; I thank them warmly for their help on that occasion. Without the patient tenacity of Amy Powell, my part in this project would have been indefinitely stalled. Sacvan Bercovitch has graced me with kindnesses professional and personal, and I am grateful both for his generosity and for his editorial virtuosity. As for Frank Lentricchia, from whose writing, teaching, talking, and life I have learned a lot, and who remains my mentor even as he has become my friend, I would like to thank him for associating himself with one he knows well to be a felon of the mind.

Andrew DuBois

POETRY IN THE MACHINE AGE

I would like to thank Sacvan Bercovitch for having challenged me with this project and never failed to support it. His kind encouragement and expert guidance were crucial at all stages of my work. Many scholars in the field whose work justifies my own are my creditors, as are colleagues and post-graduate students on both sides of the Atlantic for many stimulating discussions. Special thanks are due to Isabel Caldeira, Doris Friedensohn, and Susan Stanford Friedman for their careful reading of parts of the manuscript. The University of Coimbra granted generous leaves during two fall terms while I was writing this project. The University of Wisconsin-Madison graciously provided hospitality in the Department of Comparative Literature and ample access to the collections in the Memorial Library. I am grateful to Mary Layoun, Jane Tylus, and Keith Cohen, who chaired the Department of Comparative Literature during the time I was working on this project, and particularly to Próspero Saíz, who liberally shared his fine insights on lyric poetry with me. Financial support from the Luso-American Foundation for Development (FLAD) and the Center for Social Studies of the University of Coimbra (CES) made it all possible.

Irene Ramalho Santos

LITERARY CRITICISM

I am grateful to my wife, Barbara Leah Harman, and my daughters, Julia and Isabel, for their love and support. I also want to thank my colleagues and friends at Wellesley College for their helpful comments on earlier versions of the material presented here. And I appreciate as well the encouragement and guidance that I have received from Ray Ryan and Sacvan Bercovitch.

A number of years ago, I met and spent time with Irving Howe and Alfred Kazin during visits they made to Wellesley. I stayed in touch with them afterwards and I continue to reread and feel inspired by their passionate, provocative work. I dedicate my section of this volume to their memory.

William E. Cain

CHRONOLOGY

I am grateful to Irene Santos and Rafia Zafar for their valuable suggestions and corrections to the Chronology. I also owe thanks to the many colleagues and students at Harvard University who have made teaching, learning, and writing about literature and history a pleasure, particularly Tim McCarthy. More so than anyone else, Sacvan Bercovitch has been instrumental in my progress as a scholar. His high standards and his patience continue to inspire me. Most of all, I thank my wife, Elizabeth, for her constant support and companionship.

Jonathan Fortescue

INTRODUCTION

THIS MULTIVOLUME *History* marks a new beginning in the study of American literature. The first *Cambridge History of American Literature* (1917) helped introduce a new branch of English writing. The *Literary History of the United States*, assembled thirty years later under the aegis of Robert E. Spiller, helped establish a new field of academic study. This *History* embodies the work of a generation of Americanists who have redrawn the boundaries of the field. Trained in the 1960s and early 1970s, representing the broad spectrum of both new and established directions in all branches of American writing, these scholars and critics have shaped, and continue to shape, what has become a major area of modern literary scholarship.

Over the past three decades, Americanist literary criticism has expanded from a border province into a center of humanist studies. The vitality of the field is reflected in the rising interest in American literature nationally and globally, in the scope of scholarly activity, and in the polemical intensity of debate. Significantly, American texts have come to provide a major focus for inter- and cross-disciplinary investigation. Gender studies, ethnic studies, and popular-culture studies, among others, have penetrated to all corners of the profession, but perhaps their single largest base is American literature. The same is true with regard to controversies over multiculturalism and canon formation: the issues are transhistorical and transcultural, but the debates themselves have often turned on American books.

However we situate ourselves in these debates, it seems clear that the activity they have generated has provided a source of intellectual revitalization and new research, involving a massive recovery of neglected and undervalued bodies of writing. We know far more than ever about what some have termed (in the plural) "American literatures," a term grounded in the persistence in the United States of different traditions, different kinds of aesthetics, even different notions of the literary.

These developments have enlarged the meanings as well as the materials of American literature. For this generation of critics and scholars, American literary history is no longer the history of a certain, agreed-upon group of American masterworks. Nor is it any longer based upon a certain, agreed-upon historical perspective on American writing. The quests for certainty and agreement continue, as they should, but they proceed now within a climate of critical decentralization – of controversy, sectarianism, and, at best, dialogue among different schools of explanation.

This scene of conflict signals a shift in structures of academic authority. The practice of all literary history hitherto, from its inception in the eighteenth century, has depended upon an established consensus about the essence or nature of its subject. Today the invocation of consensus sounds rather like an appeal for compromise, or like nostalgia. The study of American literary history now defines itself in the plural, as a multivocal, multifaceted scholarly, critical, and pedagogic enterprise. Authority in this context is a function of disparate but connected bodies of knowledge. We might call it the authority of difference. It resides in part in the energies of heterogeneity: a variety of contending constituencies, bodies of materials, and sets of authorities. In part the authority of difference lies in the critic's capacity to connect: to turn the particularity of his or her approach into a form of challenge and engagement, so that it actually gains substance and depth in relation to other, sometimes complementary, sometimes conflicting, modes of explanation.

This new *Cambridge History of American Literature* claims authority on both counts, contentious and collaborative. In a sense, this makes it representative of the specialized, processual, marketplace culture it describes. Our *History* is fundamentally pluralist: a federated histories of American literatures. But it is worth noting that in large measure this representative quality is adversarial. Our *History* is an expression of ongoing debates within the profession about cultural patterns and values. Some of these narratives may be termed celebratory, insofar as they uncover correlations between social and aesthetic achievement. Others are explicitly oppositional, sometimes to the point of turning literary analysis into a critique of liberal pluralism. Oppositionalism, however, stands in a complex relation here to advocacy. Indeed it may be said to mark the *History*'s most traditional aspect. The high moral stance that oppositional criticism assumes – literary analysis as the occasion for resistance and alternative vision – is grounded in the very definition of art we have inherited from the Romantic era. The earlier, genteel view of literature upheld the universality of ideals embodied in great books. By implication, therefore, as in the declared autonomy of art, and often by direct assault upon social norms and practices, especially those of Western capitalism, it fostered a broad ethical–aesthetic antinomianism – a celebration of literature (in Matthew Arnold's words) as the criticism of life. By midcentury that criticism had issued, on the one hand, in the New Critics' assault on industrial society, and, on the other hand, in the neo-Marxist theories of praxis.

The relation here between oppositional and nonoppositional approaches makes for a problematic perspective on nationality. It is a problem that invites many sorts of resolution, including a post-national (or post-American) perspective. Some of these prospective revisions are implicit in these volumes, perhaps as shadows or images of literary histories to come. But by and large "America" here designates the United States, or the territories that were to become part of the United States. Although several of our authors adopt a comparatist trans-Atlantic or pan-American framework, and although several of them discuss works in other languages, mainly their concerns center upon writing in English in this country – "American literature" as it has been (and still is) commonly understood in its national implications. This restriction marks a deliberate choice on our part. To some extent, no doubt, it reflects limitations of time, space, training, and available materials; but it must be added that our contributors have made the most of their limitations. They have taken advantage of time, space, training, and newly available materials to turn nationality itself into a *question of literary* history. Precisely because of their focus on English-language literatures in the United States, the term "America" for them is neither a narrative *donnee* – an assumed or inevitable or natural premise – nor an objective background (*the* national history). Quite the contrary: it is the contested site of many sorts of literary–historical inquiry. What had presented itself as a neutral territory, hospitable to all authorized parties, turns out upon examination to be, and to have always been, a volatile combat-zone.

"America" in these volumes is a historical entity, the United States of America. It is also a declaration of community, a people constituted and sustained by verbal fiat, a set of universal principles, a strategy of social cohesion, a summons to social protest, a prophecy, a dream, an aesthetic ideal, a trope of the modern ("progress," "opportunity," "the new"), a semiotics of inclusion ("melting pot," "patchwork quilt," "nation of nations"), and a semiotics of exclusion, closing out not only the Old World but all other countries of the Americas, north and south, as well as large groups within the United States. A nationality so conceived is a rhetorical battleground. "America" in these volumes is a shifting, many-sided focal point for exploring the historicity of the text and the textuality of history.

Not coincidentally, these are the two most vexed issues today in literary studies. At no time in literary studies has theorizing about history been more acute and pervasive. It is hardly too much to say that what joins all the special interests in the field, all factions in our current dissensus, is an overriding interest in history: as the ground and texture of ideas, metaphors, and myths; as the substance of the texts we read and the spirit in which we interpret them. Even if we acknowledge that great books, a few configurations of language raised to an extraordinary pitch of intensity, have transcended their time and place (and even if we believe that their enduring power offers a recurrent source of opposition), it is evident upon reflection that concepts of aesthetic transcendence are themselves timebound. Like other claims to the absolute, from the hermeneutics of faith to scientific objectivity, aesthetic claims about high art are shaped by history. We grasp their particular forms of beyondness (the aesthetics of divine inspiration, the aesthetics of ambiguity, subversion, and indeterminacy) through an identifiably historical consciousness.

The same recognition of contingency extends to the writing of history. Some histories are truer than others; a few histories are invested for a time with the grandeur of being "definitive" and "comprehensive"; but all are narrative conditioned by their historical moments. So are these. Our intention here is to make limitations a source of open-endedness. All previous histories of American literature have been either totalizing or encyclopedic. They have offered either the magisterial sweep of a single vision or a multitude of terse accounts that come to seem just as totalizing, if only because the genre of the brief, expert synthesis precludes the development of authorial voice. Here, in contrast, American literary history unfolds through a polyphony of large-scale narratives. Because the number of contributors is limited, each of them has the scope to elaborate distinctive views (premises, arguments, analyses); each of their narratives, therefore, is persuasive by demonstration, rather than by assertion; and each is related to the others (in spite of difference) through themes and concerns, anxieties and aspirations, that are common to *this* generation of Americanists.

The authors were selected first for the excellence of their scholarship and then for the significance of the critical communities informing their work. Together, they demonstrate the achievements of Americanist literary criticism over the past three decades. Their contributions to these volumes show links as well as gaps between generations. They give voice to the extraordinary range of materials now subsumed under the heading of American literature. They express the distinctive sorts of excitement and commitment that have led to the remarkable expansion of the field. And they reflect the diversity of interests that constitutes literary studies in our time as well as the ethnographic diversity that has come to characterize our universities, faculty and students alike, since World War II, and especially since the 1960s.

The same qualities inform this *History*'s organizational principles. Its flexibility of structure is meant to accommodate the varieties of American literary history. Some major writers appear in more than one volume, because they belong to more than one age. Some texts are discussed in several narratives within a volume, because they are important to different realms of cultural experience. Sometimes the story of a certain movement is retold from different perspectives, because the story requires a plural focus: as pertaining, for example, to the margins as well as to the mainstream, or as being equally the culmination of one era and the beginning of another. Such overlap was not planned, but it was encouraged from the start, and the resulting diversity of perspectives corresponds to the sheer plenitude of literary and historical materials. It also makes for a richer, more intricate account of particulars (writers, texts, movements) than that available in any previous history of American literature.

Sacvan Bercovitch

Every volume in this *History* displays these strengths in its own way. This volume does so by finding a common paradox at the heart of the projects of modernist American poets and critics: their determination to escape from history even as they passionately engaged it. In other words, these men and women championed the human potential for unfettered artistic genius, but they also believed that the strongest art makes an exacting response to the culture in which it arises. This paradox takes many forms. Andrew DuBois and Frank Lentricchia see it in the plight of the individual writer bereft of patrons. For them, the conditions of literary production in a democratic, market-driven society forced the boldest of the era's poets to try to reconcile their need for a remunerative career with the knowledge that their commitment to high art might never pay. Irene Ramalho Santos sees the paradox in the kinds of subjects and materials that were no longer available, or else were newly available, for poetry in the industrialized world. She describes the daunting prospect poets faced of preserving an authentic lyric voice in what Walter Benjamin called the age of mechanical reproduction. And William E. Cain writes about the effort of American scholars and critics to institute the study of a distinctively nationalistic literature even while they borrowed many of their literary terms and tastes from English predecessors.

Together, the narratives in this volume establish a tacit genealogy. It unfolds through the lives of four major figures – Robert Frost, T. S. Eliot, Wallace Stevens, and Ezra Pound – who came of age when the roles of poet and critic were still intertwined. These "philosopher-poets" were selective and self-contradictory in the building of their family tree. They looked back to classical Greece for aesthetic models as readily as they rejected their immediate predecessors, the genteel Fireside Poets, for keeping aloof from the hurly-burly nastiness of modern life. The social and cultural scope of the genealogy broadens as the volume progresses. Santos's central figures – Gertrude Stein, William Carlos Williams, Hart Crane, H. D., Marianne Moore, and Langston Hughes – appear as proponents of a literary tradition who are less conflicted about the celebration of demotic voices in their work. They understood the modernist imperative, "make it new," to apply not only to the best remnants of Western civilization but also to previously unrepresented aspects of the present, such as local vernaculars and the latest material goods.

DuBois and Lentricchia invoke the life stories of Ezra Pound and Robert Frost to personify the contrary cultural forces that gave rise to American modernist poetry. Pound represents the rebel in exile, a self-expatriated gadfly who saw no way forward in the mainstream culture of the United States. Disgusted with what he considered the pabulum that passed as poetry in such popular publications as *Ladies' Home Journal* and *Scribner's*, he worked tirelessly to promote the cause of *Poetry* and *Little Review*, magazines where avant-garde poets like himself could find an outlet if not a broad audience. Frost represents the high-minded careerist. Rather than reject the dominant commercial system of literary production, he aimed to take it over. He eschewed fractured poetic forms and overt political content, typified by *The Cantos*, in favor of a deliberately homespun, democratically open poetry that could be read for pleasure as well as plumbed for its subtler (often darker) themes. DuBois and Lentricchia see in this pairing an epitome of the conditions driving the writing and reception of all the major poetry of the period, including the variously conservative but popular anthologies of then contemporary verse. Thus a reaction against consumer culture was basic to the formation of the modernist literary imagination. But DuBois and Lentricchia are far from being cultural determinists. They carefully differentiate Frost, Eliot, Stevens, and Pound by temperament and style. They discuss "Prufrock" and *The Waste Land*, for example, within the context of Eliot's mandarin interest in ancient literary narratives, French symbolism, and his brooding disaffection from the masses. And they read the self-conscious play with gender roles and poetic form in *Harmonium* in the light both of Stevens's epicurean indulgences and of his lament for a bygone America. Throughout the narrative, key letters from the personal correspondence of the poets serve as *artes poeticae* in prose, further shaping the account of the relationship between their lives and works.

Santos surveys a more diverse coterie of poets. In some cases, her analysis implicitly touches upon the opposition outlined by DuBois and Lentricchia. She notes the profound but negative influence that *The Waste Land* had on Williams and Crane; like Frost, they thought it effete. Her account of Moore's fascination with commercial advertising recalls the example of Pound. So too does H. D.'s classicism. But Santos's explicit focus is on a crisis in literary form.

She unites the six poets she treats through their efforts to reinvent poetry for the modern, mechanical age. Stein experimented with complex repetitions to estrange her readers from the language they thought they knew. Williams introduced simple material objects, and previously marginal American vernaculars, into the realm of high art. H. D. renovated Greek myths in search of an analogue to her experience as a self-possessed woman and lover in a man's world. Moore insisted upon a scientific rigor in her art, endlessly researching and revising (in one case, she reduced a well-known thirty-line poem to three lines and a footnote). Crane pushed the epic form to its limits in an effort to capture the fragmentary experience of modern life. And Hughes brought the formal innovations and structures of the blues into the poetic mainstream. In general, Santos shows how the increasingly dizzying circulation of people, objects, and money imbued the work of all six poets – and beyond them, the poetry of the period as a whole (for her analysis ranges to include virtually the entire spectrum of poetic production) – with a cosmopolitan challenge to the nation's faith in the concrete, the quotidian, and the traditional.

Cain tells the other half of the story. He traces the rise of the profession that would take charge of transmitting modernist literary values to subsequent generations. His approach combines social and intellectual history with literary biography; and in doing so it reveals the many influences, indigenous and foreign, highbrow and reactionary, that shaped the increasingly specialized role of the literary critic in the United States. His narrative begins with the invention of the idea of a distinctively American literature, a revolution in scholarship that accompanied the revolution in American poetry. The parallels between the two projects are as numerous as are the ironies. The same scientific, technological, and economic advances which Pound saw as a challenge, an obstacle to the future of high art, emboldened men like Van Wyck Brooks to discover in the national past a cultural heritage worthy of a new world power. Cain builds from this insight to extended readings of the progressive politics of Jane Addams and Randolph Bourne and the cultural aesthetics of Alain Locke. He also places V. L. Parrington, F. O. Matthiessen, Perry Miller, Emma Goldman, W. E. B. Du Bois, and Edmund Wilson, among others, within a larger institutional context: in effect, the consolidation of a field of scholars dedicated to the study of American literature. Here Cain makes a significant recovery of his own. The self-conscious nationalism of the critical project, he shows, obscured how profoundly indebted many of these critics were to the work of Thomas Carlyle and Matthew Arnold. Finally, Cain turns to the rise of New Criticism, again finding English antecedents, and offering a lucid explanation of the success of the New Critics in the setting of the university. That pedagogic triumph, which marked the rout of the genteel tradition in

America, may be seen as the culmination of the aesthetic movement that began with Pound's "Patria Mia."

In a sense that triumph also marked the limits of the modernist achievement. For the effort to free the poem from its context risked making it irrelevant to future readers, and, with the advent of a new generation of critics, feminists, Marxists, post-structuralists, and others assailed the New Criticism for its narrow aesthetic preferences: lyric over epic, poetry over prose, white males over everyone else. The modernist poets themselves ran the same risk. Pound and Eliot took great pride in the obscurity of their poetry. They meant to inspire their readers to rediscover the density of human existence that they believed had been vitiated by modernity. But their exclusiveness could be seen to have robbed their work of its vitality. The result is a troubled legacy. The three narratives in this volume provide a rich overview of its implications. They capture the historical arc of the modernist project, from its bold swerve away from the genteel tradition to its apotheosis at mid-century in the university classroom. They interrogate and re-evaluate its successes and failures (reflecting the poets' and critics' own self-awareness in this regard). And they delineate its abiding achievements of the mind and imagination. Considered together, they convey the aesthetic, intellectual, and cultural complexities embedded in the "modernism" we have inherited.

Sacvan Bercovitch
Jonathan Fortescue

MODERNIST LYRIC IN THE CULTURE OF CAPITAL

Andrew DuBois and Frank Lentricchia

PROLOGUE

THE American literary culture that Frost, Stevens, Eliot, and Pound grew to know, and despise, as young men of great literary ambition was dominated by values that hostile commentators characterize as "genteel." The names of the genteel literary powers are now mostly forgotten: R. H. Stoddard, Bayard Taylor, G. H. Boker, Thomas Bailey Aldrich, E. C. Stedman, Richard Watson Gilder (Boston, Philadelphia, but mainly New York); at Columbia, Harvard, and Princeton, the academic reflectors G. E. Woodberry, Barrett Wendell, Henry Van Dyke. These were the men who shaped and ruled the literary culture of modernism's American scene of emergence. They represented, in their prime, the idea of poetry and true literary value. What Willard Thorp said about them more than forty years ago still cuts to the heart of this matter of literary politics: "As the years went by, connections which the group formed with magazines and publishing houses multiplied until their names were spoken and seen everywhere, and they formed a kind of literary interlocking directorate." In other words, they policed Parnassus by capturing and controlling the modes of literary publication. And not only did they "represent" the idea of poetry ("represent" is too weak, and they would have said the *ideal* of poetry): they enforced that representation from the 1880s through the first decade or so of the twentieth century; in particular, they enforced it by editing, in those pre-little magazine times, the period's dominant magazines of culture – *Scribner's,* the *Atlantic,* and *Century*.

America's looming genteel directorate unleashed a culture-saturating wave of literature and criticism: appreciations, recollections, histories of English and American poetry, numerous volumes of their own verse, some novels, one major translation (Taylor's of Goethe), travel books of considerable popularity, social reflections and criticism, decisive taste-making anthologies of American literature, coffee-table books of photos, illustrations, and light essays on great American writers "at home," including one such volume featuring one of the group's own, E. C. Stedman. The volume on Stedman ensured that his face, as well as his name, would be seen everywhere. And when his poems, like those of his "Fireside" predecessors, finally made their way into a Houghton Mifflin "household" edition, Stedman's cultural power received its ultimate enhancement.

"Household": there's a key word, an index to a culture that modernist writers would bury in scorn. "Fireside" poets, "schoolroom" poets (Bryant, Whittier, Longfellow, Holmes, Lowell): poets for the whole family, to be read around the fireside, sometimes out loud, with children and grandparents in comfortable attention. "Genteel" poets, successors to the Fireside group: nothing abrasive to family values here, either, but probably not much read around the fireplace. For bad reasons, they were difficult of access.

These genteel poets and critics formed our poetic nineties, not to be conflated with the Paterian nineties of British aestheticism. Our aesthetes valued purity above all, the rigorous evacuation from poetry of sensuousness and the sensual, and of any tendencies to social representation. Our aesthetes were ascetics of the circumambient gas. They flew from the world that capital was making (but so would the modernists), from what one of them called the "modern industry of prose fiction" (the metaphor reveals almost everything), a denigrating reference to the (then) avant-garde presence of realist and naturalist fiction and all the repulsive social references of this new writing: the classes, middle and lower, in uneasy relation and movement, America's new (and swarthy) immigrants, business, money, power, sex, divorce, and other distinctly nonideal preoccupations of a post-aristocratic literary world. The new fiction carried the news of radical social change, and Thomas Bailey Aldrich, editor of the *Atlantic*, poet and novelist, took notice:

> The mighty Zolaistic movement now
> Engrosses us – a miasmatic breath
> Blown from the slums. We paint life as it is,
> The hideous side of it, with careful pains,
> Making a god of the dull commonplace.

Of course, they were attacked for being out of touch: hopelessly nostalgic, prudish, feminine, all enervated lyric inwardness. They certainly *felt* themselves to be attacked. Aldrich's easy slip from a defensive "us" to the "we" which was painting the "hideous side" is a grammatical hint at how inexorable the poetic genteel believed the realist movement to be, an astute if inadvertent prophecy. Here was the progress of a post-Enlightenment elite giving way to social and aesthetic regress, from the pure breeze of poetic inspiration to the ghetto's sweaty stench. The verb telling of the realist absorption of the genteel also tells of the genteel reaction to uncouth art – they were being "engrossed," and it grossed them out.

So they refused to swallow such unwashed fare. Maybe – in Santayana's unfair phrase for Emerson – they digested vacancy. (A great lyric poet, Wallace Stevens, could make such an act the poignant and persistent substance of his work, a lyric drama of inwardness.) In fact, it's hard to say what the genteel poets digested. They would have agreed, at any rate, that they were out of touch: they intended to be out of touch; it was the nature and function of poetry to be out of touch. Thus: "Language is colloquial and declarative in our ordinary speech, and on its legs for common use and movement. Only when it takes wing does it become poetry." Invested with the Swinburnean "trinity of timebeat, consonance, and assonance," language manages to "rise to the upper air," free of the vernacular voice in worldly situation, afloat over a dimly perceived pastoral terrain:

The Woods that Bring the Sunset Near

The wind from out the west is blowing
The homeward-wandering cows are lowing,
Dark grow the pine-woods, dark and drear, –
The woods that bring the sunset near.

When o'er wide seas the sun declines,
Far off its fading glory shines,
Far off, sublime, and full of fear –
The pine-woods bring the sunset near.

This house that looks to east, to west,
This, dear one, is our home, our rest;
Yonder the stormy sea, and here
The woods that bring the sunset near.
                          Richard Watson Gilder

The genteel poets reduced the limited virtues of their Fireside predeces-sors to forceless gestures. The formal strength of Longfellow becomes in the hands of Gilder a dullness of form that overdetermines the content – cows whose "lowing" is no doubt elicited by the "blowing" of the western wind (that tired cause of predictable lyric "effects"); the distinct topography of Bryant's American pastoral is now generic landscape; Whittier's sharp aboli-tionist stance becomes a weak cultural politics of "fading glory," complete with nostalgic trope (the declining sun). In a characteristic finale, Gilder sequesters himself and a "dear one" from "yonder" stormy sea amidst the walls of a restful domestic space: "our home." "Far off, sublime, and full of fear," indeed – were the irony of "sublime" intentional, the phrase as self-assessment would be both accurate and (grudgingly) admirable.

Genteel poetry was a poetry of willfully dissociated sensibility; its odor was distinctly one of mildewed and dusty old books. The library needed proper ventilating, but these poets didn't know it, and would never know it. The initial chapter of this part of the volume surveys two important turn-of-the-century fields on which the battle for cultural centrality was being waged, two sites of cultural production – anthologies and magazines – which give strong evidence in material form of the aesthetic and ideological differences between the genteel powers and the burgeoning avant-garde. Through the examples of Pound and Frost, the first chapter offers a view of a key inaugural moment: the founding of the so-called "little magazines" in the setting of emergent mass culture. Just as these little magazines offered a space for the dissemination of what would become known as modernist poetry, a space which had been denied by the era's dominant magazines of culture, so did Louis Untermeyer's groundbreaking anthology offer a challenge to the cultural dominance of the exceedingly popular genteel anthologies of Francis Palgrave and Jessie Belle Rittenhouse. The first chapter concludes in studying the commercial pressures and personal commitments driving the taste-making arguments manifested in these important anthologies, and in telling the story of the literary histor-ical effects of Untermeyer's editorial success. The chapters that follow – on Frost, Stevens, Eliot, and Pound – are intended to give four angles of vision on modernist experiment; the inclusion of Frost in modernist company will seem odd only if the heterogeneity of modernist literature is forgotten: Ibsen, Strindberg, Chekhov, Hardy, Shaw, the Joyce of *Dubliners*, and Frost, as well as the usual (and glorious) suspects who knew how to ventilate the library. In the setting of four "modern" lives, these chapters present four individual efforts to create a new poetry against the restrictive standard established by the poetics that encouraged the practice of a writer like Richard Watson Gilder. These chapters on the poets, though multi-intentioned, are united in the purpose to evoke the genteel environment as cultural origin of modernist reaction, one important (though not the only) historical ground of experiment.

I

ANTHOLOGIES AND AUDIENCE, GENTEEL TO MODERN

WRITING in self-willed exile to an ex-student from a cottage in Beaconsfield, England, which he called "The Bung-Hole"; still deep in literary obscurity – though not quite as deep as the obscurity he had experienced in America in the previous twenty years; writing in November 1913, with his first book out and warmly reviewed by the right sort of people, Ezra Pound among them, and with a second and maybe even a third book waiting in the wings, Robert Frost hatched the plot of his return to the United States as the first step in his cunning pursuit of the fame that would eventually become the means of supporting himself and his family. And more: he would court fame because it would provide the material base for the realization of a desire he publicly announced in the 1930s and to which critics on the Left might have responded sympathetically – but didn't. (Frost came up through some pretty joyless conditions.) That desire, at once induced by and mainly prohibited in Frost's American culture, Yeats called the desire for "unity of being." Other high modernists would weigh in with other, equally romantic, phrases for a need that represented not only longing for another and better – because integrated – kind of life, but also criticism of the social ground on which they stood. With crafted American homeliness, Frost called it his "object in living" to unite "My avocation and my vocation / As my eyes make one in sight": pleasure, play, doing whatever you want – in 1913, at thirty-nine years old, Frost had done little of the latter – fused with work, what you had to do if you were someone like Frost. The object of Frost and many other twentieth-century writers was to sustain a commitment to their art in the daunting knowledge that their lives would be pressured by relentless economic need to which their art could bring no surcease.

So the definition of modern American poetry demanded by its economic circumstances is just this: the craft of nonremunerative writing pursued by those who cannot afford to pursue the craft of nonremunerative writing. The American literary dream in the twentieth century is to reconcile aesthetic commitment and economic necessity beyond the storied opposition that had more or less inescapably haunted writers ever since the eighteenth century, the more or less of nightmare depending on the more or less of cash a writer might lay easy claim to from an inheritance, say, or possibly a patron. But where was an American writer going to find a patron? And how many American writers in the twentieth century inherited leisure-class conditions?

Reflecting on the strong critical reception that his first book, *A Boy's Will*, had just won for him, Frost, in November of 1913, wrote to his ex-student John Bartlett:

> You mus[t]n't take me too seriously if I now proceed to brag a bit about my exploits as a poet. There is one qualifying fact always to bear in mind: there is a kind of success called "of esteem" and it butters no parsnips. It means success with the critical few who are supposed to know. But really to arrive where I can stand on my legs as a poet and nothing else I must get outside that circle to the general reader who buys books in their thousands. I may not be able to do that. I believe in doing it – don't you doubt me there. I want to be a poet for all sorts and kinds. I could never make a merit of being caviare to the crowd the way my quasi-friend Pound does. I want to reach out, and would if it were a thing I could do by taking thought.

This ambition of Frost's to stand on his legs "as a poet and nothing else" – he had been barely standing as a teacher and reluctant farmer – is an outrageous ambition inside the emerging context of literary and social ideals that would be codified as "modernist" in the 1950s, and that Ezra Pound was doing so much to help bring into existence in the year that Frost wrote this letter.

In 1913, Pound was pursuing his intention to shape a career that would violate the literary values incarnated in the guise of contemporary poetry, which many young American writers, who (like Pound) would become important modern poets, were reading and despising while still youths in the first decade of this century. In so violating established literary culture, Pound would inaugurate another intention, not separable from his literary desire, to make social change: the transformation of the economic structure itself, which (Pound was convinced) had produced the literature he would displace – the very literature that was, he would argue, nothing less than his society's symptomatic expression, in the realm of culture, of its totalitarian direction. In 1913, Pound's radical leanings found public display in one of the most decisive pieces of social and literary criticism he would compose, a monograph-length essay whose Italian title, "Patria Mia," simultaneously reflects his American attachment and longing and – in his refusal to state it in English – his distance and alienation.

Pound's divided feelings are expressed in "Patria Mia" in his hopes for what he called an "American *risorgimento*" and in his savaging of our foremost literary disease, that "appalling fungus" which is the commercial system of magazine publishing and circulation, "dry rot, magazitis." But the stakes in Pound's criticism of America were not primarily literary; the suppression of idiosyncratic artistic impulse was for him symptomatic of a more general extinguishment in America of all possibilities for human "individuality" (perhaps Pound's key synonym for freedom). Pound believed he could see the drift toward political slavery vividly on display in the mass-circulation magazines, which marked the aesthetically realized perfection of the cultural division of labor and the poem as commodity: "As the factory owner wants one man to make screws and one man to make wheels and each man in his employ to do some one mechanical thing that he can do almost without the expenditure of thought, so the magazine producer wants one man to provide one element, let us say one sort of story and another articles on Italian cities and above all, nothing personal."

Pound's extended comparison insists on the equivalence of cultural and economic production, not in order to make some roughly Marxist point about the relations of culture to the economic base of American society (though he does in effect make that point) but in order to decry the economic condition that transforms cultural agents into mindless and selfless producers who turn out poems, articles, and stories as their factory counterparts turn out screws and wheels, virtually without thought, certainly without personality, all in the service of the magazine-factory's finished product. The economic setting of capitalist culture is the index of cultural degradation under capitalism and our severely diminished capacity in such conditions – here Pound's idealism comes ringingly through – to be human. And by "human" he means something other than an economic being. But his criticism of capitalism is not issued nostalgically on behalf of some other social context, historically now out of reach, where it was once presumably easier to be human ("individual") rather than some cog in a machine. It is a criticism directed against capitalism for what subversion it had done to the promises of freedom in his country, especially the freedom of writers.

The commodity form of art is the death of what Pound thought literature essentially to be, the essence of real literature a nonessence, historical contingency itself, always surprising and unpredictable, "something living, something capable of constant transformation and rebirth." What the commodity form of art threatens to remove from the historical stage for the first time – this belief is the source of all critical urgency in Pound – is the avant-garde author himself, who is no contemporary phenomenon but a perpetual possibility, the creative traces of whom Pound spent a lifetime recording and preserving in his essays and in *The Cantos*. The avant-garde author as the exemplary "individual": not God's gift to society, but a recurring historical phenomenon motivated by various tyrannizing social contexts, and his best paradoxical example may be Pound himself, whose sensibility was born with specific historical density, or so "Patria Mia" would indicate, as an emerging counterstatement to the society and culture of the commodity which he was so concerned to excoriate.

Inside Pound's context of avant-garde literary production and manifesto, Frost's desire for a parsnips-buttering poetry can hardly help but be read as contemptible evidence of complicity. By virtue of its deliberate strangeness of structure and discourse and its flaunted hostility to everyday life in capitalist culture, emerging high modernist literature was finding its honor precisely in its economic unviability, and in the distance that separated it from the tradition of popular verse which Frost had in mind when he entitled his first book in echo of Longfellow. Frost would woo that tradition's mainstream audience – the "general reader who buys books in their thousands," even books of poetry; a reader who is no figment of Frost's fame-hungry imagination but the material force that had made the books of Longfellow and other Fireside poets, as well as a number of women poets, best-sellers in nineteenth-century America.

Within Pound's avant-garde context, Frost's desire to make it economically as America's poet places him outside the pale of modernist company, unless literary memory recalls that Frost was the oldest of the American poets with whom he is usually compared, commonly to the denigration of his reputation with those university intellectuals who invented and sustained the official phenomenon called modernism. Frost was formed in the 1890s and early years of the twentieth century when, in the United States, no poetic company existed outside the mainstream. His letter to Bartlett is not the inauguration of an ambition against what would be called modernism, or, finally, what it most immediately is, an expression of enmity born in his important and difficult relationship with Pound. The letter reiterates, in the face of new opportunities for literary publication – the recently launched little magazines – an ambition generated in him by a poetry scene exclusively controlled by mass-circulation magazines (like the *Atlantic*, *Harper's*, and *Century*), which were actually supporting the lives of a few genteel poets well known in the young manhood of Frost and Pound, though now passed from canonical memory, and who were models for poetic success after the examples of Bryant, Longfellow, and Whittier. For the young Robert Frost, popular success in the mode of the Fireside Poets represented not "mainstream" literary life (a term that presupposes an avant-garde margin of opposition) but the only "stream."

But Frost wanted it both ways ("I want to be a poet for *all* sorts and kinds"). His literary identity was in some part shaped by the critical ideas of the emerging avant-garde. He wanted to get to those who read the *Atlantic* with pleasure, but he also wanted to get to Pound himself, whose approval he painfully sought, who reviewed Frost's first two volumes with guarded admiration, who pushed Frost to *Poetry* editor Harriet Monroe in Chicago and to editors of new-wave literary magazines in London, and who once punned the *Ladies' Home Journal* right into the *Ladies' Home Urinal.*

Frost returned to the United States in early 1915 in part because he thought he could work within its dominant commercial system of literary production. Making it at the level Frost wanted to make it would, however, require more than the ideal action of his intellect thinking its thoughts, writing its poems; he would have to do more on his own behalf than "take thought." He would have to become practical in a way long forbidden by the anticapitalism of romantic literary models. He would need to become his own best public relations adviser, the first broad-scaled poetic media star, the ordinary man's modernist. And even better, if he could actually become a poet for all sorts and kinds, then he would succeed not only in making the commercial system work on his economic behalf but also in having his literary way with it. Pound saw it otherwise: he saw no way of living here and boring from within, no way of slyly subverting, much less seizing, the system of literary publication, so he expatriated himself to a place outside, from which he hurled at his native country relentless charges of human betrayal, finally to return after World War II, against his will, as fascism's brightest modernist star.

In modernism's scene of emergence and triumph in America, "Frost" and "Pound" may turn out to be not so much names of authors who quarreled over basic issues as they are signs of cultural forces in struggle, whose difference presented itself to Frost in 1913 as a choice between mass circulation and avant-garde little magazines, forces whose persistent difference would constitute the scene of what would be called modernism. "Frost" against "Pound" as the American way of making it new against the European avant-garde, those producers of aesthetic caviar so culturally inaccessible to the American masses; "Frost," then, as bearer of a democratic rhetoric, suspicious of everything from the wrong side of the Atlantic, including and perhaps most especially the political radicalism of the aesthetic vanguard. Frost's 1913 letter to John Bartlett is a prefiguring of an aesthetic and social argument within modernism that would shape the movement of the new poetry from 1912, when the inaugural issue of *Poetry* appeared, to 1930, the close of its most fertile phase of literary innovation and negative political critique. By 1930, the major documents of modern American poetry – *North of Boston*, "The Love Song of J. Alfred Prufrock," *Hugh Selwyn Mauberley*, *Spring and All*, *The Waste Land*, *Harmonium*, *A Draft of XXX Cantos*, and *The Bridge* – not only had all been published but also, with unpredictable speed, had become the textual conscience of our poetry and a controversial, internally conflicted core of social reimagination whose most radical question had to do with the political experiment called "America," and whether that experiment was a qualified success or a sham and a failure. The aesthetic arguments within modernism were simultaneously arguments over what shape the American social future should take.

Less than a month after writing to Bartlett from England about his ambition to be a best-selling writer, Frost expressed doubt about his own capacity to bring it off and about the generic suitability of poetry for the task. In a letter to another old American friend, in which he wrote, "At most poetry can pave the way for prose and prose may or may not make money," he admitted not having much stomach for the moneymaking side of writing and that he wasn't, at any rate, all that inclined to prose. In his bad old American days, he told Ernest Silver, he would try prose for two or three days at a time, "having resolved it was the thing for a man with a family to do. But just when I bade fair to produce a novel, right in the middle of chapter three or four I would bring up in another inconsequential poem . . . It remains to be seen whether I shall take hold and earn a living as a writer."

Frost's novelistic energies in fact came to some consequence as they were rechanneled into poetic narratives, dialogues, and monologues, into those longer poems, outside his lyric mode, which dominate his second volume, *North of Boston*, published in 1914, about a year after he had uttered his true confessions of econo-poetic need to Bartlett and Silver. Frost returned home in 1915 to find himself famous, still poor, and wondering in a letter written in April of that year what he might have earned had he had freshly in hand, in the moment of his newfound poetic notoriety, those longish *North of Boston* poems ready to be sent off to the very magazines that had routinely rejected him before: "The thought that gets me," he writes, "is that at magazine rates there is about a thousand dollars worth of poetry in N.O.B. that I might have had last winter if the people who love me now had loved me then. Never you doubt that I gave them the chance to love me." Just a few days later in another letter, in more expansively embittered mood, he wrote: "These people once my enemies in the editorial offices are trying hard to be my generous friends. Some of them are making hard work of it. Some are making very hard work . . . Twenty years ago I gave some of these people a chance. I wish I were rich and independent enough to tell them to go to Hell."

Now that he was home, however, and being made such a fuss over "in a country where I had not one [friend] three years ago," he found that he really could get up some stomach for the moneymaking part of writing: "While the excitement lasts you will see that it would be affectation for me to pretend not to be interested in it. It means nothing or next to nothing to my future poetry." He then adds an afterthought that would predict the scornful high-brow modernist reaction to him, while showing how even he, the ordinary man's modern poet, had internalized Pound's avant-garde perspective on the necessary antagonism of mass-cultural values and authentic aesthetic value, the idea of the modern being perhaps unintelligible outside that antagonism of commercial and aesthetic. Frost himself would never forget that his first two volumes were brought out by a small London publisher. The new American excitement over his English success fueled his interest in his own fame, the pursuit of which would shortly become virtually his vocation.

By June 1915 all had changed. He told another correspondent that his "rage has gathered considerable headway," that Ellery Sedgwick, editor of the *Atlantic Monthly*, "has just written me a beautiful letter and sent me fifty-five beautiful dollars for poetry." In August 1915 Frost made the first of his many appearances in the *Atlantic* with a group of short poems that included "The Road Not Taken," likely the most anthologized poem of the important modern American poets. "The Road Not Taken" would soon become the lead-off poem of his first American volume, *Mountain Interval* (1916), and eventually would lend its title to all manner of books and articles, including a biography of Frost, a study of US race relations, at least one work of feminist scholarship, a study of US social conditions, an essay that excoriates American literary theorists for not going the way of the Italian Marxist Antonio Gramsci, a proposal for alternatives to prison for nonviolent felons, a biography of an eighteenth-century Jesuit, a self-help text which occupied the *New York Times* best-seller list for over seven years, and an analysis of a crisis in highway repairs and maintenance in Connecticut. The poem is also a chestnut of high-school teachers of American literature and a frequent citation on greeting cards of rugged American sentiment. All in all, a veritable American adage, a pithy concentration of our proudest wisdom of self-reliance from Emerson to John Wayne: the very idiom of American desire. Ellery Sedgwick apparently knew what he was doing when he welcomed Frost into the pages of the *Atlantic*. Frost was well on his way to selling books "in their thousands," to standing on his legs "as a poet and nothing else," but not, apparently, to being "a poet for all sorts and kinds."

Frost once said about his basic strategy as a poet in search of mass cultural impact that he would "like to be so subtle at this game as to seem to the casual person altogether obvious," a remark that decisively clarifies the split between mass and modernist cultural desire which marked the difference of Frost (and Robinson, Lindsay, Masters, and Sandburg) from the company of the high modernists, Stevens, Pound, and Eliot. For who could ever imagine for Stevens, Pound, and Eliot a "casual" reader who could respond to *The Cantos*,

Notes toward a Supreme Fiction, and *The Waste Land* as if they were "altogether obvious"? Frost's desire to reach a mass audience by becoming, among other things, acceptable to mass-circulation magazines like the *Atlantic*, shaped his rhetorical literary relations to his imagined ordinary reader. He could become a poet for all kinds, but only by favoring the ordinary reader, by fashioning an accessible and seductively inviting literary surface that would welcome the casual reader of poetry (as opposed to the intellectually armed scholar of modernism), while burying very deep the sorts of subtleties that might please those accustomed to Pound's aesthetic caviar. And judging by the reaction to him from high modernist quarters, Frost buried his subtleties right out of sight. For by choosing to fashion a transparent instead of a forbidding surface, he succeeded in telling his highbrow critics that his writing was undergirded by no challenging substance. If obscurity of surface in high modernist writing has typically been received in standard accounts of modernism as an index to complexity of social analysis, then the fact that the "easy" Frost looked like no modernist poet meant, in modernist context, that he required no effort of engaged reading.

The stylistic difference between Frost and Pound may in some part be a difference in temperament (style is the man), but it is also a historical difference, one conditioned and driven by the difference, say, between the *Atlantic* and the *Little Review*, an engendering sort of difference, moreover, which conditions and drives alternative means of literary reception – a popular as well as an elite academic canon – and, therefore, alternative accounts of the history of modern American poetry. In 1920, the arguments within modernism in the United States were fully engaged and unresolved, with Conrad Aiken taking the side of Pound, Eliot, and the avant-garde, and Louis Untermeyer taking the side of Frost and the native tradition, the low modernists out of Whitman. Frost's side lost. Our recent chief accounts of modernist poetic history find him anomalous, a poet of the twentieth century but not a truly "modern" poet. Yet if modernism out of Pound means an attack on official genteel poetic culture, then the poet who wickedly links the beautiful with money rather than poetry (as in "fifty-five beautiful dollars") may be making not only a comment that no modern American (male) poet could be out of sympathy with, since no modern American (male) poet could help worrying about securing the means of his and his family's subsistence; he might also be launching a sneak attack on the airy ideals of conventional accounts of poetry (with a capital P) and "the beautiful" which had descended to Frost through the genteel generation that preceded him.

"The Road Not Taken" might actually be the best example in all of American poetry of a wolf in sheep's clothing, a hard-to-detect subversion of both the principal American myth – that of autonomous selfhood – and the deeply abiding Fireside poetic form within which, in this poem, Frost chooses to embody his dramatization of cardinal liberal principle and his reflections thereon.

> Two roads diverged in a yellow wood,
> And sorry I could not travel both
> And be one traveler, long I stood
> And looked down one as far as I could
> To where it bent in the undergrowth;
>
> Then took the other, as just as fair,
> And having perhaps the better claim,
> Because it was grassy and wanted wear;
> Though as for that the passing there
> Had worn them really about the same,
>
> And both that morning equally lay
> In leaves no step had trodden black.
> Oh, I kept the first for another day!
> Yet knowing how way leads on to way,
> I doubted if I should ever come back.
>
> I shall be telling this with a sigh
> Somewhere ages and ages hence:
> Two roads diverged in a wood, and I –
> I took the one less traveled by,
> And that has made all the difference.

Self-reliance in "The Road Not Taken" is alluringly embodied as the outcome of a story presumably representative of all stories of selfhood, and whose central episode is that moment of the turning-point decision, the crisis from which a self springs: a critical decision consolingly, for Frost's American readers, grounded in a rational act when a self, and therefore an entire course of life, are autonomously and irreversibly *chosen*. The particular Fireside poetic structure in which Frost incarnates this myth of selfhood is the analogical landscape poem, perhaps most famously executed by William Cullen Bryant in "To a Waterfowl," a poem that Matthew Arnold praised as the finest lyric of the nineteenth century and that Frost had by heart as a child thanks to his mother's enthusiasm.

The analogical landscape poem draws its force from the culturally ancient and pervasive idea of nature as an allegorical book, in its American poetic setting a book out of which to draw explicit lessons for the conduct of life (nature as self-help text). In its classic Fireside expression, the details of landscape and all natural events are cagily set up for moral summary as they are marched to the poem's conclusion, like little imagistic lambs to slaughter, for their payoff in uplifting message. Frost appears to recapitulate the tradition in his sketching of the yellow wood and the two roads and in his channeling of the poem's course of events right up to the portentous colon ("Somewhere ages and ages hence:") beyond which lies the wisdom that we jot down and take home:

> Two roads diverged in a wood, and I –
> I took the one less traveled by,
> And that has made all the difference.

If we couple such tradition-bound thematic structure with Frost's more or less conventional handling of metric, stanzaic form and rhyme scheme, then we have reason enough for Ellery Sedgwick's acceptance of this poem for the *Atlantic*: no "caviare to the crowd" here.

And yet Frost has played a subtle game in an effort to have it both ways. In order to satisfy the *Atlantic* and its readers, he hews closely to the requirements of popular genre writing and its mode of poetic production, the mass circulation magazine. But at the same time he has more than a little undermined what that mode facilitates in the realm of American poetic and political ideals. There must be two roads and they must, of course, be different if the choice of one over the other is to make a rational difference ("And that has made all the difference"). But the key fact, that on the particular morning when the choice was made the two roads looked "about the same," makes it difficult to understand how the choice could be rationally grounded on perceptible, objective "difference" (the poem's key word). The allegorical "way" has been chosen, a self has been forever made, but not because a text has been "read" and the "way" of nonconformity courageously, ruggedly chosen. The fact is, there is no text to be read, because reading requires a differentiation of signs, and on that morning clear signifying differences were obliterated. Frost's delivery of this unpleasant news has long been difficult for his readers to hear because he cunningly throws it away in a syntax of subordination that drifts out of thematic focus. The unpleasant news is hard to hear, in addition, because Fireside form demands, and therefore creates the expectation of, readable textual differences in the book of nature. Frost's heavy investment in traditional structure virtually assures that Fireside literary form will override and cover its mischievous handling in this poem.

For a self to be reliant, decisive, nonconformist, there must *already* be an autonomous self out of which to propel decision. But what propelled choice on that fateful morning? Frost's speaker does not choose out of some rational capacity; he prefers, in fact, not to choose at all. That is why he can admit to what no self-respecting self-reliant self can admit to: that he is "sorry" he "could not travel both / And be one traveler." The good American ending, the last three lines of the poem, is prefaced by two lines of story-telling self-consciousness in which the speaker, speaking in the *present* to a listener (reader) to whom he has just conveyed "this," his story of the *past* – everything preceding the last stanza – in effect tells his auditor that in some unspecified *future* he will tell it otherwise, to some gullible audience, tell it the way they want to hear it, as a fiction of autonomous intention.

The strongly sententious yet ironic last stanza in effect predicts the happy American construction which "The Road Not Taken" has been traditionally understood to endorse – predicts, in other words, what the poem will be sentimentally made into, but from a place in the poem that its *Atlantic Monthly* reading, as it were, will never touch. The power of the last stanza within the Fireside teleology of analogical landscape assures Frost his popular audience, while for those who get his game – some member, say, of a different audience, versed in the avant-garde little magazines and in the treacheries of irony and the impulse of the individual talent trying, as Pound urged, to "make it new" against the literary and social American grain – for *that* reader, this poem tells a different tale: that our life-shaping choices are irrational, that we are fundamentally out of control. This is the fabled "wisdom" of Frost, which he hides in a moralizing statement that asserts the consoling contrary of what he knows. But perhaps (in another reading of the poem's trickiest lines) Frost's wisdom will be too much for even him to bear. He imagines a future in which he forgets his harsh knowledge and yields to sentimentality by telling himself that once, long ago, he made a life-shaping, a rational choice.

In the American situation for poetry in 1915, when "The Road Not Taken" was published, Frost's poem is a critical expression (that manages, for a few readers, to have it both ways) issuing from the very source (the mass circulation magazine) that Pound condemned, and in so condemning launched modern poetry. The poem is an instance, famous at that, of what mass-cultural media demanded from American poets and simultaneously what Frost, like Pound, wanted to say against that mode, a savage little undoing of our mainline literary and political sentiments. So "The Road Not Taken" is an internalization of that opposition within the mode of poetic production – mass or little magazine? – which was, in 1915, becoming the sign of the modern.

Nonetheless, over the years "The Road Not Taken" has attested to the power of convention to withstand those who would subvert it from within. It remains a famous poem, one of the "best loved of the American people," not for its irony, but for the sentiments that make its irony hard to see. Frost wanted to be a poet for all kinds, but mainly he failed. He is the least respected of the moderns. Pound wanted a few, fit readers, and he got them. Thus far, the alternative means of literary publication in American culture prohibit, in either direction, crossover poetic careers because they engender two different and mutually hostile readerships.

By 1919, Louis Untermeyer – Robert Frost's most assiduously cultivated literary operative – could declare in the opening sentence to the first edition of his soon-to-be influential anthology, *Modern American Poetry*, that "'America's poetic renascence'" was more than just a bandied and self-congratulatory phase of advanced literary culture: "it is a fact." And on the basis of that fact, or wish (it hardly matters which), Untermeyer and Harcourt Brace made what turned out to be a lucrative wager on the poetry market through seven editions of the anthology, the last of which entered the university curriculum and stayed there through the 1940s and 1950s, bearing to more than one generation of faculty and students the news of the poetry of modernism and at the same time establishing, well into the sixties, a list of modernist musts: Frost foremost, together with strong representations of Pound, Eliot, Stevens, Williams, Hart Crane, and a long list of more briefly represented – and now mostly forgotten – poets. What Untermeyer had succeeded in presenting in his later editions was a stylistic texture of modern American poetry so varied as to defy the force of canonical directive. If the poetry of modernism could include Frost, Stevens, Pound, Marianne Moore, and Langston Hughes, then perhaps the phenomenon of modernism embraced a diversity of intentions too heterogeneous to satisfy the tidy needs of definition.

But the 1919 first edition of Untermeyer's book offered no such collage-like portrait of the emerging scene of modern American poetry, no Eliot, Stevens, or Williams, only a token of Pound and the avant-gardists. Untermeyer's anthology of 1919 was in fact heavily studded with names that had appeared a few years earlier in the *Little Book of Modern Verse* (1912), the anthology of his chief genteel competitor, Jessie Belle Rittenhouse. The economic interests of Untermeyer and his publisher ensured that his declaration of the new be accompanied not by an avant-garde act of rupture but by a conciliating act that veiled his departures from the popular taste that Rittenhouse, then in her second edition, had so well played to. The first edition of her anthology had sold over one hundred thousand copies, a fact never apparently lost on Untermeyer, who through all of his editions managed to include poems that Rittenhouse would have admired and that, through no stretch of the imagination, would be included in anybody's definition of modernism.

Rittenhouse was a major literary journalist in America in the first two decades of this century, and she published in 1904 what must have been the first book to attempt a characterization of *modern* American poetry (*The Younger American Poets*), though not one writer she took up has survived in recent accounts of American literary history (not even for a sentence). She made it her business to get to know the literary powers of the day in New York and Boston, became chief poetry reviewer for the *New York Times* and a founder, in 1910, of the Poetry Society of America. In her various writings and anthologies she could say who was in and who (usually by omission) was out, and though recent historians have not ratified any of her choices and do not know her name, she was a force who, both in her female person and her taste, represented the grain against which the emerging modernist male poets were working: the principle of "the Feminine in literature," as Eliot put it, which he was none too anxious to give space to in the *Egoist*; one of those Pound charged with turning poetry (for serious people) into "balderdash – a sort of embroidery for dilettantes and women."

The animosity Pound directed at genteel anthologists begins to be explained by a story he told in the *New York Herald Tribune* in 1929, with the literary revolution won and modernism fully in place. It was to become the representative anecdote of his literary career, the substance of the larger tales that his poetry and his literary and social criticism would ceaselessly tell and retell of epiphanic revelation: the dawning upon him that aesthetic and economic production were insidiously related. Literary expression in America and England was the effect of an economic cause deadly to all individual identity (whether political or literary), a cause whose aesthetic products were not different in kind from those we conventionally know as commodities. Pound had had his definitive encounter with the culture of capital and had emerged a badly bruised romantic – poetry, he learned, was an expression of the marketplace, not its critique, as idealists since Kant had desired – badly bruised, but more than ever a romantic whose will was newly steeled for social change.

It struck him that if "the best history of painting in London was the National Gallery," then the best history of poetry "would be a twelve-volume anthology in which each poem was chosen not merely because it was a nice poem or a poem Aunt Hepsy liked, but because it contained an invention, a definite contribution to the art of verbal expression." With this in mind, he approached a respected agent who was impressed by his plan for an anthology but apparently too indolent to recast Pound's "introductory letter into a form suited to commerce." The agent made contact with a "long-established publishing house"; two days later he summoned Pound in order to ask him, in astonishment, if he, Pound, knew what he had said about Palgrave, the editor of the most famous anthology of poetry in the English language. Pound: "It is time we had something to replace that doddard Palgrave." The agent: "But don't you know that the whole fortune of X & Co. is founded on Palgrave's *Golden Treasury?*" From that day on, Pound wrote, no book of his received a British imprimatur "until the appearance of Eliot's castrated edition of my poems. I perceived that there were thousands of pounds sterling invested in electro-plate, and the least change in the public taste, let alone swift, catastrophic changes, would depreciate the value of those electros . . . against a so vast vested interest the lone odds were too heavy."

Pound's anecdote clusters together, at the site of literary production, issues that shape the larger story of his career, as well as (they are not easy to separate) the career of modernism. If a poetry anthology ought to function like the National Gallery – as a space for exhibits – then who or what will provide the economic wherewithal to sustain such space? Who or what will play the role of patron of the arts? And why should the patron, whether national agency or private agent, agree to underwrite a culture of invention ("Swift catastrophic changes") implicitly at odds with an economic system so heavily invested in aesthetic repetition, not change, precisely the system that sustains the would-be patron? A specific anthology of poetry, Pound learns – Francis Palgrave's *Golden Treasury of the Best Songs and Lyrical Poems in the English Language* – in fact functions not as the space for the exhibition of original literary talents and their inventions but as a commodity requiring heavy investment in electroplates, the sole purpose of which is to help make the fortune of those who control the means of its production, Macmillan Company, whose goal is best realized by monopolizing the market and thereby avoiding the costly production of new plates.

Palgrave had hoped that his anthology, the poems themselves, would assist in liberating the spiritual life of the capitalist subject from the everyday life of getting and spending. Instead, contrary to his hopes, his anthology would actively reenforce the life of capital at the cultural level by normalizing taste (this is a poem), then taste's appetite (this is what I want more of), and finally taste's evaluative purpose (this is what a poem should be like). From out of its material economy – the mass-produced object, the system of its distribution – Palgrave's widely circulating text (in the 1860s alone it sold almost 300,000 copies in the USA) performs the cultural ("civilizing") work of a capitalist society. *The Golden Treasury* inaugurates and sustains taste immune to competitive versions, to other ideals of poetic shape and function. The major economic enemy of Palgrave's anthology, whether small or catastrophic, is therefore change; and not economic change, but change of the cultural sort, aesthetic change of the kind indicated and longed for by those hallmark words of modernist critical vocabulary, "originality" and "creativity," what Pound calls "invention" and what Eliot, in a simple but telling phrase, calls "the individual talent."

Like Palgrave's *Golden Treasury* and aesthetic imitators like E. C. Stedman's *An American Anthology, 1787–1900*, Jessie Belle Rittenhouse's *Little Book of Modern Verse* sustained an innocent ideal of sweetness, the voice of unadulterated song. Nothing in her anthology contradicted the literary principles announced earlier by Palgrave and Stedman in their respective prefaces, where they characterized lyric by what they excluded – no narrative allowed, no intellect at meditation, no description of local reference, no didacticism, no personal, occasional, or religious material, no humor, no speaking voice, no dramatic texture, no realist novelistic detail. Eliot would say that a real poet can amalgamate his experiences of falling in love and reading Spinoza because a real poet's sensibility is not dissociated; a real poet does not shrink from the impurities of experience. Palgrave, Stedman, and Rittenhouse were champions of the dissociated lyric of exclusion, the homogeneity of the unmixed feeling, and their books sanctioned and perpetuated that lyric ideal through the young manhoods of the modernists-to-be, who would in large part learn how to write a "modern" poetry by writing against "poetry" as it was sponsored by these major tastemakers and the mass circulation magazines that gave space to genteel lyric, and precious little else.

Stedman summed up genteel America's poetic ideal when – in an I-told-you-so aside – he noted that the Civil War had motivated no "little classics of absolute song." Democratic cultures are not, of course, supposed to venerate heroic ideals and their "big" epic literary vehicle: we have only the little or lyric classic; but even that is imperiled by the forces of social environment, the penetration of lyric interiority by the immediacies of Civil War history. The unhappy result, in the embedded logic of Stedman's lament, is the birth of the impure or "partial" song not quite emptied of worldly interests and pressures – lyric too much with the world.

Joyce Kilmer thought Rittenhouse had "raised anthology-making to a fine art." Frost thought otherwise. He told one correspondent that her title was "silly." He didn't explain what he meant, but he must have meant that she had no right to the word *modern*; and, of course, by the governing aesthetic dicta of genteel anthology making, she didn't. In the world of Palgrave, Stedman, and Rittenhouse, "modern lyric" was a contradiction in terms, not to mention a besmirching of the category of lyric. Lyric practice by male and female writers seemed to Pound and Frost an effeminate business, and cultural authority in the female person of Jessie Belle must have made it seem doubly so.

Aside from needing to make a buck, Untermeyer needed to make a point or two. For him the modern moment was peculiarly American, its progenitors his benign versions of Whitman and Dickinson, its vision hopeful and democratic, its formal manner always submissive to its human content: art with positive social function. The decadence of Stevens, the assiduous internationalism of Pound, the tenuous inwardness of Eliot, all represented to Untermeyer an unhealthy foreign strain, an elitist art-for-art's-sake plying of the craft for a coterie audience: in fact, undemocratic to the core, he believed, because it was an art that only the culturally privileged could make any sense of. Untermeyer's *Modern American Poetry* was aimed at a mass audience for economic reasons, but its democratic point of view also demanded a mass audience, and as a perfectly blended capitalist/populist venture, the book stood against the coterie anthologies only recently issued by the New York avant-garde, by Pound, and by Wyndham Lewis (*Others, The Catholic Anthology, Blast*). So, upon the economic success of *Modern American Poetry* hung Untermeyer's version of the future of the new poetry: his desire for a poetry rooted in diverse American cultures, his hopes for the writing, reading, and dissemination of poetry in a democratic society. Upon the economic success of Untermeyer's anthology hung the cultural authority of the party of Van Wyck Brooks's nativist intellectuals, the cultural politics of "America's coming-of-age," of which *Modern American Poetry* was the anthological representative.

Untermeyer went polemically further in his companion critical volume *The New Era in American Poetry* (also published in 1919), in which he characterized the work of Pound, Stevens, and their aesthetic companions published in Walter Arensberg's *Others* as "mere verbal legerdemain," effeminate and morbid. Conrad Aiken, Eliot's college mate and longtime correspondent, counterattacked in a review of the book in *The New Republic* with the charge that Untermeyer's celebration in American poetry of "the unflinchingly masculine" (which he glossed with the words "Americanism" and "lustihood") was unwittingly a celebration of the most conservative of poetic and political values. After all, poetry with the right message – the carefully monitored poetry of the ideal state, good for the education of soldiers – had been welcomed by Plato, poetry's most celebrated historical enemy. Aiken argued that Untermeyer's soft socialist politics, grafted onto a happy version of Whitman, blinded him to the force of the true revolutionaries who were "throwing their bombs into the aesthetic arena": not Frost, Sandburg, Masters, Robinson, and Lindsay (those low modernists who dominated the first edition of *Modern American Poetry*), but the formal innovators, the high modernists of "absolute poetry" to whom Untermeyer had given such short shrift.

Untermeyer never managed to, or could, say why the stance of virility or the politics of social democracy required poetic representation, or what difference it could make to virility or democracy that they be imagined in an aesthetic rather than in some other medium. Aiken, who declared himself on the side of literary experimentation as the agency of art for art's sake, never managed to, or could, say what connection, if any, obtained between literary and social experimentation, or why he should be taken seriously when he described the literary avant-gardist as a bomb-throwing radical. Surfacing within this early argument within modernism is one of the most ancient topics in literary theory, that of the relationship of art and the commonweal, here, in the Aiken–Untermeyer clash, given what would become its definitive framing in the critical literature of modernism, where aesthetics and politics are typically forced by rhetorical heat to stand in opposition even as that same rhetoric of modernist polemic causes them suspiciously (because protesting too much) to lean toward one another, as if revolution in poetry and social change could not be imagined outside a relation of strong interdependence.

But if, in Aiken's view, Untermeyer's introduction to *Modern American Poetry* seemed in its immediate polemical context to cherish too chauvinistically the peculiarly American possibilities for poetic renascence, and too eager to court insulation from European traditions; if Untermeyer appeared to be replaying Emerson's call in "The American Scholar" for an American literature free from servility to British aesthetic rule, rooted in the American commonplaces, and therefore worthy of the American social experiment, then on Untermeyer's behalf it ought to be remembered that his distinguishing heritage was not Emersonian New England but German-Jewish immigrant stock, and that his revision of Emerson's ideas on the relations of literary expression to their cultural matrix was worked out at the high tide of our heaviest period of immigration. What Untermeyer needed to see in the new poetry was aesthetic responsiveness to voices that were never heard at the cosmopolitan finishing schools of genteel America, voices that were virtually unrepresented in poetic traditions before Wordsworth because they were unworthy of the memorialization provided by traditional producers of literature, whose typical objects of representation were people like themselves, with privileged routes to the acquisition of literacy. Alongside genteel authors Untermeyer published a black poet, Paul Laurence Dunbar, several Jews, a Philadelphia Irish American journalist, T. A. Daly, whose specialty was Italian-American dialect, and numerous poets from outside the northeast corner of the United States. In his critical book he devoted an entire chapter to the Italian immigrant socialist admirer of Whitman, Arturo Giovannitti.

America was changing and, as an untraditional literary voice himself, Untermeyer, the revisionist literary historian as anthologist, found himself in the sensitive political position to disseminate his vision of an America in which poetry emerged not from one or two culturally elite centers but from everywhere; a poetry which, in refusing legendary, traditional, and classical sources, was fashioning itself as a revolutionary literature standing against what literature had been. From the traditional perspective, the new poetry was an antipoetic poetry that even the "conservative *New York Times*," as Untermeyer put it, had to acknowledge had dislodged poetic traditions in this country in favor of a writing that insisted on prosaic everydayness, not only as subject but as its very medium of expression: a poetry which would spell the demise of genteel aesthetic ideals and at the same time signal a larger death, that of genteel America's cultural and political authority.

Although Louis Untermeyer, a keen observer of the literary scene, probably tuned on his own into much of the cultural and social change in America, his sensibility was nevertheless being shrewdly coached by his correspondence with Robert Frost, his favorite poet of the new school, who by the time he returned home from England in 1915 had set himself against the self-conscious avant-garde and was fully engaged in the entrepreneurial process of staging his own image as a different, an American, kind of modernist. The Frostian directives that found their way into both Untermeyer's anthology and the critical volume of 1919 must have sounded to Aiken like Wordsworth's Preface to *Lyrical Ballads* revisited, an effort to finish off a poetic revolution that had gotten sidetracked by Tennysonian aestheticism and the various moods of the 1890s. Untermeyer thought he saw in the new American poetry the discarding of a "stilted" (he meant a rare, rhetorical, *writerly*) vocabulary in favor of what he called a sincere, simple "daily vocabulary" (a vocal language of everyday situation): a radical realism of diction which appears to overcome the very mediation of print itself, so that we can virtually hear the speaker on the printed page; a stylistic sea change whose most powerful effect would lie in the illusion it creates of its unliterariness – an illusion born from its refusal to borrow its verbal modes and tics from official poetic history, from Poetry with a capital letter under the imprimatur of Francis Palgrave. Modern American poetry, Untermeyer thought, would be recognizable by its unliterary (vernacular) borrowing directly from life itself: like Frost and the realists, by "life" he meant the lives of the historically unsung. Therein lay the radical, the "modern," and the "American" character of "modern American poetry."

ROBERT FROST

I N its relation to the genteel poetic mode of the early years of the century, Louis Untermeyer's reconception of modern American poetry was not merely an attempt to achieve, on slightly different grounds, the popularity of the anthologies of Palgrave and Rittenhouse (though popularity was doubtless a prized reward). Instead, the driving force of Untermeyer's editorial and critical effort was a radical American populism that would welcome to its ranks any and all comers, but most significantly would welcome the kinds of people who had been hitherto excluded from the ranks of the published and read. A truly modern American poetry, in Untermeyer's strong opinion, would be closer to life as it was daily lived, allowing with no condescension and with veiled political intention the inclusion of vernacular voices, the unliterary, the (according to genteel standards) anti-poetic.

What this account of the new poetry left out is that such radicality is mainly perceptible only to those with keen awareness of the history of English poetry, because only those readers (not the unlettered man celebrated by Untermeyer's Whitmanesque ideal) are in a position to grasp shifts in literary history, to grasp, not a change from "literariness" to "life-likeness," but a change from established kinds of literariness, and the social bases that supported such writing, to a new kind of literariness, presumably an organic expression of a new kind of social arrangement: literary change, in so many words, as index of social change, glimpse of and push in the direction American society might be heading – a culturally diverse democracy unheard of in human history. The historically startling idea is that social change might be reflected in and directed by lyric poetry, of all things, as well as in the grungy bourgeois forms of prose fiction, where accounts of social conflict are to be expected – reflected in a novelized poetry which (Untermeyer's words) "explores the borderland of poetry and prose" and thereby, at that generic crossing, explores fundamental social differences. This activist conception of poetry was perhaps the most deeply buried issue of the relation of aesthetics and politics that lay unexamined between Untermeyer and Aiken.

In his battle with inherited poetic diction, Frost believed that in *North of Boston* he had scored a decisive victory in literary history, because there he had "dropped to an everyday level of diction that even Wordsworth kept above"; he had performed "in a language absolutely unliterary" and had barred from his writing all "words and expressions he had merely *seen*" (in books) and had not "*heard* used in running speech." "Words that are the product of another poet's imagination," as he declared in his strongest avant-garde moment, "cannot be passed off again . . . All this using of poetic diction is wrong." This, he explained, was the essence of his "war on clichés," which he later described as a war on all systems and system-building. But he didn't want to be misunderstood, as he believed Pound had misunderstood him, as "a spontaneous untutored child," because he was not "undesigning." What Frost's design amounted to was an antinomian intention to undo all design (all intention, all structure) in its institutional incarnation and sanction. "What I suspect we hate," he wrote in 1937, "is canons, which are no better than my guidances insisted on as your guidances." Canons are on the side of stabilization and tradition, and would give the rule of the dead over the living, once and for all. But literature, Frost thought, is the very spirit of insubordination, and as such the anticanonical spirit verbally incarnate. If nothing is "momentous," if "nothing is final," then, he concluded, literary canons and the critical generalizations which produce and sustain them are instruments of literary repression wielded by professors in Frost's constant institutional target of literary repression, the university or college.

The logic of Frost's poetics equates literary insubordination with literature itself, and literature with modern literature, not as some specific historical style evolved in the early twentieth century but as something very like the spirit of literature finding its fullest incarnation in an American scene that provided its true (because democratic) political directive: no literature except in radically individualized expression. In his arguments on behalf of the vernacular as locality, intoned and intransigent, the basis of a vital and living literary voice, "entangled somehow in the syntax, idiom and meaning of a sentence," Frost named the multiheaded enemy of literary insubordination – that is to say, the enemy of *literature* – as the professorial sentence, the dead, grammatical discourse taught at school; the poets of classical tradition, fawned over by professors who teach them as literary models but whose sentences in living speech are not accessible to us; and the reiterated poeticisms of English tradition preserved and sustained by contemporary anthologists like Stedman and Rittenhouse: all those enemies of a living, genuinely "modern" literature who come at us from the feminized crypt of manliness, the book.

"Words," Frost said in a striking proverbial moment, "exist in the cave of the mouth," their masculine origin, "not in books," their effeminate emasculation.

He told his son Carol, in a startling letter of sexual-poetic self-evocation, that Carol had written "No sissy poem such as I get from poetic boys..." And note "poetic boys": the provocatively gendered responses of Frost, Pound, and other male modernists were to a literary style, a cultural feminization, at work in the writing of both sexes. It seems that Carol (who, with a name like that, maybe needed to hear this) had managed to "ram" his writing "full of all sorts of things"; the poem he sent his father had been "written with a man's vigor and goes down into a man's depth." The mark of Frost's own "prowess" lay (this is a frequent boast in his letters) in the success he had in breaking through the genteel lyric as if through a cultural chastity belt, in "bringing to book" vernacular tones from the cave of the mouth, tones hitherto unheard in poetry books.

Frost's struggle against canonical forces was a struggle carried out on behalf of a new lyric diction and therefore new (and low) lyric social materials (below even Wordsworth), for the purpose of reengendering lyric for "masculinity," a word in Frost's and other poetic modernists' lexicons signifying, not a literal opening of the lyric to actual male voices and subjects, but a symbolic shattering of a constrictive lyric decorum that had the effect, in Frost's America, of denigrating poetry as the province of leisured women in their land of cultural irrelevance. The accolade of manliness that Frost gave his son and his desire to get rid of poetic diction altogether are the related acts of insubordination and resentment of an economically marginal American college dropout, who enjoyed none of the social privileges of the great English poets he admired, whose class formation denied him even the easy pleasures of idealizing the life of his womenfolk. Frost's experiments in fact often featured at their center economically disadvantaged females, and the women he knew best knew only the hardest of times. Neither Frost's mother nor his wife were working-class in the term's technical sense, but both were tied to toiling joylessly and without hope of respite in jobs of no glamor and to lifetime grooves of family obligation that permitted no life in high cultural activity for themselves; no life, certainly, in the leisured-class work of cultural promulgation – the taming of the materially driven spirit of men via the values of religion, poetry, and domestic commitment; no life, in other words, in the cultural work enshrined in America's sentimental nineteenth-century feminine tradition.

For Frost, the fashioning of a new lyric mode was an opening to all that his social identity had declared out of bounds. Unlike the old lyric, the modern lyric (like modern America itself) would be (should be) indecorously open ("full of all sorts of things"). The old lyric, which Frost talked about as if it were coextensive with poetry itself and what it had been, "left to its own tendencies" "would exclude everything but love and the moon" from its decorous world.

Frost's struggle against the traditional lyric was simultaneously a struggle against both social and literary exclusion. The new lyric would be "modern" because it would implicitly stand as a political rebuke to traditional literature: revolutionary because heterogeneous in form, style, diction, subject, social origin, and social reference. In Untermeyer's and Frost's vision, the new lyric would be an expressive medium of the collage of cultures America was fast becoming, the literary resistance to the cultural melting pot, a genuinely American creation.

Frost made his points in letters, not in essays, but those points reappeared in Untermeyer's critical prose, and they functioned as the hidden genius of his anthology. Untermeyer was the conduit of Frost's critical ideas. Concurrent with Frost's socially expansive efforts to rethink and rewrite lyric, Pound and Eliot pursued parallel efforts to open up the lyric to all sorts of things, but in more public ways, in essays of immediate critical impact which eventually gave rise to a codified theory of poetry, the critical reflection of modernism that came to be known as the New Criticism. In one of its most elegant expressions, Robert Penn Warren, in "Pure and Impure Poetry" (1943), provides at once a focus for the issues of the emerging new lyric around 1912 and the ironic costs of the institutional prestige it had achieved by the late 1940s, when Warren, Cleanth Brooks, John Crowe Ransom, and Allen Tate had secured the domination of T. S. Eliot's poetry and criticism.

Like Frost, and in a gesture typical of the drastically narrowed idea of poetic types that had taken hold early in the nineteenth century, Warren – following Poe's pronouncement that a long poem is a contradiction in terms – identifies poetry with the singular intensity of the short lyric and its tendency to exclude everything but feeling anchored in its own self-regard. In a key allegorical moment of alliance with the aesthetic ideals that he wanted to revise, Warren says, "Poetry wants to be pure, but poems do not." The impurity that lyric would exclude – and that Warren would put back into poems – turns out to be coextensive with the world of "prose and imperfection," by which Warren means the everyday world represented in realist fiction – "unbeautiful, disagreeable, or neutral materials," "situation, narrative," "realistic details, exact description, realism in general." In Frost's example, even "the axe-handle of a French Canadian woodchopper."

Warren's list of excluded impurities is notable for its aesthetic conservatism. If there are such things as inherently unbeautiful or disagreeable materials, then there must be (as Poe believed) an inherently beautiful object toward which "poetry" might properly yearn. And his list is notable as well for its interesting confusion of realms, with some elements in the list referring to the realist literary medium of their representation. The oddity of Warren's effort to liberate Poe from the strait-jacketing decorum of "poetry" is that it must grant the genteel aesthete's point – that there is a realm of the beautiful which is poetry's proper object – precisely in order to establish the identity of the "poem," whose character would lie in its act of avoiding "poetry." Strong mixtures of subject, diction, tone, and allusion are the trademarks of the tough-minded modernist poem that Warren and other New Critics admired in Eliot, and which they theorized in their essays as signs of highest literary value. But these signs of the new poetics often bear a haunted quality – an uneasy consciousness (ironic, nostalgic, sometimes both at once) of the way things used to be, of what can no longer be written but which is nevertheless evoked in gestures of modernist farewell.

Warren's account of traditional lyric would appear to identify lyric sub-stance with unsituated feelings of love, a subjectivity whose object knows no history. Poe's beautiful dead woman would be something like the logical object and fulfillment of this aesthetic and affective drive, the essence of lyric idealism, not its deviation. Frost calls the traditional lyric object "love and the moon"; Warren's examples of lyric are almost all drawn from the litera-ture of love. So Frost and Warren pursue, because they understand, the issue of lyric purity in its late-nineteenth-century embattled context in which the contemporary genteel lyric was being pushed gleefully into the grave by the polemical defenders of realism. They implicitly define the modernist moment for poetry as the moment of realist pressure upon the lyric. Both castigate a late-nineteenth-century lyric impulse drained of historical specificity, because they are exceptionally sensitive to the generic dominance of a kind of writing (realist fiction) whose central claim to cultural value was precisely its empirical and historical density. The struggle for literary liberation in the early mod-ern moment of American poetry was directed against genteel idealism and its Victorian and Romantic sources, but the seductive pull of that idealism in the embryonic moments of modernist literary culture turned out to be greater, more insidious, and more invasive than might appear at face value in modernist polemic and manifesto.

Frost's effort to destroy what Poe, Tennyson, and Swinburne had wrought (and Palgrave, Stedman, and Rittenhouse had institutionalized) by dramati-cally adapting the rhythms and aural qualities of the traditional lyric to the cacophonous, speaking rhythms of voices in worldly situations is an effort to come to terms with the novel, as is his theory that everything "written is as good as it is dramatic – even the most unassuming lyric," which must be heard as "spoken by a person in a scene – in character, in a setting." His desire to be known as a poet who had "summoned" (not created) tones and rhythms from actual speech is as good a sign as we have of how far down in prestige traditional notions of "poetry" had sunk in the rankings of the literary genres by the early twentieth century. If in middle-class societies the novel had displaced the epic of traditional culture, and if classic forms of drama were increasingly being "replaced" (Pound's acidic reflection) by more popular and economically feasible forms of theater, then what meaningful role could possibly be imagined for the lyric?

In his earliest efforts to open lyric practice by rejecting the Anglophilic heritage of official poetic diction, Frost in effect predicted the shape that his literary career would take. It was to be a career committed to nativist values. The struggle of any young American poet who would be an original, he argued, must be against those custodians of culture who betray the American scene by directing him to write in a banalized, special language found only in books (and English books at that), a language with no sources in the "cave" of the "mouth," a language that "everybody exclaims Poetry! at." The American sounds and rhythms in running speech were to constitute Frost's newfound virgin land, the uncanonized territory that gave him the refuge of aesthetic freedom because he could refuse, as "no one horse American poet" after Keats could refuse, the mimetic idolatry of Keats's yearning, romantic diction. Frost proffered the endlessly echoed word *alien* from "Ode to a Nightingale" as the exemplary piece of ironic evidence of American self-alienation, a denaturing of the American thing by poets who could not help but indenture themselves to Keats and a continuing display of aesthetic servitude to British rule that Emerson and many others had lamented in the 1820s and 1830s, in their call for literary emancipation.

The generally conservative lyric practice of Frost's first volume, *A Boy's Will* (1913), was followed by the dramatic and narrative experiments in the blending of dialogue, storytelling, and a vocality "lower" than Wordsworth's, in his second volume, *North of Boston* (1914), which was in turn followed by his final major transformation into the sententious poet of public fame who came to dominate most of what he wrote after the publication of his third volume, *Mountain Interval* (1916). These neat divisions of Frost's career tell the familiar modern American tale of youthful genius emancipated from convention only to be seduced by money and heavy media attention. But in this case it is a story that partially misrepresents, because it segregates what at Frost's most original was the fusion from early on, in a single literary impulse, of lyrical, narrative, dramatic, and didactic moods. His most radical moment as a new poet is discernible, not in the dramatic and narrative successes of *North of Boston* ("Mending Wall," "The Death of the Hired Man," "A Servant to Servants"), but in the deceptive poems of *A Boy's Will*, where, in a context of tame, historically recognizable lyric practice, which won him (before he traveled to England) some acceptances in mass-circulation magazines, we come across "Mowing," a poem in which he thought he had come so close to getting down everything he wanted to get down, that he despaired of ever matching that effort again:

> There was never a sound beside the wood but one,
> And that was my long scythe whispering to the ground.
> What was it it whispered? I knew not well myself;
> Perhaps it was something about the heat of the sun,
> Something, perhaps, about the lack of sound –
> And that was why it whispered and did not speak.
> It was no dream of the gift of idle hours,
> Or easy gold at the hand of fey or elf:
> Anything more than the truth would have seemed too weak
> To the earnest love that laid the swale in rows,
> Not without feeble-pointed spikes of flowers
> (Pale orchises), and scared a bright green snake.
> The fact is the sweetest dream that labor knows.
> My long scythe whispered and left the hay to make.

Frost plunges us into a poetry of literary satisfaction wrested from a context of labor that is at once the antagonist of the literary moment and the trigger of its gratification. Labor is the grudging basis of poetry for those who have no traditional means of economic and cultural support for the writing of lyric – those whose lyricism, like Frost's, had better somehow be supported by and in the course of the actual tasks of daily work because there is no alternative system of literary support available, those who somehow must be simultaneously poets and laborers. Frost's penchant for titles featuring the present participle promotes the biographically telling fiction that his writing is coincidental with the actual processes of work it describes ("Mowing," "Going for Water," "Mending Wall," "After Apple Picking," "Putting in the Seed"). These poems obliquely focus the biography of a writer who, from his childhood, was required by circumstances to work: between eight and eighteen as newspaper carrier, waiter, gatekeeper at a mill, farmhand, and more than once, as assembly-line worker – first at twelve years old in a shoe factory, the second time at a woolen mill, at age seventeen, for sixty-three hours per week.

Wordsworth often composed in his head, wandering at his leisure in the Lake District, and Stevens did likewise, walking purposively through the districts of Hartford, Connecticut to his executive desk at the insurance company.

Frost's most intriguing poems imply the fiction that he created his poems as he worked, that their written forms are unnecessary – the gratuitous recordings of an act, antecedent to writing, an act of labor aesthetically intersected for a laborer who may never actually write, either because he will have no time for it or because he will have no skill to do so. The poetics of Frost's lyric poetry of work implies the statement that this is a kind of writing which claims nothing special for its being written or for the values of writing as such: an antipoetics of work for those who may never have heard of poetics or read a poet; a highly literate poetry, nevertheless, that needed, in sly guilt, to efface itself as literature – as if poetry were a high-falutin' indulgence, yet for some reason necessary – and in such effacement gives us access to life in the here and now; access, in other words, to "modernity."

Unlike Wordsworth's "The Solitary Reaper," upon which Frost's "Mowing" mounts a criticism empowered not a little out of resentment, there is no separation in Frost's poem of poetic and laboring voices. Wordsworth, a third-person observer, coolly notes "yon" Highland lass, reaping and singing. His poem's key rhetorical directives ("Behold her . . . Stop here or gently pass!") tell us that his physical distance from the reaper is an aid to the distance required for imaginative reflection. And distance, physical and contemplative, is a figure for the class hierarchy and privilege that define Wordsworth's relation to the working presence named in his title. These social distances produce the very possibility of this poem and also this, its pivotal question: "Will no one tell me what she sings?" Frost, a first-person participant, answers Wordsworth's innocent question with a parodic allusion to it that amounts to a workingman's joke on a comfortable outsider, whose purpose is manipulation of pastoral conventions, not knowledge of labor: "What was it it whispered? I knew not well myself." The reaper is the occasion for Wordsworth's imaginative excursion; Wordsworth is in part recollecting his experience as a literal tourist who doesn't speak the language, but it hardly matters. In fact, his outsiderly perspective (linguistically, economically, and educationally inflected) is all to the good: he is not obligated to communication, only to searching his own inwardness. So, just as fast as he can, and while seeming to honor the mesmeric power of the reaper's song, Wordsworth moves in his second stanza from the site of the reaper's work to faraway romantic places, "Arabian sands," "the farthest Hebrides." Through Frost's lens, Wordsworth's poem is everything that Frost's is not: "a dream of the gift of idle hours." Frost's poem, in this dialogue of literary history, claims that this man who writes *is* working, he *is* the solitary reaper.

Wordsworth's polished displays of rhythm and intricate rhyme pattern, sustained flawlessly from beginning to end, sound monological next to Frost's equally intricate sonnet, which moves between the effortless lyric grace of its opening two lines (with anapests, trochees, and iambs fluidly integrated), to the sudden interruption of a rough talking (not singing) voice at line three ("What was it it whispered?") and its playful, prosy surmises (perhaps, perhaps), then on to the flat declarative and epigrammatic moment for which he will become famous in the penultimate line: "The fact is the sweetest dream that labor knows." Never a poet of discontinuities and fragments in the sense synonymous with modernist collage and made famous by Pound and Eliot, Frost is yet, in his subtlest vocal experiments, a maker of the quiet vocal collage which, more than anything else in his repertory of strategies, is the mark of his mixed identity as writer-worker, his difference from the traditional poet represented by Wordsworth.

Frost did what Wordsworth never had to do (worked at lower-class jobs) but also what all those represented by Wordsworth's female reaper were not likely to do (write poems of literary sophistication). Frost's virtuoso vocal changes, worked through a heavily Anglo-Saxonate diction, flaunt his difference from Wordsworth, whose nondramatic, smooth song voice, bodied forth in high literacy, highlights the critical social difference between the poet who imagines and the object which is the cause of his imagining. The socially and economically comfortable male poet builds visionary stanzas tranquilly upon his recollection of a female laborer, who becomes a peculiarly modern muse for a socially sympathetic English lyricist, the very same who had gone officially on record, in his famous polemical Preface, as intending to honor ordinary voices, but who is himself no ordinary voice, and whose poem "The Solitary Reaper" unintentionally acknowledges his privileged relation to the base of rural labor that inspired him.

Although the poverty and the sex of the solitary reaper doubly and drastically preclude her access to the ease of literacy that might eventuate in a career like Wordsworth's, and although Frost's male mower performs roughly the solitary reaper's kind of work – therein lie the connections of class across gender – at the same time Frost's male mower can do what Wordsworth's female reaper cannot (this is Frost's pact with Wordsworth): make knowing allusion to literary tradition, in this instance, a Shakespearean song in part about work: ("Perhaps it was something about the heat of the sun"), thereby revealing his learned, bookish ways in the very voice of the ordinary worker. This laborer is an American who has had the advantage conferred by democratic commitment to mass education. And his whispering scythe talks not only Shakespeare but also more than a little Andrew Marvell, whose "Damon the Mower" Frost recalls in order deftly to send up – in his critical allusion to "fey or elf" – a patently literary device, an artifice out of touch with the quotidian of farm labor

("The deathless Fairyes take me oft / To lead them in their Danses soft"). No fairies are taking Frost's poet-laborer anywhere.

Closer to literary home, Frost's whispering scythe implies, through a criticism of W. B. Yeats, the dominant living poet in English in the first decade of the twentieth century, Frost's own self-criticism: in denying "dream" and the work of "fey or elf," Frost, in the directness of his vernacular voice, mounts an internal commentary on the nineties-ish poetic diction of a number of his own early dreamy lyrics in *A Boy's Will*, while forecasting the colloquial richness and unpretentiousness of *North of Boston*. Frost stakes his claim to difference, not only from Wordsworth's elite position, but also from Yeats and his overt celebration of dream in his early poetry and plays, which Frost knew intimately, having produced the plays of heart's desire while a teacher at Pinkerton Academy in 1910 – a claim to difference from the Yeats who had famously declared, in flight from the world of fact, that the "dream" of the poets "alone is certain good." So "dream" becomes, in Frost's poem, a doubly burdened term of criticism signifying both the leisured idleness of the British poetic classes and a contemporary aestheticist fashionability, a world-fleeing imagination whose diction Yeats would purify from his writing with the help of Pound's editing, but which Pound himself would have trouble getting out of his own system until after Frost had succeeded in doing so – though Frost, in his early-century obscurity at the Derry, New Hampshire farm, was without the proper critical organs at his disposal to declare his triumph of having made it new.

Boring from within Wordsworth's pastoral territory and Yeats's domain of dream-as-imagination, Frost reduces visionary dream to vision (as in visual) and imagination to a pure act of perception (as in image-making), an act that yields a precious because fleeting knowledge of fact, and fleeting because labor will not permit leisurely lingering in aesthetic pleasure of natural detail strictly irrelevant to the task of labor. It is a knowledge that Frost comes to have not as independent agent – the laboring agent knows little freedom – but as agent of labor's action. Labor, not Frost, in Frost's most radical identification of literature with work, "knows" "the fact," which is also and at the same time the ultimate dream of imagination; Frost may know only insofar as he labors. The act of labor as an act of imagination rescues dreaming (Yeats's synonym for poetry) from both Wordsworth and Yeats, in this context impractical "dreamers" in the worst sense of the word.

Frost dreams in riveted attention to the incidental fact unveiled in work: a glimpse of fact for itself alone opened briefly, in a throwaway moment of syntactical subordination, as if it would be a desecration of work to permit those images of flowers (only parenthetically named) and the "bright green snake" to take over center stage and distract the laborer from his real task. This moment of syntactical subordination in "Mowing" is the expressive sign of a culturally subordinated aesthesis, an American guilt of poesis: the image garnered for no profit, stolen from the process of work which opens the possibility of aesthetic experience for a laborer momentarily out of the groove of the job at hand. Work, a ruthless end-directed activity, not in hostile opposition to an activity valuable in itself – as the story of nineteenth-century idealist aesthetics would have it – but work as both constraining and productive context, necessary economic ground of the aesthetic for those, unlike Wordsworth and Yeats, who find work inescapable, whose own labor, not someone else's, is their peculiarly modern muse.

Yet what comes seeping through this effort to write out of a sympathetic antipastoral of work is a social arrangement similar to the object of Frost's criticism of Wordsworth. Social distance and its corollary attitude, the sentimentalizing of common country labor – an attitude virtually demanded by traditional pastoral – make a subversive return in "Mowing" in order partially to trip up Frost's intention and to reveal the duplicity of his would-be realist antipoetics. This literate farmer is more literate than farmer, but uneasily so. This is guilty pastoral, written not out of leisure-class privilege but out of American social constraint by a man who wanted his work to be writing, not those other jobs he did that qualify officially in our culture as work and that he found so dissatisfying. The "earnest love" of this farmer's "long scythe" that "laid the swale" (not just any meadow but a low-lying, moist depression of a meadow), this farmer's productive phallic love throws into even greater subordination the moment of aesthetic vision as an interior moment of pathos, a moment freed from the act of labor (which makes hay while the sun shines) – productive, masturbatory, the indulgent feminine moment; in "Mowing," the literal parenthesis of lyric impression.

The didactic point of Frost's difficult penultimate line becomes clear and sharp against the background of the huge cultural claims for poetic function made by traditional theories of poetry from Aristotle to Wordsworth. The role of poetry for a poet who is constrained by inescapable labor is perhaps a diminished thing in light of the portentousness of those earlier claims. But perhaps poetic function is newly enhanced, after all, in this kind of modern setting of work. Poetry now is a pragmatic personal urgency, an aid to getting by in a social setting which, for Frost (in this he is representative of the modern American writer), doesn't make getting by very easy. Frost's implied comparative and his explicit superlative in "Mowing" condense a complex story of literary and social history: dreams sweet and sweeter, the dreams of Marvell, Wordsworth, and Yeats – the easy poetic gold of idleness – yield to dreams sweetest. Sweetest dream – the best dream of all – is a form of laboring consciousness, somehow and oddly identical with "fact" – what is presumably raw, informational, objectively there. But "fact," in that ordinary sense, is turned by this poet into an extraordinary thing; this constricted laborer just happens (an American happening) to be schooled in Latin etymologies of English ordinariness. *Factum*: a thing done, or produced, a matter revealed by and for a laboring consciousness, for no end beyond the momentary refreshment of its own act. *Factum*: a feat, a kind of performance, a display of prowess, virtuosity, the poetry of work, but also (how could aesthetic contemplation be otherwise for a practical American male?) a kind of crime, as in an accessory after the fact.

When the poet who worked working-class jobs as a teenager and farmed and taught as an adult took his family to England in September 1912, he was virtually unknown, verging on forty, but willing to gamble his modest resources on one last effort to achieve a literary breakthrough – so that he might farm and teach no more. In short order, he made his way into the London literary scene; published his first two books there to excellent notices; impressed many writers, including William Butler Yeats; and came to the attention of Ezra Pound, tireless and superbly effective entrepreneur of the modern, who touted him, perhaps no more usefully than in a review of *A Boy's Will* in *Poetry*, Harriet Monroe's new but immediately influential little magazine. Two and a half years later, in February 1915, Robert Frost returned home to find himself on the eve of his American fame.

Whatever pleasure Pound's review must have given was more than matched by the political anxiety it caused. Pound said that Frost had been ignored by the "great American editors," who had also ignored, not incidentally, many new-wave poets (for example, Ezra Pound). Better to seek out English publishers, as Frost had, whose sensibilities were not yet fatally shaped by the new symbiosis of conventional taste and mass-market lust, and who had somehow found a way to balance economic necessity with the love of good letters. Frost wrote to his friend John Bartlett that he objected "chiefly to what [Pound said] about the great American editors. Not that I have any love for the two or three he has in mind. But they are better ignored – at any rate they are better not offended. We may want to use them some time."

On the eve of his American fame, Frost knew who he was and knew what he must do. Although he was writing against the grain of prevailing genteel standards, he believed (correctly, it turned out) that he did not require the little magazines to see the light of literary day because his style was not shockingly

new – it never called openly for a coterie of specially armed readers. His sharpest effects were easily as subtle as they were unsettling, but his verbal surfaces were accessible, even kindly. Maybe he could bore subversively from within while doing what countless avant-garde writers could not do: make a living from his writing. But until those anglophilic American editors learned of his English triumphs, he would not be acceptable to them, and he would not make a living from his writing.

What made the great American editors change their minds? Frost raised that question to Bartlett in another letter, confessed he didn't have the answer, though he had his suspicions:

Doubtless you saw my countenance displayed in The [Boston] Herald one day. The Transcript will [do] me next. The literary editor of The Chicago Post writes to say that I may look for two columns of loving kindness in The Post in a day or two. It is not just naught – say what you will. One likes best to write poetry and one knew that he did . . . before one got even one reputation. Still one can't pretend not to like to win the game. One can't help thinking a little of Number One . . . I need money as I suspect you may yourself.

After he came back from England, and with driven application to the end of his life, Frost played to win. With the possible exceptions of Ernest Hemingway and Norman Mailer, no important American writer in the twentieth century promoted himself more successfully to wider celebrity. After Henry Holt brought out the American editions of his first two volumes within weeks of his return, Frost's career took off. From 1916 to 1963, the year of his death, almost no year passed without the conferring upon him of some major honor: in the USA and abroad, more than forty honorary degrees; four Pulitzers and one Bollingen Prize; a slew of gold medals for literary achievement from various colleges, universities, and civic organizations; the prestigious Norton professorship in poetry at Harvard; and, toward the end, like the giants of nineteenth-century American literature whom he admired and whose cultural force he coveted, he acquired political recognition and function as a literary ambassador, first for Dwight D. Eisenhower and then for John F. Kennedy (who was once photographed reading one of Frost's volumes). And anyone who saw it will never forget the conferring of his greatest honor, which co-incided with his greatest performance before an audience of many millions who watched it on television. With a mean January wind blowing through the fabulous thatched white hair of America's poet, and a harsh sun-glare making it impossible for him to read what he had written for Kennedy's inaugural, he righted himself like a great actor avoiding disaster without missing a beat and recited "The Gift Outright," from memory.

In his last years Frost's poetry sold in numbers that not even the combined sales of his powerful modernist company could match. Joyce, Pound, Eliot, and Stevens have their fame, but it is pretty strictly enclosed in the small pond of other writers, critics, and our sometimes reluctant students. Just a few months after his first book appeared, Frost, writing from England, told Bartlett that he would never be satisfied with the snobby pleasures of avant-garde renown, "success," as he put it, "with the critical few who are supposed to know," because "really to arrive where I can stand on my legs as a poet and nothing else I must get outside that circle to the general reader who buys books in their thousands." To the delight of their publishers and inheritors, Frost and the other famous names of modernism now sell "books in their thousands," but Frost did it while he was alive, and he did it long before he and the others became fixtures in the captive market of the university curriculum in English and American literature.

In the same letter to Bartlett, he said he wanted "to reach out, and would if it were a thing I could do by taking thought." In 1913, Frost was apparently something of an idealist. He wanted to get to a mass audience, but only on his own terms: by thinking, by writing poems, by being appreciated for what he was. His instincts were democratic; he believed that the people could "know," that the "critical few who are supposed to know" probably don't. After he returned to America, he must have come to the realization that in this culture, in this time, to stand on your feet as a poet and nothing else is a hope of utopian order. If he wanted to reach those who buy books in their thousands, he would need to do more than toil away in his writer's room. In 1915, he found himself on the eve of his American fame; in his later years, he found himself about as famous as a serious poet can ever hope to be; in between – and now the passive voice must be dropped because it obscures the truth – he spared no effort to bring his fame to its high noon, as he became his fame's shrewdest agent.

Getting one's picture in major dailies in Boston and Chicago wasn't just nothing if one needed money. Frost was never innocent about the power of the press, but until he returned to the United States with two books under his belt and a budding reputation he was in no position to seize the engines of publicity. But then seize them he did: alongside his career in poetry-making, he forged a complementary career in fame by granting in the neighborhood of one hundred interviews, including one to television's Sunday must of the fifties and sixties "Meet the Press"; by frequenting, and working – really working – writers' conferences, including the prestigious one held at Breadloaf, Vermont, for which Frost played, year in and year out, the role of genius in residence; and, most

of all, by mastering the poetry business, the reading circuit for which he performed (that is the word) brilliantly and indefatigably. In a prejet age, he spent on the average of three to four months per year on the road, doing readings and riding on trains to and from engagements all over the country. In other words, he learned quickly that although he couldn't, in the strict sense, stand on his feet as a poet and nothing else, in a looser sense he could do so by selling himself and his poems as the complete product. He learned that his poems sold better as he sold Robert Frost, famous American poet who, far from scorning average people (as Pound and his avant-garde friends were doing), actually spoke to them, or at the least dearly loved to give the impression of doing so.

In 1921 fame brought Frost to the university as writer-in-residence, only the second in America to hold such a position: an industry-inaugurating moment at the University of Michigan, his legacy to serious American writers who couldn't make a living by writing alone. His appointments at Michigan and, later, on and off, at Amherst and Dartmouth contributed heavily to the livelihood set up by the sales of his books and by his fees on the reading circuit. In a country without patronage, it was the American way: "I've never had to write a word of thanks to anybody I had a cent from," he boasted to the *Paris Review*. "The colleges came between."

According to the myth of artistic authenticity conceived and disseminated relentlessly by writers, artists, and critics since the late eighteenth century, real writers are supposed to be alienated, difficult in person and style, and expected to take a stand as their cultures' most withering critics. They are supposed to be all these things because they come to us (they tell us) bearing alternative values. Frost instead put himself on constant public display as the people's poet, the antithesis to all avant-garde ideals of the writer. In an interview published in the *New York Times Book Review* on the occasion of the publication of *New Hampshire*, the volume that won him his first Pulitzer Prize, he said that inspiration "lies in the clean and wholesome life of the ordinary man." "Men have told me, and perhaps they are right, that I have no 'straddle' . . . That means that I cannot spread out far enough to lie in filth and write in the treetops. I can't. Perhaps it is because I am so ordinary." In another interview, he said that a "poet should not include in his writing anything that the average reader will not easily understand." The shocking word is "easily." No doubt that's why Frost chose it – as the signal of his democratic nativism, the mark of a poet who not only didn't write according to the norms of the avant-garde (so full of contempt for the bourgeoisie), but who would so define and proudly advertise himself as ordinary to those who might buy books in the thousands, if only they could be confident that those books would speak to them, coming from one of their own. If we try to imagine Pound or Joyce saying the things

that Frost said about being wholesome and ordinary, much less performing publicly as Frost did, according to such dictates, we shall come quickly to Frost's difference from high modernist company.

Frost succeeded so well in selling his greatest poem, his self-creation as Mr. Ordinary – kindly, wise, and readable – that, after his death, when Lawrence Thompson's three-volume tell-everything biography appeared, revealing him to be Mr. Ordinary in some unkindly ways, an overreaction set in that was surprising only for its orgy of selfrighteousness. (Frost was a "monster," said one reviewer; "a more hateful human being can not have lived," said another.) But his greatest feat of self-creation and promotion lay in his ambidextrous ability to pass himself off as cracker-barrel Rob, all the while dramatizing himself (in Randall Jarrell's phrase) as The Only Genuine Robert Frost in Captivity. Frost told us openly, in countless ways, that he was ordinary and not to be feared. He also told us, in countless covert ways – by standing before us in public, for example, a famous man – that he was different from us, that we should love and venerate him for his difference and fear and envy him a little for having what the ordinary don't have: charismatic power.

If the freshness of Frost's manner in a few of his earliest poems lay in his creation of a lyricism indigenous to (and jostling with) the vernacular voice of an ordinary man engaged in ordinary tasks (so it goes in Frostean theater), and whose extraordinary flirtations with literary history are submerged, not flourished in poetic self-consciousness; if the poetry of "Mowing" would thereby sponsor the sprezzatura of an American democrat (and college dropout) who only incidentally happened to be a poet, then we have to say it is a poetry not much in evidence in *A Boy's Will*. Frost's first book was heavily marked by the tone of the fin-de-siècle – the ambience of unanchored grief, the moodiness of autumnal sorrows (the youth of the poet notwithstanding); here and there by an unaffected plainness of song lyric; and, more than here and there, by a style whose diction and syntax refer us not to the writer who draws his power from the unassuming, but to one too much in love with books of elevated, antique voice, from which he picks up words and phrases whose origin is not living speech but the graveyard of bookish eloquence: "o'er," "e'er," "wend," "vainly," "tremulous," "zephyr," "whither," "thine," "thou," "misty fen," and (the Tennysonian theft) "in airy dalliance." The paradox of "Waiting: Afield at Dusk," a characteristic performance in *A Boy's Will*, is that it was written by someone with the right sort of disruptive aesthetic for his time (his desire to freshen Palgrave's *Golden Treasury*: "the worn book of old-golden song," as he calls it), whose own voice is nonetheless still indentured to his memories of earlier

poets; who is willing to give away his poem's opening words to *A Midsummer Night's Dream* ("What things for dream there are . . . "), and then its closing lines to an imitation of the Shakespeare of the sonnets: "But on the memory of one absent, most, / For whom these lines when they shall greet her eye."

Set in the context of the main drift of his early practice and the banal lyric norms of the early century, *North of Boston* is radical stuff. With a couple of splendid exceptions ("After Apple-Picking" being one of them), most of the poems in Frost's second book are mid-size narratives, carried mainly by dialogue seemingly gathered without mediation (this is their subtlest art) directly from the lives of the suffering rural poor, whose only psychic leavening occurs in moments of lyric burst that come as if from out of nowhere, their discontinuity with the narrative flow of depressed rural existence being perhaps their ultimate point: as if Frost's sudden jump from storytelling and dialogue into lyricism were the literary sign of lives that could not support and sustain lyric imagination and therefore had to snatch it desperately when its time came, at the least excuse.

What Frost sees in New England's rural poor are images of the poet-laborer he had debuted in "Mowing": figures of himself. *North of Boston* is the objectification, in a series of little dramas and stories, of the central (econo-aesthetic) issue of Frost's early life and poetry. In "The Death of the Hired Man," "The Mountain," "The Black Cottage," "A Servant to Servants," and "The House-keeper," the rare but shrewdly placed lyric passage often stops domestic working time and redeems for a brief space lives that are by turns lonely and boring and horrifying and dull; relationships that bespeak little relating; tales of the coldness in the heart, stupefying routine, sexual betrayal, and madness. Far from banishing his lyric impulses to the margins, *North of Boston* places them at the psychological center, where they function as release mechanisms for freedom, however constricted, however brief.

The radically realist aesthetic that drives the writing of *North of Boston* is on uncompromising display in "A Servant to Servants" (a monologue) and "The Housekeeper" (mainly a monologue), two plotless narratives that resist summary, come to no epiphany, yield no detachable wisdom. In these poems what is put on display is voice itself, too long pent up. Frost's craft encourages us to imagine life before these poems begin, to imagine it as a time of long, female silence. These poems begin as a sudden breaking of silence, with vocal energy released in a torrent of plain speaking – reflective, anecdotal, lyrical, mercilessly self-descriptive – to a stranger who happens by into the lives of two housekeeping and housebound women, a stranger who gives audience to these two talking writers, the housekeeper in the poem of that title literally housebound, who tells us she's so fat that they won't be able to get her through

the door: "I've been built in here like a big church organ." These women talk as if the sole point of talking were to produce more talk. What they know, without ever quite knowing it, is that narrative shapeliness and closure, perfectly concatenated beginnings, middles, and ends, only hasten the death of talk and a spirit grimly hanging on; a thousand and one nights, New England country style.

If Frost has a point, it is to say: Behold, these too exist, they suffer, and there is nothing you or I can do about it. This is the way it is *North of Boston*, a title he said was inspired by the real-estate section of the classifieds. The success of his radical realism in *North of Boston* depends for its strongest impact on our hearing his volume as a whole as a rebuke; as a book with a critical agenda, set slyly into literary history and pitched, with great deviousness, to readers of urban sophistication; a sharply sardonic commentary on conventions of sentiment concerning the supposed simplicities and therapies of the pastoral life.

Nothing in either volume but the change itself from *A Boy's Will* to *North of Boston* suggests a portrait of the writer in the act of finding his true material and medium (Frost's art makes it difficult to make the distinction), now practicing his craft confidently, no longer looking over his shoulder at those who came before. In fact, though, a new kind of self-consciousness stirs embryonically in *North of Boston*, born in literary obscurity and economic need, in imagination of the fame and consequent cultural authority that might come to be his, and we experience this form of self-consciousness as the sound of a voice: this time a sophisticated poet's voice taking pleasure in its own writerly presence, the poet once again looking over his shoulder, now in order to observe, with pleasure, the act of his writing in the act of doing it. In such moments of self-observation he creates the image of the writer he wanted to be and the major subject and style of what he wrote and became after *North of Boston*. The image of Robert Frost, famous American poet, is the source and authentic substance of much that is very good and very bad in the poems of Robert Frost, famous American poet. Frost inaugurates an early but rigorously postmodern phase in the history of American literature, preceded by similar efforts in image-retailing made by Whitman and Twain.

This poet who imagines his emergence into fame can be heard even in *North of Boston*, as if he were always lurking in Frost's heart, in what will become one of his best-known poems, "Mending Wall," which Frost placed as the lead-off, misleading tone-setter of *North of Boston*. Here, desire for the therapy of conversation becomes just another poetic subject. The playful narrator, all

self-possession and aplomb, addresses himself to an audience focused on the delightful peregrinations of his voice, not on his dramatic situation; on the narrator as a poet, not on the narrator as a character with a crippling problem, a poet who talks to us about conversation, a topic among other topics, how he'd rather his stolid neighbor wouldn't introduce the conversation-killing proverb into a discussion that he'd like to get rolling. "Mending Wall" is laced with jokes and puns, all shared with us, all at the expense of that Johnny-one-note who is deaf to Frost's deft play. The poem's secret subject is the bond that a writer would like to forge with his audience; the writer-speaker's true need is to perform successful literary seduction on his possible public. He tells us between the lines that we're no blockheads; we've been honored by his confidence. He assumes, so generously, that we get his game. This wily rhetorical note – it's the presiding tonality of "Mending Wall" – is one of the keynotes of Frost's later career, and it sounds prophetically in "The Road Not Taken" (the properly placed lead-off poem of his third volume, *Mountain Interval*), whose deepest subject is the sentimental American fiction of self-making that the speaker imagines pitching (that is the word) to a gullible audience sometime in the future. This gullible audience, which will need to hear it, will also need to be distinguished from those who get his poem's quietly unnerving point, those honored by his rhetorical embrace as elect readers. But this distinction between audiences in fact can be made only by the elect – here is the brilliant deviousness of Frost's rhetoric; because in making the distinction they prove themselves to be the elect. So do the self-defined elect, with Frost's subtle prodding, separate themselves from the American masses who must get him wrong, who must read him sentimentally, and who must make him famous.

In the persistent, ever-renewed moment of self-creation (its power will shape his future), the modernist writer typically defines himself against the standards of mass-market literary expression as the champion of radical originality and the maker of a literary text that's a one-of-a-kind phenomenon (in other words, no "kind" at all). This severe ideal of modernist aesthetic demands constant experimentation, the creation of writing forever refreshed and refreshing (to writer and reader both, like an injection of radical individualism), never repeating itself. Frost and T. S. Eliot are the modernists who, only partially against their wills, made themselves into deluxe commodities, poets whose poems are unreadable unless we grasp their true subject: the poet in the act of talking, as a poet, to audiences not assumed to be hospitable. *Four Quartets* cannot have its strongest impact unless we accept it as the meditation of the world's most famous man of letters, reviewing his journey to date and taking further steps

in the private spiritual adventure which, by the time of *Quartets*, was, thanks to Eliot's efforts, a public text. The modernist desire in Frost and Eliot – to preserve an independent selfhood against the coercions of the market, a self made and secured by the creation of a unique style – is subverted by the logic of the market, not because they wrote according to popular formulas, but because they give us their poems as delicious experiences of voyeurism, illusions of direct access to the life and thought of the famous writer, with the poet inside the poem like a rare animal in a zoo. This was the only commodity Frost and Eliot were capable of producing: the modernist phenomenon as product, mass culture's ultimate revenge on those who would scorn it.

But in spite of his contempt for the self-conscious avant-garde and his will to self-commodification, the poetry Frost made from *Mountain Interval* onward is more varied in tone and style than any of the poetries made by the canonical modernists whom he is not supposed to resemble, Ezra Pound perhaps excepted. The later poetry of Frost is riddled with the warmly humorous sayings of cracker-barrel Rob: rambling pontifications on the world that we are to imagine as spoken from deep in the heart of Yankeedom, pleasing takes on country matters, poems concluding so many times with proverb-like turns, epigrams, the wise insights of the bard ("trust my instincts – I'm a bard") – all those vaguely optimistic lines we're supposed to remember, write down, refer to when the going gets tough. This public poetry of uplift connects Frost firmly to those Fireside poets who played cultural minister to America's nineteenth century and whose rhetorical role was inherited and restaged in different ways by Frost and Eliot: a vein of writing particularly rich in Frost after *Mountain Interval*, the kind of writing for which he is best known, best loved, and best deprecated by champions of the high modern. And this new Fireside poet did not hesitate to reach for the dead metaphor, not in order to refresh it but in order to foreground it: "It's when I'm weary of considerations / And life is too much like a pathless wood." That's from "Birches," a *Mountain Interval* poem about the one-on-a-side sport called poetry, a celebration of the wholesome, self-reliant background of the country-bred poet, too far from town to learn baseball as a boy, a team sport that the real Robert Frost learned early and loved late – he was commissioned by *Sports Illustrated* to write on the 1956 All-Star game. But baseball is here put down in favor of birch-riding, a game of invention (like poetry writing) one plays alone.

The mythical Robert Frost who never played baseball gives us, in "Birches," the oft-quoted "Earth's the right place for love," an unanswerable, moralizing line followed by this answer: the not often quoted, "I don't know where it's likely to go better" (a chuckle-stimulator from the bard, until we think about it twice and feel the total and delightful nastiness of Frost's humor). The

mythical Robert Frost in "Hyla Brook" gives us a last (you must remember this) line of ethical nobility, phrased with vernacular elegance: "We love the things we love for what they are." But "Hyla Brook" is an even cagier *Mountain Interval* poem about poetry whose easily detachable last line (what "things"?) will seem calculated to make happy those readers who desire Fireside comforts. In the concluding, pithy didactic moments of his writing, Frost gains entry to that traditional kind of audience, to the dismay of those who want their modern writers obscure and antididactic. But, in context, the line "We love the things we love for what they are" makes virtually no sense because its referent is a brook that exists only as a series of rapidly turned figures, a dried up non-brook that lives only in imaginative metamorphosis, in the guise of poetic "things," including one, most unvernacular poetic "thing": "Like ghost of sleigh bells in a ghost of snow." So the traditional figure with which Frost opens "Hyla Brook" ("By June our brook's run out of song and speed") is transformed into an unthinglike "thing" hard to see unless we can dance with Frost through styles of figurative remembrance, in high literary and vernacular alternation. The detachable wisdom of the last line of "Hyla Brook" does not come cheaply and is not really detachable from its context. It is a rarified literary joke that depends on an occulted allusion to Tennyson. But Robert Frost, famous American poet, always encouraged us to think him easy and made a living from a readership he schooled to think him so.

Alongside such self-consciously literary performances in *Mountain Interval* the stark manner of *North of Boston* persists in "An Old Man's Winter Night," a portrait of encroaching physical and mental decrepitude in which Frost's blank verse of ruthless detail strips bare the blank end of life:

> All out-of-doors looked darkly in at him
> Through the thin frost, almost in separate stars,
> That gathers on the pane in empty rooms.
> What kept his eyes from giving back the gaze
> Was the lamp tilted near them in his hand.
> What kept him from remembering what it was
> That brought him to that creaking room was age.
> He stood with barrels round him – at a loss.

The pun on "pane in empty rooms" itself is painful in its hard-edged plainness, as are the poem's late lines in which the horrifying repetition of a simple verb extinguishes the human difference: "The log that shifted with a jolt / Once in the stove, disturbed him and he shifted." Here is a poetry of unrelievable depression that makes a mockery of Frost's better-known poems of uplift.

In the even less varnished "Out, Out – ' " whose title is a quotation from Macbeth's despairing last soliloquy, Shakespeare is brought down from heroic altitude to the grinding rural level and its routine tragedies. Frost tells a story about a boy who loses his hand to an electric saw when he's distracted by the call to supper. At the awful moment of severance, Frost turns his usual benign whimsy to the work of gruesome humor: The saw "Leaped out at the boy's hand" as if to demonstrate that "saws knew what supper meant." At the end of the poem, which coincides with the boy's unexpected but not much grieved death, Frost turns harshly self-conscious in order to say something about local-color writing, something about how to end poems that depend for life on local incident, as if to reflect on the sawlike nature of his own art of feeding off unheralded catastrophe (anything for a poem); this from a poet renowned for his warmth and "old saws." Like those relatives of the boy who carry on with their affairs, he, too, must move on, find new matter for poetry: "No more to build on there."

With a few strong exceptions ("The Witch of Coos," "The Subverted Flower"), the vein of harsh narrative writing pretty much peters out, as Frost proceeds through his long years of acclaim. More and more, the poet who had played hard for, and had been granted, cultural centrality takes over and begins to speak. His own cultural authority becomes the grounding assumption of his speaking, the reason why we listen. One of the dominant tones struck in his later career, beginning in his fourth volume (*New Hampshire*, 1923) with "Fire and Ice" and continuing through later volumes – in "Spring Pools," "Once By the Pacific," and "Sand Dunes" – is the tone of bardic apocalypticism: the prophetic voice of decisive upheaval telling us that fearful change is at hand, which upon closer analysis rather unbards itself by being unable to specify the causes of apocalypse. In these poems, fear floats free of its objects, becoming all the more fearful for its vagueness, and more fearful still when we consider that its vocal vehicle is exactly the sort of poet who is supposed to have himself well in hand. How else shall he be capable of consoling us in our hour of crisis? How else shall we know him as a bard, a famous man, an authority, not one of us? For what other reason would we bother to listen? What could be more unsettling than an insecure bard? And it doesn't help, not at all, to remember that the last instance of the poetry of reason undone, "The Draft Horse" – Frost doing Kafka – occurs in a volume, Frost's last, called *In the Clearing* (1962).

Often, the later Frost is a poet who writes as if he were running out of energy, looking back to his earlier work in order to mine in cold blood materials that once gave off an existential glow (whether they had actually been lived through is beside the point). The poetry of work, so richly done in "Mowing," becomes in "Two Tramps in Mud-Time" an exercise for the purpose of making the utopian point that it's better when work and play are the same activity (and when you're a famous writer, they are). Sometimes this famous Frost seems to need to measure his prowess against Eliot, as in the awesome "Directive"

(*Steeple Bush*, 1947), which gathers up elements in the poetic landscape he had been fashioning since *A Boy's Will*, as if to rewrite, in a single sweeping and triumphant gesture, both *The Waste Land* and *Four Quartets*: as if he were saying he could do it better than Eliot had – more economically, more accessibly – and with a lightness of touch beyond Eliot's ken. "Drink and be whole again beyond confusion," directs the bard in the last line, after having told us that the drinking goblet he's hidden is broken (the goblet, like the Grail, hidden in a native chapel perilous, a ruined farmhouse in an America gone urban). With that gesture, Frost plays a joke on his mythic projection as the speaker of maxims, and on anyone not used to reading him with close slowness of attention, any reader who takes Frost in once only, for the bardic impression, as if Frost were speaking to him from the platform like a media phenom.

And it is that sort of passive auditor of Frost the famous writer, precisely the sort of reader he cultivated in the press and from the platform, who will be unequipped to take in one of the most sustained and varied stretches of virtuosity in American poetry, some eight or nine poems in *A Witness Tree* (1942) that share nothing but independent brilliance, as they survey the prime topoi of modernist concern: the linguistic self-sufficiency of a love poem sustained by a single, generative conceit ("The Silken Tent"); the vicious narrative of repressed sexuality ("The Subverted Flower"); myths of origin political, religious, and aesthetic ("The Gift Outright," "Never Again Would Birds' Song Be the Same"); the epistemological priority of subjective consciousness, and the toying with such heaviness ("All Revelation," "Come In"); and the modern poet's anxious relationship to literary history ("Carpe Diem"), rendered with an ease that bespeaks little, perhaps no, anxiety.

A Boy's Will in 1913, *North of Boston* in 1914, *Mountain Interval*, his first American volume, in 1916: an illusion of creative renaissance. All of the first two and much of the third volume had in fact been written in obscurity, over the twenty-year period before he left for England. Once back home, the obligations of an emerging and seductive fame consumed him. At a time when he could have published virtually anything, anywhere he wanted, he had little to give: from 1917 through 1920, only four of his poems appeared in periodicals; his fourth volume, *New Hampshire*, came out seven years after *Mountain Interval*. In its title poem, which is also its lead-off poem, the man who had been working the circuit hard – fashioning and plying the image of himself, to the point of distraction – transmutes his labors in the disciplines of fame into poetic substance. The famous poet steps forward in full dress.

The center of interest in "New Hampshire" is a speaker who identifies himself as a writer, showing us his mind and manner (and manners) in the act of turning over Subjects of Importance, from a site of speaking, rural New England, presumed to give him a unique point of view. The binding rhetorical contract that Frost makes with his readers in the poem will guarantee that the speaker is special because he is organically connected, the authentic voice of a place whose values are different. And that difference gives the voice authority of judgment because the difference is one of superior values. And we listen because we are not where Frost is, because we are living lives we wish would be shaped by the values that shape him and his place. The contract presumes an insider and an underprivileged outsider. If we listen attentively, Frost promises to ease our deprivation. The local-color aesthetic is at the same time an ethic, and in "New Hampshire," Robert Frost – a new and important force in the literary scene – offers himself as representative and incarnation of it. To read him is to partake of him (like partaking of communion) and all he stands for.

The poem itself is all cunningly controlled ramble, full of pleasant, funny, and very chummy stretches, carried in a colloquial voice that (typical Frost) breezes through the allusion to Shelley's "Ozymandias" in its anecdotal style: "I met a lady from the South who said . . . "; "I met a traveler from Arkansas / Who boasted . . . ":

> I met a Californian who would
> Talk California – a state so blessed,
> He said, in climate, none had ever died there
> A natural death, and Vigilance Committees
> Had had to organize the graveyards
> And vindicate the state's humanity.

The point of these anecdotes is that everyone, except those who live in New Hampshire, is in the market selling or buying, and that the market is unavoidable – except, of course, in New Hampshire. Poets sell ideas; Californians, their climate. If modernist poets want to define themselves against the market, then New Hampshire, which doesn't have enough of anything to sell, is their unexpected land of heart's desire, not London or Paris (take heed, ye high modernists). The search for the sometimes guilty pleasures of the aesthetic – pleasure for its own sake – which preoccupied Frost early and late, from "Mowing" to "Two Tramps in Mud-Time" (and beyond), is here in "New Hampshire" a theme, a vantage point, a seat of judgment, that which gives structure to the rambling voice.

Having hooked us with the genial comedy of his opening sections, the poet quickly expands his aesthetic criticism of America, sparing neither New Hampshire nor himself. He offers us a mythic history of the founding whites of New Hampshire as a tale of primal imperialism. An unnamed reformer, who would reform the world in order to make it hospitable for artists, sounds suspiciously like Frost, taking a page from Pound's text while reflecting upon his recent rise in literary and economic fortune, splashing bitters into his genial style. Where was the attention when I needed it most? We need a world reformed so as to be acceptable to artists, "the minute they set up as artists, / Before, that is, they are themselves accepted . . . "

The poet who embodies the good way feels compromised. New Hampshire produces nothing in serious enough quantity and quality to have to worry the producers about disposing of the surplus – except for writing itself. The poet reveals himself a reluctant merchant, more assiduously businesslike than the genuine article:

> Do you know,
> Considering the market, there are more
> Poems produced than any other thing?
> No wonder poets sometimes have to *seem*
> So much more businesslike than businessmen.
> Their wares are so much harder to get rid of.

At the end, having declared himself to be – and having performed as – a "creature of literature" rather than of any region, Frost concludes with these self-ironic lines, which pretty much invalidate the terms of the contract he's made with us:

> I choose to be a plain New Hampshire farmer
> With an income in cash of, say, a thousand
> (From, say, a publisher in New York City) . . .
> At present I am living in Vermont.

The games Frost plays with his readers in "New Hampshire" are unsettling but benign (more or less: perhaps less than more; it's hard to tell). Later poems tell a different story. Who, for example, is Frost imagining as his ideal reader in "Neither Out Far Nor In Deep"? Not those referred to, certainly, by the first two words in the poem, and then again referred to in the third quatrain, not "the people." Not those who all "along the sand" will "look at the sea all day," and whose act of looking in this plain-styled allegory (not a word here that couldn't "easily" be grasped by "the people"), whose ability to know anything, including themselves, is coldly evaluated by Frost's title and by his fourth and final quatrain:

> They cannot look out far.
> They cannot look in deep.
> But when was that ever a bar
> To any watch they keep?

Lines to remember, wisdom spit forth (but for whom?) about "the people." Has anyone ever pronounced "they" with more deadpanned contempt? "We" who are implicitly addressed, "we" truly understand, "we" are not "they." But wasn't it precisely "they," not "we" (the "critical few who are supposed to know") whom this ordinary American, who happened to be a poet, was courting all along, who made him famous?

"Neither Out Far Nor In Deep" occurs in *A Further Range* (1936), which also contains "Provide, Provide" (among other strong performances), separated by only a few pages from "Neither Out Far Nor In Deep," this one addressed, seemingly, to "the people," a lacerating analysis of fame's basis and likely course:

> The witch that came (the withered hag)
> To wash the steps with pail and rag
> Was once the beauty Abishag,
>
> The picture pride of Hollywood.
> Too many fall from great and good
> For you to doubt the likelihood.
>
> Die early and avoid the fate.
> Or if predestined to die late
> Make up your mind to die in state.
>
> Make the whole stock exchange your own!
> If need be occupy a throne,
> Where nobody can call *you* crone.
>
> Some have relied on what they knew,
> Others on being simply true.
> What worked for them might work for you.
>
> No memory of having starred
> Atones for later disregard
> Or keeps the end from being hard.
>
> Better to go down dignified
> With boughten friendship at your side
> Than none at all. Provide, provide!

The entire tone and manner is that of the public poet speaking to his democratic culture. The diction is appropriately drawn from the accessible middle level, with the exception of "boughten," a regionalist trace of the authentic life, meaning "store-bought" as opposed to "homemade": no major problem if the subject is ice cream or bread, but with "boughten friendship" we step into an ugly world. The bardic voice speaks, but now in mock-directives ("Die early and avoid the fate," "Make the whole stock exchange your own"), counseling the value of money and power; how they command fear; how fear commands, at a minimum, a sham of decency from others (better that than the authenticity of their meanness). Genuine knowledge? Sincerity? Devices only in the Hollywood of everyday life. Try them, they might "work."

But who, really, is Frost talking to? Who is this "you"? He appears to be addressing the audience he had been reaching (for twenty years at this point) through the press and from the platform: "For you to doubt the likelihood" is a bardic reminder to the masses. "What worked for them might work for you" is cynical and contemptuous counsel offered to the same. The penultimate stanza, however, whose triplet rhyme condenses the entire poem, makes no sense in that rhetorical scheme:

> No memory of having starred
> Atones for later disregard
> Or keeps the end from being hard.

Who among the ordinary, the unassuming, the obscure from fame, has any memory of having starred, of having lost it, of having to find a way to make up for later disregard? From a rhetorical point of view, the poem becomes incoherent here, but the incoherence is interesting and, I believe, calculated: an expressive sign. We know who has this problem: Hollywood's poet, talking contemptuously to and at himself, looking down the road at a possible fate that he would not be able to say he hadn't chosen, were it to turn out to be his – because he had made the decision to commit himself to fame's course, within the cruel range of choices our culture offers to its serious writers, whose wares are so hard to unload. America's serious writers are all like the biblical Abishag, who, though young and beautiful, could not warm King David: she could not arouse him, and her trying only degraded her.

3

WALLACE STEVENS

I N between his time at Harvard (1897–1900), when he published
frequently in undergraduate magazines, and his move to Hartford,
Connecticut, in 1916, when he was beginning to appear with regularity in the newly emerging little magazines of avant-garde writing, Wallace
Stevens led a double life in New York City, with the lion's share of his waking
hours spent trying (and failing) to earn a wage good enough to enable him to
resume the comfortable upper-middle-class style he had been accustomed to
in Reading, Pennsylvania, where he grew up, and in Cambridge, where he was
supported by his father's faithful checks. In the late hours of evening during
his New York years he read and occasionally wrote verses. On weekends he
became the part-time exemplar of Teddy Roosevelt's ideal of the "strenuous
life," taking marathon walks in the country of twenty to thirty miles.

While his son was still at Harvard, Garrett Stevens – successful lawyer,
small businessman, and poet himself – had sent Wallace this letter, which
haunted the younger Stevens for the rest of his life:

Our young folk would of course prefer to be born like English noblemen with Entailed
estates, income guaranteed and in choosing a profession they would simply say – "How
shall I amuse myself" – but young America understands that the question is – "*Starting
with nothing, how shall I sustain myself and perhaps a wife and family – and send my boys
to College and live* comfortably in my old age." Young fellows must all come to that
question, for unless they inherit money, marry money, find money, steal money or
somebody presents it to them, they must *earn it* and earning it save it up for the
time of need. How best can he earn a sufficiency! What talent does he possess which
carefully nurtured will produce something which people want and therefore will pay
for. This is the whole problem! and to Know Thyself!

A few years after he received this letter, while toiling unhappily in the competitive world of New York journalism, Stevens in fact requested guaranteed
income from his father so that he might pursue another kind of career in writing, one which could not sustain himself, much less a wife, family, a college
education for his sons, and a comfortable old age. His father refused. The

son of Garrett Stevens had begun to understand, but apparently had not yet learned to live with, the primary lesson in American history that was to be his burden, as it was the burden of most of young America's males. His father was passing on the wisdom of Poor Richard and Horatio Alger that to be born an American is typically to be born without a sustaining economic past: to start with nothing, even if your father (like Garrett Stevens) has supported himself, a wife, and has sent his boys (not his daughters) to college, because such a father in achieving such accomplishments was likely to have exhausted most of what he had earned. What little he might leave would never be enough for his son to support himself, his wife, and so on. To be born an American is to be born into a situation where literary patronage virtually does not exist and where your father cannot be your patron. I have done it, Garrett Stevens was saying to his son, now prove your manhood by imitating me to the letter.

Stevens's move to New York in 1900 forced him to bear witness to the thinness of his middle-class insulation. Shortly after getting there, he entered into his journal a reflection on a Harvard graduate whom he had never met, but of whom he had heard much, one Philip Henry Savage. This journal entry echoes the Poor Richard letter his father had sent to him at Harvard, and it touches a new theme. This would-be ruggedly independent new American man would somehow, if he could, join his aesthetic sense, already heavily cultivated as a teenager and at Harvard, to what he was beginning to see as the unavoidable economic plot of his existence:

Savage was like every other able-bodied man – he wanted to stand alone. Self-dependence is the greatest thing in the world for a young man & Savage knew it. I cannot talk about the subject, however, because I know too little about it. But for one thing, Savage went into the shoe business & still kept an eye on sunsets and red-winged blackbirds – the summum bonum.

Very soon, Stevens would know much more about the subject. His New York years (1900–16) quickly became an effort to achieve Savage's sort of balance between necessity and pleasure, work and art, because that sort of contradictory balance ("the summum bonum") was the very thing that his upbringing as the son of Garrett Stevens taught him to desire. But the story of his New York years was mainly one of Stevens's failure to achieve the summum bonum, or of his success, if weekend aestheticism must suffice. The means of self-dependence were pursued Monday through Friday; things for themselves pursued and savored on Saturdays and Sundays: "I doubt if there is any keener delight in the world than, after being penned up for a week, to get into the woods . . . every pound of flesh vibrates with new strength, every nerve seems to be drinking at some refreshing spring."

One way of mitigating this solution of the "weekend" – a therapeutic as well as a temporal concept in bourgeois life – and of joining his vocation with his avocation, or so it seemed to Stevens, lay in his first choice of career in journalism, a field he tried as soon as he got to New York. The guiding principle behind his choice seems to have been: Write all the time, write sometimes because you want to, and write when you must, for a living, but write. He quickly learned, however, that the monetary rewards of journalism were erratic, the writing assignments mainly a grind, and his future as a journalist just too chancy. All of which was brought sharply into focus for him in the depressing spectacle of the funeral of a fellow journalist, who also wrote fiction that he respected. Stevens found the affair "wretched"; hardly anyone went to the church. Those in attendance were obviously lower-class. A few literary types showed up, but in appearance it was impossible to distinguish them from the nonliterary and merely poor. Stephen Crane's funeral gave him a glimpse of a possible writerly future. He entered law school.

Three years later, in August 1904, about a month after being admitted to the New York bar, he brooded in his journal on the perilous comforts of middle-class life as he had known it. Theodore Dreiser couldn't have done it better. It is a meditative moment that marks the birth of Wallace Stevens as self-conscious economic man for whom the American dream was no longer an abstraction; Wallace Stevens – real-life brother of some of the most compelling figures in modern American fiction: Carrie Meeber and G. W. Hurstwood in *Sister Carrie*, Thomas Sutpen in *Absalom, Absalom!*, Jay Gatsby. What made Stevens different and maybe more typical – neither Dreiser nor Faulkner nor Fitzgerald would tell his story – was his sense that he had been expelled from Eden, that his particular form of the American dream involved the recapturing of a lost social and economic status that he had never earned but which he had nevertheless enjoyed, the resumption of a life that had fashioned the mode of his desire and had given him a taste of the good life. Suddenly he felt a shocking solidarity with the poor, who had hitherto only repulsed him in their filth and poverty (the sight of Italian immigrants had once made it impossible for him to finish a snack of clams on the half shell); he was coming to know a new sort of closeness with those who had hitherto made him feel faintly disgusted when they sat too near him on commuter trains.

At the age of twenty-five Stevens came to the existential knowledge of economic difference and the peculiar privilege of middle-class life in America. The Italian immigrants he saw in Greenwich Village, like the bums in the Bowery he observed on his walks through the city, might dream the dream of upward mobility: they could sink no lower economically. The fabulously wealthy of his time, legends even then – the Carnegies, Mellons, Rockefellers, the class Fitzgerald called, simply, "the very rich" – could pass out dimes in the streets if they liked (and they did). Their children, whatever spiritual descents they might experience, could look with impunity upon the poor: they would never be one of them. But Stevens, and those like him, knew better than to dream the dream of upward mobility. Passage into the realm of the Rockefellers was not realistic; a repetition of one's father's economic status was more likely, and it was clearly preferable over that other possibility which is the special privilege of the middle class: the possibility of economic descent. The dream of the middle class in America is the nightmare of downward mobility: Stevens's version of the nightmare concluded with an effort to resist it, with what in his writing is an almost never expressed impulse, the utopian urge toward classless society: "There was a time when I walked downtown in the morning almost oblivious of the thousands and thousands of people I passed; now I look at them with extraordinary interest as companions in the same fight that I am about to join."

For this middle-class professional, endowed with capitalist values through his father, in part against his literary desires, the inescapable question pressed upon him first by family and then by his New York experience was: How can I turn some part of myself (my "talent") into a commodity that people will want and "therefore pay for"? The choice of profession need not "amuse," it need not give pleasure, but (as Father said) it must pay. To Know Thyself, according to Garrett Stevens, is to know yourself as economic man, fit for the hurly-burly of the marketplace where the big boys slug it out. To Know Thyself for Garrett Stevens's son meant that in finding his productive talent he would prove his masculinity in general and prove it in particular as equal to his father's. But knowing himself also meant knowing that he derived pleasure from his verse-writing talent, and to know himself that way as a young man meant to know himself as the potential subverter of his official role as a young American male. Only leisured women and leisured men could do what he wanted to do. Modernist poetics in the United States began with the great problem of the bourgeois world: the antagonism between duty and happiness. Modernist poetics in the United States is sexually and economically framed (in both senses) from the beginning.

Garrett Stevens was by most standards an unsuccessful poet, and in the end his failure in business was so disastrous – he went bankrupt – that his son had no choice but to stand on his own. His son's life and career as poet and superb man of business were therefore at once an imitation and stunning transcendence of the father. A brilliant success in two areas (he rose to the vice presidency of a major insurance company), Stevens, with his bifurcated career, was the perfect realization of the contradictory values of his society.

In the period between Harvard and his appearances in the little magazines fell his courtship of Elsie Moll. It went on for about five years, because Stevens was not about to be married until he felt himself economically secure as his father had defined economic security for him. Part of his courting of Elsie Moll involved sharing with her his passion for poetry. In a letter written to her about a year and a half before the appearance of "Sunday Morning" (his famous early poem), and with a deceptively light tone, Stevens touched upon an issue central to the course of modernism in the United States:

I sit at home o'nights. But I read very little. I have, in fact, been trying to get together a little collection of verses again; and although they are simple to read, when they're done, it's a deuce of a job (for me) to do them. Keep all this a great secret. There is something absurd about all this writing of verses; but the truth is, it elates and satisfies me to do it. It is an all-round exercise quite superior to ordinary reading. So that, you see, my habits are positively lady-like.

Stevens's designation of verse writing as "positively lady-like" feminizes in the direction of the leisured class, and, in spite of the effort, which marks many of his letters to Elsie, to fend off issues of gender, vocation, and money with flippancy of tone, Stevens registers and unmasks, against his desire, what proved to be the unmasterable situation that he would prefer to submerge in "the gaiety of language," which is supposed to, but cannot, redeem his social *malheur*. His "absurd" habit of verse writing embodies this unavoidable contradiction of his culture: as it brings forth feelings of pleasure ("it elates and satisfies me to do it"), while engaging him in the sort of exertion synonymous with work ("a deuce of a job"), it triggers at the very moment of pleasure the negative judgment of his superego, because this job can bring no economic support, cannot earn the characterization "work" – hence is really no job at all. His "absurd" habit of verse writing forces upon him a feeling at odds with his maleness – the feeling of the sexual other within, in the mask of poetic culture: the lady poet. So when we ask, just who is this "me" made happy by verse writing, the implicit cultural logic of his letter to Elsie makes us answer that Stevens's "me" is in some fundamental sense a ladylike, economically unproductive "she."

It is a figure with which Stevens will enter into troubled dialogue to the end of his career, and which appeared early on in his first major poetic success:

> Complacencies of the peignoir,
> And late coffee and oranges in a sunny chair
> And the green freedom of a cockatoo
> Upon a rug . . .

The "she" of the opening lines of "Sunday Morning" is represented as a comfortable woman of class, whose expensive and leisured femaleness Stevens insists upon: By their peignoirs ye shall know them. In its atmospherics and in its ideas, "Sunday Morning" appears to be a conventional poem, very much of its intellectual period: a late-nineteenth-century set piece on behalf of the religion of art that happened to be written in New York City in 1914 and published a year later in Harriet Monroe's *Poetry*.

"All New York, as I have seen it, is for sale – and I think the parts I have seen are the parts that make New York what it is." Stevens wrote that in a depressed mood shortly after moving from Cambridge. He found everyday life in New York an exhibition of consumer capitalism, a frustrating spectacle, surreal and narcissistic, with "Everybody . . . looking at everybody else – a foolish crowd walking on mirrors." In this setting, all commodities become promises of romance, whispers of fulfillment quite beyond the explicit use of commodities: vehicles of an imagined entrance into an existence (with ourselves as heroes and heroines) definitively more pleasurable than one's own, and available for a price. The world of New York, a "field of tireless and antagonistic interests," is the ultimate marketplace: Stevens called it "fascinating but horribly unreal" – he meant "unfortunately real" because so destructively tempting. Nature is sometimes exempted from this economy of desire, but only because (he notes sardonically) winds and clouds are not "generated in Yorkville" or "manufactured in Harlem."

"Sunday Morning" came at the end of almost fourteen years of mostly unhappy New York life. We cannot locate the elegant interior and woman of "Sunday Morning" there, but we can place Stevens in New York, in shabby elegance, inside a room of his own. The interior decoration in Stevens's apartment bore pictures of what he thought "most real" and (in the heart of the city) out of reach.

The carpet on the floor of my room is grey set off with pink roses. In the bathroom is a rug with the figure of a peacock woven into it – blue and scarlet, and black, and green, and gold. And on the paper on my wall are designs of fleur-de-lis and forget-me-not. Flowers and birds enough of rags and paper – but no more. In this Eden, made spicy with the smoke of my pipe which hangs heavy in the ceiling, in this Paradise ringing with the bells of streetcars and the bustle of fellow boarders heard through the thin partitions, in this Elysium of Elysiums I now shall lay me down.

The contentment and control Stevens communicates in this journal entry about his protected little apartment veils his feeling of being out of place in a world he can't help but encounter daily on the streets of New York. The world of aesthetic enjoyment, often identified in his journals with experiences of art exhibits and nature – not nature in a vacuum, but nature as a motivated negation of New York: what he walked away from on weekends – this aesthetic world of the weekend is not enough in itself to alleviate the dissatisfaction he felt throughout the workweek. His radical desire was for the aesthetic Monday through Friday, and he got it at night in the privacy of his apartment, in the middle of the city, where decor and furnishings appeared to be freed from the "field of tireless and antagonistic interests." Commodities like rugs and wallpaper, so cherished, are the image of heaven – Stevens called it Eden – and their delights are even more keenly felt thanks to the thinness of partitions that do not block out the sounds of the city.

In Stevens's early letters and journals we are taken into the social kitchen of his poetics, where Ezra Pound's modernist shibboleth "make it new" becomes "make it private": the aesthetic as a lyric process of moving toward the interior, from the real space of the streets of New York to the private space of his room, and then into the psychic space of consciousness (now perilously sealed to the outside); lyric aesthesis, the formation of sensuous impression, as the repression of the seedier side of New York – a process that first transforms the bums in Washington Square into "crows in rainy weather" before taking the final leap into subjective freedom – the atmosphere of an impressionist painting, color abstracted from all objects:

The other morning as I came home I walked up to Washington Square to take a look at the trees ... I was surprised to find the large number of people who were sleeping on the grass and on the benches. One or two of them with collars turned up & hands in their pockets shuffled off through the sulphurous air like crows in rainy weather. The rest lay about in various states of collapse. There must have been a good many aching bones when the sun rose. The light was thin and bluishly misty; by the time I was in my room it had become more intense & was like a veil of thin gold.

In light of the vocational anxieties Stevens experienced in New York, the journal passage on the rug with the peacock woven into it and the opening lines of "Sunday Morning," placed side by side, unveil a decisive scene for modern American poetry: the author imagining himself as sexual as well as economic transvestite: a liberating impulse that he feels (the impulse, as he wrote in his journal, to be "all dream") but that his male obligations tell him he must not choose. The apocalyptic seventh section of "Sunday Morning" returns us to the world, now phallically renewed:

> Supple and turbulent, a ring of men
> Shall chant in orgy on a summer morn
> Their boisterous devotion to the sun,
> Not as a god, but as a god might be,
> Naked among them, like a savage source.

> Their chant shall be a chant of paradise,
> Out of their blood, returning to the sky;
> And in their chant shall enter, voice by voice,
> The windy lake wherein their lord delights,
> The trees, like serafin, and echoing hills,
> That choir among themselves long afterward.

As a vision of the future this passage is absurd, but Stevens's absurdity is important because it joins mainline American literary visions of male utopias, realms of delicious irresponsibility: certain raft passages in *Huckleberry Finn*, the "Squeeze of the Hand" chapter in *Moby-Dick*, Rip Van Winkle's fantasy in the Catskills of men at play, many things in Whitman and, more recently, the Brooks Range conclusion of Norman Mailer's *Why Are We in Vietnam?* What Stevens imagines for the social future is a place without women; men who work, but whose work cannot be distinguished from homoerotic pleasure; men who work nakedly – and in their nakedness bear no signs, as the peignoired woman bears signs, of social difference. Their nakedness and their arrangement in a ring speak the classless language of fraternity (brothers, but no sisters) and equality. And they chant: collectively they create a fundamental poetry – a devotion to a "lordly" nature that is spun out in the sentimentality of choiring angels, a metaphor wrested from traditional Christianity and transvalued with outrageous deliberation into the music of pagan naturalism. The contradictions of Stevens's early life and poetry are fused in an image of masculine power: Father Nature.

In his Harvard journal Stevens makes this incisive remark, whose immediate target might appear to be then-popular women poets like Frances Osgood and Lydia Sigourney, but whose true object is genteel culture in America: "Poetry and Manhood: those who say poetry is now the peculiar province of women say so because ideas about poetry are effeminate. Homer, Dante, Shakespeare, Milton, Keats, Browning, much of Tennyson – they are your man-poets. Silly verse is always the work of silly men." Yet the power of those silly men to affect the cultural conscience of their time might be measured precisely there, with Stevens saying, in so many words, that he knew better, and yet while knowing better nevertheless played out his literary youth as if he feared that he just might be one of those silly men who would be denied poetic manhood.

As a student at Harvard, Stevens (in a thickening fin-de-siècle atmosphere) came to despise aestheticist theory – "the sensuous for the sake of sensuousness" – which he deemed "the most arrant as it is the most inexcusable rubbish." "Art," he argued, "must fit with other things; it must be part of the system of the world. And if it finds a place in that system it will likewise find a ministry and relations that are its proper adjuncts." Stevens also learned to distrust overtly moralizing art. He recoiled from Bryant and the Fireside group because, as he put it, the "New England school of poets were too hard thinkers. For them there was no pathos in the rose except as it went to point a moral or adorn a tale. I like my philosophy smothered in beauty and not the opposite." Yet philosophy smothered in beauty is philosophy nevertheless; a discipline with which Stevens, and a surprising handful of other now-famous modernists, had a significant and historically propitious relationship.

When George Santayana was appointed to the philosophy department at Harvard in 1889, just a year after finishing his doctorate there, he became the junior colleague of William James and Josiah Royce, and the three together, over the next two decades – in relationships supportive, competitive, and critical – collectively defined the shapes and limitations of what would come to be understood as modernism in the United States: its desires and values, its literary, social, and philosophical genesis and ground, and the sometimes stinging antithetical force of its cultural and social commentary. Stevens, Frost, and E. A. Robinson were all "special" (non-degree candidate) students at Harvard in the period in question: Robinson from 1891 to 1893, Frost from 1897 to 1899, Stevens from 1897 to 1900. Eliot, from 1906 to 1914, was the genuine article at Harvard, taking a B.A. in 1910, an M.A. in 1911, and doing advanced work for the Ph.D. in languages and philosophy before settling in London in 1914, dissertation completed but, by choice, no Ph.D. in hand. So the apprenticeship of what we know as modern American poetry coincides with the big bang of modernist American philosophy. And the site of emerging modernist poetic idioms and of an authoritative philosophical discourse was Cambridge, Massachusetts, at the turn of the twentieth century. Both in personal ways and in the prescribed academic fashion, Robinson, Frost, Stevens, Eliot, and Radcliffe's modernist, Gertrude Stein, encountered the Harvard philosophers. In the conventional sense of what we mean by the terms, these philosophers were "influences" and "sources."

Stevens knew Santayana personally, read and was moved to a lifetime of meditation by his *Interpretations of Poetry and Religion*, and evoked him in the moving late poem "To an Old Philosopher in Rome." Stevens celebrated Santayana for his consistent elegance of irony that found the real inadequate to our needs but still the constant and necessary corrector and deflator of our visionary projections. Yet, of the Harvard philosophers, it is not Santayana but James to whom Stevens's poetics owes the greatest debt (if in ways sometimes antithetical). To James, Santayana was a moribund Latin, rotten to the core, because, unable any longer to believe that there was an eternal morphology of the real, he cultivated *fictions* of eternal morphology – a position that Stevens grappled with his whole career and to which he assented both aphoristically in "Adagia" and apocryphally in his deathbed Catholic conversion. James, for whom the metaphysical argument over structure was intellectually and existentially empty, saw such structure in pragmatic light as political instrument and force: "The bigger the unit you deal with, the hollower, the more brutal, the more mendacious is the life displayed. So I am against all big organizations as such, national ones first and foremost . . . System, as such, does violence whenever it lays its hands upon us."

In James, modernism was born in America as an anti-imperialist project. His pragmatist vision is irreducibly a vision of heterogeneity and contentiousness – a vision strong for criticism, self-scrutiny, and self-revision that never claims knowledge of a monolithic human narrative because it refuses belief in such narrative and the often repressive political conduct resulting from such belief. The lectures James delivered in Boston and New York in late 1906 and early 1907, and then shortly after published as the book *Pragmatism*, bear the mark of a decisive moment in United States history: our first fully launched imperialist adventure, in the last years of the nineteenth century, in Cuba and the Philippines.

Against the immediate background of Twain's and Howells's inspiring example, James became the first in a hidden history of oddly connected refusers of imperialism. The second was Wallace Stevens, in his 1919 "Anecdote of the Jar" as read by a third, Michael Herr, in his 1970 book on Vietnam, *Dispatches*, in which the entire focus of American military power concentrated in the fortification of Khe Sanh was evoked by his citation of Stevens's poem. Stevens is made by Herr to speak directly against the ideology of imposition and obliteration coactive in Vietnam with a strategy of defoliation. The textual expression of that strategy is the literal remapping of a country – "the military expediency," in Herr's ironic reflection on the sometimes deadly relations of sign and referent, "to impose a new set of references over Vietnam's truer, older being, an imposition that began most simply with the division of one country into two and continued . . . with the further division of South Vietnam into four clearly defined tactical corps." Herr concludes by glossing Khe Sanh via the imaginative imperialism that was activated and subtly evaluated in "Anecdote of the Jar": "Once it was all locked in place, Khe Sanh became like the planted jar in Wallace Stevens's poem. It took dominion everywhere."

James had written his own anecdote of the jar in the opening lecture of *Pragmatism*:

The world of concrete personal experiences to which the street belongs is multitudinous beyond imagination, tangled, muddy, painful and perplexed. The world to which your philosophy professor introduces you is simple, clean and noble. The contradictions of real life are absent from it, its architecture is classic. Principles of reason trace its outlines, logical necessities cement its parts. Purity and dignity are what it most expresses. It is a kind of marble temple shining on a hill.

Philosophy so conceived, James says, is not, despite its claim, an "account of this actual world." It is an "addition built upon it": a "sanctuary," a "refuge," a "substitute," a "way of escape," a "monument of artificiality" – all negative qualities, of course, and quite harmless, until we add one other characteristic which gives ominous point to all the others – James's shining marble temple of philosophy, like Stevens's jar of imagination, like Khe Sanh, is also a "remedy."

In this dismantling of the classic project of reason, what James wishes to show is that the product of rationalist method is not cool, contemplative representation – "theory" above the battle: it is *purity in action*. The shining marble temple is "round upon the ground"; it does not give "of bird or bush." Like the defoliating jar in Stevens's Tennessee, classical reason (the desire for theory) becomes, under James's corrosive scrutiny, a "powerful ... appetite of the mind," the need for a "refined object." Reason as theory-desire, the desire for refinement, gets expressed as the *will to refine*: a chilling process when considered in the political contexts within which James writes. In an eerie foreshadowing of both Stevens's poem and Herr's Khe Sanh as the "planted jar," James evokes his sense of the perversity of the American presence in the Philippines by describing it as an effort to "plant our order." Stevens, against an often expressed desire, knows such presence is a threat to reality and the self, knows early in his "Anecdote" and late in his *Notes*, when, moving toward a Supreme Fiction, he stops to warn himself not to "impose," but to "discover." He says (he hopes, he urges) it must be possible.

In 1941, in a lecture Stevens gave at Princeton, called "The Noble Rider and the Sound of Words," when he was well beyond what his earliest reviewers took to be – not without the poet's partial assent – the self-conscious and insouciant aesthetic experimentation of his early period, in a surprisingly blunt passage on the meaning of one of his key words, he defined the genteel social base from which his avant-garde sensibility had improbably emerged and the social change – so traumatic to genteel culture – to which the styles of his first book, *Harmonium* (1923), were caustic, comedic, elegiac, and verbally prodigal responses. The key word is "reality"; it peppers his essays, letters, and poems as some ultimate ontological portent, and it is constantly coordinated with two other major obsessive terms, "imagination," Stevens's inherited word of high romantic desire, and "transparency," this latter bearing his American intellectual and social past.

In a striking passage from Emerson's "Nature" (1836), notorious even in its own day – that of the transparent eyeball – the eye pure and unmediated itself becomes a medium. In moments of transparency, Emerson says, "standing on the bare ground," his head "bathed by the blithe air and uplifted into infinite space," he becomes "part or parcel of God." Stevens's terms are antitranscendental and naturalistic, atheistic and aestheticist; but with Emerson he tends to believe that these moments of vitality cannot happen in the streets of our cities, and that when they do happen, our fundamental social relations, even those obviously hinged on power, are made meaningless. Emerson again: "The name of the nearest friend sounds then foreign and accidental: to be brothers, to be acquaintances, master or servant, is then a trifle and a disturbance." Such moments of the "real" are urgent and final because they are presumably uncapturable by history's various forms of social gravity. In these moments we are most ourselves, wonderfully alone, cut loose from tradition and community.

That most surprising passage on the "real" in Stevens's Princeton lecture makes reference, however, not to nature but to history and society as twin forces of gravity, powers of determination which are almost irresistible and which the poet's imagination does not cherish. The social real, which rarely makes center-stage appearances in Stevens, is revealed in his Princeton lecture as the repressed monster, the unsuccessfully negated condition of his being – this "real," Stevens's most haunted word, is given, in the lecture, the most precise historical boundaries. There is the "reality," he says, that is "taken for granted"; it is "latent and, on the whole, ignored." This reality "is the comfortable American state of life in the eighties, the nineties, and the first ten years of the present century," a period that pretty much coincides with the first thirty years of his life, a period – though he doesn't say so in his essay – in which he lived unreflectively in comfort given and protected by his mother and father, and when he could with impunity take life for granted, until he left Harvard and went to New York to live on his own, cut loose for good (but not without regret) from his father's economic support. At which time "reality" changed for him personally (and painfully) and personal change triggered new social vision. "The Victorians had been disposed of," he says, "and the intellectual and social minorities began to take their place and to convert our state of life to something that might not be final."

At the actual moment when Stevens came to know this social change in an existentially pressing way – some thirty-five years before he composed the Princeton lecture – he had seen himself suddenly cast out among New York's unprivileged, exiled from comfort, and forced to worry (somehow unfairly) about economic survival, even though he was graced with an educated sensibility, a predilection for reading, writing, and the things (elegant paintings, gourmet food, oriental rugs) that the working-class types he feared might be his new mirrors could never claim for their own interests or talents. At the actual moment when he was learning that the state of existence, and innocence, that his father had maintained for him was not final, that there was a life outside "the comfortable American state" being lived by millions who did not share "our state of life" – who could take little for granted – at the actual moment when he was learning that he might have to become one of them, at this moment of class-consciousness, his ethnic consciousness was rudely awakened by what he saw on his frequent walks through Greenwich Village and the Lower East Side, the radical demographic change whose impact would upset America for good, the flooding mass of new immigrants.

This new reality, at once economically and ethnically disturbing, Stevens calls in the Princeton lecture "tense" and describes as "instinct with the fatal or with what might be the fatal." In this new reality, a "possible poet" must set aside his romantic imagination of sympathy and in its place put an imagination capable of "resisting or evading," but without illusion, because tomorrow's reality might be even deadlier for those like himself whose existence had been put in jeopardy by these new Americans. By "possible poet" he means a poet like himself, who might have gone to Princeton or Harvard in the days when only the blue eyes went to those schools: working-class and immigrant poets of the early twentieth century in fact wrote sympathetically of the new Americans; evading them was not part of their aesthetic or social agendas. Stevens's Princeton audience would not likely have questioned the clubby rhetoric of "our state of life"; his Princeton audience would not have found his rhetoric xenophobic: "The minorities began to convince us," he says, "that the Victorians had left nothing behind." Stevens's "possible poet" must hear this futile injunction: resist if you can, but probably you can't, this distasteful new world; try to remember the world you loved and that has been replaced, and that through the lens of your nostalgia begins to "look like a volume of Ackerman's colored plates or one of Topfer's books of sketches in Switzerland" – remote and irretrievable for those who had lost it, who had found it so comfortable, and who used to take it for granted as the way things would always be.

The social and cultural change Stevens lamented late in his career in his Princeton lecture he also lamented very early when still a Harvard dandy and publishing in the *Advocate* a poem he called "Ballade of the Pink Parasol," which mirrors an aestheticist vogue for Villon ("where are the snows of yester-year?" in Rossetti's translation) with questions that mourn half-playfully, with decided triviality, the passing not of natural but of social time: "where is the old-time wig?" "the lofty hat?" "the old calash, the light sedan?" "the coat of yellow and tan"?

> ... these baubles are far away,
> In the ruin of palace and hall,
> Made dark by the shadows of yesterday –
> But where is the pink parasol?

The lament is mostly light-toned, a little gaudy in rhetoric in Stevens's early manner, and half-ironic (half-irony being the master timbre of his voice, early and late), and yet – this, too, a mark of the early manner – it is a genuine lament, only half-ironic and surprisingly poignant in that unlikeliest of refrains, "where is the pink parasol?" The parasol: the apt, quintessential figure for a departed aristocratic context, a shield against the sun which keeps white ladies' complexions free of those darker tones that used to tell the tale of class difference.

In his Princeton lecture, the problem is not the absence of an aristocracy, which Stevens, like other American writers, could not have known, but the "expansion" of the middle class in the twentieth century, with its little bit of learning, thanks to mass education, with its "ideas," thanks to "liberal thinkers," and with "its realistic satisfactions," by which he means its mass-produced way of life. The realistic satisfactions of the middle class involve, not only its appetite for realist fiction and art, but also its vast apartment-house complexes and its kind of food (no doubt from the A&P, Stevens noted). "We no longer live in homes but in housing projects ... We are intimate with people we have never seen and, unhappily, they are intimate with us." In other words, by "realistic satisfactions" Stevens intends something like "commodity culture." His taste for gourmet food, the search thereof being one of the reasons for his frequent New York excursions from Hartford, and a recurrent theme in his letters; his pursuit of avant-garde paintings from France and the precious handcrafted artifact from far-flung places on the globe; his desire for the unique thing to be cherished for itself, are all indications of a sensibility in revolt against the middle class and its satisfactions and the mass culture of capitalism that ministered to those satisfactions.

Stevens's avant-garde sensibility was doubly engendered: on the one hand by the demographic change propelled by the massive influx of the new minorities, and on the other by the power of mass culture to dominate everyday life at the material level to such an extent that it was difficult for those like Stevens, who wanted to, to avoid its affective impact. The distinctive, the one-of-a-kind, where are they gone if not with the old-time wigs and pink parasols to their proper places in museums? Living in a world of repetitions (whether in groceries, popular genre fiction, or apartments: "the ennui of apartments," as he phrased it in *Notes toward a Supreme Fiction*) had the effect of withering Stevens's aesthetic sensibility, which inclined him to want precisely that rare thing which his commodity culture by intention does not produce. In a late metapoem, he wrote that the motive for metaphor is the exhilaration of change that verbal figuration introduces into consciousness: verbal surprises are experiential surprises. It is also the motive for money. Stevens's supreme fantasy was an aesthete's utopia and an interior decorator's dream: to have so much cash that he could completely renovate his home every autumn. For those who have it, monetary wealth, like verbal wealth, also produces experiential change, the new, the exhilaration that gives life to the life that wanes and dulls.

So the search for originality in poetic and life styles is a search for the pleasure of the original, a pleasure sought in reaction to a culture of numbing sameness. Everyday life in the culture of the commodity represented nothing less than a phenomenological police state from which his lyric muse, his Ariel, would rescue him, or so he hoped. He would go to a watercolor show and see "the same old grind of waves and moonlight and trees and sunlight and so on." He would walk up Sixth Avenue after dinner looking in the store windows and see "millinery, postal-cards, shoes and so on." Back in those leaner days in New York, he took "shabby tea" (Stevens knew his teas), ate corned beef, dry biscuits, and chopped pineapple. From this, the prison house of "and so on" – "and so on" is a verbal tic in his letters which registers his feelings of perceptual and emotional death, the boredom of *la vie quotidienne*, the social texture which threatens his sensibility and drives it in an aestheticist direction – from this social nightmare he is pressed (of course) into his nature walks. But once there, with a sensibility already hammered by repetition, the sentimental pleasures of pastoral landscape are not to be found. There is no nature except what is shaped by a social experience that makes nature over into just another boring arena of "and so on": "the truth is . . . that it is chiefly the surprise of blossoms I like," meaning not the blossoms themselves. "After I have seen them for a week (this is great scandal) I am ready for the leaves that come after them," meaning not the leaves themselves but the change from blossoms; he takes some complacent pleasure in his unconventional view, but not before trying to cover up another truth: that he had gone to the country precisely to find what his conventional expectation had longed for, a change of scene.

Nature walks, like those on Sixth Avenue, are a bore, because walks in the woods and walks on Sixth Avenue are alarmingly similar – and a walk through conventional literature will give no relief. What is wanted is the "quick" and the "unaccountable," the true means of escape from all manner of police (economic, literary, and natural) and their prison houses of replication. What is wanted is a radical deviancy of experience that only literature in its most committed avant-garde form can provide: a radical deviancy whose home must be "literary" because Stevens, with his social experience, could not imagine (hope) that it could be "social" or "natural."

Stevens's rejoinders to the various kinds of police may take the form in *Harmonium* of "The Snow Man," a moving, plain-dictioned search for an impossibly pure plainness of vision: a desire for unmediated vision, a seeing for the first time, put in the appropriate form of the infinitive ("to regard," "to behold"), verbal form of desire itself; or it may take the form, in "Disillusionment of Ten O'Clock," of a sympathetic satire on middle-class life, sadly colorless (literally so), undecorated by distinctive sartorial imagination, and therefore (an aesthete's logic) utterly without joy; or it may take the form of the life-affirming directive for a funeral, "The Emperor of Ice Cream," a poem which bares the driving fear of Stevens's aestheticist urge for sensuous experience and for gaiety of language and dress: death itself; or it may take the form of playfully analytical metapoems like "Metaphors of a Magnifico," which imply the story of the epistemological and ethical necessity of the image (they are inseparable), of the need for the perceptual clarity and individuality of the image freed of all habitual thought, even reason itself: "On the image of what we see," he wrote in *Notes toward a Supreme Fiction*, "to catch from that / irrational moment its unreasoning"; or it may take the form of bawdy critiques of middle-class Christian piety in "A High-Toned Old Christian Woman," "The Plot Against the Giant," and the poem about Saint Ursula and the virgins – all outrageous sexualizations of Christianity.

The forms and styles of counterstatement in *Harmonium*, though not literally numberless, give the impression of a writer capable of endless inventive reactions, willing to try anything to ward off the torpor of repetition that his culture imposed. And should that effort take the form of too much seriousness, waxing pompous, then he will turn on himself: "Hi! the creator too is blind." But all of these maneuvers, in the end, are haunted by what Santayana said of Emerson, a writer who, though he could not retail the genteel tradition, had really nothing to put in its place, a writer of interiority, finally, and of inner play, attempting to digest vacancy. Stevens knew the individualistic pleasures of merely circulating in his interior world, but he also knew that the life of the mind of a modern poet, a "disbeliever in reality" who assiduously courts the unrealistic literary satisfactions of avant-garde alienation, may be the "skeleton's life," or so he feared in the late poem "As You Leave the Room" (1954).

In (for him) a remarkably direct apostrophe to his lyric muse, "O Florida, Venereal Soil," he left us a record of his response to what Emerson in his journal had called "the black eyes and the black drop" (*drop* in this context is horticultural, meaning "fallen fruit"; *black drop*: "rotten fallen fruit"). What drove Stevens inward, in his characteristic lyric direction as a disbeliever in "reality" who desires to free himself from the social impediments of his lyricism, he tells us, with no punches pulled, is the "dreadful sundry of this world," the social minorities he would allude to in his Princeton lecture some twenty years later:

> The Cuban, Polodowsky,
> The Mexican women,
> The negro undertaker
> Killing the time between corpses
> Fishing for crayfish

Unusual for its bluntness of revulsion from non-Anglo America, this apostrophe to Florida, site of his winter vacations, is as typical of Stevens's literary posture as anything he would write, early or late, with its lush diction and sensuous atmosphere marking it as a poem of his early career, and with its cerebral, metapoetic quality pointing to where Stevens would later go as a writer for whom lyricism was essentially problematic, less a poetic mode than an object of agonized reflection and quest: a writer whose lyricism consists in the desire for a lyrical purity of feeling untouched and untouchable by social context, a writer whose place is at the painful brink of a consummation impossible to consummate.

Florida is "venereal," under the sign of Venus: stock lyric subject and inspiration. Florida – site of potential erotic relation of poet and landscape – is the muse of modernist aesthesis: sensuous experience of "things for themselves," approached in a lover's mood, with no ulterior motive, and preserved in crystalline freshness by what T. E. Hulme and Ezra Pound were polemicizing as the "image." But Florida's social "black drop" breaks into the poem, as if from outside, with disjunctive effect, as some hostile force, as the disease of love, "venereal" in the other sense, an effect of invasion Stevens achieves by giving these "dreadful sundry" no proper grammatical habitat. They come in the form of a sentence fragment and an aside, a parenthetical moment indecorously forced upon him, a diversion of the poem's proper lyric course, rendering him incapable of the kind of consciousness that can attend to a thing for itself: as if lyric aesthesis, the object of Stevens's love, had met its ultimate match in Florida's minorities, spoilers of his holiday mood, as if the mere presence of the minorities makes lyric (holiday of the spirit) impossible, as if they heralded, these venereal mediums, the death of poetry.

The minorities will become sources of "character" in the realist fiction that Stevens alluded to so condescendingly in his Princeton lecture ("the realist satisfactions" of the middle class); they will offer the realists new subjects of vernacular speech; they will give blue-eyed America strange new cultures. In short, the minorities will provide a motive for Stevens's avant-garde imagination, because with their realist needs they will propel an ever-expanding market for realism. In Stevens's youth, lyric was the prized and imperiled (prized because imperiled) genre of genteel literary America, then under pressure from realist fiction, genre of the vernacular. Lyric utterance – a writing that would be historically free and socially uncontaminated – in Stevens and the genteel tradition of which he is reluctant and culminating heir, stands in specific combat with the minorities and their culturally rooted vernacular. With erotic urgency Stevens writes:

> Swiftly in the nights
> In the porches of Key West,
> Behind the bougainvilleas,
> After the guitar is asleep,
> Lasciviously as the wind,
> You come tormenting,
> Insatiable . . .

Underneath the romantic conventions newly pressured by his social scene speaks the poet who is driven by a longing that cannot be satisfied by his lyric muse's splendid social indifference ("You might sit, / A scholar of darkness, / Sequestered over the sea"). Stevens, a tormented lyricist, sporting an erotics of diction no genteel poet could abide, could not hide the causes of his unhappiness. He desired either full aesthesis or full banishment of his lyric muse ("Conceal yourself or disclose / Fewest things to the lover"), was granted neither, and in this tension made in *Harmonium* a modern lyric poetry out of genteel crisis, a sexy lyricism resonant with trouble, that could not successfully suppress the lost social ground of its emergence and its despair of social relation in America.

Probably no subject is more conventionally dear to the aesthete than death, since death is the antithetical instigator of various aestheticist pursuits of pleasure. In *Harmonium*, Stevens tapped the convention with dazzling virtuosity in the improvisational poetry of "Thirteen Ways of Looking at a Blackbird," where various styles of perspective and experiment are trailed, and scarily organized, by the blackbird, at first appearance a mere literary prop, but by the poem's end a menacing and insidiously omnipresent final fact. Social death in the Princeton lecture (the new social reality is "instinct with the fatal") and existential death in the blackbird poem blend, in the Florida poem, in a single, punning image: "The negro undertaker / Killing the time between corpses."

The myth that Stevens promoted about himself in letters to friendly critics seeking help with his difficult poetry is that he actually grew up as he grew

older, and that the proof of his maturity lies in his later long poems, where
he at last achieved the requisite (churchly) tone of high seriousness and important human reference. That myth of personal growth is important because
it is strongly echoed in a wider cultural dimension in the self-reflexive song
of canonical modernism, in the full terror that modernists feel for what they
fear is their own social irrelevance. Beginning with aestheticist principles,
modernists ask – with an art that presumably turns its back on the world,
turns inward to sensation and impression, as Pater urged – how can we put
art back in, give it connection, power, or, in Stevens's words, "a ministry in
the world"? Georg Lukács's storied excoriation of the subjective and plotless qualities of high modernist literature is perfectly just, as far as it goes.
What it leaves out is one of the most interesting things about high modernists: their discomfort with what they suspect is their own self-trivializing
ahistoricism.

Reviewers of Stevens's first volume said over and over again that he was
a precious aesthete – that he had nothing to say and, worse, that his poems
were, on principle, mindless: maybe gemlike, but also without point. These
negative assessments bothered Stevens but not for the usual reasons. The fact
is he had heard it all before. His reviewers had only uttered publicly what
he was telling his friends in letters during the months when he was deciding
on the contents of *Harmonium*. He was saying, in those self-conscious days,
that his poems were "horrid cocoons from which later abortive insects had
sprung," that they were "witherlings," "debilitated." At best, "preliminary
minutiae"; at worst, "garbage" from which no "crisp salad" could be picked.
Stevens, at forty-four, would not be one of those writers who could gather
sustenance by reading over his old works. He was one of those modernists
who suffered from a severe originality neurosis whose sources were equally
literary, social, and economic, and whose obsessive force was determined by
equally decisive experiences of the literary avant-garde and the moneyed edge
of consumer capitalism.

As his master category of value, originality simply made nonsense of the
conventional modernist opposition of aesthetics and economics, because it not
only prized the new as the different, the rare, and the strange, but could and
did find triggering releases of pleasure equally in original poems and exotic
fruits. Stevens was one of those writers who find their old things just old – and
psychically unprofitable to reencounter. And given the significant social role
he had imagined and would imagine for poetry from his Harvard years on to
the end of his life, his judgment upon what he had actually managed to produce from his late twenties through his early forties must have been difficult to
take. But even as he condemned himself, he was allowing himself the hopeful

fiction of organic growth. He might be looking at abortions, but he could imagine and believe in the possibility of full-term birth and teleological perfection, both for himself and for his poetic project – a distinction which became harder and harder to make as he absorbed the failure of his marriage to Elsie Moll.

Stevens's beginning as an aesthete, if only a beginning, in the delights of pure perception and linguistic riot was yet the right sort of beginning. The aesthetic was an isolated moment, withdrawn from the social mess and forever free from didactic and political translation. As he grew older and more critical of the modernism he partly endorsed, he began to believe that if the autonomous aesthetic moment was to become the urgent and compelling moment he always felt it inherently to be, then it would somehow have to carry its purity beyond itself, back into the social mess, to his rhetorical target: those culturally and economically privileged readers who, like himself, needed to transform the basic joyless conditions of their existence. "It Must Give Pleasure" is the title of the final section of *Notes toward a Supreme Fiction*. It must give pleasure because little else does. He declared, in a characteristic moment in the essays he wrote in the later years of his career, that poetry helps us to live our lives, and lucky for us that it does – we get so little help from any place else. He once told his wife that the nine-to-five working-day Wallace was nothing – the sources of his authentic selfhood were at home, quite literally: the site of his marriage and (for this aesthetic burgher) the site of poetic activity. But when love and marriage parted, his writing became the final source of selfhood: his last resort. The fate of his poetic project turned out to be indistinguishable from the fate of pleasure.

The idea of the long poem became attractive to Stevens in the prepublication period of *Harmonium* because it promised to resolve the painful and difficult-to-disentangle questions of his literary stature and his marriage, neither of which he could separate from his economic role as a male, from the social disease of econo-machismo. The long poem, not the small pleasures of minutiae – those little things of Thomas Campion and Verlaine he had once praised – could be the signature at once of his maleness and cultural prowess. "Witherlings," that coinage for his early poems, was just right. Real men like Gainsborough, Stevens once wrote, paint landscapes and portraits, not decorations on fans; real men, if they write poetry, go for the long poem of public (epic) import, not the small lyric of bourgeois delight. The poet who in his thirties felt himself marginalized by his social context as a ladylike dabbler in after-hours verse-writing would become, in his imaginative life at least (or is it at most?), a Latin lover courting what has to seem for the male modernist a forbidden woman, the epic muse who not only inspired but also had been possessed by a special sort of man, the sort embodied in Homer, Virgil, Dante, Milton. Could ladylike Stevens become one of those he had once called "your man-poets"? He wasn't sure, and he expressed his doubts with a humor that is always the sign (if we can trust Robert Frost's surmise about this) of virtually unbearable and unshareable inner seriousness: "I find this prolonged attention to a single subject has the same result that prolonged attention to a senora has according to the authorities. All manner of favors drop from it. Only it requires a skill in the varying of the serenade that occasionally makes one feel like a Guatemalan when one particularly wants to feel like an Italian."

In the time between the publication of *Harmonium* (1923) and his second volume, *Ideas of Order* (1935), in the period between 1923 and 1930 or so, Stevens wrote hardly anything. His literary sterility during those years cannot be explained by the largely indifferent and hostile reception of *Harmonium*; bad reviews did not silence him, because he was their virtual author. In "The Comedian as the Letter C," his first attempt at a long poem, Stevens was a previewer of *Harmonium*'s reception, harsher than any of his actual reviewers. The "Comedian" is a tough and hilarious reflection on a poet, like himself, who seemed to him to deserve the deflating mockery of epithets like "lutanist of fleas" and "Socrates of snails," as well as sexually caustic allegorization as a skinny sailor trying to conduct the sublimely frightening music of a sea-storm with a pathetically inadequate little baton: as if poetic and sexual inadequacy were somehow each other's proper sign.

Self-disappointment and the need to think through self-revision are better but not sufficient explanations of Stevens's literary silence: if he was experimenting with new longer forms and new ambition, he was doing it in his head, or in drafts which no one will ever see. He certainly wasn't trying out his new self in the little magazines, whose editors constantly requested his work and would have published pretty much anything he might have given them. By 1923 he was a respected avant-garde writer whose attractiveness was enhanced by his privacy and mysteriousness. He turned down many requests for poems; he had nothing to give. And while he was imagining but doing very little about earning his poetic manhood, he was living out and doing a great deal about earning the sort of manhood that his middle-class superego had taught him to desire or pay the price in guilt.

In this post-*Harmonium* period Stevens seems to have made his greatest effort – in which he succeeded – to rise to the corporate top of his business world: the right sort of thing to do for a man with family responsibilities, who was the sole source of the family's income, who wanted his own home, and who liked oriental rugs. Poetry was power and freedom over circumstances – Stevens, like most writers since the late eighteenth century, needed to believe that – and the more financially unstable the modern writer, the more he has tended to believe that proposition of aesthetic idealism, the promise that there will be refuge even in the filthy prison house of capitalism. Stevens undefensively knew and admitted and even celebrated another, more commonly held proposition: that money is power and freedom, too. Cultural capital, money of the mind, is good, even if it is the opium of the intellectuals: it is a *kind* of money. But money itself, whatever it is, certainly is not a *kind* of money. The logic, which Stevens never resisted, which he put down as aphorism in his "Adagia," is that "money is a kind of poetry."

In 1935, the middle of the Great Depression, when he was earning $25,000 a year (roughly the equivalent of $200,000 a year in our terms), when, in other words, he had made it financially – after 1935 his poetic production simply mushroomed – he wrote this to a business associate:

Our house has been a great delight to us, but it is still quite incomplete inside . . . It has cost a great deal of money to get it where it is and, while it is pleasant to buy all these things, and no one likes to do it more than I do, still it is equally pleasant to feel that you are not the creature of circumstances, but are (at least to a certain degree) the master of the situation, which can only be if you have the savings banks sagging with your money and the presidents of the insurance companies stopping their cars to ask the privilege of taking you to the office. For my part, I never really lived until I had a home, say, with a package of books from Paris or London.

Unlike most writers in the romantic and modernist tradition, Stevens knew that feelings of power and freedom in imagination were precisely the effects produced by a capitalist economic context in those writers and intellectuals who hate capitalist economic contexts; he seemed to know that aesthetic purity was economically encased; that imaginative power was good, to be sure, but that economic power was a more basic good because it enables the aesthetic goods (books from Paris and London) that he required. Can poetic power, however acquired and whatever its origin, turn on its economic base, become a liberating and constructive force in its own right? Stevens constantly chewed over the idea, and though he rejected the notion that literary force is also political force – the artist has no social role, he said more than once in his letters and essays – it may be that the deep unity of his later career was in part shaped by his encounter with radical thought in the thirties. Stevens emerged from that encounter thinking that Stanley Burnshaw's Marxist critique of his work was probing; he emerged believing in the social responsibility of his poetry, everything he says to the contrary notwithstanding. How much more responsible (and guilty) can you get than, on the one hand, writing the rarefied lyric that Stevens wrote, and, on the other, asserting that poets help people live their lives?

What Burnshaw's critique of *Ideas of Order* did was clarify for Stevens his own class position and at the same time that of his ideal and, as it would seem to him, inevitable audience. Stevens found Burnshaw's review "most interesting" because it "placed" him in a "new setting," the "middle ground" of the middle class, the socio-economic space of those who are both potential allies and potential enemies of class struggle. Burnshaw's statement of this contradiction of the middle class is matched and one-upped by Stevens in a letter written shortly after he read Burnshaw in *The New Masses*: "I hope I am headed left, but there are lefts and lefts, and certainly I am not headed for the ghastly left of Masses. The rich man and the comfortable man of imagination are not nearly so rich nor nearly so comfortable as he believes them to be. And, what is more, his poor men are not nearly so poor." In the United States, Stevens suggests, the middle ground is vaster than Burnshaw thinks, and the high and low grounds are narrower and not as melodramatically in opposition as the Manichean metaphors of Communist Party rhetoric would make them out to be. As the poet of the middle ground, of those not subject to revolutionary hunger, whose basic sustenance was more or less assured (the "more or less" assuring also a conservative anxiety, a willingness to rock the boat ever so gently), it was Stevens's "role to help people" – people: the middle class is easily universalized in American discourse – "to help people live their lives. [The poet] has had immensely to do with giving life whatever savor it possesses." To supply savor is to supply aesthetic, not biological, necessity: what Marx in *The German Ideology* called the "new needs" (or felt lacks) of women and men after their life-sustaining necessities have been met and they begin to produce not only their sustenance but also the means of reproducing their sustenance. At the point at which leisure becomes real, "we" – those for whom leisure is real – need a civilized poet.

Even in 1938, when he had behind him *Ideas of Order, The Man with the Blue Guitar*, and the difficult period (1923–30) following the publication of *Harmonium*, when it seemed he might be finished; even in 1938, when he was beginning to experience a personal literary renaissance and an onset of personal affluence dramatically highlighted by the collective disaster of the Great Depression, at fifty-nine years old, Wallace Stevens continued to speak, as he would speak to the end of his life, in the contradictions and with the denigrating self-consciousness that had shaped his early sense of himself. He was a writer who had to be responsible to his role as married, middle-class male citizen – his father's son:

The few things that I have already done have merely been preliminary. I cannot believe that I have done anything of real importance. The truth is, of course, that I never may, because there are so many things that take up my time and to which I am bound to give my best. Thinking about poetry is, with me, an affair of weekends and holidays, a matter of walking to and from the office. This makes it difficult to progress rapidly and certainly. Besides, I very much like the idea of something ahead; I don't care to make exhaustive effort to reach it, to see what it is. It is like the long time that I am going to live somewhere where I don't live now.

The new note in this rehearsal of his old and definitive conflict comes in toward the end, and it brings uneasy resolution. He feels desire for nothing in particular, desire without an object exterior to itself, the sheer feeling of desire as the ground of pleasure. Not quite: he needs to posit an object of hope beyond longing that will bring longing to an end, but he doesn't care to make an "exhaustive effort to reach it" because he doesn't really care "to see what it is." The object that he won't go all out to reach is ostensibly the poetry that he might write, those poems that will not be preliminary, will not be a bourgeois affair of weekends, holidays, and those few hours just before and after work, walking to and from the office. One way of phrasing the odd theme of Stevens's later life and poems, the odd and necessary game he plays with himself, is to say that it is constituted by a double desire: to *want* to write poems of real significance and, at the same time, not to want to *write* them.

The tone of this entire passage from a letter written in 1938 is shaped by its last sentence: "It is like the long time that I am going to live somewhere where I don't live now." The pain in that remark should be called structural, because the "It" that is like "living somewhere else," the writing he would do had he sufficient world and time, would be embedded in a social context that would be "its" enabling, "its" nourishing ground. *Would*: the entire passage is marked by an implicit subjunctive mood and is itself an example of the kind of writing that it tries to characterize – writing that is preliminary to the realization it imagines but does not quite want: preliminariness being the condition that Stevens wants to transcend and yet which is necessary to sustain if fulfillment, the problematic object of his hope, is to be deferred.

What, more specifically, can be said about the imagined social context of an imagined writing that would bring utter fulfillment? It is a place ("where I don't live now") that would not subject him to demands that now rob him of time and force him to give his best (make him feel "bound") to others. But if the imagined context is a place to live without constraints, it is also and most quintessentially time itself in the sense of a delicious process of living his life in such a way that fulfillment will be "long." Not the ecstatic arrest of desire's movement once it gets what it wants – culmination, and then what nobody wants, the aftermath of anticlimax – but ongoing ecstasy. The pathos communicated in the passage derives from Stevens's desire not to be resigned and his implicit admission that he must be resigned to a life of quiet despair because his life and writing feel contained and dominated. The title of one of James T. Farrell's novels (via A. E. Housman) is almost perfect here: *A World I Never Made.*

Not that Stevens wouldn't have wanted to unmake and then remake his world. But no one will accuse him of being a revolutionary writer – even to say the words *Wallace Stevens* and *revolution* in the same breath seems ridiculous, extremely so, yet what shall we call the urge that is being expressed in that key sentence ("It is like the long time that I am going to live somewhere where I don't live now"), and specifically in the analogy that says in so many words that writing the way you really want to write is like living in the way you really want to live, and you are doing neither, nor will you ever do either as long as the course of your everyday life continues to run as it always has. Underlying the analogy is the proposition that writing is the expression of a material ground at once personal and social. The particular mix of feeling in this passage, desire and fatality, might have been a kind of subjective political nitroglycerin. But it never went off. Stevens was never able to believe that the social ground of his life and writing was itself unstable, that the personal subjects it contained and restrained (like himself) might in their discontent make it unstable, explode its structure by refusing the very thing that keeps in place social structures which produce unhappiness: the acceptance of social structure as unalterable fact, like a thing of nature; by refusing, therefore, resignation to the structure.

Stevens's writing tends to wander unhappily between criticism and utopia. If his desire is without clear utopian object, so is his dissatisfaction without sharply viewed critical object. Resignation to unhappiness is a massive repression in Stevens, from his young manhood to his last years, of the personal choice that affirmed commitment to the system of his unhappiness. *Repression,* an easy word to use in literary circles, does no justice to the devious rhetoric of repression which manipulates its subjects by giving them a discourse for saying "happy" when they mean unhappy:

If Beethoven could look back on what he accomplished and say that it was a collection of crumbs compared to what he had hoped to accomplish, where should I ever find a figure of speech adequate to size up the little that I have done compared to that which I had once hoped to do. Of course, I have had a happy and well-kept life. But I have not even begun to touch the spheres within spheres that might have been possible if, instead of devoting the principal amount of my time to making a living, I had devoted it to thought and poetry. Certainly it is as true as it ever was that whatever means most to one should receive all of one's time and that has not been true in my case. But, then, if I had been more determined about it, I might now be looking back not with a mere sense of regret but at some actual devastation. To be cheerful about it, I am now in the happy position of being able to say that I don't know what would have happened if I had more time. This is very much better than to have had all the time in the world and have found oneself inadequate.

If "repression," better than "resignation," captures the psychological quality of this letter of 1950, then "rhetoric of repression" is better than either, because "rhetoric" suggests that Stevens is caught up in a situation in which he is both target and speaking subject, the self-subverting speaker of a kind of newspeak in which regret over not doing what you most want to do – and what, really, is "mere regret"? – and willed superficiality (choosing not to go to your depths, your "spheres within spheres") all somehow add up to a "happy and well-kept life." But we have to say that not even "rhetoric of repression" can do justice to the lucid and self-stinging consciousness that says "well-kept" and "To be cheerful about it," to the man who is not cheerful, knows he is not, and knows precisely the costs of his life and can somehow bear those costs because he believes ("of course") that he has chosen them. And perhaps that is the Supremest of all of Stevens's American fictions: the sustaining feeling that the life he so often felt he suffered, he chose; that necessity is, in fact, freedom.

When Stevens said in the letter of 1938 that he would like to do something of "real importance," he was alluding both to his negative feelings about *Harmonium* (a book mainly of little things) and to the desire that he felt, in the months when he was preparing *Harmonium* for press, to write the long poem, a desire in great part propelled by his assessment of his early work. The course of his intention as a poet can be traced in two letters written forty-two years apart; the change is from self-deprecating lyricist and a poetry of decorative frivolity, to philosophical consciousness of his age and a poetry of necessary knowledge; the change can be charted in the recurrence of a single word. Consider this passage from a letter to Elsie written in 1911: "I swear ... that it's a great pleasure to be so poetical. – But it follows that, the intellect having been replaced by the emotions, one cannot think of anything at all. – At any rate, my trifling poesies are like the trifling designs one sees on fans." Compare that with this response to Renato Poggioli, who needed some clarification about certain stanzas of *The Man with the Blue Guitar*, a poem Poggioli was translating for an Italian edition: "I desire my poem to mean as much, as deeply, as a missal. While I am writing what appear to be trifles, I intend these trifles to be a missal for brooding-sight: for an understanding of the world." This comment was intended to serve Poggioli as an explication of *Blue Guitar*, stanza 24:

> A poem like a missal found
> In the mud, a missal for that young man,
>
> That scholar hungriest for that book,
> The very book, or, less, a page
>
> Or, at the least, a phrase, that phrase,
> A hawk of life, that latined phrase:
>
> To know; a missal for brooding – sight.
> To meet that hawk's eye and to flinch
>
> Not at the eye but at the joy of it.
> I play. But this is what I think.

The change in the career of a "trifle" appears radical: from effeminate "trifling poesies" to missal; from a trivial thing in the hand of a comfortable lady to the book of books in the hand of a fevered young man; from decorative nonsense to world-penetrating knowledge – the original trifle somehow become sacred text.

How more dramatically could Stevens have elevated his conception of poetic function? Yet note that he really insists on the importance of trifling things ("I intend these trifles," these poems, these playful stanzas of *Blue Guitar*, "to be a missal"), as if the aborted purposes of his "horrid cocoons" (metaphor for his earlier poems) might somehow still be redeemed, the miscarried insects reimplanted in the nourishing environment of a longer meditative form, so that their potential might finally emerge. The passage from *Blue Guitar* catches Stevens in his later manner: it enacts, not the sensuous immediacies of perception, or erotic linguistic festivity, but the immediacy of a kind of thought indistinguishable from desire: pleasure now reimagined as something almost final, almost ultimately good, the fruit of fulfillment yet to be enjoyed; the pleasurable object of desire semiobscure, barely but forever out of reach. The effect of later Stevens, especially in the long poems, is of someone discoursing on some tremendous urgency, the thing most needed – poetry, the poem, the supreme fiction – without ever being able to make it clear what the thing is, though getting close, and without ever experiencing the fulfillment that the thing might bring, though getting tantalizingly close. If poetry is the object of Stevens's desire, then the central fact about Stevens in his later manner is that he was not writing "poems," according to the implicit definition of the poem we find in *Harmonium*, a book in which he delivered and did not just hope for poetic payload. What he is writing is a kind of pre-poetry, a tentative approach to the poem, an enactment of desire, not as a state of mind, with all the inert implications of the phrase "state of mind," but as movement, and not movement in a straight line, as if he could see the end of the journey, but a zigzag sort of motion: desire as improvisational action, a poetry that gives us a sense of starting, stopping, changing direction, revising the phrase, refining the language, drafting the poem and keeping the process of drafting all there as the final thing because the finished thing cannot be had ("The very book, or, less, a page / Or, at the least, a phrase, that phrase . . . that latined phrase").

Riveting later Stevens draws his reader into the improvisational music of desire, a writing about itself in the sense that the "itself" is longing as language eking itself out, each phrase a kind of blind adventure going nowhere, an infinite and exquisite foreplay. So what precedes foreplay? His version of the bourgeois quotidian, "the effect of order and regularity, the effect of moving in a groove . . . railroading to an office and then railroading back." Above all, the police, who "are as thick as trees and as reasonable. But you must obey them. – Now, Ariel, rescue me from police and all that kind of thing": as if the police were not only who they are but also a kind of thing, a metaphor of the social world for which only "books make up. They shatter the groove." But only in books. And what follows foreplay, anyway? Necessarily the end of desire, the police and all that sort of thing: reasonableness, the groove, no play.

In *Blue Guitar* 24 Stevens shapes a doubled image: at the base, the figure of the young man in a maximum agony of desire – ecstatic need matched by ecstatic book. The figure of the young man, the scholar finding the book, discarded like detritus in the mud, not writing the book; a figure at all points repeated by the figure of the poet writing of the young scholar, the poet leaning in late with mounting anticipation, looking for the poem, not writing it in the sense of planning it out or intending to write it by realizing a pregiven structure ("perish all sonnets"), but having it come upon him, out of nowhere – a surprise, like the poem that Stevens wanted to fly in through the window. This second image, of Stevens himself brooding over the scholar of brooding sight, rhythmically replays the scholar's hungriest hunger (his wanting to know) in a lurching rhetoric not only improvisational but repetitively so (that book, the very book; a phrase, that phrase, that latined phrase), a rhetoric verging on stutter – an excitement that would extinguish all language – then modulated without warning into the metaphor of the hawk of life – improvisation resolved into major chord.

That hugest banality of literary modernism – that poetry is a substitute for religion – is openly affirmed only to be radically reduced, shaved almost to nothing (from book to page to phrase): a missal for the purpose of brooding upon the mouse in the grass. At that very point of minimalist pathos comes an abrupt shift to maximalist grandeur (who could have predicted this escape from the literary police of repetition?), a shift embodied in the infinitive form of the verb which, in Stevens, is often the linguistic shape of desire in itself, a mode of transcendence, the sacred text of longing without end: to know without a subject of knowing; to know without an object of knowing, purely to know; not conjugated, not in time.

Turning from the "joy" of such purity of consciousness, away from the hawklike eye that broods over living detail, you "flinch," not at the eye, the vehicle of aesthesis, but at the joy of aesthesis. To have joy is not to have the joy of anticipation. "I play. But this is what I think." Those flat declaratives of the last line, made even flatter by the heavy caesura which separates them, speak with a staged yawn of the poet's withdrawal from joy and of his imagining of joy that he knows will go stale, because all joy eventually does.

Where does this poetry of the desire for poetry finally go? Nowhere at all, as it mustn't. To write a long poem out of such intention, without plot or historical subject or philosophical system, is to write the epic of bourgeois interiority, wherein the life of the spirit is hard to distinguish from the special sort of desire stimulated in the time and place of first-world consumer capitalism: when the life of the spirit is subjected to endless need for the new which alone can break us out of the grooves of boredom. What we want is to be thrilled: "What I want more than anything else in music, painting, and poetry, in life and in belief is the thrill that I experienced once in all the things that no longer thrill me at all. I am like a man in a grocery store that is sick and tired of raisins and oyster crackers and who nevertheless is overwhelmed by appetite." Stevens gourmandized with epicurean delight – he frequented gourmet grocery stores in search of the most expensive, the most exotic, the most sumptuous; he saw, he bought, he ate. His later poetry is a masochistic form of gourmandizing, deliberately teased out and emptied of satisfaction, a sustaining of overwhelming appetite. At the poetic, if not at the economic, level of existence, he found a way to supply the spirit by resisting consumption: a life of indulgence, a poetics of asceticism tempted.

Stevens on the grocery store is Stevens expressing desire in old age – that's what it feels like to be old and still to desire. Grocery stores of the sort that he frequented are not timeless objects of experience: "To enjoy the fine things of life you have to go to $438\frac{1}{2}$ East 78th St., two floors up in the rear, not three floors, and pay \$6.00 a pound for Viennese chocolates. One of the men in the office here got talking to me about tea the other day. I asked him what kind of tea he used. Oh, he said, anything that the A&P happens to have." What Stevens felt about supermarkets he also felt about department stores, labor unions, social classes, apartment houses, and any and all forms of life and literary expression that partook in the slightest of generic regularity. Generic forms, schools of writing and music ("There is no music because the only music tolerated is modern music. There is no painting because the only painting permitted is painting derived from Picasso or Matisse"), mimesis, literary modes, standardized and disciplined production of all kinds – in a word, the generalization of everyday life and the generalization of literary life, for Stevens, all added up to one thing: the potential destruction of an original life of one's own and of an original literature of one's own, the twin goals he announced in a letter long before he wrote his meditation on old age and desire. For Stevens to imagine himself satiated on raisins and oyster crackers, in a grocery store where only raisins and oyster crackers are available, is for Stevens to imagine himself without thrills, locked in the ennui of old age – but old and without thrills in a specific way, in a gourmet consumer's version of hell: not just anyplace, but here and now, for a man who thought that buying a pair of pajamas at Brooks Brothers was a partaking of the "bread of life," "better than any soufflé." His late poetry of deferred desire is not the escape of gourmandizing, it is its perfection.

To write the long poem, then, is to string together a collocation of moments and to create a book of moments which hangs together by the force of desire for moments – the moving into the moment, the moving out. Such a long poem, so called, is only delusively different in scope from his earlier works. Stevens did not advance in scope, ambition, or high seriousness. Of course, like his critics, who take their cue from him, he liked to think he had. He wanted to call his collected poems "The Whole of Harmonium," a wonderfully resolved, teleological construction of the life of a writer who had once toyed with calling *Harmonium* "The Grand Poem: Preliminary Minutiae." He even considered, in his later years, the idea that his sort of poetry could be theorized, become an object for study; he spoke with friends of the possibility of an endowed chair at Princeton in the theory of poetry. But Stevens knew that the one thing you cannot do with surprises that fly in through the window is to theorize them. He knew that improvisation formalized is something else.

What Stevens seeks, early and late, is a mode of consciousness which (after Emerson) he calls, in the introductory poem to *Notes toward a Supreme Fiction* (1942), "vivid transparence" (with punning insistence on the latinate resonance of "vivid") – vision washed clean of all that has been said, a freeing from history:

> How clean the sun when seen in its idea,
> Washed in the remotest cleanliness of a heaven
> That has expelled us and our images . . .

This supreme, because unmediated, consciousness would effect original relation to things, face to face, abstracted from all tradition. Vivid transparence would yield access to what Stevens called, in urgent redundancy, "living changingness," the medium of escape from granite monotony, the culturally enforced repetitions of what has been thought and said. The pleasure achieved would be "peace," a moment attendant upon a "crystallization of freshness": vivid, living changingness aesthetically trapped, as in a crystal, known in and for its uniqueness, then quickly lost in its freshness, having been hardened in verbal form. Vivid transparence is both medium and substance of authentic literariness: avant-garde of perception and perpetual ground of the new, perpetually imperiled by the forms of cultural habit, an imperative constantly to reimagine.

In several poems of 1938, most strikingly in "The Latest Freed Man," Stevens fully entered into his late phase. The aesthete, who had his metapoetic moments of reflection in *Harmonium*, becomes in these poems insistently the meta-aesthete poised at the edge of escape from all life-deadening structures of perception, whose language tries to render not the moment of the sensuous image in itself but its psychic preconditions. The moment is dawn, when the "latest freed man" (the irony of the phrase is wicked), trying to be "Like a man without a doctrine" – trying "To be without description of to be," "For a moment on rising, at the edge of the bed" – becomes movingly inarticulate, his excited dumbness the sign of his original access to presence without doctrine and beyond speech.

The latest freed man's desire to be without a past, merely to be, his desire for original relation, unmediated by tradition, is the revolutionary desire for an American origin announced in the opening sentences of Emerson's "Nature" essay of 1836: the hope of rupture with Europe in the cultural as well as the political realm, revolutionary hope become a way of being in the world, down to, and perhaps most essentially including, revolutionary freshness of perception. Freshness of perception is phenomenological rupture in the wake of political rupture; it is the medium of a revolutionary everyday life. The transparent eyeball passage in Emerson is father to the moment of vivid transparency in Stevens. Between Emerson and Stevens falls, not the struggle of fathers and sons, but a thorough commodification of everyday life. The appetite for American newness, in Emerson transcendental, antihistorical, nature-oriented – become like the roses outside your window, he urges, they are wholly themselves, they make no reference to past or future roses, they are above time – that sort of desire for freshness of natural encounter, always driven in Emerson by social pressure (which is why he urges it), is translated by later Stevens into hope for the freshness of an original relation to the commodity. Consumption in Stevens, literary or gastronomical, is always to be understood under the sign of the gastronomical: his gourmand's idea of fruit becomes the gastronomical equivalent of his avant-garde pleasure in producing exotic literary fare for our savor, so that he might help us to live our lives. In Stevens, capitalism and avant-garde poetics are not opposites but symbiotic complements, the basis of an integrated life, a unified sensibility quite unlike anything dreamt of in the utopian imagination.

"When I get up at 6 o'clock in the morning," he wrote to his friend Henry Church, "(A time when you are first closing your novel, pulling the chain on the lamp at your bedside), the thing" – the idea of a supreme fiction – "crawls all over me; it is in my hair when I shave and I think of it in the bathtub. Then I come down here to the office and, except for an occasional letter like this, have to put it to one side. After all, I like Rhine wine, blue grapes, good cheese, endive and lots of books, etc., etc., etc., as much as I like supreme fiction." Dawn, the time of the supreme fiction, is also the time when, having consumed the night away in fiction, Henry Church – who is really rich, who buys what he wants, reads when he wants, all night if he likes – can go to sleep. Henry Church doesn't have to report to the office. He doesn't work, he doesn't have to wish for a life "somewhere where I don't live now." Dawn, for Stevens, is an intersected moment: the awakening to the desire for supreme fiction and the transition period when supreme fictions must be deferred as soon as they are contemplated, not in order to forget them but in order to do what he must do in order to lay up their representations, the substitutes for supreme fiction that money can buy: good cheese, blue grapes, lots of books, etcetera – especially, perhaps, etcetera: the endless substitutes that money can buy, the specialty market of supreme fictions he loves almost as much as the imaginative thing for which commodities like Rhine wine substitute.

Work, after all, is the site of his writing to Henry Church; work not only enables the purchase of substitutive satisfactions, it enables reflection on the difference between real and substitute supreme fictions, and on why he has to be concerned with that difference, why he must work, and on what the difference between being Wallace Stevens and being Henry Church actually consists of. Work might have shed light on his difference from Henry Church (an aristocratic émigré) as a class difference – work might have been the site of an embryonic class-consciousness – but I see no evidence that Stevens ever got to that point; although perhaps mentioning to Henry Church that he can put out the lights when others, like Stevens, are turning them on is a gentler form of class-consciousness, with all hostility either utterly absent or civilly repressed. *Notes toward a Supreme Fiction* is appropriately dedicated to Church; in another time, another place, he would have been the patron of Wallace Stevens. In this time, this place – the poem was published in 1942 – the dedication to Church functions doubly: first, it refers to a person living everyday life as Stevens dreamed of living it, as an aesthetic totality; second, it signals the difference between a European leisured aristocrat (a traditional recipient of poetic dedication) and an American (an untraditional writer of poems) whose economic status and literary ambition created difficulties that Church would never experience. The dedication of *Notes* to Church is an idealization, a little self-ironic, a little (how could it not be?) hostile.

Very late in his life, in a poem called "The World as Meditation," Stevens returned to the figure of the poet not as virile youth (a figure of the persistent anxiety he felt for his masculinity) but as a woman, Homer's Penelope as himself, without a trace of the self-consciousness that had accompanied his earlier, ladylike poses as the versifier of the trivial. The world as field of heroic action belongs to Ulysses; the world as meditation is Penelope's creation. Penelope's poetry is her special kind of writing, her active passivity; she is his final representation of desire as a capacity for reception rather than an agitated seeking of desirable objects, a traditional female image with which Stevens identifies completely, without the safe distancing effect that the character of Penelope provides in "The World as Meditation." It was what, as writer and collector of objets d'art, he had wanted all along; the position, poetical and sexual, that he courted all along; his way of saying "no" to the life he felt forced to lead.

If Ulysses is the male principle expressed as the epic genre of action, then Penelope is the female principle expressed as the lyric genre of contemplation. Ulysses is quickly and tellingly reduced as the "interminable adventurer": a comedic sort of epithet which has a very different, undercutting kind of effect in the context of the heroic style that is being recollected. This is not Homer's man skilled in all the ways of contending; this Ulysses is closer to Bill Bailey, whom Pearl of the same surname importunes, in a low musical genre of domestic relations, "Won't you come home?" Penelope is drawn into the poem's center of consciousness: Stevens's *Odyssey* is not the famous middle books of adventure but wholly its beginning, from the perspective of Penelope, who imagines maximum distance, absence, and uncertain return – a radical reduction of *The Odyssey* to domestic anecdote (Will he ever return?). Ulysses is an exterior figure, quite literally, outside the room which is the universe of her waiting; just as the sun, with whom Ulysses is strategically confused, is outside. The division of the genders (and genres) is starkly projected in the antithetical figures of male energy and female enclosure, public and private spheres, "fire" and "cretonnes":

> Someone is moving
> On the horizon and lifting himself up above it.
> A form of fire approaches the cretonnes of Penelope,
> Whose mere savage presence awakens the world in which she dwells.

The "savage presence" in this poem of his last years retrieves through self-quotation the self-conscious, primitive moment of forced phallic music from "Sunday Morning." This "savage presence" implicitly grants, without anxiety, what Stevens anxiously desired in his youth to grant himself, as poet and economic actor: autonomy of the male principle figured as the energy of a system, the sun itself (in appropriate pre-Copernican vision) like a self-sufficient hero "lifting himself above" the horizon. (Stevens's father might have liked that phrase: it came so close to his kind of cliché, like lifting yourself up by your own bootstraps.) Stevens grants to Ulysses what males have typically claimed for themselves but what he does not wish to claim for himself now, and in the same act grants to canonical Homer an authority of epic mastery for which he no longer yearns through the disguises of sexual self-irony and self-styled minority.

It is the sun (or the thought of Ulysses) which stirs Penelope's consciousness from sleep to vision; she depends upon it (him), it (he) motivates her meditation. The sun lifts itself over the horizon, Ulysses approaches (perhaps), Penelope both dwells in and creates a dwelling place. Her power, located literally within the domestic dwelling place, is the power of lyric meditation, whose actual domestic site is a figure for a site and dwelling that she makes and that is impervious to male presence: it needs no real Ulysses to fill her desire, for there, in the dwelling she makes, she is the composer of selves, the single artificer of the world in which she dwells, the principle of high formalist imagination so revered by modernist writers, now (unlike its earlier canonical evocation in "The Idea of Order at Key West") unequivocally rendered and accepted as a female principle, the autonomous goddess of radical creativity whose function is much more than formal. She composes selves – his as well as hers – and she places them in a shelter beyond violation. She creates them – in that sense she composes them. She consoles them – in that sense also does she compose them – gives them poise in the face of unassuaged grief. She gives deeply founded stability – not a "shelter," but a "sheltering"; not a place but a process of mind, in never-ending meditation, whose security is inviolable; perfection of lyric internalization, Penelope's poetry:

> She has composed, so long, a self with which to welcome him,
> Companion to his self for her, which she imagined,
> Two in a deep-founded sheltering . . .

Penelope's meditative process is "so long" because its object is absent – and though in the end, in Homer's story, Ulysses is brought home, in Stevens's version he is kept away; in Stevens's version there is no plot, no culmination of touch. Erotic fulfillment is imagined ("His arms would be her necklace / And her belt"), and imagined as an alternative to the worldly booty he might bring but which she doesn't want ("She wanted no fetchings" because "His arms" would be "the final fortune of their desire"). Note: not "*her* desire," which might seem logical, but "*their* desire," which is correct because the world as meditation is wholly hers: Ulysses has no say in it; there, she is the arbiter of all desire, what she wants is what he wants. In Stevens's lyricizing of Homer's narrative, in his draining of plot and time, Penelope is placed in the suspension of an interminable imagining because knowledge of the end is denied her: no narrative climax, no sexual climax.

The trajectory of the long poem Stevens compared to the trajectory of love: prolonged attention to a single subject is like prolonged attention to a forbidden woman, and success in the longer forms is like success in love – if one can write/love like an Italian. Both trajectories were denied to Stevens, and he likewise denies them to Penelope. Lyric longing is no more a choice than erotic longing; they were historically fated impositions, and so he imposes them on Penelope, who "accommodates" her circumstances, what she does not choose, with a tenacity and force that answer Ulysses' savage presence and absence with her own "barbarous strength" that "would never fail." Stevens's Penelope is a revision of Whitman's agonized voyeur ("Song of Myself," section 11), whose desire to be male, painfully described in her fantasy of assuming the classic male sexual posture, only underscores what she really is: a proper and properly repressed lady. Stevens's Penelope refuses all male posture, but she is no "lady" – her sexual and poetic identity is "within her"; it is not imposed by a male superego, it is primitive. Penelope's meditation sustains her life; Stevens is of no mind to designate it "trifling poesy," as he had once designated his early work.

But Penelope, though the poem's center of meditation, is not the poem's voice: this Stevens reserves for himself, as a kind of frame meditator and would-be storyteller, reduced to brooding over one moment of *The Odyssey*. With all narrative action denied him, the long poem that he attempted repeatedly in the thirties and forties now frankly beyond his possibilities, Stevens here pens his farewell to the Homeric text which he can in no way rewrite in the epic spirit but can appropriate in his kind of lyric mode, converting Ulysses' world as a field of action into Penelope's world as interior moment of reflection: the world not as object of meditation but the world as meditation – victory over the canonical principle of epic bought at the heavy cost of idealization. Poetry at the interior, lovers at the interior, both set by the frame meditator into a natural context large and inhuman ("an inhuman meditation, larger than her own"), which he insists is itself a creative process of meditation, yet so figured as to render the inhuman domestic, a process of Penelope's mind: the grand natural cycles a reflection of household work, mending and washing ("The trees are mended. / That winter is washed away"), as if Penelope herself were what she never was, a dutiful bourgeois wife. And then, having adopted Penelope's metaphors as his own, Stevens reduces his lovers to greeting-card sentiment: "friend and dear friend." Here, at last, is a Homer for the little things, the small tasks and pleasures of the sort of house that Stevens knew so well because he lived in it. Stevens, who was never confident of his ability to stand with "your man-poets," here, in this poem of 1952, has made over the canonical of canonical poets into an image of himself as writer: the frame meditator becomes Penelope.

If Penelope's isolation is terrible, that is because her lyric idealization fails to compensate perfectly for her exclusion from her husband's world. Hers is an incantatory poetry, dependent on its absent male object of focus: "She would talk a little to herself as she combed her hair / Repeating his name with its patient syllables" (Ulysses, Ulysses). Ulysses is at home in the Greek universe, taken care of by such as Aeolus, even recognized by his dog after all those years. Penelope does not belong: "No winds like dogs watched over her at night." What she has, in the end, is what Stevens had as a young man in New York, his room; what she has is what is left over when all "fetchings" have been refused: purified lyric longing, painful perfection of interiority, her room. And what a miracle of creation "fetchings" is, even for this poet who performed them as second nature. *Fetch*: to reach by sailing, especially against the wind or tide; to go or come after and bring or take back. *Fetching*: attractive, pleasing. Thus *fetchings*: attractive or pleasing things, which bring a price, as in the price a commodity will fetch, brought back over water, defined as commodities by the act of fetching that brought them home, valued as fetchings in the homeland of the actor who fetches: an etymology of imperialism. She wanted none of that.

The poet has been in love, illicitly, for a very long time. He can't remember when he wasn't. The end is now near, and only his beloved will speak, because in this affair the beloved alone speaks. For this last time, what will be said is all that it is possible to say. In other words, we inhabit the world of Stevens's last phase, the poems collected in *The Rock* and presided over by "Final Soliloquy of the Interior Paramour," logically, though not chronologically, the final speaking of Penelope, Stevens's own imaginative capacity, as if she were a person distinct from yet uncannily intimate with the writer himself, looking back, summing up, but centrally speaking in praise, with intense poignant plainness, of ground value, what persists to the end, what will suffice, even at the end.

"Final Soliloquy" (1950) affirms the nourishing value of an affair whose vital boundary is in the mind, meditative consummation without foundation.

What sustains is love's enactment of itself, the actual writings, even though no particular enactment can secure the future of love unless it should provoke – and, in Stevens's case, it always does – desire for future consummation. One rendezvous leads to another, because the one just previous was sufficiently satisfying to spur further journeys in desire. The tone is urgent – this much is what must be said (it says), this much, at least (it says), must be acknowledged.

Quickly, urgency shades subtly into desperation. Final loss will need to be faced; it cannot be far away, Stevens is in his seventies. But the great good is still available. This amorous intensity cannot diminish, it can only die. And though this great good is minimal – like a "single shawl / Wrapped tightly round us," in our poverty, in the cold – by the agency of this love, this good, Stevens feels completed, "collected" from his fragments into a wholeness of self, whose sole mode of existence is writerly consummation. So good is this good that the poet will say of it much more than he has the right to say. He will say "knowledge," he will say "miraculous influence," he will say "The world imagined is the ultimate good," and he will say "God and the imagination are one." Need, not reason, propels such mounting phrases, from the very base of poverty, our single shawl against the cold, to impossible richness: "a warmth, / A light, a power, the miraculous influence."

Yet the poet has never been more sober, he knows that his poverty will not be escaped; but he knows, too, that the rendezvous is good enough, if no miracle. So he imagines without support, not imagining *something*, but taking "to imagine" as an intransitive verb. The process itself without object, *that* is enough, this sublimest narcissism, this happiness that cannot be taken from him, except by his death.

4

T. S. ELIOT

T. S. Eliot grew up knowing he was privileged and obligated. One of his biographers, Peter Ackroyd, remarks that "the Eliots were the aristocrats of nineteenth-century America (family motto: *Tace et fac*), part of that rising mercantile class which offered moral leadership to those who came after them; their self-imposed mission was to administer and to educate": to educate by leading and administering; most of all, to educate. The poet's grandfather, William Greenleaf Eliot, left the Harvard Divinity School in order to establish the Unitarian faith in the frontier town of St. Louis, Missouri, in 1834, where he founded a church and (as Ackroyd puts it) "three schools, a university, a poor fund, and a sanitary commission." His father, Henry Ware Eliot, grew wealthy from the proceeds of the Hydraulic-Press Brick Company, of which he was president. His mother, Charlotte Stearns Eliot, was (one wants to say "of course") a poet, some of whose verses were published in newspapers, most of which were pasted into her scrapbooks.

Social versus cultural responsibility, striking business prowess versus aesthetic sensibility: in America, these historically opposed domains were the heritage of the twentieth century's most famous and powerful taste-determining man of letters. Thomas Stearns, a chip off the old family block, became a poet, a literary critic, a stalwart at Lloyds Bank and Faber and Faber, a Nobel Prize winner, and, in the peak years of his fame, the author of a prose of heavy concern (the cultural equivalent of his grandfather's sanitary commission).

The man-of-letters-to-be stepped forward early, as the boy of letters, age eleven, when he wrote and illustrated at Smith Academy in St. Louis fourteen numbers of a weekly magazine, *The Fireside*, containing "Fiction, Gossip, Theatre, Jokes, and all interesting." He entered Harvard in 1906, began publishing poems in *The Harvard Advocate* the following year and regularly thereafter. In 1909, Eliot joined the editorial board of the *Advocate* and added book reviews to his repertory. In other words, the patterns of his literary life were pretty much fixed in his undergraduate days.

In his junior year (1908), Eliot enjoyed a transformative literary experience that radically revised the shape of his early poetry. He read Arthur Symons's *The Symbolist Movement in Literature* and a new world was suddenly opened to him. Rimbaud, Verlaine, Corbière, and, most of all, Jules Laforgue presented him with an unconventional way of standing in the world of literature. Sentences and phrases in Symons's chapter on Laforgue will leap out at readers (even those only casually familiar with Eliot's early poetry) as a preamble to "The Love Song of J. Alfred Prufrock," a poem unimaginable in the landscape of American and English verse in 1908. Here is Symons on Laforgue:

> "The old cadences, the old eloquence, the ingenuous seriousness of poetry, are all banished"
> "the sickly modern being, with his clothes, his nerves"
> "it plays, somewhat uneasily, at disdainful indifference"
> "there is in it all the restlessness of modern life"
> "it is part of his manner not to distinguish between irony and pity, or even belief"
> "He composes love-poems hat in hand"
> "how much suffering and despair, and resignation to what is, after all, the inevitable, are hidden under this disguise"

After reading Symons, a few months later Eliot read the complete poems of Laforgue, and he became himself. Laforgue did for him, as he would put it years later, what no "single living poet in England or America, then at the height of his powers," could do: "point the way to a young poet conscious of the desire for a new idiom."

"The Love Song of J. Alfred Prufrock" was written in part during Eliot's senior year (1910) and completed the following year in Europe. In 1910–11, he had as possible outlets in America for his new poem (excepting the *Advocate*) only the mass-circulation magazines. Eliot understood that in 1911 "Prufrock" was unpublishable. He committed it to his notebook and then seems to have given up on it. In the fall of 1914, in London, he met Pound, who read "Prufrock" (by then three years in manuscript). Pound promptly sent it on to Harriet Monroe, whose newly founded *Poetry* was presumably the sort of place intended for things like "Prufrock." But Monroe sat on it, and only after hard prodding by Pound (she wanted an upbeat ending) did she publish the poem, in June 1915.

Before his Laforgian conversion, Eliot was writing some poems that might have appeared in Richard Watson Gilder's *Century* magazine; with "Prufrock," he burst upon the avant-garde scene and became a presence to reckon with. The poem would shortly inspire work as independently brilliant, and important, as Pound's *Hugh Selwyn Mauberley* and Stevens's "The Comedian as the

Letter C." Eventually, "Prufrock" would become a performance for the high school textbooks, the most recognizable voice in twentieth-century literature and the implicit definition of modernism, the embodiment of a self-conscious style that poets in Eliot's generation (Hart Crane, William Carlos Williams), and after, would need to learn to reject if they were to chart their own course.

Symons's chapter on Laforgue describes the shell of "Prufrock," the gestures and the poses, and it explains all there is to know about the Laforgian imitations that Eliot chose not to preserve, and the one he did keep for his first volume ("Conversation Galante"). Even the title of Eliot's first book, *Prufrock and Other Observations* (1917), is a Laforgian deflation of conventional lyric piety: coolness, objectivity, and analytical precision, not the gushing nonsense of popular poetry, the title says, were to be the marks of the new poetry that Hulme and Pound would polemicize into existence in the London where Eliot moved in 1915, a poetry whose tone and texture would implicitly function as criticism of the lyric styles it would replace. A "modern" poem was to be an observation recorded, not a feeling expressed.

The now legendary and too familiar, but in 1915 historically fresh and strange, opening simile of "Prufrock" implicitly announces a revolution against poetry as Eliot's readers would have known it. In the opening lines of the poem, a stock lyric subject is aggressively reversed by a poet interested, as a poet, in the hospital operating room, and that old poetic evening, with its soft, subjective tone, opens onto odd subjective terrain ("like a patient etherised upon a table"). Who sees evenings in this way? Whose sick love song is this? In "Prufrock," Eliot seizes upon the studied wit and artificiality, the subterfuges and shocks of Laforgue's antiromanticism, in order to enter the lyric world again, but on new (in historical context), antipoetic terms. The layered gestures of irony, indifference, and tiredness, the (self-)mock-heroics of the persona, the projected face of neurasthenia – all of these Laforgian mannerisms are not ends but strategies for the slyer reclaiming of inward space, lyricism in the company of the relatively new science of anesthesiology.

So "Prufrock" is a poem of feeling and sensibility masquerading as an observation, delivered, famously, as a dramatic monologue without auditor, in rhythms that forecast a voice of search and longing, teased out over a career which, by *Four Quartets*, is a much scrutinized public text: search and longing in the cadences of incantation, waiting for grace, but often (especially early, but late too) encased in embarrassment (no, he is neither St. John the Baptist nor Prince Hamlet), weariness and fatality ("I grow old ... I grow old ... "), and hesitation, always hesitation, on the verge of acting, not acting ("Do I dare ... ?"). What poem in the English canon proceeds so insistently through the crippling interrogative? The rhythms speak desire of apocalypse, but the tones, the sound and sense of the startling rhymes, the grandiose allusions that diminish the self before memories of the past, the lacerating self-consciousness, especially in the company of women, all play from the interior the muse of despair. "Prufrock" is the first major showcasing of Eliot's persona, the voice that simultaneously hopes and retreats, wanting new life ("Let us go then"), but instead waking, the effect of ether now worn off, into a death of consciousness ("human voices wake us, and we drown"); wishing for power, but believing in its impotence (lacking the "strength to force the moment to its crisis").

But "Prufrock" is most of all a drama of literary anguish, a writer's drama, played through the mask of a character (like the poet himself) who is well-born, prim, even prissy, in self-dialogue, telling himself that a walk on the wild side is just what he needs as the proper prelude to really letting go of all that he knows as himself, in order (like a hero from the later fiction of Henry James) to relinquish himself to a life of impulse and instinct ("I should have been a pair of ragged claws"), sex and violence appearing as the other domain of a consciousness at some level barely human, buried but faintly stirring, and titillating. The gestures, the manners, and the desires that find speech, the poem itself – this is perhaps one of Eliot's strongest and most characteristic effects – are all glimpsed as if from an emanating point the other side of the poem and language, from a subjectivity that sees itself, defines itself, as oppressed, threatened, and hurt by language, a self that nevertheless sees the world through language: as in "streets that follow like a tedious argument / Of insidious intent"; as in "the works and days of hands / That lift and drop a question on your plate"; as in "time" itself experienced as the permission of "a hundred visions and revisions" and (fatal rhymeword) "decisions" revised. The central act of choice for this self is the literary act of rewriting. The eyes "fix you in a formulated phrase," the phrase punctures and pins him to the wall. Traditional texts (always looming) pressure and get inside the voice, capturing its rhythm, turning it into someone else's writing, diminishing and debunking its puny urges. The famous alienation of "The Love Song of J. Alfred Prufrock" is grounded in a young man's fear of impotence, sexual and literary (what could possibly, for him, be the difference?). Eliot's poetry, from the start, gives off whiffs of decay and death. "Prufrock" is the first in his series of portraits of the artist as the old man of youth.

The celebrity of "Prufrock" has obscured the virtuoso variety of performance in Eliot's first volume. "Prufrock" is the work of a sensibility that has pared itself out of existence, but in "Portrait of a Lady" and "La Figlia Che Piange" the dramatist enters his play. These are the poems of a writer who enjoys seeing himself in dramatic light, so much the better to luxuriate in his manipulative power and take pleasure in his own dramatizing sensibility, his self-consciousness as arranger, producer, director, god of his imagined world, not indifferent to his creation, but a specially privileged character within – he alone, T. S. Eliot, there, in literary space, free, who felt himself free nowhere else.

"Portrait" is part narrative and part character sketch, featuring slices of reverberating dialogue, a poetry, as its title suggests, inspired by Henry James, and it is partly a self-portrait of the writer with vampire-like relations to real life (a late Jamesian theme here), which he needs to convert into material for composition (composition alone having the power to compose him): the vampire who knows but cannot change himself, who must compose (suck blood) at any cost. He says to himself: "You have the scene arrange itself – as it will seem to do – "; "Well! and what if she should die some afternoon . . . die and leave me sitting pen in hand . . . " This vampire-writer has a knack for the distilling comic phrase: "We have been, let us say, to hear the latest Pole / Transmit the Preludes, through his hair and finger-tips"; he takes satirical relish in the democracy of the newspaper, with all manner of data placed side by side; he has an eye for the new ethnic details of Boston circa 1910:

> An English countess upon the stage.
> A Greek was murdered at a Polish dance,
> Another bank defaulter has confessed.

With its ruling subjunctive tense and correlative moods of yearning and emptiness, the director (in "La Figlia") becomes his actors in a strategic confusion of pronouns ("I" becomes "he," "he" and "you" become "we"), and the dramatist speaks lyrically, thereby undoing the fiction of selfpossession that belongs to writers who choose the dramatic mode. To what extent does this observer want to stay outside, under the cool control of his reason? Or is his reason a repression of a desire to give himself, blessedly to lose himself? The virtuosity of performance in Eliot's first book is a mark of his literary prowess, but it is also a mark of uncertainty and struggle in a writer who has not yet found a mastering voice, because he does not yet know who he is.

And the satirical performances in *Prufrock and Other Observations* only reinscribe the problem: "The *Boston Evening Transcript*," "Aunt Helen," and "Cousin Nancy" are exercises, studied and flat, sporting unsurprising, pro forma ironic contrasts. The poetic voice sounds self-possessed, but there has been no challenge; Eliot dominates his material too easily. Only in the last of the satirical group, "Mr. Apollinax," does he let us inside his imaginative process in a kind of poem (topical satire) that would ordinarily prohibit revelations of this sort.

In "Mr. Apollinax," mythic sexual energy is set against effete contemporary social material ("Priapus in the shrubbery" against "the teacups"). This time ironic contrast provides the framework, not the substance of the poem. A few years later Eliot would begin reading *Ulysses* in manuscript, and would find, as he thought, a "method" for writing significantly in a world where frameworks are hard to come by honestly. "Mr. Apollinax" is his first, and perhaps independent, stab in that direction, a comic evaluation of a desiccated society from the perspective of an anciently rooted yet still possible vitality. This satirical poet finds personal urgency in his memory of myth, urgency that seems not yet clearly understood by himself: the surprising nexus of myth, sexual force, contemporary emptiness, satirical judgment – the heterogeneous poetic substance, really, of *The Waste Land* – is here handled in nascent form. And in the center of the poem is an extended conceit, hard to figure into the poem's satire but easy to figure into the work that will come: coral islands and a worrisome death by drowning, a death that may not be the end, constitute elements of a complex image that allures as it unfolds, unfolds perhaps because it allures, pursued by a poet who may have no choice but to pursue it:

> His laughter was submarine and profound
> Like the old man of the sea's
> Hidden under coral islands
> Where worried bodies of drowned men drift down in the green silence,
> Dropping from fingers of surf.

The title of Eliot's first volume appropriates the naturalist rhetoric of Zola and the prestige of late-nineteenth-century positivist science, so much the better to wage cultural war: to kill off and bury the enervated spirit of lyric that ruled the scene in Eliot's young manhood in England and America. Against the background of Eliot's youth, the notable thing about the group of poems made up by "Preludes," "Rhapsody on a Windy Night" (these two written in the "Prufrock" period), and "Morning at the Window" (written shortly after his move to London) is the novelistic character of their patterns of imagery, a poetry of realist texture – inspired by Baudelaire – which anchors itself in the lower echelons of society, in urban scenes of the down-at-the-heels, the grungy, the unsavory. In its time, this is also the kind of poem (like "Prufrock" but in a different register) that proclaims itself against Poetry with a capital letter. Broken blinds, newspapers blowing down the street, faint stale smells of beer, dingy shades, furnished rooms, yellow soles of feet, soiled hands, vacant lots, a dress torn and stained, a spring broken and rusty, a cat licking rancid butter, body parts but rarely whole bodies – such are the defining images of a scene strolled through and brooded over by a consciousness alternately repulsed and hallucinated by what it takes in, a consciousness willing to let in all that the standard lyricism of its time had excluded from poetry, but a consciousness, nevertheless, whose own lyric needs for transformation and transcendence remain incorrigibly romantic (in Eliot, a lyric self always lurks). Laforgian and Zolaesque conversions are useful; they bring surprising literary change to the domain of poetry. Eventually, though, another kind of conversion will come to seem necessary, one that lyric writing can long for but cannot itself accomplish.

Three events set the shape and texture of Eliot's everyday life through the publication of *The Waste Land* in 1922. In 1915, he decided to move to London; in the same year, he met and married (in rapid succession) Vivienne Haigh-Wood; in the month they were married, *Poetry* published "Prufrock." Thanks to "Prufrock," Eliot entered the avant-garde with a splash, as a writer of such originality that, on the basis of this single poem, he was established as the new poet to watch, a tone-setter. But *The Waste Land* brought him out of the alluring literary underground for good, where Pound remained as a writer's writer, to the riveted attention of the literary world at large. *The Waste Land* made Eliot at once the towering poet of modernism and its public face, the figure to whom those who cared (and those who did not care) for modernism would need to pay attention, an awesome image, idolized and detested. Very quickly, *The Waste Land* ceased to be a poem to be read and became a phrase to be intoned, the essence of a perspective and an attitude, the signature of a lost generation: in other words, a cultural event that got beyond Eliot's intention and control. The scandalous success of the poem, the reams of commentary it has spawned, its centrality for the teaching of modern literature, all have had the double effect of making Eliot a major force in world literature while obscuring the specific narrative of his life and poetry.

Marriage to Vivienne Haigh-Wood brought his much-agonized-over condition of virginity to an end, and marriage plunged them both into chaos. They suffered endless emotional and physical troubles, the former promoting the latter, but they supported each other unstintingly and selflessly. He took devoted care of her during her hard times; she was a fiercely loyal supporter (and keen reader) of his writing, a great believer in his talent, who did all she could to gain him the time that he almost never had to write poems.

They suffered collapses; more than likely, no change of circumstance could have saved their life together. Nevertheless, their circumstances were damaging. Eliot's family was wealthy but did not approve of his choice of career. His parents had expected him to return from his graduate studies in England, philosophy dissertation in hand, ready to assume a position at a distinguished American university. But he wanted a career in writing, not in teaching, and, like Frost, knew that London was the capital of the English-speaking literary world, the place to be. The early London period of the Eliots was marked by a steady stream of requests to St. Louis for understanding and financial aid. Eliot, Vivienne, Pound, and Bertrand Russell all wrote. Vivienne, for one, did not stand on pride: she told the poet's mother that she was darning her husband's underwear. Eliot's father and brother responded with frequent, though modest, gifts. And Eliot spared himself not at all: he taught at night (at jobs that often entailed immense commutes); he steadily wrote reviews for philosophy and literary journals that paid; he became assistant editor of the *Egoist* (a position which required, in addition to the usual dreary chores, that he write, anonymously, when sufficient copy was not at hand, almost entire issues); he produced a huge number of still mostly uncollected essays; he took on a regular job at Lloyds (which meant that his evenings were reserved for editing, writing essays and reviews, and personal correspondence) – all the while conceiving of himself as a poet whose budding reputation and promising future he was squandering, here and there finding the time to do what he believed he was meant and most needed to do. And so the leitmotifs of Eliot's correspondence of the period: too much work, too little time, too little money, too nervous, too tired to write poems – in Vivienne's phrase: "that inexorable pile of work piling up against him." He "dried up" (his phrase); he "collapsed" (his word); she collapsed.

Eliot's views of what "literature" ought to be and how it ought to function were influenced in large part by his reading, and they were expressed on numerous celebrated occasions in critical writings that span his career. But these views were also driven by the economically constrained life he felt forced to lead in London – and "forced" is half right and half wrong. "Right" because it would be difficult to imagine anyone, with foreknowledge, choosing the misery in which he lived; "wrong" because Eliot believed that the life we get – he got – was a matter of desire, if not choice: "everybody gets the kind of life he wants," as he put it to his brother in 1916.

From all manner of sources Eliot knew the romantic claim that poetry was radically different from all other kinds of writing: it presumably resisted utilitarian manipulation, it was autonomous, a unique thing working only for its own ends. Despite declaring himself to be against romanticism on various occasions, he tended to accept these staple propositions of literary theory in the romantic mode, especially in his early career. But the truth of the theory that authentic poetry has no function in the world of profit and loss he learned from experience. It would not feed him and Vivienne or pay the rent, unlike, say, editing, or writing for the popular press, or teaching literature at night to working-class people who taught *him*, to his delight, that they too took a disinterested view of literary experience, they too valued it for itself. The autonomous nature of art, his art in particular, had economic effects in life, his life. Other kinds of writing might pay the rent – Frost and Pound had tried their hand at fiction, because with fiction you might get lucky – but poetry of the high modernist moment, Eliot's poetry certainly, was economically hopeless, which, of course, it was supposed to be (he got the life he wanted).

And so the more his time was eaten up by economically necessary pursuits, the less time he had for writing poems, the more deeply special those moments became, because they opened up an alternative space of consciousness, another level of living. Of the likelihood of pay raises at the bank, Eliot said (at the time he was also lecturing at night), "at my present rate of increase of salary I can reasonably look forward to a time when they [the lectures] will be unnecessary, and I shall be able to spend all my spare time exactly as I please. When I can earn all the money I need out of one thing, and be able to read and write in the rest of my time without thinking of the financial reward of what I do, then I shall be satisfied." His conception of his poetry ("my own serious work," my "independent writing") was virtually forced upon him by the literary work he did to help sustain his and Vivienne's existence. In this personal setting, the famous description of the poet's self-sacrifice in "Tradition and the Individual Talent" – "What happens is a continual surrender of himself as he is at the moment to something which is more valuable" – tells the story of Eliot's need to enter into the poetic process in order to achieve a new life beyond the struggles of "himself as he is at the moment," the man who is trying to get by, transcended for "something" – what exactly is it? – "which is more valuable."

After securing a position at Lloyds, for a time (it will be brief), on his own testimony and that of the one best able to corroborate it, Eliot, as Vivienne put it, "*writes* better, feels better and happier and has better health when he knows that money (however *little*) is assured, and coming in regularly – even tho' he has only a few hours a day to write in, than when he has *all* day – and nothing settled, nothing *sure*." A couple of weeks later, in another letter to her mother-in-law, she wrote: "not one of his friends has failed to see, and to remark upon, the great change in Tom's health, appearance, spirits, and literary productiveness since he went in for Banking." Eliot's father, naturally, approved: his son had finally taken on real work and had confined to his "spare time" – his son's phrase – the useless activity of writing poems. Naturally, his father's emissary, Tom's conscience, also approved. He had gotten the life he wanted, or was supposed to have, a difficult distinction at best.

Like Stevens, Pound, and Frost, Eliot was a modern American man, with all the problems that the world imposes upon one who chooses to become a poet.

Eliot, too, was a full-fledged citizen of the bourgeois world, a modern writer in a sense that Yeats was not. Yeats had fired away at similar social enemies of poetry, but from a position that the American modernists could not assume, with memories of a hospitable aristocratic (Anglo-Irish) past, a real Coole Park become a Coole Park of the mind, a bitter but delicious nostalgia that was poetically productive, a memory which no American could share.

The modern American poets (Stevens is the exception: he would never lift a finger on his own literary behalf) cultivated literary schizophrenia: they pursued poetry as an alternative culture yet worked mightily to make their poetry and themselves, as figures of the poet, important, influential, and, in a word that Eliot never shied away from, *powerful*. In the process of composition, a poem was to put one on another plane of existence, beyond the reach of the reason that reigned in the culture of capital. Once in public, however, Eliot did all he could to make his writing an "event" in that very culture ("event" is his word). An Eliot poem, as he knew when barely thirty years old, was and always would be a rare thing. He early knew himself as a man who would write little. He would therefore cultivate a mystique: isolation, detachment, an enigmatic persona. At the same time, he would cultivate his connections in the world of letters, and when he came with a poem, he would come with a thing literally *remarkable*, a happening, something to be discussed and debated but never ignored.

Before 1922, the year of *The Waste Land*, even before 1920, the year of his first critical book, *The Sacred Wood*, Eliot had decided – this writer known for one poem and a handful of strong essays – that he could become a force in English letters. He believed himself on the verge of assuming literary power, more than any American had ever enjoyed in England, with the possible exception of Henry James. His first critical book would need, therefore, to deliver "a single distinct blow," so that his criticism, like his poems, could also become an instrument for wielding "influence" and "power" (his words) in the literary capital of the English-speaking world.

The essays collected in *The Sacred Wood* project a unified and supremely self-confident voice; at times, as Eliot saw in retrospect, a voice shading into solemnity and pomposity, a tone and persona precisely the reverse of Prufrock, hiding that side of himself. Here is the man, the voice implies, who knows literary history since Homer with the detail and ease of an elder statesman of letters (in fact, the essays of *The Sacred Wood* were written by a young man between his twenty-eighth and thirty-second years, not that well schooled in literary history, who had worked up his knowledge for the occasion). And the composure never cracks. At his most winning, Eliot writes sentences of luminous insight and agile wit that seem to demand to be copied out because they embody a literary wisdom – often much more than literary – which, the voice implies, will prevail.

The essays possess vocal unity but not the intellectual unity of the systematic thinker: it is easy, but pointless, to hunt for and find contradiction in *The Sacred Wood* (it has been done). One of the purposes of Eliot's dissertation on F. H. Bradley seems to have been to undermine the classical project of philosophy. He told his classmate Norbert Weiner that in order to stay inside the boundaries of common sense one would need to avoid taking any theory to its conclusion – an act which always violates our experience – and to avoid consistency. Thematic recurrences in the essays seem to well up from an inductive engagement with particulars, seem never to be imposed, and perhaps that is why his major themes and ideas are so compelling. He gives us the impression (this, perhaps, his shrewdest rhetorical effect) that his ideas emerge naturally, that they come because they must, not because he wants them to. In his approach to literary criticism he was himself a case-by-case pragmatist who avoided "foolish consistency."

Yet Eliot never had any use for Emerson; among the Harvard philosophers he took the side of Josiah Royce against William James, the side of the theorist of community against the Emersonian celebrant of freelancing individualism. Royce's later work established a context of social issues in compelling terms for his most famous student, who as poet, dramatist, critic, and social theorist brought his own (arguably authoritarian) inclinations and his philosophy teacher's (arguably democratic) preoccupations to the center of literary modernism. Royce's *The Problem of Christianity* was published almost simultaneously with Eliot's participation in Royce's graduate seminar on comparative methodology (and only five years before "Tradition and the Individual Talent"). In the book's second half, Royce explored in broader terms than Eliot would the difficult proposition that we all, not just the professional writers among us, need (in Eliot's words) to "surrender" our private selves to "something which is more valuable," and that, paradoxically, such surrender will result not in slavish conformity and all loss of selfhood but in the discovery of an enriched and more satisfying self within a "living whole." By "living whole" Eliot meant, in 1919, when "Tradition and the Individual Talent" appeared in the *Egoist*, the Western literary tradition since Homer. After his conversion in 1927, he would embed that literary "living whole" in an idea of Christian community. Emerson asks, "Why should not we also enjoy an original relation to the universe?" and Royce and Eliot reply that Emerson has no right to say "we" because the ground of "we" is history and community, or precisely everything from which Emerson's isolated visionary seeks to sever himself in quest of "original relation."

Eliot's complex spirit of community-minded, literary critical pragmatism is matched and motivated by the cosmopolitan character of his sources: Laforgue and the French symbolists, Charles Maurras, Remy DuGourmont, Paul Claudel, the Elizabethan and Jacobean dramatists, Dante, Donne and the Metaphysical poets, T. E. Hulme, Pound, Henry James, Ford Madox Ford, and, later, when he no longer felt it necessary to muster the weapons of antiromanticism, Coleridge's definition of imagination ("the balance or reconciliation of opposite or discordant qualities"), in which he recognized a kindred spirit. But it was yet another Harvard presence of Eliot's undergraduate years who bent his attitudes in antiromantic directions, and who encouraged him to look to French thinkers, well before those encounters with Hulme and Pound, which confirmed but did not shape him. Irving Babbitt's *Literature and the American College* (1908) now reads like a primer for T. S. Eliot's thought.

In the late 1920s, Eliot would pen his distance, writing, in effect, that Babbitt's neohumanist "inner check" of restraint turns out to be grounded on nothing but the individual's own innerness. Nevertheless, much of Eliot's social and literary criticism, from beginning to end, assumes both Babbitt's classical values and their animus toward Bacon and Rousseau, and everything those cultural gods of modernity have come to represent. With Babbitt, he stands against humanitarianism and the enthusiasm that all men are worthy of a promiscuous sympathy and benevolence; against the belief in the kingdom of man through the interventions of science (the religion of "progress"); against the rule of impulse ("one impulse from a vernal wood"); against the "inordinate exaltation of the individual," the democratic spirit, the "pedantry of individualism," and the "free play of one's individual faculties." He stands for discipline, constraint, and the ideals of community; for tradition and classical literary values that stress impersonality and the universal life (as opposed, in Eliot's dark imagery from Dante and Bradley, to the prison of self); for the muses of memory over those of inspiration and genius. And, always, Eliot believes in the social centrality of literary experience: in Babbitt's words, "that golden chain of masterpieces which link together into a single tradition the more permanent experience of the race." The golden chain of masterpieces (an inspiration here for the future author of "Tradition and the Individual Talent") invites not "servile" but "creative imitation," a "balance" of the "forces of tradition and the claims of originality." Finally, in the language of Babbitt, we see the return of the poet's paternal grandfather, William Greenleaf Eliot: social obligation in attendance on the "minds and characters of future citizens of a republic." Now mix in the authoritarianism of Maurras, and the Eliot who would declare himself in 1927 "classicist in literature, royalist in politics, and anglo-catholic in religion" is virtually formed more than a decade before he will make the much quoted declaration that Babbitt himself had urged him to make, in the "open."

The major ideas of *The Sacred Wood* are the major and often recurrent ideas of Eliot's career (they will set the foundation of the New Criticism): (1) *the integrity of poetry* ("a poem, in some sense, has its own life," and note "in some sense," a qualification usually ignored by his formalist inheritors); (2) the need to cultivate awareness of *literary tradition*, not as a repository of rule-bearing repressors, harsh father-figures, but of "masters" who persist as "living forces" of inspiration and historical community (Eliot always speaks negatively of the tyranny of the dead, the canonical standard); (3) the value of *unified sensibility* and the need for its recovery, a sensibility that he finds in Dante and Shakespeare but not in Massinger and Milton, who mark its breakdown, whose intellects are not "immediately at the tips of the senses"; (4) the celebration of *dramatic form*, for its power to express social variety, and (5) the kind of *dramatic character* (absent in modern drama) which delights in seeing itself in dramatic light; (6) the *music-hall artist* as an inspiration for modern literary form, a figure for the potential recapturing of the organic ideal of the performer-artist integrated with a performer-audience; (7) the need for a *framework* – stabilized habits of response, a "culture" evident in the overall "preparedness," the receptivity of an audience, a "temper" which a writer does not create but assumes as a basis of his rhetorical contract with his readers; (8) the value of inheriting a *literary form* ("no man can invent a form, create a taste for it, and perfect it, too": Eliot, unlike Wordsworth and Pound, was an unhappy, a reluctant experimentalist); (9) the ideal of *impersonality* ("The progress of an artist is a continual self-sacrifice, a continual extinction of personality").

But for all his avowed classicism, Eliot stands, as a poet, closer to Blake than to his beloved Dante: "He was naked," he says of Blake, and exposed to the "dangers to which the naked man is exposed" – "formlessness" in particular. In his brilliant phrase for Blake, he became the creator in *The Waste Land* of an "ingenious piece of home-made furniture," more in the romantic and the American grain than he wanted to be, or could admit, desiring "a framework of accepted and traditional ideas," but never (like Dante) in confident possession of it. In his essay on Blake, we come up to the edge of "Gerontion" and *The Waste Land*. Eliot, like Royce and Santayana, is critical of the sweeping modernist tide (perceptualism, hedonism, imagism, the poetry of fragments, "odds and ends of still life and stage properties"); he struggles against the tide, but is at its mercy nevertheless. He did not want to stand between Dante and Blake, but that's where he found himself, and that is his drama.

Most of the poems in Eliot's small second volume were composed between 1917, when *Prufrock and Other Observations* appeared, and 1920, a period that also saw the publication of a number of his most provocative essays, including

"Tradition and the Individual Talent," "Hamlet and His Problems," and a piece about Henry James: three essays that give us discursive entry to the poetic obsessions which propelled him, especially in "Gerontion," into a literary territory hostile to critical commentary, a poetry virtually alien to the generalizing power of ideas.

In James's fiction Eliot saw the expression of the sort of sensibility he found and admired in Dante, Shakespeare, Donne, and certain Jacobean dramatists; a tradition interrupted, so he thought, around the time of Milton, who represented both a major divergence and a major (damaging) influence throughout the eighteenth and nineteenth centuries; a tradition resumed by the French symbolists, James, and (he hoped) himself. What went wrong around the time of Milton? Was the problem primarily literary or social in nature? A literary breakdown caused by a social breakdown? Eliot liked to hint at theories (particularly the latter one, because he believed that a healthy literature could not be written in a sick society), but he never argued for or even asserted an explanation with any detail or clarity. He would suggest teasing theories of a Fall, but nowhere in his work does he speak of a lost social Eden. Around 1920, Eliot was piecing together (making up) a tradition (like an ingenious piece of home-made furniture) of integrated sensibilities (the writers he was most drawn to), and, at the same time, feeling a ruling desire to become part of that tradition, to join that company in beloved literary community.

As the modern representative of this tradition, James is "a mind so fine no idea could violate it," the "last test of a superior intelligence" being its "baffling escape from Ideas." The point is to avoid, somehow, thinking with the intellect (as if it were autonomous) because ideas, once abstracted from the totality of the healthy personality, became Ideas, and "run wild and pasture on the emotions." The writing of James represents, not a fusion of equal portions of "idea" and "feeling," but a capacity for generating thought, as a derivative, from the irrational matrix of personality. But once abstracted from a whole within which the distinction between idea and emotion cannot arise, then ideas ("Ideas") in themselves will take on a malevolent life of their own: they will reenter the personality in violent fashion, in a kind of rape – or, in another of Eliot's figures, as preyers on emotion, desiccators, vampires at the throat of personality.

Hamlet (and its title character) presents the problem of dissociated sensibility from the other end. The play represents a different kind of violation of personality, with Shakespeare unbalanced and his emotions become autonomous, preying on his ability to create rational design, to conceive and develop an "objective correlative," a "set of objects, a situation, a chain of events" that, once given in literary form, will evoke emotions adequate to and expressive of the object, the situation, the event; the emotion and its correlative should ideally be interdependent, another image of the wished-for wholeness which *Hamlet* presumably does not achieve. This failure to produce an objective correlative in *Hamlet* results in the expression of feeling in excess of everything. *Hamlet* is characterized by an "unmistakable tone" (like a distinctive person? a distinctive literary style?), tantalizing (the "'Mona Lisa' of literature") but impossible to localize in any quotation, or set of quotations, or any action. The play fails, thinks Eliot, except that toward the end of his essay he indicates that this presumed lapse in Shakespeare's dramatic power may be something more interesting: an experience any person of sensibility has gone through and then (usually) repressed. This terror of excess, this shock of finding out that what it means to be human is to experience feelings corresponding to nothing in the world. Eliot would rather have been like Henry James than the Shakespeare of *Hamlet*, but he didn't get his wish. He was, instead, an "unmistakable tone," difficult to localize, a style, a literary presence, Mona Lisa-like, impossible to shake from consciousness once he has been encountered.

In this context, "Tradition and the Individual Talent" is less a pronouncement about the nature of literary history than it is an expression, in literary-historical language and analysis, of Roycean desire for community-in-history: the desire to "surrender," to yield "himself as he is at the moment to something which is more valuable," a process of "continual extinction of the personality." By "personality" Eliot means something we possess painfully, in isolating individuality; and those who have a personality know what it means to want to escape it. By "extinction" he means the death of that; the "something which is more valuable" is not a no-self but a self-in-historical-community. "Community" meant for Eliot, in 1917, the literary tradition since, and proceeding from, Homer. In the following well-known passage, change "order" to "community," change "novelty" to "self," and Eliot's vision of organic mutuality, his social hunger, is clear:

> The necessity that he shall conform, that he shall cohere, is not one sided; what happens when a new work of art is created is something that happens simultaneously to all the works of art which preceded it . . . The existing order is complete before the new work arrives; for order to persist after the supervention of novelty, the whole existing order must be, if ever so slightly, altered . . .

Like his first collection of poetry, Eliot's second features considerable tonal range, although such range is again obscured by a lead-off poem ("Gerontion") whose familiar sound marks it as both a relative of "Prufrock" and a forecast of the voice-over of *The Waste Land*, the poem for which "Gerontion" was to serve as preface until Pound convinced Eliot not to use it. "Gerontion" is daunting and unrelentingly intense; other poems in the volume are satirical and playfully humorous, or satirical and not especially playful or good-hearted; still others are written in French (playfully and otherwise: an exercise that helped him to get over a dry spell).

"Burbank with a Baedeker: Bleistein with a Cigar," an instance of Eliot's satirical intention going for mock-heroic effects, defines American Jews as exemplary degenerates of contemporary culture, the invaders of Venice. The debunking allusive context of high culture, Shakespearean moments from *Othello*, and the glance at Byron's Venice at the end of the poem, cannot contain the extended expression of repulsion in the middle of it, where Eliot, full of rhetorical savagery, writes in a virulent rhetoric for which no objective correlative is possible, in excess of everything except anti-Semitism.

In "Sweeney Erect" Eliot hears the urgent imperative of tradition, which he may not be able to answer ("Paint me a cavernous waste shore / Cast in the unstilled Cyclades"); he experiences the memory of the Homeric past surging into consciousness, virtually taking it over: "Morning stirs the feet and hands / (Nausicaa and Polypheme)." In "Sweeney Among the Nightingales" he transforms his allusive technique into an interpretive principle, a way not only of evaluating the present, but of understanding the present as an expression of the past, not so much diminished as it is luridly continuous, gross realist texture undergirded by mythic narrative. Allusion is the acknowledgment of the presence of the past; allusion says cultures are haunted.

"Gerontion," the strength and fascination of Eliot's second volume, is the poem which joins "Prufrock," *The Waste Land*, "Ash Wednesday," and *Four Quartets* in establishing the major poetic episodes in the narrative of Eliot's career and life. In method and tone (though not in range of materials) "Gerontion" could certainly have been a preface to *The Waste Land*. In this poem, Eliot enacts a central proposition of "Tradition and the Individual Talent": he is "aware that the mind of Europe – the mind of his own country – a mind which he learns in time to be much more important than his own mind – is a mind which changes, and that this change is a development which abandons nothing *en route* . . . the difference between the present and the past is that the conscious present is an awareness of the past in a way and to an extent which the past's awareness of itself cannot show."

It is the mind of Europe that Eliot, in "Gerontion" and *The Waste Land*, surrenders himself to, and in so surrendering enters a literary community of long historical duration, as the "conscious present." This consciousness attaches epigraphs to its poems (in a language not necessarily English: the mind of Europe) and tends to express itself in associative leaps (embodied

in the discontinuities of collagelike formations) – leaps that defy logic and
chronology because the "conscious present" is aware of the past all at once, as a
totality, not as a linear series of events. Allusion for this kind of consciousness
is not a simple literary strategy, a knowledge of the past manipulated in
the present by a writer dispassionately distant from the past, but a mode
of consciousness whose nature is historical. However difficult it may be to
grasp the rationale of the allusive network in "Gerontion," or the reason for
the particular jumps that this consciousness makes in this poem, the art of
Eliot here and in *The Waste Land* is to make us feel that all the allusions and
associative jumps are inevitable.

And who is this speaker? He is ("of course" one wants to say; this is Eliot's
world) old, self-dramatizingly so: "Here I am, an old man in a dry month";
he is a stranger to the world of heroic action; he evokes the Jew once more
in a dehumanizing rhetoric; he yearns, via Blake, for "Christ the tiger" to
consume him away, into a new life; he desires Christian communion but cannot
help himself from evoking delicious pre-Christian pagan parallels, via Henry
Adams – another guilty, self-styled, cold man fascinated by the displays of lusty
spring below the Mason-Dixon line ("In depraved May, dogwood and chestnut,
flowering judas"). And the memory of Adams in the fecund South somehow (we
don't know how) leads into the swift internationalist evocations of character
weirdly at play, participating in some black mass full of vague sexual innuendo,
with Eliot's verbs doing precisely perverse work ("Mr. Silvero / With caressing
hands . . . Hakagawa, bowing among the Titians . . . Fräulein von Kulp / Who
turned in the hall, one hand on the door"). Then follows the major passage on
history as an overwhelming woman, confusing, full of brutal ironic reversals
("Unnatural vices / Are fathered by our heroism") and the impossibility, in this
poem, of separating the public flow of history from the private disasters and
humiliations of an unhappy sexual alliance: the mean self-lacerations ("I have
lost my sight, smell, hearing, taste and touch: / How should I use them for
your closer contact?"), and the futility ("What will the spider do, / Suspend its
operations . . . "). Eliot's famous sentences about "surrender" and "the mind of
Europe" do no justice to the thick specificity of his mind's interaction with that
larger entity, or to the surrender that does not extinguish his individuality, or
to the thinking that he does through his nerves, the artful illusion sustained
in "Gerontion" that his mind is never violated by Ideas.

The job at Lloyds Bank brought the Eliots some security, but their tran-
quility was short-lived. The family psyche quickly resumed its precipitous
downward course; the marriage became a disaster. Eliot's overly taxed daily
work life – he was at it virtually all of his waking hours – did not permit him
much contact with his self-conceived, deepest core of identity as a poet. After

his doctors recommended a three-month rest away from home and all work, he took off, ending up in a Swiss sanatorium. He got his rest; he got his vacation; and by the end of his break from home and London, all the while apparently not thinking of his poetry as "work" in the sense that his doctors must have meant the word, he found that he had almost begotten *The Waste Land*. The breakdown was just what he needed. I say "almost begotten" because he also needed Pound's midwifery. It is not probable, given the evidence of the poems written before and those written after, that *The Waste Land* would have assumed its modernist collage form, sporting such sharp and brilliant discontinuities, had Eliot not sought Pound's reaction and had Pound not been willing (but Pound was Pound) to wield an unerring editorial red pencil. That, in brief, is the personal narrative behind the poem which probably led Eliot to describe it, long after its appearance, as a "personal and wholly insignificant grouse against life; . . . a piece of rhythmical grumbling."

The literary narrative is more familiar, and more devious. *The Waste Land* is the fullest working-through of the impulses, and the voice of those impulses, driving Eliot's major early work, a poem that needed to be written after "Prufrock" and "Gerontion." Its formal and spiritual inspirations are complex and difficult to discriminate, but nevertheless in rough presence they are clear. James G. Frazer's *The Golden Bough* and Jessie L. Weston's *From Ritual to Romance* are the anthropological sources Eliot names in his notes to the poem, the books that gave him stories of ritual pagan religious practices – hints, as he took them, for literary form and a possible narrative of redemption (personal and collective, a distinction not much admired by Frazer, Weston, and Eliot). Frazer and Weston were sources for a deep structural underpinning of *The Waste Land* that, thanks to Eliot and a number of his explicators, have been made too much of (both the sources and the deep structural underpinning). Whatever else they are, the notes are the work not of a personal grouser but of a socially responsive interpreter intending to set his own work in "significant" light.

Eliot's reading of *Ulysses* constituted another major inspiration and culminates in his essay "'Ulysses,' Order, and Myth" (1923), the most important early, if indirect, critical reflection on *The Waste Land*, in which he saw Joyce's book as the expression of a need for "method" that he imagined to have given more shape to *Ulysses* (and to his own poem) than really obtains. This essay gives us not the slightest glimpse of the inventiveness and surprises, the unpredictable leaps and changes, that mark both *Ulysses* and *The Waste Land*. Joyce's continuous manipulation of a parallel with *The Odyssey* and Eliot's use of Weston's anthropological narrative or of several classical literary texts are alike in tact of deployment, lightness of structural presence, and the gentleness with which deployed structures do not control their respective deployers' imaginations, or the unexpected and unexpectable vivid particulars of texture that cannot be dominated by structure, or indeed other methods of prereading and prewriting. The main point of Eliot's essay is that the present is an opaque fragment unless set inside the framework of a classical literary narrative which will restore the context of significance, the fragment-redeeming whole. There is no understanding except through the lens of literature; Wilde would have approved. Together with his notes to the poem, the essay on Joyce sets in motion the solemn traditional take on high modernist experiment, often to the detriment of that experiment.

And, finally, the essay "The Metaphysical Poets" (1921) is an elegant summary of Eliot's critical preoccupations to that point, an indirect anticipation of the vast literary-historical ambition of the epochal poem he would publish the following year. In light of that essay's argument, the history of poetry in English, the main current of authentic poetry, as Eliot believed, interrupted around the time of Milton, would find its grand resumption in *The Waste Land* thanks to the unified sensibility of this proper heir of Dante, Shakespeare, and Donne. Of course, Eliot never said that publicly, maybe never said it privately, even to himself. But given the drift of his critical and poetic writing to 1922, that was what he desired, personal grouse or no personal grouse.

The notes to *The Waste Land* are prefaced by a paragraph that begins, "Not only the title, but the plan and a good deal of the incidental symbolism of the poem were suggested by Miss Jessie L. Weston's book on the grail legend." And he adds, "so deeply am I indebted, Miss Weston's book will elucidate the difficulties of the poem much better than my notes can . . . " Anyone familiar with Frazer and Weston, Eliot concludes, "will immediately recognize in the poem certain references to vegetation ceremonies." The statement is unremarkable in its demands. If you wish to understand the poem, it says, you will need to read other books first. Yet in his essay on Dante of 1929, he would say that "genuine poetry can communicate before it is understood," implying that "understanding" might not be our primary way of deriving pleasure and even significance from "genuine poetry"; and, indeed, Eliot's aesthetic always seemed less in favor of understanding than it was in favor of entering, through poetry, reading or writing it, another and rarer level of experience, a substratum of feeling shut off from the purity of reason. In Eliot, a romantic always lurks.

Readers of Milton (the younger Eliot would have detested the comparison), to cite only one spectacular example of difficulty, have long known the problem. The fact that Milton leaned hard on the Bible and other widely known Western classics makes a difference, but not a difference in kind. (Joyce leaned on Homer, but *Ulysses* persists in its strangeness.) Milton and Eliot not only make reference to other texts, those texts are taken in, or perhaps "make an invasion" is the way to put it, become part of the complex weave of their writing, in the case of *The Waste Land* the poet being almost perfectly covered by a canvas crowded with allusion, quotation, and pastiche. Eliot's poetry, like Pound's and Milton's, is a poetry of reading (for writer and reader alike), and – again like Pound's, but not like Milton's – a poetry of reading that could take for granted no fit audience, however small. Who among Eliot's readers, at the time of publication, could pick up on the allusions to Shakespeare and Virgil and Weston, particularly when the allusions to central writers are not necessarily to central moments or lines in their texts? Maybe none, probably not even Pound or Joyce. The notes were necessary, first of all, because the printer demanded more pages in order to fill out a signature for the book version of the poem. But they were also aids necessary to all readers; they comprise Eliot's tacit admission that he would need to introduce and train his readers in his curriculum of cultural literacy in order to make them ready to grasp his diagnosis of cultural disease.

Somehow, Eliot would refer to the tradition and teach it all at once, although "the tradition" is not correct, since it would be difficult to know, on the basis of what he quotes and alludes to, from Virgil to Verlaine, Buddha to F. H. Bradley, Webster to Weston, of just what this tradition could possibly consist, if not of Eliot's fabrication: a piece of ingenious home-made furniture, Blakean through and through. His tradition is (never mind all his schooling) the idiosyncratic imagination of an enthusiastic autodidact, trying, like Pound, to impart his treasure to readers (not a readership) who haven't the foggiest, and in the main do not care. (Autodidact may be another word for American.) *The Waste Land* represents the bizarre case of an unorthodox writer, leaning hard on his personal odyssey as a reader, his education be damned, trying to do the impossible – to invent orthodoxy – precisely the literary situation that Eliot would castigate a few years later in *After Strange Gods*, a text written after his conversion, when he, no longer a free-thinking agnostic, could go after celebrated modern writers and suggest that no coherent community (i.e., no real community) could accept them or, for that matter, too many "freethinking Jews."

In *The Golden Bough* and *From Ritual to Romance*, Eliot read of certain vegetation ceremonies, the rituals of fertility cults of very wide geographic distribution (the lure of a "universal" story), dating back to 3000 BC or more, some of whose practices and symbols survive in the Tarot cards, are represented in numerous medieval quest romances, and in, and *as*, Christianity itself (whose presence in *The Waste Land* is always in tandem with pagan myth). It is a basic narrative of the birth, fruition, decay, and death of nature – the autonomous cycle of seasons unknown and a parallel and symbiotic narrative of human fertility, the waste and regeneration of the land and the loins, the latter process being represented in a ruler, a king of semidivine origin, who is himself representative of the life principle and is subject to the vicissitudes of declining sexual powers, death, and rebirth; the life principle periodically endangered; the fate of king, community, and nature indistinguishable; the fate of king and land nevertheless subject to control in the ceremonies described by Frazer and Weston: a community empowered by itself to save itself.

The basic narrative, its rituals and symbols, provides, Eliot says, "the plan" of his poem: plot, intention, design, and the attendant values of "the plan." Knowledge of the plan is useful if we are going to grasp Eliot's historical consciousness, his playing against the anthropological plan with contemporary characters, situation, and dialogue (the living theater of the plan). The counterpointing and the setting up of diminished and truncated (and sometimes comic) contemporary parallels constitutes "the mythic method" of the poem, which other writers could learn from Joyce, Eliot thought, and would need to follow, as if *Ulysses* were a scientific model, if they were to write in a form appropriate to the modern world, and if they were to control – give order, "a shape and significance" – to what he called, in the essay on Joyce, "the immense panorama of futility and anarchy which is contemporary history." He meant contemporary history viewed and evaluated from the prospect provided by "the plan" – or at least he should have meant that.

Milton leaned on the Bible and on all those who had read it or had absorbed its myths without necessarily reading it, not having to read it because they lived in the culture of the Bible – these readers comprised his potential readership and gave Milton a chance at cultural centrality and immortality. Eliot, by leaning on still rather obscure texts in anthropology, would appear to have had no chance to make *The Waste Land* a readable text outside the modernist coterie. Nevertheless, *The Waste Land* has achieved a certain diminished centrality by finding a readership of insiders, other poets whose careers were in part formed by negative reactions to the poem or what they thought the poem stood for: Hart Crane, William Carlos Williams; a movement of antiformalist poets in the 1950s and 1960s; and, most crucially, university readers, academic literary critics and the generations of their students who were taught what they needed to know in order to avail themselves of the insider's pleasures; they were taught not only Frazer and Weston but the classic texts of the Western literary tradition, the university being perhaps the last place where those texts may be systematically and rigorously read. As the keeper of what are called canonical texts, the university has become what Eliot would never have approved of for his idea of a healthy society: the cordoned-off preserver of literary culture, the institution that unavoidably puts at the margin what it preserves; the literary department, in other words, as upscale bohemian enclave, site of the last serious readers of the major literature of the West. "Alienated readers" is understood.

For all those so armed with special decoding devices, the poem, beginning (obviously now) with its title, becomes a radiant series of organic fragments, survivals or traces, in a minor key, of ancient ritual and deep persistent myth. In its first section, "The Burial of the Dead" (an echo of the Anglican burial service), are found the imagery from the desert, the brown fogs of Dickens and Robert Louis Stevenson, the stony rubbish, the dead tree, and the dry stone which gives no sound of water; the references to the Tarot cards, and particularly the reference to The Hanged Man, figure of a dead God, a Christ-like being who may be reborn, but which the fortune-teller cannot find, and the gruesome but thematic humor of the planted corpse beginning to sprout. In the second section, "A Game of Chess," are counterpointed scenes of marriage, impotence, and abortion; in "The Fire Sermon," variations on the theme of infertile love, and again the brown land, the river "sweating" oil and tar (a startling figure of the perversions of nature, human and otherwise); in the fourth, the ambiguous "Death by Water," the title itself as reference to a central nature-cult ceremony of rebirth; and, lastly, in "What the Thunder Said," are the references to Gethsemane, the journey through the desert, the approach to the Chapel Perilous, and the anticipation of life-renewing rain. With the aid of Frazer and Weston, *The Waste Land* reads as an ironic quest-romance, filtered through a modernist aesthetic of collage whose effect is to deny narrative progression and change and to insist on a nightmare of temporal simultaneity.

The pleasures of knowing the plan, pleasures attendant upon structural understanding and getting the real story – secret allegory, decoding, riddle-solving, secret translation – are never the pleasures of texture, sensuous pleasures of aesthetic encounter, delights of the surface – values of reading *The Waste Land* that have, oddly, receded over time, that familiarity has not enhanced. It is the pleasure of the *plan*, the primacy of structure, that has been enhanced over time. It is hardly possible anymore to read the poem without passing through scholarly mediation: the explanations of anthropological sources, the fixing of literary sources, echoes, allusions, and their skillful annotation. No university reader can do otherwise, or would think of doing otherwise, or maybe should do otherwise. The cultural centrality of *The Waste Land*, as *the* pessimistic expression of the lost generation, is the centrality that critics and scholars, with Eliot's boost, have made. Yet the plan, though it underlies the poem, does so faintly and obscurely, tactfully so, despite all the academic labor to make the plan "obvious," an unavoidable structural presence in constant control of the details of the surface. And the elucidated literary allusions and quotations also now sit there "obviously," as if Eliot had written his poem standing up, notebook in hand, in front of his library shelves, yanking off the proper texts, putting in the telling quotations.

The Waste Land made by scholarship is largely cold and willful – an image of Eliot that the anti-Eliot movement in poetry and criticism, from the fifties through the seventies (it seems to have tapered off) was happy to seize upon in efforts to write and promote a new antiformal poetry (as though Eliot's work were not a formal oddball) and to promote the reputations of Hart Crane, William Carlos Williams, Wallace Stevens, and the romantic literary tradition, broadly defined, back to Spenser, that the young Eliot at times, and his inheritors in the New Criticism very often, had trashed. The countertrashing of Eliot and the New Critics helped to refocus our vision of literary history, reinstating movements and figures necessarily excluded by Eliot's and his New Critical inheritors' notion of authentic literary tradition. The countertrashing, so richly deserved, was also useful.

In any effort to encounter a more immediate incarnation of *The Waste Land* we might be helped by what Eliot said about Ben Jonson in *The Sacred Wood*: "Though he was saturated in literature, he never sacrifices the theatrical qualities – theatrical in the most favorable sense – to literature or to the study of character. His work is a titanic show." *The Waste Land*, quintessence of modernist experiment, a poem loaded with learning and "literature," is never sacrificed to "literature."

By "theater" and "theatrical," Eliot intended several things: first, the literary form he thought best suited down through the eras to meet, engage, and capture the life of the writer's times (the historicality of theater); second, a writer's literary self-consciousness of being *in performance* while writing, seeing himself in a dramatic light, in the act of creating himself as a character; third, a music-hall show, a series of entertainments, or the music-hall performer himself, represented for Eliot best by *her*self, Marie Lloyd, the entertainer whose death moved him to cultural mourning in a short essay published in the year of *The Waste Land*, in which he extols her organic genius, that special connection she activated with her audience, whom she led to discover and know itself as contributing, on-site artist in support of her (in several senses) *living* art.

The Waste Land as theater is attested to by Eliot's own recorded performance and by the frequency with which it turns up as a text for readers' theater on college campuses – persuasive testimony to the poem's dramatic character and possibilities, with its five parts functioning as five separate shows, replete with characters from all classes, language "high" and "low," jokes, dialogue, playlets, gossip, sex, popular and operatic song (something for everyone) – "and all interesting." *The Waste Land* is a titanic variety show (a *satura*, a mixture) offering the pleasures of the theater, pleasures independent of deep structure and myth, analytical intellect, or literary knowledge, pleasures one need not be an insider to enjoy and that cannot be excited by attention to "plan" and "mythic method."

One of Eliot's notes in particular, however, throws up an insuperable barrier to the experiencing of such various pleasures. It is the note on Tiresias which states that Tiresias ("I, Tiresias, though blind, throbbing between two lives"), who makes his initial (overt) appearance in "The Fire Sermon," is "the most important personage in the Poem, uniting all the rest." Various figures, Eliot says, "melt" into one another; "all the women are one woman, and the two sexes meet in Tiresias. What Tiresias *sees*, in fact, is the substance of the poem." This note does the same kind of texture-obliterating (melting) work that Eliot's comments on Weston, Frazer, and "the plan" had already done. Once again we are encouraged to plunge below the surface, so variegated, to a deep structural principle, by definition homogeneous, essential, and reductive. Whether via Weston, or whether via Tiresias-the-unifying-voice, the poem's presumably presiding consciousness, we come to the same place, where all theater and theatricality, all particularity, vanishes into thin air. No music hall that operated on such principles would last for more than a night. We are not entertained; we are bored when all the women are one woman and all the men one man.

The misleading (and self-misled, if Eliot believed it) note on Tiresias is useful if taken to suggest a less reductive principle of reading, the author's helpful hint for encountering his poem's aesthetic (sensuous, vocal) cohesion in the face of a collection of fragments that might seem unifiable only at the level of deep structure (unity apparent to intellect, not ear or eye). The note on Tiresias, so understood, becomes an instrument for the unveiling of *The Waste Land*'s persistent vocal presence, a presiding but not devouring voice that intones the poem's opening lines, a voice authoritative, prophetic, elegiac, moral, and, via "Prufrock" and "Gerontion," always soul-weary: "April is the cruelest month." This voice, so strongly "written," quickly disappears in "The Burial of the Dead" into characters like the insomniac Marie, the fortune-teller, Madame Sosostris, and the unnamed joker who madly teases Stetson about his blooming corpse – disappears, that is, into "speech," the conversational rhythms of contemporary characters; then into the formal dialogues, the diptych that comprises most of "A Game of Chess"; then into the music, bawdy and stately, that appears in "The Fire Sermon"; then, transformed, as the voice which sings the formal lyric of "Death by Water" and drives the incantation of "What the Thunder Said."

This persistent voice, this would-be voice-over, which would stay above and outside, giving moral perspective, delivering judgments dour and covert, in effect falls inside, becoming itself frequently a subject of waste when, for example, toward the end of its introduction of the first dialogue in "A Game of Chess," we suddenly find it inside the suffocating interior it describes, falling from its perch, the safety of the simple past tense, down into the entrapment of the present participle and the room of desiccation: "Staring forms / Leaned out, leaning, hushing the room enclosed." Or, in other telling moments, when we feel the rhythms of the voice-over duplicated as the rhythms of the unnamed man who fails in the hyacinth garden; or when the persistent vocal presence is spoken *to*, made a sexual offer, *made* a character, in effect, by the proposition of Mr. Eugenides; or when, in perhaps as telling a moment as we will find in the poem, the voice-over becomes another of the walking urban dead, lured by the mandolin playing in a workers' pub on Lower Thames Street, a pub adjacent to the splendid church of Magnus Martyr, adjacent institutions neither of which he can participate in. The mandolin sounds in his mind in tandem with the music of Ariel, heard by Ferdinand in *The Tempest*, Shakespeare's late play of transformation and redemption. This voice-over, this contemporary Ferdinand (searching for his Miranda, in a poem of numerous failures of love), this head full of echoes and memories of rebirth, who will not himself be reborn, does not go into the pub he wants to go into, where, or so he imagines, life is not lived in the mind: pub and church, side by side, an image of the unified, organic community for which Eliot longed. This lyric moment from "The Fire Sermon" (257–265) is perhaps the most telling in the poem because it incarnates, in a plain-styled diction, the driving desire at work in *The Waste Land*: to get out of the waste land. Desire so framed – the passage sits virtually at the center of the poem – is critical desire. The problem is not being able to come to terms with the modern metropolis, whose scene provides the details of the poem's setting, the debilitating context for a shape-changing urban stroller in the financial district, trying to forget the profit and the loss, a consciousness that would preside over the waste land with moral clarity, but more often than not finds itself losing its authority, becoming resident within. Eliot does not find his "Miranda," that "something which is more valuable" to which he would sacrifice his "self."

But the immediacy of this voice is not the immediacy of sound by itself, cut off from intellect. It is the immediacy of a total sensibility that takes in the London scene all at once as sensuous datum (of mainly repulsive detail) and as object of knowledge. This is a mind that looks at the world and does not think,

London is "like" Dante's *Inferno*; this is a mind that looks at London and *sees* Dante's *Inferno*; a mind that imagines the sexually indifferent typist and doesn't think, "In Oliver Goldsmith it would have been different" (Eliot counts on us getting the difference), but more importantly cannot experience the real except through literary mediation; as a literary voice yielding itself constantly to other literary voices; a mind that looks at "life" and sees "literature" in action. The experience of voice in this poem is dramatically concrete, like the experience of a playgoer who, through the medium of the actors' voices, gains access to a presiding mind that functions as the "conscious present," and "awareness of the past in a way and to an extent which the past's awareness of itself cannot show," a mind not *with* a perception, but *as* a perception, "not only of the pastness of the past, but of its presence." But this presiding consciousness, heterogeneous and impure, this "conscious present," this head full of memories of literature and ancient ritual, is also the conscious past, in a way and to an extent which the past, as past, could never be conscious – that is, as an awareness of the present from the point of view of the past.

The Waste Land is finally a traditional poem, not because it looks like any poem that was written before it (it does not), but because its experiments in form, its splintered negotiations of a poetic consciousness in full flight from subjective stability (escaping its personality), make sense only as they engage and revivify traditional writers in ways that those writers could never have imagined or desired, in a world that those writers did not imagine. *The Waste Land* is not a monument of literary history. It is an image of literary history itself in the act of undergoing difficult transformation, abandoning, as Eliot put it in "Tradition and the Individual Talent," "nothing *en route*."

We can see *The Waste Land* conceived as its anthropological substructure, a "plan" now not so obscure; or *The Waste Land* as sensuous embodiment and narrative of a voice constantly reincarnating itself in surprising tones, characters, and in other writers, shattering its substantial unity; or, better, *The Waste Land* as some deep-set plan contacted only through particulars of texture. And as one more version, this one suggested by terms from (for young man Eliot) the new art of moving pictures and the newly revolutionized art of painting: "montage" and "collage," recently deployed by critics to characterize the poem's surface (that is, "aesthetic") impact.

In *The Waste Land*, Eliot, a man of his aesthetic times, created a kind of painting in five panels, which must be grasped by the mind's eye all at once, as a spatial form, taken in as if the poem were a single complex image, not a work to be read through time, from beginning to end, but a work to be "seen" in a glance. This version of the poem can be contacted only by readers of veteran status who know the allusions like the back of their hands, who have read the poem so many times, in frustration and pleasure, that, in effect, they hardly need a text because they have made themselves into viewers. *The Waste Land*, so encountered, becomes the literary equivalent of a work of analytical Cubism, a series of layered "planes" transparent to each other, whose overall effect is the fracturing of the traditional literary unities of time (1922), place (London), and continuing, binding representations of character (many of them sordid and neurasthenic).

Eliot's experiment does not welcome questions about when, where, and who. And it constantly overrides the distinction between real and representation. So that contemporary London (the poem's "real," the poem's "present"), Baudelaire's Paris, and the scene of *The Inferno* stand co-presently in "The Burial of the Dead"; so that lovers from *The Aeneid* and *Hamlet* stand in co-presence, as if they all existed in the same space with contemporary couples in "A Game of Chess," the panel of couples; so that *The Tempest*, Spenser, and Marvell provide gestures of love side by side with various contemporary enactments of the flesh in "The Fire Sermon," where Buddha and St. Augustine speak, side by side. The old unities are replaced by what an active reader must bring together in a reconciling glance: not, finally, the past and present in ironic juxtaposition (though such juxtapositions stud many local textures of the poem), but past and present, "literary" and "real," in immediate painterly presence, a wall of pictures, a horror of simultaneity for a consciousness that knows too much and for which freshness of experience is impossible. In lines from the first of the *Quartets*:

> If all time is eternally present
> All time is unredeemable . . .

But the metaphor of spatial form does not quite hold all the way. In the fifth and final section, time leaks ominously out of space, painterly panel becomes narrative, and the fixed and repetitious seem about to undergo change. A key Shakespearean moment ("Those are pearls that were his eyes") is worked and reworked consciously in the poem's voice-over and unconsciously in characters who say it, not because they know Shakespeare (they do not) and enjoy displaying literary sophistication, but because the line must be spoken, because this longing for transformation must be felt. Section V, then, is seen through a veil of hallucinatory rhetoric: Gethsemane, the road to Emmaus, the whirlwind tour of exploding European capitals, and the approach to the Chapel Perilous, where the grail-quester might ask the right question, so much the better to facilitate redemption of land and impotent king, so that we might live in a new world, forgetting "the profit and the loss" (Eliot's sole but insistent political gesture, his revulsion from the world of capital). The tone is apocalyptic; some revelation, the much longed-for change is at hand, but what is it that lurks just over the horizon?

Eliot ends the poem in the mode of a desire (half-fearful) expressed, just a year before *The Waste Land* appeared, by Yeats in "The Second Coming," a desire revisited several years later by Frost, most notably in "Once by the Pacific." "Someone had better be prepared for rage" is how Frost puts it, and Yeats would have agreed. Eliot is prepared for rage and hopes for salvation. Like Yeats and Frost, he defines his modernity in *The Waste Land* as that intuition of being on the verge of upheaval – the breakup, the smashing, and the sinking of a whole era: not the new, but the verge of the new, for better or for worse. Probably, these writers fear, for worse.

Ezra Pound knew another *Ulysses*: a book, he believed, "presumably as unrepeatable as *Tristram Shandy*; I mean you cannot duplicate it; you can't take it as a model." Pound's *Ulysses* is a liberating force, the spirit of invention and a spur to the imaginations of succeeding writers to search out the springs of originality: make your own world, make yourself. So Pound's Joyce is the figure of modernist artistic selfhood, incarnating itself in a distinctive, virtuoso style, itself constantly reimagined in *Ulysses*, almost from chapter to chapter. Joyce the artist, then, as the exemplary instance of the radical individual, repeating not even his, much less someone else's form, a figure of freedom in a world of various tyrannies (artistic, economic, social), the high modernist inventor as political hero whose motto is, and must be, *non serviam*; the figure of Joyce: the anarchic self, trusting in nothing.

But a "model" is precisely what the young Eliot took Joyce's book to be, a display of narrative method which he thought had the force of a "scientific discovery," a form to be assented to and a paradigm to work within. Young Eliot, the reluctant experimentalist and unhappy individualist, thought he had found in *Ulysses* reason enough to give up his adventures in form. For if Joyce was the founder of a new literary tradition, then Eliot might become the new Shakespeare, working infinite refinements on a form given to him, bringing to culmination what had existed, so it goes, in Joyce, in a cruder state. Writers who came after *Ulysses* should be members of the literary community of *Ulysses*, finding their literary individuality inside the Joycean form, which makes possible variant and original selves, variations within a norm, without subverting the communal ground of variation.

The reasoning, which his teacher Josiah Royce would have admired, is the foundation of Eliot's literary and social thought, early, middle, and late.

"Tradition," "existing order," and the "supervention of novelty" were the terms he used in "Tradition and the Individual Talent." The point is to "sacrifice" yourself to "something which is more valuable," to lose one kind of isolate, disconnected "self" in order to find a self organically connected to a whole for which you do not have the responsibilities that would devolve upon its inventing God and sole sustainer.

Early on, the terms are literary, but in hindsight they teasingly suggest a great deal more than literary selfhood inside a magnificent community comprised of "the whole of the literature of Europe from Homer" to the present, Joyce having revived Homer for the literary present. The early literary essays, like many of his later major prose pieces, are expressions of Eliot's desire for relation inside an ideally cohesive culture. The poetry, in the meanwhile, "Ash Wednesday" and *Four Quartets* not excluded, is an expression of the actual, Eliot's life inside an incoherent and resolutely secular culture. *The Waste Land*, in this perspective, is not the mourning of an absence of values but the staging of a consciousness overwhelmed by fragments of literary forms and values as well as religious frameworks and values, a consciousness disheartened but nevertheless fascinated by a jumbled world of cultural variety that it tries to hold together in a single glance, a world in which everything is in play but nothing takes root, nothing commands, except the twin foci of Eliot's contempt: the profit and the loss and the casual sex, which is our fate, which is what Tiresias foresees.

Although his concern for literary form and the embracing social form he called a "framework" is in evidence before *The Waste Land*, after the publication of that poem, and while critics were debating its mood, meaning, and problematical unity, Eliot moved insistently in the direction of exploring "framework," the form of forms for writers and other wandering pilgrims. His literary essays continue to speak of the advantage to the writer of a "coherent traditional system of dogma and morals," "allegiance" to "something outside," and the necessity for an alternative to the vapidity of the "inner voice" and the climate of liberal opinion. But these essays (for example, "The Function of Criticism," 1923; "Dante," 1929; "Religion and Literature," 1935) move boldly out of the aesthetic arena when they argue that the writer's deepest relation to something outside, his union with that something, is "unconscious" or (in an intriguing phrase) "mostly unconscious." "Form" and "framework" acquire highly specific content: tradition, region, family, parish, community, and the gathering terms, Christian society and Christian culture, are the key words of value in the later Eliot, the signs of a doctrinal context that give clarity to the struggle evident in *Four Quartets* but never resolution, and never sectarian narrowness.

The intention driving Eliot's later career – all that he did after he joined the Church of England in 1927 – is public, socially involved, intellectually activist. Eliot, editor and intellectual, founded *The Criterion* in 1922, and for seventeen years thereafter worked to nourish a mostly conscious cosmopolitan culture, rooted in diverse national ground but unified beyond the borders. In the early 1930s, he turned to the theater, because he wanted "to have a part to play in society as worthy as that of the music-hall comedian," because, though he never said it explicitly, he wanted to be the Marie Lloyd of high modernist literature. His career in theater is a would-be farewell to the social disdain of the high modernist coterie. The modest Broadway success of *The Cocktail Party* thrilled him for more than reasons of financial gain (which was not negligible); he would have loved *Cats*; he packed a basketball stadium at the University of Minnesota with a lecture on criticism. These were some of the significant external signs of a conscious will to join and sustain "something which is more valuable," but to live at a "mostly unconscious" level.

Eliot's later major social criticism – *After Strange Gods* (1934), *The Idea of a Christian Society* (1939), and *Notes Toward the Definition of Culture* (1948) – is controversial for its harsh disposal of central modern assumptions and pieties (liberalism, secularism, and democracy; the latter mere rhetoric, he believed, veiling financial oligarchy), for its counterstatement of a Christian religious framework, and for the anti-Semitism of a much cited passage in *After Strange Gods*. In the jargon of our day, Eliot believed "multiculturalism" to be a contradiction in terms if intended as a description of any given and genuine culture and a banality if intended as a description of the human world. In *After Strange Gods*, Eliot argued that culture could neither exist nor persist except in small, out-of-the-way pockets, free from the impact of modernization, close to the soil, and, particularly in the United States, free from the influx of foreign races, far from New York City (let us say, in and around Charlottesville, Virginia). In *The Idea of a Christian Society* and *Notes*, he dropped his nostalgia for rural life and made no hostile references to Jews.

Eliot's anti-Semitism in *After Strange Gods* is exactly what it seems to be, but it is something more when set in the context of the Israeli experiment in society and the troubles in Northern Ireland. "Anti-Catholic," "anti-Islamic," and "anti-Semitic," in such contexts, miss a significant point. Efforts to establish and sustain a cohesive culture and society ("cohesive" is redundant in Eliot's analysis, a synonym for "real") are bound, at a certain level, to be exclusionary, to desire "cleanliness," ethnic, religious, or both, and to be hostile to self-differentiating elements ("dominant," in the realm of culture, is another synonym for "real"). Such efforts need not be violent and xenophobic, though the Israeli and Irish examples, mild as they are alongside some others in the twentieth century, remind us that violence and intolerance often attend the projects for cohesive culture. Eliot worked in *The Criterion* for a cosmopolitan effect because he believed that national cultures need constant transfusions from outside in order to stay vital; he cherished above all a multicultural world, cultures differently and deeply rooted. But he feared that liberal and secular modes of thought and US cultural imperialism would obliterate that diversity, and homogenize the world's cultural texture, and he had contempt for societies that by intention or thoughtless drift might become multicultural. Eliot clearly could not admire the multicultural diversity of the United States, and did not believe that such diversity could become a "culture" in any sense of the word that he understood. On Eliot's behalf it may be said that the charge of anti-Semitism leveled at *After Strange Gods* is spurious in the context of his traditional analysis of what culture is, and that the jury is still out concerning the American experiment in diversity. In a couple of places in the poems, and in several places in his published letters, "anti-Semitic" is an accurate description – and that, too, needs to be acknowledged if we are to get on with the projects of literary criticism and literary history, which do not require that writers be models of decency.

Eliot's much desired, "mostly unconscious" relation is to culture conceived as "habitual actions, habits and customs, from the most significant religious rite to our conventional way of greeting a stranger." Culture, as the "blood kinship of the 'same people living in the same place,'" is an expressive totality, a "way of feeling and acting which characterizes a group throughout generations." Culture, in other words, is necessarily mostly unconscious. Inside culture, behavior constitutes belief, and behavior is mostly not chosen. The "individual," thoroughly enmeshed in and dependent upon the group and its traditions, is released into "individuality"; the "individual" is permitted by "tradition." In such a vision, and it is a vision (recalling his early vision of literary totality and tradition), the necessary values are conservation, stability, and resistance to change – values to be managed and cultivated by the culture's intellectuals (in a Christian culture, the community of Christian elite who presumably mediate the pattern laid up in heaven in its relation to actual society). It was Eliot's hope that culture would have no use for the cult of personality, would not encourage the artist to nourish his alienation, his deviance, and his difference, would not permit itself to be a proving ground for avant-garde thought and expression, would not desire to position its artists and intellectuals as agents of social change, much less revolution. Eliot never lived in such a cultural place, which exists, for him, only in the ideal projections of his prose.

He was doubtful that the real world could be so transformed, but thought it important, nevertheless, to imagine, argue, and work (in his prose life) for a world so transformed.

The major poetic episodes in Eliot's career after *The Waste Land* include: "The Hollow Men" (1925), in effect, an epilogue to *The Waste Land*; "Ash Wednesday" (1930, with sections published over the three previous years), his initial and still major expression of Christian commitment; the opening of his career as verse dramatist with *Murder in the Cathedral* (produced and published in 1935); and the crowning achievement both of his Christian turn and his poetry after *The Waste Land*, the four meditative poems that appeared in collected form in 1943 as *Four Quartets* ("Burnt Norton," 1935; "East Coker," 1940; "The Dry Salvages," 1941; "Little Gidding," 1942). The site of *Four Quartets* as a meditative venture, its constraining cultural ground, is precisely the cultural place that Eliot had excoriated in his prose, the actual culture he lived in ("No place of grace"), not the one he dreamed of in *The Idea of a Christian Society*. The essential themes and tones of *Four Quartets* are sounded in "Ash Wednesday": resignation and fear in the context of encroaching age; crippling self-dialogue and the plea, the prayer for patience, humility, and deliverance; sumptuous and pressingly sexual memory and the desire for the ascetic life – all, and always, in the tone of the pilgrim requiring transformation, waiting for grace.

"Burnt Norton" was a gift, grace from the literary gods, an accident that grew from some discarded fragments of *Murder in the Cathedral*. Only with "East Coker" did Eliot hit upon an intention for a suite of four poems for which "Burnt Norton" would provide a model of structure in five parts – or movements, as his musical metaphor would demand – sections to be repeated and varied in ensuing poems, so much the better to achieve an effect of spatial form periodically interrupted by an effect of temporality. In the thematic expression of his musical shape: constricting order, suffocating enclosure, suddenly opened and redeemed by a surprising infusion of grace; meaningless flow, one damned thing after another in the shifting world, suddenly punctuated and thrown into perspective by a fixed presence, a center, the endlessness of flow becoming elegantly geometric. In the language of his master metaphor, consciousness seeks to be "at the still point of the turning world," a reality that human kind can bear (at best) only in rare, ecstatic doses. The Reality is Incarnation, neither flesh nor fleshless; the fixed Presence, everpresent, is Christ, who may be sought, occasionally contacted, everpresent but mainly not present.

Because *Four Quartets* follows *The Waste Land*, its fate, despite all the literary pyrotechnics of the earlier poem, is to seem even more literary, a poem that requires knowledge of the earlier poem if its place in Eliot's inner journey is to be grasped in proper context. In addition, because of its open personal references to its author as a literary man in the middle of the way, and just because this man, when he writes and publishes it, is the leading man of letters of his time, who is making substantial references to *The Waste Land* (the third movement of each of the poems, with one exception, is a retrieval of the scene of *The Waste Land*, without the technical difficulties), it is assumed that the reader of course knows who he, T. S. Eliot, is – knows his fame, has long sensed his ambition for high place in literary history, knows about the conversion of 1927 to the Church of England. Despite its relative ease of access, *Four Quartets* is a poem for a literary insider who (the final limiting factor) is no reflex secularist.

The structure of the *Quartets* consists of an initial section which presents the sort of large view of things that tends to be called "philosophical." In each of the poems the problem is time itself: in "Burnt Norton" evoked abstractly; in the others, with concreteness, in the styles of lyric meditation and biblical prophecy and the imagery of generations, natural force, and miraculous eruptions of spring in winter (the rise and fall of houses, the great brown god of the Mississippi, "spring time / But not in time's covenant"). The initial section is then broken by extra spacing, the indication of a leap to a passage of visionary memory whose object is personal. The second sections begin with a lyric of cosmological vision, followed by a reflection and elaboration again personal, this time concerning the trials of a poet in grave doubt about all that he has accomplished. The third sections (with the exception of "Little Gidding") are revisitations of waste-land scenes; the fourth are all doctrinal in weight, Christian allegorical lyrics of agonized (never complacent) tone. And the concluding sections deal with the question of poetry itself – the nature of its language and values. As a whole, the *Quartets* present an alternation of voices lyrical and discursive, the expression of a writer who must always be questioning the worth and place of his expression. Underneath everything, the persistent vocal substance is meditative, the tone is measured, stoically at peace, the voice of a poet trying to care and not to care, trying to sit still.

The unresolvable tension of *Four Quartets* is that Eliot, a reluctant experimentalist, who wanted to (but did not) inherit viable traditional form, who wanted to (but did not) bury isolate selfhood in a community ("which is more valuable"), who could not finally hide his life entirely in Christ, nevertheless committed himself in this poem to the most uncompromising implications of avant-garde aesthetic. Knowledge of the past, he tells us, imposes falsifying pattern onto the present, falsifying because "the pattern is new in every moment / And every moment is a new and shocking / Valuation of all we have been." Knowledge of one's craft, likewise, imposes falsifying pattern. The triumph of literary form and language is its radical mimesis of the new and shocking moment. It is a triumph over literary history, over the falsity of received pattern, over convention. What we have already perceived, yesterday's perception caught in yesterday's poem, is yesterday's triumph – good only for yesterday and who we were yesterday. Today we are dumb, and every effort to write and live freshly is necessarily a "raid on the inarticulate / With shabby equipment always deteriorating."

Yesterday's equipment is shabby, and so is yesterday's self. Shabby but comfortable, comfortable but a lie. Old men, or older men, as he should have written (the *Quartets* were composed between his forty-seventh and fifty-fourth years), would rather not be explorers. They would rather repeat themselves as writers and repeat themselves as selves. They would rather repeat than create; rather not chance possession because they do not wish to bear any Reality, or be borne by it. The courage to "make it new" as a writer is not a metaphor: it is Eliot's path to regeneration.

The other side of Eliot is never avant-gardist, is the very antithesis of the spirit of the avant-garde. The two sides coexist, always uneasily but always through necessity, in Eliot's writing, life being a truncated travesty if imagined otherwise. I refer, of course, to his commitments to tradition, literary history, the past. The urgent way to put it is the best way: his life, and ours, with the dead. Not the dead letters of texts, but those familiar, compound ghosts haunting texts. Here, at last (in an echo of Pound's "The Return"), he contacts Joyce's great orthodox theme. And this is how he says it in "Little Gidding":

> We die with the dying:
> See, they depart, and we go with them.
> We are born with the dead:
> See, they return, and bring us with them.

That is Eliot's grandest expression of communitarian vision, the voice least likely to be heard in the modern secular and liberal state.

The Waste Land will remain the singular aesthetic event of modernist poetry in the English language; and its stance, however we construct it, seems one we can live with because, however we construct it, it seems one that suits our sense of ourselves. But Eliot after *The Waste Land* will continue to be another matter: an event unabsorbed because, in the context of advanced Western values, it is unabsorbable.

5

EZRA POUND

A MONG modernists of the English-speaking world, not even Joyce achieved the infamy and authority of Ezra Pound, who inaugurated his career with an act of expatriation in 1908 after being fired earlier that year from his teaching post at Wabash College in Crawfordsville, Indiana. One bitter winter night (so it goes in Pound's telling), Pound gave his bed to a homeless male impersonator, so that he might "bring warmth to her frozen body," while he slept on the floor, fully clothed, wrapped in his topcoat. The president of Wabash and Pound's landlady were not amused.

About two years later, in the summer of 1910, Pound returned home in an unsuccessful effort to acquire another teaching post, this time at his alma mater, the University of Pennsylvania. That winter he spent considerable time in New York City pondering the literary scene and gathering the impressions and notes for "Patria Mia," his single most important piece of literary and social criticism, which he would publish in 1913 in the *New Age* when he was twenty-eight. Early in 1911 he left America for good, returning to London until 1920, a period during which he became the leading international instigator of a new poetry and poetics, the unofficial agent and publicist for Frost, Eliot, Joyce, H. D., and Wyndham Lewis (among others), and the foreign editor and correspondent of arguably the two most important of the little magazines of the period, *Poetry* (Chicago) and *The Little Review*.

In late 1920, Pound left London for Paris, marking his departure with the satirical autobiographical and cultural retrospective he called *Hugh Selwyn Mauberley*. While in Paris he served as editor-in-chief of *The Waste Land*, a poem whose famous modernist form we owe to Pound's excellent, merciless advice. He left Paris in 1924 for Italy, where he lived until 1945, when he was arrested and brought back to the United States to face charges of treason for his wartime Rome Radio broadcasts on behalf of fascism. Thanks to a judgment of madness, he escaped execution and was incarcerated at St. Elizabeth's Hospital in Washington, DC, for thirteen years. Meanwhile, his *Pisan Cantos*, composed while he was detained under harsh conditions in Pisa at a makeshift military prison, were published in 1948 and awarded the first Bollingen Prize for Poetry, an act which touched off one of the fiercest storms of cultural controversy in this century, only recently surpassed in rhetorical heat and existential consequences, as it was replayed in a different religious context, by the scandal of Salman Rushdie's *Satanic Verses*. Can a traitor and an open anti-Semite write worthy poetry even as he expresses traitorous and anti-Semitic sentiments? Or, as the maximum Ayatollah might have put it, who would not have raised the question because he had the answer: a traitor and an open anti-Muslim cannot... and so on. In 1958, thanks to the efforts of numerous writers, Pound was released from St. Elizabeth's, whereupon he returned to Italy to live out his final years, mainly in silence. He died in Venice, November 1, 1972: the high modernist who lived the longest.

The Rome Radio broadcasts, whatever else they were, were an act of criticism – and as such, a shocking (when not totally incomprehensible) expression of the central, career-defining act of expatriation with which Pound began his official literary life in 1908. "Patria Mia," the essay engendered on native ground in the winter of 1910–11, was the archetype of the kind of indictment of American culture that Pound pursued indefatigably. And, for Pound, the critical act was indistinguishable from the teaching act. *How to Read*, the *ABC of Economics, Jefferson and/or Mussolini, America, Roosevelt, and the Causes of the Present War* – all were exemplary sorts of cultural interventions whose titles tell us how basic (and how grandiose) his ambitions were. His efforts in anthology-making in *Des Imagistes* (1914), the *Catholic Anthology* (1915) – which gave Eliot his first international press – the *Active Anthology* (1933), whose title says it all, and *Confucius to Cummings* (1964) were the efforts of an incorrigible educator for whom the lack of a conventional teaching post was never any hindrance. Seeing to it that the right sorts of writers were published, properly reviewed, and remunerated; getting out the right sorts of collections, in timely fashion, as representations of the right sort of literary way; working cunningly for the magazines – seeing to it that their editors published according to his, not their, wishes; himself publishing a mind-boggling number of critical pieces (over three hundred in one year alone) – all of this is saliently glossed by his primal act of criticism, the choice to live outside his country but not (as he noted in "Patria Mia") outside his American identity, a consummation he would not have wanted, even if it were possible.

All appearances to the contrary notwithstanding, Pound was from the beginning an American writer. His driving energy was critical, totally devoted to the goal of an "American *risorgimento*" (a phrase he liked) which he eventually concluded would never come to pass without fundamental economic renovation. As the poet of *The Cantos*, the project that occupied him from

1920 on – a work that grew to more than twice the length of *Paradise Lost* –
Pound's critical energy assumed the form of a poetry whose intention was the
retrieval and resuscitation of all that had been lost to the modern world; a
poetry whose goal was to provoke literary and social change by providing its
essential curriculum.

With the generalizing wit of the satirical diagnostician, Pound gave some
telling names to the literary culture he found in force as a young man, none
more quintessential than that of "Tennyson," whose poetic tone exemplified a
Victorian rage for expurgation and exclusion. What made Tennyson the god
of expurgative desire, a sensibility willfully and desperately dissociated, was
the fact that there never was nor ever could be, Pound wickedly predicted,
"an edition of 'Purified Tennyson.'" The problem was not Tennyson himself,
whose actual life suggested saltier possibilities. The problem was cultural,
"that lady-like attitude toward the printed page ... that ineffable something
which kept Tennyson out of his works." Pound was not identifying what he
thought of as the badness of his literary culture with women, as if the origin of
Tennysonian badness were a contagious female psyche. Pound's libertarianism
was in fact radical: "Our presumption," he meant the American presumption,
"is that those things are right which give the greatest freedom, the greatest
opportunity for individual development to the individual, of whatever age or
sex or condition." His support for H. D. and Marianne Moore, among other
women writers, was unswerving. Sappho's lyrics were one of his consistently
touted corrective models of the genteel attitude whose literary victims were
male and female alike.

Pound's most unmerciful criticism of American literature was reserved for a
"certain [male] versifier," who seemed to him especially worthless in a society
that values more than anything else the adventurous spirit whose ability to
make things happen, literally to "make it new," captured his admiration in spite
of everything he had to say against capitalist culture. The entrepreneurial spirit,
Pound thought, constitutes America's most interesting cultural force, because
its heroes of nineteenth-century capital make the country "a different place
each decade." These innovators of capital who scorn all stasis, not the American
poets, are the American models of the avant-garde sensibility, exemplars of
identity for those (like Pound) who would make it verbally new and who
believe that "no good poetry is ever written in a manner twenty years old."
In a country whose actual poetic models were Tennyson, the genteel version
of Keats, and the versifiers regularly appearing in the commercial magazines,
the entrepreneurs of capital represented to Pound forces whose power to effect

palpable social change in America made genteel poetry, in its flight from the world that capital dominated, seem simply irrelevant.

The entrepreneur ensures that the country will not look the same in two successive decades; no genuine poet writes in a manner twenty years old: by Pound's logic the successful entrepreneur and the genuine poet are twin images of creative force, makers of social and literary change, and proof of the possible harmony and even interchangeability of culture and power. Pound's criticism of genteel culture is not, moreover, directed to a phenomenon confined to late nineteenth-century America. His is a criticism of what he thought culture had always been in the USA, a decorative couch, an ability to quote the oracles of wisdom – Emerson and Mrs. Eddy – and he thought Americans incapable of distinguishing between the two.

Nowhere more dramatically does Pound make clear his hope for a unified social and literary practice than in an anecdote he relates in "Patria Mia." In the winter of 1910–11 he found himself in New York, spending too much time in the company of a "certain versifier," and in his boredom thought he might do the man some good by taking him to see what he called – in destructive comparison – two "full men," who had "fought in battles and sailed before the mast and lived on everything from $2.50 per week, precarious, to $7,500 per annum" – *and* they commanded literature between Rabelais and Shakespeare, *and* they wielded "a racy, painted speech that would do no shame to an Elizabethan." In the course of the evening this versifier, believing himself in the company "of the representatives of hated commercialism" (Pound's phrasing notes in acid the knee-jerk genteel response to capitalism), suddenly became (the simile is deliberately, savagely inappropriate) "bold as a lion" and decided to grace the hardened spirits of his hosts with a poetry reading – "a bad poem – of someone else's . . . from a current magazine."

Pound and his friends sat it out in devastating silence. The conclusion of his anecdote sweeps up his linked concerns in a single breath: "that is 'art in America,' that is why 'the American' cannot be expected to take it seriously, and why it is left to the care of ladies' societies, and of 'current events' clubs, and is numbered among the 'cultural influences.'" If that is literature and culture in America, says this twenty-five-year-old American briefly home from Europe, then so much the worse for literature and culture in America. An original literature would take poetry away from a trivializing contemporaneity (literature as a "current event") and the newly founded Poetry Society of America, where it had been safely tucked away in cultural impotence under the direction of Jessie Belle Rittenhouse. A new literature would belong to "full men" like Pound's two business friends, who were the type of the socially vital poet, men skilled, like Ulysses, in all the ways of contending.

His insistent, career-long attacks on "rhetoric and frilled paper decoration"; his desire to get poetry closer to "the thing" (as if poetry had wandered far away into the stratosphere of abstraction, far from thingness or *Dinglichkeit*, as the New Critic John Crowe Ransom would say in echo years later); his embarrassment as a male lyricist feeling out of place in a lyric territory that he believed his culture had feminized so much the better to trivialize it: these are some of the reactive gestures that became standard in the early modernist period in America and that link Ezra Pound to any number of his contemporaries, not so much in aesthetic solidarity on behalf of a new poetics as in cultural negation. Pound's better publicized efforts – first by himself, much later by the academic Pound industry – to reimagine lyric look at first remarkably like Robert Frost's. He also set himself the project of escaping the demand put upon him by official literary culture that he glean his diction from the lyric masters collected by Francis Palgrave. But if with Frost he shared a target of cultural critique, then against Frost's democratic antipoetics of vernacular voice, which worked toward a novelized lyric of character in the American tradition of local-color realism, Pound worked toward the formal voice of traditional literary culture – a voice he called "curial" with no American shame, at a time when James Whitcomb Riley may have been the most popular poet in America.

So in his critical project he set himself against the poetry in dialect mode descended from Wordsworth ("so intent on the ordinary or plain word that he never thought of hunting for *le mot juste*"); set himself against the aestheticist poetics of the dreamy line, with all its archaisms and inversions, which he criticized in the early Yeats but which he himself had trouble avoiding; set himself against the tradition of masculinity out of Whitman, the school of self-conscious red-bloods like Richard Hovey and Bliss Carman founded upon "the insight that possession of the phallus differentiates human kind from the lower animals" – an insight that Pound himself seemed to enjoy waving with some frequency from early on; and finally set himself against "the school of normal production" (a phrase of considerable resonance for his analysis of the lyric marketplace of capital), the school that fills the pages of the commercial magazines with "nice domestic sentiments inoffensively versified." Pound's dictum that poetry be at least as well written as Flaubert's prose would stand, in this context, as a counterstatement against contemporary poetry as he knew it. It urges not narrative in poetry but a turn toward the elegant ideals of economy, precision, and hardness – a turn toward Flaubert and Ford Madox Ford as stylistic models for lyric poetry and a rejection altogether of the contemporary poetry scene wherein such models for writing, he was convinced, were not to be found.

With these evocations of the Roman Catholic curia, Flaubert, and various European masters as models of elevated vocal authority in poetry, Pound launched, in his early career, a voyage toward an avant-garde whose essential nourishment would be drawn, not from alliance with some presumably (American) revolutionary and contemporary moment, but from the past. With the epigrammatic flair of the avant-gardist looking for attention, he wrote that line, "No good poetry is ever written in a manner twenty years old." But this avant-gardist had gone to graduate school in comparative literature and philology: "yet a man feeling the divorce of life and his art," he says in the next breath, "may naturally try to resurrect a forgotten mode if he finds in that mode some leaven, or if he thinks he sees in it some element lacking in contemporary art . . . " Pound's aesthetic preferences would be polemically international and antiquarian, the politics of those preferences apparently authoritarian, though even here, at the outset of his career, his admiration for the novels of Henry James muddies these political waters and sets up his most interesting contradiction.

As the "author of book after book against oppression, against all the sordid petty personal crushing oppression of modern life," James represented for Pound the greatest hatred of tyranny imaginable. And the historical wonder of James lay in the fact that he embodied his critical intentions in the novel, modern form of forms, "not in the diagrams of Greek tragedy, not labeled 'epos' or 'Aeschylus.'" Pound's explanation of the implicit politics of James's fiction is as fully in the American grain as his literary preference for the curial voice is not. In one of the most American of his many American moments, the man from rural, small-town Idaho, of modest cultural patrimony, writes with the democratic ease of camaraderie this ringing endorsement of James, high-toned American of immense cultural advantage: "What he fights is 'influence,' the impinging of family pressure, the impinging of one personality on another; all of them in the highest degree damn'd, loathsome and detestable." When Pound lamented, in the most deeply felt metaphor for his politics, a loss of respect for "the peripheries of the individual," he feared for his literary life. His analysis of the hostile economic context of his desire to write against the formulas demanded by commercial magazines in the USA culminated in his strongest poetry of criticism outside *The Cantos*, the small literary history, semiautobiography, and social critique he called *Hugh Selwyn Mauberley*. This poetic sequence fuses his complex impulses: a politics of and for the radical individual, an admiration for Flaubertian realist experiments in fiction, a veneration for older poetic modes out of step with the times, and a criticism of the one certifiable poetic avant-garde of his youth – the aestheticism of the 1890s, the turn inward which he thought disabled writers like Lionel Johnson and Ernest Dowson in the face of the social evil that culminated in World War I.

Henry James's fictional representations of individuals insidiously destroyed by invisible impingements of social arrangement is reflected politically in the anti-imperialism Pound shared with his generation of American modernists who grew up in the shadow of the American incursion into Cuba and the Philippines. Encounter with the anti-imperialist movement at the turn of the century was the trigger of political initiation and commitment for any number of modern American writers, their chief form of protest against invasion of the individual's boundaries and a protest, as well, on behalf of the integrity of discrete cultures now newly imperiled by the expansionist desires of American power and capital. It was an anti-imperialism whose moral, epistemological, and political themes were eloquently played for the emerging modernists in William James's writerly activism at the turn of the century.

Pound's distrust of the political horror of abstraction was every bit as deep-seated as that of William James, who had excoriated with the term "abstract" our imperial impositions of value, our intrusions into organic systems of culture, far from our shores. Like James, Pound believed that the world we live in "exists diffused and distributed, in the form of an infinitely numerous lot of eaches," a collection of stories expressed from a collection of discrete localities of value that cannot be unified into a single narrative. And, like James, Pound believed that the diversity of the world's cultures needed to be cherished because, far from being an irreducible and impervious fact of human ontology, cultural diversity was at the mercy of abstractionist modes of writing and thinking; a criminal form of behavior that William James accused Theodore Roosevelt's party of indulging as foreign policy, and that Pound accused the popular poets of the day of indulging as a cultural policy whose human costs were equally unacceptable. And both James and Pound used the word *criminal* to describe the effects of "abstraction."

If the James brothers together fathered American modernism's vision of individuals and diverse cultures under siege, then what Pound did in his early literary essays was to focus that vision on the imperiled literary individual, the would-be author who would survive economic assault on his desire to protect his writing's artistic individuality from the imperial processes of abstraction that American culture imposed upon writing. "The point toward which I strive," Pound wrote in 1910, "is that at no time was there such machinery for the circulation of printed expression – and all this favors a sham." In his social criticism in prose, in *Mauberley*, in many of the *Cantos*, he goes after the machinery itself, the material conditions of cultural production; all those, he imagines, who stand to profit from it; and, most harrowingly, its death-ray effects on language, the sustenance and fabric of a healthy (i.e., individualist) culture. Pound explored the possibility of a corrective: a refusal of the literary culture ruled over by "Mr. Nixon," satirical representative of the culture of capital he invented in *Mauberley*, who counsels young writers to butter up reviewers and never to kick against the pricks.

In March of 1913, Pound published, in Harriet Monroe's *Poetry*, what quickly became the classic manifesto for a new ("imagist") poetics. The theory of the image he announced there ("an intellectual and emotional complex in an instant of time") was fresh in its immediate historical context because it demanded a *complex* for the lyric – a heterogeneous texture that fused the traditional image (the sensory object) with intellect as well as feeling – a lyric texture in opposition to the conventional lyric *simplex* implicitly demanded and promoted by Palgrave, among other anthologists with whom Pound was at war, whose lyric exhibits and critical commentary thereon would banish everything but abstracted feeling from the lyric mode. But Pound's "image" as "complex" nevertheless remained at its core fully lyric, even visionary in function: "It is the presentation of such a complex instantaneously which gives the sense of sudden liberation; that sense of freedom from time and space limits." This new lyric, with its stress on the poet's psychic integration, would be the verbal index of a thoroughly associated sensibility, a poet recalling Coleridge's romantic ideal who brings the entire personality ("the whole soul of man") into an articulated expressive act, with all faculties in perfect coordination; a poet something like Pound's entrepreneurial friends (a "full man") or like his Renaissance soldier-patron of the arts, Sigismondo Malatesta ("an entire man"), who dominated several early cantos, or like Bertran de Born, war-mongering troubadour, who appears in the early poetry. The reception of the new lyric of the image would release the reader from the constraints of circumstance, so that he could feel transported in an experience of "sudden growth," what Pound had called several years earlier, in *The Spirit of Romance*, "delightful psychic experience," by which he meant an experience akin to what is recorded in ancient myth: the feeling of walking "sheer into nonsense." Like the image, myth was the trigger of that sort of feeling, the occasion of a subjective moment of liberation from common sense. The "image" is lyric, it tells no story. Its existence lies wholly in an eternal present (the "instant"), with no past or future encumbrances attached.

The manifesto on the image was not new for Pound in 1913: he had been at work earlier on a similar conception (he then called it the "luminous detail") and he would continue to press his idea of the image through its revised incarnations in the Chinese ideogram (thanks to Ernest Fenollosa), the theory of the vortex, and into the practice of many of the *Cantos*. The heterogeneity of the new image implies a lyric practice reimagined in the ambience of Ford

Madox Ford's fiction and the polemical theorizing of T. E. Hulme on behalf of what Hulme had called a "classical" poetics, a series of characterizations for a new poetry that recalls Pound's technical directives for the new image: "dry hardness," the "accurate, precise, and definite description" that comes only after a "terrific struggle" to bend the generic character of language to the unique perceptual possibility (the radical individuality that defines human difference), so much the better to produce a "visual concrete language" that prevents the reader from "gliding through" to "an abstract process," a language of images which "are not mere decoration, but the very essence of an intuitive language."

But despite the revolutionary character of Pound's novelistic insistence on "exact treatment" – a worldliness of lyric, an early urge to write a poem that would include history – in fact his theory of the image looks back to the Paterian 1890s. The image is for release, for an inward turning away from the world, for dream in the manner of the earliest, world-weary Yeats ("dreams alone can truly be," is the major Yeatsean echo from Pound's first volume, *A Lume Spento*), and for brief but vitalizing contact with visionary splendor. In his metapoetic declaration of principle in the opening poem of *A Lume Spento* (1908), Pound prays (from on high) that his songs will be granted the power to light up with divine fire the lives of "grey folk":

> As bright white drops upon a leaden sea
> Grant so my songs to this grey folk may be:
> As drops that dream and gleam and falling catch the sun,
> Evan'scent mirrors every opal one
> Of such his splendor as their compass is . . .

In post-symbolist fashion in the wake of Poe, Pound offered the lyric as the normative literary form, the subjective center of all forms. "Even the Divina Commedia,' he wrote, "must not be considered an epic . . . It is . . . the tremendous lyric of the subjective Dante . . . "

Even so, at the outset of his career, in his early twenties, Pound had wedded his apparently disengaged lyric disposition to social obligation, to the presumed benefit of those he called "grey folk," and to this end (until his end) he pursued the role of the lyric "instant" in society on the assumption that the poet has something so special to contribute that society could not possibly function healthily without him. In the lyric fragments for Canto 117, he wrote: "For the blue flash and the moments / benedetta." In that same fragment of a canto, he wrote, in one of his purest lines of desire: "To have heard the farfalla gasping / as toward a bridge over worlds." In 117, the last of the cantos printed in the collected *Cantos of Ezra Pound*, in this image of the butterfly in transcendent movement, appropriately rendered in a sentence fragment,

Pound, last of the living legendary modernist poets, was enacting the very attitude that he and his friend T. E. Hulme had worked so hard to debunk on behalf of the imagist practice that would replace it. As Hulme put it, "the whole of the romantic attitude seems to crystallize in verse round metaphors of flight." One of the genteel enemy, E. C. Stedman, had portrayed Keats, in the quintessential genteel image of the poet's (dis)relation to the world of capital, as a "superb blue moth." Not only did Pound never escape from the romantic literary culture he became famous for criticizing; that culture would constitute one of the most important ingredients of his poetics of obligation. Shelley had called the poet the unacknowledged legislator of the world; Pound wanted him acknowledged, not for the laws that poetry would embody, but for the freedom from law imposed, from the loathsome oppression that follows when the individual's boundaries are not respected.

But more even than its definition of the image, Pound's manifesto of 1913 was powerful for the negative directives that cast light on what he meant by the image and on the conventional lyric practice the new writing would displace. Several of his directives (like those of Hulme) amount to a single warning against everything that the image was not – "ornamental" discourse in the service of "abstraction." The image, like the "luminous detail" Pound had theorized before it, and like the ideogram and vortex that came after, was the exemplary figure of concentration and totality, the essential texture of a new poetry that would necessarily appear difficult in the context of the diluted practice where "abstraction" reigned. By "abstraction" Pound meant not only too much generality but also the act of dislodging an element from an integrated complex. This prescription for a concentrated complexity – a poetic whole "rammed full," as Frost put it, with "all sorts of things," or a "rag-bag," as Pound described the form of *The Cantos* in a suppressed version of his first Canto – though followed faithfully in the practice of the short lyrics of Pound and Eliot, and though it would appear to be a prescription for the modern genre of poetic genres, the intellectually demanding short poem, was also the driving structural imagination behind the writing of the modernist long poem – *Mauberley, The Cantos, The Waste Land, The Bridge,* and *Paterson* – and nowhere is this made more evident than in the radical editorial compression that Pound urged, and that Eliot accepted, for a transformation of the bloated manuscript version of *The Waste Land* into the classic modernist collage of sharp discontinuity that we know.

As verbal equivalent of the poet's undissociated self, Pound's "image" – a way of seeing as much as a new thing seen – is an honorific figure of perceptual concreteness in opposition to the method of "abstraction"; a figure for a truthful discourse in opposition to "rhetoric"; a figure of intellectual as opposed to sentimental control; of aesthetic necessity and social relevance as opposed to aesthetic "ornament" and social uselessness. "Ornament," "sentiment," "abstraction," and "rhetoric" are the various terms Pound makes synonymous and which he employs, early and late, to describe the literary practice he deplored: the hated conventional textures of American poetry, the soft post-symbolist practice in vogue in England since the nineties, the immoral relation to the world that he believed those textures mediate for readers. Pound's criticism of those literary textures is at once aesthetic, epistemological, and political. The luminosity of the detail; the natural adequacy that he claimed for the image and the ideogram – an ornamental and abstract discourse is the earliest instance of what he meant in Canto 45 by *contra naturam*; the "radiance" of the vortex (a dynamic conception of the image, not a static complex but a "node from which, and through which, and into which, ideas are constantly rushing"): all are urgent theories for a new poetry that would not look like the poetry represented by Pound's cunning exhibit of the old in his manifesto of 1913 – "dim lands of peace" – a phrase that embodies the thematic abstraction it refers to, and whose major effect is to double the obscurity of the abstraction ("peace") with an adjective stressing the obscurity (dimming) of vision.

Pound often glosses the proper relation of particulars to generals with references to Aristotle and scholastic philosophy ("generalities," as he put it in Canto 74, must be "born from a sufficient phalanx of particulars"). But his connection with Hulme must have reminded him of what he more typically believed: that there is no proper relation of particular to general, that the particular is not the cognitive base of the general but the desired entirety of knowledge, all else being dangerous illusion. The issue for Pound was never how to adjudicate the argument between realists (like Aristotle) and nominalists (like Hulme) as if he had some stake in the discipline of philosophy. The issue was pragmatic: a function of his needs in an actual historical situation. Aristotle and Hulme were names-as-weapons in a contemporary cultural war that he was fighting independently of the epistemological status of their claims. The image, the vortex, and the ideogram are three names for poetic media of particularity that would ensure an aesthetic renovation of abstract writing; an epistemological renovation of that same sort of airiness; and – in the renovated relation of reader to world promoted by a writing sufficiently phalanxed with particularity – a political renovation, a renewed respect for the peripheries of the particular individual, who for Pound is the subatomic foundation of locality, his value of all values ("Humanity is a collection of individuals, not a whole divided into segments or units").

As image, or ideogram, or vortex, the poem would function like an "inspired mathematics" – a special kind of notation for the subjective life of feeling, a "new word" beyond the existing categories of formulated language. Pound's mixing of symbolist dicta via Mallarmé with scientific ideals of exactitude, routinely caricatured by the symbolists and aesthetes whom he only partially admired, his evocation of a poetic language become as precise as mathematical equation, bespeaks the fruitful contradiction in his critical thought to wed the culturally trivialized urge of the poets with a socially honored activity (the language of science). In another rhetorical rescue mission, he would charge the lyric impulse, feminized in capitalist culture, with the masculine dimension of social involvement; his aim was to join the feminine with pragmatic energy, not to do away with the lyric feminine but to make it "harder," give it "shock and stroke." "The poet is a centaur"; his entrepreneurial friends commanded Shakespeare *and* capital. The poet is doubly sexed.

Pound's theory of the image came rather quickly to seem to him inadequate. The image was static, too lyrically disengaged and inward in its emphasis to match his ideal of the poet as a man supremely engaged and worldly. Hence his revisions of the image in the theories of ideogram and vortex that stressed the image in action, the image as including its situation, particulars in provocative juxtaposition. The ideogram is the image which knows not the distinction between noun and verb. The vortex is the image conceived as the whole poem; the vortex-poem a composition of juxtaposed planes, after the mode of analytical cubism, a spatial construction of elements in superposition, not a *representation* of particularity but a *phalanx* of particularity – the military etymology is important: a cultural weapon, something like a body of infantry in close array, an idea in action, working in the social arena. Far from being an ornament for ladies and alienated aesthetes, such a poem would be the proper expressive complement of Pound's idea of the poet – his culture urged him to think it "masculine" – the proof that poetry and power were not the antithetical properties of the half-humans called women and men in the culture in which he grew up.

But the issue of poetic function is no issue at all so long as "the practice of literary composition" is carried out in secluded domestic space, "like knitting, crotcheting, etc." For such practice can never "transgress the definition of liberty we find in the declaration of the *Droits de l'Homme*" as "the right to do anything which harms not others. All of which," Pound concludes, "is rather negative and unsatisfactory." Aesthetic or any other sort of practice so sustained, in privacy, can do others neither harm nor good: it is trivial. But literary composition carried on in public will bear directly on the freedom of others. It may constitute a transgression of someone else's liberty, the worst sort of criminality in Pound's universe. The poet, like the corrupt doctor who makes false reports, may become "responsible for future oppressions." Hence Pound's insistence on clarity, in his prescription for the image – "exact treatment of the thing" – for any "thing" ("whether subjective or objective") may be falsified, at which point the classical ideals of poetics – teaching, moving, and delighting – become their demonic counterparts: we "obscure" so much better to "mislead," and we "mislead" in order to "bamboozle." At the base of such rhetorical criminality is not so much a criminality of persons as a criminality of the literary medium and the institutions that sustain it; a criminality of a discourse gone "slushy and inexact," out of touch with "things," where the "application of word to thing" has gone "rotten." The social relevance of Pound's ideal poet would lie in his power to keep the medium clean, precise, and exact, because the "individual cannot think and communicate his thought," and "the governor and legislator cannot act effectively or frame his laws without words and the solidity and validity of those words is in the care of the damned and despised *literati*."

The politics of Pound's image is close to the politics of Pound's Henry James, with this difference: Pound's imagist (his vorticist, his ideogrammist) would not be charged with writing a poetry against the penetration by the usual social influences of the individual's peripheries. In his commitment to an individuating clarity and exactitude of presentation, the poet would under-write the health of language by defusing its transgressive power – that power whereby, via the means of an insidious because obscuring abstractness, one individual crosses cunningly, under linguistic cover, into the space of another, so much the better to control him. Language, poetic or ordinary, is above all, for Pound, a medium of communication and exchange, and that is why it is his constant target and obsession. To let it go abstract – this perilous media-tor of all identity, this medium of influence, manipulation, bamboozling, and control – is to set the conditions for a reasonable paranoia. Pound's belief that it lies within the power of the writer to keep language healthy and therefore culture safe for the individual is an index of his high social hope; in his Hell Cantos (14–16) he shows us in detail just what his hope must work against, just how powerful the betrayers of language are.

So Pound's various equations for the poet – Odysseus, Malatesta, de Born, the associated sensibility, the full Renaissance man in his American capitalist incarnation; his figures of poetic function, early and late (luminosity, clarity, and radiance); his attacks on aesthetic ornamentation; his insistence on getting accurate representation of "the thing" (he found the decorative verse of his time worthless because it was a language apropos of no*thing*) – these clustered motifs in his poetics make sense in the ambience of his social intentions and against the immediate literary backdrop of his thought. Pound increasingly emphasized the image as an irreducible aesthetic monad. More and more, he would think of the image as the poem, not part of the poem, an organic whole whose function is defined from Coleridge and Shelley to Pound as a unique unveiling, a moment of radiance in which the film of familiarity is stripped from the world around us. Such mainline romantic theory about aesthetic autonomy, and the value of "the poem itself," feeds the modernist avant-garde but is differentiated and politically turned by Pound's insistence that we see "the poem itself," not as a medium of pure contemplation and imagination, standing in aloof alienation from what Yeats, in constant contempt, called the world of the journalist and the money changer, but precisely as a way of engaging that world. Pound's attacks on the aesthetic of the ornament were not made on behalf of an isolated aesthetic autonomy but on behalf of the necessity of the aesthetic within the human economy: an avant-gardism with a rhetorical, a Victorian and Fireside conscience.

As a rhetoric against the trivializing of literature in capitalist context, Pound's anti-ornamentalism is not really what it seems to be – a mystical theory of a naturally necessary language – but a coded plea for a writing of relevance. Just as his ideal poet refuses to stand off in a domestic space as a figure of contemplative removal, so in the ideogrammic and vorticist stages of his thought Pound's luminous image is a figure of epistemic action: it is no longer a moment in which readers are propelled into a subjective realm, in the mode of *A Lume Spento*, in order to find their liberation from the gray world of capital, but a heightened moment of new consciousness through which that world's human "things" are revealed in definitive profile. It is as if Pound believed that abstraction, a form of consciousness motivated and fed by a form of abstract writing, once renovated, would spell the end of imperialism, the politics of abstraction; as if the respect of human difference in actual social relations were a necessary consequence of its representation in a writing properly phalanxed with particularity. The unity of Pound's ad hoc theorizing is the unity of a mind seeking to reestablish in a hostile context the old honorable role of the poet as the good cultural doctor, a rearguing, because his environment demanded it by demeaning that role, of the premises of a classic apology: "It is curious that one should be asked," he says, "to rewrite Sidney's *Defense of Poesie* in the year of grace 1913." Pound's career shows us just how curious, necessary, and fated to failure.

As a social and literary critic, Pound is a celebrant of the intensely peculiar, the apparently primordial, autonomous force which he believed stood under and propelled everything that is expressed: what rescues Homer or Dante, Chaucer or Shakespeare – his chief examples – from what would otherwise have been their certain aesthetic and political fate as rank imitators, the lackeys of someone else's mind. Pound's word for this substance of substances was *virtu*.

In his populist American logic, *individuality*, therefore *virtue*, and therefore (the aesthetic turn on his politics) *virtuosity*, were threatened at their virile heart by the culture of capitalism and its commodity-based economy. The virtuous artist was Pound's persistent emblem of the free individual and his representation of a generous ideal of culture that he would see translated into the social sphere at large. "Having discovered his own virtue," Pound wrote, "the artist will be more likely to discern and allow for a peculiar *virtu* in others." This, Pound's live-and-let-live company of literary worthies, is his measure of actual social decency at any given time and the basis of his political criticism of what he thought American capitalism had done to our fundamental political ideals.

When Pound told his story of *virtu*, a story he retold obsessively, he was talking the ahistorical psychology of genius; when he talked the dilemma of the artist in modern America, he told another story: that of the vulnerability of genius to social pressures, the curious inability of the primordial and the autonomous to stay primordial and autonomous. This second story is the backbone of Pound's career – the backbone, in other words, of high modernism. The necessity of reimagining the social sphere is initially a literary necessity, social change pursued in order to ensure the life of the artist. Later, and more grandly, in Pound's theorizing of the 1930s, in an odd utopian echo of a famous passage in Marx, social change is pursued in order to ensure that every man may fish in the morning for his sustenance and pursue criticism and poetry in the afternoons; social change on behalf of the artist in us all; society totally reimagined from the aesthetic point of view.

But if it is precisely as a celebrant of a linked literary and political *virtu* that Pound achieved his own *virtu* as a critical voice – he became the polemical engine of high modernism – then the oddity of Pound the poet is that he was haunted for his entire career by the suspicion that he was not original, that he was a poet of no *virtu* whatsoever. Out of this haunting by the spirits of literary history's virtuous powers he fashioned a practice, from *A Lume Spento* through *The Cantos*, more continuous than the usual views of his poetic evolution (including his own) have generally allowed.

If no *virtu*, then no self; if no self, then nothing to express. Like Stevens, Pound's life as a poet was in constant, if implicit, dialogue with the archetypal and revolutionary American desire for radical origination in a new land ("new land, new men, new thoughts"), a desire for self-creation that Emerson thought would be realized only if we could forget history, rid ourselves of the old man of old thoughts from the old land. In order to kill himself off as an expression of history and simultaneously re-birth himself as the first man living utterly in the present, a man must "go into solitude," not only from society but also from his "chamber" – the place where "I read and write," where though no one is bodily present, "I" am "not solitary," because "I" have the unwanted company of all those represented selves who populate my books. The "I" must therefore be emptied of everything, including its literary company. And the virgin American woods, Emerson thought, is the context which might induce the necessary ascetic action, the place where "I" may escape all mediation and confront nature "face to face" – the place where "I" can say, at last, "I am nothing." With the historically layered self presumably so negated, the "I" – this urgent and almost passive emptiness which is not quite nothing – becomes a capacity for reception ("a transparent eyeball"), a hollowed-out space anxious to be filled: desire in its purest form – in Emerson, a no-self gratified, become filled up, and so rescued at the last moment from nothingness by the inflowing currents of the Transcendental Self.

Pound's effort to rethink lyric practice is inseparable from Emerson's dynamic of American desire, which in its turn is an expression of the quintessence of the immigrant imagination on its neverending crossing of a real or metaphoric Atlantic, the immigrant who would leave "I" behind in the suffocating ghetto of a real or a metaphoric Europe (say, some small town in the Midwest), leave behind the "I" that *is* for a magically fulfilling self that we are not but would become – Vito Andolini become Vito Corleone, James Gatz become Jay Gatsby. In Pound, the Atlantic crossing is reversed and (in the trajectory of his biography) taken all the way back, from Idaho to Philadelphia to Italy. An American expatriate who left his country because he believed its cultural and economic system denied him literary selfhood, Pound took his American desire to make it new, the "nothing" that "I am," back to European ground, and in a cluster of his earliest poems figured himself precisely as a determinate emptiness of literary longing seeking writerly identity in recontact with international literary tradition, which is what he achieved in glamorous substitution for Emerson's Transcendental Self. What Pound learned very early was that the Emersonian promise of selfhood couldn't be delivered; Emerson's American woods, after all, were only natural, there was no literature there, no *selva oscura*, no Yeatsean mythological mystery. Our so-called virgin land was a nightmare to Pound precisely because of its solitude and its purity.

So, as a reverse immigrant, Pound fled the literary death whose name was natural immediacy, fled an America where he enjoyed the sorts of freedoms and comforts that classic immigrants coming to America sought. He went to Italy – his twenty-third birthday still several months off – seeking cultural life in the very period when millions of Italians from the south were fleeing their homes (such as they were) for America in the hope of improving an economic base that Pound's family had already secured, and upon which (thanks to his father's generous understanding) he could – and did – modestly draw during his expatriation. In effect, Pound replayed Henry James's criticism of America as a place whose cultural newness made a certain kind of literature improbable. James's core judgment of American society – he thought it "denuded" – signifies what, for him and for Pound, had been lost in the new world. James's solution was to drop the innocent American into the context of European experience: "one might enumerate the items of high civilization," James wrote, "as it exists in other countries, which are absent from the texture of American life until it should become a wonder to know what was left." The effect of such absence on an English or French imagination "would probably," he surmised, "be appalling." On himself and on Pound, the impact of such absence provided the energy for and often the structure of the writing they would do.

In a brief poem from *A Lume Spento*, Pound stages the predicament of his empty American "I" gazing into the mirror of desire; he sees "I" represented as a series of incompatible images; the denuded "I" who *is* comes before the mirror and presumably "before" what is represented in the mirror as the foundation of representation. But this "I" is represented as somebody else, a multiplicity of selves, the constantly metamorphosing consciousness Pound would take on: "O strange face there in the glass! / O ribald company, O saintly host!" "On His Own Face in a Glass" stages the moment of self-awareness as a moment of some shock and anxiety ("I? I? I?"), a moment of self-awareness in which he comes to know that there is no self anterior to representation to be aware of and that all the self (selves) that can ever be exists in the magical medium of representation, in literature now envisioned, as the pilgrims and other immigrants imagined America itself, as a mirror of transforming desire. Pound's primary poetic tone for such knowledge was mainly confident, even grateful, as if in one stroke – the shape his entire career would take bears heavily upon the point – he had discovered a role to play which coordinated all of his impulses as poet, literary historian, critic, anthologist, and translator, with this last activity providing the cohesion which made the role unified, lent it identity, so that he did become a self of sorts.

In the concluding poem of *A Lume Spento*, Pound represents his soul as a "hole full of God" through which the "song of all time blows . . . As winds thru a knot-holed board." And in his first English volume, *A Quinzaine for This Yule* (1908), he represents the "I" similarly as a "clear space":

> 'Tis as in midmost us there glows a sphere
> Translucent, molten gold, that is the "I"
> And into this some form projects itself:
> Christus, or John, or eke the Florentine;
> And as the clear space is not if a form's
> Imposed thereon,
> So cease we from all being for the time
> And there, the Masters of the Soul live on.

These early poems about poetry – so stilted, so unmodern in diction – escape mere conventionality by the extremity of their representation of the self seeking inspiration and poetic selfhood. As Pound figures it, his pre-poetic self is much less than that favorite romantic figure of self at home in the world, unanxiously dependent, self as aeolian harp awaiting the winds of nature that will stir it into music. Pound's pre-poetic self is in possession of no resources of its own. In what sense it is a self is hard to say: "Thus am I Dante for a space and am / One François Villon." But when not Dante or Villon, what then? Just who is this "I" who ceases to be when the virtuous and manly masters of his soul fill the hole of self? The self as translator, the self of no virtue, becomes a medium of the *virtu* of others, and Pound's poems, *The Cantos* most especially, become a kind of international gallery, a hall of exhibits of the originality that he lacked and that without his heroic retrieval would be locked away in a cultural dead space, of antiquarian interest only. Pound's famous avant-garde directive, "make it new," really means "make contemporary what is old." Pound is a man without a center, in whom the old masters can "live on"; his poetry is the lifeline and medium of their persistent historicity. His poetry's "modernity" would lie in its creation of a usable literary and political past, exemplary in force: a model to live by and a cultural community to live in.

If the absence of *virtu* is no condition to be overcome in a search for an original self of his own but the durable basis of everything Pound did as a poet – an absence of identity that he came comfortably to accept as his identity, a trigger of poetic production, early and late – then in one important sense Pound never really "evolved" as a poet. The numerous and dramatic shifts in style we can note from *A Lume Spento* to *The Cantos* – and not only from volume to volume but often within a given volume – are not evidence of the dissatisfied, self-critical young writer groping toward his one and only true voice, but the very sign of his voice and all the maturity he would ever achieve. The word Pound frequently used to describe this persistent mark of change in his poetic writing was *metamorphosis*, from "the tradition of metamorphoses," as he explained in 1918, "that teaches us that things do not always remain the same. They become other things by swift and unanalysable process." Pound's theory of myth was based on an attempt to explain the moment when a man, after walking "sheer into nonsense," tried to tell someone else about it "who called him a liar." The man was forced to make a myth, "an impersonal or objective story woven out of his own emotion, as the nearest equation that he was capable of putting into words."

Among the manifestations of Pound's obsession with protean energy there is his radically avant-garde idea of literature as "something living, something capable of constant transformation and rebirth"; his doctrine of the image, which asserts that in the presence of the genuine work of art we experience "the sense of sudden liberation; that sense of freedom from time and space limits; that sense of sudden growth"; and his statement in *The Spirit of Romance* that myth takes its origin subjectively, in a moment when we pass through "delightful psychic experience." In the period spanning the many stylistic changes from his earliest poems to his early *Cantos*, Pound changed not at all on the value of metamorphosis for the sort of writer (himself) who explained the process of writing to himself in his earliest poems as an experience of walking sheer into nonsense – becoming Christ, Villon, or Dante, God or a tree – a writer who would project the psychic value of his own aesthetic experience as the real value of *reading* his poems. Pound's reader would also be freed from the self of the moment, liberated into some strange and bracing identity, joining the writer in mythic experience in order to take on, with Pound, what he, like Pound, does not possess.

The unstated assumption of Pound's poetics is that his typical reader is not everyman but an American like himself, in need of what he needs – a reader, in other words, not only with no *virtu* of his own but who does not want to be fixed with a "self," a reader for whom avant-gardism, though not known as such, is the ruling philosophy of everyday life in the land of opportunity and infinite self-development. From the delightful, because liberating, psychic experience of the poet and the parallel experience of his American reader comes this projection: the reformation of literary history in his own (and America's) image via the bold antidefinition of literature as writing without historically prior and persistent identity, writing without a prior "self" to rely on, a nonidentity of sheerest possibility, an absence of essence – "constant transformation," constant rebirth into a newness of (these are equivalents) an American and a modern literary selfhood. Never mind that "constant transformation" also describes the dream of consumer capitalism, avant-garde of capitalist economics.

Metamorphosis is the unprecedented master category in Pound's literary theory. And in spite of the explicit Ovidian allusion, the theory is not Ovidian. Nor does Pound draw upon a notion of biological metamorphosis: the man who comes "before" the glass cannot be traced, not even obscurely, as a surviving form in the new self (hence Pound's shocked "I?"). But if there is to be metamorphosis in any recognizable sense of the word, there must be a prior something which undergoes transformation. If the prior "something" is, as in Pound, a determinate nothing, a hole needing filling and fulfilling, valuable ("golden") precisely because of its amorphic condition, then Pound has pushed metamorphosis to the edge of its limiting boundary: the classic American dream, self-origination ex nihilo. Pound theorizes metamorphosis, a process of self-emergence, as Emerson had theorized it: as a condition of potential-for-self only, not the transformation of one self into another, a condition without a memory out of which a self might emerge that is nothing but memory, and thus – the irony and paradox of Pound's career – no self at all.

When some of his earliest poems were republished in 1965, Pound dismissed them as a "collection of stale creampuffs," a judgment that obscures his true target, toward which he would always feel a residual and unresolvable ambivalence: the fin-de-siècle literary scene that had energized him by lending him masks of identity. By 1908, when he left America for Venice, those masks marked the existence of an avant-garde solidified by its rejection of the world that young writers had found fully in place in England and America in the last decades of the nineteenth century. The distinction of what is called high modernism may be that no literary movement ever had less respect for its social situation.

The exemplary literary rejectors – Swinburne, Rossetti and the pre-Raphaelites, the decadents of the 1890s, and the most famous poet writing in English when Pound left for Venice, W. B. Yeats – were isolationists of the aesthetic who desired to fashion a self-contained world of art, not in order to celebrate the wonders of aesthetic autonomy, but in order to win their freedom from a world they detested and feared they could not escape. Thus the hankerings after apocalypse, the hope that the body of all that is world and worldly had entered its autumnal phase, those poetic landscapes enshrouded in mists and shadows, that nostalgia for pre-capitalist societies, those extraordinary investments in the magic of word color, the newly revitalized interest in the mythological imagination which represents the world as an enchanted place frequented by the gods, and, most of all, and presiding over everything, the monolithic tonality of mournfulness. Hulme, surveying the scene, said that a poem couldn't be a poem unless it was "moaning or whining about something or other." The children of Swinburne (the young Pound was one of them) could not achieve escape from the disenchanted world made by capital and its agents – those money changers, journalists, and literary realists who were Yeats's relentless representatives for what, in a telling gesture of aestheticist despair, he called, in the opening poem of *Crossways* (1889), "Grey Truth," a code term signifying all the forces against the aesthetic, particularly the politics of democracy, capitalist economics, and science. These are the forces opposed by "dream" ("Dream, dream, for this is also sooth"), another key code word in the literary context of the young Pound, signifying poetry as a mode of contemplation, vision, and revery, all in the service of world-weariness turned inward, subjectivity pursued ("Then nowise worship dusty deeds"); an affirmation of the word over the act; poetry as a fragile haven off the route where history was too obviously tending.

The retrospective embarrassment Pound felt for his earlier work aside, the poems themselves taken as a whole present considerable evidence of the sort of energy for aesthetic experiment and variety that would mark *The Cantos*. Even *A Lume Spento* (1908), all by itself, is an image of the various energies at work in late-nineteenth and early-twentieth-century English poetry. The mythological imagination he recovered via Greece, Ovid, and Yeats's Celtic twilight gave Pound a nature not virgin and sensuous, a nature not natural, but bookishly mediated, alive with the sort of culture that a modernized, skeptical, and secular world was coming thoroughly to disrecognize: "By the still pool of Mar-nan-otha / Have I found me a bride / That was a dog-wood tree some syne"; "I stood still and was a tree amid the wood / Knowing the truth of things unseen before, / Of Daphne and the laurel bow." Snugly alongside such bookish lyricism from the other world, a voice much in evidence in the early Pound, was the robust earthiness of Browning: "Bah! I have sung women in three cities, / But it is all the same"; "Aye you're a man that! ye old mesmerizer"; there was also the lament of the decadent all too aware of his victimization and the lateness of his arrival: "Broken our strength, yes as crushed reeds we fall, / And yet the art, the art goes on"; the voice that speaks through the stylish troubadour mask of Bertran de Born: "Tho thou cost wish me ill / Audiart, Audiart"; and the poet who would animate genteel diction with infusions of a native diction, not directly but through the mask of another poet (Villon) who Pound thought had found a speech "unvarnished," and who came to Pound thanks to a late-nineteenth-century vogue as much for his persona as for his writing – via Rossetti's translation. Villon, a poet "without illusion," would "revive our poetry in the midst of mid-Victorian desiccation."

"A Villonaud for This Yule" bears Pound's characteristic habits as a poet: the fashioning of a poetic discourse out of pastiche and translation, one of whose effects is to root lyric impulse historically, draw it through layers of tradition, as a writing done over other writing ("palimpsest" was one of Pound's key words for *The Cantos*). Thus to write lyric was to write the history of lyric in a kind of scholarly act graced at the same time by a poet's sort of footnote – allusion – and thereby to embed lyric feeling in a long tradition, to make lyric into an emotional and intellectual "complex," to engage spontaneity with reflection. Thus to write lyric is to fashion a composite of borrowings and inspirations whose effect is to suggest that the poet's intention is to create single-handedly a traditional culture out of his welded fragments and bring it home to his time.

De Born's "borrowed lady" or, as the Italians translated it, *una donna ideale*, is also a figure of Pound's lyric practice and his desire to instigate cultural *risorgimento*, for America in particular. *Una donna ideale* is the image of the tradition – his true Beatrice – that, particularly in *The Cantos*, Pound would invent by piecing together a new writing characterized by allusion, quotation, translation, adaptation, pastiche, even original writing in another language. This new poetry would be open to the inclusion of history by way of the incorporation of half-acres of document, the brute prose of chronicle that Pound jammed into the intimate rooms of his elegant lyricism. This is lyric impulse forced to live with what the commercial enforcers of lyric taste in Pound's young manhood refused to live with: a heterogeneity of discourses often not only unlyric but positively, at times, antilyric.

In *Personae* and *Exultations* (both 1909) Pound added a new voice to his ensemble, one that threw into sharp relief the mask of the languorous and passive aesthete. *Personae*, with its Yeats-echoing epigraph ("Make strong old dreams lest this our world lose heart"), contains Pound's adaptation from D'Aubigne, an anti-aestheticist mask which stresses the muscular and martial involvement of the poet who writes "From the Saddle," whose lines necessarily bear the stress and strain of the active life. "From the Saddle" may be Pound's first incarnation in the mask of the fully integrated sensibility, a lyric expression traced by the sounds of battle. Nevertheless, "From the Saddle" continues to flourish turn-of-the-century manners ("with gin and snare right near alway," "Ever on word," "Tis meet my verse"). "Sestina: Altaforte" is more direct – "Damn it all! all this our South stinks peace. / You whoreson dog, Papiols, come! Let's to music!" – though it is a highly literary directness, sounding with the voice of some forceful Shakespearean hero. Gaudier-Brzeska's creative misauditing of this poem (for the repeated "peace" he heard, repeatedly, "piss") is true to Pound's macho spirit and led to Gaudier-Brzeska's sculpting of the phallic bust of Pound, with the ironic caveat that it would not look like Pound; the phallic bust which was the very image of the poet as red blood that Pound would later criticize in the inheritors of Whitman, not seeing it in himself, perhaps, because when he looked in the glass of his poetry he saw no self there he recognized as his own, because these masculinist masks were just that, masks.

But they were masks of critical point, yearning portraits of medieval vigor. Here is Pound's unusual, because for once positive, connection with mass culture – the popular romance fiction of his day; here is his implicit criticism of his own decadent manner and a high culture whose neurasthenia was being medically reported on in the magazines of the day and would be definitively dissected in "The Love Song of J. Alfred Prufrock." In his "Ballad of the Goodly

Fere," Pound adopted a dialect voice out of Robert Burns in an effort to savage the conventional, whispy Christ of the herd mentality with an antithetical "man o' men was he," a man like the seafarer and Ulysses ("Wi' his eyes like the grey o' of the sea") – a man of the deed ("They'll no' get him a' in a book I think . . . No mouse of the scrolls was the Goodly Fere / But aye loved the open sea"). Pound's vitalist Christ was a criticism not only of the virtually disembodied mainstream representations of Christ that had infuriated him, but an attack (like Frost's) on the bookish flight he saw everywhere in contemporary poetry – a critical image not only because of His masculinity but also because of the sound of His speech; no sophisticated ennui there.

By title and by vocal attitude, "Francesca," one of the poems Pound placed toward the end of *Exultations*, forecasts the mode that preoccupied him in a volume that would prove to be a turning point, *Canzoni* (1911), which caused Ford Madox Ford to roll on the floor in didactic laughter – a response that made a decisive impact on Pound's style, or so Pound said. *Canzoni* was saturated with medieval colors from Dante and Cavalcanti: poem after poem was a hushed adoration of a lady of ladies (*donna non vidi mai*), Pound's own version of Beatrice enfolded in a light not of the sun: "A splendid calyx that about her gloweth / Smiting the sunlight on whose ray she goeth." Apparently Ford thought that Pound had captured his neoplatonic vision all too well, in a poetic manner also "not of the sun." Pound took the point to heart – and would pass it on to Yeats in another and similarly significant act of literary history.

Beginning with *Ripostes* (1912) and then *Lustra* (1916), Pound managed to reform his phrasing to a prosier (though elegant) mode while forsaking conventional decorum. He began to write a poetry that could live up to the theoretical principles he and Hulme were forging in tandem. The impulse to write lines like "Guerdoned by thy sun-gold traces" or phrases like "eke the Florentine" would be purged. But in "Francesca" Pound had already begun to break that habit and managed to produce a voice at once plain (by the standards of educated conversation), formal, and elevated – a "curial" voice that he would come to rely on for the numerous lyric passages that stud *The Cantos* and that provides striking contrast to his self-conscious masculinity. Thus, "Francesca":

> You came in out of the night
> And there were flowers in your hands,
> Now you will come out of a confusion of people,
> Out of a turmoil of speech about you.

And in *Canzoni* itself there are other vocal presences, including a satirical one, which would bloom in *Lustra* and beyond:

> O woe, woe,
> People are born and die,
> We shall also be dead pretty soon
> Therefore let us act as if we were
>   dead already.

If it is the case that the poetry of *Canzoni* is more various than the poet of *Canzoni* (and Ford) would allow, it is also true that the dominant mood of the volume is sustained by Pound's visionary portraits of the Beatrice-like woman who is the model of self-generating originality which Pound praised in the male poets he most admired, and which he learned, from his glimpse in the glass, that he could not claim for himself. His adoring tone is not for some imagined ineffectual angel, placed on a pedestal because (according to ancient fantasy) she is safe nowhere else, but for the female representation of a power of self-possession and independence that underwrote his basic values in politics (anti-imperialism, individualism) and in poetics (the autonomous genius, the active soul). This visionary woman will reappear in numerous passages of *The Cantos* as a goddess from out of ancient myths, brought back to life, in Pound's meditations, as a sudden new visitor to modern Italy, a breakthrough of the gods:

> And the cities set in their hills,
> And the goddess of the fair knees
> Moving there, with the oak-wood behind her,
> The green slope, with her white hounds leaping about her . . .

The awed tone (Canto 17) of one who has been gratuitously blessed, privileged with the ultimate surprise, is the mark of Pound's relation to visionary women in *Canzoni* and *The Cantos*. But the difference between her earlier and later appearances is important. In *The Cantos* she stands not alone, as she does in *Canzoni*, a pure presence vulnerable to Ford's ironies – Ford was Pound's Mercutio – but as an element in an integrated complex, a lyric moment of praise placed in a poetic texture thick with many other things, most of them not lyric. She is an element in a complex writing who is protected from skeptics by her unprepared-for appearances and quick disappearances. In *Ripostes* (1912) she is present briefly in a Dantean metamorphosis ("Apparuit"), a change from ordinariness ("Thou a slight thing") to visionary splendor ("I saw / thee. . . . then shone thine oriel and the stunned light / faded about thee"). And she is present powerfully by her absence in the volume's most riveting poem, "Portrait D'Une Femme," a picture of the culturally privileged but desiccated female of no force, pathetically dependent, a collector of objects of aestheticist delight and utter inconsequence ("Idols and ambergris and rare inlays"), not an independent power of light that stuns the light of the sun but a metaphoric Sargasso Sea. The poem's opening and scandalous first line ("Your mind and you are our Sargasso Sea") horrified at least one famous genteel American editor: "I sent them a real poem, a modern poem, containing the word 'uxorious,' and they wrote back that I used the letter 'r' three times in the first line, and that it was very difficult to pronounce, and that I might not remember that Tennyson had once condemned the use of four s's in a certain line of a different meter."

Pound's deliberate antilyricism in "Portrait D'Une Femme" is the vehicle of his narrative intention to tell a story, implicated in the details of useless junk that clogs a sensibility afloat, of a self without a center; not a trashed female antithesis of his manly seafarer, but a figure of the aesthete within that he would exorcise in its male incarnation in his literary farewell to London, *Hugh Selwyn Mauberley*. "Portrait D'Une Femme" is also, and most importantly, a riposte in form as well as in theme: a concentrated narrative that exorcises bad lyric and all its sentimentality with this kind of conversational piquancy:

> You have been second always. Tragical?
> No. You preferred it to the usual thing:
> One dull man, dulling and uxorious . . .

The distance Pound traveled between *A Lume Spento* and *Lustra* can in part be measured by the titles of those volumes: the first in the self-pitying mood of the fin de siècle ("with quenched tapers"); the second in the worldly and interventionist mode of the social criticism that he would increasingly be loath to segregate from the project of his poetry ("Lustrum: an offering for the sins of the whole people, made by the censors at the expiration of their five years of office"). *Lustra* contains roughly two kinds of poetry: one borne by an insouciant plainness of antilyric voice, direct in syntax and satirical in intent, with the object of heaping hostile criticism on the bourgeois order that has no use for what Pound called "the serious artist." This voice is funny but often tiresomely insistent in *Lustra*, marking poem after poem with the (even then) conventional postures of bohemian scorn out of the garret: "Will people accept them? / [i.e. these songs] . . . Their virgin stupidity is untemptable . . . " Or this: "Come, let us pity those who are better off / than we are . . . " The second kind of poem, with ancestry in *Canzoni* (though in plainer syntax), presents the adored vision of female *virtu* ("She passed and left no quiver in the veins"), now grounded in the earthier poetics implied by "The Study in Aesthetics," an anecdotal reflection set in Sirmione. And Pound's choice of the Italian "Sirmione" rather than the Latin "Sirmio," which he favored in

Canzoni, tells us that his literary reveries with tradition are feeling the gravity of contemporary life.

Even as he turned out small poem after small poem and a shocking number of pages of prose, Pound was all along – perhaps as early as 1904, while a student at Hamilton College – working himself up to writing a long poem of epic size, "long after" (Pound speaking) "mankind has been commanded never again to attempt a poem of any length." He apparently began work in earnest on this poem sometime in 1915, published his first three "cantos," as he called them, in *Poetry* in 1917, only soon thereafter to suppress them and began anew. After an initial volume appeared in 1925 as *A Draft of XVI Cantos*, gatherings of cantos were published with regularity, to the end of Pound's life, including the infamous *Pisan Cantos* in 1948 and two volumes, in 1955 and 1959, written in the insane asylum. The least taught of the famous modernist texts, the collected volume, *The Cantos of Ezra Pound* – one hundred and seventeen cantos' worth – appeared in 1970 and has been reprinted thirteen times as of this writing, this latter fact strong testimony on behalf of our continuing fascination with the high modernists, including this one whose major work is widely assumed to be unreasonably difficult, often pure gibberish, and, in its occasionally lucid moments, offensive to most standards of decency.

Just what kind of literary work he was writing Pound had trouble deciding. He was keenly conscious of his epic predecessors and often glossed their intentions as his own: to give voice to the "general heart," to write "the speech of a nation" through the medium of one person's sensibility. Yet for all his classic desire and expressed contempt for romantic poetry, Pound was also marked by its contrary aesthetic: "the man who tries to explain his age instead of expressing himself," he writes, "is doomed to destruction." In Pound, the poetics of *The Odyssey* and *The Divine Comedy* are complicated by the poetics of *The Prelude* and *Song of Myself*: refocused by Pound in the lens of Wordsworth, Whitman, and Poe, *The Divine Comedy* becomes Dante's "tremendous lyric."

Classic ambition and romantic impulse would surface constantly through the long publishing history of *The Cantos*. An "epic is a poem including history," Pound wrote in 1935, in the midst of a decade during which he was writing cantos that "included" history and chunks of the historical record with stupefying literality: redactions of Chinese history in Cantos 52–61, extract after extract from the writings of John Adams in Cantos 62–71. In 1937, in *Guide to Kulchur*, he declared (with a nod to Kipling) that his long poem would tell "the tale of the tribe," but in the same book he also described *The Cantos*,

with analogy to Bartók's Fifth Quartet, as the "record of a personal struggle."
Then, in the middle of the journey, in 1939, he struck a new note, this one
neither epic nor romantic: "As to the form of *The Cantos*: All I can say or pray
is wait till it's there. I mean wait till I get 'em written and then if it don't show,
I will start exegesis. I haven't an Aquinas-map; Aquinas *not* valid now." And
with that nostalgic glance back at the cultural context of his beloved Dante,
Pound approached the clarity he achieved in 1962 in his *Paris Review* dialogue
with Donald Hall.

With over a hundred cantos done, he gave Hall a definition – anti-definition,
really – of the poem's form that marked it "modernist" in strictest terms.
Not Homer or Dante, but Joyce and Eliot stand behind Pound's search for
a form "that wouldn't exclude something merely because it didn't fit." With
this gesture Pound declares the classic concern of aesthetics for the decorous
relationship of genre to subject matter beside the modernist point. He tells us
that the literary form that can include what doesn't fit is the authentic signature
of modern writing, the sign that the literature of our time has adequately taken
the measure of its exploded culture.

Like Wordsworth, Pound felt himself an outsider in his society, a literary
radical who knew that his poetry was unrecognizable as such by mainstream
culture. As a consequence, he set himself the task (in Wordsworth's phrasing)
"of *creating* the taste by which he is to be enjoyed." His project was to provide
epic substance for a culture grounded in none of the assumptions that typically
had nourished the epic poet: a culture no longer capable of issuing a valid
rhetorical contract between writer and reader. In a culture that cannot read
him – here is the motivating contradiction of *The Cantos* and much high
modernism – Pound would write a poem that his culture needs to read in order
to make itself truly a culture. "The modern mind contains heteroclite elements.
The past epos has succeeded when all or a great many of the answers were
assumed, at least between author and audience. The attempt in an experimental
age" – he means socially as well as aesthetically experimental – "is therefore
rash."

Rash or no, Pound persisted in epic intention because, as he told Hall,
"there are epic subjects. The struggle for individual rights is an epic subject,
consecutive from jury trial in Athens to Anselm versus William Rufus, to the
murder of Becket and to Coke and through John Adams." So the poem that
Pound had mainly written by 1962 found its home, not in a specific Western
culture and place, as classical epics had done, but in Western culture as a
whole, as the grand story of struggle, not yet won, for individual rights; and
it found its strange literary form in an age of experiment that demanded he
invent his own. The form he invented is at once the representation of a culture

he thought to be in fragments and an offering of hope for a different kind of future, rooted in the narrative of common lineage and destiny.

Pound knew that in order to tell the tale of the tribe he needed a tribe to tell it to, knew he didn't have one, and in *The Cantos* – a poem without unifying epic hero or stability of cultural scene – he gave us the unlikely record of one poet's effort to create through means unclassical a new classical situation for writing. What he ended up achieving was a poem whose experimental character overwhelms all cultural and social goals except those that bear on the welfare of writers. *The Cantos* would resuscitate a community of letters for modern writers, in order that they might join a tradition of radical experimenters and their noble patrons, all those who waged their struggle for individual (largely aesthetic) rights against the grain; a tradition brought to life for an age (our own) cut off from nourishment and patronage, a home for our contemplative, but only our contemplative, life.

In this light, Pound's title, *The Cantos*, is tellingly odd. It is the nontitle of a writer who apparently never saw the need to make up his mind – who, if he could have lived forever, would probably not have endowed his experiment with a crystallizing title (like *The Waste Land* or *The Bridge*). Calling a poem *The Cantos* (and shall we say *The Cantos* "is" or *The Cantos* "are"? – to decide that question is to claim much) is like calling a novel *Work in Progress* while writing it and then publishing it under that title, or perhaps *The Chapters*, like a Renaissance sonneteer deciding to call his sequence *The Sonnets*. To publish sections of this poem, forever in progress, with the words "a draft of" included in the title only underscores the tentativeness of the writer's intention. Unlike all the epics we know, *The Cantos* names as its substance aesthetic form itself, without ever claiming, as Wordsworth and Whitman had in their romantic versions, the substantial coherence of a binding subjectivity.

Not that there isn't a discernible subjectivity afloat in the poem: there is, but it doesn't congeal as a "self" whose autonomous presence is projected in the autobiographical narrative of a poet's mind. For much of the way, "Ezra Pound" appears to us in the shape of a desire: as a generous capacity for reception, a virtually transparent subjectivity, a facilitating vehicle, a literary producer (in the theatrical sense of that word, a gatherer of artistic forces), a man, by his own account, of no *virtu*, an absence of selfhood, a hole, a mirror for others. This tissue of masks, this incessant scholarly quoter – translator, alluder, medium of pastiche, tradition's own ventriloquist – this poet as anthologist, poet of the specimen, patron and exhibitor of styles, heroes, and cultural contexts which are given space in the literary gallery and curriculum called *The Cantos*, is an active and empathetic memory trapped in the dead present of his culture, casting a long lifeline into the past (as tradition's own lifeguard) in order to rescue by transmitting tradition, and in so transmitting bring his own culture back to life again.

The Cantos approached as if they were written by a poet-without-a-self unveil themselves as a vast texture (text, textile, interweaving) of discourses lyric, satirical, narrative, dramatic, and nonliterary (historical, epistolary, technical); Pound's influential idea of the heterogeneous image (an "intellectual and emotional complex in an instant of time") writ very large; an immense vortex; or, in the perfect metaphor from the discarded first canto (drafted in 1912), a "ragbag," best form of all for a poet who didn't want to exclude something merely because it didn't fit – the form of a poetry by and for the culturally homeless.

And hence the centrality for *The Cantos* of those storied modernist metaphors drawn from the visual and spatial arts: like montage, a stark juxtaposition that yields its significance in some third, unnamed thing to be construed (imagined, created), by an active reader in the process of interpretation, whose own imaginative life will be the force which brings Pound's cultural hope to realization, and who is charged with voicing the poem's otherwise unvoiced vision, with making the diagnosis, distributing Pound's medicine; a reader who appreciates Pound properly and therefore earns his own entry into the community of letters by transforming himself from passive consumer in the culture of capital into resourceful, self-reliant free agent; Pound's critic become the reader as modernist, co-maker of *The Cantos*, and co-worker in the enterprise of culture-making. And of course the metaphor of collage, surrealist version of the ragbag, a composition whose diverse and incongruously placed fragments – drawn from all manner of media – asks us (as does montage, but now on the scale of the entire work) to take the thing as a whole, not as a narrative but as a form hung in space, in order to "view" it in its entirety. Under the pressure of these metaphors, *The Cantos* become a difficult structure of fragments signifying not the imitation of fragmentation by means of fragmentation but some missing total vision (or the desire thereof), whose presence in any given canto must be supplied by an engaged reader. So read, *The Cantos* emerge as a vision of social and cultural health sporadically in evidence and constantly threatened by the historical process; a vision of the free individual gathering himself against history's gloom of diseased economics; a vision contemplated and disseminated by those who must read Pound in a thickening contemporary cultural darkness that is almost complete. *The Cantos* may be the clearest example we have of the doubled character of Pound's literary desire, to pursue aesthetic innovation for the purpose of instigating social change, a poem whose unparalleled formal sumptuousness – a cornucopia of literary texture – calls forth those mediators who would join Pound's lifelong experiment in cultural hope to a world of possible readers.

"And then went down to the ship / Set keel to breakers, forth on the godly sea..." That is how *The Cantos* begin, in a strange world modified by gods, with Pound translating from the eleventh book of *The Odyssey*, the descent into the underworld. Assuming the mask of an epic hero already written, Pound voyages, "Heavy with weeping" (the tone is elegiac, the subject is cultural loss), to a place of darkness, dimly lit with torches, for a colloquy with the dead, the prophetic Tiresias in particular. Ezra Pound, Odyssean poet, makes his descent into the West's literary underworld in order to conjure the ghosts of writers past in a poetry of reading. Homer's hero summons the dead with the ritual blood of sacrifice; Pound, with the blood of scholarly poetic labor, would summon Homer via a Latin translation made by Andreas Divas in the Renaissance, period of classical recovery; he presses his Latin Homer through the alliterative strong rhythms of Anglo-Saxon poetry and then into modern English, thereby producing the effect of a triple translation for the benefit of the modern English reader, an illusion of three literary traditions simultaneously present in culturally mixed traces of diction and proper names, a palimpsest, writing over writing for a period – his own – which Pound hoped would also be a time of cultural recovery.

The first of *The Cantos* begins the project of a new *risorgimento* as if it were already in progress: the first word of the first canto is *and*. We are offered a stylistic exhibit of heroic endeavor, by a poet-patron, toward the end of which the stylistic exhibitor himself comes forward, breaking out of the mask of Odysseus. In an abrupt comic descent from the heroic decorum of his tone and diction, Ezra Pound speaks – "Lie quiet Divas" – so revealing himself in that moment as a haunter of libraries and old bookstores – in the dramatic fiction of Canto 1, a man poring over a rare book – searching for the traces of a usable tradition, and finding them in the text of Divas's translation.

In the eleventh book of Homer's epic, Odysseus's youngest companion, Elpenor, asks Odysseus to provide him proper burial, lest he restlessly and forever wander the earth's surface, and he requests a memorial so that he may enjoy an afterlife in his culture's collective memory. Just so does Pound grant Divas, another unhappy ghost, similar (if imagined) requests in order that Divas may "lie quiet." And Pound's autobiographically aggressive translation of Homer's epitaph for Elpenor ("A man of no fortune, and a name to come") links him to Elpenor and Divas both, and to a literary history that merges ancient, Renaissance, and modern cultures in an overarching triplet rhyme of tradition-making, the point of literary history being its own transmission; the immortality of writers depending on other writers who remember long.

Pound, a bibliophile and cultural genealogist, gives the citation as a kind of epitaph: "I mean, that is Andreas Divas, / In officina Wecheli, 1538, out of Homer." Divas and Wecheli (the bookmaker), those, too, are names of heroes in the commemorative world of *The Cantos*, heroes as significant as Odysseus. For one more line and a half Pound returns, now in his own voice – the spell of recovery is broken – to the Homeric narrative, then (as it were) flips the pages to the back of the book that Wecheli made, this time quoting the Latin of Georgius Dartona of Cyprus, whose translation of the Homeric hymns was bound in with Divas's work: some enamored phrases about Aphrodite ("thou with dark eyelids"), who was assigned the defenses of Crete, phrases whose Latin will be strange to the modern reader, but much less strange than the idea they contain, absurd to the modern mind (Pound knows this), of art active in the world, beauty in defense of the city. At the end of Canto 1 Pound comes forward as a voice among old books, trying to breathe life into voices he feared had been silenced by his culture. In that act, he creates a voice of his own.

> Two mice and a moth my guides –
> To have heard the farfalla gasping
>   as toward a bridge over worlds.
>   That the kings meet in their island,
>   where no food is after flight from the pole.
>   Milkweed the sustenance
>   as to enter arcanum.
>
> To be men not destroyers.

That is how *The Cantos* end, with Pound writing lyric notes: on the forms of his confusion ("M'amour, m'amour / what do I love and / where are you?"); on his regrets ("Let the Gods forgive what I / have made / Let those I love try to forgive / what I have made"); on his econo-aesthetic obsessions ("La faillite de François Bernouard, Paris" – Bernouard, unsung, unknown in poetry until this moment in *The Cantos*, a contemporary version of Wecheli, a hero in the cultural struggle for *risorgimento*, a French bookmaker who went bankrupt printing the classics and who functions here as an incarnation of history's truth, Pound-style: the destruction of the honorable by a dishonorable economic system that will not permit the valuing of beauty and beauty's patrons). Notes, too, on his unceasing hatred for the human costs of war and the cold-blooded calculation of the secure-from-battle ("the young for the old / that is tragedy"); notes on his sustaining confidence in the liberating power of the image as the bedrock of personal redemption, aestheticist life-preserver of Pound's youth coming in handy at the end of a life of failed larger design ("For the blue flash and the moments / benedetta"); notes on his grandiose ambition ("I have tried to write Paradise"), his anchoring modesty, his disavowal of ambition ("Do not move / Let the wind speak / that is paradise"); notes on his cultural deprivation, having to go it, as Dante did not, without a Virgil-like teacher for his guide ("Two mice and a moth my guides – "). All his notes are the verbal condensation of desire, and desire, the gathering ambience of *The Cantos*, become palpable, the real subject of his last collection, *Drafts and Fragments* (1969).

In this final fragment of the final canto (117), a collage representative of virtually everything Pound thought about in *The Cantos* as a whole, the striking note sounded is not in some final revelation for poet and reader but in the variegated sounds of the poet's voice – in Pound's tonal agility, his compression of a range of vocal attitudes: the desperate old man, speaking painfully in the dark, sometimes in the curious mixed tones of prayer and imperative; sometimes in gentle self-directive; sometimes in fragments of amazement ("That I lost my center / fighting the world"; "That the kings meet in their island / where no food is after flight from the pole"); sometimes in desire's timeless infinitive ("To have heard the farfalla gasping / as toward a bridge over worlds"). Fragment follows fragment, in a poem heavy with sharply etched perceptions and feelings freed (largely) from reason's habitat of correct English syntax: a poem of reason undone, and in its unravelment of reason displaying the constituents of a mind trying to strip itself of the authoritative power of utterance it used to command (half-wanting to fail, still desiring authority), wanting to enter the realm of the unspeakable with the Monarch butterflies in need of no food – those kings that are figures of the soul entering the last mystery. The final line is the one with which Pound (according to his lover, Olga Rudge) wanted to end *The Cantos*, a line impossibly poised in tone and form, hung between yearning and self-confident imperative: "To be men not destroyers."

Between the first and the last of *The Cantos*, in a cluster which occupies the virtual center of the entire work – approximately fifty lie on either side of it – fall the Chinese and American history cantos (52–71), a section nearly one-quarter the length of the complete cantos, and presenting the one continuous stretch of writing to be found in *The Cantos of Ezra Pound*; a chronological span recounting some five thousand years of Chinese history, from 3000 BC through the eighteenth century AD, mediated for America by the French Enlightenment (when Chinese texts began to be translated), an era in European thought that eventually passed formatively into the social theories of John Adams and the founding fathers.

There's a point to Pound's history, but the point is not easy to grasp because his history is told in a rush of names, dates, references, and events presented largely without explanation or narrative connection. The effect is one of relentless obscurity, which was perhaps Pound's intention: to rub our noses in the fact that we have been cut off from the sources of what he imagined to be social vitality, that we have no tradition, that we need to make another Odyssean journey back to another cultural underworld, one not Western, and that we can do it, but it will take scholarly work. Such work itself would, presumably, be salutary, a sign that we are recovering (in both senses of the word), for in doing the work that Pound asks, we begin the process of self-healing. And if enough of us who do this work of recovery will only disseminate its findings, we shall be on our way to cultural and not just personal healing as the active readers whom Pound needs in the corporate effort to make the bridge between the isolated island of the modern world and the mainland of cultural history. The payoff will be a renovated economics, with justice for all, and a renovated language in which the word will bear the right name. Like an honest currency (in Pound that means an imagist economics), the word will not go the way of abstraction because it will be ligatured to real goods extant. And economics and poetics alike will be underwritten by a benevolent totalitarian (Confucius being a more perfect totalitarian than Aristotle; Mussolini, the hopeful modern instance), who protects money and words, properly ligatured, from manipulation by usurers, gun manufacturers, the fantastic international Jewish conspiracy, and other corrupters, financial and aesthetic, real and imaginary.

So do the Chinese and Adams cantos work in theory; in practice, and by the measure of Pound's aesthetic, they are a disaster. The aesthetic and the great majority of cantos insist on heterogeneity in texture, voice, and form; the Chinese and Adams cantos present a homogeneous voice of didactic intent. The aesthetic and the great majority of cantos insist on fragments and the surprising and delightful juxtapositions of montage which invite creative reading; the Chinese and Adams cantos progress by a principle of deadly smooth continuity that puts the reader into the passive position of a student listening to a lecturer with no dramatic talent. The literary project of *The Cantos* is modernist, but Cantos 52–71 fulfill no one's idea of modernist writing, or even, perhaps, of interesting writing.

The Chinese/Adams cantos fail because they lack the vivid presence of cultural poverty that motivates Pound's project for redemption. They give us a portrait of the poet comfortable in his views, speaking without duress from nowhere. But at their most riveting *The Cantos* evoke as their true speaking subject, however minimally, the presence of a writer – *The Cantos* are "about" a writer as much as they are "about" anything – a writer engaged in struggle, working against the grain, under the inspiration of the muses of memory, those muses being his only hope in a culture without memory; as in Canto 1, for example, where, at the end, we finally see Pound, book in hand, meditating on ancient ideals of heroism and beauty from a place where those ideals are not honored. Or in Canto 2, where Pound fictionalizes himself, Whitman-like, as a brooder at the seashore, a man for whom all mythologies of the sea are simultaneously present, from Homer to Ovid to Picasso, but with no mythology of his own to be at home in. "And" – the linguistic sign of Pound's consciousness, eager to bind together – here in Canto 2 becomes the sign of a mind which says "and" because it cannot say "because" – because it cannot trace a logical path to its leap into Ovid's *Metamorphoses*, the presiding cultural exhibit of Canto 2.

"And by Scios": Pound becomes a first-person participant in the story of the kidnapping of the young Dionysus by sailors who would sell him into slavery (not knowing who he was). The episode retold from Ovid is a story whose chief characters, in many variants, dominate *The Cantos*, a story of money lust and mythic power: poetry turned against and vanquishing greed (usually the story ends badly in *The Cantos*, but not here); Dionysus is unleashed, and Pound in attendance, awestruck, retelling the consequences for the ears of worldly power ("Fish scales on the oarsmen," "Arms shrunk into fins"): "And you Pentheus, had as well listen . . . or your luck will go out of you." Canto 2 concludes with a return to the brooding poet in his place on the shore. With his vision lapsed into the desolation of the present, and the Ovidian memory fading fast, now only an after-image mediating his experience of the sea, Pound presses Homer's epithet of the wine-dark sea through Ovid's Bacchus ("wave, color of grape's pulp"); Pound, a writer whose detailed and life-endowing memory of literary tradition unsettles him for life in his own world.

Can these, or any of Pound's literary exhibits, make our dry cultural bones dance again? Can his specimens of cultures past make any difference? Do Pound's heroes from ancient and Renaissance worlds (forerunners all of *Il Duce*?) translate as our heroes, or do they best remain where they are, exemplars for his imaginative life, beacons in his struggle through cultural darkness? In his last canto Pound says, "I have tried to write Paradise": a line whose force lies not in the vision glimpsed, or even in the vision glimpsed-and-then-lost, but in the effort of writing a paradise that can be lived only in the act of writing, sustained in and by a writing that cannot sustain it for very long. The quintessential fact about Pound's paradise is that it cannot be culturally transported outside *The Cantos*. The most moving (if implicit) image of *The Cantos* is that of a writer working mightily at the retrieval of the West's great cultural highs, who believes that if he can only talk eloquently enough, incessantly enough, about what he loves, the subjects of his love will spring to life before him, talked back to life – if only he does not lose heart (as so frequently he does), lose vocal energy and intensity (this, too, is part of the image) – and in so doing remind himself and us where we all are.

One of the strong, comically pathetic moments of *The Cantos* occurs in the Pisan group when Pound admits defeat and in the same breath tries to build out of defeat's humble gifts a new paradise. If *Il Duce* is the summation of the heroic tradition, then what can Pound save of tradition with "Ben and la Clara *a Milano* / by the heels at Milano"? And he answers in Canto 74:

> Le Paradis n'est pas artificiel
> but spezzato apparently
> it exists only in fragments unexpected excellent sausage,
>   the smell of mint, for example,
>   Ladro the night cat

And the reader's equivalent, the unexpected excellent literary sausage of a broken paradise, lies in scattered but numerous moments of individual elegance, sudden interventions of Pound's virtuosity in the midst of his historical labor of recuperation; as in Canto 13, where he presents in doctrinally constrained dialogue the Confucian ethic and social ideal – a canto intended to make a point about order, personal and public, and who underwrites it:

> If a man have not order within him
> He can not spread order about him;
> And if a man have not order within him
> His family will not act with due order;
>   And if the prince have not order within him
> He can not put order in his dominions.

Pound assigns those lines to Kung himself, the man whose authority stems from the wisdom that cannot be questioned, an oriental voice drawn through Western timbres of biblical propheticism: the constant Poundian conjunctive ("and") now marking unshakable certitude ("And if a man," "And if the prince," and you'd better believe it). And we shall hear that supremely self-possessed voice again, whenever Pound sows his doctrinal oats. But in the midst of this canto about the origin and dissemination of right political authority, dictatorial power, we watch the poet in pursuit of something else, like a bloodhound after the irrelevant detail, in a long aside off the doctrinal tract, seduced by the unfolding, self-pleasuring movement of his own conceit; the familiar Poundian conjunctive now marking lyric momentum:

> And Tian said, with his hand on the strings of his lute
> The low sounds continuing
>   after his hand left the strings,
> And the sound went up like smoke, under the leaves,
> And he looked after the sound . . .

Within the doctrinal program of Canto 13 these lines move with a grace that passes beyond the reach of doctrine; they are the unexpected and unexpectable gift of cantabile, for no ends beyond the singing itself.

Elsewhere – strikingly so in the Malatesta group (Cantos 8–11) – Pound's minor beauties engage major preoccupations, not as food for isolate aesthetic indulgence but as medium of historical work. Cantos 8–11 concern the exploits of an obscure fifteenth-century Italian professional soldier of fortune, Sigismondo Malatesta, a complete political cynic with a singular passion for art and artists – just the sort of passion for which Pound will forgive anything (and with Malatesta there is, apparently, much to forgive), a type of the Poundian hero who achieved what he achieved "against the current of power" and found his truest expression of selfhood as patron par excellence, in unswerving devotion to the building of the Tempio Malatestiano in Rimini: Malatesta, in other words, as figure of the poet Pound would be in *The Cantos*, building in the Tempio, as Pound would build, a "little civilization," part pagan, part Christian.

Pound's method in the Malatesta group is cagily documentary: he quotes heavily from chronicles, letters, legal documents, papal denunciations; inserts his own retelling, sometimes as on-site narrator, in recreation of scenes for which no documentation exists. These cantos take the shape of a boiling polylogue, some voices friendly, most not, to Sigismondo's person and desire; they give off an ambience of thickest treachery, of men (including Sigismondo) willing to do anything – he for the love of art, they for the love of power. The arrangement of the documents is dramatic: Pound's purpose is to conjure his obscure hero (Canto 8 opens with incantatory rhetoric), to show him in the act of emerging from corruption, his voice freeing itself, soaring, somehow uncontaminated; a voice elegant, dignified, gracious, lyrical, and promising violence, a man whose passion rescues him even from the evil that he does. The strength of Pound's showing lies not in the narrative of Sigismondo – its confusions overwhelm even Pound – but in the rhetorical effects he manages in honor of his hero. Pound loves the man, and his love creates a verbal habitation that insulates him from the garbage of his circumstances. We know not Malatesta but Pound "writing Malatesta" – not "of" or "about" Malatesta, but writing Malatesta as in "writing poetry;" or "writing Paradise," or in this translation of one of Malatesta's letters concerning what he would do for Piero della Francesca:

> So that he can work as he likes,
> Or waste his time as he likes
> (*affatigandose per suo piacere o no*
> *non gli manchera la provixione mai*)
>   never lacking provision.

The prose meaning of Pound's English captures the prose of Malatesta's Italian, but with its arrangement into a versified parallel, like two lines of poetry with a full caesura at the end of each line, the translation adds an eloquence beyond the touch of its prose sense. Pound's translation becomes a stylistic index, the verbal maneuver that directs us by dint of its phrasing alone to the generous soul of Malatesta. And the sandwiched Italian original proves Pound's fidelity of translation, his capacity for living transmission:

> With the church against him,
> With the Medici bank for itself,
> With wattle Sforza against him
> Sforza Francesco, wattle-nose,
> Who married him (Sigismondo) his (Francesco's)
> Daughter in September,
> Who stole Pésaro in October (as Broglio says
>   "*bestialmente*"),
> Who stood with the Venetians in November,
> With the Milanese in December,
> Sold Milan in November, stole Milan in December
> Or something of that sort,
> Commanded the Milanese in the spring,
> The Venetians at midsummer,
> The Milanese in the autumn,
> And was Naples' ally in October ...

From this swamp of political confusion, this comic litany of the months and seasons of byzantine betrayal – spoken, no doubt, in some smoke-filled backroom – comes a line from another level, elevated in syntax and tone, with a Latin phrase at the end (like an anchor of final authority) telling us what Malatesta did – the Latin working for Pound (as languages other than English often did) as some talismanic discourse, the facilitator of magical transcendence from politics to the plane of art: "He, Sigismondo, *templum aedificavit.*" "He, Sigismundo" – a phrasing repeated often in the Malatesta group – not only clarifies just who it is among these obscure political actors that Pound is talking about, but adds the sound of awe, like an epitaph which registers the shock of the memorialist, that in the midst of all this, he, Sigismondo, did what he did: "In the gloom, the gold gathers the light against it."

In his introduction to the *Active Anthology*, Pound says that experiment "aims at writing that will have a relation to the present analogous to the relation which past masterwork had to the life of its time." He insists, "without constant experiment literature dates." He means that literary experimentation is the response to the challenge, posed by social change, that writers come to terms with a new world. The implication is that the true history of literature is the discontinuous nonhistory of experiment, a series of modernist revolutions (what Pound means by "masterwork") in evidence across the ages, whose relations to one another lie not in content, form, or value, but in the incomparable fact of radical originality – radical as in "root"; originality as in deriving from an "origin": a literature rooted in an origin, the origin here being the writer's salient historical situation. The severe discipline of a modernist aesthetic relegates "literature" as such, or "literariness" as such, to the status of empty concepts, because no writer who would be modern (original) in any age (rather than the voice of some other time) has anything to lean on. Original writing (the essence of which is that it has no essence) proceeds, as always, in the dark, driven by difficult questions the answers to which are never known in advance: What is it like to be alive now? What strange new forms has human being assumed here, in this place? Would we, if we could, do some social experimentation? New World writing – the project of an "American" literature – is the exemplary moment of modernist literature.

Pound thought Eliot insufficiently moved by the experimental spirit. Of Eliot's modernist benchmark, "Tradition and the Individual Talent," he wrote: "This kind of essay assumes the existence of a culture that no longer subsists and does nothing to prepare a better culture that must or ought to come into being." If Western culture, as Pound told Donald Hall, is the struggle for individual rights, beginning with jury trial in Athens, then ever since the late eighteenth century we have been living in an age of revolution for individual rights in relation to which Eliot's "existing monuments" of literary tradition can have no organic significance. Pound thought "existing monuments" a contradiction, thought we needed "something living," and might have sought (he would have been stunned by this suggestion) support from Emerson for his political reading of the course of the West: the necessity, as Pound put it, to respect the "peripheries" of the individual.

The chief sign of the times, Emerson wrote in "The American Scholar," is the "new importance given to the single person. Everything that tends to insulate the individual – to surround him with barriers of natural respect, so that each man shall feel the world is his, and man shall treat with man as a sovereign state with a sovereign state – tends to true union": he meant, tends to just community. Emerson thought the revolutions of democratic change he was witnessing had implications for revolutions of cultural freedom, the individual and national rights of intellect and imagination. "Our day of dependence, our long apprenticeship to the learning of other lands, draws to a close . . . We have listened too long to the courtly muses of Europe." Or, in the equally clarion call from the opening paragraph of "Nature": "Why should not we have a poetry and philosophy of insight and not of tradition . . . ?"

Emerson, in the optative mood, spoke on behalf of the American cultural achievement he hoped would come to pass, an aesthetic birth that would, in Pound's words, bear a relation to its present which past art bore to the life of its time. Pound's criticism of Eliot sounds suspiciously like the criticism of a nativist leveled against an expatriate, who in fleeing his country has also fled Emerson's challenge to American writers (whether here or abroad) to resist the seductions of Old World culture, to make the cultural journey over the Atlantic to America, to come home, not in order to embrace the American imagination but in order to create it.

But Pound, like Eliot, was a reverse American immigrant, an unlikely ally of Emerson, who seemed all along to have intended to seek out those courtly muses who inspired no revolutions on behalf of any individual. Emerson probably had Longfellow in mind when he wrote the following, but the implied stricture seems to fit Pound even better: "I ask not for the great, the remote, the romantic; what is doing in Italy or Arabia, what is Greek art, or Provençal minstrelsy; I embrace the common, I explore and sit at the feet of the familiar, the low." Pound's theory of experimentation is in the American grain, but his practice in *The Cantos*, his pamphleteering of the 1930s, his Rome Radio broadcasts during World War II – are they not betrayals? Had not Pound written, in the outrageously entitled *Jefferson and/or Mussolini*: "The heritage of Jefferson . . . is HERE, NOW *in the Italian peninsula* at the beginning of fascist second decennio, not in Massachusetts or Delaware"?

Perhaps, though, the failure was less Pound's than Emerson's, whose visionary essays of the 1830s and 1840s on the future of the American writer, who would be nourished in experimental freedom by an original culture, do not come close to comprehending what would become the crisis of the modern writer, whose classic situation in the age of revolution is one in which he feels himself irremediably outside, in uncertain relation to the culture of his time.

Pound in New York, in 1910, on the eve of decisive expatriation, gathers his data for his first and most sustained critical meditation on American culture ("Patria Mia"). He reflects upon life in a democratic culture and concludes (in effect) that there has been no improvement in the situation of cultural deprivation Emerson had observed in the 1830s. He leaves America, confirmed in his judgment that its people are committed to the exigencies of the practical life and the cash nexus; with a sense that the cost of a new land was severance from the cultural past of Europe, a loss evidenced by the dry imitations of English verse he has read in the organs of the literary marketplace; and with a belief that the marketplace is the instrument of amnesia, the great barrier to the past, which would seem to ensure, for those who did not take Pound's expatriate option, the permanent triviality of American writing. For those like Pound, who would not or could not write to market demands – for all writers of modest middle-class means (or less) – America's post-aristocratic culture could offer only perennial anxiety about economic survival; the choice of the literary vocation was a choice for poverty and the contempt of mainstream society.

The exciting new culture Emerson had prophesied turned out to be mass culture, engineered by a culture industry feeding its commodities to democratic man, not a culture, as Emerson had hoped, organic with the life of the ordinary man. Pound, not alone among modern American writers, believed that the American common man was of no literary interest except as he might serve as the object of the ridiculing satirical gaze.

Far from being the expression of an American who had forsaken his culture, *The Cantos* are the work of an American experimenter standing at cultural ground zero. This experimenter is a man not unlike Henry James's archetype of the American, who works himself furiously up to cultural snuff – the archetypal modern as major autodidact of no cultural patrimony, who by sheer effort of discipline acquires all there is to know, and whose typical vocal posture before the great European cultural treasures is one of stunned awe; who will address Homer, Ovid, and Dante, talk to them in worshipful apostrophe, speak their names as only an adoring American could speak them, as the names of gods; an American who will find certain moments in these writers so excellent that he will repeat them over and over in *The Cantos*, as if he were recording them in a notebook of the most important quotations of great writers I have read. For all their complexity, *The Cantos* often resemble the book of wonders of a precocious American student.

By the measure of the ambitious desire to create culture that moved their writing, *The Cantos* are a failure. They engender (or recover) no unified vision or single narrative, rest upon no stable foundation of concepts, offer no odyssey of character; and for these failures we probably should be grateful. *The Cantos* "are," not "is." *The Cantos* narrate, quote, translate, dramatize, sing, and rant – as literary montage and collage they invite readers to supply the missing totality that would make sense of all the fragments; but what is missing, or only subtly present, is not some deep-seated story that binds all the pieces together into a social whole, but the writer in the act of trying to make sense of his circumstances. In Wallace Stevens's words: "the poem of the mind in the act of finding / What will suffice." It may be that there is a sense in which every age is an age of experiment, and that all writing proceeds in the dark in an effort to find the socially companionable form, but the modernist believes (in this believing is being) that he proceeds in a darkness apparently total. Dante and Milton had the cultural gift of the Christian map: Joyce, Eliot, Stevens, and Pound believed that their cultures had little to give, that they were living in a time when all the stage sets (again Stevens's figure) were being struck (*being* struck: they were witnesses to various dissolutions). They found that the privilege of living in an age of revolution was more than matched by the burdens of modernist culture; they found that they could take nothing for granted; that every thing would need to be reimagined.

The world of *The Cantos* is close to the world of the later Yeats, who saw the destruction of the great country house as the socially symbolic moment of modernism's inauguration: the end of the politically and socially privileged class and all the artistic life (in all senses) that it ensured and supported (in all senses), the end of the writer's security, the underwriting of his vision blotted out in social upheaval. Adrift in a new world, Yeats is left with his memories, and Pound, passionate American reader of the classics, is left with the desire for memory within a new social system – secular, democratic, capitalist – that has no use for the past and offers no structural support for its artists, whom it does not believe can defend its cities. And it is much worse for Pound, because unlike Yeats he never saw the gracious old American estate, which is also cultural matrix – there is no American experience of this; we have no exemplary Coole Park for memory to cherish in the lineage of our American cultural blood, no Coole Park which, in unforgiving recollection, can be the measure of modernist loss. Unlike Yeats, Pound nurses no delicious and bitter nostalgia (no return-pain), unless we choose (as I do) to credit his longing as a paradox of nostalgia – a New World desire to return to the cultural home he never had.

In the notorious *Pisan Cantos* (74–84) the poet as modernist steps forward, holding back nothing. Written in a military detention camp in Pisa at the end of the war and awarded the first Bollingen Prize for Poetry in 1949, to the shock and anger of at least half the English-speaking literary world, these poems, as well as any in the modernist tradition, figure forth the modernist writer as the quintessential outsider. Now in prison, which is just about where the modernist has always thought he was, literally old, which is what modernist poets often feel even when they're young (as if they had never experienced vaulting zest for life: culturally desiccated from the start, Prufrocks all – a figure Eliot invented as an undergraduate), an old man without a country whose subject now is openly himself incessantly in conversation with himself, in elegiac remembrance of writers ancient, Renaissance, and contemporary, friends all (the literal ones also now all dead: Ford, Joyce, Yeats "to earth o'ergiven"); and talking his favorite opinions (how economic justice can be ensured through just distribution and reform of the money system; how to collar the "buggering banks"; the role of the "yidds" in the world's exploitation; the cattlelike nature of the "goyim"; the death of Mussolini and the failure of fascism; the desire to build the ideal city): Pound, an old man quoting his favorite phrases, poetic and political, and then quoting them again and again; remembering his earlier cantos, alluding to the heroic figures therein; quoting his own lines, especially the one in the first canto about losing all companions: all this talk as if (Robert Frost's phrase) "the talk were all" – and it is.

The *Pisan Cantos* are jail-talk from solitary confinement (who at Pisa could Pound talk to?), jail-talk gone about as far as the modernist can take it. In the saying of his memories, in their linguistic retrieval and preservation of cultures past (especially the cultures made by writers, recalling what they wrote and sometimes what they did), Pound projects an image of the modernist writer working from the shards of tradition and frustrated political obsession, but not working them up into a new culture – placing them, instead, side by side, as he counts the losses. Pound-the-modernist is a writer in extremis because extremity is his norm – a writer who creates in his experiment a poem precisely adequate to the cultural circumstances of a man, unlike Homer, without a story to tell.

No one will take Pound, after what he has revealed, as hero or moral guide. The Pound in the *Pisan Cantos* is the best answer to the Pound who venerated heroes and thought Mussolini would underwrite economic justice and the independence of the individual. *The Cantos* are a poetry full of heterogeneity to the point of chaos, an indescribable mixture whose ingredients of anti-Semitism and fascism are not of the essence because, in this experiment, nothing is of the essence. The most typical moments of *The Cantos* are those which defy the expectations of typicality: like the moment when out of nowhere we hear a black man speak (blacks in *The Cantos* appear as "coons," "niggers," and "negroes") and we learn that Pound has been done (by this black man) a risky act of charity – against regulations, he has been spoken to, and, more, has been built a box upon which to set his typewriter: "doan you tell no one / I made you that table," words that will be repeated throughout the *Pisan Cantos*, in the same way that phrases from the literary giants are repeated, until Mr. Edwards-who-made-the-box assumes the status of Sigismondo-who-made-the-Tempio. Mr. Edwards takes his commemorative place with Malatesta because, like Malatesta, he achieved what he achieved against the current of power. (What Mr. Edwards calls a "table," Pound calls a "box"; Mr. Edwards is an imaginative writer of another order.) He, Mr. Edwards, *boxum aedificavit*. And the significance of this act of patronage and charity for the whole of *The Cantos*? Only that a poetry which was written with no encouragement from its culture, and with no possibility of gaining cultural centrality, was helped along its way a little by a patron of the arts who couldn't read it, and who could have had no intention, surely, of helping this particular poem come to life and to print.

EPILOGUE

G. H. BOKER, Thomas Bailey Aldrich, Bayard Taylor, E. C. Stedman, R. H. Stoddard, Richard Watson Gilder – names which now mean nothing, not even to the diligent reader of poems. But to many appreciative American readers at the end of the nineteenth century, these names were synonymous with poetry. Other readers – Eliot, Frost, and especially Pound among them – saw things differently, saw these displaced late Victorians, this genteel cabal, filling the day's major magazines of culture, saw these fat old hens styling themselves as wise old owls and taking roost in the impossibly successful anthologies of Palgrave and Rittenhouse; from there, and from deep inside cultured America's heart, they saw these men squatting out the inadequate eggs of the day, their boring poems.

Against this intolerable situation, the modernists made their attack. When the feathers finally settled, a handful of expatriates and the scattered nativist and homebody had already proved that the young century might be an American century, for poetry at least. Of course, the new movement was international in scope, its contributions coming from the artists of various lands. But who a few years before the explosion would have been perceptive or bold enough to predict the American abundance of Eliot, Stevens, Pound, of Frost and Moore and Crane and Hughes and William Carlos Williams?

So the day was won by this historical movement, this *modernism*. And what of its particular aesthetic successes, its lasting objects of art, its major poems? R. P. Blackmur weighed in fifty years ago with a partial assessment that would still garner partial assent from a wide range of critical judges: "It is a striking and disheartening fact that the three most ambitious poems of our time should all have failed in similar ways: in composition, in independent objective existence, and in intelligibility of language. *The Waste Land*, the *Cantos*, and *The Bridge* all fail to hang together structurally in the sense that 'Prufrock,' 'Envoi,' and 'Praise for an Urn' – lesser works in every other respect – do hang together." So intelligibility of language, independent objective existence, and composition are the elements that produce "hanging together structurally," or coherence;

lesser works are works that "do hang together," and the major monuments are greater than the lesser works in every way except the way of coherence: the greater works cannot claim intelligibility of language (otherwise they would make more sense to more people), they are failed in their composition (an internal imbalance persists among the various elements which constitute the object), and they fail to achieve independent objective existence. This final criterion was perhaps *the* New Critical shibboleth, edged into prominence by summary slogans – the heresy of paraphrase, the poem as artifact – which help mark the fact that the New Criticism was both a critical theory and an interpretive method doubling as a definer of taste.

After years of New Critical dominance, new structuralisms from the Continent swept through the land; new minds, like the archetypalist Northrop Frye's, asserted new and ever expansive versions of literary coherence. And then, in 1966 at Johns Hopkins University, the dashing *philosophe* Jacques Derrida delivered the frequently coherent "Structure, Sign and Play in the Discourse of the Human Sciences" (criticism, like poetry, has its cherished breakthrough narratives). There he gave pointed warning to a burgeoning critical community: "coherence in contradiction expresses the force of a desire." His sensible poststructuralist standard is generally taken to mean that the desire for coherence *in spite of* the contradictions that make coherence impossible is a shaper of reality and simultaneously constitutes, as critical doctrine, a misapprehension of reality. At the same time, the desire may be *not* for coherence in spite of unrecognized or repressed contradiction, but for coherence *in the midst of* an admitted contradiction – "coherence-in-contradiction" as a totality of the critically self-aware.

As for the academic vehicle of poetic modernism, as for the New Criticism, it can in retrospect hardly have a better slogan than "coherence-in-contradiction," placing as it did a premium on internal tensions and ambiguities and their organic resolution. At the time it may have seemed "disheartening" (to use Blackmur's word), and may now seem ironic given certain methodological edicts, but critical valuation finally smiled most sweetly on those modernist works in which coherence and contradiction form a productive dialectic. It was, and is, a dialectic the contrary poles of which can be substituted without diminishing the conflictual energy that is the essence of the modernist canon: belief and skepticism, desire and self-denial, success and failure, tradition and originality, ambition and inadequacy. After the tepid scratchings of the genteel mind, the modernist ethos brought a Blakean vigor back to the writing table. That such ambitious contrariety brought also to the table the specter of failure was a necessity, an *excitement*. The modern marriage of heaven and hell, of the avant-garde artist and the culture of capital, would be both for better and for worse. As such, better and worse would be harder than ever to distinguish, though Pound for one was still trying as late as Canto 116: "But the beauty is not the madness / Tho' my errors and wrecks lie about me." What was the properly-hoped-for result in the collision of art with wrecks both cultural and (inevitably) personal? What now was to be the proper relation between beauties and errors both old and new?

As early as 1917, T. S. Eliot imagined a quasi-religious "ideal order" of literature. In remembering the structure of desire of the religious believer, in re-remembering coherence-in-contradiction out of the church and on to the poem and, with help, into the classroom, Eliot was finding a degraded category compelling. The missing term in modernist thinking – Eliot stands by himself on this point – is community: something larger, something more valuable than isolate selfhood, that would include original selves, nourish and sustain them, while also nourishing and sustaining a network of connection, a wholeness (greater than the sum of selves) which the thinker of community believes makes healthy selfhood possible. In literary terms, in the cultural ground zero of the young Eliot, this "wholeness" was *tradition*, which was reliant for its survival on a new and active remembrance. As he later put it pragmatically in *Four Quartets*:

> This is the use of memory:
> For liberation – not less of love but expanding
> Of love beyond desire, and so liberation
> From the future as well as the past.

Of course the memory of a fabled coherence never moved the major modernists beyond desire – not Pound, neither Frost nor Stevens, certainly not Eliot – and in fact the *use* of memory was motivated by the very desire that Eliot proposes such use will move us beyond, resulting in the paradoxical privileging of a tradition which reaches perfection in its own effacement. The central paradox of the classic modernist writers is that the adversarial stance they typically took, the kind of experimental writing they typically did – in so many words, what made them, in *this* world, original and famous – would become, in the transformed world of their desire, unnecessary and even unimaginable. Had Eliot been able actually to live all his life in the "community" of desire he projected in his later prose, he would never have written *The Waste Land*. He could not have written it. There would have been no fragments to shore against his ruins; there would have been no ruins.

Against the ruins that most certainly *are*, desire or no desire, Pound with brusque lucidity put on frequent display the key value terms in the modernist lexicon: *originality, creativity, individuality, freedom*. Pound's radical point is that these terms are synonymous, and that, together, they comprise the index of an authentic selfhood of which the artist is both rigorous champion and superb representative, and of which the artist's culture is rigorous and superb denier, marginalizer, and (Pound feared) destroyer. The major political assumption of the modernists is that people in advanced Western societies desire, or would desire were they sufficiently intelligent about their circumstances, the originality and freedom of an authentic selfhood; that people should want what they, the modernists, want; that the serious artist is, or should be, the exemplary individual. Wanting to make the world possible for themselves – and why shouldn't they? – modernist writers believe that everyone would be happier if only they could become artists. The world would then be a decent place.

Of course, they see that all the evidence points in the other direction. Virtually nobody wants what they want. In fact, given the flow of things, the possibility of (noncommercial) art and freedom, as they envision it, will simply be rubbed out of human possibility. That is what they tend to believe. Hence, apocalypse; modernists tend to be apocalypticists. So Yeats, in "The Second Coming": the blood-dimmed tide is loosed, and what rough beast is this, slouching to be born? So Eliot, in the last section of *The Waste Land*: the hallucinatory images of exploding European capitals, and the sullen and hooded and swarming hordes. So Frost, in "Once by the Pacific": "Somebody had better be prepared for rage." What is the fate of the artist in modern society and culture? The role of art in a world shaped by the economics and ethos of the commodity? Fretting over those familiar questions, writers and critics of modernism have achieved well-known consensus. The role is alienated and constantly critical, and the fate of the artist is dire.

POETRY IN THE MACHINE AGE

Irene Ramalho Santos

PROLOGUE

L ITERARY history gives voice even as it inevitably silences. Voicing and silencing are determined by the very processes of literary history itself. Or rather, voicing and silencing in literary history are conditioned by historiography. As is the case of any other scientific inquiry, archeology being perhaps the best example, the writing of literary history inevitably changes the object it purports to present "objectively." Since by its very nature literary history involves canon making, the writing of literary history implies exclusion even as it aims to include. A perfunctory survey of literary histories and anthologies produced roughly during the last hundred years gives a fascinating account of the oscillations of poetic relevance and cultural preeminence in the period: which poets are included and how many of their poems are quoted or discussed; which poems from which collections are mentioned or anthologized; which poems never collected in book form continue to be culled from the wealth of little magazines that circulated in the period; how the literary scene changes, when unpublished material is suddenly unearthed and a new poet discovered. One might also consider in this regard which poets have been most taught and dealt with in academic dissertations at different times and in different schools; which poets crop up more frequently in theoretical discussions of the lyric, and which poets make it into the common discourse of daily life. It may be, as Harold Bloom has argued, that only "strong" poets last and that poets themselves are mainly responsible for canon formation. Nonetheless, we need to ask which poets go on being potently *rewritten* by younger poets of different persuasions.

Poetry anthologies, usually organized by poets, already tell us a great deal about this. It would be interesting to see, for example, which poets are left out, and why, of the most recent and probably the most inclusive anthology of twentieth-century American poetry, the Library of America *American Poetry: The Twentieth Century* (2000). Counting several distinguished poets on its advisory board, this two-volume anthology aims to map the territory of poetry in the United States in the twentieth century, from Henry Adams to May Swenson (since no poet born after 1913 – Swenson's birthdate – is considered, one assumes that a third volume is being prepared). Frost, Stein, Stevens, Williams, Pound, H. D., Moore, and Eliot are amply represented in volume I, which also includes "The Preacher and the Slave" ("you'll get pie in the sky when you die") by the *Little Red Song Book*'s Joe Hill (1879–1915), Ma Rainey's "Southern Blues" (1886–1939), and three lyrics by Cole Porter (1891–1964). Bessie Smith (1894–1937) and Blind Lemon Jefferson (1897–1927) have one poem each in volume II, alongside far larger selections of Crane and Hughes. Inclusiveness appears to be the anthology's implicit criterion, but the amount of space allotted to each poet is highly significant. Omissions, too, whether of poets or poems, betray unmentioned, but inescapable, time-bound and value-laden judgments.

"Poetry in the Machine Age" does not claim to be inclusive. Gertrude Stein, William Carlos Williams, H. D., Marianne Moore, Hart Crane, and Langston Hughes comprise six angles of vision on the phenomenon that we have come to know as American modernist poetry. They are six of the most relevant poets in the dynamic picture of a changing culture in the first half of twentieth-century America; together with Robert Frost, Wallace Stevens, Ezra Pound, and T. S. Eliot, they represent the major landmarks of what we call modernist poetry. But of course the poetic achievement itself is far broader. Even were we to mention only poets born in the nineteenth century (and claim Hughes, born in 1902, as the only exception), many other poets come to mind, some of them winners of the Pulitzer Prize, in a few cases more than once. What follows is a brief chronological survey of those "other poets" who contributed in different, often remarkable ways to give shape to early twentieth-century poetry in the United States.

Edgar Lee Masters (1868–1950) is remembered for his large gallery of over two hundred free-verse portraits of small-town characters in his *Spoon River Anthology* (1915), a volume that became a popular and critical success. Born in Kansas and brought up in Illinois, Masters was firmly rooted in the Midwestern society he both praised and criticized. The poems of *Spoon River Anthology*, modeled on the Greek Anthology, are as many epitaphs spoken from the cemetery of the town of Spoon River. The dead characters' view of their and other people's lives is at times so grotesquely cynical that the picture of the human comedy offered by Masters ends up being a ruthless report of small-town inhuman relations in middle America ("praise not my self sacrifice," says the woman who reared her two orphaned nieces; "censure not their contempt," she adds, and concludes: "I poisoned my benefactions / With constant reminders of their dependence"). Although the impact of Masters's work, mostly lauded for its truthfulness and directness, had more to do with scandal than poetry, it nonetheless introduced what has since come to be known as the Chicago Renaissance, a group of writers that also includes Carl Sandburg, Vachel Lindsay, and Theodore Dreiser.

Edwin Arlington Robinson (1869–1935), generally considered the first important American poet of the twentieth century and certainly one of the most prolific, devoted all his life to poetry writing. A New England poet who lived in New York most of his life, Robinson was raised in Gardiner, Maine (the "Tilbury Town" of his poetry) and is also famous for memorable portraits of small-town characters. His first two books (*The Torrent and The Night Before* [1896] and *The Children of the Night* [1897]) were published at his own expense. His breakthrough came when Theodore Roosevelt, who admired his poetry, persuaded Random House to republish *The Children of the Night* and wrote a glowing preface for it. In 1910, Robinson reciprocated by dedicating *The Town down the River* to the President. Robinson's voluminous *Collected Poems* (1921) earned him the first of his three Pulitzer Prizes (his poems, amounting in the end to nearly 1,500 pages, were collected again in 1930 and, posthumously, in 1937). The other two Pulitzers were awarded for *The Man Who Died Twice* (1924) and *Tristram* (1927), two long narrative poems that drew good reviews. *Tristram*, inspired by the Arthurian legends, even became a popular success. *The Man Who Died Twice*, a long narrative poem that tells the story of a musician whose masterpiece is lost when he collapses after a night of debauchery, is characteristic of much of Robinson's work. His poetry deals mainly with the emptiness of life, pain, failure, and frustration, but also the playful ability of common people to deal with them. Although he excelled in the long, blank-verse narrative poem, like "Isaac and Archibald" (included in *Captain Graig* [1902]), anthologies, for obvious reason, tend to canonize his shorter poems, like "Miniver Cheevy" (1910). In the introduction he wrote for Robinson's last book of poems, *King Jasper* (1935), Robert Frost best sums up Robinson's place vis-à-vis modern American poetry: "[In] this . . . our age . . . wild in the quest of new ways to be new . . . Robinson stayed content with the old-fashioned ways to be new."

Amy Lowell (1874–1925) entitled her first book of poems *A Dome of Many-Coloured Glass* (1912), a phrase taken from *Adonais*, Shelley's elegy for Keats. Heavily influenced by Keats's poetry (whose biography Lowell was to write later [*John Keats*, 1925]), *A Dome of Many-Coloured Glass* abounds in conventional themes and traditional forms. Born into a wealthy family of New England founding fathers, Lowell had all that money and status could afford: social preeminence, a fine education, and the opportunity do travel extensively. This and her physical appearance (she was a heavy-set, domineering woman not blessed with beauty) often came in the way of her readers. Malcolm Cowley is reported to have said once, no doubt having the poet's physical appearance in mind as well: "It is hard to be a true poet when one is rich, blanketed with 4 percent debentures and rocked to sleep in a cradle of sound common stocks." Lowell won public recognition with her second book of poetry, *Sword Blades and Poppy Seed* (1914). About that time, she read H. D.'s imagist poems on the pages of Harriet Monroe's *Poetry* and decided, not entirely without grounds, that she had always been an imagist poet. She would later provoke Pound's resentful scorn for her major role in consolidating *his* "invention" of *imagisme* in her three anthologies of *Some Imagist Poets* (1915, 1916, 1917). Her last volume of poems, *What's O'Clock* (1925), was awarded the Pulitzer Prize posthumously in 1926. Lowell's poetry is uneven. Among her most successful poems are the love songs addressed to her companion of more than ten years, the actress Ada Dwyer Russel: "Tell me, / Was Venus more beautiful / Than you are . . . Was Botticelli's vision / Fairer than mine. . . . ?" ("Venus Transiens" [1919]). Also effective is her meditation on poetry, gender, and creativity in "The Sisters" (1925): "Taking us by and large, we're a queer lot / We women who write poetry . . . "

Carl Sandburg (1878–1967), the Midwestern poet of politically motivated urban themes, yields contradictory responses. Some critics speak of the "illusion" of poetry in his works and say it depends more on the arrangement of the lines than on the lines themselves. But his admirers disagree. Sherwood Anderson said, "among all the poets of America [Sandburg] is my poet." Amy Lowell called *Chicago Poems* (1916), Sandburg's first collection of poetry, "one of the most original books this age has produced." His other major books of verse are *Cornhuskers* (1918), *Smoke and Steel* (1920), and *The People, Yes* (1936). His range of literary interests covers, besides poetry, history, biography, fiction, and music. His monumental two-volume *Abraham Lincoln*, for which he earned a Pulitzer Prize, appeared in 1954. Sandburg was a compelling reader and performer of his poetry, which he liked to recite to the sound of his guitar (he studied under Andrés Segovia for a while). Many of his poems deal with modern, industrialized, mechanized America. The most memorable of them is "Chicago" (1916), where the paradigm of the modern city is described with an eloquent string of virile epithets: "Hog Butcher for the World / Tool Maker, Stacker of Wheat, / Player with Railroads and the Nation's Freight Handler; / Stormy, husky, brawling, / City of Big Shoulders."

Vachel Lindsay (1879–1931), poet, performer/reader, and popularizer, won general recognition with his *General William Booth Enters into Heaven* (1913). His reputation rests today on this and three more books of poems: *The Congo and Other Poems* (1914), *The Chinese Nightingale and Other Poems* (1917), and *The Golden Whales of California and Other Rhymes in the American Language* (1920). In his own day, Lindsay became famous as a traveling bard whose theatrical performance in public readings helped to keep appreciation for poetry as a spoken art alive in the American Midwest. The title poem of *General William Booth Enters into Heaven*, a celebratory elegy for the revivalist soldier-founder of the Salvation Army (William Booth, 1829–1912), has instructions for the musical accompaniment of its delivery: "To be sung to the tune of the 'Blood of the Lamb' with indicated instruments," the indicated instruments being the bass drum, banjo, flute, and "tambourines to the foreground" for the grand finale. "The Congo," too, has a gloss with directions on how the poem must be read and dramatically performed. Lindsay's Whitmanian and compassionate inspiration, as that of Sandburg's, had great impact on the poets of the Harlem Renaissance.

The poetic achievement of English-born Mina Loy (1882–1966) is contained in *The Last Lunar Baedeker*, published in 1982, sixteen years after the poet's death. Though she published very little during her lifetime, this multifaceted poet and artist, author of exquisitely lyrical poems, often with a satirical ring, first collected in *Lunar Baedeker* (1923), was greatly admired by some of the major American poets and critics of the time, including Pound, Eliot, and Yvor Winters. When he reviewed *The Last Lunar Baedeker* for the *New York Times Book Review* in the early 1980s, Hugh Kenner expressed his perplexity at the poet's absence from the literary canon. A friend of Gertrude Stein and Marcel Duchamp, Loy lived in Paris during the 1920s and was actively involved in the avant-garde experiments. Her interest in the nature of artistic creation is reflected in the surrealist mode of her poems. Here is Song IX of her "Songs to Joannes" (1917): "When we lifted / Our eye-lids on Love / A cosmos / Of coloured voices / And laughing honey // And spermatozoa / At the core of Nothing / In the milk of the Moon." Loy penned a number of perceptive poems on other poets. Her poem on Gertrude Stein is quoted on p. 215 below. Her uncanny "Poe" reads like this: "a lyric elixir of death // embalms / the spindle spirits of your hour glass loves / on moon spun nights // sets / icicled canopy / for corpses of poesy / with roses of northern lights // Where frozen nightingales in ilix aisles // sing burial rites."

Unlike Loy, Sara Teasdale (1884–1933) published several books of poetry during her lifetime and was highly praised for her mastery of conventional form and romantic topics. *Sonnets to Duse and Other Poems* (1907), published at her parents' expense, was her first book of poems, followed by *Helen of Troy and Other Poems* (1911) and *Rivers to the Sea* (1915). With her next book, *Love Songs* (1917), a collection of delicately crafted lyrics of love, longing, and pain, Teasdale won the first Columbia (later Pulitzer) Poetry Prize. The poems gathered in *Flame and Shadow* (1920) and *Dark of the Moon* (1926) follow the same pattern of structure and sentiment, with increasing disenchantment.

After she committed suicide in 1933, her late poems were published as *Strange Victory* (1933). The following ominous "Lines" are taken from there: "These are the ultimate highlands, / Like chord on chords of music / Climbing to rest / On the highest peak and the bluest / Large on the luminous heavens / Deep in the west."

The trajectory of Elinor Wylie (1885–1928) as a poet is similar to Teasdale's. Showered with praise in her lifetime, Wylie fell rapidly from literary grace after her death only to be somewhat revived by feminist criticism. Today, discussions of Wylie's poetry, as of that of several women poets of the period (including Teasdale), are to be found almost exclusively in essays devoted to twentieth-century women writers. The first book of verse by Wylie, who authored several novels as well, was privately printed (*Incidental Numbers*, 1912). *Nets to Catch the Wind* (1921) was her first commercially published book. Other major collections of poetry are *Black Armour*, 1923, *Trivial Breath*, 1928, and *Angels and Earthly Creatures: A Sequence of Sonnets*, 1928 (posthumously printed). Wylie's decorous poetic forms contrast sharply with the course of her unconventional life (three marriages, one of them after a dramatic elopement). Her well-crafted romantic lyrics, however, pose all kinds of questions about a woman's thwarted life in a profoundly sexist society. One of the most distinguished of these is "Self-Portrait," where "woman" emerges as a flint-like powerful "mind" and an emptied out "little rest": "Instead of stone," the poem closes, "instead of sculptured strength, / This soul, this vanity, blown hither and thither / By trivial breath, over the whole world's length."

Long before environmental studies and ecocriticism became fashionable, Robinson Jeffers (1887–1962) was writing environmental poetry. From his first (privately published) book of poetry (*Flagons and Apples*, 1912) onwards, Jeffers emerges as the nostalgic singer of the ecological balances of nature threatened by human destructiveness. Lucretius, Schopenhauer, Nietzsche, Vico, and Spengler are some of the sources for his "inhumanism," as he himself termed it, variously expressed as a faith in the perennity of nature as opposed to the futility of the human race. "The extraordinary patience of things!," the poet marvels in "Carmel Point" (1954), "people are a tide / That swells and in time will ebb, and all / Their works dissolve." Much earlier, in "Credo" (1927), the poet had already stated memorably: "The beauty of things was born before eyes and sufficient to itself; the heart-breaking beauty / Will remain when there is no heart to break for it." Jeffers's many collections of poetry include *Californians* (1916); *Tamar and Other Poems* (1924) (expanded the following year as *Roan Stallion, Tamar and Other Poems*, this book, a combination of short lyrics interspersed with long narrative poems, became a critical and popular success); *The Women at Point Sur* (1927); *Cawdor* (1928); *Dear Judas* (1929);

Descent to the Dead (1931); *Thurso's Landing* (1932); *Give Your Heart to the Hawks* (1933); *Solstice* (1935); *Such Counsels You Gave Me* (1937); *Be Angry at the Sun* (1941); *Hungerfield and Other Poems* (1954). *The Beginning and the End*, a collection of final poems, appeared posthumously in 1963. The three-volume *Collected Poetry of Robinson Jeffers* was published in 1988–91. Born in Pittsburgh, Pennsylvania around 1910, Jeffers went to the West Coast to do graduate work at the University of Southern California and lived in Carmel, California the rest of his life. Carmel and the "Tor House" he built there for his wife, Una, with his own hands are a constant presence in, and symbol of, his poetry.

As a young girl, Edna St. Vincent Millay (1892–1950) wanted to be a concert pianist, but her piano teacher dissuaded her because her hands were too small. The talented young woman turned to poetry instead. Educated at Barnard College and Vassar, Millay evolved into a cultured and learned author. Besides lyric poetry, Millay is noted for a handful of dramatic works, including an opera libretto. She also translated, with George Dillon, and wrote the introduction to, Baudelaire's *Fleurs du mal* (*Flowers of Evil*, 1936). Millay's poetic career started with "Renascence," a poem submitted to the *Lyrical Year* contest in 1912. Although it came fourth in the contest, "Renascence" was praised by influential critics at the time and made her reputation. *Renascence, and Other Poems* was published in 1917. Several other collections of poetry followed, including *A Few Figs From Thistles: Poems and Four Sonnets* (1920), *Second April* (1921), *The Ballad of the Harp Weaver* (1922), winner of the Pulitzer Prize, *The Buck in the Snow, and Other Poems* (1928), *Fatal Interview* (1931), *Wine from These Grapes* (1934), *Conversation at Midnight* (1937), *Huntsman, What Quarry?* (1939), *Make Bright the Arrows: 1940 Notebook* (1940), *Collected Sonnets* (1941), and *The Murder of Lidice* (1942). Millay's *Collected Poems* appeared posthumously in 1956. Her involvement with the Provincetown Players in Greenwich Village in the late 1910s encouraged her left leanings. Her nonconformism is, however, best expressed in her poetry in her treatment of love and the relations between men and women. Some of her poems, like "Second Fig" (1922), firmly reject the conventional female realm of domestic security: "Safe upon the solid rock the ugly houses stand: / Come and see my shining palace built upon the sand!" In others, a deidealized vision of passion is made problematic by the acute pain of its want. "First Fig" (1922) ("My candle burns at both ends; / It will not last the night; / But ah, my foes, and oh, my friends – / It gives a lovely light") and the sonnet that begins "Love is not all; it is not meat nor drink" (1931) gain if read one against the other. The latter poem ends like this: "I might be driven to sell your love for peace, / Or trade the memory of this night for food. / It well may be. I don't think I would." A fine self-reflective lyricist in the romantic mode, Millay excelled in the sonnet form like few other poets of her generation.

Dorothy Parker (1893–1967), iconoclast poet of wry humor, had little regard for her own poetry (and probably even less for Millay's). Late in life, she told an interviewer about her "verse:"

> I cannot say poems . . . Like everybody was then, I was following in the exquisite footsteps of Miss Millay, unhappily in my own horrible sneakers. My verses are no damn good. Let's face it, honey, my verse is terribly dated – as anything once fashionable is dreadful now. I gave it up [her last published poem was written in 1944], knowing it wasn't getting any better, but nobody seemed to notice my magnificent gesture.

Parker had slightly more respect for her work as a freelance writer, author of short stories, and magazine editor, reviewer, and abrasive columnist (*Vogue*, *Vanity Fair*, and especially *The New Yorker* are the magazines she worked for). Of her experience as writer of screenplays in Hollywood in the 1930s and 1940s she had nothing pleasant to say. A socially committed woman (supporter of Sacco and Vanzetti, member of the Joint Anti-Fascist Refugee Committee, anti-war protester, supporter of the National Association for the Advancement of Colored People), Parker had to answer to the House of Un-American Activities Committee in 1951. Her body of poetry, though slender, and regardless of her own self-irony, is remarkable. Her collections of poems include *Enough Rope* (1926), *Sunset Gun* (1928), *Death and Texas* (1931), and *Not So Deep as a Well* (1936). Parker's humor and satirical wit, features usually considered not very "feminine," became legendary. She herself once complained that "it got so bad that they began to laugh before I opened my mouth." Satirical, unsentimental demystification describes her poems best. "A Pig's Eye View of Literature" (1928) is a witty caricature of a dozen nineteenth-century authors. Here is "D. G. Rossetti": "Dante Gabriel Rossetti / Buried all of his libretti, / Thought the matter over, – then / Went and dug them up again."

Poet, painter, novelist, and playwright, E. E. Cummings (1894–1962) made his debut in American letters with *The Enormous Room* (1922), a fictionalized account of his captivity in France during the Great War on charges of espionage. The book was very well reviewed at the time and remains to this date one of the most compelling narratives of the kind. As a poet, Cummings is arguably the most technically innovative author of twentieth-century America. He experimented radically and profusely with grammar, typography, spelling, word invention, and social commentary in several collections of poetry. In subject matter, his poems range from eroticism to denunciation of social injustice, commercialism, intellectual massification, and group conformity. After the eccentric shapes of Cummings's poems on the page, with their defamiliarization effect, the American poem could no longer be read the same way again. His graphic disruptions may be said to have inaugurated what has recently been called disjunctive poetics. The first of his books of poetry was *Tulips and Chimneys* (1923) immediately followed by *it. &* (1925), which contained the poems that the publisher had deleted from *Tulips and Chimneys* (Cummings wanted it to be *Tulips it. & Chimneys*). That same year, *XLI Poems* came out. In 1926, *Is 5* was published, with an introduction in which Cummings explained his conception of poetry, quite in tune with modernist poetics, as "a process" rather than "a product." These volumes established Cummings's reputation as an avant-garde poet (in 1925, Cummings was awarded the coveted Dial Prize; in 1958 he would get the Bollingen). Later collections of poetry include *No Thanks* (1935), *Collected Poems* (1938), *50 Poems* (1940), *1 X 1* (1945), *XAIPE* (1950), and *95 Poems* (1958). "i like my body when it is with your" (1925) and "I sing of Olaf glad and big" (1931) illustrate the two major trends in Cummings's poetry: erotic lyricism and political protest. Cummings's poetry has always drawn praise and dismissal. He has been assessed contradictorily both as a "daringly original poet" of "uncompromising talent" and as a case of "arrested development," clever but with little lasting value beyond a few technical innovations.

Louise Bogan (1897–1970) was one of the most distinguished American women of letters of her generation. Poet, critic, editor, translator (of Goethe among others), Bogan contributed verse and criticism to many magazines, including the *New Republic*, *The Nation*, *Poetry: A Magazine of Verse*, *Measure: A Journal of Poetry*, *Atlantic Monthly*, and *The New Yorker*. For almost forty years she was poetry editor for *The New Yorker*. Her poetry, rich with conceptual imagery struggling between thought and feeling, has been praised for its metaphysical qualities, and many have compared Bogan to the likes of George Herbert, John Donne, and Henry Vaughan. Her first book of poems, *Body of This Death*, appeared in 1923. It skillfully combined mastery of traditional techniques with the constructed immediacy of contemporary language to speak of a woman's experience in a changing culture. In twentieth-century America, how is a woman to reconcile her intellectual professionalism with her desire? "I burned my life," she writes in "The Alchemist" (1923), "that I might find / A passion wholly of the mind, / Thought divorced from eye and bone, / Ecstasy come to breath alone." The poem's second stanza reveals that the alchemy doesn't work at all. Once life is consumed in the experiment's fiery crucible, the poet is left with "unmysterious flesh" and the overwhelming power of passion. Occasionally, her poems remind readers of Marianne Moore. "Dragonfly" (1937) is a precise animal poem that reveals deep truths about the human condition: "You are made of almost nothing / But of enough / To be great eyes / And diaphanous double vans; / To be ceaseless movement, / Unending hunger / Grappling love." Bogan's other collections of poetry were *Dark Summer* (1929), *The Sleeping Fury* (1937), and *Poems and New Poems* (1941), *Collected Poems, 1923–1953* (1954), and *The Blue Estuaries: Poems, 1923–1968* (1968).

The preceding paragraphs suggest that other stories could have been told in this history. Some other poets not mentioned there are also part of ever-changing historical emphases in descriptions of the period. Claude McKay (1890–1948), Jamaica-born Harlem poet who made the Shakespearean son-net sing accusingly of racial violence, as in "If We Must Die" from *Harlem Shadows* (1922) ("If we must die, let it not be like hogs...O let us nobly die"), is briefly discussed on pp. 338–341 below, along with Sterling Brown and Countee Cullen. Noteworthy are also Charles Reznikoff (1894–1976), who authored a handful of brief free-verse lyrics of striking precision, dealing with experiences of everyday life, and privately printed in collections like *Poems* (1920); Genevieve Taggard (1894–1948), who started her poetic career with poems about love and courtship (*For Eager Lovers*, 1922) but was soon writing vibrant indictments of social inequality; Jean Toomer (1894–1967), whose masterpiece, *Cane* (1923), narratives of the American South interspersed with powerful lyrics, tells of the beauty and violence of African-American life in a deft combination of poetry, prose poetry, fiction, and dramatic dialogue; Melvin Tolson (1898–1966), a black virtuoso of traditional European forms, whose first book of poetry, *Rendez-vous with America*, appeared as late as 1944; Janet Lewis (1899–1998), whose first book of poetry, *The Indians in the Woods* (1922), trans-lates the author's fascination with Indian experience in America into imagist poems of great clarity; Allen Tate (1899–1979), one of the "Fugitives," who published his first book of poetry, *Mr. Pope*, in 1928 and is more often sum-moned today for his role as a Southern Agrarian, co-author of *I'll Take My Stand* (1930), and intelligent shaper of new critical taste than for his pleas-antly competent poems (Tate and other Southerners, like Robert Penn Warren [1905–89], perhaps the most accomplished poet of them all, are discussed in volume VII); Yvor Winters (1900–68), a moralist of the imagination, who published his first book of poetry, *The Immobile Wind*, in 1921, and was, like Tate, a fine craftsman, yet more frequently invoked for his opinionated, often devastating criticism of other authors. Winters and Tate are particularly im-portant, in the context of the history written in "Poetry in the Machine Age," for their literary exchanges with Hart Crane.

The poets selected for lengthier study here, however, can be said to incor-porate best the rich diversity of early twentieth-century American poetry, and particularly the intricate web of often contradictory poetic and cultural features that the concept of literary modernism signifies. Most modern American poets responded, in one way or another, to the dramatic changes that occurred in the period. Some of them were fully part of those changes. Indeed, they were instrumental in making those changes happen. As Pound would say, they were news that stayed news. They are still news. That is why the designation of modernist poets best fits them. Not modern in a particular time, or in the sense of having a critical relation to *their* present (which, of course, they do as well), but modern in the sense that they have not yet stopped urging questions about "the present" (or "the past" and "future," for that matter).

Stein, Williams, H. D., Moore, Crane, and Hughes are thus brought together, along with Frost, Stevens, Pound, and Eliot, because their accomplishments as modernist poets make them representative, not only because they do represent, and are represented by, the culture, but also because their originality renders problematic the very idea of representation itself. Resorting to Stein's memorable phrasing, we might say that, in spite of their being indisputably classics today, they continue to surprise and shock the literary establishment as outlaws, as witness the many and different uses that poets, interpreters, theoreticians, and cultural commentators make of them. Yet in very different ways, Stein, Frost, Stevens, Williams, Pound, H. D., Moore, Eliot, Crane, and Hughes never allow us to forget that they, themselves, are primarily part of, and give eloquent voice to, the revolution in knowledge, feeling, and mores that radically changed society and culture in the early twentieth century. Their being lyric poets is part of the issues in question. Poetic modernism intimates a crisis in the lyric in the Western world that is contemporaneous with, and in part the result of, the anxiety, uncertainty, and disquietude of a post-Darwinian, post-Nietzschean, post-Freudian, post-Marxian *Zeitgeist*. The shattered lyric subject that modernist poets reinvented in the concept of depersonalization parallels the fragmentation of self and society first laid bare by Freud and Marx.

Modernist poets are thus one with the crisis of modernity brought about by transformations in art and mores, economy and politics, and, above all, science and technology. Modernist poets write in a machine age, and they are critically aware of that. Their stance is international and cosmopolitan, and they are attentive to the early processes of what we call globalization today. Their poetry interrogates the crisis of modernity and invites further interrogation. Modernist poets understand the crisis of modernity as mainly a crisis of language. Their poems speak the language of rupture and give finest expression to the abyss between thing and word. In their poems, the apparent transparency of language gives way to the maddening opacity of words-that-are-like-things. With these poets' innovative performance in mind, a more appropriate title for Roy Harvey Pearce's *The Continuity of American Poetry* (1961) would be *The Discontinuity of American Poetry*.

The first half of the twentieth century was witness to unprecedented social and political changes in Western society and culture. The Great War, the Bolshevik Revolution, the artistic avant-gardes, the Second Industrial Revolution, the Great Depression, the Second World War, and the gradual emergence of new nations in the African continent transformed the geopolitics of the West completely. The United States of America, no longer a mere metaphorical last hope for humanity and a rising imperial power to be reckoned with, gradually became part of "The West" in its own right, on a par with Europe. Its position in the world system as a country of immigration with continuing flows of peoples of many different origins, its rapid incorporation of capital and industry, its incredibly fast developments in science and technology, its increasing weight in world affairs, as well as its many social and racial problems (however muted by the dominant culture), soon turned the American nation into the paradigm of social, scientific, and cultural, even artistic transformation in the modern world. American modernist poets were confronted with unheard-of ambiguities of language in a constantly moving culture that were as many linguistic possibilities. They were dazzled by modernity as technology, mass communication, mass production, advertising, consumerism, and efficiency. They felt exhilarated and threatened by speed, the rapid circulation of people, objects, and money. They wondered at the apparent instantaneousness of times, places, and lives. They were surprised by the shifting roles and relative positions of men and women in society. They were excited by the sudden perception of language-as-repetition without original. At the same time, their poems were displaying, as if on a stage, all these interruptive transformations. "The scene was set / Then the theatre was changed," sings Stevens's "Of Modern Poetry" in 1940.

This was the time when "modern" began to be synonymous with "American," as Whitman had predicted and Hart Crane acknowledged in the 1920s. Poets were faced with the need, as Crane said, to "acclimatize the machine." The American poet, modern by definition, could not but compose "in the machine age." The American poem might even present itself, Williams proclaimed, as "a machine made of words." Distinctions became blurred and yet never so important. The beautiful and the "unbeautiful" (H. D.) were being redefined. And so were the genres and the very forms of the poem on the page. How do the verbal and the visual relate? How does prose relate to lyric poetry? How does the lyric poet relate to the communal? Is modernist poetry lyric or epic? What are the modern melodies of the lyric? Could lyric poetry truly sing in the machine age? The tradition had to be challenged to be reinvented. If pictures wanted "to leave their frames," as Stein said of Picasso, lyric poetry could not but be totally immersed in the materiality of the modern culture, be witness to the nation, and yet speak the whole wide world. Often, this was best accomplished in America by poets who chose to live outside the country: Stein, Pound, H. D., and T. S. Eliot. It was as if the New World had decided to strike back and make the Old World anew. But the expatriates were no less the intelligence of their native soil than Frost, Stevens, Williams, Moore, Crane, and Hughes. On both sides of the Atlantic, modernity and the tradition were face to face at last in the American poem.

It was the American modernist poet's self-appointed mission to reinvent the tradition for the machine age. The lyric threatened to interrupt the epic, and thus Crane's "epic of the modern consciousness" emerged as a new genre – the modernist long poem whose lyric "I" voices the collective ethos of a nation-transcending culture: *New Hampshire*, *The Making of Americans*, *Notes toward a Supreme Fiction*, *Paterson*, *The Cantos*, *Helen in Egypt*, *Marriage*, *The Waste Land*, *The Bridge*, *Montage of a Dream Deferred*. Often these poets, Stein foremost among them, made English sound like a "foreign" language made of objects. Occasionally, like H. D., they went back to "the Greeks" and their primordial myths only to "completely express" the "complete actual present," as Stein urged. The actual present, in H. D.'s case, included the tension between a professional and gifted woman poet and the sexist society that continued to impinge on her writing. Other poets resorted to the vernacular culture for inspiration, whether by listening to the colloquial sounds and rhythms of the "western dialect," as Williams chose to do, or, as Hughes did, by moving center stage the neglected rich culture of African-American blues, or still, as Moore did, by simply reenacting in the poem the possible genuineness and timelessness of a culture obsessed with the fleeting advertising slogan. All of them lived "between worlds," as H. D. said, and Hughes experienced the predicament the most.

In the age of capital and market productivity, the American modernist poet is a producer that yet defies the culture of production. The American modernist poet challenges the nation's myths in the concreteness of the quotidian, be it the geography of the land, the form of objects, the production of goods, the sound of words, the gender or race of people – or that miracle of science, technology, and industry, herald of the twentieth century, the Brooklyn Bridge.

I

GERTRUDE STEIN
THE POET AS MASTER OF REPETITION

WHEN *The Autobiography of Alice B. Toklas* was published in 1933 by Harcourt, Brace and Co. of New York, Gertrude Stein (1874–1946) became instantly famous. At that time, her house in Paris was packed with some of the most innovative of her manuscripts that no publisher wanted to touch. However, Stein's first published book, *Three Lives* (1909), was generally well received, if only by a limited audience. The book impressed readers for its original handling of language, narrative form, and character, as well as for the mesmerizing effect of its repetitive style. Its first reviewers praised it as "a very masterpiece of realism" with "extraordinary vitality" and "sense of urgent life." Written, according to Stein's own account, under the influence of Flaubert's *Trois contes*, which she had been translating, and inspired by Cézanne's portrait of his wife then hanging in Stein's sitting room, *Three Lives* gathers together three long stories focusing on three working-class women: "The Good Anna," "Melanctha," and "The Gentle Lena." Stein's power of character observation and her ability to capture the speech of common people get the highest praise from Richard Wright, who was later to recount how delighted he was when he first read the story about the black woman, Melanctha. Troubled by "one left-wing literary critic'"s denunciation of Stein as a "decadent" writer, Wright says that he had even read "Melanctha" to "a group of semi-literate Negro stockyard workers" who "understood every word:" "Enthralled," concludes Wright, "they slapped their thighs, howled, laughed, stomped, and interrupted [him] constantly to comment upon the characters."

But the more abstract, language-focused, and not so easily "readable" writing that Stein was producing at the same time rarely made its way into print. When it did, the publication was self-subsidized, brought out by non-commercial or even private (poets') presses with a very small audience, and the response beyond the narrowest group of Stein admirers was, with few exceptions, one of dismissive bewilderment. The two "Portraits" published by Alfred Stieglitz in the August 1912 issue of *Camera Work* ("Picasso" and "Matisse") were greeted in artistic and intellectual circles by ridicule and satire.

That was the case, too, when *Tender Buttons* (1914) was brought out by Claire-Marie, the publishing house founded by poet Donald Evans to publish his own work. In fact, just about all of Stein's publications in the 1920s and early 1930s followed this pattern closely: *Geography and Plays* (1922), published by the avant-garde Four Sea Press of Boston; *The Making of Americans* (1925), by Robert McAlmon's Contact Editions at Hemingway's recommendation; *Composition as Explanation* (1926), by Leonard and Virginia Woolf's Hogarth Press of London; *Useful Knowledge* (1928), by Payson & Clarke of New York.

By the time *The Autobiography of Alice B. Toklas* appeared in 1933, with the commercial imprimatur of Harcourt, Brace, Plain Editions, of Paris, had brought out five more books by Gertrude Stein: *Lucy Church Amiably* (1930); *Before the Flowers of Friendship Faded Friendship Faded* (1931); *How to Write* (1931); *Operas and Plays* (1932); *Matisse Picasso and Gertrude Stein with Two Shorter Stories* (1933). Stein and Toklas picked the name Plain Editions when they first decided to underwrite Stein's unpublished works by selling a Picasso, *Femme à l'éventail* (1905). The objective was to accomplish what no publisher before had been adventurous enough to attempt: to make Stein widely known as an innovative modern writer and create an audience for her original and demanding work. But where Plain Editions did not succeed, *The Autobiography of Alice B. Toklas* did – with a vengeance. The author of *Three Lives*, *Tender Buttons*, *The Making of Americans*, and *Geography and Plays* suddenly became an important, serious "author" whose oeuvre could no longer be ignored. By her own definition in "Composition as Explanation" (1926), *The Autobiography* made "a classic" of "outlawed" Gertrude Stein. It would take fifty more years for critics to begin to read in expatriate Stein's work as a whole an intelligent and creative response to concerns about the possibility of a true American culture, expressed at the beginning of the century by such influential American intellectuals as Van Wyck Brooks, Harold Stearns, Randolph Bourne, H. L. Mencken, and Lewis Mumford. Stein's work never appeared in *The Seven Arts* (1916–17), the little magazine founded by some of these intellectuals and to whose circle Stein's brother, Leo, also belonged. Leo Stein himself considered his sister's writing "abominable."

Excerpts of the *The Autobiography of Alice B. Toklas* had been published in *The Atlantic*, whetting the reading public's appetite for sensational information about bohemian life in Paris. Perhaps for this reason the book rapidly became a best-seller in the United States. It didn't take long for Paris-based Stein finally to agree to go back to the United States for a series of lectures on literature and art (published as *Lectures in America* in 1935). *The Autobiography* continues to this day to be an engaging book, not so much because of its gossipy content (though the angry reactions of some of the artists mentioned in it still enhance this aspect ["Testimony against Gertrude Stein," *transition*, February 1935]), but because it is a highly interesting, witty, and entertaining piece of narrative, constructed in a complex, sophisticated, and compelling manner. Although its form and language structure are closer to literary and grammatical conventions, or precisely for that very reason, *The Autobiography* provides important clues to Stein's notorious idiosyncrasies as a modernist verbal artist. The subtlest of such clues may well be the circular inscription of Stein's most quoted tautology, already used in *Geography and Plays* (1922), on the front cover of the first edition: "Rose is a rose is a rose is a rose" (the "device," as "Toklas" explains in *The Autobiography*, had earlier been taken by herself from one of Stein's manuscripts ["Sacred Emily," 1913] to be used on Stein's letter paper and linen). Moreover, while being ostensibly an informative chronicle of a famous epoch, the book's writing subbornly resists straightforward, transparent description, even as it subverts the subject's identity and goes on to problematize, in its ventriloquist mode, the authority of perspective and authorship. Almost any passage of *The Autobiography* would do as an example but none so emblematically as its two last paragraphs. The first paragraph is, in Stein's typically paratactical and repetitive style, the author's omissive tribute to the woman who, wife-like, made her writing possible (there is no indication of the depth and intimacy of Stein's relationship with Toklas); the second one is "Toklas"'s consecration of "pretty good authorship" in the author's self-fiction of "Gertrude Stein." Throughout the book, "Toklas" refers to Stein consistently as "Gertrude Stein"; at its closure, in a gesture that renders problematic the distinction between "autobiography" and "narrative fiction," while reinforcing the dominant culture's gender stereotypes (Toklas's housekeeping vs. Stein's writing, Stein-the-creator vs. Toklas-the-created, or muse), "Toklas" ends up presenting herself as Robinson Crusoe to "Gertrude Stein"'s Daniel Defoe. Here is "Toklas"'s commentary on "Gertrude Stein"'s suggestion that she write her autobiography:

I am a pretty good housekeeper and a pretty good gardener and a pretty good needle-woman and a pretty good secretary and a pretty good editor and a pretty good vet for dogs and I have to do them all at once and I found it difficult to add being a pretty good author.

About six weeks ago Gertrude Stein said, it does not look to me as if you were ever going to write that autobiography. You know what I am going to do. I am going to write it for you. I am going to write it as simply as Defoe did the autobiography of Robinson Crusoe. And she has and this is it.

The Autobiography renders explicit what remains implicit in Stein's more language-centered writing, namely, that literature is its own literary

construction, and that "Gertrude Stein" is also its name (and no mere synecdoche). We see the same conception at work in different ways in all the other
major modernists, such as Williams, Moore, and Pound, but no other poet
flaunts her self-contained "genius" in such an unabashedly witty manner as
Gertrude Stein. "I may say that only three times in my life have I met a genius,"
says "Alice Toklas" at the start of "her" autobiography, "and each time a bell
within me rang and I was not mistaken, and I may say in each case it was before
there was any general recognition of the quality of genius in them. The three
geniuses of whom I wish to speak are Gertrude Stein, Pablo Picasso and Alfred
Whitehead." In *The Autobiography* "genius" is semi-facetiously displayed in the
irony of Toklas's voice. However, in *Lectures in America* (1935) it is expressed
by the seemingly unassuming, yet irrefutably Olympian stance of Stein's own
discourse. Thus she keeps repeating, in "What Is English Literature," "you
will have to see what I mean," or "Oh yes you do see this," or "you completely
see what I mean," or, more interestingly still, "you do see what I say." As
for herself, she can only arrogantly assert, "I know quite completely what I
mean."

The Autobiography* brought Gertrude Stein public acclaim, fame, and financial success. These delighted the writer. However, she was dismayed at the
contrast between her self-conception as the avant-garde American poet who
single-handedly reinvented English literature as *writing* (as she explains in
"What Is English Literature"), and the public view of herself as a marketable literary personality and self-advertising popular chronicler of an eventful epoch.
Identity, a concept that had troubled her since she had started working on
Q. E. D. (first published as *Things As They Are* in 1950) and *The Making of
Americans* (1925) in the early 1900s, was once again in question. Not surprisingly, then, although she continues to compose pieces that challenge all
traditional modes and conventional styles, Stein also proceeds to meet the
demands of the expanding literary marketplace by writing more overt self-
narrative. *Stanzas in Meditation*, her coded intimate autobiography, of which
only parts were published during her lifetime, and *Four in America* (1947), her
brilliant meditation on personality and creativity, were composed at the same
time that *The Autobiography* was being written. The sense of who one is and
how external circumstances affect one's identity is at the core of *Everybody's
Autobiography* (1937), a modest sequel to *The Autobiography of Alice B. Toklas*,
which vividly records life in the 1930s as Stein experienced it. But, again, the
impossibility of proper perspective in autobiography is immediately signaled
by the paradox of the book's title. By shifting the perspective from self-writing
to objective seeing, the title of the last piece of autobiographical writing Stein
published, *Wars I Have Seen* (1945), has the same effect as well.

A poet's identity as it is constantly challenged by all kinds of otherness cannot but be that poet's major poetic theme, however obliquely. In *Three Lives* and *The Making of Americans*, Stein deals with Americanness as dislocation and reinvention of identity, whether it be the fictionalized saga of her own family's immigration across the ocean to generations of success in America or the short, pointless lives of three working-class women, two German servant girls recently arrived from the old country and an African-American woman who dies of her own split psychology and culture. In both works, but perhaps more strikingly in "Melanctha," identity is presented as utterly vulnerable in its unavoidable interrelatedness. In the earlier novel, *Q. E. D.* [*Quod Erat Demonstrandum*] (written in 1903), Stein had already dealt with the same problem, though focusing rather on love, sexuality, and lesbianism. After the flattering reception of *The Autobiography*, as she continues to explore the advantages of market success as an American exile who finally makes it the American way, Stein goes back to a concern that had been with her from the very beginning. In her lectures, which, along with the earlier *How To Write* (1931), can actually be read as the life story of her writing, Stein draws an important distinction between "identity" and "entity."

The distinction is made explicit in "What Are Master-Pieces and Why Are There So Few of Them" (1940). "Identity" pertains to "human nature." It is what you are in the mirror of society and of yourself, the way you are seen and understood by others as well as the way you, yourself, see and understand how you are perceived by others. Identity is a relational concept and implies remembrance and recognition. "Entity," on the other hand, pertains to the "human mind." It is what you do as a creative being rather than what you are in the context of your own and others' memory and acknowledgment. "Identity" is, then, part of necessity (of what is, as Stein keeps saying, "necessary"), it is what you are under the pressure of what happens around you in the world and in society (what Stevens calls the "pressure of reality"). "Entity," on the other hand, is closer to "genius." It is the freedom that enables you to make things happen, or to create. Creation only occurs, or "happens," when "identity" is suspended or emptied out and "entity" becomes free to act. Keats's Negative Capability cannot be too far behind. "Happening," as Auden would repeat later, is a good way to refer to the poet's act of creativity. Indeed, if Stein, Stevens, and Auden could be conflated here, we might say that "entity" alone allows for the act of the human mind to happen. "The thing one gradually comes to find out," Stein argues in "What Are Master-Pieces," "is that one has no identity that is when one is in the act of doing anything. Identity is recognition, you know who you are because you and others remember anything about yourself but essentially you are not that when you are doing anything." And then she elaborates on the much-quoted phrase from *Geography and Plays* (1922) and "Identity A Poem" (1935): "I am I because my little dog knows me but, creatively speaking the little dog knowing that you are you and your recognising that he knows, that is what destroys creation." In order to create the new word, the logical conclusion seems to be, Stein's poet must stand alone and unecumbered, like the rugged American individual bringing about a new world.

We might say that Stein's poet still competes with the sublime, but the sublime is now the modern (American) sublime – or emerging mass culture. "[R]adios cinemas newspapers biographies autobiographies," Stein specifies in "What Are Master-Pieces." Mass communication, mass production, speed, the fast circulation of people, objects, consumerism, and money, the instantaneousness of times, places, and lives – such are the encroachments of modern necessity on the poet's imagination (or "entity"). How is modern identity to suspend itself and allow entity to engage with the American sublime? The answer is in "Composition as Explanation," a lecture Stein gave in Oxford and Cambridge in 1926. Using herself as an example, Stein explains modern poetry (she calls it "composition") in terms of "time-sense." The two key, interrelated concepts are *authenticity* and *contemporaneity*. "No one is ahead of his time," Stein says, meaning, "no one is outside of his or her time" (Stein's masculine pronoun is for "genius" as defined in *The Autobiography*). Quite in tune with the most recent developments of modern physics, Stein's time includes space (her name for this Einsteinian articulation is "geography"). To compose authentically is to compose in, from, and for the contemporary present. And what more contemporary and present than American culture?

"The business of Art as I tried to explain in Composition as Explanation," writes Stein in her lecture on "Plays," "is to live in the actual present, and to completely express that complete actual present." *Three Lives*, with special mention of "Melanctha" (written in 1905), is described in "Composition as Explanation" as a "prolonged present." *The Making of Americans* (completed in 1911), as a "continuous present." The sheer size of the latter book, almost one thousand pages of continuous present, add a Whitmanian dimension to Stein's epic of the American consciousness. In "The Gradual Making of *The Making of Americans*" (*Lectures in America*), we further learn that this "very American thing" (and "thing," thus irrupting of stammering repetitiousness, is Stein's way of suspending the abyss between signifier and signified), this "essentially American book," makes a "whole present" of human history. As she tries to explain the difficulty she felt in *The Making of Americans* of putting human being into words, Stein resorts to the Poesque parable of the butterfly that she tells early in the book. For Stein as for Poe, the butterfly is a symbol for writing. But while Poe's exquisite artificial butterfly is so perfect that it threatens to undo art by becoming alive, Stein's dead and pinned butterfly – belonging to a collector – is the paradoxical symbol of living art. Both stories speak the abyss between art and life which artists and poets have attempted to bridge since the beginning of creative time. Continuously repeating the continuous present, so as "to make a whole present of something that it had taken a great deal of time to find out," is one of Stein's ways of dealing with the problem. Stein's poet fits to perfection Stevens's definition of "master of repetition."

The poetic identity of Gertrude Stein, who lived in Paris almost all her life, turns out to be entity made in America. Her way of avoiding the modernist "anxiety of contamination" is by boldly writing America-as-modern-mass-culture. Of course, she was never, nor will she ever be, a mass-cultural writer, but her simple vocabulary and her maddeningly repetitious and self-interruptive style, so resonant of the rhythms of common modern living, may well strike its readers as the paradox of originality-as-mass-production. Paraphrasing Stevens once again, we might say that Stein, writing doubly from the outside, as an American Jew in exile, still is the intelligence of America's soil. Her art is the creation of contemporaneity, the romantic unmediated vision replaced by instant perception. But while industry, capital, and technology do give the illusion of instant perception (train, airplane, automobile, newspapers, telephone, telegraph, radio, cinema, television), poetry, as in the little boy's dead butterfly, bespeaks, perhaps ever romantically, its *impossibility*.

Stein's apt name for the phenomenal presentness which her writing wishes to grasp is "being existing." Other modernist images of time captured in an instant come to mind: Eliot's simultaneous order and still point of the turning world, Pound's vortex, Stevens's hour, Williams's gist, and Crane's day. *The Making of Americans*, Stein's large, multitudinous book about American identity and difference, a continuous present using everything and beginning again, "irritating annoying stimulating" that it is, can be said to be, like the American nation itself, "unreadable," as so many competent readers have testified (Edmund Wilson, Paul Bowles, Truman Capote), including Gertrude Stein herself in "Composition as Explanation:" "I . . . was a little troubled with it when I read it. I became then like the others who read it . . . I lost myself in it again." The contemporaneity of American time that *The Making of Americans* wishes to depict *happens* in unbearable successions of paragraphs made up of repetitive sentences that seem to repeat themselves only because they stumble on each other, constantly interrupting themselves. One of the effects of Stein's self-interruptive repetition is the utter foreignness of language, as if stuttering repetition alone could erase all foreign languages and bring about a totally new and impossibly nonforeign, finally intelligible language. Here is Stein on being's acculturation in America:

Certainly some were certain that any one understanding the meaning in his being existing would be liking that thing. Some were certain and then later were certain that this was not what every one understanding the meaning of his being one being existing would be feeling. Some were certain that any one understanding the being in him would be liking his being one being existing. Some of such of them were learning in being ones going on being living that some could be understanding the being in him and would then be ones not liking that thing not liking his being one being existing.

Besides being a description of "everyone who is, or has been, or will be," *The Making of Americans* is the story of the rising of Stein's immigrant family in America, including the story of herself as a writer, written from the vantage-point of the author as reverse immigrant. The youngest child of an affluent Jewish American family, Gertrude Stein lived outside the United States most of her life. The very same year she was born, her family moved to Austria, where she learned German along with English. In 1878, her mother took her and her siblings to Paris, where she also learned French. In the 1880s and 1890s, Stein lived in the United States, and became immersed in the English language. But the first English she heard there would often have been incorrectly spoken by some of the members of her immigrant family. This early contact with different languages and the sense of what can or cannot be "correctly" done with them no doubt affected her development as a verbal artist. Later, to her great annoyance, publishers would often comment on the English "errors" made by this American author writing in France, and candidly offer to have her syntax and grammar revised. Stein's concept of "language" and "culture" was, therefore, closely related to her sense of her own identity as a citizen of the newest nation in the world, not in search, as in Williams, of an autochthonous idiom, but in the process of making it happen.

Although she had never received her diploma from Oakland High School in California, she earned her B.A. from Radcliffe in 1898. There she studied under some of the intellectuals that helped to shape modernism in America: George Santayana and Josiah Royce (philosophy), William James and Hugo Münsterberg (psychology), William Vaughn Moody (literary composition). She frequently referred to William James as her "big influence" (his brother Henry James, whose long, intricate sentences in his late work she much admired, was the subject of a "portrait" in *Four in America*). In the summer of 1897, Stein studied at Woods Hole Marine Biological Laboratory in Massachusetts with her brother Leo, to whom she had always been very close and on whom she became heavily dependent after the deaths of their mother (1888) and father (1891). In the fall of 1897, following William James's advice to get a medical education in order to do advanced study in psychology, Gertrude Stein entered Johns Hopkins School of Medicine, where Leo Stein was already studying biology. Meanwhile, two articles of hers, written in collaboration with Leon Solomons, and the result of their research on automatic writing at the Harvard Psychology Laboratory under Münsterberg, came out in *Psychological Review* ("Normal Motor Automatism," 1896, and "Cultivated Motor Automatism," 1898). "Cultivated Motor Automatism," we learn in *The Autobiography of Alice B. Toklas*, "is very interesting to read because the method of writing to be afterwards developed in Three Lives and the Making of Americans already shows itself." The "method of writing" was a "marked tendency to repetition," which Solomons had observed in the writing produced by Stein as the subject of the experiment that led to "Normal Motor Automatism." At Johns Hopkins, although she enjoyed some of her clinical practice in Baltimore's black neighborhoods (where the idea for Melanctha's story first came to her), Stein was not very successful in the classroom. Neither she nor her brother ever earned a degree from Johns Hopkins.

As with William Carlos Williams and Marianne Moore, Stein's scientific training and her attentiveness to modern science and technology play an important role in her work. At the beginning of the twentieth century, the scientists, philosophers, poets, and artists who suddenly realized that "the reality of the twentieth century is not the reality of the nineteenth century," as Stein writes in her essay on Picasso (*Picasso*, first published in French in 1938), were those that mattered to her. The three "geniuses" identified in *The Autobiography* are "Gertrude Stein," "Picasso," and "Alfred Whitehead," and they represent Stein's major intellectual and interrelated interests: poetry, painting, and science. But if "Picasso" and "Gertrude Stein" seem obvious choices to signify the modernist revolution in painting and poetry, "Alfred Whitehead" somehow doesn't quite fit. A friend of Gertrude Stein's, Alfred North Whitehead was an important English mathematician noted for his early collaboration with Bertrand Russell in *Principia Mathematica* (1910). As a philosopher of science and an educator, Whitehead also played an important role as popularizer of modern science. His *Science and the Modern World* (1925), with chapters on "Relativity" and "Quantum Theory," was extremely influential in bringing concepts of modern physics to bear on intellectual, artistic, and literary discourse in the first half of the twentieth century. Edmund Wilson refers to *Science and the Modern World* frequently in *Axel's Castle* (1931), his study of the tendencies of contemporary writing since Symbolism, which includes a perceptive chapter on Gertrude Stein (the others deal with Yeats, Valéry, Eliot, Proust, and Joyce).

A better candidate for the "genius" of modern science would have been Einstein. In the first decades of the century, Einstein's name was often loosely invoked as a metaphor for modern physics and its radical change of paradigms, conflating quantum theory, relativity, the uncertainty principle, and even complementarity, with little regard for or much ignorance of the theoretical differences between Max Planck, Einstein, Heisenberg, or Niels Bohr. In an essay titled "The Poem as a Field of Action" (1948), William Carlos Williams (resorting to Wilson's essay on Proust and modern physics) makes perhaps the clearest connection between Einstein's "theory of relativity" and "the relativity of measurements" with the modern American poet's search for a "new measure," of which his own "variable foot" is an experiment. Moore, like Williams, was prone to link the newest developments in science to the United States as the nation of industry, technology, and experimentation par excellence, and the consequences of all this for the practice of modern poetry in America. Moore's poem, "The Student" (1932), concerned with American ideals and institutions, quotes Einstein as having said that science and the experiment are never finished, as if the common feature of science, poetry, and America were that they were all always *in the making*. Thus, Stein's famous title, *The Making of Americans*, comes back to us. Indeed, in *Everybody's Autobiography* Stein immodestly links herself with Einstein: "Einstein was the creative philosophic mind of the century and I have been the creative literary mind of the century."

Like many other poets and artists, Stein must have felt that she was confirmed, rather than inspired, by modern science. If modern science was raising questions about the reality of science itself, modern art was raising questions about clear-cut distinctions between art and not art. Post-symbolist experiments with time, space, and perspective, Primitivism, Cubism, and the promiscuity of art and consumption as in Duchamp's ready-mades turned the distinction between high art and mass culture, elite production and bourgeois consumption, gratuitous art and advertising, once and for all, into a matter of social convention. In other words, pictures "commenced to want to leave their frames" (Stein in *Picasso*). As scientists were discovering troublesome new relations between the subject observing and the object observed, a painter like Picasso was struggling, according to Stein, "not to express what he could see but not to express the things he did not see, that is to say the things everybody is certain of seeing, but which they do not really see." Stein claims to have been the only one to understand Picasso in his Cubist period, "because [she] was expressing the same thing in literature." Stein explains this congeniality between Picasso and herself, a congeniality which tends to suspend another important distinction of modernity – the distinction between modern scientific progress and pre-modern lack of it – by reference to their respective nationalities. "Spain because of its lack of organization," explains Stein, "and America by its excess of organization were the natural founders of the twentieth century." The places, colors, and rhythms of Spain, which Stein visited with

Toklas in 1912 and, at greater length, in 1915, were indeed very inspiring for Stein, perhaps also because of the growing love relationship between the two women at the time. Many of the pieces in *Geography and Plays* (1922) were written in Spain. Nevertheless, Stein's deep appreciation of Picasso is rooted in her life-long interest in and study of painting, and in her discovery confirmed in Cézanne that a painting does not have to be representation (or "look like anything," as she puts it in "Pictures").

A passionate taste for travel, self-cultivation, and cosmopolitanism, as well as the excitement of the post-symbolist artistic milieu in France at the turn of the century had lured Leo and Gertrude Stein to Paris, where in 1903 they made their home together at 27 rue de Fleurus. A comfortable income made all this possible. In the years that followed the Steins were busy visiting art galleries; admiring and buying paintings by Cézanne, Gauguin, Renoir, Delacroix, Bonnard, Manet, Toulouse-Lautrec, Degas, Matisse, Picasso, Bracque, Picabia, Juan Gris, Duchamp, Marie Laurencin; holding Saturday-night salons for modern and avant-garde painters and poets (among the latter Picasso's friends Max Jacob and Guillaume Apollinaire); and shaping the artistic taste of their time. In this they were helped by their older brother Michael and his wife, Sarah, who had moved to Paris at about the same time. The Steins' collection of paintings were part of the famous 1913 Armory Show in New York – the exhibit that made such a strong impression on Stevens and other American poets and artists. Though Picasso was admired by all the Steins, Gertrude alone developed an intense friendship and intellectual relationship with him that was to last for life. Their conversations on art and literature became the subject of each other's artistic performance: Picasso painted the well-known Stein portrait just before *Les demoiselles d'Avignon* and the emergence of Cubism, and Stein's verbal "Portraits" (Picasso's included), "Plays," and *Tender Buttons* are her own Cubist counterpart to his Cubist paintings.

Stein's reference to a controversial Picasso painting as "a composition that had neither a beginning nor an end, a composition of which one corner was as important as another corner, in fact the composition of cubism" applies equally well to her own exacting and equally controversial writing. "Picasso," the portrait, is a fine example of a kind of poetic writing that entitles the author to state categorically, you do *see* what I *say*. Consisting of twelve paragraphs of variable length, in which the same words, often one gerund after another, the same phrases, and the same sentences repeat themselves with exasperating circularity, "Picasso" sensuously depicts a remarkable subject collapsed into the complex, unavoidable object of his own making. Stein's Picasso emerges as "one" who was either always working or not ever completely working, "one" whom some were certainly following, "one" who had meaning coming out of him (the child-bearing metaphor is explicit). Though the portrait has no beginning or end, the ninth paragraph sums it all up:

This one always had something being coming out of this one. This one was working. This one always had been working. This one was always having something that was coming out of this one that was a solid thing, a charming thing, a lovely thing, a perplexing thing, a disconcerting thing, a simple thing, a clear thing, a complicated thing, an interesting thing, a disturbing thing, a repellent thing, a very pretty thing. This one was certainly one being one having something coming out of him. This one was one whom some were following. This one was one who was working.

By Stein's own account, French writing never caught her attention the way French painting did. Although she used a quotation from Jules Laforgue as epigraph for *Three Lives* ("Donc je suis un malheureux et ce n'est ni ma faute ni celle de la vie"), she claimed that only literature written in the English language was important to her, and indeed she was widely and deeply read in English literature (by which she meant American literature as well). However, the French poets Guillaume Apollinaire and Max Jacob were also very much part of her Paris scene during the first two decades of the century. Stein produced a "Portrait" of Apollinaire in 1913, published in *Dix portraits* (English and French, 1930), suggesting that she could not have been totally uninterested in his work or, for that matter, in the progress of French poetry from Rimbaud, Verlaine, and Baudelaire (who introduced Edgar Allan Poe's conception of poetry as verbal music to France) to Mallarmé (who also hosted poetic salons) and later poets. Though Cubism is a painter's invention, Mallarmé had already anticipated it in his emphasis on the plastic and sound value of words disconnected from reference, connotation, suggestiveness, and sentiment. In their insistence on the "poetic value" of words "freed from their literal meaning" (Paul Reverdy), post-impressionist poets may have been more immediately influenced by Cubist painting than by Mallarmé, but they could not have been unaware of *Un coup de dès* (1897). Considered by many a fine example of Stein's most disconcertingly opaque writing, the five lines of "Guillaume Apollinaire" (the title must be counted in) defy interpretation as they invite daring play of word sounds in more than one language:

Guillaume Apollinaire

Give known or pin ware.
Fancy teeth, gas strips.
Elbow elect, sour stout pore, pore caesar, pour state at.
Leave eye lesson I. Leave I. Lessons. I. Leave I lessons, I.

Starting with the homophony of "eye"/"I" in the last and perhaps least shocking line, and having in mind Apollinaire's visual, calligrammatic poetry, the poem, in its Cubist circularity, with no beginning or end, strikes the eye: I, Guillaume Apollinaire, give eye lessons. Then, the juxtaposition of "lessons" and "leave," in a portrait of a French-writing poet drawn in words by an English-writing poet, conjures up the French homophone of "lessons" (leçons), "laissons" (we leave/let's leave), thus establishing the complicity between the portraitist and her subject, both of them foreigners in Paris. Guillaume Apollinaire (1880–1918) was not a Frenchman but a Pole (Guglielmo Alberto Wladimiro Apollinare de Kostrowitzky) whose first language was Italian. His mother always called him Wilhelm, like the German Kaiser. To consider the way people hear an unknown language and awkwardly repeat orally or in writing, often transliterating, a foreign, strange-sounding name, not simply the Frenchified "Guillaume Apollinaire" but the Latinate German-Slavic "Guglielmo Alberto Wladimiro Apollinare de Kostrowitzky," may be one key to enjoying Stein's poetic strategy, not only in this most provocative of her "Portraits" ("Guillaume Apollinaire" and all its possible sounds, "native" and "foreign," grotesquely translated into "Give known or pin ware"), but also in her writing as a whole. Stein's poetic practice exemplifies to perfection Stevens's insight that only when we realize that we are all foreigners, can we be natives in this world.

The lives of the Stein siblings followed different paths. While Leo had decided he wanted to be a painter (he never succeeded), Gertrude was totally committed to writing. Growing tensions between brother and sister determined their separation in 1913, when Alice B. Toklas, Stein's life-long companion, lover, homemaker, secretary, typist, and at times her only admiring audience, was already living at 27 rue de Fleurus. Except for a time during World War II when the two women took refuge in the country, some short trips to London and her America lecture tour in 1934–35, Paris was their permanent residence. During all these years, young, aspiring American writers flocked to Stein's salons for encouragement, intellectual stimulation, or sheer curiosity. Among the Americans was the critic and creative writer Carl Van Vechten, who had arranged for the printing of *Tender Buttons* in 1914, and was to edit, in collaboration with Stein herself, the first and influential *Selected Writings of Gertrude Stein* (1946). With some exceptions, the incredible number of manuscripts produced by Stein and painstakingly typed by Toklas remained unpublished during her lifetime. However, her poetic genius was acclaimed by such fellow writers as Sherwood Anderson and Thornton Wilder (both of whom wrote admiring introductions to her work), E. E. Cummings, Jean Cocteau, Mina Loy, Ernest Hemingway (who would later resent her influence), F. Scott Fitzgerald, and Richard Wright. William Carlos Williams, whose first encounter with Gertrude Stein at rue des Fleurus in 1924 as recounted in his *Autobiography*

(1951) was not auspicious, wrote a very perceptive and comprehensive essay about her work for the first issue of *Pagany* in 1930. "The Work of Gertrude Stein," which may have been prompted by Stein's great admirer and Williams's friend Louis Zukovsky, is Williams's response to the American scholars' silence about Gertrude Stein. In accord with his own modernist conceptions and appreciations, Williams compares Stein's innovative aesthetic experiments to those of Laurence Sterne and Johann Sebastian Bach, states approvingly that her "theme" is "writing" and praises the way she reinvents words as objects of integrity in the text, and highlights her capacity for "unhampering" and "unburdening" "writing" of the extraneous "affairs" of science and philosophy. In a later essay, in which he deals with the revolutionary nature of Stein's and Pound's writing, Williams praises Stein for "smashing every connotation that words have ever had, in order to get them back clean" ("A 1 Pound Stein" [*Pagany* 1934], *Selected Essays*, 1954).

Perhaps the best tribute to Stein's exasperatingly exacting writing came from Marianne Moore, another "high modernist" highly admired by Williams for qualities he also finds in Stein (both women poets, like Williams himself, had training in science). Moore entitled her 1936 review of *The Geographical History of America* in *The Nation* "Perspicuous Opacity." Stein's is indeed a kind of writing, with its repetitive and self-interruptive character, which many readers find repellent and fascinating at the same time. The limpid transparency, or *perspicuity*, of endless variable repetitions of simple words that structure her texts speak nothing more than the obscurity, or *opacity*, of their claiming to be the visible sound of clear solid words. This is precisely how Stein explains she wishes to be read: "I found that any kind of a book if you read with glasses and somebody is cutting your hair and so you cannot keep the glasses on and you use your glasses as a magnifying glass and so read word by word reading word by word makes the writing that is not anything be something" (*The Geographical History of America*, 1936). Until this is understood, many Stein readers with intense interpretive cravings may find themselves in the position of Ahab, insanely wishing to strike at knowledge through an impenetrable epistemological mask. As Stein says in "What is English Literature," "knowledge is what one knows."

Thanks to the posthumous editions published by Yale in the 1950s, followed by several Selections and Readers (as edited by Patricia Meyerwitz for Peter Owen, 1967; Ulla E. Dydo for Northwestern, 1993; and, more recently, Catherine R. Stimpson and Harriet Chessman for The Library of America, 1998 [2 vols.]), the main body of Stein's work has now been available for quite some time. A wealth of criticism, interpretation, and commentary (in several languages) has helped to place Stein firmly on the canonical map of modern literature. Feminist and lesbian criticism, in particular, have opened new perspectives on Stein's writing. And yet, to assess Stein's achievement together with that of her contemporary women writers, who often at the time earned more public recognition than she, may not be very productive. Her writing does not yield the kind of female sensibility – overtly defiant and vulnerable, intense and disenchanted at the same time – that is readily associated with the work of Sara Teasdale (1884–1933), Elinor Wylie (1885–1928), Edna St. Vincent Millay (1892–1950), Dorothy Parker (1893–1967), Genevieve Taggard (1894–1948), and Louise Bogan (1897–1970). Many of these poets' poems deal explicitly with the impingement of unequal power relations on women's identity, emotions, and sexuality. Bogan's negative description of "Women," in *Body of this Death* (1932), actually sounds like a reverse portrait of a powerful woman like Stein ("Women have no wilderness ... they do not see ... they do not hear ... "). Taggard's "Everyday Alchemy" (*From Eager Lovers*, 1922), demystifies the traditional image of women as men's source of solace ("peace ... poured by poor women / Out of their heart's poverty"), while Millay's "Second Fig" (*A Few Figs from Thistles*, 1922) scornfully rejects domestic security and respectability ("Safe upon the solid rock the ugly houses stand: / Come and see my shining palace built upon the sand!"). Teasdale's "After Love" (*Rivers to the Sea*, 1915) or Wylie's "Confession of Faith" (*Trivial Breath*, 1928) are miles apart in mood, form, and style from Stein's love poetry in *Tender Buttons*, published the year before. Parker's "One Perfect Rose" (*Enough Rope*, 1926), however, could be read, metaleptically, as an ironic commentary on Stein's celebrated foursome rose. "A single flow'r he sent me," Parker's poem begins, only comically to deflate this incipit in the last stanza: "Why is it no one ever sent me / One perfect limousine, do you suppose? / Ah no, it's always my luck to get / One perfect rose."

Stein will be always difficult to categorize, as a perfunctory look at any history of modern American literature will show: is she better discussed under narrative fiction, lyric poetry, drama, or perhaps the theoretical essay? Can one, in Stein, rigorously distinguish one genre from the others? Is *The Geographical History of America* a work of prose or poetry? (*écriture* and *Dichtung* are better descriptions). And how useful are the categories of gender, class and ethnicity, biography and autobiography to discuss Stein's work? In the recent Library of America two-volume *American Poetry: The Twentieth Century* (2000) Stein is canonized as a modernist poet, but at least one reviewer was shocked by the amount of space (forty pages) granted to excerpts from *Tender Buttons* and "Lifting Belly."

Students and readers in general will continue to have trouble not only classifying Stein's writing but also counting her in. Like many modernist poets, but in a far more radical way, Stein's practice not only challenges the conventional categories of the literary tradition, but also subverts English grammar and questions cultural and social mores. Although she often designates her works by such well-established nomenclature as "novel," "play," "poetry," "poem," "story," "lecture," or even the less common "portrait," the truth is that any resemblance between Stein's works so designated and the genres and subgenres of literary convention as normally taught in school may well be deemed pure coincidence. Take the concept of "play," for instance, as it appears in *What Happened, A Five Act Play* (written in 1913, first published in *Geography and Other Plays* [1922]). Even though the text is appropriately divided into five acts and called "A Play," the scanty four pages of the piece have no dramatic content whatsoever and bear no resemblance to any known theatrical composition. There are no characters, no stage directions, no dialogue, no action. But there is certainly the play *act-ing*, or rather writing-as-acting. "What Happened," indeed, except the play-full written text on the page?

Apparently in lieu of identified or identifiable speakers, on the left-hand side of the page the text provides italicized numerical indications as if to identify or specify parts of the discourse: "(*One.*)," "(*Five.*)," "(*Two.*)," "(*Two.*)," "(*Three.*)" (in Act I); "(*Three.*)," "(*The same three.*)," "(*The same three.*)" (Act II); "(*Two.*)," "(*Four.*)," "(*One.*)" (Act III); "(*Four and four more.*)" (Act IV); "(*Two.*)" (Act V). But what are these signs, these stage nondirections, signaling? The number of paragraphs that follow? This hypothesis makes sense if you count the paragraphs in Acts I, II, III, and V. Then, it does seem as if words, language, discourse dressed up as and impersonating paragraphs are the characters in the play (in *How to Write* [1931] Stein "made a discovery that [she] considered fundamental," as she explains in her lecture on "Plays," "that sentences are not emotional and that paragraphs are"). But, in Act IV, what the reader has managed to construct as a comforting convention, after what she begins to believe Stein's peculiar private conception of a literary genre might be, falls apart. "(*Four and four more.*)" contains indeed four paragraphs, which are followed, not by four more paragraphs, but by one long single paragraph that is made up of one long single sentence. There is a certain impudence in Stein's demonstrations that literary conventions and conventional literary namings are precisely that: mere literary conventions. Since there is no right correspondence between the sounds and the meanings of the word that designate them, they must be reinvented for the sheer pleasure of poetic making. Readers faced with a composition that has "neither a beginning nor an end," who wish to know "what happened," have to fall into the trap of Stein's whimsical playfulness and, as before a Cubist painting, yield to the temptation to "reconstruct" the "play."

In a short piece titled simply "Play" (1923), later included in *Portraits and Prayers* (1934), Gertrude Stein plays with all possible meanings and implications of the word "play" (including those of its French equivalent, *pièce*) suggesting that life is merely repetitive, fragmentary, play-as-enactment. Its first three sentences read like this: "Play, play every day, play and play and play away, and then play the play you played to-day, the play you play every day, play it and play it. Play it, and remember it and ask to play it. Play it, and play it and play away." Then, the text offers different kinds of justification for the repeated imperative: "Certainly every one wants you to play," "That's the way to play," "This is the way to play," "Every one is very glad to have them play." Next, comes the act of playing, convened by Stein's famous present participle, as what is surely happening:

Every one is certain that some of them are playing, playing and playing and playing every day and all day and to-day. Every one is certain that some of them are playing and remembering and playing again again what they were playing. Some of them are certainly playing, playing, playing. Every one is wanting some of them to be playing and playing and playing, to be playing to-day, to be playing all day, to be playing every day, to be playing away.

In this light, Stein's *What Happened, A Five Act Play*, presenting itself as static play-on-the-page, is a challenging invitation to theatrical production: the production must make the piece perform, not what happened, but the happening in the present that it wishes to be. We realize that *What Happened* is a play only because Stein says so ("I think and always have thought," Stein writes in her lecture on "Plays," "that if you write a play you ought to announce that it is a play. And that is what I did. What Happened. A Play"). *What Happened* is indeed paradigmatic of Stein's modernist reinvention of the genre by minimizing character and story or action, and putting all the emphasis on what she calls "geography" or "landscape" (Stevens calls it "climate") and some would call "the lyric." Here is an alliterative paragraph from Act II, rich with suggestions of travel and linkages: "A connection, a clam cup connection, a survey, a ticket and a return to laying over." The poetic, playful quality of the text disengaged from immediate meaning is what is important and has paradoxically inspired productions. For obvious reasons, stagings of Stein's plays have not been abundant. While there have been successful productions of the more ostensibly dramatic plays, such as *The Mother of Us All* (on Susan B. Anthony) or *Four Saints in Three Acts*, Stein's static plays have attracted such innovative directors, with an interest in the dramatic potential of essentially lyric texts, as composer Virgil Thompson, Living Theatre's Julian Beck, and Obie prize-winner Lawrence Kornfeld. A memorable production of *What Happened* was the "Dance Drama" performed by the Judson Poet's Theatre at The Judson Memorial Church in New York City in 1963, directed by Lawrence Kornfeld, with music by Al Carmines, and design by Larry Siegel. In *Against Interpretation*, Susan Sontag describes this production as "the closest thing" to "the theater of cruelty" in America.

The pieces (or "plays") in which Stein comes closest to conveying the immediacy and authenticity of "being existing" are her love poems. In her lecture on "Poetry and Grammar," quite in tune with modernist perplexities, Stein finds it difficult to distinguish prose from poetry. Prose, she says, is the balance of sentences and paragraphs composed mainly of verbs, articles, and pronouns. Not nouns or adverbs. Poetry is just the opposite. Poets, she says, have always been "drunk with nouns." The concept is traditional enough ("think of Homer, think of Chaucer, think of the Bible"). Poetry is naming: In the beginning was the Word. For Stein, too, poetry is not so much a fixed form, but the awesome "discovery" of love by giving it a name, or names: *Tender Buttons*. As she was writing *The Making of Americans* and balancing the life of people and generations of people, "something happened," she says. She discovered, her wording in "Poetry and Grammar" leads us to conclude, the wonder of being in love. She discovered that things were finally made visible to her as sensuous things, and all of a sudden there was no balance in her writing, only passion. The poetic passion of naming. Not the passion of inventing new nouns for names that have been names for a very long time (that's the job of slang), but the passion of naming anew the proper names of things. All of a sudden, she was, Cratylus-like, conjuring up, not a vocabulary of thinking (as in *How to Write*), but a vocabulary of *thinging*. The sensuous thinging of "Objects," "Food," and "Rooms" in *Tender Buttons*:

> I began to discover the names of things, that is not discover the names but discover the things the things to see the things to look at and in so doing I had of course to name them not to give them new names but to see that I could find out how to know that they were there by their names or by replacing their names. And how was I to do so. They had their names and naturally I called them by the names they had and in doing so having begun looking at them I called them by their names with passion and that made poetry, I did not mean it to make poetry but it did, it made the Tender Buttons, and the Tender Buttons was very good poetry . . .

While slang finds new nouns to freshen up the old names of things, poetry names the proper-noun-names of things in such a way as to make them both new (things and names). Nowhere is Stein more eloquent regarding the belatedness of modern poetry and the possibility of its reinvention than in her remarks to the student who once asked her about her celebrated repetition of the rose. In order to reinvent the "excitingness of pure being" in the "wornout literary words," Stein argues after Pater, the poet has "to put some strangeness, something unexpected, into the structure of the sentence in order to bring back vitality to the noun." In that particular line of one particular poem, "Rose is a rose is a rose is a rose," the rose, Stein rounds off triumphantly, "is red for the first time in English poetry for a hundred years." Likewise, each paragraph-poem in *Tender Buttons* (literally "emotional" because, being "buttons," they fasten and unfasten passion, like women's nipples) is a naming indistinguishable from a sensuous thinging, a domestic still life, somewhat like one of Stein's portraits:

> A petticoat.
> A light white, a disgrace, an ink spot, a rosy charm. ("Objects")

> Potatoes.
> In the preparation of cheese, in the preparation of crackers, in the preparation of butter, in it ("Food")

> Sugar any sugar, anger every anger, lover sermon lover, center no distractor, all order is in a measure. ("Rooms")

In the paragraphs isolated above from each of the three parts of *Tender Buttons*, each one with its own dream-like ambience, several threads of meaning can be woven into the domesticity already announced by the three titles ("Objects" "Food" "Rooms"). Female underwear and the abandonment of bedroom intimacy. Cooking and the kitchen. Emotions and sentiment, this last one to be easily connected metaphorically with the previous two. For example: the juxtaposition of sweet and bitter loving with measuring spoon suggests sexuality wishing to escape regulation. It would not be difficult to trace other lines of the same kind of signification. Clothing and sewing, eating and drinking, pecking and petting. *Tender Buttons* places English lyric poetry in the tranquil geography of trivial – yet joyful, playful, pleasurable, and caring – quotidian living in the feminine. The poetic closure of *Tender Buttons* does away with bucolic sentiment only to make it strangely new inside the woman's sitting room:

> The care with which the rain is wrong and the green is wrong and the white is wrong, the care with which there is a chair and plenty of breathing. The care with which there is incredible justice and likeness, all this makes a magnificent asparagus, and also a fountain.

Stein, writing not only like a woman but *as* a woman, thus reinvents erotic poetry. In a far more exuberant and explicit manner than *Tender Buttons*, "Lifting Belly" (1915–17), which was not published in Stein's lifetime, speaks a new language of sexual love and love-making never heard before: "What did I say, that I was a great poet like the English only sweeter." "Sweeter," she means, than "sweet Will," who in the sonnets puns on sexual desire and gourmandise in a manner that is comparable to Stein's in her erotic poetry: "Lifting belly this. / So sweet. / To me. / Say anything a pudding made of Caesars. / Lobster. Baby is so good to baby" (A whole paragraph in the first few pages of "Patriarchal Poetry" reads like a parodic menu for the week). "Lifting belly is a language," a coded language, to be sure, that savors and delights in the elliptical, syncopated dialogues of two women's intimate living together and its many private double meanings. It is a language full of the tastes, sounds, smells, and rhythms of female domesticity, yet fully aware of the world outside as well (including the Great War). While Stein's language here is crisscrossed by enigmatic references, such as "a cow" and "two caesars," it is charmingly decodable in repeated readings of its self-interruptive and cross-referential repetitiousness. "Cow" refers to the woman's sexual organs (punning on the vulgar French term), "caesars" to her breasts, and what they can accomplish together: orgasm ("as a wife has a cow, a love story," in "A Book Concluding with As a Wife Has a Cow. A Love Story" [1926]).

It would be tempting to approach the poem biographically (some people called Stein "Caesar" because she looked like a Roman emperor) and discover a "fatty" Gertrude, a "thin" Alice, and their "Ford" (or "Aunt Pauline"), or the hymeneal ménage of husband-Gertrude and wife-Alice as "jew lady" ("my little Hebrew" was one of Stein's endearing names for Alice). But, as always, biographism adds little to the erotic effect of the poem, beyond the envious titillation of peeping into the joyfully gratified life of two famous lesbian lovers. "Lifting belly" is the poem's major character and single plot: "Lifting belly means me," "Lifting belly is . . . the only spectacle." It is each of the lovers as they engage in their love-making and the reciprocal climax of pleasure itself: "Lifting belly is so kind." Traditionally enough (think of "The Song of Songs," or Shakespeare's sonnets), for Stein, too, sex and love-making are the perfect metaphor for the wondrous complexity of life. The ecstasy of "being existing."

Some of Stein's male colleagues resented her power as a *woman* writer. T. S. Eliot is reported to have once said that Stein's writing

is not improving, it is not amusing, it is not interesting, it is not good for one's mind. But its rhythms have a peculiar hypnotic power not met with before. It has a kinship with the saxophone. If this is the future, then the future is, as it very likely is, of the barbarians. But this is the future in which we ought not to be interested.

There is a "we," associated with the hegemonic culture, and an implicit "other," explicitly identified by race and perhaps obliquely by gender as well ("the sax-ophone" and "the barbarians"). For Eliot, Pound, Wyndham Lewis, and others, the professionalization of poetry at the beginning of the twentieth century, countering the popular poetesses' "embroidery" and the threatening emergence of other traditions, called for the full concentration and total dominion of the (white) masculine genius. "Masculine genius" would even sound somewhat pleonastic.

Stein herself, who around 1909 had read Otto Weininger's *Sex and Character* approvingly, had to transcend being a woman, as well as a Jew, in order to become a genius and a true literary professional. Hadn't she once told Dr. Williams that writing was not really *his* métier? Stein's income had, after all, allowed her to write like a man (though not as a man) and thus escape the condition of a Veblenian bourgeois wife in a consumer culture. However, even as her writing denounces the dominant culture and severely interrogates the literary tradition, what Stein claims above all is a prominent place amongst their "geniuses." The hilariously inscrutable "Patriarchal Poetry" (written in 1927 and never published in Stein's lifetime) can be read as the poet's parodic dissection of the literary construction of the literary tradition in order to earn a place in it. Indeed, Stein succeeded, and the admiration of her work by younger poets is also proof of her achievement. Foremost among these are the so-called L=A=N=G=U=A=G=E poets, whose language and literary experiments pay constant tribute to Stein's work (see volume VIII).

The idiosyncratic work of Charles Bernstein, for example, both his poetry and his scholarly essays, as well as his theoretical reflections, is best understood in light of Gertrude Stein's literary innovations and disruption of tradition. Bernstein's poems combine words in a way that is similar to Stein's provocations of readerly passive comprehension. "There is not a man alive who does not / admire soup. I felt that way myself / sometimes, in a manner that greatly / resembles a plug," begins his "Claire-in-the-Building" (1993). Like art, language is not to say things but to make them with meaning. The Preface to Bernstein's collection of essays, playfully entitled, after Frank Sinatra, *My Way. Speeches and Poems* (1999), opens with a series of questions that parallel the perplexities provoked by Stein's own oeuvre: "What is the difference between poetry and prose, verse and essays? Is it possible that a poem can extend the argument of an essay or that an essay can extend the prosody of a poem? Whose on first, or aren't you the kind that tells?" *My Way*, like an earlier collection entitled *A Poetics* (1992), combines poetry and prose, theory and commentary in such a way that makes the traditional distinctions totally irrelevant. Indeed, the subtitle, *Speeches and Poems*, points to a suspension of poetic conventions that only the authority of the poet's originality justifies ("my way"). An essay on "Stein's Identity" (1996) confirms Bernstein's conception of the poet, in the manner of Stein, as arrogant master-transgressor.

These ideas are shared by Bruce Andrews, co-author (with Bernstein) of
The L=A=N=G=U=A=G=E Book (1984). Both poets conceive of poetry
(or art) as Steinian nonreferential "playing," and write by constantly putting
in question the "correction" of language, or what can or cannot be "correctly"
done with language. The Steinian *thingness* of language is what stimulates these
poets to experiment with linguistic impossibility and poetic deformation and
transformation. The compositions included in Andrews's *Wobbling* (1981) are
fine examples of the poet's radical exploration of "the limits of language." The
title poem, a series of words linked, paradoxically, by their being unyoked
by syntax or semantics, may well bring to mind Stein's anecdote of a reader
using her glasses as a magnifying glass to read word by word. "[R]eading
word by word," says Stein, and Andrews evidently concurs, "makes the writing that is not anything be something." But perhaps the most interesting
experiment with language in America after Stein, whether she considers herself a L=A=N=G=U=A=G=E poet or not, appears in German-born Rosemarie
Waldrop's *A Key into the Language of America* (1994), a dazzling reinvention of
the nation's language based on Roger Williams's book of 1643 with the same
title. By their own insistence on the materiality of language and on exacting
experimentation, L=A=N=G=U=A=G=E poets would no doubt acclaim Stein's
genius enthusiastically in modernist Mina Loy's "Gertrude Stein":

> Curie
> of the laboratory
> of vocabulary
>   she crushed
> the tonnage
> of consciousness
> congealed to phrases
>   to extract
> a radium of the word

Stein often spoke of herself, without irony, as "a genius." "Slowly and in a
way it was not astonishing but slowly," she writes in *Everybody's Autobiography*
(1937) about her increasing self-confidence as an "authentic" artist in the
1910s, "I was knowing that I was a genius and it was happening and I did not
say anything but I was almost ready to begin to say something." And a genius
she was, indeed, in the romantic sense of the ability to encompass and articulate
instantly life, art, time, and the mind as a universal whole (Novalis): Genius,
therefore, conceived of as "reason in her most exalted mood" (Wordsworth),
the finest faculty of the imagination, the most radically inventive capacity
to grasp, interrogate, and transform the world in a singular way, make new
discoveries in science, and create original works of art. Another Steinian word

for "genius" is "entity." As Stein explains in "What Are Master-Pieces and Why Are There So Few of Them," "entity" is the ability *to hear what one says*, rather than *what the audience hears one say*.

Stein's writing is a constant indictment of conformity and consensus as they threaten to become naturalized and seemingly inevitable in language use. "Everybody knows it," she denounces in "Composition as Explanation," "because everybody says it." And yet, "not to know" can be also "troublesome." The singularity, or "authenticity," of "genius" is that, regrettably, and although she writes in, from, and for contemporaneity, the genius has no "contemporaries." "The creator of the new composition in the arts," she states memorably, "is an outlaw until he is a classic." It would be "so very much more exciting and satisfactory for everybody," Stein goes on to argue, "if one [could] have contemporaries, if all ones contemporaries could be ones contemporaries." But the nature of the writing genius is precisely to interrupt and surprise time so that her readers at all times can really *see* what she says. "I once said," we read in "What are Master-Pieces and Why Are There So Few of Them," "that nothing could bother me more than the way a thing goes dead after it has been said." Stein's entire oeuvre is a continuing demonstration of Emily Dickinson's poem that places the beginning of composition-as-life in the spoken and written word ("A word is dead / When it is said / Some say. / I say it just / Begins to live / That day"). The boldest of Stein's exercises in freeing language of fixed meanings may well be "Yet Dish" (written in 1913 and never published in her lifetime). The first of its forty-nine pun-laden fragments of English, "American," and Yiddish reads like this:

> Put a sun in Sunday, Sunday.
> Eleven please ten hoop. Hoop.
> Cousin coarse in coarse in soap.
> Cousin course in soap sew up. soap.
> Cousin coarse in sew up soap.

Deconstruction *avant la lettre*? Or theory (and, for that matter, and quite literally, L=A=N=G=U=A=G=E poetry) confirmed as *posterous*?

2

WILLIAM CARLOS WILLIAMS
IN SEARCH OF A WESTERN DIALECT

CHAPTER 25 of *The Autobiography* (1951) of William Carlos Williams (1883–1963) begins with the following startling remarks about the first two decades of the twentieth century:

These were the years just before the great catastrophe of our letters – the appearance of T. S. Eliot's *The Waste Land*. There was heat in us, a core and a drive that was gathering headway upon the theme of discovery of a primary impetus, the elementary principle of all art, in the local conditions. Our work staggered to a halt for a moment under the blast of Eliot's genius which gave the poem back to academics. We did not know how to answer him.

Later in the book Williams elaborates on this topic in more detail. According to him, during the first two decades of the century young American poets just starting their careers, Williams foremost among them, were experiencing an exhilarating excitement about reinventing art and poetry in America to which the publication of *The Waste Land* (1922) somehow put an end. Evidently, one gathers, after Eliot's classical, erudite, and cosmopolitan gesture, the other young American poets, whose conception of American poetry claimed to have everything to do with a primary understanding of the elemental locality of America as a new nation, did not know what to do about inaugurating a "new order." Even Marianne Moore, one of the poets whom Williams believed to be in the right direction (we might call it the "nativist" or "vernacular" direction), was "no luckier" than all the others.

Williams's disappointment and resentment at the publication of *The Waste Land*, however facetiously expressed, does tell us something about Williams's view of the development of American poetry during this crucial period in literary history, the important role he ascribed to himself in that development, and the greater importance his role might have had but for Eliot's sudden emergence as a poet of success and acclaim. It tells us, too, that poetry and poetry writing, publishing and readership are also a question of power and influence: the poets' power and influence to shape the imagination of the

community, locally and globally, for a common understanding of individual and collective identities. In chapter 30 of *The Autobiography*, Williams returns to the subject of Eliot's interruption of a certain project for American poetry, a project which Williams clearly believed had to be properly localized and situated in the specific American reality. Here is the relevant passage:

Then out of the blue *The Dial* brought out *The Waste Land* and all our hilarity ended. It wiped out our world as if an atom bomb had been dropped upon it and our brave sallies in the unknown were turned to dust.

To me especially it struck like a sardonic bullet. I felt at once that it had set me back twenty years, and I am sure it did. Critically Eliot returned us to the classroom just at the moment when I felt that we were on the point of an escape to matters much closer to the essence of a new art form itself – rooted in the locality which should give it fruit. I knew at once that in certain ways I was most defeated.

Eliot had turned his back on the possibility of reviving my world. And being an accomplished craftsman, better skilled in some ways than I could ever hope to be, I had to watch him carry my world off with him, the fool, to the enemy.

If with his skill he could have been kept here to be employed by our slowly shaping drive, what strides might we not have taken! We needed him in the scheme I was half-consciously forming. I needed him: he might have become our advisor, even our hero. By his walking out on us we were stopped, for the moment, cold. It was a bad moment. Only now, as I predicted, have we begun to catch hold again and restarted to make the line over. This is not to say that Eliot has not, indirectly, contributed much to the emergence of the next step in metrical construction, but if he had not turned away from the direct attack here, in the western dialect, we might have gone ahead much faster.

It was fair enough, I had to admit. But to have the man run out that way drove me mad. I have never quite got over it in spite of Pound's advocacy and the rest of it. *The Criterion* had no place for me or anything I stood for. I had to go on without it.

A few concepts and ideas strike us most in these passages. First of all, the provocative notion that the publication of *The Waste Land* was a "catastrophe" for the American imagination. Second, the belief that the "catastrophe" could not be dissociated from the idea that Eliot had turned his back on "American" poetry. Third, Williams's emphasis on "locality" and the "western dialect", that is to say, the American common scene and the sounds of colloquial American English, as the things that Eliot had forsaken in writing *The Waste Land*. Fourth, Williams's genuine admiration for Eliot as a poet of genius and his ungrudging recognition that Eliot was a superb, indeed a superior craftsman, a fact that makes Eliot's supposed desertion even more unacceptable. After all, Eliot's art of metrical construction was deeply needed, as Williams puts it, to help make the American line over. Eliot's "treason" was evidently that he had lost "contact" with the accomplishments of American technology and industry, thus enumerated by Williams in the third issue of his own little

magazine *Contact* (Spring 1921): "American plumbing, American shoes, American bridges, indexing systems, locomotives, printing presses, city buildings, farm implements and a thousand other things [that] have become notable in the world."

The instant success of *The Waste Land* no doubt nettled Williams as well. Barely a year later, Williams would send Eliot an essay on Marianne Moore for the *Criterion*, which Eliot never even acknowledged. Moreover, Williams writes his *Autobiography* at a time, in the late forties and early fifties, when he himself is already reasonably acknowledged, the winner of various awards and recipient of honorary degrees, a regular college lecturer, and a Fellow of the Library of Congress, but Eliot's reputation as an *American* poet is unparalleled, both in Europe and in the United States. This is even truer of *I Wanted to Write a Poem*, a book of interviews published in 1958, where Williams confesses to having felt that everything he believed in had been "betrayed" by Eliot when "Prufrock" appeared in the pages of Harriet Monroe's *Poetry* in 1915:

He was looking backward; I was looking forward. He was a conformist, with wit, learning which I did not possess . . . I felt he had rejected America and I refused to be rejected and so my reaction was violent. I realized the responsibility I must accept. I knew he would influence all subsequent American poets and take them out of my sphere. I had envisaged a new form of poetic composition, a form for the future. It was a shock to me that he was so tremendously successful; my contemporaries flocked to him – away from what I wanted. It forced me to be successful.

But what most strikes us in Williams's half-comic accusations in *The Autobiography* is his conception of a revival of American art and poetry that Eliot could have had a hand at but failed to participate in, simply by uprooting himself from the American soil. Of course, it is not the fact of Eliot's voluntary exile in London that is at stake here, although that circumstance also has (at least) symbolic relevance. What is really important to note is Williams's assessment of *The Waste Land* as a fine and thoroughly skillful American poem which nonetheless fails to answer to the call of the American idiom and experience in their elementary principles and local conditions.

One is reminded of the famous question Pound addressed to Harriet Monroe at the beginning of the *Poetry* project:

Are you for American poetry or for poetry? The latter is more important, but it is important that America should boost the former, provided it don't mean a blindness to the art. The glory of any nation is to produce art that can be exported without disgrace to its origin.

Not long after this, Williams himself was also challenging Monroe, who had rejected some poems and accepted others after tampering with them as was

her wont, on the proper role of her little magazine in helping to bring about a "revolution" in American poetry. At issue in these and similar exchanges at the time are clearly two rival, though by no means irreconcilable, conceptions of poetry, as Williams's essay on Poe in *In the American Grain* (1925) so well demonstrates: on the one hand, Poetry with a capital "P," a timeless, universal, and transcendent concept; on the other, poetry with a small "p," a contingent, experience-bound, historically situated concept, and hence, seemingly paradoxically, a concept envisaging poetry as capable of true originality and universality. In an important essay entitled "Against the Weather: A Study of the Artist" (1939) and later included in *Selected Essays* (1954), Williams insists that "the universality of the local" is what the "sensuality" of the "world of the artist" manages to achieve. The way Pound, Eliot, and Williams view Edgar Allan Poe in the tradition may, in fact, best clarify for us their divergences of conception and, indeed, commonality of goals. Curiously enough, both Williams and Eliot stress the importance and influence of Poe as a poet, but in strikingly different ways. Pound didn't seem to have much use for Poe, "the cult of Poe" being, as he puts it in his 1914 essay "The Renaissance," "an exotic introduced via Mallarmé and Arthur Symons." For Eliot, on the other hand, Poe is at the root of the poetic tradition he most admires and enjoys. In Eliot's own phrasing, Poe is the "germ" of the "*art poétique*" that "represents the most interesting development of poetic consciousness *anywhere*" (italics added), whose best accomplishments Eliot most applauds in the work of Paul Valéry, and whose demise he mournfully regrets in *From Poe to Valéry* (1948).

For Williams, on the contrary, Poe, "a genius intimately shaped by his locality and time," is the paradigmatic American poet precisely for his deeply felt sense of a "*new locality*" and "genius of *place*" (Williams's emphasis). Williams's "Edgar Allan Poe" sounds at times like a re-writing of Mallarmé's "Le tombeau d'Edgar Poe" on the American side of the Atlantic. For Williams also, Poe is the original poet, *literally* original in his being a poet of the *beginning*, in the sense of "going back to the ground," like Mallarmé's "angel" fallen from the stars, and whose "strange voice" speaks the purity of the "tribe" and grounds the truth of the "soil" – in Williams's own terms, "time" and "locality." "Locality" (the very last word of the essay, except for the closing sentence summing up Poe's poetic excellence in "To One in Paradise") or "local" are repeated at least fifteen times in Williams's short essay, not to mention the use of such related expressions as "place," "ground," "native vigor," "time," "beginning," "fresh beginning." What Poe's theory and practice teach us, according to Williams, is that the newness and originality of American poetry must stem from its locality. This basically implies using a language, that is admittedly not new, in such an "elemental" way as to make it say the "soul" anew. Not surprisingly,

at this point Williams compares Poe's rhythms and figure-like words with Gertrude Stein's playful probings of language (in 1930, Williams's perceptive essay on "The Work of Gertrude Stein" was published in the first issue of Richard John's little magazine, *Pagany*). Again not surprisingly, Williams is very careful to distinguish, after Poe himself, "locality" from "nationality in letters." Pound's letter to Monroe in 1912 comes to mind again ("art that can be exported without disgrace to its origin"). In *Spring and All* (1923) Williams was to say of Poe that he is "[t]ypically American – accurately, even inevitably set in his time."

On the other hand, as a willed, learned, metrically accomplished, and original poem, yet, to Williams's mind, evidently a *placeless* poem in its originality, *The Waste Land* was food for academics and students, rather than "primary impetus" for the renewal of "American" poetry. In other words, in Williams's opinion, *The Waste Land*, having ostensibly divorced itself from America's autochthonous idiom, or "western dialect," and rather "conforming to the excellencies of classroom English" (as Williams was to say later in conversation), was no firm stride toward "the essence of a new [American] art form." If Williams had chosen to evoke Emerson, he might have said of *The Waste Land*, too much craftsmanship merely to court the muses of Europe. Or, if he were inclined to paraphrase Whitman, he might have said, *The Waste Land*, magnificent poem that it is, only proves that Eliot has not heard America sing.

In 1922, when *The Waste Land* first appeared in *The Dial*, William Carlos Williams had already published three slim volumes of poetry – at his own expense, to be sure (*Poems*, 1909, though this was a volume Williams was later to reject; *The Tempers*, 1913; and *Al Que Quiere!*, 1917). Many of his poems had meanwhile been accepted by such influential avant-garde little magazines as *The Egoist*, *Poetry*, *The Poetry Review*, *The Little Review*, and *Others!* To have a sense of what Williams believed, however misguidedly, Eliot's "Prufrock" and *The Waste Land* had interrupted and perhaps jeopardized, we might want to look at an early poem that was to occupy a privileged position in Williams's own view of his evolution as a poet. "The Wanderer: A Rococo Study" was first published in *The Egoist* in 1914, then included, in a slightly revised version, in *Al Que Quiere!* (1917); it eventually stimulated, in Williams's own account in *The Autobiography*, the inspiration, mode, and tone for the poet's later major poetic achievement, the five-book *Paterson* (1946, 1948, 1949, 1951, 1958).

"The Wanderer" is the poem of the poet's advent into poethood, the poem in which the poet finds, or rather, "creates" his place. As a poem of initiation, "The Wanderer" performs a number of identifications that in the end encompass poet, poem, poetry, poetic calling, and the nation, in anticipation, as it were, of *Paterson*, the poem that is a man and a city. The natural environment, the city, the social conflicts, the people, the glories and sorrows of modernity, all have to be grasped and reinvented by the poet for a new poetry to emerge, a poetry that is expected to be universal in its being most localized and situated. For poetic calling, or inspiration, the poem proffers the traditional muse, even if somewhat transfigured. A "she" that is desired before she manifests itself, the feminine "mind" of poetry that becomes the poet's mind of "clarity," the "woman in us that / makes us write," as Williams says in a poem of the same period ("Transitional" [1914]). The woman in the poem is the wanderer made wonder, the surprise of discovery as ageless lover and mother, transgressor and instructor, guide and prophet, inciter and comforter, "harlot" and "mighty." In contrast to Eliot's poetry (as Williams read it), Williams's poetry aims to be a "mirror" to "modernity."

Thus, as early as 1914, "The Wanderer" already establishes the coordinates of all Williams's future poetry: the female principle of poetry, woman as virgin and whore; the poet's Whitmanian grasp of the American reality and myths, as in his ritual immersion in the "filthy" Passaic River that brings him the knowledge of identity ("And I knew all – it became me"); the poet's acute, almost "clinical" awareness of the social scene with all its inequalities, as well as his sad acknowledgment of the dehumanizing effects of capital's exploitation and workers' struggle alike (the grotesque "sagging breasts and protruding stomachs" of the strikers in the bread-line); the personal and the political conspiring to bring poetry about. The year before "The Wanderer" was published, in 1913, Dr. Williams, obstetrician, pediatrician, and general practitioner in Rutherford, New Jersey, had been no doubt aware, in his practice too, of the effects of the strike of silk workers in nearby Paterson, indeed, one of the many workers' strikes that shook the country during the decade ("I was permitted by my medical badge," Williams acknowledges in *The Autobiography*, "to follow the poor, defeated body into [the] gulfs and grottos [of the self and the colloquial language of the people]"). Furthermore, the woman in the poem is also Williams's paternal grandmother, Emily Dickinson Wellcome, who crops up at least twice in *Paterson* and of whose heroic self-fashioning in a harsh country yet a country full of promise Williams has written elsewhere ("Dedication for a Plot of Ground" [1917]; "The Last Words of My English Grandmother" [1924; 1939]), and whose resounding name cannot but have struck the poet's imagination as a good omen for his vocation as well.

"The Wanderer" is thus an example of what Williams thought he had to offer in terms of a poetic project, the poet's primordial *hearing* of modernity in America, before "Prufrock" and *The Waste Land* came to distract and disturb him, and Eliot's sudden success, a success which Williams's dear friend Ezra Pound had militantly helped to make possible, shattered Williams's expectations of leadership in American poetic modernism. He needen't have worried. On the one hand, Eliot and Williams (or Pound) were not desiring or indeed trying to do completely different things as regards poetic form and technique, or even *subject matter*. They were all intent on reinventing poetry for modernity and the machine age, even if not all of them were fully aware, as Hart Crane was, that the first step would be to "acclimatize the machine," or even to conceive of the poem as a "machine made of words," as Williams himself did. On the other hand, if Eliot's influence was unquestionably much stronger immediately and in the decades that followed (although as early as 1932 Williams was already anouncing wishfully in a letter to Kay Boyle that "Eliot is finally and definitely dead – and his troop along with him"), in the sixties and after Williams was duly acknowledged as one of the most innovative, prolific, and versatile of the modernist poets, and easily became a source of inspiration, or proper "sphere," for a wide variety of distinguished poets, such as Charles Olson, Robert Duncan, Louis Zukofsky, Robert Creeley, Allen Ginsberg, Denise Levertov, Robert Lowell, Adrienne Rich, George Oppen, Michael Palmer, and, closer to us, the so-called L=A=N=G=U=A=G=E poets. Long before that, however, the opening imaging that goes on to shape "The Wanderer" can be heard in Hart Crane's *The Bridge* as well: the question about the woman in the dawn which turns the woman into the age-old poetic principle, the flying bird subsuming the principle, the bird's flight as imagination's crossing, bridging, and plunging. Later, Crane's suicidal plunging into the sea in 1932 – the poet's self-destructive gesture in despair of his creativity, as Williams understood it – would also haunt Williams as he wrote *Paterson* I. Sam Patch's leap into the abyss, as if in response to the roaring call of the Falls, in a gesture that dares Tim Crane's flimsy bridge over the chasm, dramatizes Williams's view of poetry as the proper hearing of the local language, as does, in a different way, Mrs. Sarah Cumming's uncanny fall.

Crane and Williams never really got together to exchange ideas on poetry and poetics, as Crane had wished and Williams never felt inclined to do. As a highly praised young poet in the late 1920s, Crane was obviously threatening to Williams. Strangely (or significantly) enough, Williams was later to confess that he didn't quite remember having ever actually met Crane, although they had had "a lively correspondence for a year or so." It seems clear today that the kind of creative harvest that Crane's poetry and craft yield left Williams uneasy. He couldn't tell whether Crane's poetry had captured the rigor and clarity of the "western dialect" ("If what [Crane] puts on the page is related to design, or thought, or emotion – or anything but disguised sentimentality and sloppy feeling – then I am licked and no one more happy to acknowledge it than myself," Williams says in a 1928 letter to Pound). Crane, however, admired Williams's work very much. He would at times resent the older poet's "constant experimentation" seemingly for the sake of experimentation alone, but he found Williams's conceptions regarding American culture and art, particularly as expounded in *In the American Grain* (1925), very congenial. Perhaps too congenial for the integrity of his own imagining of "America" in *The Bridge*, as his letter to Waldo Frank of November 21, 1926 clearly reveals:

> Williams' – American Grain is an achievement that I'd be proud of. A most important and *sincere* book. I'm very enthusiastic – I put off reading it, you know, until I felt my way cleared beyond chance of confusions incident to reading a book so intimate to my theme. I was so interested to note that he puts Poe and his 'character' in the same position as I had *symbolized* for him in the 'Tunnel' section. (Crane's emphasis)

Indeed, the two poets have a great deal in common, namely in the way they both distance themselves from Eliot's views of American culture and problematic role in the development of American poetry.

Williams's obsession with marking his difference from Eliot as an American poet is painfully present in his production of the twenties and particularly explicit in some of the prose poetry of that period. *Kora in Hell: Improvisations* (1920) presents itself as, precisely, an exercise in *improvising* "novelty," as Williams puts it in The Prologue (where he also says provocatively of Pound and Eliot both that they were "content with the connotations of their masters"). Improvising novelty is, therefore, a mode that aims at breaking with the long-established European tradition and decorum, rather than insisting on Eliot's "exquisite" "rehashing" and "repetition," thus opening up the desired space for a genuine American form and diction. There is certainly a freshness in *Kora in Hell* in Williams's bold handling of subjects not usually dealt with in poetry up until then (except by Whitman).

Still, the real novelty of *Kora in Hell* resides not so much in Williams's adoption of vernacular topics and use of colloquial and even vulgar language and funny innuendoes ("When Beldams dig clams their fat hams . . . "), but rather in the strange poetic beauty and rhythm of the prose, and particularly in the very *fiction* of improvisation that structures the text. As Marianne Moore pointed out in her review printed in *Contact* (1921) when the book first came out, Williams's art of "compression, color, speed, accuracy" and "instinctive craftsmanship" is what accounts for his "ability to see resemblances in things that are dissimilar." Pieces that record free and loose imaginal and ideological associations in a densely poetical manner, very often bordering on the surrealistic, are as ostensibly paralleled by prosier, more discursive and reflective pieces purporting to "explain" the previous ones. However, the "explanations," to which Williams refers in The Prologue as "more or less opaque commentar[ies]," in their very sententiousness often border on the surrealistic as well, and do little more than add to the surprise of the fragmentariness, arbitrariness, and inconclusiveness of the poetic experiment. The distinction between "improvisation" (lyric poetry?) and "commentary" (critical prose?) is thus put in question in a way that points forward to the more overt strategy of *Spring and All* (1923). Several other works published mainly in little magazines during the twenties, of which the most interesting one is *The Descent of Winter*, printed in Pound's *The Exile* in 1928, and particularly the more complex and varied hybrid gestures of *Paterson* are also already *in nuce* in *Kora in Hell*. In fact, in *Kora in Hell* commentaries could easily be switched around and made to pair with different improvisations with no major alteration of the work's poetic effect. Here is an improvisation:

Such an old sinner knows the lit-edged clouds. No spring days like those that come in October. Strindberg had the eyes for Swan White! So make my bed with yours, tomorrow? . . . Tomorrow . . . the hospital.

And here is a commentary that could well "belong" to the improvisation just quoted, but does not, in the sense that it is not attached to it, and also in the sense that neither does it properly "belong" to the one it is attached to:

Buzzards, granted their distrusting habits in regard to meat, have eyes of a power equal to that of the eagles'

There are some ironies in relation to *Kora in Hell* by which Williams, who had a fine sense of humor, could not but have been amused. The title, suggested by Pound ("the best enemy that United States verse has"), legitimizes Williams. It renders Williams as fit a subject for academics and the classroom as his two more erudite colleagues. Moreover, by invoking the myth of the rape of Kore (Persephone) – abducted by Hades and half-rescued by her inconsolable mother, Demeter, goddess of fertility, but still compelled to live in the land of the dead one-third of the year – it allows Williams, the self-appointed all-American poet, to fashion himself as an Orpheus-like figure plunging into the abysmal and formless American reality only to return from his discovering catabasis with the authentic poetry of America. And, finally, the self-appointed all-American poet, unlike Pound or Eliot, is really only a second-generation American, born in Rutherford, New Jersey, of English father and Puerto Rican mother of French ancestry, as Pound reminds him in a hilarious letter reproduced in The Prologue. If the "improvisations," of which Pound had read a few as first published in Margaret Anderson's *Little Review*, claimed to be about America, Pound suggests, Williams had better give "some hint" about what he was trying to get at. Williams's problem, according to Pound, was that he didn't know anything about the country: "And America?," Pound cries out, "What the h—l do you a blooming foreigner know about the place. Your *père* only penetrated the edge, and you've never been west of Upper Darby, or the Maunchunk switchback." However, it could be argued that Williams's cultural stance from his early writings, and particularly *In the American Grain*, to *Paterson* amounts to a daring problematization of, precisely, such a unified notion as all-Americanness.

In Williams's next book, *Sour Grapes* (1921), the poet's self-conscious progress in search of the American lyric is quite noticeable. This is no longer Williams's "Keats period," when, by his own account, he wrote only "bad Keats," after having discovered the English romantic poet in his father's Palgrave's *Golden Treasury of English Verse*; but a certain melancholic mood which it would not be totally inappropriate to call Keatsian pervades the entire volume. Time, the inexorable passage of time, and nostalgia for earliness and beginnings make up its major theme: the seasons, the years, the months, day and night, the natural elements and geography, trees and flowers, and even quintessentially romantic nightingales that turn out comically to be the poet's shoes, are summoned to portray the poet as "late singer." The underlying structure of the poet's oblique self-portrayal in *Sour Grapes* is the romantic confrontation of the poetic self with the sublime. But even when the context of the poems is not clearly that of the doctor's physical intimacy with his everyday clinical experience, and often it is ("the round and perfect thighs / of the Police Sergeant's wife / perfect still after many babies"), their mode and bravado, sounds and rhythms are decidedly modernist, as in the Shelleyan reverberations of "January":

> Again I reply to the triple winds
> running chromatic fifths of derision
> outside my window:
> > > Play louder.
> You will not succeed. I am
> bound more to my sentences
> the more you batter at me
> to follow you.
> > > And the wind,
> as before, fingers perfectly
> its derisive music.

Halfway through the volume, a piece in prose that runs a page and a half, titled "The Delicacies," abruptly interrupts the sequence of lyrical poems. Commenting on *Sour Grapes* in *I Wanted to Write a Poem*, Williams says:

"For some reason I included a short prose piece called 'The Delicacies' – an impression of beautiful food at a party, image after image piled up, an impression in rhythmic prose." "Reason" is surely not a good way of putting it, but "straight observation," the expression the poet uses to refer to four flower poems immediately after his perplexity concerning the insertion of "The Delicacies," is quite telling. The piece manages to be an impression, in rhythmic prose, of image piled up on image of beautiful food at a party, as Williams claims, but it is also a representation of the somewhat ludicrous amenities of social life in the bourgeois parlor ("Ice-cream in the shape of flowers and domestic objects: a pipe for me since I do not smoke, a doll for you"), a representation that is slightly and subtly overshadowed by intimations of social needs in the outside world (" . . . it is the little dancing mayor's wife telling her of the Day Nursery in East Rutherford, 'cross the track, divided from us by the railroad . . . "). But mostly the interruption "in rhythmic prose," while going back to the structure of *Kora in Hell*, anticipates rather Williams's great experiment of this period, *Spring and All* (1923). This work, announced as "Poems interspersed with 'disturbed' prose," was evidently meant to be *disturbing*, as was *The Great American Novel* (1923), a parody ("travesty" is Williams's word) of that much-talked-about notion of conventional writing, cleverly set in the technological context of American modernity. In his *Autobiography*, Williams describes *The Great American Novel* as "a satire on the novel form in which a little (female) Ford car falls more or less in love with a Mack truck." However, having both been published in Paris the same year in expensive, limited editions, neither *Spring and All* nor *The Great American Novel* had much circulation or immediate impact.

Spring and All represents Williams's parodic style at its best. Considering the form in which it is presented – some of Williams's most limpid and memorable lyrics framed by provocative non-sequential outbursts of half-meditative, half-critical prose – the thought that comes to mind is that the poet's scattered notes and loose poems on his desk have been blown away by a sudden draft. The next person in the room, perhaps an illiterate cleaning woman, has proceeded to put the papers back on the desk, but the sheets that by chance had landed in the waste basket have been duly discarded. There is no way of knowing how many poems may have disappeared but obviously many prose passages are missing. The end product is just a bunch of loose poems, though carefully numbered from I to XXVII, and a series of chunks of prose, some of the prose passages headed by chapter numbers, now in roman now in arabic figures, all out of order, with one chapter heading even playfully inscribed upside down. It amounts to a display of destructiveness as the source of creativity, and suggests Williams's critical attentiveness to the latest controversies in

America about the European artistic avant-garde, on which Williams also wrote on the pages of *Contact*: the Armory Show of 1913; the visits of Francis Picabia to New York on that occasion and again in 1915; Marcel Duchamp and the scandal of his *Nude Descending a Staircase* and readymades; the impact of Dada; the appearance of the experimental journal *291* (1915–16), inspired by Guillaume Apollinaire's *Les soirées de Paris* (1912–14) (issue no. 1 of *291* carried Apollinaire's *idéogramme* "Voyage").

The iconoclastic prose writing of *Spring and All* is comically disconnected and outrageously violent at times, perhaps Williams's parody of that violence he says "America adores" in "Jacataqua" (*In the American Grain*), but it does yield meanings about life and literature, mostly about literature, that were dear to Williams throughout his life: a half-serious concern with the tradition and literary conventions that insists on bringing back Eliot's ghost ("THE BEGINNING" resoundingly opposing "THE TRADITIONALISTS OF PLAGIARISM"); the imagination as the most destructive thing, as Stevens also says in a less parodic manner; the exhilaration of total erasure or the New World travestied as the clean slate of origin, for which the spring is the best metaphor; oblique allusion to contemporary intellectual issues and controversies (e.g., *The Egoist*'s "Dora Marsden's philosophic algebra"); play with early twentieth-century obsession with typographical form (to which the recent art of advertising added a new dimension); problematization of clear-cut distinctions between prose and poetry, and even more so of distinctions between poetry and not poetry or lyricality and commentary; parody of the rational, well-structured, persuasive essay on life and poetry; demystification of contemporary literary criticism, namely the amusing "vermiculations of S.[hakespeare] criticism." Now and then, a sharp aphorism occurs, such as the following one concerned with the integrity of poetic form: "prose has to do with the fact of an emotion; poetry has to do with the dynamization of emotion into a separate form"; or a fairly solemn statement on the poet's conception of poetry and poetic value: "What I put down of value will have this value: an escape from crude symbolism, the annihilation of strained associations, complicated ritualistic forms designated to separate the work from 'reality' – such as rhyme, meter as meter and not as the essential of the work, one of its words."

The most rewarding part of *Spring and All*, most commentators would agree, consists of a number of amazingly fresh lyrics that do indeed seem to arise out of nowhere if not from the poet's musings on the nature of writing itself (the most anthologized, but not necessarily the most accomplished, of them being "Spring and All" ["By the road to the contagious hospital..."] and "The Red Wheelbarrow" ["So much depends..."]). Dedicated to Williams's friend the painter Charles Demuth, whom the poet had met as a student, along with Pound and H. D., at the University of Pennsylvania, and who was largely responsible for introducing Americans to the European avant-gardes of the early twentieth century, *Spring and All* highlights Williams's lifelong interaction with the other arts, and especially with painting. Many painters find their way into the text, including Marsden Hartley, the American painter with a keen eye for the "common thing" and another friend of Williams's. If a particular feature were to be emphasized in the interspersed lyrics of *Spring and All* it would be no doubt their painterly quality, the color and sharply distinctive shape of the objects (Blake called it, *contra* Sir Joshua Reynolds, "Correct & Definite Outline"). Occasionally, when the poem's setting involves a compassionate look at the sordidness of daily hospital work, the intense visual presence of objects is uncanny, as in Poem IX, where John Marin plays Reynolds to Williams's Blake. "John Marin: skyscraper soup – ," the poem reads early on; and, further down, "beds, beds, beds / elevators, fruit, night-tables / breasts to see, white and blue – / to hold in the hand, to nozzle // It is not onion soup . . . " If most of these lyrics seem to border on ekphrasis and are best read as descriptions of paintings, some even aspire to the very condition of painting, and later will be given painterly titles: "The Pot of Flowers" (II) or "Composition" (XII). The latter, depicting a "red paper box" that is now a sewing kit, now a tool-box filled with trivial odd objects, may well strike the reader as a perfect figure for the entire composition known as *Spring and All*: a portable, usable whole that is irrelevant beyond the tidbits that make it up.

As in Gertrude Stein and Marianne Moore, Williams's attentiveness to avant-garde art is paralleled by his interest in modern science, technology, and Einstein's new physics ("It may seem presumptive to state," Williams was to write to John C. Thirlwall in 1955, "that such an apparently minor activity as a movement in verse construction could be an indication of Einstein's discoveries in the relativity of our measurements of physical matter is drastic enough, but such is the fact"). In Williams also, experiment with form and theme is related to early training and continuing practice in science, and pleasure in absorbing the contradictory textures and speedy paces of material America in his poetry. Some of the poems in *Spring and All* present themselves as fast moving combinations of art, technology, and even finance, with idealized nature and myth. Poem VIII, for example, convenes "sunlight," "song," and "varnished floor" together with "fifty pounds pressure," the "faucet of June," and "Persephone's cow pasture," apparently for no other reason than to invoke J[ohn] P[ierpont] Morgan. The American financier who best represents American capitalism at the beginning of the twentieth century, one of the founders of corporate America, was a supporter of the motor industry and great collector

of old masters, like Veronese or Rubens (and perhaps not so much a Maecenas
for young American artists, the poem seems to imply). John Pierpont Morgan,
Jr., his "son" (with a comic pun on "sunlight"), continues the father's work
in market investments, a reality that is clearly disturbing to the poet but
which he cannot afford not to take into account ("Impossible // to say, impossible / to underestimate – "). Here is the central section of Williams's kinetic
poem:

> When from among
> the steel rocks leaps
> J. P. M.
>
> who enjoyed
> extraordinary privileges
> among virginity
>
> to solve the core
> whirling flywheels
> by cutting
>
> the Gordian knot
> with a Veronese or
> perhaps a Rubens –
>
> whose cars are about
> the finest on
> the market today –

By the end of the 1920s, Williams had evidently reconsidered the effect of
his experiments with genre hybridity, and preferred to sort prose from verse.
Spring and All, for example, was not reprinted in its original form in Williams's
lifetime, although the lyric poems, with titles added then, were included in
all subsequent collections of Williams's poetry. It was reprinted by Frontier
Press in 1970, the same year that it was made part of the collection of *prose*
edited by Webster Schott in the volume titled *Imaginations* (1970), and later
properly included, as *a book of poetry that renders problematic the very notion of
poetry*, in A. Walton Litz and Christopher MacGowan's edition of the first
volume of *The Collected Poems* in 1986. *Collected Poems, 1921–1931*, published
in 1934 by Louis Zukofsky at the Objectivist Press with a Preface by Wallace
Stevens, was Williams's much-longed-for first book of poems after *Sour Grapes*
had appeared in 1921. Some of the excluded prose (which, Williams once said,
"can be a laboratory for metrics") went into Williams's *Selected Essays* (1954),
as was the case with "Notes in Diary Form," taken from *The Descent of Winter*.
Williams's last attempt at prose and improvisations interspersed with lyrical
verse was *The Wedge*; however, with the expert assistance of Louis Zukofsky,

the volume came out (1944, a beautiful Cummington Press edition) with just the lyrics and all the prose reduced to the "Author's Introduction." Adapted from a talk given at the New York Public Library in 1943, when the war was at its peak, Williams's Introduction to *The Wedge* is a prose counterpart to Stevens's Coda to *Notes toward a Supreme Fiction* (1942, also published by the Cummington Press): poetry is not a diversion from the war, both poets, of such different political outlooks, concur; poetry is a different kind of war, a war that never ends.

The composition of *The Wedge*, spreading out from the late thirties, is contemporaneous with Williams's conception of *Paterson*, and includes poems which, together with many short lyrics published in the early forties, are part of what we might call Williams's Paterson Project. All along, Williams had also been writing and publishing novels, short stories, plays, and critical essays, attempting, no doubt, to grasp the whole world about him in the locality of America. But he soon came to the realization that he would only be able to accomplish that much with any degree of profundity in poetry (or "the poem," as he would say). The sequence titled "For the Poem Paterson," from *The Broken Span* (1941), is clearly at the very genesis of *Paterson* (it opens with the well-known prose epigraph: "A man like a city and a woman like a flower – who are in love. Two women. Three women. Innumerable women, each like a flower. But only one man – like a city"). Reading it through carefully we reach the conclusion that the Paterson Project started out by being a project about and an experiment with the lyric, not only Williams's ongoing attempt at making "the line over" but also and mainly his "digging" into the "archaic forms" down into the utmost "bottom" in order to hear, in twentieth-century America, the primordial lyric cry ("digging," "archaic forms," and "bottom" are Williams's own terms in "Against the Weather"). Paterson, the city, was at the beginning a mere mask for the man-poet, whose first avatar is the slightly ridiculed "great philosopher" of Williams's first "Paterson" poem (published in *The Dial* in 1927 and awarded the *Dial*'s Prize for that year).

But even then the man and the city are not easily distinguishable: in a passage that would become later part of *Paterson* I, the city is Mr. Paterson's "thoughts sitting and standing." More decidedly, in the sequence of fifteen numbered poems of "For the Poem Paterson," the city is like the man poet; the woman, like the woman in "The Wanderer," a woman that is many women, all flower-like, and all of them making up the heterosexual man poet's genial muse; the fifteen lyrics that follow seem like attempts at voicing the earliest, most elemental cry of poetry. Here is the first, sprightlier version of "2. Sparrows among Dry Leaves" (the second version, in a far more controlled verse form, appeared later in *The Wedge*):

The sparrows
by the iron fence-post
hardly seen

for the dry leaves
that half
cover them —

stirring up
the leaves — fight
and chirp

stridently
search
and

peck the sharp
gravel
to good digestion

and love's
obscure and insatiable
appetite

In Williams's project, however, Paterson — city, man, and poem — soon becomes the hybrid complexity of theme and form that constitutes the "new locality" that the poet wishes to hear *and* speak (one of his three poems for Horace Gregory in 1941, "The Fight," closes with the phrase "overheard by William Carlos Williams"). Meanwhile, the "new locality" had been absorbing the events in history that caught the concerned attention of Dr. Williams, ever politically alert and of left leanings: the Depression, the Scottsboro Trial, the Spanish Civil War, the rise of Mussolini and Hitler, World War II and its consequences for a mill town like Paterson, NJ, as well as the ongoing debate among artists and intellectuals about the apparent conflict between aestheticism/internationalism and *art engagé*/nationalism. Williams never had any patience with art as propaganda but he always believed that the work of art had to be true to the "place" that "bred" it (as he put it in reviews of Muriel Rukeyser's poetry and Walker Evans's photographs in *The New Republic* in 1938). Until he died, in 1963, Williams went on writing some of the most rhythmical and luminous lyrics of contemporary American poetry, culminating in the acclaimed last collection, *Pictures from Brueghel and Other Poems* (1962), a book that would earn him the Pulitzer Prize just a few months after his death in 1963. A delightful series in the collection, playfully alluding to Williams's lifelong experiments with prosody and caesura, is titled "Some Simple Measures in the American Idiom and the Variable Foot." Poem no. IV,

"The Blue Jay," sings like this, the kinetic enjambement from line 4 to line 5 winking at Marianne Moore's daring verse acrobatics:

> It crouched
> just before the take-off
>
> caught
> in the cinematograph-
>
> ic motion
> of the mind wings
>
> just set to spread a
> flash a
>
> blue curse
> a memory of you
>
> my friend shrieked at me
> – serving art
>
> as usual

Meanwhile, all the exciting and innovative promiscuity of form, style, genre, and even theme, in the manner of Pound's *Cantos*, was being reserved for *Paterson*. However, more so than *The Cantos*, *Paterson* cannot but strike the reader, after Crane's *The Bridge* (and though Williams would have no doubt strongly disliked the association), as the newest epic of the modern (or American) consciousness. On the other hand, like *Leaves of Grass*, *Paterson* would prove to be an ever unfinished poem.

Williams had originally planned a four-book poem, which he did in fact complete in the course of five years, between 1946 and 1951, each book bearing a different title (*The Delineaments of the Giants*, *Sunday in the Park*, *The Library*, and *The Run to the Sea*). When he later decided to add a fifth book, Williams took seven years to rest contented with the results of his efforts, having at some point rejected for that purpose his work on a very remarkable lyrical poem resonant of the Cold War period, a long poem about love (*eros* and *agape*), history, time, and the atomic bomb, which was meanwhile to be published as "Asphodel, That Greeny Flower" (*Journey to Love* [1955]). How the actual Book v (which does not bear an independent title of its own) does or does not fit *Paterson* as a whole organically is still matter for critical debate (whether *Paterson* is at all "organic" is another question). In the last years of his life, Williams started to work on a sixth book. In 1963, the five books of *Paterson* and the fragments of the sixth were first published together, as they still appear in Christopher MacGowan's carefully revised edition of 1992. But *Paterson* v and the scanty four pages we have of *Paterson* vi may well indicate that the Paterson Project was only to attain full poetical fruition in the great lyrics of the fifties included in *Pictures from Brueghel and Other Poems* (1962).

From *The Desert Music* (1954) and *Journey to Love* (1955) onwards, Williams, without forsaking "locality," had managed to sound in the American idiom the purer strains of the primal music of the subject's objectivity which Nietzsche had claimed for lyricality over a century ago in *The Birth of Tragedy*. In 1951, Williams had written to Louis Martz about his search for a "new measure" and how he had been misguided in listening too exclusively to the colloquial measures of present-day America. A contemporary prose translation of *The Iliad*, along with "articles in *The New Mexico Quarterly* and elsewhere," which he had been reading at the time, helped him "'place' the new in its relation to the past much more accurately." In his Preface to the *Selected Essays*, written just three years later, Williams is more precise. He tells of having "discovered certain rules," "ancient rules, profoundly true but long since all but forgotten." The "new measure" is language at the origin of time, the myth of origin that all poetry aspires to be. Of poetry thus conceived, language-as-we-know-it is, according to Emerson, a "fossil." Williams's variable foot and triadic form, which he claims to have discovered while writing Book II of *Paterson*, that is to say, the graphically and rhythmically three-step broken line of the passage that was later to be reprinted as "The Descent" in *The Desert Music*, is how Williams finally hears America sing. A primordial time and tempo which, though it cannot be fully understood outside the "new locality" that voices it in the "western dialect," is not exclusively dependent upon it. We hear it ringing beautifully in "Asphodel That Greeny Flower":

                        All appears
            as if seen
                        wavering through water.
                                We start awake with a cry
            of recognition
                        but soon the outlines
                                become again vague.
            If we are to understand our time,
                        we must find the key to it,
                                not in the eighteenth
            and nineteenth centuries,
                        but in earlier, wilder
                                and darker epochs.

The best introduction to *Paterson* is, together with Williams's remarks on Books I and II in *I Wanted to Write a Poem*, chapter 58 of his *Autobiography*, where the poet also explains why he chose Paterson, and not New York City, for example, "to find an image large enough to embody the whole knowable world about [him]." He had thought "of other places upon the Passaic River" but Paterson "won out." As he explains, at some length, how Paterson won out, we understand that Paterson, the situated city, with its "falls, vocal, seasonally vociferous," as it speaks the nation from colonial times onwards, and in its being in turn spoken by the poem, *Paterson*, becomes indistinguishable from the city in the poet's no less situated voice. "I had taken part in some of the incidents that make up the place," the poet claims,

I had heard Billy Sunday: I had talked with John Reed: I had in my hospital experiences got to know many of the women: I had tramped Garret Mountain as a youngster, swum in its ponds, appeared in court there, looked at its charred ruins, its flooded streets, read of its past in Nelson's history of Paterson, read the Dutch who settled it.

In the city's busy noises and images heavy with time and pregnant with meaning, as well in the reverberating roar of the Passaic Falls, the poet hears at last the sounds and rhythms that make possible American poetry, the new speech that he himself speaks, the many registers of the multivocal western dialect of the history of America he had been in search of ever since "Prufrock" and *The Waste Land* supposedly distracted him some twenty years ago. "Paterson: The Falls," another poem included in *The Wedge* that explicitly refers to the conception and structure of the future *Paterson*, begins by asking a question about language, later repeated in *Paterson* I, and replying to it unhesitantly with poetry writing itself ("What common language to unravel? / The Falls, combed into straight lines / from that rafter of a rock's lip. Strike it! the middle of // some trenchant phrase, some / well packed clause . . . ") and then builds a subject matter around the natural places, sights, and sounds, as well as the historical sites, scenes, and characters that make up modern America, only to conclude with poetry's capacious ear generously opening itself up to the "roar" of the country's being (Dickinson's "just an ear" to the heavens' huge "bell" can't but come to mind ["I felt a funeral in my brain"]). One can see why the historical-poetical essays of *In the American Grain* make for enlightening parallel reading to *Paterson*.

In *Paterson*, the strikingly original lyrics that make up the consciousness of the modern poet's epic are constantly being interrupted by prose fragments, often written by Williams himself but more frequently his adaptation of documents with factual information or personal opinions and feelings, whether letters from poets and friends (John Thirlwall, Edward Dahlberg, Ezra Pound, Marcia Nardi, Allen Ginsberg), pieces of news or articles from newspapers, excerpts from historical tracts (including a passage from Columbus's journals), financial ads, medical case reports, census data, statistics, which together bring alive the physical, palpable existence as well as the intelligible reality of the city/nation. Geography, history, religion, politics, economy, the rise of capitalism, the challenge of communism, social unrest, local anecdotes, Indian lore and the plight of Native Americans, the woman's question, forms of public events and images of domesticity, the shared ideas of the community and the private opinions or sentiments of individuals, as well as Dr. Williams/Paterson's and the poet's life trajectory – all combine to highlight the poetry and, at the same time, as in *Spring and All*, to make problematic the distinctions between poetry and not poetry, reality and the imagination, life and art, word and thing. As the Passaic runs through Paterson, the city, so this aspect of Williams's poetics runs like a river all along *Paterson*, the poem, and is heavily underscored in Book v by the insertion, at the end of section II, of an amusing dialogue between the poet and his interviewer on what is or is not poetry. That the lyrics themselves, while firmly holding the poem together, are often related to documentary sources, though not always or necessarily those printed closest to them in the poem, only adds to Williams's problematization of the poetic process throughout the entire work. The note at the end of Book I, taken from John Addington Symonds's *Studies of the Greek Poets*, on the ancients' preoccupation with balance between "meter" and "common speech," is a commentary on Williams's conception of *Paterson*. Another, much more subtle commentary is the period mark, which, as later in Robert Duncan (theorized as the "stress" of "silence" in the Introduction to *Bending the Bow* [1968]), punctuates the entire poem. Christopher MacGowan tells us that these "periods" indicate omissions from Williams's earlier drafts, but in the graphic materiality of the poem as a work of art they function rather as a kind of emphatic suspension dots that bespeak the Poundian condensation (*dichten*) of the poetic. The powerful effect of Williams's poetic method in *Paterson*, whether we like it or not (apparently, John Thirlwall and Edward Dahlberg never did), is the suspension of the abyss, dreaded of all poets, between word and thing. "I have been actively at work . . . in the flesh," Williams had written in the early 1930s, "watching how words match the act, especially how they come together."

Predictably in a heterosexual male poet of his age, class, and upbringing in the first half of the twentieth century, Williams's conception of his poem of the "new" locality is explicitly and stereotypically gendered, as are his images, metaphors, and language. Williams's "universal," like Eliot's or Pound's (whether altogether unlike contemporary women modernist poets' remains to be seen), depends heavily on the particulars of the subsuming male principle. Thus, right at the beginning of *Paterson*, the city or culture is Paterson, the man, whereas the mountain or nature is the woman. But the man, or culture, encompasses the woman, or nature, as we learn in "The Delineaments of the Giants." One giant is the city-as-man-as-poet; the other is the mountain-as-woman-as-muse (or the American soil, like Crane's Pocahontas). At the beginning of Book II ("Sunday in the Park"), we read:

> The scene's the Park
> upon the rock,
> female to the city
>
> – upon whose body Paterson instructs his thoughts
> (concretely)

Masculinity is physical strength, action, intellectual power, and prowess; femininity is physical passivity and vulnerability, in need of male protection, and intellectual openness as stimulus for the male mind. In *Paterson* I–IV, and even more so in *Paterson* V and the later poems in *Pictures from Brueghel* that are so close to *Paterson* V in conception and subject matter, we learn that man's imagination yields the aggressive daring of creativity, invention, and ever renewed discovery; whereas the best that woman's imagination can yield is constancy and forgiveness. Which is not to say that there are no disruptions of this neat imaginal and ideological pattern, as witness the use Williams makes of Marcia Nardi's letters to himself in the poem. Moreover, if Paterson/Williams is the Odysseus-like poet constantly reinventing himself in his wanderings, to conceive of the woman-his-Penelope the poet needs constantly to reinvent his imagining of her – not merely the faithfully expectant wife, though her also, but the woman who wields power like a man, and so challenges him even as she inspires and arouses him ("Curie : woman (of no importance) genius : radium / THE GIST" – *Paterson* IV): Beautiful Thing, the erotic object of desire that is parallel to the poet's creative urge; Marie Curie, the woman scientist who turns pitchblende into luminous radium, just as the poet turns Paterson, the city, into *Paterson*, the poem ("the radiant gist that / resists final crystallization"); Sappho, the woman poet whose very life and work suspend the conventional distinction between "masculine" and "feminine"; Gertrude Stein, who makes "vocables" dance in her "writings"; Emily Dickinson Wellcome, Williams's paternal grandmother, in whose brave life and daring language his imagination captured the very source of poetry as the "sensuality" of the "poet's world."

As *Paterson* V reaches its closure and Paterson, the poet, has grown "older," all forms of art seem to inundate the poem – Brueghel's "authentic" painting; the melodious texture of Chaucer's writing; the embroidery of the ancient tapestries in the Cloisters which provided Williams with his basic theme of life and poetry, the Unicorn-poet betrayed by the Virgin-sham-of-innocence – only to culminate in the figure of dance, the measure that sums up Williams's definition of poetry and finally discovers *Paterson* as a whole as ingenious choreography:

> We know nothing and can know nothing
> but
> the dance, to dance to a measure
> contrapuntally,
> Satyrically, the tragic foot.

Although Williams's most-quoted phrase is "no ideas but in things," what *Paterson* ends up saying in its deft collage of sounds, rather than images, is "no poetry but in the rhythms of language."

3

H. D.

A POET BETWEEN WORLDS

UGH Kenner once said that to identify H. D. (Hilda Doolittle [1886–1961]) as an imagist poet would be the same as to select a few of the shortest pieces in *Harmonium* (1923) and make them stand for the life's work of Wallace Stevens. However, as one would not wish lightly to dismiss "The Snowman," "Fabliau of Florida," or "The Anecdote of the Jar," neither would one want to slight the importance for the literary history of American modernism of H. D.'s emergence as "H. D., Imagiste" on the pages of Harriet Monroe's *Poetry: A Review of Verse*, in January 1913. Although a very young Hilda Doolittle had already used the initials as a signature (to sign an early letter to William Carlos Williams), it was Ezra Pound's privilege (according to H. D. herself in *End to Torment* [1979, written in 1958]) to make them famous by thus presenting the author of the three poems which he, in his capacity of foreign correspondent, sent off to the little magazine in Chicago in October 1912.

This graphic gesture – Hilda Doolittle reinscribed and thus reinvented as H. D. – can be seen as a dramatization of the "impersonal," "objective" poetics of modernism, which Pound and Eliot were soon to conceptualize and theorize. Pound, H. D., and Eliot were then living as expatriates in London, a city teeming with little magazines, poetry readings and exchanges, poetic gatherings in tea-and-bun-shops or at The Poetry Book Shop of Harold Monro (*Poetry Review*). Pound, always in the limelight of the poetic scene in London, was determined to influence the course of American poetry in the United States by getting the avant-garde work of his friends and his own published in poetry journals back home. H. D. had recently met the young poet Richard Aldington, whom she was shortly to marry. H. D. and Aldington, who had also been struck by the revival of classical studies at the turn of the century and shared a keen interest in ancient Greece, had been busy exchanging poems and comparing translations of Greek poetry.

The poems by this new American poet that were published in the second issue of *Poetry* – "Hermes of the Ways," "Priapus, Keeper-of-Orchards" (later retitled "Orchard"), and "Epigram: After the Greek," generally announced as "Verses, Translations, and Reflections from 'The [Greek] Anthology'" – can be said to perform to perfection the conception, soon to be developed by Pound, of an imagist poem as being presided over by "an image" embodying an "intellectual and emotional complex in an instant of time" ("A Few Dont's by an Imagist," included in the March 1913 issue of *Poetry*). Elsewhere, Pound further defines "an image" as a "radiant node or cluster" of "luminous detail." If, regardless of the less distinguished course of imagist poetry in the hands of other poets of the "movement" (Richard Aldington, F. S. Flint, John Gould Fletcher, Amy Lowell), the "image" was to remain always "vital" for Pound, the same can be said of H. D. Although for years she was annoyed at being too closely identified with the "imagist" label, later in life she would recognize the importance of that earlier conception for her own identity and development as a poet. All her life, in her poetry and self-probing (rather than merely self-indulgent) autobiographical prose, H. D. strove to conjure up the energy, economy, and stark precision – or "vortex" – that would make her lyric poems "breathe" (we might say after Emily Dickinson). As in Pound, in H. D. the lyric had to be reinvented as a new complex of individual sensibility, personal commitment, historical depth, and mythical density.

There are other affinities between Pound and H. D., beyond the romantic fact of their youthful engagement in Pennsylvania around 1909. For both, poetry was a solemn vocation. They were both serious artists who admired and respected each other. They both conceived of poetry as a way of achieving social change: Pound as an indefatigable intellectual activist and cultural educator, H. D., in a more personal and intimate way, as a subtle and troubled questioner of the culture and the tradition, and the hegemonic (male) intellect, imagination, and sensibility that sustained them. And they both succeeded in giving epic dimension to the lyric mode, Pound in his *Cantos*, H. D. in *Helen in Egypt* (1960), her own "cantos," as she called them after Norman Holmes Pearson. But there are many differences, too, between these two highly gifted American poets in Europe, writing in English at the beginning of the twentieth century, at a time of revolutionary changes in the various fields of cultural and social life. Assumptions about the individual and collective identities of men and women, long taken for granted in the hierarchical order of the patriarchal tradition, were being challenged by science and technology, the intensification of commerce, and the unprecedented acceleration of travel and communication. By suddenly upsetting notions of which tasks could go on counting as private or public, domestic or political, the Great War was to highlight all these changes in a brutal way.

Perhaps the most important difference between Pound and H. D. was the obvious one: gender. H. D.'s intense emotional and erotic attachment to Frances Josepha Gregg at the time of her amorous and poetic involvement with Pound, as well as Gregg's and Pound's "betrayal" by becoming also romantically involved, may have played a role in the woman poet's understanding of herself as a poet, and not just as a muse who also writes poetry. Theoretically, both Pound and H. D. would agree, sexual difference was irrelevant for the *art* of poetry. They would both, no doubt, endorse Nietzsche's view of the lyric poet as "objective," but they would add Sappho to Archilochus as examples of what is meant by "poetic objectivity" ("Direct treatment of the 'thing,' whether subjective or objective," F. S. Flint recommends in the March 1913 issue of *Poetry*). Nonetheless, as poets and intellectuals in a changing world, both H. D. and Pound had to deal with the fact that "being a man" or "being a woman" was changing rapidly in the culture at large. The way H. D. perceived the affinities and differences between Pound and herself can be found in her memoir of their relationship, *End to Torment* (written in 1958, when Pound was still in St. Elizabeth's Hospital). "[Pound] wanted to make them [women artists], he did not want to break them; in a sense, he identified himself with them and their art." Two worlds, male and female, are implied in H. D.'s phrasing, as are the dangers, for women, and the rewards, for men, of crossing them. Art transcends these two worlds, but it is not genderless, let alone sex-less, as the beautiful poem of her old age, "Winter Love" (1972, written in 1959), so movingly acknowledges. Lyric poetry speaks the poet's solitude, and so in the end the woman poet cannot but feel that she is "deserted utterly." But she knows that love alone "kindles the flame." The best account we have of H. D.'s determination to be recognized by the dominant culture as a self-fashioned poet *who is a woman*, is her own record of her sessions of psychoanalysis with Sigmund Freud in Vienna in the mid thirties, which she wrote in London during the Second World War: *Tribute to Freud* (1956), originally titled "Writing on the Wall," and "Advent" (the latter was assembled from her original notes made during the first weeks of her first analysis with Freud in March 1933 and was not published until the second edition of *Tribute to Freud* in 1974).

H. D. saw Freud on two different occasions (in the spring of 1933 and late fall of 1934), both as an analysand and as a student of psychoanalysis. She saw several other psychoanalysts in the course of her life (Havelock Ellis, Mary Chadwick, Hanns Sachs, Walter Schmideberg, Erich Heydt), but the really important encounter was with Freud, to whom she was referred by Hanns Sachs (the psychoanalyst of her friend and lifelong supporter, the historical novelist Bryher [Winifred Ellerman]). The letters she addressed to several friends at the time give further information on the extent to which H. D.'s exchange with Freud was crucial to help her redefine and confirm her role as a woman poet. Her sessions with the distinguished and famous Professor, particularly their discussion of her dreams, perceptions, and visions, clarified for her her understanding of the hegemonic culture and its pervasive sexism, however subtly sexism might present itself in the context of an intellectual relationship between a renowned male scientist and a woman student and patient of great talent and means. The pattern had been there before, when Ezra was the poet-teacher and Hilda the tree nymph, or "dryad" (as Pound called her), who suddenly started producing poems of her own.

As she learned with Freud, being a woman poet eventually meant, for H. D., to reconcile herself with her Moravian mother, Helen Wolle Doolittle, a musician and an artist who had sacrificed her talents for her husband and children, and whose example of self-abnegation H. D. did not wish to follow. But however apt as a model her scientist father might have been for her (Charles Leander Doolittle, a mathematician and an astronomer at the University of Pennsylvania, became the Director of the Flower Astronomical Observatory in 1895), during all her life and poetic career H. D. was in search of the female model, or muse, that would justify her and her dedication to her work as a poet. When, in "Writing on the Wall" (1945–46), later published as *Tribute to Freud* (1956), she wrote that "the mother is the Muse, the Creator," she was fully aware of how much she had disappointed her father by not becoming the "Madame Curie" he had wanted her to be. Although, as she perceived the Doolittle household, she was her father's favorite (her mother's was H. D.'s brother Gilbert), it was the artist-mother she longed for, not the scientist-father. And yet, the two are inextricably linked together in her poetic self-creation, or "legend," as she terms it. In *Tribute to the Angels* (1945), written the same year as "Writing on the Wall," the poem's persona asks midway through the alchemical process that transmutes her into a poet: "what is this mother-father / to tear at our entrails? // What is this unsatisfied duality / which you can not satisfy?"

H. D.'s insistence, in her account of her analysis with Freud, that "The Professor was not always right" points clearly to her rejection of Freud's theory of male primacy and female secondariness. *Tribute to Freud* records H. D.'s reinvention of the mother as muse, woman as bearer of light. H. D understands her "dream of the Princess," with *Moses in the Bulrushes* from the illustrated Doré Bible in its background, to mean, ultimately, that she as the dreamer contains in herself all the other figures and signs: Miriam, who brought the baby to be saved; the Princess, who will find, protect, and shelter the baby like a real mother; the baby Moses himself, the founder of a new religion; and the dreamer, the bearer of the language, or poetry, that reconciles and speaks all meanings.

In "The Master," a poem probably written in 1935 but never published in her lifetime, H. D. comes to terms with her admiration for Freud's intelligence, knowledge, and wisdom, on the one hand, and, on the other, her disappointment at the Professor's incapacity to overcome and denounce the gender prejudice in the science and culture of the time. Paradoxically (or perhaps appropriately, given the ideological stereotypes of the culture), it is through the thwarted "wisdom" of the old "beautiful" male sage that the woman rediscovers she is a poet with a mission ("he . . . set me free to prophesy"). It is through his wisdom and in spite of his wisdom that she knows that *woman is perfect* and lacks nothing (the same "message" is charmingly conveyed in the children's story *The Hedgehog* [1936] written about the same time). The triumphant, speaking authority of the Professor (Sigmund = Sieg Mund; Freud = Freude, she playfully muses in *Tribute to Freud*) reveals and justifies for H. D. her own personal career as a woman poet, reconciler of different worlds and words. Although the personal and historical course of H. D.'s life was to make her falter many times and even paralyze her with writer's block, this poetic conception was there from the very beginning.

Of the three H. D. poems sent to *Poetry* by Pound from London in October 1912, only "Epigram" was to be excluded from her first collection of poetry, *Sea Garden* (1916), perhaps because in this short lyric the "image" affects exquisitely only by its very absence, or abstraction – the death of beauty and music. "Hermes of the Ways" (the poem supposedly trimmed down by Pound before being sent out) plays deftly with the mirror-image of the ample ways of nature: on the one side, sea, wind, and sand; stream, trees, and fruits; the magical joining of "sea-grass" and "shore-grass" – and, on the other, the wanderer-messenger, he "of the triple path-ways," Hermes Trismegistus and Psychopompos. But "Orchard," H. D.'s hymn to Priapus, is by far the most effective of the three, and the one that best contains, in the bud as it were, the modernist theory and practice of her entire poetry. The "image" is the phallic god himself, embodying, in the poem's spare, terse diction and classical resonance, the age-old complex articulation of life and death, love and violence, pleasure and pain, Keatsian abundance and imminent destruction: "This is the sort of American stuff" (Pound wrote to Monroe, in his cover letter from London) "that I can show here and in Paris without its being ridiculed. Objective – no slither; direct – no excessive use of adjectives, no metaphors that won't permit examination. It's straight talk, straight as the Greek!"

The publication of these poems by H. D. in *Poetry* in January 1913 and the arrival of Francis Picabia in New York that same month, just before the opening of the Armory Show, may be seen as an interesting coincidence in the history of American poetry. At exactly the same time that American poets were sailing for Europe in search of the newest manifestations of the most ancient tradition, European avant-garde artists were arriving in the United States determined to find in the American machine – and mass-culture's mixture of primitivism and technology – justification for their escape from tradition and confirmation of the necessary renovation and reconceptualization of art. Marcel Duchamp and his "ugly" readymades were very much part of the American scene that Eliot, Pound, and H. D. apparently wished to escape. And yet, H. D.'s choice of "rough-hewn," "unbeautiful" Priapus is a curious one, and what the poet insistently asks of the oversexed god in return for her "offering" even more so: "spare us from loveliness," "spare us from the beauty / of fruit trees," "spare us from loveliness." Though in a completely different register, H. D.'s rejection of "beauty" and "loveliness" has the same desentimentalizing motivation and effect, vis-à-vis the ornate and florid poetry of late Victorian poets, that the debunking provocations of Picabia's "New Art" were trying to achieve in the visual arts. But while the "anti-Art artists" were looking for inspiration in the sharp aggressiveness of modern quotidian objects, H. D. was construing her own peculiar vision of the "old Greeks," often by translating them from the Greek Anthology, in search of new synthetic meanings for a fast changing world. In a much later poem, written during the Second World War ("May 1943"), H. D., who almost thirty years earlier had also witnessed the ravages of the Great War, sees the poet in herself as the "mender" of "a break in time." The hyphenated epithets that often sprinkle her poems speak eloquently to this desire to bridge rifts in time, space, and mores.

"Orchard" combines a harsh, "unbeautiful" version of the "Greeks" with paradise lost reimagined, and writes anew the myth of the origin of life and its first curse, the death that comes with it. The "first pear / as it fell" resonates with the first pair fallen from edenic bliss, as the "son of the god [Dionysus]," to whom the poem's prayer is addressed, cannot fail to invoke the Christian son of God, Christ the Savior. The lush autumnal imagery of harvest time is literally imagery of the fall as well, which defiantly flouts redemption ("fallen hazel-nuts, / stripped late of their green sheaths," "berries / dripping with wine, / pomegranates already broken," "shrunken figs"). Save us from "loveliness," the poet provocatively pleads, and take this "fallen" fruit "as offering," she bargains. The gap between antiquity and modernity, and between the Greek and the Judeo-Christian traditions (pagan living and divine transcendence), is bridged by the heretical cult of the uncouth, hyphenated "rough-hewn" god of sex, in whom the myth of salvation is suspended. But since the poem is interrupted at its closure by the act of offering itself, before the god is given the opportunity to answer, hope (or meaning) is not altogether precluded. After all, the "quinces" are brought "untouched," as if offering themselves for the repetition of that first fruit-bite in the original garden, perhaps promising a new outcome. Could *agape* and *eros* ever be reconciled? Or, as Stevens, in "Sunday Morning" (1915), formulates this same question, to which however he gives an unequivocally earthier reply, "Shall our blood fail? Or shall it come to be / The blood of paradise? And shall the earth / Seem all of paradise that we shall know?"

The oxymoronic mode of the title of H. D.'s first book of poems, *Sea Garden*, repeats itself in the titles of several poems in the book ("Sea Rose," "Sea Lily," "Sea Poppies," "Sea Violet," "Sea Iris") and prepares the reader for the strange creativeness of the clashes of words that characterize this poetry. "Sea Rose," the poem that opens the collection, presents an image of the rose that is the reverse of what is traditionally associated with this symbol-laden flower. Rather than imposingly beautiful and seductive, sweet of scent, and lush of petal and leaf, H. D.'s "sea rose" is "harsh" and "acrid," "meagre" and "stunted." And yet, this "marred," unbeautified rose, the poem insists, is more "precious" and sensuous than all the others. The sexual innuendoes are clearly there. The rose, a traditional symbol of love, sexuality, and the female body, is "flung on the sand" and "lifted / in the crisp sand." It is as if Blake's romantic rose were found even more inebriatingly valuable after the worm made her "sick" (Blake's rose will often appear again in H. D.'s later poetry). As in the culture at large, in poetry too, sexual identifications and proprieties are in a state of fluctuation.

> Rose, harsh rose,
> marred and with stint of petals,
> meagre flower, thin,
> sparse of leaf,
>
> more precious
> than a wet rose
> single on a stem —
> you are caught in the drift.
>
> Stunted, with small leaf,
> you are flung on the sand,
> you are lifted
> in the crisp sand
> that drives in the wind.
>
> Can the spice-rose
> drip such acrid fragrance
> hardened in a leaf?

The angry voice in another poem in *Sea Garden*, "Sheltered Garden," could belong to this harsh sea rose entrapped in the wrong kind of beauty, caught by a "beauty without strength" that "chokes out life." "I have had enough. / I gasp for breath," the poem begins, and the urgency of this impatience ("I have had enough") is repeated in the third stanza. The irritated statement is justified by a description of the loathed "[good] place" of "scented pinks" and fruit "protected from the frost," on the one hand, and a projection of the voice's defiant utopia of "a new beauty / in some terrible / wind-tortured place," on the other. Again, the ideal of beauty and desirability is being put upside down. Firmly rejected is the sheltered garden of paradise, where images of life seem perversely perfect in their arrested ripeness ("pears wadded in cloth, / protected from the frost, / melons, almost ripe, / smothered in straw . . . "). Rejecting the life that is contained in perfection and completion, or what Stevens calls, in "Credences of Summer" (1942), the "barrenness / Of the fertile thing that can attain no more," the voice in "Sheltered Garden" craves rather the violence and destruction that come with the full power of lived experience. The wind becomes the dominant image, but not the romantic "corresponding breeze" of gentle cross-fertilization between nature and poet's imagination. Rather, "Sheltered Garden" presents the wind as the poet's own imagination engaging in "valiant" fight with nature to understand its function anew:

> I want wind to break,
> scatter these pink-stalks,
> snap off their spiced heads,
> fling them about with dead leaves –
> spread the paths with twigs,
> limbs broken off,
> trail great pine branches,
> hurled from some far wood
> right across the melon-patch,
> break pear and quince –
> leave half-trees, torn, twisted
> but showing the fight was valiant.

The poem's imagery unveils an underlying narrative of gender difference and the desire to transcend the binary conception. The poem clearly rejects the "feminine" beauty of sweet-scented pinks, the stereotypically predictable and socially sanctioned beauty of decorous femininity. The poet's prayer to Priapus in "Orchard" was also aimed at sparing the poet from the suffocating sentiment of such "loveliness." The beauty that the poem craves is the "masculine," unsentimental, resin-scented beauty of rough strength, sharp boldness, and power. But though the poem ends by wishing to "blot out" and "forget" "this garden," the poet has to go on imagining and writing it by continuing to use such concepts as "garden," "beauty," "scent." Moreover, in forgetting there is much remembrance, as Crane reminds us; blotting out is not the same as erasing utterly, and H. D. knew all about scrapbooks and palimpsests (her own three-layered novel *Palimpsest* was published in 1926). What the poem ultimately wants is the dynamic inclusiveness of beauty *with* strength, a garden redolent of astringent aromas, a beautiful place exposed to the wonderful terribleness of life. But what the poet as mender of rifts could often accomplish in her poetry was perhaps harder to reach in the woman's social and personal life – not to mention the difficulty of reconciling the two, woman and poet. It comes as no surprise that H. D. saw herself sometimes as "a between-worlds person."

At the beginning of the twentieth century, it had become more difficult than ever before to be a woman in a man's world, precisely because all three – woman, man, and world – were being transformed in many subtle and complex ways. H. D.'s troublesome "free" marriage to Aldington ended disastrously only a few years after their wedding in 1913 (although they did not actually get a divorce until 1938); her miscarriage in 1915 had deeper consequences for their relationship beyond the sad loss of their child; the exhilaration of her intense spiritual relationship with D. H. Lawrence after 1914 ended in utter disappointment and frustration in 1918; her experience of motherhood and her relationship with Perdita, the daughter she had in 1919 with musicologist Cecil Gray (who never took any responsibility for either mother or daughter), were never easy to internalize; nor was H. D. ever comfortable with her bi-sexuality, whether in body or in mind. The appearance of Bryher in her life at this time was a blessing. H. D.'s brother had been killed in the last few months of the Great War, and her father died, presumably from the shock, shortly afterwards. When H. D. was most in physical and emotional need, Bryher brought back to her the reassurance of love, admiration, and compan-ionship (*eros* and *agape*), and offered her the peace of mind and easy comfort that caring generosity and a very large fortune can provide. In the Isles of Scilly, during her healing trip with Bryher in 1919, H. D. had her "jelly-fish" or "bell-jar" experience, one of the visonary experiences on the conditions of artistic consciousness that she would later discuss with Freud. The notes she wrote about it at the time are themselves like "flickering lights" that read like a meditative prose poem in the process of creating itself ("Notes on Thought and Vision" [1982; written in 1919]). Musing about life and poetry, body and mind, male and female, creativity and eroticism, thought and feeling (or, as she puts it, "Sphynx" and "Centaur"), H. D. expresses a hard-earned under-standing of life's extremes of joy and pain as inspiration, to which her poetry had already been pointing from the very beginning: "If you cannot be seduced by beauty, you cannot learn the wisdom of ugliness." This "wisdom" the poet had already grasped in "Cities," the poem at the closure of *Sea Garden*. Here, too, beauty and hideousness, "honey" and the "seething life" of larvae make up the inescapable reality of existence.

H. D. tells the story of her painful war years in "Madrigal," an autobiographical and historical record of the period that reads like a *roman à clef*. Written and revised over a number of years, including the Second World War, it was only published in 1960 as *Bid Me To Live*. The book traces the intricate emotional and sexual, as well as poetical and intellectual relationships among H. D., Aldington and the women he was involved with, Lawrence, Pound, John Cournos, and Cecil Gray. Aldington entered the army in 1916, and perhaps the single most important factor in H. D.'s changing perception of life at this time was the effect of the war on her husband. Intensely personal as her fictionalized memoir is, in *Bid Me To Live* H. D. is, like Virginia Woolf, acutely aware of the role of history, and war in particular, in giving meaning to, while shattering, people's lives ("The past had been blasted to hell, you might say; already, in 1917, the past was gone. It had been blasted and blighted, the old order was dead, was dying, was being bombed to bits, was no more").

Bid Me To Live parallels H. D.'s poetic production of the years 1916–21. Her poems of these years best speak of the impact of experience on her development as a poet. After her "imagiste" emergence in Monroe's *Poetry* in 1913 and *Sea Garden* in 1916, her second volume of verse, *Hymen* (1921), begins to strike a stronger narrative and mythmaking note. The same is even truer of the collections that followed, *Heliodora* (1924) and *Red Roses for Bronze* (1931). Although what H. D. once wrote in a letter to John Cournos remains valid throughout her poetic career and should give her readers pause ("I do not put my personal self into my poems"), after *Sea Garden* her poems begin gradually to tell the story of *her persona* as a woman poet finding a credible voice in a time of social and personal turmoil. The war trilogy, published separately in the 1940s (*The Walls Do Not Fall*, 1944; *Tribute to the Angels*, 1945; *The Flowering of the Rod*, 1946), *Helen in Egypt* (1960), "Winter Love" (written in 1959), and *Hermetic Definition* (1972) present the culmination of this poetic process of mythic self-discovery and self-narration. All these later poems depend, for their effect, on H. D.'s construction of a female persona that has to cope with a powerful male imagination, whether as regards the conception of poetry sanctioned by the tradition or the male poets she admired and loved (Pound inspires "Winter Love," as Saint-John Perse inspires *Hermetic Definition*). These poems also reflect H. D.'s increasing interest in the occult and hermetic traditions in search of a transcendent and absolute meaning beyond the merely aesthetic.

H. D. dedicated *Hymen* to Bryher and Perdita. The dedication poem opposes love to ruthlessness and celebrates the healing power of kindness and compassion against the callous indifference sprung from war and death. The title poem, a modernist combination of verse and prose which H. D. was to resort to again in *By Avon River* (1949) and *Helen in Egypt* (1960), appears immediately after the dedication. The masque-like epithalamium that alternates melodic lyrics with narrative stage directions prolongs the celebration of the dedication poem in a symbolic bridal ceremony of music, dance and beautiful song (the word "symbolic" is repeated more than once in the prose passages). The figures are all female, except for the flame-like "tall youth" and his "band of [singing] boys" that make their appearance at the end. Tall, dignified, queen-like matrons sing the opening song of salutation promising a gift "beyond the cry of Hymen"; young maidens and "boyish" little girls praise the bride's beauty and sing bridal farewell songs, but the sadness of loss is tempered by the beauty of the ceremonial celebration. The flower imagery is delicately, not aggressively, phallic (gladiolus, hyacinth, cyclamen). The fiery "tall youth" impersonates Love and sings the figurative, ritualized song of hymeneal consummation ("There with his honey-seeking lips / the bee clings close and warmly sips, / And seeks with honey-thighs to sway / And drink the very flower away"). Love's "band of boys," Puck-like, sing the epilogue in honor of Love and clean up the stage "with symbolic gesture." The concluding song praises the irresistible power of love: "Where love is come / Our limbs are numb / . . . / Before his fiery lips / Our lips are mute and dumb." However, the position of the poem at the beginning of the volume and its inscription to Bryher and Perdita, as well as its dramatic and narrative structure, fictionalized mode, and subtly androgynous ambience, encourage the counter-hymeneal interpretation that love is overwhelmingly "beyond" Hymen. "Ah! love is come indeed!" is the last line of the song. The lights are put out and the music ends. The last image left is the "purple curtain" that only in fiction hides the thalamus. Beyond the poem and its symbolic meanings, Hymen, or conventional heterosexual love, is not. Love is.

Read in this way, "Hymen" sounds like a well-crafted song for love lost and found, or death-as-part-of-life. This is what many of the poems in *Hymen* and *Heliodora* are about. The setting is Greece and the Greek islands, where Bryher took H. D. in 1920 and where the poet experienced the wondrous and awesome "vision" she called the "writing-on-the-wall." One day, on the island of Corfu, H. D. saw flickering light pictures projected on the wall: a soldier's head, a chalice, a Delphic tripod, swarming black creatures (that seem threatening), a ladder of light, the figure of winged Nike (which H. D. associates with herself) flying free and being beckoned by the sun to a disk of light. As she "reads" the flickering lights, first with Bryher's help and later with Freud's, and perhaps stirred by her interest in film as well, H. D. begins to understand that the mystery and strength of her creativity are equally embedded in her own life experience of joys and sorrows, and the glory of Greek myth (Hellas). Hellas she associates with Helios, the sun god of poetry, and with Helen, the name of her mother, as well as a name for her persona, particularly in her late poetry. The poet's inspiration is thus grounded on the cinematic "dots of light" of her "writing-on-the-wall" converging to signify mortal woman, Greek myth, and the power of prophecy. Looking back at the classical world from the viewpoint of her modern world and reinventing the ancient myths anew, H. D. recreates in her poems the exhilaration and torture of living between worlds. The voice of H. D.'s Demeter, in *Hymen*'s poem of the same title, evokes the Great Goddess's loss of her daughter, Persephone, to Hades, the death god, but also the fate of Dionysus' mother, Semele, burnt to ashes by the god's full glory. Such is the tragic fate that H. D.'s woman poet must avoid in her exchanges with the male poet of tradition. As "Demeter" speaks of the mother, creator of life in spite of death – her "slim fingers" turned into iron to retrieve Persephone from the underworld – this mother goddess begins to be like the figure of a woman poet who is reinventing the old songs by herself, and whose fingers, too, are "wrought of iron / to wrest from earth / secrets."

Other poems in *Hymen* and *Heliodora* are dramatic monologues or portraits that give women from Greek mythology a new kind of life. H. D.'s modernist reinvention of the old myths becomes more powerful when, as in "Demeter," the language of the poem suggests that H. D. has the statues of the deities in her mind or even in front of her, providing her with the "image" she needs to convey her emotions: "Ah they have wrought me heavy / and great of limb – ," says Demeter with her "wide feet on a mighty plinth"; but what the poem ultimately sings is the vulnerability of human love, caring, and sexual passion as H. D. experienced them too in her own life. One of H. D.'s most interesting recreations is "Cassandra," first published in 1923. The poem – an urgent apostrophe to Hymen, the god of love-as-marriage, and structured by a series of insistent rhetorical questions – is poignantly ironic, for Cassandra, the never-to-be-believed seer and prophet, wants desperately to hear from Hymen, reconciler of opposites but no seer or prophet, the comforting word that would appease her tormented heart. Does she, who knows the fate of all, really know her own fate as being hopelessly interrupted and incomplete? Will she really be denied the fulfillment of consummation? ("may Love not lie beside me / till his heat / burn me to ash? / may he not comfort me then, / spent of all that fire and heat . . . ?").

It would be tempting to read H. D.'s whole emotional and sexual life into this poem, regardless of its date, as if the poet, Cassandra-like, were seeing her whole fate in Cassandra's fate in an imagist instant of time: her early romantic

involvement with Pound and Gregg, her failed marriage to Aldington, her intense poetic relationship of sentiment and intellect with Lawrence, her sexual
encounter with Gray, her severe illness at the term of her pregnancy and the
survival of mother and daughter against all odds, Aldington's desertion and
hostility, Gray's indifferent stepping aside, the timely, soothing love of Bryher,
and H. D.'s many other romantic and sexual encounters throughout her life.
But this would be reductive. The rich intertextuality, or "palimpsestic" quality, of H. D.'s poetry demands another kind of reading. Far more productive
is, therefore, to observe how H. D. projects into her poem the complexity of
human feelings and relationships, and the social, economic, and even artistic conditions that control them, be it "after Troy" (the title of the poem
that precedes "Cassandra" in *Heliodora*) or after the Great War. Love, passion,
marriage depend on class, "race," and gender (as well as many other far more
banal circumstances of life). Troy's defeat, Cassandra's abduction by the foreign
conquerer, and her "bitter power of song" deprive an enslaved Cassandra of
love, passion, marriage. Wealthy Bryher's gender drives her to a marriage of
convenience (to Robert McAlmon in 1921) for the sake of freedom. "Love,"
or "Hymen king," is no more than a fiction, particularly for the woman poet.
And though it breaks her heart, she cannot but know it: "to sing of love, / love
must first shatter us" ("Fragment Forty").

A much earlier poem, which was left out of *Hymen* and *Heliodora* but included
in H. D.'s premature *Collected Poems* (1925), had already touched powerfully on
the subject. "Eurydice," H. D.'s indictment of Orpheus as the archetypal (male)
poet who feeds on the woman-as-muse, appeared in *The Egoist* in May 1917.
The voice is Eurydice's, and it upsets the myth. Eurydice is now the singer,
Orpheus the object of the song. By angrily invoking the poet and denouncing
the self-centered rashness of Orpheus, Eurydice's voice depicts the self-portrait
of a woman muse whom pain has turned into self-sufficient singer. The poem
begins in a kind of deductive mode that rings somewhat contemptuously, as
if suggesting that Orpheus could not have helped himself: "So you have swept
me back . . . So for your arrogance / I am broken at last." The series of seemingly
anguished questions that Eurydice addresses to Orpheus in the second section
of the poem turn out to be mere rhetorical devices to convey Eurydice's correct
assessment of the situation: by looking at her face, she accuses, Orpheus only
wanted to see himself confirmed:

> why did you turn back
>   [. . .]
> why did you glance back?
>   [. . .]
> what was it that crossed my face

> with the light from yours
> and your glance?
> what was it you saw in my face,
> the fire of your own presence?

But Eurydice's bitter experience of abandonment and loss, described in the sections that follow as the loss of the light and flowers of the earth, is actually the (woman) poet's utter gain. It is as if Orpheus had finally been reinvented in Eurydice and *she* had now the power of her own light to open up the darkness of hell, and redeem poetry. Many years later, another woman poet, Adrienne Rich, may have had H. D.'s "Eurydice" in mind when she wrote "I Dream I'm the Death of Orpheus" (1968). In her dream, the woman poet becomes the death that drives Orpheus to the underworld, where the *Ur*-poet learns how to walk backwards on the wrong side of the mirror. H. D.'s much earlier poem remains a little more ambiguous, for the defiant wording of the last stanza can't but ring with piercing regret ("at least"):

> At least I have the flowers of myself,
> and my thoughts, no god
> can take that;
> I have the fervour of myself for a presence
> and my own spirit for light;
>
> and my spirit with its loss
> knows this;
> though small against the black,
> small against the formless rocks,
> hell must break before I am lost;
>
> before I am lost,
> hell must open like a red rose
> for the dead to pass.

"Eurydice," like "Cassandra," reverberates with the circumstances of H. D.'s life in the earlier stages of her poetic career, when she was struggling to become a poet on her own terms, with, or in spite of, the support, attention, or betrayal of the men poets she loved (Pound, Aldington, Lawrence). But H. D. knew only too well that a poem is not a slice of life. Even as regards the details of her autobiographical fiction and self-reflective prose (some of it still unpublished) she is subtler than that. However, she was fully aware (and wary) of the reader's "biological approach," as Crane called it. She knew that "Amaranth," "Eros," and "Envy" would be read as telling the "story," her own story, of a woman abandoned by her husband for other women, and so she did not publish them. H. D. left the three poems bound together in a typescript under a flyleaf bearing the following inscription in her own hand: "Corfe Castle – Dorset – summer 1917 – from poems of the *The Islands* series – " Unlike the other three, "The Islands," which can also be said to "tell the story," though rather more obliquely ("What are the islands to me / if you are lost – "), was published in *North American Review* in 1920, and later included in *Hymen*. In her review of this volume for *Broom* in 1923, Marianne Moore, who knew her friend's "story" well enough, resists the biographical approach and rather singles out this poem to highlight H. D.'s modernist "objectivity" ("Direct treatment of the 'thing,' whether subjective or objective," according to Flint). Moore praises H. D.'s "wiry diction, accurate observation and a homogeneous color sense," as well as her "faithfulness to fact." But Moore is aware, also, of her own sensitivity to the gender implications of H. D.'s evolving self-consciousness as a woman poet, struggling with the image of "woman" in a man's world:

Talk of weapons and the tendency to match one's intellectual and emotional vigor with the violence of nature, give a martial, an apparently masculine tone to such writing as H. D.'s, the more so that women are regarded as belonging necessarily to either of two classes – that of the intellectual free-lance or that of the eternally sleeping beauty, effortless yet effective in the indestructible limestone keep of domesticity.

"Amaranth," "Eros," and "Envy" (now available in Louis Martz's edition of the *Collected Poems, 1912–1944* [1982]), were refashioned as fragments after Sappho for publication in *Heliodora* ("Fragment Forty," "Fragment Forty-one," and "Fragment Sixty-eight"). The major difference between the two versions is not that the poems from "*The Islands* series" are autobiographically more explicit than the "Fragments," but that the "Fragments," by the very Sapphic device, present themselves as more carefully crafted. Stevens once said that though poems may very well happen, they had rather be made. Perhaps H. D. felt that "Amaranth," "Eros," and "Envy" – particularly for those readers who knew the "story" – would sound as having happened rather than as having been made. In fact, the two versions of each poem differ only slightly as far as "content" goes. All poems deal with love, both heterosexual and lesbian, both carnal and spiritual, and they all speak, despairingly, the impossibility of reconciling passion and permanence, *eros* and *agape*. Amaranth, the mythical purple flower that never fades, is mythical indeed. At the end of "Fragment Forty-one," the poet offers to Sappho's goddess, Aphrodite, no more than the lyric cry of the unbearable impossibility of myth:

> I offer you more than the lad
> singing at your steps,
> praise of himself,
> his mirror his friend's face,

more than any girl,
I offer you this:
(grant only strength
that I withdraw not my gift,)
I give you my praise and this:
the love of my lover
for his mistress.

During the late 1920s and through the 1930s, H. D. experimented with different kinds of writing. *Hippolytus Temporizes*, a three-act verse drama, was published in 1927, and *Hedylus*, a novel, in 1928, both to scanty critical attention. Most of the prose fiction she was writing then, often under a pseudonym, remained largely unpublished during her lifetime. The fact that these writings are intensely autobiographical and that H. D. resorts to masculine as well as feminine pseudonyms emphasizes her stance as a modernist poet forever in the process of reinventing her own persona as a poet between worlds. A notable exception is *The Hedgehog* (1936), an engaging story ostensibly for children but clearly meant for adult understanding, published, with charming illustrations by George Plank, in Bryher's Dijon series, after having been rejected by Houghton Mifflin. Meanwhile, H. D. had also become involved in cinema, an art she considered quintessentially modernist, and was also writing film reviews for *Close Up*. The avant-garde film journal, to which Gertrude Stein also contributed, was founded and funded by Bryher and edited by Kenneth Macpherson (H. D.'s lover at the time and Bryher's second husband of convenience for appearance's sake). Macpherson was also the director of *Borderline*, the 1930 movie dealing with interracial sex and violence and featuring Paul and Eslanda Robeson, H. D., and Bryher. H. D.'s essay *Borderline*, a pamphlet published annonymously to promote the film, reveals much about H. D.'s version of modernism as an interplay of different worlds from the vantage point of their margins.

At the same time, H. D. continued to write poetry, but the poems in her next book, *Red Roses for Bronze* (1931), display less aesthetic power than the previous ones. The setting is still Greece, with several translations from choruses (*Bacchae*, *Morpheus*, *Hecuba*), and the mode is the love portrait or self-portrait "after the Greeks" that had appeared previously. The effect of the poem often depends on the visual presencing (or even "making") of Greek art, as in the title poem ("If I might take a weight of bronze / and sate / my wretched fingers / in ecstatic work / if I might fashion / eyes and mouth and chin, / if I might take dark bronze / and hammer in / the line beneath your underlip"). But some stridency of repetition creeps into the love poem to signify the poet's incapacity to accomplish the "magic" of "peace," or perfection, whether in art or love ("If I might ease my fingers and my brain / with stroke, / stroke, / stroke, / stroke, / stroke at – something [stone, marble, intent, stable, materialized] / peace, / even magic sleep / might come again"). The poem ends by insisting on "jealousy" and resorting to the conditional mode ("I would"), thus denouncing love as the Pygmalionian power to "make" the beloved. The inclusion of a quite effective brief "Epitaph" in the volume may signal the poet's malaise and disatisfaction with her poetry writing at this time, because of which she was soon to consult with Freud in Vienna. And yet, the volume includes one of H. D.'s best shorter poetic sequences ever. "Let Zeus Record" is a poem about "Love's authority" as opposed to the authority of the Father or Law or Religion (Zeus). It presents itself in the vocative mode and its wry tone sounds rather impatient and matter-of-fact throughtout ("I say, I am quite done," the first line reads). The voice is one in an implied dialogue on love that deigns to expect any response. The poem's seven beautifully balanced, delicately musical lyrics of different formats, combining sections of compactly phrased quatrains of two- or three-stress lines with sections of ampler stanzas where the traditional pentameter predominates, resoundingly speak the authority of love and love poetry. Love is not easy in difficult times, the poem keeps intimating, it can't always be kept at the height of beauty and desire, and sometimes it cannot even be invoked but by the lack of it. Nonetheless, the poem concludes with a note of unsentimental self-confidence and defiant affirmation: "let Zeus record this / daring Death to mar."

When the Second World War broke out in 1939 H. D. and Bryher were in London. Ever since 1922 they had been moving back and forth between their residences in London and in Switzerland. But they remained in London throughout the conflict, witnessing and suffering the nightmare of a city being devastated by continuous air raids and bombings. During this time, H. D. became more and more interested in theosophy, esoteric and occult traditions, and spiritualist interpretations of reality, as if in search of an all-encompassing center that would hold. She also developed a close friendship with Norman Holmes Pearson, who encouraged her to resume writing poetry and who was to play an important role in collecting her manuscripts at the Yale Beinecke Library and later editing and providing for the publication of some of them. In the midst of the harrowing experience of war, H. D., who had been writing hardly any poetry at all for some time, rediscovered her poetic voice in the longer modernist myth-making sequence. *Trilogy* is comparable to Crane's *The Bridge* (1930), Pound's *Cantos* (1925–48), Stevens's *Notes toward a Supreme Fiction* (1942), Eliot's *Four Quartets* (1944), and Williams's *Paterson* (1946–59).

Trilogy, brought out by Pearson in 1973, gathers together three long sequences which were published separately in the mid 1940s but which H. D.

herself came to see as a coherent whole: *The Walls Do Not Fall* (1944), *Tribute to the Angels* (1945), and *The Flowering of the Rod* (1946). *Trilogy*, as a whole, is a woman poet's self-conscious re-inscription of Western culture at a time when Nazism and the war were threatening to reduce Western culture to utter ruin. *The Walls Do Not Fall* is once again dedicated to Bryher. H. D. and Bryher had visited Egypt together in 1923, at the time of the Tutankhamen excavation, and seen the ruins of the temple at Karnak. The encounter with the ancientness of culture and art, more ancient indeed than "the Greeks," and their "palimpsestic" permanence, made a strong impression on H. D. "To Bryher / *for Karnak* 1923 / *from London* 1942" parallels the epigraphs that preside over the other two books. The real epigraphs are taken from the two previous books (from *The Walls Do Not Fall* in the case of *Tribute to the Angels*, and from *Tribute to the Angels* in the case of *The Flowering of the Rod*), as if signaling the coherent meaning of the sequence and its climax in the third book. But the inscription to Bryher lays the foundations of the whole sequence on H. D.'s lifelong indebtedness to her friend and points to the sequence's construction of the center as a syncretic "image" of female divinity that transcends the ruins of war ("Love, the Creator" is invoked in Section XXXIV of *The Walls Do Not Fall* as a goddess; and the last image of the sequence, in *The Flowering of the Rod*, is that of an uncanny childless Virgin venerated by the Magi).

Written during the Blitz and with the memory of the Nazi book-burning in 1933 (the year H. D. began her analysis with Freud, whose books were also burnt), *The Walls Do Not Fall* points the way to reinvention by becoming the re-writing of culture itself. As if to confirm that indeed "eternity endures" in spite of the rubble and ashes, the poet is called upon not to escape, let alone erase the culture of pain and sorrow (or "scratch out" "past misadventure"), but rather to write anew upon the "old parchment." Section IX syncretically convenes culture as re-writing (or as poetry and art) – from Egypt to Greece to contemporary Europe – and underscores what power of construction and destruction both there is in art and poetry:

> Thoth, Hermes, the stylus,
> the palette, the pen, the quill endure,
>
> though our books are a floor
> of smouldering ash under our feet;
>
> though the burning of the books remains
> the most perverse gesture
>
> and the meanest
> of man's meanest nature,

yet give us, they still cry,
give us books,

folio, manuscript, old parchment
will do for cartridge cases;

irony is bitter truth
wrapped up in a little joke,

and Hatshepsut's name is still circled
with what they call the *cartouche*.

H. D.'s prosody in this first book and throughout the *Trilogy* reflects the palimpsestic conception behind her poetry: poetry as layers and layers of language dismembered and re-membered. The poet exorcizes destruction and ruin by showing how meaning must be created out of them. "I know, I feel / the meaning that words hide," she cries out in Section XXXIX; and in the sections that follow she exemplifies: "Osiris equates O-sir-is or O-sire-is." Further down, she continues: "O, Sire, is this the path? / . . . / O, Sire, is this the waste? / . . . /O, Sire, / is this union at last?"

The answer to this rather gnostic question about "the path" is never given. *The Walls Do Not Fall* records the resistance of language to meaning and understanding in times of war ("Still the walls do not fall / . . . / there is zrr-hiss, / lightning in a not-known"). And so the poem ends in mere Dickinsonian "possibility," with a sentence that will become the epigraph of *Tribute to the Angels*: "possibly we will reach haven, / heaven" (could the "irrational moment" of Stevens's "heaven-haven" in *Notes toward a Supreme Fiction* [III, i] be on H. D.'s mind here?). Alchemy and occultism are now crucial strategies in H. D.'s poetry writing. In order to show "the path," *Tribute to the Angels* begins by invoking Hermes Trismegistus, "patron of alchemists." The power of alchemy to melt without melding, and so transmute, not really fuse, matter, the elements, and language itself, is enacted in Section VIII:

Now polish the crucible
and in the bowl distill

a word most bitter, *marah*,
a word bitterer still, *mar*,

sea brine, breaker, seducer,
giver of life, giver of tears;

now polish the crucible
and set the jet of flame

under, till *marah-mar*
are melted, fuse and join

and change and alter,
mer, mere, mère, mater, Maia, Mary,

Star of the Sea,
Mother.

H. D.'s alchemical theory and practice of poetry evolves in the following sections. Different traditions and cults, as well as different forms of art, are distilled in the crucible of poetic language. The figure of woman as "Mother" that the crucible yields is pregnant with meaning, a meaning which however remains unreachable. The alchemical process must go on endlessly. The concrete images by which woman is made manifest – jewel, star, shell – or the supernatural entities that put her in perspective – goddesses, angels, the Mother of God – must in turn be distilled in the alchemical bowl. It is as if the whole world of cultures and traditions were a crucible, and quicksilver, Hermes' slippery metal, the perfect metaphor for the inscrutability of meaning.

The Flowering of the Rod rewrites the myth of resurrection in woman-as-mother. Mary-Mother-of-God, rather than Christ-Son-of-God, holds the meaning of life and death, but only after the poet's distillation of images of woman from all traditions has reinvented her and nativity itself as the ultimate image of a totally self-contained, all-encompassing new beginning-and-end:

> But she spoke so he looked at her,
> she was shy and simple and young;
>
> she said, Sir, it is a most beautiful fragrance,
> as of all flowering things together;
>
> But Kaspar knew the seal of the jar was unbroken.
> he did not know whether she knew
>
> the fragrance came from the bundle of myrrh
> she held in her arms.

This scene of a finally resolved and creative oppositional exchange between the male and female principles had long been in H. D.'s imagination. Like Yeats's "Leda and the Swan" (1924), H. D.'s "Leda," published for the first time in 1919, reinvents the myth of origin (or, as we learn in *Helen in Egypt*, the "first-cause 'of all-time, of all-history'"); but it casts a much denser shadow upon the mystery of woman, to which Yeats also refers at the end of his poem ("Did she put on his knowledge with his power / Before the indifferent beak could let her drop?"). In H. D.'s poem, Leda is no longer there. There is only the lily and the reeds and the water, and the red swan floating elegantly with no "regret" or "memories." History is now happening in Leda, beyond "his" knowledge and power. Helen is about to be born and bring in the beauty and terror of a new world. In *Helen in Egypt* (1960), H. D.'s greatest achievement, the beautiful, much-loved, and much-hated Helen, the Greek, is transformed into the most adequate symbol of poetry ("she herself is the writing") and the most perfect image of the woman poet ("she [brings] the moment and infinity together"). Throughout the poem, whether in the prose introductions or in the lyrics themselves, it is often difficult to tell the world of Helen, the poem, from the world of H. D., the poet, weaving its myth. Helen, the myth, and H. D., the myth-making poet, are bound together to "reconstruct the legend." Together they are the hieroglyph; together they are "the undecipherable script" only they know.

Greece and Troy, the Trojan War, and the dramatic clashes of humans and gods parallel the social and political scene in Europe during the first half of the twentieth century, the two devastating wars, and H. D.'s personal encounters at the time. H. D.'s complex life and relationships find their way into the poem (the personal is the political is the poetical); they bring to the poem the poignant vulnerability of the poet's heart, what Yeats so movingly called "the foul rag-and-bone shop of the heart"; but they are not the poem, and should not condition its reading. *Helen in Egypt* is really an American "epic of the modern consciousness," with Helen of Troy as its main character and focus. The poem retells Helen's story and the creative/destructive effect of her extraordinary beauty from and beyond its many different recorded versions – Homer, Stesichorus, Euripides, and many other poets closer to H. D.'s own time – versions in which Helen is vilified as the cause of war and tragedy because of her seductive and irresponsible beauty, and versions that exonerate her as merely an innocent character in the drama. *Helen in Egypt* denies no facet of the various Helens variously recorded by the tradition. Thus, to the extent that it envisions new possibilities for the relations between men and women in the culture, *Helen in Egypt* becomes the reinvented "script" as "the thousand-petalled lily." In its epistemological quest for "Helen," the poem incorporates all the complexities of the myth in order to translate Helen into "Hellas," H. D.'s metaphor for origin, culture, art, and poetry. Like Crane's "For the Marriage of Faustus and Helen" (1923, 1924), H. D.'s *Helen in Egypt* remembers, forgets, and recreates the very idea of myth as it shapes all history and culture in the poetical.

Helen in Egypt is H. D.'s most carefully conceived and composed work. It is divided into three parts: "Pallinode" (*sic*); "Leuké (*L'isle blanche*);" and "Eidolon." Each part is composed of "Books," seven in the first two, and six in the third one. Each book is made up of eight lyrics of varying length, composed of three-line unrhymed stanzas, the lines having usually no more than two to three stresses. As often in H. D., the lyric's music relies on assonance and rhythm, occasional rhyme being also used here and there. Each one of the lyrics is anteceded by a brief prose introduction. The prose recounts and reflects upon the story, allowing each individual lyric poem to be read and enjoyed as such. Consider, for example, the lyric toward the end of "Leuké" quoted below. It sums up in "Helen," a figure that is like a newly refashioned "radiant node or cluster" or "luminous detail" of an image, H. D.'s conception of poetry as reconciliation of opposites, though not without strife and violence. The fast pace of the poem, with its short lines of parallel concepts bound together by sense and sound, underscores the instantaneous, flash-like concentration of meaning in the image of "Helen." The two opposite versions of the myth are brilliantly reinscribed in Blake's "sick" rose at last restored to eternal life and beauty. H. D.'s Helen is where the "paths" meet, and she has now the power (of poetry) to be beauty for ever:

> Thus, thus, thus,
> as day, night,
> as wrong, right,
>
> as dark, light,
> as water, fire,
> as earth, air,
>
> as storm, calm,
> as fruit, flower,
> as life, death,
>
> as death, life;
> the rose deflowered,
> the rose reborn;
>
> Helen in Egypt,
> Helen at home,
> Helen is Hellas forever.

H. D. has often been called a poets' poet. When she died in 1961, after having been the first woman to receive the Award of Merit Medal for Poetry of the American Academy of Arts and Letters in the previous year, she was by no means a widely read and acclaimed poet. But younger poets were beginning to respond to her poetry with the same admiration and sense of discovery that had struck her modernist colleagues at the beginning of her career. In 1925, William Carlos Williams, then struggling to have his own *Collected Poems* published (Zukofsky was to bring the book out only in 1934), wrote an enthusiastic review of her *Collected Poems* for the *New York Evening Post*

Literary Review. Just before he died in 1972, Ezra Pound reiterated in a letter to James Laughlin his early admiration for the more than "Dryad," expressing his conviction that H. D. is the "finest woman poet in America since Emily Dickinson." But even before Pound's judgment, poets of the younger generation, like Denise Levertov and Robert Duncan, had fallen under the spell of H. D.'s poetry and poetics. "[H. D.] showed a way to penetrate mystery," wrote Levertov in 1962, and she explains: "which means, not to flood darkness with light so that darkness is destroyed, but to *enter into* darkness, mystery, so that it is experienced." However, the greatest poet's tribute H. D.'s poetry has received so far comes from Robert Duncan. *The H. D. Book* is what Duncan calls his series of meditations on poetry and poetics, life and existence, that read like an "autobiographia literaria" of modern poetry, and which he went on writing from the mid-sixties through the eighties. If the poetry of H. D., as one of the great modernist poets of the English language, grounds Duncan's thoughts in *The H. D. Book*, it powerfully inspires his poetry writing as well. *Roots and Branches* (1964) includes "A Sequence of Poems for H. D.'s Birthday, September 10, 1959" that ends by invoking the female principle of knowledge, "Sophia," under the appearance of "a divine human radiance."

4

MARIANNE MOORE
A VORACITY OF CONTEMPLATION

P ERHAPS no major poet of American modernism attained more public recognition in the United States during her or his lifetime than
Marianne Moore (1887–1972). Even taking into account Eliot's international consecration as the foremost (Anglo-)American man of letters of the
period, or the notoriety of Pound's treason case after World War II, Moore's
public acclaim in American letters and society at large as a prize-winning
poet, critic, and translator (especially of the *Fables of La Fontaine* [1954]) in
the fifties and sixties is quite remarkable. While still at Bryn Mawr (1905–
09), Moore started publishing poetry in student journals. In 1915 and the
years immediately following she was already having poems accepted by some
of the most interesting avant-garde little magazines at the time: *The Egoist*,
Poetry, Others, Bruno's Weekly, Chimaera, Contact. Between 1921, when her first
collection of poetry came out in England, and 1967, when *The Complete Poems*
were published, Moore's bibliography counts more than thirty books, whether
of poetry, prose, or translation. By then, too, Moore had been awarded all the
major prizes for poetry in the United States, including what Randall Jarrell
called her "Triple Crown": the Bollingen Prize, the National Book Award,
and the Pulitzer Prize, all awarded in 1952. But the real proof of her high
public reputation as a verbal artist in the American scene was the invitation
she received in 1955 from the Ford Motor Company to propose an attractive
and suggestive name for a new series of cars. Moore, who was fascinated by
advertising all her life, promptly accepted.

The episode is significant in more than one way. The course of Moore's life
of eighty-five years spans the fast changes undergone by American culture in
the course of the twentieth century. Moore saw the expansion of market capitalism and the rise of consumer culture in the United States, was witness to
the appearance of corporate finance and managerial professionals in the various departments of the American society, and could not but have marveled at
the extraordinary development of commerce and national advertising throughout the decades. An omnivorous reader and meticulous gatherer of information

("I would be lost without the newspaper"), and a self-defined "observer," Moore was fully aware of the impact of the nineteenth-century industrial and market revolutions that led on to technologies of information, entrepreneurial enterprise, and corporate advertising of factory-produced goods in the twentieth century. The debate, by mid century, about advertising as technical expertise to inform the public objectively on the one hand or as a seductive art to promote consumption and stimulate commerce on the other could not have escaped the attention of a poet who referred to her own poetry writing as "exercises in composition." In Moore we can best observe how poetic modernism conflates with modernization. Although her favorite authors were "the classics" ("ignorance of originals is suicidal"), Moore was deeply immersed in the American culture of her own time, of which New York City was the uncontested capital. "I was born in Missouri in 1887" (she wrote in 1951 for the *New York Herald Tribune Book Review*'s "Some Authors of 1951 Speaking for Themselves" [October 7]), "graduated from Bryn Mawr in 1909 and live in Brooklyn in a six-story yellow brick and lime-stone apartment house on what is known as The Hill." As for "recreations," she indicated that her tastes were varied and eclectic. Resorting to the advertising rhetoric of the time, we might say that her likings privileged the scientific mind and efficient professionalism of modernity without relinquishing the romantic appeal of nature. She delighted, she said, in "the theater, tennis, sailing, reading and the movies – animal documentaries, travelogues, an occasional French film, and the newsreel." She also liked "country fairs, roller-coasters, merry-go-rounds, dog shows, museums, avenues of trees, old elms, vehicles, experiments in time . . . [and] animals." In Moore's poetry, *physis* and *techne*, nature and art(ifice), are skillfully articulated. She herself viewed her poems both as mechanical objects and as natural organisms. Natural organisms, in turn, often appear in her poems as made mechanisms of precision. In the informative, story-telling mode of "The Jerboa" (1932), for example, the "small desert rat" seems no less "contrived" than the pine-cone fountain at the beginning ("with the tail as a weight, / undulated out by speed, straight"; "pillar body erect / on a three-cornered smooth-working Chippendale / claw"). Contrivance, or technology, is here also the African ingenuity of putting "baboons on the necks of giraffes to pick / fruit." Moore's work clearly contributes to and comments on the reassessment of poetry in a culture dominated by science, technology, and the ideas of the practical and the useful.

The Ford invitation could not but have delighted Marianne Moore. The gesture in itself signified corporate concern with refining the methods and objectives of publicity for best results: how best to inform the public "honestly" (or with "authenticity"), while seducing consumers efficaciously; how best to encourage and take commercial advantage of the functional equilibrium, expounded by Talcott Parsons, between production and consumption; how best to combine, in advertising, the professionalism and managerial technology capable of reconciling private needs with capital and public interests, with the "magic" of creativity and art. By the invitation they addressed to Moore in 1955, the Ford Motor Company recognized that poetry had a role to play in contemporary American culture (as modernist poets had been arguing since the beginning of the century), while paying tribute to the power of the poetic word to persuade the public and mobilize consumers. Moore willingly obliged. A modest choice of Moore's fanciful suggestions would include The Ford Silver Sword, The Resilient Bullet, The Intelligent Whale, The Mongoose Civique, The Aeroterre, The Pastelogram, The Utopian Turtletop. That none of these resounding appellations was found compelling by the managerial experts of the Ford Motor Company, is proof that, in this little anecdote in the history of American advertising, the "plain speech" of "objectivity," "honesty," and "authenticity" prevailed upon "imagination" and "enthusiasm," though not entirely upon "sentiment" and "originality." The new car was finally called The Edsel, Edsel being the not-so-common given name of Ford's oldest son. The authenticity of the company was thus safeguarded by its origins in an honest American family, mindful of its true values.

But the episode has implications as well for our understanding of the history of modernist poetry. The publication of the Ford Motor Company correspondence with Moore in *The New Yorker* three years later turned a reputed woman-of-letters into a celebrity. More interesting still is Moore's inclusion of this correspondence in *A Marianne Moore Reader* (1961). Moore's extravagant play with names, whether already existent or made up, destined to identify a new car, is thus called upon as well to define "Marianne Moore" as an "American Poet." As for most poets of the period, the very notion of "poetry" is for Moore under constant revision, and her own "Foreword" to *A Marianne Moore Reader* leaves no doubt about that. Though the "Foreword" has often been praised for its author's humility and self-effacement, the concept of poetic arrogance is rather in order. In *A Marianne Moore Reader*, including its introduction, Moore boldly recreates herself as "Marianne Moore" and sets her own poetic terms for the reading of herself as a modern American poet, at the same time giving clues as to how poetry in general ought to be read. Poetry is part of the culture, and as such it must be read. Modern American poetry is part of the culture of modern America, and as such it must be read. Of her poem "Marriage" she says in the "Foreword," "The thing (I would hardly call it a poem) is no philosophic precipitate; nor does it veil anything personal in the way of triumphs, entrapments, or dangerous colloquies. It is a little anthology of statements that took my fancy – phrasings that I liked." Moore's "verse," she insists in the same place, is always "observations" and her "prose" "will always be 'essays.'" What is, then, the role of the Ford Motor Company correspondence in *A Marianne Moore Reader*? A possible answer is to show the poet's delight in what Stevens called the "gaiety of language" and display her dexterity at verbal reinvention ("dexterity" is a quality which, like Frost, she praises, particularly in "animals" and "athletes"); but also to question further and reestablish her own terms for the definition of "the poetical" in modern American poetry, not in opposition to but taking into account the rhythms and achievements of the material culture. All the other modernists were trying to do the same, one way or another. William Carlos Williams, for example, in *Spring and All* (1923) had already challenged conceptions of poetry that continued to distinguish poetry from not-poetry in ways that were damaging to both. He thus rejects the traditional distinction between poetry and prose, while invoking "Marianne Moore" as the best example of the "American" poet. Williams praises Moore in particular for her sense of "the purpose of poetry" in avoiding the conventional forms of verse (image, meter, rhythm), and endowing each word with its own opacity and power of concentration. "Marianne's words remain separate," says Williams, "each unwilling to group with the others except as they move in the one direction." Williams may also have had in mind an earlier, more technical attempt at poetic reinvention on Moore's part. The concept of the accented syllable, first mentioned in her essay of the same title, "The Accented Syllable" (*The Egoist*, 1916), is a conception for a new poetics of the line that is indeed somewhat analogous in its objectives to Williams's "variable foot."

If American poetic modernism, particularly the version of it that has been at times designated as "high modernism," can be said to be a fine web of intellectual, imaginative, and even personal relationships, Marianne Moore emerges as one of its foci, if not its strongest fulcrum. Sooner or later she would write reviews of Eliot, Pound, Stevens, H. D., Williams, Cummings, Stein, often more than once, and all these poets would eventually write about her as well. Two of the most important critical appreciations of Moore's work at the beginning of her career were Eliot's review of *Poems* (1921) and *Marriage* (1923) for *The Dial* (1923), and Williams's essay dealing with the same two works and also published in *The Dial* two years later. Given the intellectual scene and lively social life around literary and artistic events in New York City of which all of them were part, even if not physically present (as was the case with the London exiles, Pound, Eliot, H. D.), the relationships soon became friendly and personal rather than merely professional. Though the letters they exchanged among themselves in the course of years are also revealing of these relationships, the best source for their steady development is to be found in the letters written by Moore's mother, Mary Craig Moore, to her son, John Warner Moore (a Presbyterian clergyman), and Moore's own letters to her brother. Mary Moore had separated from her mentally unstable husband before her daughter was born. Mother, son, and daughter eventually became a very close family even after Warner's marriage in 1918, welded together by religion, a vast intellectual and moral curiosity, a great love of books, an interest in animals, and Moore's poetry. Their deep emotional intimacy and good-humored solidarity best express themselves in the nicknames they gave one another, animal names right out of Kenneth Grahame's *Wind in the Willows* (Rat [Marianne], Mole [Mary], and Badger [Warner]). "Dear Badger," Moore writes her brother in 1923 to tell him about her stimulating exchanges with (or about) Monroe Wheeler, William Carlos Williams, Kenneth Burke, Gorham Munson, Ezra Pound, David Lawson, and Lola Ridge; the letter closes "with love" from Rat, not without delivering a message from Mole. The family's solid Presbyterian background and deep ethical concerns also find their way into Moore's poetry. In an early response to Pound's questions about her influences (January 9, 1919), Moore confesses to knowing no Greek and having not read the French symbolists, but finds it relevant to mention "Gordon Craig, Henry James, Blake, the minor prophets and Hardy," as well as her "purely Celtic" ancestry (Irish and Scottish) and Presbyterian upbringing. In an autobiographical mode that is not at all characteristic of Moore's poetry, her "purely Celtic" becomes the explicit topic of "Spenser's Ireland" (1941).

Moore's first critical intervention of relevance for the history of modernist poetry and poetics was her brief review of Eliot's *Prufrock and Other Observations* in Harriet Monroe's *Poetry* in 1918. It is notable not for its substance (nothing much is said about the poems, though Moore inspires some respect for the firmness of her opinions), or for its skillful balance of serious attention and humorous nudging (when she calls for a "fangless edition" of Eliot's first book of poetry "for the gentle reader," it is hard to decide whether she is faulting the author or poking fun at his readers), but rather because it inaugurated a wide network of critical relationships that remains one of the high marks of American poetic modernism. Moore's review of Williams's *Kora in Hell* (1920) in *The Caravan* three years later is a far more substantial and perceptive piece of critical writing ("The sharpened faculties which require exactness, instant satisfaction and an underpinning of truth are too abrupt in their activities sometimes to follow; but the niceness and effect of vigor for which they are responsible, are never absent from Dr. Williams' work and its crisp exterior is one of its great distinctions"). Her detailed, carefully documented reading of Stevens's *Harmonium* (1923) for *The Dial* in 1924 is likewise full of insightful, sensitive, and rigorous appreciation of the poet's "riot of gorgeousness," while noting his occasional "acrimonious, unprovoked contumely" as well. Ten years later, Moore's review of Pound's *A Draft of XXX Cantos* (1932) for *The Criterion*, quoting extensively and sensitively from the author and work under review and making intelligent associations with other works and other arts in order to stress the poetics of the poem in question, confirms her learning, critical acumen, and reading skills ("There is many a spectacular concealment, or musical ruse should one say, in the patterns presented of slang, foreign speech, and numerals – an ability borrowed as it were from 'the churn, the loom, the spinning-wheel, the oars': 'Malatesta de Malatestis ad Magnificum Dominicum Patremque suum, etc.' about the gift of the bay pony. We have in some of these metrical effects a wisdom as remarkable as anything since Bach"). No wonder Moore came to be one of the American modernist poets most admired, respected, and loved by her fellow poets, of both her own generation and the next.

Elizabeth Bishop, whose "Efforts of Affection: A Memoir of Marianne Moore," written probably around 1969, is one of the most sensitive and suggestive portraits a poet ever sketched of another poet, once called Marianne Moore "The World's Greatest Living Observer." Bishop was no doubt remindful of "The Paper Nautilus" (1940), the poem she received from Moore in return for her gift of a paper nautilus shell. In the poem, the poet is as observant of the nurturing power enshrined in the delicate shell as of the supportive yet free relationship between older and younger poet. Bishop's appellation, which appeared in her contribution to the 1948 all-Marianne Moore issue of *Quarterly Review of Literature* under the title of "As We Like It," could not but have flattered Moore. She would have liked to have had "Observations" as the title of her first book of *Poems* (1921), published at the Egoist Press by the good efforts of her friends H. D. and Bryher [Winifred Ellerman] and allegedly without Moore's knowledge. Moore's second book of poems, however, was entitled precisely *Observations*. It was published by The Dial Press in 1924 and announced as a "reprint" "with additions" of the London edition. The book earned Moore the prestigious Dial Prize for 1924. The following year, The Dial Press put out a new edition of *Observations* with only one more poem added ("The Monkey Puzzler," first published in *The Dial* that same year).

In a far more rigorous way than is ever to be found in *Prufrock and Other Observations* (1917), each poem in *Observations* is indeed an "observation," in all possible senses of the verb "to observe." To watch attentively, to perceive, to study a phenomenon scientifically, to remark, to respect, to contemplate – all these verbs illustrate Moore's intellectual stance and actual performance as a verbal artist. Eliot once told her that the term "observations" was more rightly hers as a poet than his. The intense precision of Moore's attentiveness to things – from objects, conceptions, or sentiments to words, sounds, images, or forms – is a characteristic of her poetry from the very beginning. It is related to her early training in biology and continuing devotion to the rigor of science. Around 1920, disturbed by blatant scientific inaccuracies in contemporary poetry, she thought of sending a letter to Harriet Monroe's *Poetry* suggesting the creation of "a Poet's Handbook of Science." Moore herself revised "Four Quartz Crystal Clocks" (1940), a poem that celebrates technological accuracy, to avoid a possible technical imprecision concerning the temperature at which clocks were maintained in the Bell Telephone Laboratories in New York. The way this characteristic of hers was promptly acknowledged by her readers tells us something also about the intellectual climate of the age. Fellow poets, admirers, critics, and commentators have never failed to highlight the quality of precision in her writing, whether by defining her as "accurate" (T. S. Eliot) or "meticulous" (Robert Lowell), or by stressing her "fastidiousness of thought" (William Carlos Williams), "finical phraseology" (Wallace Stevens), "accurate description" (Elizabeth Bishop), "scrupulosity" (Donald Hall), "objectivism" (Kenneth Burke), or formal "rigor" (Hugh Kenner).

That her rigor is not at all understood by most of her readers as arid scientism can be best seen in Lowell's pairing her "meticulousness" with "lavishness." Marianne Moore herself once expressed her "envy" of the "accuracy of the vernacular" she found in the plays of Lillian Hellman, and in her criticism she made frequent analogies between the poet and the scientist, since they both "must strive for precision." But one of her favorite words of appreciation was "gusto" (her 1949 essay "Humility, Concentration, and Gusto" explains how "to heighten gusto"), and she was always delighted when she sensed "gusto" in her brother's readings of her poems. Moore's definition of poetry in her review of Stevens's *Ideas of Order* for *The Criterion* (1936) best sums it all up: "Poetry . . . is a voracity of contemplation."

A good early illustration of Moore's handling of "observation" is "To a Steam Roller," first published in *The Egoist* in 1915. Resorting to a strategy that she would use to different effects all her life, Moore singles out an object, in this case an instrument of urban modernization ("a steam roller"), and turns it into a subject, by addressing the poem to it ("to a steam roller") and by including it in the poem ("you"). She then goes on to abstract from her chosen object a subject matter ("conformity" or "congruent complement"). From abstracted theme to didactic meditation and allegorization is but a short distance. The actual function of the steam roller (to "crush all the particles down / into close conformity" or [to crush] "sparkling chips of rock" "to the level of the parent block") becomes a metaphor for the stolid single-mindedness of dogmatic judgment. The fragile, flitting image of "butterflies" in the last stanza, by creating a dramatic contrast with the steam roller's ruthless reduction of "particles" to the leveling "conformity" of authority ("parent block"), flashes back to the first stanza, where the heavy solidity of the object ironically makes "half wit" desirable in retrospect. The poem's conclusion doubly prolongs this irony, for it is "lack" of "half wit" that deprives the steam roller, turned now into an allegory for unimaginative, uncritical thinking, of the self-reflectivity needed to "question" the "congruence" that does not exist after all.

> The illustration
> is nothing to you without the application.
>   You lack half wit. You crush all the particles down
>   into close conformity, and then walk back and forth on them.
>
> Sparkling chips of a rock
> are crushed down to the level of the parent block.
>   Were not "impersonal judgment in aesthetic
>   matters, a metaphysical impossibility," you
>
> might fairly achieve
> it. As for butterflies, I can hardly conceive
>   of one's attending upon you, but to question
>   the congruence of complement is vain, if it exists.

The power of observation of a poet immersed in an increasingly visual culture consists in making her poems in turn objects of the reader's observation as well. Readers cannot but pay attention to the sharp contrast in shape between "An Octopus" and "The Fish." Observation concerns form, rhythm, and sound. The shape, or perhaps rather the "mechanics," of a Moore poem is rarely mistaken. Moore was "very interested," as she said, "in mechanical things." That was one of the reasons why she took such pleasure in collaborating with the Ford Motor Company to find catchy names for their motorcars. But she also claimed that there was nothing mechanical about the composition of her poems. Her imagery to describe her process of composition pertains rather to the romantic realm of the organism. "I never 'plan' a stanza," she told Donald Hall in an interview in 1963. Remindful of her biology minor and her pleasure in lab work, she continued: "Words cluster like chromosomes, determining the procedure." Nevertheless, she also admitted to the difficulty of reproducing successive stanzas identical to that chromosomal first one. The sequence of Moore's syllabic stanzas in a poem does convey the impression of a carefully made object, an object constructed with meticulous precision, as if manufactured by a skilled factory worker, but somehow to defy commodification. "To a Steam Roller" is made up of three similarly constructed stanzas of four lines each, of similarly equal or unequal number of syllables, and equally paired by rhyme or lack of it. The first two lines of each stanza rhyme, though they differ considerably as to number of syllables (five the first, twelve the second), the second and third lines have the same number of syllables but do not rhyme, and the fourth and last line stands alone with a larger number of syllables (fifteen) and no rhyme. Moore's deft handling of English monosyllables and Latinate polysyllables (one is reminded of Stevens's "imagination's Latin" and "lingua franca et jocundissima") brings to mind her response to her own sly question in a much later poem, "Armor's Undermining Modesty" (first published in *The Nation* in 1950). Her question and reply here – "What is more precise than precision? / Illusion" – point to her lifelong desire to reconcile the accuracy of science with the imaginings of poetry. By giving another poem of about the same period as "Armor's Undermining Modesty" the strange title of "Voracities and Verities Sometimes Are Interacting" (1947), Moore recalls her definition of poetry as a voracity of contemplation in her 1936 review of Stevens's *Ideas of Order* further to merge the rigor of concrete reference, abundant in the poem ("diamonds," "emerald," "elephant," "tiger-book"), and the suggestive fluidity of abstraction that brings the poem to closure ("One may be pardoned, yes I know / one may, for love undying").

"To a Steam Roller" also illustrates Moore's lifelong habit of interrupting her own poetic discourse by inserting in her poems quotations from other authors, usually from prose writings. Moore's technique, to be distinguished from that of Eliot or Pound who quote to evoke the tradition, produces three main effects. First, the graphically marked citation calls attention to the linguistic materiality of the poem and underscores its overt presentation as an intertextual literary construct, an object that is itself made of already made objects ("Were not 'impersonal judgment in aesthetic / matters, a metaphysical impossibility,' you"). Second, it comically demystifies the romantic notion of poetic originality, a topic with which Eliot was to deal theoretically in "Tradition and the Individual Talent" (1919) only four years after "To a Steam Roller" was published. Finally, it calls attention to a certain advertisement-like quality in her poetry, which in fact often has its source in promotional literature or informative articles in magazines (one of her favorites was *The Illustrated London News*). To leaf through Moore's *Complete Poems* and have one's eyes caught by so many inverted commas sprinkling most of the individual lyrics is also to think of Moore as a collector in a consumer culture, collecting quotations in her reading diary as she collected material objects – like the famously visible elephants on her mantelpiece. Her quotations come from a wide variety of sources, from magazines and literary texts and textbooks, or critical, scholarly, and biographical essays, to advertisements, travel brochures, government pamphlets, business documents; from important public speeches to random overheard statements or snatches of conversation (often with her mother). Moore started using notes to identify her quotations in *Observations* (1924), her first book – if we accept her claim that she had nothing to do with the publication of *Poems* in England (1921) – but she doesn't always identify all of them. The quotation in "To a Steam Roller," for example, taken from a passage in Lawrence Gilman's "Drama in Music" (*The New American Review* [April 1915]) which she had recorded in her reading diary, remains unacknowledged in her "Notes." On the other hand, she doesn't always use quotation marks to reveal her borrowings. Though Moore once explained this habit by her desire to be "honorable and not steal things" and thus avoid being a "plagiarist," a closer look at the way she uses the art of citation will tell us more about her conception of poetic truth ("verity" was a favorite word of hers) than about the accuracy of her quotations and their identifications. Eventually (at least since *What Are Years* [1941]), Moore's "Notes" to her quotation-studded poems appeared preceded by "A Note on the Notes." It reads uncannily like a clever advertisement, proclaiming its own uselessness by virtue of the intrinsic goodness of the product advertised:

A willingness to satisfy contradictory objections to one's manner of writing might turn one's work into the donkey that finally found itself being carried by its masters, since some readers suggest that quotation-marks are disruptive of pleasant progress; others, that notes to what should be complete are a pedantry or evidence of an insufficiently realized task. But since in anything I have written, there have been lines in which the chief interest is borrowed, and I have not yet been able to outgrow this hybrid method of composition, acknowledgements seem only honest. Perhaps those who are annoyed by provisos, detainments, and postscripts could be persuaded to take probity on faith and disregard the notes.

As it seems, the "Notes" are at once both important and negligible. What is really, uniquely important is "the hybrid method of composition," Moore's own way of reinventing language through intertextuality, a reinvention that alone enables the poet to bring used, deadened words back to unexpected, surprising life. A deliberate reflection on the advertising techniques of the time, this is also a further, oblique commentary on poetic originality, which Moore may skillfully render problematic but still craves, like any other major poet in the Western tradition. After Harold Bloom and his musings on the anxiety of influence, one would perhaps wonder if some of the borrowings not identified by Moore either by quotation marks or notes, and often quite "prosaic" in themselves, might not "belong" to other poets "originally." In "Efforts of Affection," Elizabeth Bishop, who had just been praising Moore's intellectual honesty in the highest terms, confesses her "slight grudge" against one of Moore's unacknowledged borrowings, which Bishop wished then to "reclaim" as her own. The "bell-boy with the buoy-ball" in the fifth stanza of "Four Quartz Crystal Clocks," a phrase that goes unmentioned in Moore's "Notes," had first occurred to Bishop in Cape Cod as she watched the hotel bell-boy carry her luggage down the corridor along with the buoy-balls Bishop was bringing home to a friend. Bishop liked the sound of it so much that, out of "vanity," she later repeated it to Moore. "It was so thoroughly out of character for [Moore] to do this," Bishop concludes, "that I have never understood it. I am sometimes appalled to think how much I may have unconsciously stolen from her. Perhaps we are all magpies."

Whether Moore had forgotten where the bell-boy with the buoy-ball came from is not the point. The point is that poets *are* all magpies (if that happens to be your preferred metaphor), and there is nothing wrong with that. Poets are "magpies" in the sense that they always write their poems in the tradition, inside poetry and out of previous poets' poems, and thus inside language and culture. What is interesting in Moore's case is that her "Notes" and "A Note on the Notes" put into question this notorious parasitism of poets, by identifying her "borrowings" as being mainly from non-poetical sources. Moreover, as the poet herself knew only too well, poets do tend to "forget" what is poetically most relevant for their creativity. No wonder she so often "forgets" to give the references of her quotations. A fine example of deliberate forgetfulness, although bearing, as Hart Crane would say, much remembrance, is Moore's "Granite and Steel," first published in *The New Yorker* in 1966:

> Enfranchising cable, silvered by the sea,
>   of woven wire, grayed by the mist,
>   and Liberty dominate the Bay –
>   her feet as one on shattered chains,
>   once whole links wrought by Tyranny.
>
> Caged Circe of steel and stone,
> her parent German ingenuity.
> "O catenary curve" from tower to pier,
> implacable enemy of the mind's deformity,
> of man's uncompunctious greed
> his crass love of crass priority
>   just recently
> obstructing acquiescent feet
> about to step ashore when darkness fell
>   without a cause,
> as if probity had not joined our cities
>   in the sea
>
> "O path amid the stars
> crossed by the seagull's wing!"

"O radiance that doth inherit me!"
– affirming inter-acting harmony!

Untried expedient, untried; then tried;
way out; way in; romantic passageway
first seen by the eye of the mind,
then by the eye. O steel! o stone!
Climactic ornament, a double rainbow,
as if inverted by French perspicacity,
    John Roebling's monument,
    German tenacity also;
    composite span – an actuality.

The "source" of the poem, according to its "Notes," is Alan Trachtenberg's *Brooklyn Bridge: Fact and Symbol* (1965). One of its marked quotations ("O catenary curve") is said to be taken directly from Trachtenberg's book (p. 69), as is the unmarked image of "Caged Circe" (no page given [137]). No other marked quotation is identified or acknowledged ("O path amid the stars / crossed by the seagull's wing!"; "O radiance that doth inherit me!"), and though these two come directly form Hart Crane's "Atlantis" in *The Bridge*, Crane's name or his poem are never mentioned. And yet, Moore knows only too well that Crane's poem is always in Trachtenberg's mind as he writes his book, whose concluding chapter is entirely devoted to the great singer of America's "evil" and "redemption." Moreover, Moore's poem, whose title is also borrowed from "Atlantis" ("Up the index of night, granite and steel – / Transparent meshes – fleckless the gleaming staves – / Sibylline voices flicker, waveringly stream / As though a God were issue of the strings . . ."), resonates with Crane's wording, music, and sense of wonder and awe before the miracle of Roebling's construction, not only in "Atlantis" but also in "To Brooklyn Bridge." Even Poe's "The City in the Sea" gets into Moore's poem filtered through Crane's "The Tunnel" by Trachtenberg's hand. "Granite and Steel" was perhaps the last major poem written by Moore. In its background there is also the establishment of Brooklyn Bridge as a national monument in 1964. As she was writing her poem at age seventy-eight, the ample span of her life almost completed, Moore evidently had the promise of "America"'s "Liberty" more in her mind than twenty-seven-year-old Crane did when he was struggling with sections of *The Bridge* in the Isle of Pines in the summer of 1926. In his letters to Waldo Frank at the time (in which, incidentally, he says at one point he hopes to sell some of his "tropical" poems to Marianne Moore for *The Dial*), Crane is often tormented that "the whole theme and project seems more and more absurd." There is no indication that Moore had access to Crane's letters, which Brom Weber first published in 1952 but, if she did, Crane's moving apology for *The Bridge*, for Whitman (whom Moore actually abhorred), and for the nation in his letter to Allen Tate of July 13, 1930, would have been on her mind as well. In the conversation that all poetry is, and American modernist poetry to a large extent explicitly is, what Moore's "hybrid method" quietly accomplishes in "Granite and Steel" is the vindication of Crane's "project" in the sixties, certainly a far more hopeful moment for the United States than the Depression thirties: faith in America's "Liberty" without losing sight of the nation's "actuality."

In 1925 Marianne Moore became acting editor of *The Dial*. The following year she took full responsibility as editor, a position she would hold until the journal's demise in 1929. During her term as editor of *The Dial*, excluding her regular contributions to the journal, Moore published very little poetry. But the mid-thirties saw the appearance of two important books: *Selected Poems* (1935) and *The Pangolin and Other Verse* (1936). The idea of a *Selected Poems* was Eliot's, who also offered to write the introduction, an enlarged and revised version of his 1923 joint review of *Poems* and *Marriage*. *Selected Poems* would be more accurately described as a gathering together of the poems included in her two previous books, the long poem *Marriage* (1923) printed separately as a chapbook in Monroe Wheeler's Manikin Press, and a few other poems that had meanwhile appeared in anthologies. Eliot was right in thinking that calling the collection "Selected," with its discreet touch of publicity, would help to consolidate Moore's reputation as an established poet. He was also responsible for having the *Selected Poems* start with poems written after *Observations*, the very first one being "The Steeple-Jack," which would later continue to initiate all Moore's collections, from *Collected Poems* (1951), *The Complete Poems* (1967), and *Selected Poems* (1969) to the more complete edition of *The Complete Poems*, published in 1980 by Clive Driver, the literary executor of the estate of Marianne Moore.

"The Steeple-Jack" first appeared with "The Hero" and "The Student" in *Poetry* (1932), under the collective title of "Part of a Novel, Part of a Poem, Part of a Play." While the first two poems went into *Selected Poems* (the collective title having meanwhile disappeared), the third one was to be included only in *What Are Years* (1941). However, the first joint publication under that encompassing title points explicitly to the presentation of the poems as very self-consciously concerning the art of fiction. The student, the hero, and the steeplejack in Moore's poems are figures for the poet. "The Student," which was not included in *Collected Poems*, suggests that poetry for Moore is also learning, knowledge, and professional literary work. The student of her poem is Emerson's "scholar," as we find out from Moore's note on the phrase "a variety of hero" and the quotations that follow in the fifth stanza ("patient of neglect and of reproach" and "hold by himself"). Here is what Moore transcribes in her notes from Emerson's "The American Scholar": "There can be no scholar without the heroic mind"; "let him hold by himself"; "patient of neglect, patient of reproach."

Emerson's "scholar" had already found its way into Stevens's poetry, at least since the "dull scholar" of "Le Monocle de Mon Oncle" in *Harmonium* (1923). Stevens's "scholar" plays a very important role as a figure for the poet in all his oeuvre, as does the "hero," who also made his appearance at the same time (in "The Comedian as the Letter C," of whose exuberance Moore had written with such gusto in her review of *Harmonium* for *The Dial* in 1924). For Moore, too, the poet is a scholar or "student." In Moore's age of increasing professionalization, the poet is also a serious professional of the arts of language, ready to risk the "dangers" of "bookworms, mildews, / and complaisancies." However facetiously put, the "dangers" that "beset" "study" link this poem to the physical peril that threatens the steeplejack in the poem of the same title. While in "The Student" the association with "languages," "mottoes," and "feeling" subtly points to poetry writing itself, in "The Steeple-Jack" and "The Hero" Moore resorts to the names of two painters to stress excellence of performance, and thus leaves no doubt that she has art and the artist in mind in these poems: Albrecht Dürer in one, and El Greco in the other. As we read in the next to the last stanza of "The Steeple-Jack": "The hero, the student, / the steeple-jack, each in his way, / is at home."

"Dürer" is the first word of "The Steeple-Jack," and thus the first word that catches the imagination when one begins to read Moore's *The Complete Poems* from the very beginning. Dürer crops up again more than once in her poetry ("Apparition of Splendor" [*Nation*, 1952]; "Then the Ermine" [*Poetry*, 1952]). We know that Moore was fascinated by the Dürers she saw in the Louvre during her summer trip to Europe with her mother in 1911. In 1928 she wrote a piece in *The Dial* calling its readers' attention to an exhibition of Dürer and his contemporaries then showing in the print room of the New York Public Library. In her writing she also mentions an earlier exhibition of Dürer's wood blocks and engraving tools at the Metropolitan Museum. Moore was evidently drawn to Dürer's sharp powers of observation, which she also desired for her own art, and the detailed accuracy of representation of the physical world in his engravings and paintings. In the *Dial* article, she acknowledges in Dürer the attraction which "originality with precision" exerts in her and admires the effort and work he puts into his art (and Moore quotes St. Jerome's "perseverance" to stress her point), whether it is a trip he takes "to the Dutch coast to look at a stranded whale that was washed to sea before he was able to arrive" (the circumstance that provides her with the opening image of her poem) or the painstaking techniques of the art of engraving itself.

Moore's poems, too, are the result of much work and craftsmanship. They yield the image of the poet as a concerned professional. It seems as if Moore conducted a scientist's research in order to construct her poems like an expert worker. "If she was willing to put in so much hard work on a review running to two or two and a half pages," Elizabeth Bishop says, "one can imagine the work that went into a poem such as 'The Jerboa,' or 'He Digesteth Harde Yron' (about the ostrich), with their elaborate rhyme schemes and syllable-counting meters." The six, symmetrically arranged, syllable-counting lines of the fourteen stanzas that make up "The Steeple-Jack" call further attention to the poem as an object made of parts, as if fresh from the assembly line. Its shape is carefully controlled by the rhyme that pairs lines 2 and 5 of each stanza, and particularly so in the fourth, eighth, and thirteenth stanzas, where "the" is made to rhyme with "sea-," "that" with "hat" and "a" with "way." What we have here is Moore's conception of the "accented syllable" in action. In the self-consciously artful way in which it combines many different images, places, and landscapes in Moore's mind ("it is a privilege to see so / much confusion") – from Dürer's etchings to seacoast scenes, from a dazzling proliferation of fauna and flora to communal references to the everyday life of urban "simple people" – the obviously made-up poem rightfully claims its status as a modern work of art alongside Dürer's. Moore's sense of place and nature, so well conveyed through Dürer's art in "The Steeple-Jack," has expression also in her fine articulation of geography and culture in such poems as "England" (1920), "New York" (1921), "People's Surroundings" (1922), "Virginia Britannia" (1935), and "Spenser's Ireland" (1941). Perhaps more so than the others, however, "The Steeple-Jack" will not close without leaving behind a discreet didactic note of prudent "living" and "hope." A more intrusive moral tone will increasingly find its way into Moore's poems as the passage of years contributes to enhance her Republican conservatism. The sixties will find her supporting the Vietnam War (which she, like her brother, does not hesitate to compare with World War II) and agreeing with those who were then affirming the values of "civilization" and conformity against the radical protesters.

Moore's radicalism best expresses itself as poetry. Moore's poems speak themselves as they interrogate modern culture. Of "The Fish" (first published in *The Egoist* in 1918) H. D. said that it was a key to the understanding of modern writing and that it changed the way modern poetry was perceived in the culture. "The Fish" inaugurated a strategy that Moore was to use until the very end, although not always with the same extraordinary poetic effect of surprise and uncertainty, as comparison with a very late poem, "The Magicians Retreat" (1970), easily shows. The strategy consists of beginning the first sentence of the poem already with the title and continuing it in the first line. One would perhaps expect the effect to be one of smooth fluidity, harmonious continuity, and serenity. This is indeed what we find in "The Magicians Retreat," whose handling of line, rhythm, and rhyme helps somehow to smooth the strangeness of the syntax. The last four lines of the later poem read like this: "A black tree mass rose at the back / almost touching the eaves / with the definiteness of Magritte, / was above all discreet." The allusion to Magritte cannot but bring to mind the celebrated anti-representational title "Ceci n'est pas une pipe," questioning, perhaps, the very existence of the magician's retreat. Not so in "The Fish," where the artificiality of the stratagem is forcefully enhanced by the visual shape of the poem, both as an obviously contrived artifact and an exquisitely shaped organism. The "fish" is/are the "poem." The most blatant example is the next to the last stanza, which provocatively taunts the reader with its strange outline of a totally disconnected thing:

> ac-
> cident – lack
>   of cornice, dynamite grooves, burns, and
>   hatchet strokes, these things stand
>   out on it; the chasm-side is

The extremely precise shatteredness of Moore's stanzaic form is here further underscored by imagery suggesting explosion and violence ("dynamite grooves"; "hatchet strokes"; "chasm"). The same can be said of the poem as a whole. By its deft use of discreet sea imagery that seems at one point to reflect the starred sky (by stanzas 4 and 5 the sea – "black jade" and "turquoise sea of bodies" – seems to become indistinct from the sky), the poem very skillfully works toward giving the impression of one single all-comprehending organism, or "defiant edifice" (something similar happens in "The Paper Nautilus," where various sea creatures have their counterparts in constellations in the sky). And yet, the swift movement of the language in "The Fish," with its gerunds and images of threatening separateness and fragmentation, leaves the poem in utter undecidability (even as regards the contradiction between what is "dead" and the age-old "sea"). So, a device that may at first seem to work toward an effect of continuity ends up being in fact an effect of discontinuity – or poetic interruption.

The Fish

> wade
> through black jade.
>   Of the crow-blue mussel-shells, one keeps
>   adjusting the ash-heaps;
>   opening and shutting itself like

an
injured fan.
    The barnacles which encrust the side
    of the wave, cannot hide
        there for the submerged shafts of the

sun
split like spun
    glass, move themselves with spotlight swiftness
    into the crevices –
        in and out illuminating

the
turquoise sea
    of bodies. The water drives a wedge
    of iron through the iron edge
        of the cliff; whereupon the stars,

pink
rice-grains, ink-
    bespattered jelly fish, crabs like green
    lilies, and submarine
        toadstools, slide each on other.

All
external
    marks of abuse are present on this
    defiant edifice –
        all the physical features of

ac-
cident – lack
    of cornice, dynamite grooves, burns, and
    hatchet strokes, these things stand
        out on it; the chasm-side is

dead.
Repeated
    evidence has proved that it can live
    on what can not revive
        its youth. The sea grows old in it.

A similar interruptive effect is achieved in "An Octopus" (*The Dial*, 1924) but by completely different means. "An Octopus" is a much longer poem than "The Fish," and visually quite different. Not made up of any of Moore's artfully shaped stanzas, it rather lets its long free-verse lines, here and there interspersed by shorter ones, sprawl luxuriously along six pages of *The Complete Poems* (only "Marriage" goes over more pages in the volume). For music, the

poem relies on its rhythmic flow of long and short lines and its well-calculated
pauses, and on internal rhyme, alliteration, and assonance. As in "The Fish,"
the poem's title runs unexpectedly into the poem, thus constituting its first line
("An Octopus // of ice."), as if suggesting a beginning that will then proceed
to flow its course unimpededly to a tranquil end. However, that abrupt first
period, preventing the first sentence of the poem from being really a complete
sentence, should already be a warning to the reader, who nonetheless cannot
but be promptly seduced by the description that follows:

> An Octopus
>
> of ice. Deceptively reserved and flat,
> it lies "in grandeur and in mass"
> beneath a sea of shifting snow-dunes;
> dots of cyclamen-red and maroon on its clearly defined
>   pseudo-podia
> made of glass that will bend – a much needed invention –
> Comprising twenty-eight ice-fields from fifty to five
>   hundred feet thick,
> of unimagined delicacy.

Description, although it seems meticulous and profuse like a catalogue
throughout the poem, is perhaps not the right word. Although she conveys
a great deal of information in her poems, Moore is hardly a descriptive poet.
Like many of her poems, "An Octopus" relies on ignorance and surmise or the
desire for surmise: "a much needed invention"; "unimagined delicacy"; "What
spot could have merits of equal importance / for bears, elk, deer, wolves,
goats, and ducks?"; "what we clumsily call happiness." Or, if description,
then, as in Stevens, description without place, for in the end the poem becomes the only "place" worth considering. A written place as exuberant as
nature, if not more exuberant in the way it heightens the pure gusto of language, reaching out its lines of discovery like the unpredictable arms of an
octopus, spreading like a vine-like tree, stretching endlessly like a long Henry
James sentence (James appears at the end, American "remoteness" strangely
contrasted with the "distrusting," hard-hearted "Greeks"). But nonetheless a
place that is so interrupted by marked quotations that, here, too, the "defiant
edifice" has all "the physical features of accident," as in "The Fish"; and even
if it cries out toward the end for "neatness of finish" and octopus-like "relentless accuracy," the poem closes in perplexity, uncertainty of syntax, and the
fragility of the simile. Poetry and "engineering" balance each other in reciprocal
interruption:

Is "tree" the word for these things
"flat on the ground like vines"?
some "bent in a half circle with branches on one side
suggesting dust-brushes not trees;
some finding strength in union, forming little stunted groves
their flattened mats of branches shrunk in trying to escape"
from the hard mountain "planed by ice and polished by the
                                                    wind" –

the white volcano with no weather side;
the lightning flashing at its base,
rain falling in the valleys, and snow falling on the peak –
the glassy octopus symmetrically pointed,
its claw cut by the avalanche
"with a sound like the crack of a rifle,
in a curtain of powdered snow launched like a waterfall."

Not that there is no "real place" that "An Octopus" can be said to refer to. In 1922, Moore and her brother Warner climbed the glacier in Mount Rainier National Park in Washington State, and that experience is there behind the poem as well. As is usually the case, Moore's papers in the Rosenbach Archives tell us far more about the various sources for the quotations in the poem than the notes provided by *The Complete Poems*. The notes do not tell us, for example, that *The National Parks Portfolio of Rules and Regulations*, mentioned by Moore, included an aerial photograph in which Mount Rainier looked like an octopus, and that the phrase "an octopus of ice" was actually used to describe it. While reading the poem, the reader may well have the impression that "An Octopus" presents itself like a parody of a "useful" tourist advertisement, some of the quotations functioning then as ironic publicity slogans ("creepy to behold"; "grottoes from which issue penetrating draughts / which make you wonder why you came"; "a mountain with those graceful lines which prove it a volcano"; "names and addresses of persons to notify / in case of disaster"). Moore's poetry, not unlike many of the articles she wrote for *The Dial*, plays frequently with the promotional: writing that enhances pleasure by the information it claims to convey. In the case of "An Octopus," beginning by having an octopus as an image for the glacier, Moore goes on to display "accurate" knowledge about one and the other (octopods both) for the construction of her own verbal artifact of complex, far-reaching associations. The natural sublime of Mount Tacoma, the Indian name for Mount Rainier, on which Moore lavishly lingers throughout the poem, culminates in "sacrosanct remoteness," best represented by Henry James (Moore's admiration for Henry James's "Americanness" is recorded in her essay on the writer, "Henry James as a Characteristic American," first published in *Hound and Horn* in 1934). In the end, the notes are irrelevant, though not the quotations. The quotations send us back to the "not poetry" of poetry making. They are like "clearly defined pseudo-podia," made of words, which enable the poet to weave her poem like an "exacting porcupine," and take pleasure in the result: a "useless" verbal *objet d'art*. "One writes," Moore claims in "Idiosyncrasy and Technique" (1958), "because one has a burning desire to objectify what is indispensable to one's happiness to express."

Though it is not, strictly speaking, one of Moore's "animal" poems, by its very title "An Octopus" cannot but remind its readers of them. "The Pangolin," which gave its title to one of Moore's volumes (*The Pangolin and Other Verse*, 1936), is one of the most remarkable and accomplished of them all. "Why an inordinate interest in animals and athletes?" By posing and answering this question herself in her foreword to *A Marianne Moore Reader*, Moore gives us culture-bound clues to her poems about animals, particularly the "armored" ones (pangolins, lizards, porcupines, hedgehogs, salamanders). Her seemingly glib reply to her self-addressed question is the following: "They are subjects for art and exemplars of it, are they not? minding their own business. Pangolins, hornbills, pitchers, catchers, do not pry or prey – or prolong the conversation . . . " What seems to relate animals and athletes in Moore's imagination is the "business" they "mind": the wondrous exquisiteness and exact purposefulness of the animal's natural morphology (*physis*), and the hard-earned perfecting of skill and proficiency (or "dexterity") of athletes (*techne*). At one point, Moore compares a player's gesture to a puma's. In "Baseball and Writing," a poem "suggested by post-game broadcasts" and first published in *The New Yorker* in 1961, the excitement of the game is said to be like the excitement of writing. Moore's lifelong interest in athletic prowess is well documented. In his memoir of the twenties (*Troubadour*, 1925), Alfred Kreymborg has a humorous anecdote to relate about Moore. Trying to find fault with her immense reading capacity or a gap in her encyclopedic range of knowledge, which all her friends genuinely admired, he once took her to a baseball game. Right at the beginning, when Christy Matthewson had just thrown a strike, Kreymborg asked Moore if she happened to know who that gentleman was. Her reply to a dumbfounded Kreymborg was that she had never seen the gentleman but that she guessed it must be Mr. Matthewson, for she had read his "instructive book on the art of pitching" and was quite delighted to "note how unerringly his execution [supported] his theories."

Moore's fascination with the professionalism and perfected technology of human "dexterity" is only paralleled by her fascination with animal morphology. Her interest in zoology, natural history, and science in general dates from her Bryn Mawr years. She delighted in illustrated books, articles, and lectures about animals all her life, and she was well known for her frequent visits to the zoo. The pangolin, however, she may never have seen in the zoo. As Robert T. Hall explains in an article on pangolins which Moore cites in her notes, in captivity it is very difficult to feed this ant-eating beast from the Asian and African forests, which renders its presence in zoological gardens in the West a near impossibility. We "seldom hear," Moore writes in "The Pangolin" (1936), of this "impressive animal and toiler." Perhaps for this reason, she wants her poem, on one level, to be an accurate, scientific description of the pangolin, a "model of exactness on four legs." A strange, non-aggressive creature covered with scales and having a long snout and a long tool-like tail, and a long, sticky tongue, the pangolin is capable of rolling itself up into a ball to escape danger quickly and quietly. It can spare its good digging claws by walking on the outside edges of its hands. Its nose, eyes, and ears are capable of complete closure to protect it from the fury of the ants it preys upon. It is capable of enduring long-term toil and exhausting, solitary trips.

But Moore also wishes her discourse on the pangolin to be more than merely skillful. "Another armored animal," the poem begins, already pointing to a world of references which the poet alone, in her poem and in her poetry as a whole, can allow to be made meaningful. Another armored animal, i.e., one more armored animal, like so many others the poet has been interested in and read and written about. The basilisk, for example, which had already appeared in "The Plummet Basilisk" in *Hound and Horn* (1933). On the other hand, the announcement made at the beginning of "The Pangolin" ("another armored animal") insists on *this* being *one other* armored animal that is distinctively different from all the others and which can perhaps, for that reason, yield meanings beyond itself as well. The analogy drawn in the first stanza between the pangolin and a miniature replica of a work by Leonardo da Vinci introduces the theme of nature competing with and imitating art (or more precisely, in this case, technology) that is also so dear to Stevens (Moore's image of the artichoke to describe the overlapping scales of the pangolin anticipates Stevens's pineapple as "a wholly artificial nature" in "Someone Puts a Pineapple Together" [1951]). But the fact that the "artist engineer" is really Leonardo suggests also the use of the pangolin as a figure for the artist and for the poet herself. *Another* armored animal, then, vis-à-vis the poet herself, who uses language as a shield behind which to construct her integrity.

> Another armored animal – scale
>   lapping scale with spruce-cone regularity until they
> form the uninterrupted central
>   tail-row! This near artichoke with head and legs and
>   grit-equipped gizzard,

the night miniature artist engineer is,
  yes, Leonardo da Vinci's replica –
    impressive animal and toiler of whom we seldom hear.
Armor seems extra. But for him,
  the closing ear-ridge –
    or bare ear lacking even this small
    eminence and similarly safe

contracting nose and eye apertures
  impenetrably closable, are not; – a true ant-eater,
not cockroach-eater, who endures
  exhausting solitary trips through unfamiliar ground at night,
  returning before sunrise; stepping in the moonlight,
    on the moonlight peculiarly, that the outside
    edges of his hands may bear the weight and save the
                        claws
    for digging. [. . .]

By using the personal relative ("of whom we seldom hear") and the masculine pronoun ("But for him"), Moore leaves the articulation between Leonardo and the pangolin open. The pangolin looks like an object created by Leonardo's engineering and artistic skills. But its own power to metamorphose its body according to its circumstantial survival needs makes it a privileged engineer as well. The poem goes on drawing various kinds of associations between nature and art, animal and human being, inevitability and intention. The pangolin, serpentining down the tree with the help of its tail, is likened to a wrought-iron vine in Westminster Abbey; the compactness of the rolled-up pangolin is compared to a fixture in a matador's hat; the gracefulness of the pangolin goes on to evoke spires of monasteries, themselves graced with animals; and man, although finally retrieved as "a mammal," is celebrated as the only animal with "a sense of humor" ("humor . . . saves years"), both ennobled and belittled by the contradictions of being human. Thus, Moore's poem rolls up on itself, like the armored pangolin, to keep alive the tension between the sheer accuracy of biological teleology and the moral design of humanly pondered, yet fallible technology (if not fallible democratic social engineering). Pangolins "are models of exactness . . . on hind feet plantigrade, / with certain postures of a man." While man slaves "to make his life more sweet," yet "leaves half the flowers worth having." Displaying some fine sense of humor herself, Moore concludes her poem with an aestheticization of the moral good to be found in being human rather than just animal.

For Moore's radicalism in the radical sense of "radical," we have to turn to her awareness of gender in some poems, of which the only potentially subversive one is "Marriage" (1923). "Radical" and "subversive" in the sense of turning a certain social given upside down by rigorously questioning its grounds (or roots): in other words, in "Marriage," marriage is forcefully put in question in its many aspects, including its current reassessments in modern culture. This is what Moore had in mind when she told her brother that she was hoping to give offense by this poem. Moore, who never got married herself (thus avoiding "circular traditions and impostures"), refers, disapprovingly, to the fact that marriage was frivolously considered to be a casual, impermanent state by so many people surrounding her. Marriage as a mere social contract for the temporary convenience of two people (like the marriage of Bryher and Robert McAlmon) must have been on her mind as well. Wasn't the marriage of Bryher and Robert McAlmon the perfect example of being "alone together" in Moore's poem? Mary Moore, in a letter to Bryher, explains that the latter part of her daughter's poem is about the indivisibility of the married couple. She also explains that the motto on the base of Daniel Webster's statue in Central Park, cited at the end of the poem ("'Liberty and union / now and forever'"), is as true of the family as the state. Moore may indeed have had in mind the conception of marriage as an ideal state bonding two people while setting them free, but the poem itself undermines the possibility of this ideal. In marriage too, Moore (who as a young woman had been active in the suffragist movement) could easily observe around her, "'some have merely rights / while some have obligations.'" The changes in values, manners, and conventions that American society and culture were undergoing in the first decades of the century, rather than grounding that possibility, added new difficulties to the relation between the sexes and to the idea and ideal of the family. Adam and Eve did not progress to a balanced bonding of new woman and new man, rather their supposedly elemental being-female and being-male was still there (along with "the serpent"), to complicate the new, would-be interchangeable roles to be played.

Marriage was subject for debate in Moore's literary circle, and Moore cannot but have taken part in it. In the same year that "Marriage" came out, Moore's friend Alyse Gregory published an article in *The New Republic* entitled "The Dilemma of Marriage." Gregory (whose husband, the English novelist Llewelyn Powys, was known for his liberal attitudes toward relations between men and women) sets out to denounce current ideologies on the subject of "marriage," which affirmed permanence and indivisibility while allowing for infidelities and adulteries that were left unspoken for the sake of maintaining comfortable relationships of convenience, economic stability, and, of course, social appearances. "It is hardly an exaggeration to say," writes Gregory while drawing to her conclusion, "that most monogamous marriages are compromises based upon mutual illusion, and maintained by fear." Then as now, "family values" could be easily adapted to circumstance.

The dilemma of marriage, a "public" "enterprise" to fulfill a "private obligation," as Moore puts it in her poem, is what grounds the structure of "Marriage"
as well. But because Moore's radicalism is also *poetic* radicalism, she succeeds,
as Williams says of her poetry in general, in separating the poem from "the
subject." Her explanation of her own "Notes" to the poem is very interesting
in this regard: "Statements that took my fancy which I tried to arrange plausi-
bly." Since the "statements" are Moore's notorious quotations, which make up
a good part of the poem, "plausibility" has to be understood as referring to the
poem's own terms. While stressing the subject, the quotations also contribute
to the swift movement of the poem, a long poem running rapidly down the
pages along its short lines, constantly calling attention to its own movement
by its constant shifts of perspective and stative framing. "Marriage" is studded
with information, like the newsreel and documentaries Moore liked so much
in the movies. This is one of the characteristics that Williams most praised
in Moore's poetry, and "Marriage" in particular. "A poem such as 'Marriage,'"
says Williams in his essay on Moore (1931), "is an anthology in transit. It
is a pleasure that can be held firm only by moving rapidly from one thing
to the next." In other words, and though it acknowledges and critiques the
politics of a socially constructed institution such as marriage, the poem resists easy semanticization and politicization. The poem's apparent declarative
beginning about marriage as a social institution ("This institution") immediately interrupts itself in the second line, as "enterprise," a concept that is both
more in accord with modern culture and more dynamic, offers itself as a more
adequate designation for marriage than stable "institution." The interrupted
declaration ends up being left unfinished as the poem quickly skips through
the mechanisms of the cultural construction of "this institution," whether
pondering the contradictory relation between the public (or political) and the
private (or personal) or invoking the first couple of protagonists in the biblical *Ur*-narrative, or even wondering about the social compulsoriness of the
institution:

> This institution,
> perhaps one should say enterprise
> out of respect for which
> one says one needs not change one's mind
> about a thing one has believed in,
> requiring public promises
> of one's intention
> to fulfil a private obligation:
> I wonder what Adam and Eve
> think of it by this time,
> this fire-gilt steel

> alive with goldenness;
> how bright it shows –
> "of circular traditions and impostures,
> committing many spoils,"
> requiring all one's criminal ingenuity to avoid!

The poem proceeds trippingly along its rapidly moving lines and disparate images and ideas, until its closure in the politically legitimating image of the American patriarch, Daniel Webster, and his motto for the nation: "Liberty and union / now and forever." But not without leaving behind an array of contradictory perspectives, often presented ironically, which problematize sexual difference and sexual identity, as well as the relations between man and woman, culture and nature, power and dependency, knowledge and ignorance – and, most importantly, the social, cultural, and literary construction of all these notions. Moore's reference to "'the Ahasuerus tête-à-tête banquet'" cannot but bring to the reader's imagination the biblical story of Vashti and Esther concerning the enduring disparate social consequences of wifely submission or rebellion. If Daniel Webster and "the Good Book" have the last word in the poem, the truth is that rebellion is right there in the cultural narrative that the poem does incorporate, but perhaps only for the purpose of "exonerating Adam." In the American 1920s culture of increasingly independent, accomplished, and professional women on the one side and ever more intensely success-driven men on the other, the emancipatory potential of marriage was clearly problematic (as it continues to be in the twenty-first century).

Moore was known for her endless revisions. The most famous of her revisions concern "Poetry" (first published in 1919), the poem that is many different poems and whose revisions in the course of years eventually turn an earlier, much longer version into Moore's "Note" to a later, much shorter version. Four versions of "Poetry" were published by Moore: a version with five stanzas, each stanza with six long lines occasionally linked by rhyme; a thirteen-line version in free verse and no stanzas; a version with three stanzas of five long lines and some rhyme; and a three-line version, to which Moore appended a revision of the five-stanza version in a footnote. Reducing a poem with five stanzas of six long lines each to a poem of only three long lines may appear like mutilation but, as Moore explains in an essay titled "Subject, Predicate, Object" (1948), the "objective is architecture, not demolition." Moore's play with architectonics can be best observed in her oscillation between syllabic stanzas and free verse, as well as in her use of the five-stanza version as a note to the three-line version. More interestingly still, in her five-stanza note to the three-line version Moore includes the original "Notes" to the longer version, which thus become the notes of a note. "I have hazarded a line,"

Moore explains in "Subject, Predicate, Object," "it never occurred to me that anyone might think I imagined myself a poet. As I said previously [e.g., regarding "Marriage"], if what I write is called poetry it is because there is no other category in which to put it."

In theoretical terms, what Moore ends up doing by playing in this way with the several versions of "Poetry," is to stage the problem of what is or is not (American) poetry, with which the impingement of culture at large (Stevens called it "the pressure of reality") was forcing all American modernist poets to struggle at the time. The conceptualization of "Poetry" and its many versions contain in themselves the consolidation of American modernist poetry, from its early need to justify itself in the "machine age" as including "useful" and "important" "raw material," to its crypt- and magic-like self-sufficiency. Between 1919, when the first "Poetry" first appeared in *Others*, and 1967, the date of *The Complete Poems*, Moore was also very actively reading and writing about other American modernist poets, all of them, in different ways, with concerns similar to hers: Eliot, Williams, Pound, Stevens, Cummings, H. D., Stein. In her review of *The Geographical History of America* for *The Nation* (1936), Moore provides a definition for Gertrude Stein's writing that applies to her own poetry as well: "perspicuous opacity." Poetry is nothing transcendent, the modernists believed, it is just "art-full" writing, a making in words, and every lasting poem reenacts in its poeming the very notion of "making" or *poiesis*. As an artifact, a made object, a "machine made of words," in Williams's much-quoted phrase, the poem can be constantly un-made and re-made (usually by its readers). This is the notion that Moore, playing the part of her own reader, dramatizes in her various experiments with "Poetry." Once demystified ("imaginary gardens with real toads in them"), and then skilfully de-assembled and efficiently re-assembled (like a factory-produced object), the poem-as-image of "speed and success" may indeed be made to appear as a "place for the genuine" – or the poetical.

> I, too, dislike it.
>   Reading it, however, with a perfect contempt for it, one dis-
>   covers in
>   it, after all, a place for the genuine.

5

HART CRANE
TORTURED WITH HISTORY

I F the American modernist poets can claim a *poète maudit*, he is Hart Crane. Born in Garretsville, Ohio on July 21, 1899, of well-to-do families of property and business, Harold Hart Crane never made it the American way. His mother, Grace Hart, was sensitive and artistically inclined but not at all prepared to work hard for what she really wanted. Frustrated and emotionally unstable, she demanded a lot of attention from her son, particularly after her marriage broke up in 1916. Devoted to her as her son was (he renamed himself "Hart Crane" to please her), he was to part with her tempestuously in 1928 never to see or be in touch with her again before his suicide in 1932. Crane's father was, by contrast, a successful, enterprising businessman, who very much wanted his son to follow in his footsteps and eventually take over the confectionery factory in Cleveland, Ohio. But Crane wanted to be a poet. In 1916, after his parents' divorce, he took off to New York City, ostensibly to prepare for college, but really to be a poet. To support himself Crane resorted to copy-editing in little magazines, advertising, even at times working for his father. But his inclinations, tastes, and orientations in life never conformed to bourgeois convention, and his needs, whether financial, emotional, or sexual, were always above his means. Excessive about his drinking and reckless about his homosexual adventures in harbors and docks, Crane ran easily into trouble with the police. He even managed to get jailed and savagely beaten at La Santé (the Paris headquarters of the French police) once for having floored a gendarme after a drunken row in a Parisian café. All along, he was writing some of the best poetry of the period. Crane's dazzling passage through his "broken world" of life and poetry is movingly captured in the "Words" Robert Lowell (1917–54) once put in the poet's mouth: "My profit was a pocket with a hole. / Who asks for me, the Shelley of my age, / must lay his heart out for my bed and board."

Born in 1899, Crane had, as he was fond of saying himself, a toe in the nineteenth century. The phrase expresses a spanning, or bridging, that is emblematic of Crane's poetry and poetic theory, as well as of the way his work was mainly received by different kinds of readers until fairly recently. Crane, some of his critics have argued and some still do, was not discriminating enough. He did not distinguish clearly poetry from life, epic from lyric, tradition from modernity, science from myth, history from fiction, reason from sentiment, country from self, self from other, perhaps masculine from feminine. Crane's poetry "fails," according to critics like Yvor Winters and Allen Tate, because the poet's Whitmanian ambition to incorporate the American nation, and even the Americas, into the subject of his poems could not but be crassly sentimental and morally, politically, ideologically, and pedagogically wrong. Some of the confusions Crane has been charged with, however, may well be only in the minds of those of his critics who use "the biological approach" (Crane's term) to read his poetry. "I'm sick of all this talk about balls and cunts in criticism," Crane replied once impatiently to Winters's single-minded idealized moral vision of "the complete [heterosexual] man" (May 29, 1927). In an earlier letter to Gorham Munson, Crane had already resented that "extra-literary impressions" of him had begun invading his friend's appreciation of his poetry (March 17, 1926).

Both Winters and Tate had praised Crane's poetry up until the publication of *The Bridge* in 1930. But by then the all too public course of Crane's tormented, unconventional life couldn't but condition the readings of friend and foe alike. Crane's faith in himself as a poet and his poetic ambition and intense longing for recognition often clashed violently with the pressure his family's conflicts put on him, with his emotional and sexual needs, his noisy fallings in and out of love or friendship, his increasingly more disagreeable and uncontrollable drinking binges, his homosexuality, his stormy one-night affairs with sailors frequently leading to brawls and to jail. The dislike Winters in particular expressed at the later development of Crane's poetry was indistinguishable from his dislike and moral disapproval of the course of Crane's personal life. In "The Significance of *The Bridge* by Hart Crane, or What are we to Think of Professor X?" (1947), Winters has no qualms about using what he thinks he knows about Crane's unconventional or controversial attitudes and preferences in life to account for the defects of his poetry. Winters grants that what he knows is by hearsay alone and so he cannot be really sure of anything. But if Crane's "weaknesses" (and Winters lumps together homosexuality, drinking habits, and Whitmanianism) can be presumed to be true, then the poet's "dissipation," as a poet, is easily accounted for.

For the way in which Crane wants to and should be read we must turn to Crane's "explication" of "At Melville's Tomb" (1926), which was his successful attempt at convincing Harriet Monroe to publish the poem in *Poetry* in spite of its "obscurities." Crane's extraordinary elegy for the author of *Moby-Dick* (soon after included in *White Buildings* [1926]), playing masterfully with alliteration, assonance, internal rhyme, and occasional end rhyme, is exemplary not only of Crane's verbal artistry but also of his "synthesis" of nation and poetry, poet and the nation's subject, epic and lyric. Crane would later call *The Bridge* (1930) his "synthesis of America." In this eight-part and fifteen-lyric long poem Crane makes his vision of the nation coincide with his vision of poetry, from the dedication "To Brooklyn Bridge" ("unfractioned idiom") and his own new prayer of Columbus in "Ave Maria" ("The word I bring") to its closure in "Atlantis" ("multitudinous Verb," "Psalm of Cathay," "Answerer of all"). From Columbus's voyage of discovery in "Ave Maria," Crane jumps forward to present-day Manhattan and its harbors only to go backwards again to rediscover America in his "handling" of its history and founding myths in the five sub-sections of "Powhatan's Daughter" ("The Harbor Dawn," "Van Winkle," The River," "The Dance," and "Indiana"). The remaining sections and poems complete the poet's double vision of poetry and nation, by combining impressions of different parts of the United States with allusions to American literature and culture (popular songs in "Cutty Sark," Whitman in "Cape Hatteras," vaudeville in "National Winter Garden," Isadora Duncan and Emily Dickinson in "Quaker Hill," Edgar Allan Poe in "The Tunnel"). However, "At Melville's Tomb" anticipates *The Bridge* in giving *lyrical* sense to the frailty and contradictions of American sea voyaging and nation building, and about the great legacy of American literature that they ground. Crane's response to Monroe's reservations about the recondite "reasoning," or lack of logic, of his poem was to offer the concept of the "logic of metaphor," which he had already used several years earlier in a letter to Alfred Stieglitz (July 4, 1923) and now associated with I. A. Richards's "pseudo-statement." As a poet, Crane explained in the letter Monroe later published in *Poetry* 29 (October 1926) along with the poem, he was (like Blake, or indeed Eliot) far "more interested in the so-called illogical impingements of the connotations of words on the consciousness (and their combinations and interplay in metaphor on this basis) than . . . in the preservation of their logically rigid significations . . . " Emerson's memorable pronouncement that poetry is meter-making argument, and not argument-making meter, comes to mind.

Here is the poem, whose title, "At Melville's Tomb," gives it its national context in American literature and culture:

> Often beneath the wave, wide from this ledge
> The dice of drowned men's bones he saw bequeath
> An embassy. Their numbers as he watched,
> Beat on the dusty shore and were obscured.

And wrecks passed without sound of bells,
The calyx of death's bounty giving back
A scattered chapter, livid hieroglyph,
The portent wound in corridors of shells.

Then in the circuit calm of one vast coil,
Its lashings charmed and malice reconciled,
Frosted eyes there were that lifted altars;
And silent answers crept across the stars.

Compass, quadrant and sextant contrive
No farther tides . . . High in azure steeps
Monody shall not wake the mariner.
This fabulous shadow only the sea keeps.

As the lyric subject constructs his viewpoint as that of the poet he sings and mourns for (thus becoming the poet he sings and mourns for ["from *this* ledge," italics added]), the poet is the sea voyager, the "mariner" that gives form to the American nation, from daring navigator envisioning a new world (somewhat like Whitman impersonating Columbus in "The Prayer of Columbus") to enterprising whaler contributing to the economic reality of the rising country. Imagination and commerce are combined in the implied figure of Captain Ahab, uncannily emerging from the shipwreck in the synecdoche of his now useless sailing instruments ("Compass, quadrant and sextant contrive / No farther tides . . ."). And yet, "bounty" continues to come from the deadly sea. How poignantly prophetic it is for the reader to realize that the sea as meaning, or "portent," of the nation is the poet's tomb, and literature the poet's sacrifice. The bequeathed treasure of "livid hieroglyph" and "scattered chapter" is the poet's poem offering itself to be forever deciphered as a *living* hieroglyph.

Curiously enough, Hart Crane, arguably the most "romantic" of the American modernist poets, displays in his poetry the clearest map for the complex and contradictory course of American culture in the twentieth century as a whole. His poems are witness to the consolidation of the emergent nation; they revisit and question the nation's myths of origin and rhetoric of legitimation; they celebrate conquest, expansion, and empire; they sing of science, technology, and material progress. But by making the poem's vulnerable subject coincide with the nation's heroic subject, by reaching out, however awkwardly, to the "other," and by presenting poetry, art, and love (*eros*) as the new faith to weld the individual and the community together, Crane's poetry seriously undermines the affirmation of its own singing. Crane's poems call powerfully for a revision of the American experience in history, its interruption of tradition and the past, and its promise of modernity and the future. Following in the footsteps of his friend and mentor Waldo Frank, Crane was forcing his readers as early as the 1920s to think of the American nation in the context of the American continent. In Crane's poems, the self-made and self-advertised America of modernization (the suspended cement and steel bridge) is also its own fiction of erasure (Columbus's "word" Cathay) which might yet offer the possibility of an alternative America in the utopian reinvention of self and nation ("Atlantis"). That Crane's "synthesis of America" is a subtle interrogation of the dominant culture (the "myth of America" he also claims to sing) can perhaps be best observed through the lenses of Winters's increasing criticism of his work. Crane evidently represented for Winters an image of "America" of which Winters totally disapproved.

Yvor Winters's harshest criticism of Crane's poetry, however, could never erase the fact that Winters, unlike Monroe, considered Crane one of the poetic geniuses, however ill-fated, of his generation. Crane's problematic impact on Winters must not be minimized. It has to do with the literary construction of American poetry in the first half of the twentieth century, with the relation of the poetry to the nation and its values, and with the various critics' self-definitions as arbiters of such matters. Crane evidently became for Winters, in Winters's capacity as a critic and moral canon maker, an *exemplum* of what an *American* poet should *not* be. On the other hand, Crane's poetic calling and single-minded dedication to poetry, as well as his generously unbiased appreciation of other poets' poetry (including Winters's), could not but haunt the poet in Winters. Not long after Crane's suicidal jump into the sea in April, 1932, Winters wrote two very moving poems about him: "Anniversary, To Achilles Holt" (1934) and "Orpheus, In Memory of Hart Crane" (1934). In both poems, Winters's self-possessed certainty about his own clear-cut intellectual and moral stance vis-à-vis what he described as Crane's lax anti-intellectualism seems to have been somewhat shaken by what must have appeared to him as a possible, and threatening, alternative vision of life, poetry, and the nation. In the Dionysiac Crane-as-Orpheus poem, subtly reminiscent of Crane's own elegy for Melville, "unmeaning," "wrung" from "the empty body" "in a bloody dream," resounds powerfully from the "lyre," the "avenging fire," the "immortal tongue." "Anniversary," in turn, closes with the following haunting lines: "Crane is dead at sea. The year / Dwindles to a purer fear."

Crane's views on poetry and poetics are to be found scattered throughout his letters, those addressed to his poet-friends in particular. All Crane's notes on poetry, whether his own poetry or that of other poets, show that he was a self-reflective poet, a very self-conscious craftsman, and fully attentive to the culture of contemporary America. His major concern as a verbal artist, as he insists in his clear-headed letter to Monroe, was with the rigorous construction of the poem according to a "predetermined and objectified" process. Crane's preoccupation with poetry as *poiesis*, or making, is not unlike Marianne Moore's, and his poems are no less carefully *made* objects than hers. As a craftsman, Crane takes pleasure in going over "the planks of the scaffolding" of his poems for the benefit of his most dedicated readers (to Waldo Frank, February 7, 1923). The way Moore received Crane's poetry was, however, always problematic. As acting editor of *The Dial*, she accepted "The Wine Menagerie" for publication (1926), but not without "changing it around and cutting it up until you would not even recognize it," as Crane complains in a letter to Charlotte and Richard Rychtarik (December 1, 1925). The exquisitely crafted three-part "For the Marriage of Faustus and Helen" was rejected (The two first parts were published separately in *Broom* in 1923 and 1924). And yet, Crane's poem, by creating a "distinctive" tone of voice and by uttering accents "flavored with artifice," is surely what Moore would call "a bouquet of vocal exclamation points" ("The Accented Syllable," 1916). The synthesis of stress and syllable in "For the Marriage of Faustus and Helen" underscores the fusion of time past and time present, tradition and modernity, that is Crane's concern in the poem. Helen-as-everlasting-beauty and the poet-as-Faustian-overreacher, the source of creativity and its potential for destruction, are reinvented in the quotidian "traffic" of the modern American city – with its arteries, streetcars, aeroplanes, and jazz rhythms – to give voice to an imagination that dares to "outpace" that of the ancients. Moore could not but have heard the poem as a "restatement" (Crane's word) of the imagination in the machine age. But she might have been disturbed by the arrogance of a poet that steals time ("thief of time") to present himself not just as the subject of lyric poetry but as the subject of the complexities and contradictions of contemporary America as well. Here is Crane's updated rhapsody of the poem's closure:

> Anchises' navel, dripping of the sea, –
> The hands Erasmus dipped in gleaming tides,
> Gathered the voltage of blown blood and vine;
> Delve upward for the new and scattered wine,
> O brother-thief of time, that we recall.
> Laugh out the meager penance of their days
> Who dare not share with us the breath released,
> The substance drilled and spent beyond repair
> For golden, or the shadow of gold hair.
>
> Distinctly praise the years, whose volatile
> Blamed bleeding hands extend and thresh the height
> The imagination spans beyond despair,
> Outpacing bargain, vocable and prayer.

Besides being an exacting writer, Crane is an attentive reader, always with sound advice to offer on the right balance of form and theme, as when he gently recommends that Tate take more time to revise his poems (February 12, 1923) or make his language more precise (January 27, 1927, a letter in which Crane comically plays "aunt Harriet" [Monroe] to Tate's "obscurities"); or as when he perceptively warns Winters against the "moral zeal" that may easily hamper the reader's "aesthetic" reception of Winters's poetry (February 26, 1927). Another important document for our understanding of Crane's ideas on poetry is "General Aims and Theories" (c. 1925), a set of notes apparently written to help Eugene O'Neill prepare the Introduction he had promised, and never wrote, for Crane's first book of poetry, *White Buildings* (1926). "General Aims and Theories" theorizes Crane's conception of poetry as a "bridge" between "tradition" and "modernity." By "modernity" Crane means "America," as another relevant essay, "Modern Poetry" (1930), further underlines. "America" in Crane is, to be sure, contemporary American culture; but also "America" in Sacvan Bercovitch's sense of an ideological consensus, a "synthetic ideal" without parallel in any other modern culture. "Modern Poetry" can be said to be "about" *The Bridge*, a justification of the poet's engagement with time and history. Although "General Aims and Theories" aims at explicating *White Buildings* for O'Neill, it deals more directly with "For the Marriage of Faustus and Helen," conceived by Crane as an alternative to Eliot's *The Waste Land* (1922), and points forward to *The Bridge*, on which Crane had already been working for quite some time.

For Crane, "modern" was synonymous with "American," if for nothing else because the American poet was in the ideal position to "acclimatize" the machine. Not to embrace the machine unconditionally, in the manner of Dada or Futurism, but to make it integral with the project of modern poetry though without ignoring its destructive potential. "Unless poetry can absorb the machine, i.e., *acclimatize* it as naturally and casually as trees, cattle, galleons, castles and all other human associations of the past, then poetry has failed of its full contemporary function" (Crane's italics). To acclimatize the machine means to acknowledge the inevitable course of time and history, and hence the substantial changes of modernity, calling for the poet's response anew. Quite in tune with New Critical principles (even if his New Critical friends were not always willing to recognize this), Crane states clearly that poetry is "an architectural art" and that the modern poet's "concern" is the same as it ever was in any great poet: "self-discipline toward a formal integration of experience." What goes on changing, Crane implies, is "experience," thus constantly challenging the poet in different ways. The modern lyric poet, for example, can no more ignore science or technology than Dante or Milton could have ignored theology.

On the contrary, the modern poet must "surrender," admittedly only "temporarily," to the challenges of urban life and the machine age, in order to achieve a new formal synthesis of experience. By the "modern poet" Crane means the American poet in tune with the rhythms and "nervosities" of modernization and the "glitter" of the technological city, perhaps himself as the "suitable Pindar for the dawn of the machine age" (to Gorham Munson, March 2, 1923). His example and inspiration is Walt Whitman, hopeful singer of the Locomotive, the Trans-Atlantic Cable, and Unity.

Crane concludes his brief reflections on "Modern Poetry" by resituating Whitman as the great earlier synthesizer of the dense complexities of the American nation – or modernity. Conceding to New Critical views that Whitman may be faulted "as a technician" and perhaps also for his "indiscriminate enthusiasm," Crane goes on to argue that the author of *Leaves of Grass* sets the example for the modern poet, for he, "better than any other, was able to coordinate those forces in America which seem most intractable, fusing them into a universal vision which takes additional significance as time goes on." What wonder, then, that *The Bridge*, Crane's "epic of the modern consciousness," includes an "ode to Whitman" (to Otto Khan, September 12, 1927) right in its middle? "Cape Hatteras," one of the few poems not published before inclusion in *The Bridge* and one of the last ones to be completed, is the "'center' of the book, both physically and symbolically," as Crane is eager to emphasize (to Caresse Crosby, December 26, 1929). Crane takes Cape Hatteras in eastern North Carolina, the site of the aeroplane experiments of the Wright brothers in 1903, as a proper synecdoche for America, the latter-day reinscription of the mythic East, or "imponderable" origin. Holding Whitman's hand, though departing on his own "way," as Whitman himself had urged in "Whoever You Are Holding Me Now in Hand," Crane pays here loving tribute to the poet who, Columbus-like, had first envisioned America as "more than India" (or Cathay). Many of Whitman's poems reverberate in "Cape Hatteras." Poems of the sea and poems of passage, poems of memory and poems of recording, poems of nation building, of course, but all of them poems of love as well, poems of reaching out and *bridging* ("Recorders ages hence [Whitman had said] . . . Publish my name and hang up my picture as that of the tenderest lover"). But many other poets and poems, including Crane's earlier ones as well, contribute to the Whitmanian "span of consciousness" of "Cape Hatteras."

By his stubborn attempt to resume Whitman's American song encompassing time and space, history and geography, geology and archeology, science and myth, fact and faith, Crane makes himself vulnerable to charges of "sentimentality." However, Crane was not oblivious (nor, to his mind, had Whitman been) of the abysmal discrepancy between Whitman's euphoric celebrations of his faith in America's universalizing role in the world and the nation's crass materialism, ruthless industrialism, and aggressive imperialism. "It's true that my rhapsodic address to [Whitman] in *The Bridge* exceeds any exact evaluation of the man," he writes to Allen Tate after his friend's not at all "admirable" review of the poem appeared in *Hound and Horn*. "But since you and I hold such divergent prejudices regarding the value of the materials and events that W. responded to, and especially as you, like so many others, never seem to have read his *Democratic Vistas* and other of his statements sharply decrying the materialism, etc., of which you name him the guilty and hysterical spokesman, there isn't much use in my tabulating the qualified, yet persistent reasons I have for my admiration for him, and my allegiance to the positive and universal tendencies implicit in nearly all his best work" (July 13, 1930).

Crane's quarrel with Eliot and "wastelandism" was, therefore, different from Williams's. It had not so much to do with the sounds and rhythms of the American "dialect," which Williams contended Eliot was incapable of hearing; it concerned, rather, the right of American poetry to its place in history. Like Williams, Crane was impatient with the lack of faith of prominent contemporary American poets not only in the continuing tradition of English poetry in the United States but also in the American nation as an adequate ground, or credible soil, for modern poetry. Not that Crane was not often tormented by serious doubts. He certainly was, as the painful writing process of *The Bridge* so well demonstrates. We might even say that what disturbed Crane's New Critical friends about his poems, and continues to disturb some of his readers to this date, is that his poetry is "tortured with history," a phrase which Crane uses in "The River" section of *The Bridge* ("The River lifts itself from its long bed, // Poised wholly on its dream, a mustard glow / Tortured with history, its one will – flow!"). Every enduring poem by Crane, from the exquisite lyrics of *White Buildings*, which Winters and Tate seemed to have admired so much, to the more complex individual lyrics that make up the whole of *The Bridge*, and beyond, is always a "lyric cry," often a love poem, and, at the same time, a poem about "modern" poetry and hence "about" the American nation as historically situated. And though Crane abided ever, against Eliot's cultural pessimism, by his faith in "America," the dark patches of the nation's history, no doubt intensified by his reading of Spengler's *Decline of the West*, could not but affect his thinking and imagination as well ("Is it Cathay . . . ?" he tremulously asks at the end of "Atlantis" and *The Bridge*).

To read Crane's letters carefully is to dispel once and for all the notion that he was an ill-educated poet. It is true that Crane never even finished high school but he was extremely intelligent and alert, an omnivorous and consistent reader, and an extremely lucid critic of himself and others. By the time he would have completed his secondary education Crane was already a published poet. "C33," a poem celebrating and mourning for Oscar Wilde, appeared in *Bruno's Weekly* in 1916, when the poet had barely turned seventeen. In the poem's *fin de siècle*, slightly decadent tone ("About the empty heart of night"; "The transient bosoms from the thorny tree") Crane's peculiar use of language, varied rhythms, and rich turns of phrase and verse are not yet to be fully heard. Like "October–November" (a more imagist-like exercise published in *The Pagan* in the same year) or other poems published in little magazines by young Crane but wisely excluded later from *White Buildings*, most poems now gathered together as "Poems Uncollected but Published by Crane" in Marc Simon's edition of the *Complete Poems* (1986) are experiments best read as songs "of minor, broken strain," as the poet says of sentimental poetry in his rather sentimental poem on Wilde. The one great exception is "The Broken Tower," which Crane never saw in print. It was published in *The New Republic* in 1932, after Crane's death. Some of the earlier poems carry symbolist modes and images (e.g., "Carmen de Boheme" [*Bruno's Bohemia*, 1918]; "To Portapovitch" [*The Modern School*, 1919]) and there is one hilarious, most unCranean parodic "homage" to E. E. Cummings ("America's Plutonic Ecstasies" [*S4N*, 1923]). The most interesting experiment is perhaps "Porphyro in Akron" (*The Double Dealer*, 1921), a poem that seems to try, not quite successfully, to construct itself in search of the appropriate synthesis of the American nation, land of rising capital, bringing together, as if anticipating some sections of *The Bridge*, "rubber workers," "Ohio hills," "Greek," "Swede," "Roumanian," and "Fords," and allusions to easily identifiable poetic traditions ("Madeleine's fair breast" and "Connais-tu le pays . . . ?"). "Forgetfulness" (*The Pagan*, 1918) concludes with a memorable, eminently quotable line resonant of Crane's preoccupation with time, history, and memory ("I can remember much forgetfulness"). A different case is that of "March" (*larus: the celestial visitor*, 1927), written after *White Buildings* was published. With its whimsical opening syntax, carefully balanced musicality, and surprising imagery of gloomy rather than bright shades, "March" reads like an accomplished compromise between Williams's "March" (*Sour Grapes*, 1921) and Stevens's "The Sun this March" (*Ideas of Order*, 1936). In all three poets, March is the month of spring and the promised renovation of life and imagination, a symbol for the desirable interruption, by poetry, of the inexorable passage of time. Williams's more celebratory poem compares and contrasts nature with art by punning with the great march of history, the intellect, and the imagination. In Stevens's poem, a minor exercise of the confrontation of the poet's "dark nature" with the sublime, March brings the threat of an early sun's "exceeding brightness." Crane's poem has a finer kind of subtlety and complexity concerning poetic genesis and process. Crane's

March, the "vagrant ghost of winter," is somehow, in the waning of winter and
its own *knowing* waning, already announcing winter once again. Poetry seems
"waveringly" to emerge from such waning knowing – or *hunger*:

> Awake to the cold light
> of wet wind running
> twigs in tremors. Walls
> are naked. Twilights raw –
> and when the sun taps steeples
> their glistening dwindle
> upward . . .
>
>   March
> slips along the ground
> like a mouse under pussy-
> willows, a little hungry.
>
> The vagrant ghost of winter,
> is it this that keeps the chimney
> busy still? For something still
> nudges shingles and windows:
>
> but waveringly,   this ghost,
> this slate-eyed saintly wraith
> of winter wanes
> and knows its waning.

Crane published only two books of poetry during his lifetime: *White Buildings* (1926), a collection of mostly previously published poems, and *The Bridge*
(1930), which may also be said to be a collection of mostly previously published poems but which aspires to be, and is, much more than its parts. A
third collection of poems, most of them published in little magazines like
transition, *The Dial*, and *The New Republic* between 1927 and 1931, was being
gathered together by Crane even as he continued to work on *The Bridge* in the
late 1920s. All these poems are now included in Simon's *Complete Poems* under
the heading "Key West: An Island Sheaf." The heading was Crane's, as was the
Blakean epigraph ("The starry floor, / The wat'ry shore, / Is given thee 'til the
break of day"), and clearly reveals the poet's desire to give some coherent form
to his "tropical memories" (to Yvor Winters, June 18, 1927). From May to late
October 1926, Crane was in the Caribbean, mainly on the Isle of Pines, where
his mother's family owned a house and some property. As a youth, in 1915,
Crane had been on the island with his parents. Though that earlier stay was
at the time painfully disrupted by serious tensions in his parents' marriage,
or perhaps for that very reason, Crane believed in 1926 that a sojourn in the
Isle of Pines would replenish him imaginatively and further his slow-paced

work on *The Bridge*. For a short period, Crane's congenial friend and mentor Waldo Frank joined him. That circumstance, as well as the fact that Crane had what seemed like a rewarding erotic experience while in the Caribbean, may account for Crane's apparently increased creativity at this time. Not only did his work on *The Bridge* progress well, but new poetic ideas and projects came to him also. Such new projects include the "Island Sheaf" poems that he had already been writing for some time, as well as a future "blank verse tragedy of Aztec mythology," of which more later.

Not all poems gathered in the "Island Sheaf" folio are "tropical" and they range very widely in form and theme. But if the "tropics" may be said to stand for a renewal of imaginative power, even such unlike poems as an elegy for Harry Crosby, Crane's wealthy friend and patron, who committed suicide in December 1929 ("To the Cloud Juggler" [1930]), and the two sonnets celebrating two great poets ("To Emily Dickinson" [*The Nation*, 1927] and "To Shakespeare" [c. 1926–30]) can be part of Crane's "Carib suite" (to Yvor Winters, July 18, 1927). With the exception of the Dickinson poem, all these poems were composed, or at least revised, under the spell of the great hurricane of mid-October, 1926, which devastated the island and nearly razed Crane's house. Whatever their subject matter, these poems deal with Crane's constant reassessment of his poetic powers, as his uncannily perceptive readings of and confrontation with Dickinson and Shakespeare in the two sonnets more explicitly reveal. The poem that bears the title of "The Hurricane" not only attempts prosodically, as Crane wrote to Waldo Frank (February 1, 1928), "to secure the ground-rhythm of the hurricane," but also grounds the whole sequence on the terrible destructiveness of creative power ("the terrific and limitless single blast of destruction, wherein even thunder is submerged," as Crane explains to Yvor Winters [August 3, 1927]). The biblical tones and elaborate phrasing – whether extremely precise or erudite or obsolete – bring a strange artificiality to the irresistible natural process that inspires the poet as if it were god-like agency ("Lo, Lord, Thou ridest! / . . . / Thy chisel wind // Rescindeth flesh from bone / To quivering whittlings thinned – // . . ."). As he was writing the quintessentially American poem that he wanted *The Bridge* to be, Crane was evidently haunted by other meanings of "America," which Waldo Frank had been discovering for some time. The seas of discovery, the western conquests following previous conquests of lands and peoples and cultures, imperialisms succeeding imperialisms, the confusion of languages vying for power – all these ideas could not but enlarge the very concept of "America" that founds *The Bridge* for Crane, and even create, however obliquely, a more complex historical setting and a wider mythical context for that poem. Crane's half-facetious remark in a letter to

Susan Jenkins Brown (May 22, 1926) on one of the poems in "Island Sheaf," "The Mango Tree" (*transition* 18, 1929), is nonetheless quite telling: "I enclose an accidental calligramme committed this morning accidentally on my way to the *Bridge*. I'm convinced that the Mango tree was the original Eden apple tree, being the first fruit to be mentioned in history with any accuracy of denomination. I've been having a great time reading *Atlantis in America*, the last book on the subject, and full of exciting suggestions. Putting it back for 40 or 50 thousand years, it's easy to believe that a continent existed in mid-Atlantic waters and that the Antilles and West Indies are but salient peaks of its surface."

As Crane's reference to Lewis Spence's *Atlantis in America* (1925) suggests, while writing his "synthesis of America" the poet was avidly looking for "justification" (as his much-admired Whitman would say), justification of America, of modern (American) poetry, and of himself as an American poet. The confrontation of the "New World," as an image of primordiality and radical origin, with the forceful invasion, penetration, and possession by late-coming humanity concerns some of the poems of "Key West," the most interesting and most "tropical" one being "O Carib Isle!" (*transition* 1, 1927). In a letter to his mother (March 19, 1927), Crane explained that the poem was written "one hellish hot day" and that "its inspiration was *Cayman*" (Crane's italics). Crane's impressions of his trip to the Cayman Islands in June 1926 are vividly reported in a letter to Waldo Frank (June 19, 1926). The unexpected duration and strenuousness of the trip, the noisy and smelly promiscuity aboard a schooner filled with "cackling, puking, farting negroes," and the extreme heat on an island infested with huge insects, left a "staggering" Crane "with a sunburn positively Ethiopian." But the experience also fired his imagination with thoughts of myths of creation, perhaps, but certainly with other poets' real or imagined sea voyages of *written* discovery and wonder before distance, otherness, the unknown or the inexplicable, such as Coleridge's "Ancient Mariner" and Melville's *Moby-Dick* (though he doesn't mention it in the letter, Crane must have had "The Encantadas" on his mind as well). In the tropical poems of "Island Sheaf" Crane is also writing, with awe and wonder, his troubled discovery of America and American poetry, to which at the same time he is trying to give coherent form in *The Bridge*. That "O Carib Isle!" is part of his "synthesis of America" becomes clear in Crane's letter to Edgell Rickword, editor of the London *Calendar* (January 7, 1927). As he sends Rickword the three poems for publication, the poet explains the "general emphasis on the *marine*" common to "O Carib Isle!" and two poems from *The Bridge*: "Cutty Sark" and "Harbor Dawn." The title of the poem itself, "O Carib Isle!" immediately conveys a sense of awesome wonder, reinforced by the cryptic syntax of the first stanza,

as if the things observed could never be what they are supposed to be, and no
regrets allowed:

> The tarantula rattling at the lily's foot
> Across the feet of the dead, laid in white sand
> Near the coral beach – nor zigzag fiddle crabs
> Side-stilting from the path (that shift, subvert
> And anagrammatize your name) – No, nothing here
> Below the palsy that one eucalyptus lifts
> In wrinkled shadows – mourns.

The poet's discovery in "O Carib Isle!" is not of pristine, timeless, unpaced land but rather a land already violated and possessed, "a doubloon
isle," yet now a land without "Captain" or "Commissioner," a land which
time and history have ruthlessly turned into a grave. As if human passage
through the earth could ever leave behind no more than deadly traces on the
ground, anagrams for the belated poet to decipher into yet "a stranger tongue."
The "pilgrim" discoverer-poet finds himself rather discovered and taunted
("anagrammatized") by the sheer physicality of the inhuman island and its
creatures (tarantulas, crabs, and terrapins) for daring to "gainsay" the earlier
language. Like a latter-day Ishmael, as he is working on *The Bridge* Crane
wonders what meanings of America his late writing (the "carbonic amulet" of
his typewriter) can still make possible. From the vantage point of a twenty-
first-century reader, Crane's Carib Isle, in its search for a distant America, "isle
without a turnstile," not only resonates with Melville's "Wandering Islands"
(remember the "greedy grave" in the First Sketch of "The Encantadas" [1856])
but also looks forward to Gary Snyder's more idealized hopes in *Turtle Island*
(1974).

Like most modernist poets, Crane made his early reputation in little mag-
azines, where all his major poems were published before being collected in
White Buildings (1926) and *The Bridge* (1930). Of these two volumes, *White
Buildings* remains a collection of discrete poems of a wide range of theme, form,
prosody, and rhetoric, and only *The Bridge* can and must be read as *one* poem.
And yet, the same "general emphasis on the *marine*" can easily be read into
White Buildings as well. In November 16, 1924, when *The Bridge* was taking
shape in his imagination, Crane wrote to his mother about a sequence of six
poems he was then "engaged in." The six poems, later to appear under the
title "Voyages" as the closing sequence of *White Buildings*, were "sea poems,"
Crane explained to his mother, as well as "love poems." And no less than *The
Bridge*, Crane's sea-voyage-and-love poems are poems about "America," too,
even though Crane's poetry both reinforces and undermines the "synthesis" of

traditional, consensual "America." In "Passage," for example, the "sea" "heard" by the poetic subject in the opening strophe subtly gives a vaster dimension to the theme of self-discovery and self-authorization that runs through the poem:

> Where the cedar leaf divides the sky
> I heard the sea.
> In sapphire arenas of the hills
> I was promised an improved infancy.

Crane's "improved infancy" points forward to "Autobiographia Literaria" by Frank O'Hara, a very close reader of Crane's poetry. Though O'Hara's prosy style clings to everyday speech where Crane's verse rings with artful poeticity, the two poets speak intelligibly to each other. Like "Passage," "Autobiographia Literaria" is a poem about becoming a poet, ostensibly in the romantic tradition but *Americanly* against the grain of that very same tradition. While the poet of "Passage" discards Wordsworthian recollection ("My memory I left in a ravine"), the poet of "Autobiographia Literaria" recollects what romantic childhood mythology tends to forget: what originates poetry is not recollection of early childhood, but interruption, or even erasure, of memory. "Memory, committed to the page, had broke," Crane's "Passage" concludes, and in O'Hara's "Autobiographia Literaria" the poet's *un*improved American infancy eventually becomes "the center of all beauty." In a later O'Hara poem, disruption of literary tradition is disruption also of the unquestioned hegemonic values of patriarchal society. "What of Hart Crane," O'Hara wonders in "Cornkind," against the background of a parody of pastoral and heterosexual bliss. O'Hara's revision of Wordsworth and Coleridge in "Autobiographia Literaria," echoing Crane's "too well-known biography" in "Passage," makes both poems disruptive not only of poetic tradition but of social mores as well. "Passage" can thus be read as an earlier instance of "autobiographia literaria," indeed, *homosexual autobiographia literaria*, to the extent that the poem's dramatic structure of protagonist and antagonist, as well as its imagery of "dangerous" disruption and "broken" "memory," cannot but raise questions about the "normalcy" of a culture that is known to be "consensually" heterosexual.

But "Passage" also echoes Whitman's sea-drift poems (in which the poet hears *the word* from the sea), as well as "Passage to India," Whitman's rather chauvinistic celebration of "America" and evolving modernity as the greatest discovery of all. "Passage" reenacts, therefore, not merely a poetic *rite de passage*, in the poet's encounter with the "thief" and argument with the "laurel," but a passage of discovery and the promise of a new beginning. In "Passage," what the poet *hears* from the sea amounts to *images* of totality and fragmentation that in the end combine to make time and distance conflate in the empty space of "unpaced beaches." "He closed the book," the last stanza begins, and from this closure the poem's conclusion irrupts in images of ancient time, abysmal mythic space, and originary *hearing*, promising perhaps a new, memory-less voice:

> He closed the book. And from the Ptolemies
> Sand troughed us in a glittering abyss.
> A serpent swam a vortex to the sun
> – On unpaced beaches leaned its tongue and drummed.
> What fountains did I hear? what icy speeches?
> Memory, committed to the page, had broke.

Thus, the poet hears from the sea not just a "new *word*, never before spoken," as he says in "General Aims and Theories," but a *new world*, never before paced, perhaps the *discovered* Cathay, Atlantis in America. Crane's poet-of-the-sea is an American poet of new beginnings precisely because he links poetry writing to ancient sea voyaging (as the image of "Anchises' navel dripping of the sea" at the end of "For the Marriage of Faustus and Helen" so beautifully suggests). Crane's voyaging always leads on to new worlds of experience and fulfillment, both personal and communal. Though the first of the six-lyric sequence of "Voyages" was already written in 1922, Crane made them into a six-poem love sequence when two years later he first fell in love with Emil Opffer, the Danish sailor with whom he had his single most satisfying and rewarding relationship. The voyages, then, are the beloved's actual sea voyages, as well as love voyages of unprecedented fulfillment for Crane as a human being and as a poet. The way he experiences this love affair, when he was living, as he liked to say, in the "shadow" of Brooklyn Bridge, reaches even beyond these two dimensions to embrace the nation, obliquely in "Voyages," fully and explicitly in *The Bridge*. The subject of love and poetry becomes the nation's subject as well. *The Bridge*, on which Crane was working all along, is also a "sea and love poem" where, indeed, the inspiration enhanced by his fulfilled love for Emil Opffer can also be seen. In its harbor scenes ("To Brooklyn Bridge," "The Harbor Dawn," "Atlantis") a lover's presence is clearly implied. "Serenely now," the poet urges his lover in "The Harbor Dawn," "before day claim our eyes / Your cool arms murmurously about me lay," that "murmurously" bringing into the love scene the softer watery sounds from the "pillowed bay." More importantly, Opffer would recall in an interview many years later that Crane liked to say to him, "The whole world is a bridge."

The "emphasis on the *marine*" in Crane's poetry points to the sea as a matrix, the cultural matrix upon which, as in Whitman, the nation-as-America is rediscovered as promise, as well as made problematic. The "great wink of eternity" at the beginning of the second of the "Voyages" lyrics bespeaks the wide conquest of time and space that it will be the role of *The Bridge* to celebrate properly. But here, too, the "paradise" promised at the end of the voyage, besides being the lovers' paradise, is reached in *"ministrel* galleons of Carib fire" through the "adagios of islands" in the West Indies on which Columbus first set eyes in the so-called New World. The sea-as-matrix thus allows Crane to reinvent "America" and to make it problematic at the same time, not only because the homosexual erotic meanings of the poems point to an "America" that brings a different "covenant" from the one that supposedly grounds the consensual nation, but because the great American shipwreck in the beautiful "monody" for Melville, "At Melville's Tomb," is there in *White Buildings* immediately preceding "Voyages." By having his Melville poem locate the nation's poet in the space between the sea and the sky ("azure steeps" and what "the sea keeps"), Crane both celebrates and suspends the "new word" of poetry and nation. And so, when we reach "Belle Isle" at the closure of the "Voyages" sequence, the "covenant" is not the promised land anymore, but merely an "imaged Word" – perhaps the rhetoric and ideology that sacralized the word, "America." For his conclusion to "Voyages VI" and the whole sequence, Crane brought over the last stanza of a love poem he never published, "Belle Isle" (c. 1923), introducing however a very telling change of wording. Where the first line originally read, "It is the after-word that holds," it was revised to read, "The imaged Word, it is, that holds." Moreover, "Belle Isle," and particularly the next to the last stanza, reverberates with the "surmise" about the promised "place," which founds the myth of America as discovery also:

> Yet, clearer than surmise, – a place
> The water lifts to gather and unfold,
> Seen always – is Belle Isle the grace
> Shed from the wave's refluent gold.

The best introduction to the thematic and structural conception of *The Bridge*, no doubt the poet's most ambitious, complex, and controversial work, is Crane's letter of September 12, 1927 addressed to his Maecenas, the banker Otto Kahn. Here, the poet explains his "general method of construction," trying mainly, and successfully, to get one more advance from Kahn, the perfect representative of American capitalism and thus a true prophet of modernity. Crane knew as well as Pound that aesthetic and economic production go hand in hand in the culture of capital. Insisting in the course of his letter that he is concerned with "handling the Myth of America" and "writing an epic of the modern consciousness," Crane lingers on some of the poems already completed and sketches some of the ones still to be composed, clearly attempting to bring author's intention and poetic effect together for the benefit of the poem's patron-reader, if not indeed for his own benefit as poet-reader-in-painful-writing-progress. To write the epic of the modern consciousness is an "indescribably complicated" task, as Crane says, only comparable to the writing of that epic of the ancient consciousness called *The Aeneid*, because, for Crane, the "modern" consciousness is the "American" consciousness: hegemonic US American consciousness, basically, and exactly as a poet of Crane's age, sex, class, ethnic background, and education could grasp it in the 1920s.

In this letter to Otto Kahn, Crane concentrates on the poem's second section, "Powhatan's Daughter," evidently eager to explain his use of the "Indian" as "first possessor" of the American soil: "Powhatan's daughter, or Pocahontas, is the mythological nature-symbol chosen to represent the physical body of the continent, or the soil . . . The five sub-sections of Part II are mainly concerned with a gradual exploration of this 'body' whose first possessor was the Indian." The poet of *The Bridge* thus reduces the "Indian" to the soil-Pocahontas and then proceeds to take possession of that soil himself, thus supplanting the "Indian." After the introductory ode "To Brooklyn Bridge" and Columbus's prayerful word for a new world in "Ave Maria," "Powhatan's Daughter" introduces the modern American man as protagonist, the poet Hart Crane expressing himself and reminiscing, of course, but mainly what his imagination encompasses, impersonates, recreates, and remembers. "Powhatan's Daughter" comprises five poems of tightly constructed, measured, and rhymed form, as well as a gloss. The first poem is "The Harbor Dawn," a love lyric with the wharves of the poet's contemporary city of New York bustling noisily in the background. Next comes "Van Winkle," heavy with remembrance and forgetfulness, both personal and communal, memories of the past and inventions of the present, literary reminiscences, and the earliest recordings of history. Then comes "The River" – the Mississippi, both real and mythic, as overt referent. Its title is a synecdoche for the nation in the swiftly running and roaring twenties, rivers, rails, and cables spanning the rural, urban, and industrial geography of an America "tortured with history." But, as already in "Repose of Rivers" (1926) and as in so many other poets in the Western tradition (Hölderlin comes immediately to mind), the river is also a metaphor for the poet's consciousness, in whose flow alone the nation is (or communal meaning emerges). Next comes "The Dance," the usurped Indian made myth by the poet, the Indian's sacrifice comparable to the poet's as he disappears in the poem, poet and Indian together making possible the perpetual music of the land (in a striking poem never published in Crane's lifetime, composed at about the same time and entitled "The Sad Indian" [c. 1926–30], the sad Indian, being the sad heart [Hart], actually performs the identification here suggested of Indian and poet, both sacrificed to the poem). Finally, there is "Indiana," the land itself, "the physical body of the continent, or the soil," that alone is left of the erased "Indian," now further ravaged by hopeful, hardworking, ordinary wandering folks, unsuccessfully pioneering from frontier to new frontier. That the protagonist has here a woman's voice (though when he wrote his letter to Otto Kahn Crane was still thinking of an Indiana farmer of the male sex) is significant. The viewpoint is that of female placedness, the possible *oikos* for the American people, of which Pocahontas herself remains the best metaphor for Crane: the woman's body as the traditional site of imagination and creativity, particularly, but not exclusively, heterosexual male imagination and creativity.

Crane's gloss was inspired by the gloss in Coleridge's "The Ancient Mariner," as he explains to Caresse Crosby (August 8, 1929), but it has a completely different function. It begins, as a real gloss, at the beginning of "Ave Maria," Crane evidently concerned that the persona and stance of that first poem be easily grasped by the reader. It continues briefly in the same historical vein at the beginning of the love poem "The Harbor Dawn" ("400 years and more") only to be immediately interrupted by surmise: " . . . or is it from the soundless shore of sleep that time // recalls you to your love . . . " Thus is history translated into time, the throbbing of life and love and the tempo and rhythms of poetry. "Who is the woman with us in the dawn?," the gloss asks, and "time's truant" is the answer. The woman in the dawn is the poet's muse, traditionally female even for the homosexual poet in the 1920s, and even if the poem itself feeds on Crane's erotic love for a man. It should come as no surprise that the muse is still Pocahontas, the physical body of the nation, what in Crane's vision is left of the mythical source of his *materia poetica*. As the leftover of the poet's vision of the "Indian," Pocahontas, or the "extinct" Indian, is the poet's focus and lens – the "'eye' in the sky," as Crane reads "the twilight's dim, perpetual throne" in the second stanza of "The Dance" for Kahn's benefit.

That "the Indian" was not really "extinct" Crane was to find out later, and then his poetry, if he ever could bring himself to write it according to his new discovery, would have to be different, for both the nation and the poetic self would have to be reinvented. A year earlier, during his very productive stay in Cuba, Crane had been eager to study Spanish. His eagerness was, to be sure, propelled by erotic desire once again, though he also gives his correspondent at the time, Waldo Frank, a more professional justification. Learning Spanish, Crane thought then, was the "necessary preparation" for his next piece, "a blank verse tragedy of Aztec mythology." After the publication of *The Bridge* – a modern *Aeneid*, truly an epic of the modern consciousness in that its bard places himself deliberately and painfully in and out of the communal meaning-making – what could the poet's major project be? What large, coherent, wide-ranging Whitmanian poetic project would be worth the poet's total dedication once again? Aztec mythology might qualify as his next project, but the truth is that, for years after his letter to Waldo Frank of September 5, 1926, Crane didn't seem to give the idea another thought. The following December, the interest in the Spanish language he also reports to "Aunt Sally" (Mrs. Sally Simpson, the caretaker of the property on the Isle of Pines, who also appears in "The River") is still nothing if not romantic (December 5, 1926).

In 1930, when the Depression was already severely affecting business and everyday life in the United States, including the Clarence Crane enterprises, the poet was shattered by disappointing reviews of *The Bridge* by the people who really mattered to him (Yvor Winters and Allen Tate). Although much discouraged, Crane was then still thinking of the stimulating advantages of another trip to Europe. In August, his application for a Guggenheim, which required candidates to live abroad for the period of their fellowship, mentions, if rather vaguely, "a desire for European study," the "characteristics of European culture," and "French literature and philosophy" as a way to understand "the emergent features of a distinctive American poetic consciousness" (August 29, 1930). In his letter of acceptance of March 16, 1931, Crane still writes of sailing "for France by the middle part of April." The poet's final choice of Mexico to spend the year of his Guggenheim Fellowship in 1931 was a last-minute, and not very considered, decision. It was only aboard the SS Orizaba, in a letter to Caresse Crosby, that the topic of a tragic Aztec "drama featuring Montezuma and Cortez" cropped up again (April 5, 1931).

Once in Mexico, Crane was dazzled by a culture he honestly found out he did not know at all, but was eager to guess would be congenial and inspiring for his poetry and the way he conceived of it. The project failed, for reasons that will never be entirely clear to us. Crane's sexual excesses and incorrigible alcoholism, some would say. Or perhaps because he trusted that his sensuous, bodily immersion in everyday Mexican culture would be enough to boost him, and so did not bother to learn Spanish or "study the obscure calendars of dead kings" (as he said he would have to when the idea of an Aztec poem first occurred to him). Or perhaps the idea of an "Aztec tragedy" was simply wrong from the start. Wrong, because a mere "tragedy" would not do full justice to the poetic possibilities of the project (possibilities that Crane could only guess at from his exhilarating experience at the *pulque* Feast of Tepoztecatl in September

1931); and wrong, because "tragedy" never was the most attractive of genres for Crane. Deeply hurt by Tate's and Winters's disparagement of *The Bridge* as being basically a sloppy, sentimental, inappropriately celebratory, genreless poem besieged by bad transcendentalism and Whitmanian optimism, Crane thought he ought to make an effort at approaching "wastelandism" and being pessimistically "moral" and "realistic" by choosing the tragic slaughter of the Aztecs by the Spanish Conquistadores as his next subject matter. It would be his way of expanding the very concept of "America," as his friend Waldo Frank had been doing for some time. But it seems that Crane could not bring himself, however unwittingly, to "possess" and exploit the "Indian" in this way, as what appears to be the first sketch of his Aztec project would suggest.

"Havana Rose" (c. 1931), Crane's prose poem inspired by an episode aboard the SS Orizaba on its way to Mexico in April 1931, is the poet's first attempt at imagining the Aztec tragedy. *"Cortez"* (the name twice repeated in italics paralleling the reiterated *"again, again"* a few lines below) is here obliquely compared to the famous scientist (Dr. Hans Zissler, a distinguished bacteriologist from Harvard) who smuggled typhoid rats into Mexico to carry out his experiments on the spread of epidemics. Or, as Crane has it in the poem, "to mix – to ransom – to deduct – *to cure...*" (*to cure* being the only other phrase in italics in the original). The poem's surrealist imagery is Crane's indictment of careless scientists, as well as of the objectification of indigenous peoples for scientific purposes, which only very recently has started to be put largely in question and condemned. Two other poems written in Mexico at about the same time and also listed in Marc Simon's edition of the *Complete Poems* as "unfinished," "Purgatorio" (c. 1931–32) and "The Circumstance" (c. 1931–32), further indicate that Crane was deeply troubled by the topic he had somewhat frivolously assigned to himself six years before in Havana. "The Circumstance" is an explicit invocation of an Aztec deity, Xochipilli, the solar "god of flowers," as the poem says (Crane must have seen the flowered statue of Xochipilli in the Museo Nacional de Antropología, in Mexico City), but also the deity of laughter, feasting, and dancing, and hence an adequate symbol for poetry. But the "you" in the poem is clearly the poet himself. The language and imagery deftly evoke some of the most salient aspects of Aztec mythology – time, nature, the sun, blood, bones, death, ritual, the sun stone, and the sacred stone of sacrifice – but the poet remains outside the scene, like a "foreign clown," suspended by the thrice repeated conditional of "If you could." Evidently, the new aspiring poet, the sacrificial victim if only of circumstance, could not give Aztec "Time" an "enduring answer." "Purgatorio," in its turn, is Crane's poetic exile in Mexico, a purgatory worse than Dante's because it grants no hopeful passage through cleansing or purging. The poet is trapped in an utterly foreign land, whose proper sounds deafen him to his own proper singing, rendering it and him useless ("the church bells . . . ring too obdurately here to need my call"). Significantly enough, the only major poem Crane completed in Mexico and sent off for publication, "The Broken Tower" (1932), one of the most compelling lyrics of Anglo-American modernism, is Crane's "call," rather than "answer," to the Mexican bells as he was capable of hearing them: "My word I poured," the poet says, but the poet's anxiety about the adequacy of the "word" ("was it cognate") has nothing to do with the "Aztec tragedy." It concerns rather the momentary and paradoxical triumph of the poet's own tragedy of mortality, the poet "healed" once again by love, this time for a woman (Peggy Baird Cowley). The poem's only precarious ground is the newly rediscovered Hart's "matrix of the heart." Here are the poem's concluding stanzas:

> The steep encroachments of my blood left me
> No answer (could blood hold such a lofty tower
> As flings the question true?) – or is it she
> Whose sweet mortality stirs latent power? –
>
> And through whose pulse I hear, counting the strokes
> My veins recall and add, revived and sure
> The angelus of war my chest evokes:
> What I hold healed, original now, and pure . . .
>
> And builds, within, a tower that is not stone
> (Not stone can jacket heaven) – but
> Slip of pebbles, visible wings of silence sown
> In azure circles, widening as they dip
>
> The matrix of the heart, lift down the eye
> That shrines the quiet lake and swells a tower . . .
> The commodious, tall decorum of that sky
> Unseals her earth, and lifts love in its shower.

Crane's interest in Aztec mythology had not so much to do with a genuine interest in a culture he considered to be "extinct." It was rather, precisely on the basis of that fiction of erasure, his attempt at reinventing the very *possibility* of poetry and his own creativity. After all, *The Bridge* is not only a poem about America; it is a poem about poetry and the poet's power to create the form of total beauty – like the Shelleyan notion of "empire." Brooklyn Bridge, synecdoche for New York City and the nation, is above all a metaphor for the imagination, "a ship, a world, a woman, a tremendous harp" – indeed, the bridge is muse, poet, and poem at one and the same time. Aztec mythology was to be Crane's next "pony" for the *possibleness* of poetry ("possibleness" is Stevens's reformulation of Dickinson's "possibility" in "An Ordinary Evening in New Haven" [1949]). In "The Havana Rose," "Purgatorio," and "The Circumstance" we have an inkling of the use Crane would have made of "The Conquest" for his own poetic project. But because for Crane the "Indian" was "extinct," not even the "proof" of his reality, beyond the ravages of "the Conquest," could bring him back for the American poet in the 1930s.

6

LANGSTON HUGHES
THE COLOR OF MODERNISM

THE first book of poetry by Langston Hughes (1902–67), entitled *The Weary Blues*, was published in 1926, at the height of the Harlem Renaissance, also known as the New Negro Movement. The 1920s were an exceptionally fertile decade for American poetry. The production of this period alone invites a reconsideration of the kind of picture that the designation "American modernist poetry" generally brings to mind: the international flow of American and European poets and artists crossing the Atlantic both ways; the "little magazines" sprouting everywhere, both in the United States and in Europe; the new and powerful articulations of poetry and life, poetry and the other arts; the intricate dialectics of tradition and modernization and of conservatism and reform or revolution; the radical innovation of form and conceptualization; the more or less overt challenges to the dominant (white) bourgeois culture; the cosmopolitanism of most American poets of the period and the materiality of their sound-, image- and language-centered texts; the ferment of new American ideas and forms rising in Paris, London, the Village, and Harlem; and many different kinds of books of poetry emerging all over the place, absorbing the newest developments in society and the culture in different ways, and changing current notions of poetry and poetics.

A brief selection of publications in the 1920s reads like a survey of poetic consciousness raising in America during the decade. *The Daniel Jazz and Other Poems*, by Hughes's soon-to-be sponsor and much-admired Vachel Lindsay, came out in 1920. Marianne Moore's first volume, *Poems*, was published in 1921. T. S. Eliot's *The Waste Land* came out in 1922, the year of publication of Jamaica-born Claude McKay's *Harlem Shadows* and James Weldon Johnson's edition of *The Book of American Negro Poetry* (with Johnson's influential essay on "The Negro's Creative Genius"). Wallace Stevens's first book, *Harmonium*, was published in 1923, as was *New Hampshire*, Robert Frost's fourth volume, William Carlos Williams's innovative *Spring and All*, and Jean Toomer's *Cane*, an even more compelling combination of poetry and prose, lyricism and poetic commentary. Edgar Lee Master's *New Spoon River* and Robinson Jeffers's *Tamar and Other Poems* came out in 1924. H. D.'s early *Collected Poems* appeared in 1925, the year of Alain Locke's *Four Negro Poets* and *The New Negro: An Interpretation*. The year 1926 witnessed the publication of Hart Crane's *White Buildings*, Ezra Pound's *Personae* (collected shorter poems), Gertrude Stein's metapoetic essay on *Composition as Explanation*, and – as already mentioned above – Langston Hughes's *The Weary Blues*, this last book bearing an enthusiastic introduction by Stein's admirer, supporter, and later editor Carl Van Vechten.

The *Weary Blues* had four reprints before the decade closed with Crane's *The Bridge*, in 1930, the year Hughes published his first novel, *Not Without Laughter*. Meanwhile, another volume of Hughes's poetry had come out under the title of *Fine Clothes to the Jew* in 1927, the year Amy Lowell's *Ballads for Sale* were published, and Countee Cullen, whose *The Black Christ and Other Poems* would appear in 1929, brought out his landmark collection of African-American poets, titled *Caroling Dusk: An Anthology of Verse by Negro Poets*. But in his Foreword Cullen argued for the aesthetic inappropriateness of such separatism ("[There] is the probability that Negro poets, dependent as they are on the English language, may have more to gain from the rich background of English and American poetry than from nebulous atavistic yearnings toward an African inheritance. Some of the poets herein represented will eventually find inclusion in any discriminatingly ordered anthology of American verse, and there will be no reason for giving such selections the needless distinction of a separate section marked Negro verse"). Eliot's edition of Pound's *Selected Poems* came out in 1928, with Eliot's influential canonization of "modern versification" in the Introduction. Eliot's glib dismissal of Whitman contrasts sharply with the importance of the Whitmanian tradition of poets like Lindsay and Carl Sandburg for Hughes and other poets of the Harlem Renaissance. But the most interesting thing about a decade in which the dominant culture was determined to confirm, by exclusion, the "distinct American type" as white, Protestant, and Anglo-Saxon, and actually managed to get the 1924 National Origins Act approved, was that it was the time of the "Negro vogue in Manhattan," as Hughes puts it in his autobiographical account *The Big Sea* (1940).

Langston Hughes is arguably the most widely traveled and cosmopolitan of American modernist poets. Before he was twenty-five and had published his first volume of poetry, Hughes had already traveled over half the globe and visited Latin America and the Caribbean, Africa, and most of Western Europe (not to mention his constant moving from one place to another within the United States themselves). He had also lived in Paris for a while. As a dishwasher at Le Grand Duc nightclub, where literary celebrities (Robert McAlmon and Nancy Cunard amongst them) came to hear the Harlem singer Florence Embry,

Hughes had the opportunity to see and hear many American musicians, artists, and intellectuals. Some of Hughes's poetry had already appeared in *The Crisis* (the monthly magazine published by the National Association for the Advancement of Colored People, subtitled *A Record of the Darker Races*). Once, Alain Locke came to Le Grand Duc to ask Hughes for a contribution to the special Harlem issue of *Survey Graphic* (later the nucleus of *The New Negro*). To be sure, Hughes's first travels in the early twenties may not easily qualify as cosmopolitan in the affluent, elite sense that the word conventionally carries, but even if he traveled mainly aboard merchant freighters as a cabin boy, Hughes was eagerly discovering the world and himself, and writing poetry all along. The sea was to haunt many of his poems ("Literature," he writes in *The Big Sea*, "is a sea full of many fish. I let down my nets and pull"). Later, having become an established author, Hughes would also go to the Soviet Union, China, Japan, and again to Europe, Africa, and Latin America (some of these trips are related in *I Wonder as I Wander: An Autobigraphical Journey* [1956]). In 1937, Hughes spent six months in Spain covering the Spanish civil war for the *Baltimore Afro-American* from a socialist perspective. And if translation can also be said to be a form of cosmopolitanism, then Hughes's credentials increase. A translator himself (of Jacques Roumain, Nicholas Guillén, Leon Damas, Federico García Lorca, Gabriela Mistral, Jean-Joseph Rebearivelo, David Diop), Hughes was one of the modernist poets most widely translated during his lifetime. However, his wide-ranging international experience only seemed to confirm the American roots of his poetic imagination and his commitment to the culture of a country deeply divided by severe racial prejudice and conflict.

Langston Hughes was born in Joplin, Missouri, in 1902, of educated African-Americans and mixed ancestry. One of the great shocks of light-brown-skinned Hughes's life was to find out in Africa, as he writes in *The Big Sea* (1940), that Africans could hardly believe he was a Negro. Later, Nicholas Guillén and other Cuban friends would express the same view. In US America, however, being a "Negro" was all he was. Hughes's work as a whole – poems, novels, short stories, essays, autobiographies, juvenile pieces, dramas, operas, musicals, and gospel-song plays – can be read both as a celebration and as a critique of the American Negro as quintessentially *American*. A celebration, because Hughes's writings insist on the nation's need to realize the crucial importance of African-Americans for its early construction and continued vitality: "Under my hand the pyramids arose. / I made mortar for the Woolworth Building," sings the first poem of *The Weary Blues*. A critique, because they also invite all Americans of all races and persuasions to view the nation as painfully yet also dynamically composite, rather than statically divided:

"I, too, sing America," proclaims the last poem in the same volume (much later, "Theme for English B," one of the lyrics in *Montage of a Dream Deferred* [1951], wonders if the page written by the "colored" student will be "colored" too). The "twoness" W. E. B. Du Bois speaks about in *The Souls of Black Folks* (1903) is not the race consciousness of blacks alone; according to Hughes, whites partake of it as well in various forms. In 1916–20, while attending Central High School in Cleveland, Ohio, then having a student body of poor white, foreign-born, and Southern black children, Hughes learned that many other "painful" words besides "nigger" can be contemptuously flung at Americans ("spick," "kike," and "hunky"). But people of African origin suffer the vilest forms of discrimination and its worst consequences. All his life, Langston Hughes was often the target of such discrimination, whether as a student at Columbia University (which he attended for a year in 1921–22 at his father's expense), or as a young man looking for jobs in New York City, or merely as a person ever aware of places for "whites only."

The deeply ingrained pervasiveness of race and class prejudice, even among members of the same group, Hughes had seen in action in his own father. Denied permission by an all-white examining board to take the bar examination, and despairing of overcoming the color line in the United States, James Nathaniel Hughes emigrated to Mexico when Hughes was a child, and there became a successful businessman after his wife (Carrie Mercer Langston Hughes) left him to return to the United States with their son. James Hughes, with his contempt for the working poor and particularly those of his own race, must have appeared to the poet like a perfect example of American double consciousness: faith in the wonderful promises of the great American nation, and despair of ever fulfilling any of them by reason of race. Later, during the time he lived in Washington, DC with his mother and half brother in 1925, Langston Hughes would see with dismay his father's attitude confirmed in the pathetic pretentiousness of the Negro aristocracy, strictly forbidden to be part of the hegemonic white culture and yet proud of their white plantation ancestry and utterly disdainful of their darker, poor working-class fellow Negroes. Hughes's close contact with the poor black proletarians in Washington, when he himself, earning $12 a week at a laundry, held one of the only menial jobs available to them, was however a much more lasting inflence on his development as a poet.

Beginning with his first book, the "Negro" becomes in Hughes's poetry the image that best conveys the most outrageous paradoxes of modernity and the rising American nation, an image all the more poignant for the brutal reality lurking behind it. The modern world, and hence modern poetry and culture (and not just the New Negro poetry), cannot be understood without taking into account the image of the disenfranchised American Negro, a creative, imaginative, and productive citizen and artist who is, however, denied full citizenship and artistic recognition in the great nation of democracy, progress, and opportunity for all. In the first part of the twentieth century, modernist poetry, and American modernist poetry in particular, had to come to terms with the consequences of European colonialism. "But could the statue stand in Africa?" Stevens wonders in "The Greenest Continent," a section of *Owl's Clover* (1936). Stevens's is, as he says, a "political" poem, which however may end up telling a different political story from that of the poet himself. Perhaps Stevens had recently seen Nancy Cunard's *Negro* anthology, just published in 1934. In her Foreword, Cunard denounced Africa's "imperialist oppressors" and lauded the African artistic "genius." In Stevens's poem there is no indication that "the statue," or art, could ever prevail upon the "tumbling green." "The marble was imagined in the cold," the poem asserts. But while the author's contrast between the aesthetic culture of white "marble" and the violent nature of dark "drenching reds," or between "angels" and "jaguar-men," easily betrays his Eurocentric ideology, the powerful imagery of his poem allows for a more complex reading. It allows for the moment when, defying "fateful Ananke," "tongues unclipped" and "throats . . . stuffed with thorns" dare to claim poetry and art for themselves.

Langston Hughes's *The Weary Blues* is a brilliant expression of such a moment of African-American self-recognition in 1926. A poem simply titled "Poem" presents that very moment, when the American black poet is positioning himself to respond to the patronizing tone of the American white poet (or artist), bypass the biased criteria of the latter's "common god," and burst into "jungle" poetry of his own. "Poem" announces itself as being "For the portrait of an African boy after the manner of Gauguin" and reads like this:

> All the tom-toms of the jungles beat in my blood,
> And all the wild hot moons of the jungles shine in my soul
> I am afraid of this civilization –
>   So hard,
>   So strong,
>   So cold.

This short "Poem" contains all the ingredients to make it a typical poem by Hughes as an African-American poet at the beginning of the twentieth century, as well as a modernist poem. The first-person voice projects the image of the "Negro" torn between exuberant "jungle" and threatening "civilization." The structure of the poem underscores the contrast between "jungle" and "civiliza-tion." The two first longer lines of the six-line poem allow the poet to linger on the African origins of his identity, not without oblique commentary on stereotypes, both black and white. The emphasis is on sound and rhythm ("the tom-toms") and the intensity of life and sensuality ("the wild hot moons"). The three last stair-shaped anaphoric short lines, of only two words each – indeed, two stressed syllables – are the succinct expression of the African-American poet's situation in the third line, dangerously sandwiched between two worlds. This motif is dealt with rather more conventionally in another poem, as regards both form and content. By invoking the consequences of early forced inter-racial sex on the plantation and the forbidden miscegenation of later days, the three four-line rhymed stanzas of "Cross" picture, in the mulatto, the predicament of African-Americans, who are considered (or rather are forced to consider themselves) neither American nor African (the identity dilemma of the mulatto as "American" recurs frequently in Hughes's works). But a far more original strategy than the fairly obvious rhetorical question in the last stanza of "Cross" ("My old man died in a fine big house / My ma died in a shack. / I wonder where I'm gonna die, / Being neither white nor black?") is the way in which the sharply hammered conclusion of "Poem" expresses itself in the "beat" of the poet's African "blood" and "soul." The two-syllable, two-stress repetitive pattern of "So hard, / So strong, / So cold," while firmly denouncing the "civilization" that cruelly discriminates against blacks, echoes the rhythmical tom-toms of the mythical African drums.

Thus, the African-American modernist poet claims his place in the poetic tradition by reinventing it after his own particular choice of lore and aesthetic models. If some had looked for the vital myths and forms of poetry in the ancient Greeks or *langue d'oc* troubadours, Langston Hughes finds them in the long-suffering lives and rich folk culture of endurance and resistance of African-Americans. If Pound had his Bertran de Born and Arnault Daniel, and H. D. had her Sappho and Theocritus, Langston Hughes had his Blind Lemon Jefferson and W. C. Handy.

When it appeared in 1926, *The Weary Blues*, for its "exquisite unusualness," struck one of its earlier commentators as an "expertly singular" book. The critic (Ormond A. Forte of the *Cleveland Herald*) was impressed by the aesthetic quality of the book as an *objet d'art* ("from the paper jacket . . . to the delicacy of its paper binding"), particularly the power and energy exuding from the cover illustration (the bold drawing of a black bluesman at the piano against bright red and yellow was by the Mexican-born caricaturist of the Harlem Renaissance, Miguel Covarrubias). The same reviewer was also interested in learning about the new author's "nomadic life" from Van Vechten's introduction better to understand the young poet's "incredible maturity" and boldness of form and content. He singles out, as "more arresting," the shorter poems because of their "strangely quickening interest," and quotes "Sea Calm" in full. Ezra Pound, who much later would praise the clear tones of Hughes's poetry against Melvin Tolson's erudite experiments, would no doubt recognize in the image of "water" in "Sea Calm" the "luminous detail" that convenes its meaning:

> How still
> How strangely still
> The water is today.
> It is not good
> For water
> To be still that way.

The *Cleveland Herald* reviewer, alluding to the "Caribbean sunset" pictured in the poem of the same title as "God having a hemorrhage," further approves of the poet's "audaciousness and utter frankness," and is elated by Hughes's defiant unconventionality in speaking of the "forbidden thing" in "Cross." By the graphic beauty of the book and its immediate association of poetry with music, by its experimentalism of form and language and its unconventionality of subject matter, by the imagistic limpidity of some of its lyrics and the epic aesthetico-political statement of some others, by the cosmopolitanism of its author and his intense dialogue with the history and myths of the culture, *The Weary Blues* emerged in 1926 very much like a modernist artifact. Beginning with *The Weary Blues*, Hughes, more than any other poet of the Harlem Renaissance, plays an important role in the ongoing modernist reinvention of the English language and rhythms for poetry, which the first imagists had explicitly reclaimed for themselves. But Gertrude Stein had started much earlier, and her experiments with black vernacular in "Melanctha" [1909], which so much delighted Richard Wright and his friends, are no mere coincidence.

Hughes's poetic inspiration comes almost entirely from the sounds, rhythms, and meanings of African-American culture: religion (although Hughes was no believer, having, as a boy, failed to see Jesus and hence to be converted), folklore, language – and music summing it all up. For his *materia poetica* Hughes draws mainly on gospel songs, spirituals, jazz, and blues. But it was in the blues that he first discovered the "black man's soul." The story of the title poem of *The Weary Blues* is told in *The Big Sea*. The poem was written in the winter of 1923, after Hughes heard a piano player in Harlem. The poet, however, was not satisfied with the poem. "Every so often I would take it out of the suitcase and do something about the ending. I could not achieve an ending I liked, although I worked and worked on it . . . " Later, after the poem had been published in *Opportunity* (1925) and won a prize, Hughes, still concerned about its ending, began to grasp the meaning it carried for him and his calling as a poet. The poem, "whose ending [he] had never been able to get quite right," had been sent to the contest at the last minute. "I thought," he explained, "perhaps [the ending] was as right now as it would ever be." And then the poem won the first prize. From then on it became Hughes's "lucky poem." And rightly so, for it skillfully combines, even if the poet was not always entirely conscious of it, the two main voices of America: the voice of the hegemonic culture and the voice of the oppressed culture. In Hughes's second account of the poem in *The Big Sea*, the poem is no longer "about a piano player [he] had heard in Harlem" but "about a working man who sang the blues all night and then went to bed and slept like a rock." This conflation of the piano player with the working man, artist with worker, further underlines the converging contrast of the two voices – the voice of the artist/narrator, detached yet sympathetically observant and in full command of the delicately rhymed and alliterated language of Western lyricality; and the original, formulaic blues song inserted in the poem, uttering the unself-conscious playing and singing of the worker/performer's life experience of endurance and resistance:

> Droning a drowsy syncopated tune,
> Rocking back and forth to a mellow croon,
>   I heard a Negro play.
> Down on Lenox Avenue the other night
> By the pale dull pallor of an old gas light
>   He did a lazy sway . . .
>   He did a lazy sway . . .
> To the tune o' those Weary Blues.
> With his ebony hands on each ivory key
> He made that poor piano moan with melody.
>   O Blues!
> Swaying to and fro on his rickety stool
> He played that sad raggy tune like a musical fool.
>   O Blues!
> In a deep song voice with a melancholy tone
> I heard that Negro sing, that old piano moan –
>   "Ain't got nobody in this world,
>   Ain't got nobody but ma self.
>   I's gwine to quit ma frownin'
>   And put ma troubles on the shelf."
> Thump, thump, thump, went his foot on the floor.
> He played a few chords then he sang some more –
>   "I got the Weary Blues
>   And I can't be satisfied.
>   Got the Weary Blues
>   And can't be satisfied –

I ain't happy no mo'
And I wish that I had died."
And far into the night he crooned that tune.
The stars went out and so did the moon.
The singer stopped playing and went to bed
While the Weary Blues echoed through his head.
He slept like a rock or a man that's dead.

The volume as a whole plays this tension throughout ("ebony hands on ivory key"), whether "the Negro" inhabits the river as one of the oldest metaphors for the poet's imagination in the Western tradition ("My soul has grown deep like the rivers," he sings in "The Negro Speaks of Rivers"); or, in a way that is reminiscent of Paul Lawrence Dunbar's dialect experiments with the lyric, lets the sparse, paratactical, nonassuming, vernacular speech of the black mother's advice to her son, in "Mother to Son," perform the poetic, cultural, and social work of the nation for black and white America alike (the image of the harsh "stair," so effectively drawn in "Poem," powerfully evoking here the upward mobility promised to all and denied to so many):

Well, son, I'll tell you:
Life for me ain't been no crystal stair.
It's had tacks in it,
And splinters,
And boards torn up,
And places with no carpet on the floor –
Bare.
But all the time
I's been a-climbin' on,
And reachin' landin's,
And turning corners,
And sometimes goin' in the dark
Where there ain't been no light.
So boy, don't you turn back.
Don't you set down on the steps
'Cause you finds it's kinder hard.
Don't you fall now –
Foe I'se still goin', honey,
I's still climbin',
And life for me ain't been no crystal stair.

The publication of *The Weary Blues* in 1926 confirmed Langston Hughes's ascendant position in the American artistic and intellectual milieu. First of all, this was confined to the African-American intellectual community of Harlem, of which the poet felt so much to be part (his reason to go to Columbia in 1921, rather than comply with his father's wish that he get an education abroad, was precisely to be in the midst of Harlem's increasingly exciting artistic scene). But the book, having been published by the prestigious and cosmopolitan Knopf, signaled the bridging of "Harlem" and "The Village" that Hughes's theory and practice of poetry actually achieve. By then, mainstream *Vanity Fair* had already published some of Hughes's poems as well. When Howard Mumford Jones wrote in his early review for the *Chicago Daily News* that the author of *The Weary Blues* was "clearly a poet with something to say," he didn't mean "a Negro poet" with something to say "to the Negro community" and for non-Negroes to overhear. In spite of the reservations he has about the volume, Mumford Jones treats *The Weary Blues* as *a book of poetry*, with due attention to the kind of life and experience that breathes through it. One of Mumford Jones's concerns is that the "vogue of Negro art" may "falsify" "genuine" "values." By the time, a few months later, he wrote his review of *Fine Clothes to the Jew* (1927), Mumford Jones's concern had evidently been dispelled by Hughes's second book of poetry.

The genuineness of values and how they can be falsified is, of course, always in question – aesthetically, historically, and sociologically. But the problem of articulating poetry and race (or poetry and gender, for that matter), when interpreting a particular poet, was as real and difficult then as it is now. Hughes himself was acutely aware of it at the time, particularly after the troubled reception of *Fine Clothes to the Jew* (1927) by African-American critics. This was after all the time when "white people began to come to Harlem in droves" to watch Negroes amuse themselves. Not content with just enjoying themselves, with no blacks watching them, at the segregated Cotton Club on Lenox Avenue, whites started "flooding the little cabarets and bars where formerly only colored people laughed and sang, and where now the strangers were given the best ringside tables to sit and stare at the Negro customers – like amusing animals in a zoo" (the scene, including an Uncle Tom "Dixie" and a sensational Negro crime of jealousy, is vividly narrated in "Death in Harlem," first published in 1935 and later included in *Shakespeare in Harlem* [1942]). The danger was there, Hughes suggests in *The Big Sea*, that Negro writers would write not "to amuse themselves" but "to entertain white people" (or to meet black people's expectations, he might have added), as the lindy dancers at the Savoy had begun to do.

The extraordinarily wide acclaim by the most refined and demanding white audiences in the US and Europe of outstanding African-American artists, like Paul Robeson, Florence Mills, Bessie Smith, Louis Armstrong, or Josephine Baker, was also disturbing at a time when Jim Crow laws and segregation were rampant, and African-Americans were being lynched in the South. Beneath the surface, the sparkling Harlem Renaissance was teeming with as many contradictions, racial conflicts, and acts of glaring discrimination as the nation at large (as the riots of later decades would tragically reveal). Carl Van Vechten's novel *Nigger Heaven* (1926), whose ironic title refers to the upper gallery in a theater, usually the only place to which African-Americans had access at the time, denounces the profound racism of the culture eloquently. So does Hughes's stridently accusatory "Advertisement for the Waldorf-Astoria," a brilliant collage of ads for the opening of the greatest hotel in New York (in 1931) on the one hand and outraged portrayals of the city's "colored" "down-and-outers" on the other (it was posthumously included in *Good Morning Revolution*, 1973).

During this period (1926–29), Hughes was a student at Lincoln University, an educational institution for black students in Pennsylvania, where only white teachers were allowed to teach. But perhaps Hughes's most painful personal experience of race relations in this white-supported jazz age was the patronage he received from Charlotte Mason, a wealthy white benefactress who expected her African-American dependents to behave exactly as such: grateful subordinate dependents. In *The Big Sea*, the unnamed "Godmother" Mason becomes a painful symbol for white America. Whites want blacks to behave according to their (the whites') own idea of blackness, and get angry when blacks do not comply. But then, so do blacks: they also get angry, perhaps angrier, when their fellow blacks present a picture of their community that defrauds their expectations of increasing acceptance by the hegemonic culture.

African-American critics, in general, did not approve of *Fine Clothes to the Jew* (1927). One of them accuses "Langston Hughes, the sewer dweller," of producing the kind of poetry that "white publishers will accept," presumably because it gives an unflattering picture of the black world. Another goes so far as to state explicitly that the poet is complicit with the current "exploitation of the Negro." Not surprisingly, some white reviewers seem to vindicate such readings by offering racist interpretations as well, and arguing for the "primitive naturalness" of the Negro's poetry. Whatever their objections, Hughes's poetry is deeply rooted in his highly self-conscious experience as an African-American in the first half of the twentieth century. His essay "The Negro Artist and the Racial Mountain," published in *The Nation* in 1926, is a personal, poetic, and political manifesto only comparable to Whitman's Preface of 1855. Language, the poet, and the poem are not distinguishable, in that only the three of them together embody the voice of the community. Only as long as he voices the community does the poet speak to all. Hughes's communal, racially confident black voice in *Fine Clothes to the Jew* (a voice which will attain its full "signifying" in *Montage of a Dream Deferred* [1951]) accounts largely for the fact that his second book of poetry must be recognized as one of the most remarkable and original achievements of American modernist poetry.

Hughes considered *Fine Clothes to the Jew* a better book of poetry than *The Weary Blues*, and he was right. Impersonating the resilient lives of poor, down-trodden blacks, and delving more deeply and creatively into the sources of African-American self-expression in the culture – folk- and work-songs, spirituals, and the blues – the poems in Hughes's second book refuse to be read by traditional and conventional criteria. More than that, by their unassuming originality of form, theme, and voice, they radically question the very stability of such concepts as "the tradition" and "the convention." The book opens with "A Note on the Blues" that reads like the poet's understated challenge of traditional poetic manners. Warning his readers that the first eight and last nine poems in the book were written "after the manner of the Negro folk-song known as *Blues*," Hughes goes on to explain the "strict poetic pattern" of the *Blues*, with its little variations: "one long line repeated and a third line to rhyme with the first two. Sometimes the second line in repetition is slightly changed and sometimes, but very seldom, is omitted." The note concludes with a brief remark on poetic mood: "The mood of the *Blues* is almost always despondency, but when they are sung people laugh." The absurd, poignant contrast between despondency and laughter echoes the tragedy of African-Americans while subjects of inhuman racial discrimination – enduring and resisting against all odds, but not without a touch of desperate contempt for the dominant culture. The sorrowful yet proud and defiant sounds of a song by Bessie Smith, so enthusiastically applauded by white audiences at the time, echo powerfully alongside Hughes's blues poems. The blues are sadder than the spirituals, Hughes explains elsewhere, "because their sadness is not softened with tears but hardened with laughter, the absurd, incongruous laughter of a sadness without even a god to appeal to." Hughes was to compose blues poems all his life, some of them more overtly protest blues, the most accomplished of these being perhaps the very last one he wrote, "The Backlash Blues," first published in *Crisis* in 1967 and soon after included in *The Panther and the Lash*, of the same year.

More perhaps than in Hughes's other collections of poetry, the structure of *Fine Clothes to the Jew* is extremely important. The modernist book of poems is an art object with a meaning of its own. Even when single poems have been published separately before in magazines, as is usually the case, the modernist poet's composition of a book is a willed act of creative art. This is why to read Hughes's books of poetry in Arnold Rampersad's comprehensive edition of *The Collected Poems* (1995), organized chronologically and regardless of the form of Hughes's own collections, is to fail to read them as they should be read. *Fine Clothes to the Jew* is carefully divided into six parts, the first and the last titled respectively "Blues" and "And Blues" and thus deliberately framing the whole volume. The book's controversial title (loathed more by African-American than Jewish readers) is taken from "Hard Luck," a poem from the first "Blues" section that is a scathing, tragicomic commentary on the multicolor racism of early-twentieth-century urban America. The poem, Hughes explains in *The Big Sea*, is about a poor, jobless black man who has to pawn his clothes to survive. Since most pawnbrokers were Jews, when blacks needed to pawn something they'd say they'd take it "to the Jew" ("Ballad of the Pawnbroker" in *Shakespeare in Harlem* [1942] dramatizes the situation at "Mr. Levy"'s pawn shop). Displaying the blues form and mood explained by Hughes in the introductory note, the one stroke of genius in "Hard Luck" is to make "you" (the poor black man with hard luck) rhyme with "Jew," thus placing the Jew and the Negro both in the broader context of racial and economic discrimination and exploitation ("Likewise," one of the lyrics in *Montage of a Dream Deferred* [1951], further pursues this topic). The only one that is really "low-down," however, is the black man, who is more deprived than some of the animals that serve humankind, as his comically unself-conscious sarcasm in the last stanza so well underlines.

> When hard luck overtakes you
> Nothin' for you to do.
> When hard luck overtakes you
> Nothin' for you to do.
> Gather up yo' fine clothes
> An' sell 'em to de Jew.
>
> Jew takes yo' fine clothes,
> Gives you a dollar an' a half.
> Jew takes yo' fine clothes,
> Gives you a dollar an' a half.
> Go to de bootleg's,
> Git some gin to make you laugh.
>
> If I was a mule I'd
> Git me a waggon to haul.
> If I was a mule I'd
> Git me a waggon to haul.
> I'm so low-down I
> Ain't even got a stall.

More often than not Hughes's blues song is like a *cantiga de amigo* (a medieval lyric written by a male poet impersonating a woman's stance and voice). It is a song sung by a woman longing for and pained by love. But whether

the love song is about betrayal and abandonment or (less often) about desire and erotic pleasure, the sheer physicality of the poem's language points
to a social context of unmitigated human relations that sets it miles apart
from the idealized images of courtly love. "Midwinter Blues," the song of a
woman deserted by her man "in the middle of the winter" and "when the
coal was low," eloquently speaks of the social conditions that turn love and
affection into the site of a fierce struggle for survival. "Suicide," in the first,
and "Ma Man," in the last blues section of the book, present two different
sides of the same theme: love and eroticism as experienced by the poor black
woman, whose life in racist and sexist America is even more dependent, constricted, and oppressed than the black man's. In "Suicide" the abandoned
woman is at the end of her life story. Loneliness and despair can only bring
about violence, whether in dreams of revenge or as the self-inflicted injury
that the poem's title announces. But the alternative is really not there. The
man has "packed his trunk and left" for good, and the woman is now all
alone. The knife with its "long" blade could only "wrong" her again where
she has been wronged before by her man, as the rhyme subtly suggests.
Deserted, disoriented, and miserable, the sorrowful woman in the last stanza
sounds like a metaphor for poor black America, dangerously on the verge of
complete oblivion as part of a wild nature not absorbable by the dominant
culture:

> 'Lieve I'll jump in de river
> Eighty-nine feet deep.
> 'Lieve I'll jump in de river
> Eighty-nine feet deep.
> Cause de river's quiet
> An' a po', po' gal can sleep.

"Ma Man" is at the other end of the spectrum. Here, the woman sings joyfully of her love for her man and is exhilarated at the intense erotic power
her banjo player holds over her. Banjo playing and love-making are one, the
woman finds her man good at both, and her delight in his music making equals
her sexual pleasure in his love-making. The poem leaves this quite clear in
the way in which the woman explains her doting on her man by being repetitive and reticent at one and the same time ("I mean plunk, plunk . . . plunk,
plunk."). There is an ironic and ominous note, however, in the reference to the
musician-lover's drinking habits ("He plays good when he's sober / An' better,
better, better, when he's drunk"). The poem's strident euphoria in chanting
the black woman's sexual pleasure thus surreptitiously carries with itself the

danger of its opposite, so mournfully portrayed in most other poems in the
book:

> When ma man looks at me
> He knocks me off ma feet.
> When ma man looks at me
> He knocks me off ma feet.
> He's got those 'lectric-shockin' eyes an'
> De way he shocks me sure is sweet.
>
> He kin play a banjo.
> Lordy, he kin plunk, plunk, plunk.
> He kin play a banjo.
> I mean plunk, plunk . . . plunk, plunk.
> He plays good when he's sober
> An' better, better, better when he's drunk.
>
> Eagle-rockin',
> Daddy, eagle-rock with me.
> Eagle rockin',
> Come an' eagle-rock with me.
> Honey baby,
> Eagle-rockish as I kin be!

The titles of the remaining sections – "Railroad Avenue," "Gloria!
Hallelujah!," "Beale Street Love," and "From the Georgia Roads" – considerably broaden the scope of the volume, while keeping the focus on the lives
of poor and abused African-Americans in early twentieth-century America.
"Laughers," the poet calls his fellow blacks, who do all the infrastructure work
of the country, in a poem included in "From the Georgia Roads" and originally titled "My People" when first published in *Crisis* in 1922. Most poems
in "Railroad Avenue," including the title poem, speak of the blacks' migration
to the North looking for work and a better life, and the racial discrimination
that keeps them away from all but the least dignifying and worst-paid jobs.
"Brass Spittoons," one of Hughes's favorite poems in the volume (he even at one
time considered giving the entire book its title), is structured like a dramatic
monologue that ironically reenacts the only kind of dialogue that is available to
blacks in a white racist society. Beginning and ending with abrupt, irrefutable
orders, the terse command of the imperative mode, though uttered by the white
man, cannot but be helplessly internalized by the black man as his only form
of survival and even salvation. "Clean the spittoons, boy," the poem begins.
And, at the end: "A clean spittoon on the altar of the Lord. / A clean bright
spittoon all newly polished, – / At least I can offer that. / Come here, boy!"

A little prayer-like poem from "Gloria! Hallelujah!" entitled "Sinner" gives a gloomy picture of the black man's predicament in a discriminatory society that credits him with no redeeming grace, whether in this or in after life:

> Have mercy, Lord!
> Po' an' black
> An' humble an' lonesome
> An' a sinner in yo' sight.
>
> Have mercy, Lord.

Along with "Red Silk Stockings" (included in "From the Georgia Roads" and discussed on p. 327 below), whose sharp irony was in general not properly understood, perhaps no section of the book shocked Hughes's African-American readers at the time more than "Beale Street Love." The center of black life in Memphis, Beale Street was famous for the blues and W. C. Handy, and its red light district. It serves as the perfect metaphor for the tortured geography and ethos of America. Using "love" as its core image, the title poem of the section gives a sparse, desentimentalized, disenchanted picture of human life when a particular community has been dehumanized by brutal relations of power, all the more brutal because in fact devoid of consequent social power. If brutality is all human relations can yield, the poem cries out piercingly, the battered woman cannot help but be wretchedly reconciled with it. The woman's voice at the closure is a gesture of arrogant self-victimization that is the satirical counterpart of the blues' paradoxical despondent laughter:

> Love
> Is a brown man's fist
> With hard knuckles
> Crushing the lips,
> Blackening the eyes, –
> Hit me again,
> Says Clorinda.

One can understand why the rising African-American bourgeoisie and its intellectuals and critics in the early twentieth century would be unwilling to see the originality and honesty of Hughes's artistry and feel uneasy with the picture of black America depicted in his poems. Although the poems' language and form leave no doubt that the source of the problem lies in the most repugnant forms of racism that have plagued American society since slavery days, the truth is that no uplifting figure or image and almost only miserable and unpleasant characters people these poems. Men are hopeless drunks and jobless philanderers who beat their wives and lovers alike; women, doubly oppressed by oppressed men, are either abject victims of humiliation and abandonment or downright whores. Nor would the image conveyed by the frank joyfulness of "Ma Man"'s erotic woman appease the concerns of respectability and propriety of the African-American community in the society at large. More offensive still was "Red Silk Stockings," a poetic miracle of language, image, and compressed meaning, whose irony was lost on its African-American readers, precisely because it evokes so masterfully the dreadest consequence of white America's most degrading exploitation of black America – the blacks' secret, unavowable desire (explicitly denounced in "The Negro Artist and the Racial Mountain") to be white:

> Put on yo' silk stockings,
> Black gal.
> Go out an' let de white boys
> Look at yo' legs.
>
> Ain't nothin' to do for you, nohow,
> Round this town, –
>
> You's too pretty.
> Put on yo' red silk stockings, gal,
> An' tomorrow's chile'll
> Be a high yaller.
>
> Go out an' let de white boys
> Look at yo' legs.

Langston Hughes's next book of poetry, *The Dream Keeper and Other Poems*, would not come out until 1932. Meanwhile, the stock market crashed, the Depression made life difficult for everybody, African-Americans had more trouble finding jobs than anybody else, and Hughes had decided he "wanted to make a living from poems and stories," as he explains at the outset of *I Wonder as I Wander* (1956). The $400 Hammond Gold Award for Literature received early in 1931 for his novel *Not Without Laughter* (1930) no doubt encouraged the poet, as did, even more so, the $1,000 grant from the Rosenwalf Fund awarded a few months later. Shortly afterwards, Hughes was touring the South on a series of poetry readings to make "poetry pay," as he puts it in his "autobiographical journey" (during one of these reading trips, after visiting the Scottsboro boys at Kilby Prison, Hughes wrote his famous angry poem, later sadly disowned by the poet, titled "Christ in Alabama" [1931], whose first line reads "Christ is a nigger").

The Dream Keeper was a commissioned book. Hughes put it together "expressly for young people" at the request of Effie L. Power, Director of Work with Children at the Cleveland Public Library, who also wrote the Introduction. The volume came out as a handsome Knopf edition with lovely illustrations by Helen Sewell. With very few exceptions, the poems are all taken from *The Weary Blues* and *Fine Clothes to the Jew*. Chosen very carefully, given the purpose of the book, and so leaving out the bitterer, more shockingly sarcastic allusions to the violence and harshness of black life under segregation laws and direst economic oppression, the poems included are aptly described in Power's introductory words as "short lyrics of great beauty, stanzas in serious vein, rollicking songs, and several typical Negro blues." Of the few poems not taken from Hughes's two previous collections, some had in fact been written for children and published in *Brownie's Book* in 1921. Hughes's publications include several children's and juvenile works (some of them in collaboration with Arna Bontemps), and he wrote many other poems for children, some of them only published posthumously (*Black Misery* [1969] with illustrations by Arouni; and *The Sweet and Sour Animal Book* [1994], with ilustrations by students from the Harlem School of the Arts). But whether by themselves or as collected in *The Dream Keeper*, Hughes's poems are no more just for children than Blake's *Songs of Innocence*, with which they have many affinities. Even such a delicately mellow poem as "Autumn Thought," for example, cannot but evoke, by its seasonal and color imagery, the broader existential context of which it is part:

> Flowers are happy in summer.
> In autumn they die and are blown away.
> Dry and withered,
> Their petals dance on the wind
> Like little brown butterflies.

It would be ten years before Hughes's next book of poetry appeared. During the whole decade he was busy writing mainly stories, essays, memoirs, and plays. *Mulatto* was staged in New York in 1935 with considerable theatrical success. The poet's clashes with its racist producer, Martin Jones, inspired one of Hughes's most quoted protest poems, "Let America Be America Again," later included in the first of the literary pamphlets for the people put out by the International Workers Order (*A New Song*, 1938). No matter how politically compelling the poems included in *A New Song* may be, Langston Hughes was decidely not a very successful proletarian poet (poets often say certain things better than politicians, Hughes once said speaking of Gwendolyn Brooks). Because of its greater artistic refinement and verbal and "imagetic" subtlety, the poetry in *Shakespeare in Harlem* (1942) is far more eloquent, even as "protest," though the book's dedicatee "Louise" (Thompson Patterson), the socialist wife of William L. Patterson, a leader of the Communist Party, would no doubt be of a different opinion.

Again, by its careful composition and presentation, and no less by its very title, *Shakespeare in Harlem* as a whole, like Hughes's previous books of poetry, claims to be an imaginative work of art. The *materia poetica* is being black – being *unashamedly* black – and the title, conflating "Shakespeare" and "Harlem," boldly calls "the tradition" into question. The somewhat flippant tone of Hughes's introductory note is deliberately misleading. "A book of light verse," the poet announces. "Afro-Americana in the blues mood. Poems syncopated and variegated in the colors of Harlem, Beale Street, West Dallas, and Chicago's South Side." And then he further specifies with apparent joyful levity, the ghost of Shakespeare vaguely beckoning in that "as you like": "Blues, ballads, and reels to be read aloud, crooned, shouted, recited, and sung. Some with gestures, some not – as you like. None with a far-away voice." The opening section, "Seven Moments of Love, An Un-sonnet Sequence in Blues," is slyly aware of Shakespeare's sonnet sequence, and the title poem, "Shakespeare in Harlem," in the last section of the book, "Lenox Avenue," is a daring appropriation, bordering on willful Negro impertinence, of a Shakespearean song:

> Hey ninny neigh!
> And a hey nonny noe!
> Where, oh, where
> Did my sweet mama go?
>
> Hey ninny neigh!
> With a tra-la-la-la!
> They say your sweet mama
> Went home to her ma.

With its eight well-conceived sections ("Seven Moments of Love," "Declarations," "Blues for Men," "Death in Harlem," "Mammy Songs," "Ballads," "Blues for the Ladies," and "Lenox Avenue"), *Shakespeare in Harlem* is *not* a trivial book of "light verse." If anything, it is a sadder book than *The Weary Blues* and *Fine Clothes to the Jew*, an unself-pitying blend of much tragedy and some comedy that conveys a deep, thought-provoking feeling of sadness and disillusionment. After years of economic depression and hardship, and seemingly useless political denunciation of racial discrimination, the "Negro Poet Laureate" (as Van Vechten once named Hughes) is once again holding the mirror up to nature, his people, and their blues – and the picture cannot be very bright. Although African-American soldiers are already fighting like heroes in the war (Dorie Miller, a black man from Chicago, shot down four enemy planes during the Pearl Harbor attack [1941]), Jim Crow laws prevail even in the army (Hughes's wishful "Jim Crow's Last Stand" [1943] notwithstanding).

Segregation, rejection, poverty, homelessness, sickness, death, impossible desires and unmentionable ambitions, and, above all, utter, heart-rending loneliness in crowded cities, pervade the entire volume. The weary blues alone provide the mood and mode of this collection. In "Songs Called the Blues," a short article published in *Phylon* in 1941, Hughes explains that, unlike "the Spirituals" (which are "group songs"), "the Blues are songs you sing alone." Whereas the "Spirituals are escape songs, looking toward heaven, tomorrow, and God," the "Blues are *today* songs, here and now, broke and broken-hearted, when you're troubled in mind and don't know what to do, and nobody cares." "Down and Out," one of the "Blues for the Ladies," read aloud, as Hughes suggested, or preferably sung in the doleful tones of Ma Rainey, best gathers the meaningful form of this book:

> Baby, if you love me
> Help me when I'm down and out.
> If you love me, baby,
> Help me when I'm down and out,
> Cause I'm a po' gal
> Nobody gives a damn about.
>
> De credit man's done took my clothes
> And rent time's most nigh here.
> Credit man's done took my clothes.
> Rent time's nearly here.
> I'd like to buy a straightenin' comb,
> An' I needs a dime fo' beer.
>
> Oh, talk about yo' friendly friends
> Bein' kind to you –
> Yes, talk about yo' friendly friends
> Bein' kind to you –
> Just let yo'self git down and out
> And then see what they'll do.

Fields of Wonder (1947), Hughes's fourth major book of poetry, was read by its earlier critics as departing considerably from the poet's earlier themes, modes, and forms. While the clear strains of its lyricism were often highly praised and its short lyrics associated with imagism and even compared to Emily Dickinson's poems, the apparent absence of "content" (meaning the plight of African-Americans in a country so severely torn apart by racial and class conflicts) was disturbing to Hughes's readers, both black and white. One at least of its eight sections ("Tearless") was often singled out for its social and racial resonance, as in "Vagabonds," the poem from which the section borrows its title ("We are the desperate / Who do not care, / The hungry / Who have nowhere / To eat, / No place to sleep, / The tearless / Who cannot / Weep"). But the book in general was thought to be more private and intimate than the previous ones. It is true that a deep personal and disengaged melancholy pervades the poems in the volume, some of them quite bucolic, as if the poet's commitment to the community had been left to such overt political poems as *Freedom's Plow* (1943) or to his prose, particularly the columns for the *Chicago Defender* featuring "Jesse B. Semple," the "Simple Minded Friend," introduced in 1943. In *Fields of Wonder* the lyric subject seems indeed to take precedence, as in "Burden": "It is not weariness / That bows me down, / But sudden nearness / To song without sound." Even "Luck," another poem from the "Tearless" section, rings with a deeply felt sense of personal abandonment and loneliness:

> Sometimes a crumb falls
> From the tables of joy,
> Sometimes a bone
> Is flung.
>
> To some people
> Love is given,
> To others
> Only heaven.

The poems included in *Fields of Wonder* range a wide temporal span that goes from the early 1920s to the date of the book's publication. "Exits" was first published as "Song for a Suicide" in *Crisis* in 1924. When it was understood by some as conveying an extremely pessimistic vision of the future of African-Americans in the country ("The sea is deep, / A knife is sharp, / And a poison acid burns – /," the short lyric begins), Hughes indignantly retorted insisting that the poem was "personal" and only spoke of the subject's occasional despondency. Furthermore, the volume includes a poem entitled "Personal," also previously published in *Crisis* in 1935, which sounds like the individual poet's defiant cry of poetic integrity:

> In an envelope marked:
>
> Personal
>
> God addressed me a letter.
> In an envelope marked:
>
> Personal
>
> I have given my answer.

One other lyric in the collection that underscores Hughes's conception of poetry as a verbal art that is closer to the freedom of music than the manipulation of rhetoric is "Songs," a "personal" poem which a particular critic did not hesitate to consider "absurd" in a poet with Hughes's political and social credentials. After all, Hughes, who was never a member of the Communist Party, was nonetheless sympathetic to the Soviet Union, though increasingly concerned about Stalin's attacks on the writer's freedom. In fact, what "Songs" ends up doing is to challenge precisely the notion of poetry as propaganda:

> I sat there singing her
> Songs in the dark
>
> She said,
> *I do not understand*
> *The words.*
>
> I said,
> *There are*
> *No words.*

Finally, what *Fields of Wonder* as a whole implies is the conception that was to be popularized by feminism in the late sixties and seventies: the personal is the political. "Motherland" (first published in the pamphlet titled *Jim Crow's Last Stand* [1943]) suspends the lyric subject altogether only to bring him back with the "bitter sorrow" of "Africa":

> Dream of yesterday
> And far-off long tomorrow:
> Africa imprisoned
> In her bitter sorrow.

Langston Hughes's next collection of poems, *One-Way Ticket* (1949), could not be mistaken for a book by any other poet. Neatly composed of ten sections with titles borrowed from poems in each one of them ("Madam to You," "Life is Fine," "Dark Glasses," "Silhouettes," "One-Way Ticket," "Making a Road," "Too Blue," "Midnight Raffle," "Home in a Box," "South Side: Chicago [A Montage]"), *One-Way Ticket* vividly recreates Hughes's poetic settings, forms, themes, characters, and moods. The harsh realities of extreme poverty, prostitution, gambling, and drug addiction add on to the continued nightmares of lynchings in the South to darken the poetry, but the poems' power and effect still derive from the contrast between their melodic lyricism and brutal realism, as in "Silhouette":

> Southern gentle lady,
> Do not swoon.
> They've just hung a black man
> In the dark of the moon.

They've hung a black man
To a roadside tree
In the dark of the moon
For the world to see
How Dixie protects
Its white womanhood.

Southern gentle lady,
Be good!
Be good!

The poems in *One-Way Ticket* again combine the tragic and comic modes with sharp irony to sing the lives of poor blacks in urban America, their oppression, exploitation, and anihilation, their economic and emotional deprivation, their frustration and alienation in the culture – but also their human determination and resiliency. There are threats of suicide that remain, comically, just threats ("Too Blue") and there is a firm decision not to die ("Boarding House" or "Funeral"). With no trace of sentimentality or moralizing, the poet refuses to project the image of African-Americans in the 1940s as a people at a dead end, an image which the political and social conditions in the United States after the war continued to reinforce. Hughes's "one-way ticket" in the poem of that title leads forward, away from "Dixie," and on to the future, even if only a stark future, devoid of empty promises, that will have to be challenged. "I pick up my life," the poem concludes, "And take it away / On a one-way-ticket – / Gone up North, / Gone out West, / Gone!" This sense of mobility and steady forward movement is beautifully reenacted in the fast pace and jazz-like rhythm of "Jitney," the poem elongated like the bus it names and that transports people to work and pleasure through the big city bustle ("Corners / Of South Parkway: / Eeeoooooo! / Cab! / 31st, / 35th, / 39th, / 43rd, / Girl, ain't you heard? . . . ").

One interesting feature distinguishes this book from the previous ones. In general, *One-Way Ticket* reads more like a book of ballads than a book of blues poems, and some of the poems sound like folk love songs in many parts of the world: "Lonesome Corner," for instance, or "Yesterday and Today." Two poems were actually rewritten for inclusion in this volume in order to erase the blues structure. "Little Old Letter" had first appeared in *Old Line* (1943) as "Little Old Letter Blues" and "Little Green Tree" had been published in *Tomorrow* (1945) as "Little Green Tree Blues," both poems abiding then by the blues formula explained by Hughes in his "Note on the Blues" for *Fine Clothes to the Jew*. In *One-Way Ticket* the blues mood is still there, as are the rhythms and vernacular sounds of poor black people, but the narrative mode and quatrain form cannot help but echo the medieval ballad and folk song, thus giving African-American experience and suffering a larger dimension. The balladesque mode is strongly emphasized right at the start by "Madam Alberta K. Johnson"'s sequence of twelve poems. "Madam" is a kind of female "Simple" in verse, black, of course, but whose stories comically illustrate the cruel economic and social absurdities that plague the urban lives of poor people in the West, whether black or white.

Hughes would put together two more collections of poetry: *Selected Poems* (1959) and *The Panther and the Lash*, published in 1967, the year of the poet's death. Hughes's last book of poetry brings no striking aesthetic novelty regarding his art as a poet. The volume includes many poems from previous collections, including *Montage of a Dream Deferred* and *Ask Your Mama*, as well as poems written at different times and previously published but not previously collected. Only sixteen poems are here published for the first time. The most recent poems, all written in the 1960s, evoke the tensions, conflicts, and violent confrontations of the time, both at home and abroad. In Africa and the Caribbean, the European colonies were slowly reaching emancipation, however problematic ("Lumumba's Grave"); but some (as was the case with Salazar's Africa) were being forced to engage in more violence and warfare with no positive results in sight ("Angola Question Mark," a poem that also resonates with opposition to the Vietnam War). In the United States, the "dream deferred" was fostering discouragement and impatience bordering on violence as well. Many of the poems, like "Frosting" or "Sweet Words on Race" or "Crowns and Garlands," record the disenchantment of African-Americans with the vain rhetoric ("the truest of the oldest lies," as stated in "Black Panther") that tries to conceal the continued ruthless oppression imposed by the dominant culture: "Freedom / Is just frosting / On somebody else's / Cake. / And so must be / Till we / Learn how to / Bake" ("Frosting"). But all poems convey the oppressed peoples' unwavering hope and threatening determination to conquer real freedom and full citizenship. That violence feeds resistance with violence and that the time of endurance is coming to an end (*The Panther and the Lash* was dedicated to Rosa Parks) is a concept that can be loudly heard amidst the contained strains of Hughes's lyricism in poems that deal with the Civil Rights movement and the ensuing white terrorism in the South ("Birmingham Sunday" and "Bombings in Dixie") or register the brutality of gratuitous police aggression in the heart of Manhattan ("Death in Yorkville" evokes the killing of young James Powell that led to the 1964 New York riots).

Hughes's most innovative contribution to the poetics of American modernism, after the initial lyrical revolution brought about by *The Weary Blues* and *Fine Clothes to the Jew*, was the composition of his two remarkable jazz poems, *Montage of a Dream Deferred* (1951; reprinted in *The Langston Hughes Reader* [1958] and *Selected Poems* [1959]) and *Ask Your Mama* (1961). Both texts rightfully claim their place amongst such long poems of American modernism as *The Bridge, Four Quartets, Paterson, Helen in Egypt,* or *The Cantos*. Like *The Bridge, Montage* is made up of short lyrics, often independently published, yet made to signify much more than their separate selves once integrated in the overall structure of the volume. Both *Montage* and *Ask Your Mama* are epics of the (modern) American consciousness, just like all the other long poems of so-called high modernism (high modernism is actually a designation that Langston Hughes's work renders absurd). Unlike them, however, *Montage* and *Ask Your Mama* offer a decentered voice, a complex, multi-toned African-American voice, that radically questions both the poem's and the nation's subject. Neither lyric nor epic, rather reinventing subjectivity in the improvisations of African-American jazz, the subject constructs the nation by deconstructing the very notions of "subject" and "nation." Blending the black vernacular with the boldest forms of modernist experimentation, and interrogating all the canonical aesthetic distinctions more radically even than the works of any other modernist poet (except perhaps those of Gertrude Stein), these two poems paved the way for the "jazz aesthetic" of Amiri Baraka, who, along with other younger African-American poets in the 1960s, turned once again to African-American music for inspiration and the consolidation of a Black Aesthetic.

Hughes often read his poems with jazz accompaniment. But *Montage* and *Ask Your Mama* go far beyond this. They do not simply require jazz accompaniment, they are part of jazz. Or rather, they *are* jazz. The best guide for readers is provided by Hughes himself. In order to begin to grasp *Montage of a Dream Deferred*, Hughes suggests in a note prefacing the poem, "jazz, ragtime, swing, blues, boogie-woogie, and be-bop" must be absorbed first. For, like bebop, the poem "is marked by conflicting changes, sudden nuances, sharp and impudent interjections, broken rhythms, and passages sometimes in the manner of the jam session, sometimes the popular song, punctuated by the riffs, runs, breaks, and disc-tortions of the music of a community in transition." Paraphrasing what Hughes's Simple says about bebop elsewhere, one might say that *Montage* is "mad, wild, frantic, crazy, and not to be dug unless you have seen dark days, too." The words in the poem register the pain of the social changes (or lack of them) in the 1940s, which African-Americans suffered more than any other group of people in the United States: for instance, the war they fought (against white supremacy in Europe), perhaps with the illusion (or dream deferred) that after the war discrimination would have to be over for ever. "World War II" is the title of one of the lyrics in the poem:

> What a grand time was the war!
>   Oh, my, my!
> What a grand time was the war!
>   My, my, my!
> In war time we had fun,
> Sorry that old war is done!
> What a grand time was the war,
>   My, my!
>
> Echo:
> *Did*
> *Somebody*
> *Die?*

Many of the lyrics highlight the economic depression, which for African-Americans in Harlem was not ended by the end of the war. "Ballad of the Landlord" narrates the plight of a destitute tenant in the hands of an unscrupulous, exploitative landlord, thus vividly speaking of the devastations of the poor in the age of capital (*"Police! Police!,"* the poem concludes in the voice of the landlord, *"Come and get this man! | He's trying to ruin the government | And overturn the land!"*). The important thing about *Montage*, however, is its claim to be a counterdiscourse just like bebop, the revolutionary, disruptive jazz form developed in the 1940s by Harlem musicians (prominent amongst them Charlie Parker, Dizzy Gillespie, Bud Powell, and Thelonius Monk), in a politically motivated attempt to resist the economic and commercial logic of "white" appropriation. But the omnivorous culture is insatiable, and its marketplace soon swallows up everything. By the early 1950s, the "marginal" gestures of bebop, if not duly coopted, were one of the many excuses for intensified police repression of racial and political protest.

Perhaps for this reason, *Ask Your Mama* goes back to the "traditional" blues model. "The traditional folk melody of 'Hesitation Blues' is the leitmotif for this poem," Hughes announces in an introductory text that combines words and musical notes. And he continues his elucidation of the aesthetic basis of *Ask Your Mama* (dedicated "To Louis Armstrong, the greatest blower of them all"): "In and around it, along with the other recognizable melodies employed, there is room for spontaneous jazz improvisations, particularly between verses, where the voice pauses. The musical figurine indicated after each 'Ask your mama' line may incorporate the impudent little melody of the old break, 'Shave and a haircut, fifteen cents.'"

The orchestration of *Ask Your Mama* is even more dazzling than that of *Montage*. While in the earlier poem the individual short lyrics, which in the original version even appeared arranged by titled sections, help keep the reader in some kind of poetic control, in the later poem, though it is also very carefully structured formally, the reader faces a work of art that switches vertiginously from verbal discourse to musical score to plastic object. The pastel pink pages unfold to reveal blue and brown lettering, the poems' capital letters dialoguing with the glosses' lower case. Each one of the twelve sections is introduced on a separate page with a Cubist design. What one might call the linguistic content is not easily distinguishable from the work itself as musically *performed*. The opening of the poem, with its hesitant, repetitive pace, powerfully recreates the unmistakable sounds and rhythms of instrumental jazz, here convened to play the never before sung history of America:

> IN THE
> IN THE QUARTER
> IN THE QUARTER OF THE NEGROES

At the same time, the marginal gloss, with its explicit reference to the German *Lieder* sung by Leontyne Price, the famous black opera singer, gives directions for a musical interpretation ("impudent," we might call it after Hughes) that is aimed at making all boundaries explode. The "Liner Notes" added at the end of the volume "For the Poetically Unhep" underscore the insolent mode of this work, the disrespectful gesture that finally desegregates poetry by composing one of the most challenging of all modernist poems. The poetically unhip, besides the conventional refinement of German *Lieder*, will have to remember not only the suffering, endurance, and resistance of black America but also the cultural work of all the great African-Americans (including Langston Hughes). Moreover, they will have to learn all about the "Hesitation Blues" (the hesitation menacingly overthrown in the poem by the intersected "ça ira, ça ira" of French revolutionists) and the dozens. The dozens is a specific African-American tradition of trading insults (usually sexual). A kind of manhood rite, it consists of a game of verbal insults usually performed before a group. It involves symmetrical joking relationships in which two or more people are free to insult each other and each other's ancestors and relatives. The mother is a favorite though not an inevitable target: "AND THEY ASKED ME RIGHT AT CHRISTMAS / IF MY BLACKNESS, WOULD IT RUB OFF? / I SAID, ASK YOUR MAMA."

That Hughes's multifaceted long poems only recently have begun to be more widely discussed as a distinguished contribution to American poetic modernism is one last comment on Hughes's deferred dream – or perhaps the sign of a positive answer, at long last, to his old angry question in *Montage of a Dream Deferred*: "*Or does it explode?*" The italicized question is the concluding line of one of Hughes's finest lyrics in *Montage*:

> What happens to a dream deferred?
>
> Does it dry up
> like a raisin in the sun?
> Or fester like a sore –
> And then run?
> Does it stink like rotten meat?
> Or crust and sugar over –
> Like a syrup sweet?
>
> Maybe it just sags
> like a heavy load.
>
> *Or does it explode?*

"*Or does it explode?*" is a closing line which, however, significantly opens up to all the contradictory meanings that are the high-water mark of Hughes's poetry: on the one hand, the half-hopeful, half-threatening tension between the aspiration of African-Americans to their rightful place in the culture – which they, too, help to shape with their specific contribution; on the other hand, the racism that prevents the dominant culture from fully acknowledging African-American specificity as a vital part of itself. What this acknowledgment implies is the recognition that the American white poet, no less than the black poet, is also sandwiched between two worlds. To speak of the pressure of two worlds, "white" or "black" (regardless of whether such categories continue to be at all operative), or male and female, popular and erudite, political and aesthetic, old and new, or even "real" and "mythical," is ultimately to point to the variety of experience that informs all poetic performance worthy of the name. American modernist poets are aware of the pressure in their poetry. Even if often, as empirical beings, some of them wished to escape from it, their poems wouldn't let them (why does Stevens describe the string of poems in "Like Decorations in a Nigger Cemetery" [1935] as African-American "litter"?). Langston Hughes made of that pressure the test of his poetic achievement. *Ask Your Mama*, his long poem of multiple cultures, modes, genres, languages, and musical tones offers "12 moods for jazz" to build not just the most complex and accomplished composition of the Harlem Renaissance, but the quintessentially American modernist symphony of poems. Its poet is right to gloat. "ME WHO USED TO BE NOBODY," boasts the persona of *Ask Your Mama*, "GOT THERE! YES, I MADE IT!"

In the context of the Harlem Renaissance, the achievement of Langston Hughes must be measured by that of other fine poets of the movement, especially Claude McKay (1890–1948), Sterling Brown (1901–89), and Countee Cullen (1903–46). McKay, no doubt because of his superb articulation of canonical forms and black themes, was the African-American poet of the period most readily accepted by the mainstream culture. He began his literary career in his native Jamaica. Walter Jekyll, an English collector of island folklore, encouraged him to write in the Jamaican dialect and helped him to publish two collections of poetry in 1912: *Songs of Jamaica* and *Constab Ballads*. These two books earned him the medal of the Jamaican Institute of Arts and Sciences, the first one won by a black. With the money award that the prize included, McKay traveled to the United States to further his education. After brief passages through the Tuskegee Institute and the Kansas State College, he went to Harlem determined to resume his call as a writer. In Harlem, McKay was befriended by such distinguished white authors as Edwin Arlington Robinson and Waldo Frank. In 1917, Frank published two of his poems in *The Seven Arts*, the "nativists'" prestigious little magazine. In 1919, several other poems were published by Max Eastman in *The Liberator*, a journal of the American literary left in the early twentieth century, to which McKay was later to contribute with essays and reviews as well as poetry. In England, where he traveled briefly in 1919–20, McKay was well received by prominent English poets and critics, including C. K. Ogden (who published several of his poems in *Cambridge Magazine*) and I. A. Richards, who wrote a preface for his third volume of verse, *Spring in New Hampshire and Other Poems* (London, 1920). In 1921, *Harlem Shadows* came out in New York. This book, McKay's fourth collection of poetry, is often credited with having inaugurated the Harlem Renaissance. The power of McKay's poetry is best illustrated by any one of his perfect Shakespearean sonnets that denounce the oppression of African-Americans with what must be described as elegant violence. In "America" (1921), one of the most anthologized of them all, the poet plays skillfully with the subject's apparent submission to the might of US America and his own unsuspected power to resist ("Her vigor flows like tides into my blood, / giving me strength erect against her hate"). As different as he is from McKay in style, Langston Hughes held the older poet, as a competent versifier and racially confident and committed writer, to be one of his major influences, along with Whitman and Sandburg.

Sterling Brown contrasts with Claude McKay in many ways. A highly educated African-American, Brown was a successful, well-published professor at Howard University for forty years. In 1945, after spending three semesters teaching at Vassar College, he was offered a permanent position there. His devotion to his black students at Howard was such, however, that he declined the flattering offer of the famed white institution. The gesture would leave him in relative isolation in academia. His important contribution to African-American studies remained largely ignored by the dominant scholarship until his books were reprinted in the early 1970s (*The Negro in American Fiction* and *Negro Poetry and Drama*, both first published in 1937, as well as the edition, with Arthur P. Davis and Ulysses Lee, of the influential anthology of African-American writing, *The Negro Caravan* [1941]). Brown's main contribution to the new black aesthetic was to insist on the validity of African-American folklore as a form of artistic expression. In this, he comes closer to Langston Hughes, even though Brown's poetic output is considerably scarcer and narrower in range. *Southern Road*, Brown's first book of poetry, appeared in 1932. Drawn primarily from material the poet had gathered during his travels in the South, the book was applauded for its fine poetic portrayals of the life, idiom, and ways of feeling and thinking of African-Americans. In spite of such an auspicious beginning, Brown could not find a publisher for his second collection of poetry, entitled *No Hiding Place*. His *Collected Poems* were published in 1980, when the rise of African-American studies made such publications commercially worthwhile, rather than risky. Brown's poems are justly praised for their fine recreations of folk stories, motifs, and rhythms. Resorting to the unmistakable sounds of worksongs, ballads, blues, and spirituals, some of his poems have an ironic palimpsestic quality, as when, in "Ma Rainey" (1932), he appropriates the singing of "the queen of the blues" to give poetic voice to the plight of African-Americans and thus strengthen them ("O Ma Rainey, / Sing yo' song, / Now you's back / Whah you belong, / Git way inside us, / Keep us strong . . . ").

Countee Cullen was perhaps the greatest unfulfilled poetic promise of the Harlem Renaissance. During his short life, he was poet, journalist, columnist, editor, novelist, playwright, children's writer, and teacher of English, French, and creative writing. His major poetry was all published between 1925 and 1935 in four slim volumes that were received with less and less favorable reviews. Having benefited from the opportunity rarely given to African-Americans to study at New York University and Harvard, Cullen excelled in his schooling and was highly praised by white academics (Irving Babbitt among them). More even than Claude McKay, Cullen cultivated faithfully the traditional forms of European poetry to sing the lives of African-Americans in the early twentieth century, and is best characterized as a genteel black poet of great merit. In his first volume of verse, entitled *Color* (1925), his fine command of form and decorum contrasts sharply and effectively with his racialized topics. In one of his most quoted poems, the elaborate sonnet "Yet Do I Marvel," the poet turns his awed wonder at the inscrutable ways of God into an understated metaphor of his outrage in the face of unjust power and racial discrimination ("Yet do I marvel at this curious thing: / To make a poet black and bid him sing!"). *Color* was followed by *Copper Sun* (1927), *The Black Christ, and Other Poems* (1929), and *The Medea, and Some Poems* (1935). In these volumes, Cullen continued to play a little too insistently with the contrast between finely controlled European forms and restrained conventional language on the one hand and the dire reality of African-American life on the other. The last collection includes Cullen's translation of Euripides' play as well as "Scottsboro, Too, Is Worth Its Song," Cullen's upbraiding of American poets, who so promptly championed the cause of two white anarchists (Sacco and Vanzetti), and yet remained mute before the predicament of the nine black youths charged with raping two white girls in Alabama in 1931. The looser, more syncopated rhythm of this nonetheless preciously rhymed poem, though pointing to a new mode, remains an exception in Cullen's oeuvre. Excellence in traditional Western forms and mastery of conventional discourse was Cullen's way of showing that black poets are as capable as white poets. In the review of *The Weary Blues* he wrote in his "Dark Tower" column in *Opportunity: Journal of Negro Life* when the book first came out in 1926, Cullen urged Hughes to avoid jazz rhythms in his poetry. In a later column, he advised black writers (no doubt having Hughes in mind) to avoid truths about African-American life "that all Negroes know, but take no pride in." This plea for black invisibility was Cullen's sincere if misguided strategy to bridge the gap between white and black art. Both his theory and his practice point to the academic distinction between form and content that all strong poetry seriously questions. Langston Hughes thought differently. In his poetry, the content is the form, and vice versa: "We know we are beautiful. And ugly too." Hughes's well-known phrase, taken from "The Black Artist and the Racial Mountain" (1926), which he in turn may have written having Cullen in mind, is a poetic as well as a sociological statement.

On one account, however, Cullen has a point. As noted earlier, Cullen argued, in the Foreword to his *Caroling Dusk* for the aesthetic inappropriateness of the separatism that presided over his own edition. Without denying that, as Adrienne Rich would say, there are "things" that need to be "known," and that history changes both "the things" and "the knowing," this literary history of American modernism aims to trace, rather than the specific characteristics of individual poets, the characteristics of this remarkable experiment in the first half of the twentieth century against (and with) the culture of capital and the age of the machine. Langston Hughes is much more than a poet of the Harlem Renaissance. He is a poet of American modernism. Like that of the other poets studied in this history, Hughes's is a poetry of contradictions that cohere, while remaining contradictions. To the modern American tensions of native and foreign, rural and urban, male and female, popular and erudite, old and new, genteel and barbarian, Gentile and Jewish, even whole and fragmentary, Hughes's poetry-as-hesitation-blues, which in itself already reenacts all these contradictions, brings in the peculiar American tension at the time, that of black and white. It could actually be argued that Hughes's "Quarter of the Negroes" in *Ask Your Mama* is what, paradoxically, makes it all cohere by making all boundaries explode. After all, isn't Leontyne Price responsible for the pot where German *Lieder* and twelve-bar blues are gently cooking with a leaf of collard green?

> IN THE QUARTER OF THE NEGROES
> WHERE THE DOORKNOB LETS IN LIEDER
> MORE THAN GERMAN EVER BORE,
> HER YESTERDAY PAST GRANDPAPA —
> NOT OF HER OWN DOING —
> IN A POT OF COLLARD GREENS
> IS GENTLY STEWING.
>
> [. . .]
> IN THE POET BEHIND THE
> PAPER DOORS WHAT'S COOKING?
> WHAT'S SMELLING, LEONTYNE?
> LIEDER, LOVELY LIEDER,
> AND A LEAF OF COLLARD GREEN.
> LOVELY LIEDER LEONTYNE.

LITERARY CRITICISM

William E. Cain

PROLOGUE

THIS study of American literary history deals with the making and breaking of boundaries in literary criticism. It focuses on literary criticism from roughly 1900 to 1950, but both the subject and the chronological period have proven hard to abide by. Many of the major literary critics of the first five decades of this century viewed themselves as *more* than literary: literary criticism was one area in which they exercised their authority as interpreters of and commentators on the culture. They addressed social, political, and cultural issues that writers and critics of the previous century had considered, and that still others explored during the 1950s and afterwards. The years from 1900 to 1950 thus mark one stage in a complex debate about the function and fate of criticism in America that began long ago and has not concluded.

The question of boundaries becomes especially important for the literary historian writing about the early 1900s and beyond because this was the period when American literature took shape as a subject and scholarly field. Before 1900, there was little organized sense of an American literature. Nor were there compelling accounts of why this literature mattered, what its chief preoccupations and traditions were, and what kinds of utility and value it possessed for the present. The case for American literature was made inside and outside the academy during the years from 1900 to 1950, and it stands as one of the most formidable achievements of modernism.

In my first chapter, I treat the process by which American literature came into being, noting the calls for American literary independence that Emerson, Whitman, and their contemporaries advanced in the 1830s, 1840s, and 1850s and that Van Wyck Brooks, H. L. Mencken, and many others echoed sixty to seventy years later during the progressive era. Here, too, I examine the work of V. L. Parrington, F. O. Matthiessen, Perry Miller, and Alfred Kazin, whose criticism and scholarship consolidated the field and established the terms by which American literature would be known.

Next, in chapter 2, I turn to intellectuals and men and women of letters, many of whom perceived their writings about American literature as a means to criticize society and culture as a whole. Brooks is again central, along with Randolph Bourne, Jane Addams, Emma Goldman, Alain Locke, Carl Van Vechten, W. E. B. Du Bois, and Edmund Wilson. In the third and final chapter, I trace the rise and institutionalization of the New Criticism, the movement that defined the role that literary studies should play in humanities education. The value of the New Criticism lay in its clarity and precision, and its limitation was its narrowed notion of the intellectual work that literary criticism should perform.

Boundaries serve useful purposes, but they can be misleading and even illegitimate. American literature is a wonderful construct, yet its formation as a scholarly subject and status as a distinctive tradition have often prompted critics to downplay or forget that this nation's literary liberty came about in large measure through a resourceful dependence on English and European writers and texts. The more one studies American literature, the clearer it becomes that this literature can best be understood in the midst of – and not separate from – the literatures of other lands. Literary nationalism is credible only within an international context.

My first chapter sets out this truth about "American" literature and literary history, and my second reinforces and extends it. Many intellectuals and men and women of letters took part in and affected literary production in America from the mid-nineteenth century to the twentieth. Yet they acquired authority because they were never provincial even when American themes and problems absorbed them. The majority of them were inspired by Thomas Carlyle or Matthew Arnold, or (as in Van Wyck Brooks's case) by both. Carlyle and Arnold showed American readers the meaning of cultural criticism, and Arnold in particular described the force that literature possessed as a criticism of life. Their influence reveals that American intellectual life, like American literature itself, strains against national boundaries that simultaneously define and distort it.

The terms and boundaries that the New Critics established for literary criticism and departments of English – the predominantly white/male canon, the intrinsic examination of the text, and the distancing of historical and biographical contexts – have few defenders today. The New Criticism has endured as a pedagogical practice, and the New Critical commitment to the study of the text is an enduring (and positive) feature of the approach that John Crowe Ransom, Cleanth Brooks, and others developed. But feminists, Marxists, post-structuralists, postcolonial critics, and gay and lesbian theorists have successfully challenged the coherence and viability of the New Criticism.

What the New Critics did in the 1930s was remarkable: they articulated the critic's job of work and stressed what it was not – not morality, politics, ethics, religion, or history. But they ruled out too much and undercut the enterprise they sought to defend. By the 1960s, literary criticism conducted according to a thinned-out New Critical theory seemed remote from the cultural issues that engaged many professors and students. It appeared to be in complicity with the status quo, a battery of techniques that equipped bureaucrats and middle managers for the business of exploitation and war. This was a gross over-simplification. But the New Critics themselves, through their theory and sometimes in their practice, exposed their approach to this attack.

Ironically, the New Criticism fell prey to teachers and critics who were raised on it. The foes of the New Criticism seized on its analytical powers – which were, and remain, impressive – in order to dismantle its prestige, and they fastened on insights about literary language that in fact already inhabited the New Critics' writings. The New Critics built boundaries that could not be sustained, and a later generation contested these boundaries with tools that the New Critics had prepared for use.

As this brief overview indicates, I have tried to sketch broad themes as well as provide coverage. There are significant figures, such as Lionel Trilling, Richard Chase, Irving Howe, Northrop Frye, Ralph Ellison, and Albert Murray, whose important work lies temptingly over the edge of the period from 1900 to 1950 that I have addressed. Though I have singled out Brooks, Bourne, Addams, Locke, J. Saunders Redding, R. P. Blackmur, and a few others for extended notice, I left out many more. I regret my omissions, and would have wished for space to discuss A. O. Lovejoy, Joseph Wood Krutch, James Weldon Johnson, and Austin Warren, and, even more, William James, John Dewey, Franz Boas, Thorstein Veblen, Charlotte Perkins Gilman, George Santayana, Charles Beard, and Reinhold Niebuhr, all of whom would merit detailed attention in a full-fledged intellectual history of the period.

My conception of what it means to write history is old-fashioned, deriving from progressive definitions of the enterprise that still seem meaningful to me. The historian Frederick Jackson Turner (1861–1932) observed that history is "the self-consciousness of the living age acquired by understanding its development from the past"; the historian and political theorist Carl Becker (1873–1945) noted that "the business of history is to arouse an intelligent discontent"; and the philosopher John Dewey (1859–1952) proposed that "the intelligent understanding of past history is to some extent a lever for moving the present into a certain kind of future." These words do not prescribe a method, but evoke a goal for which methods are found. Consequently I have studied the movements and ideas in the past that illustrate what I think needs to be better known and acted upon in the decades ahead.

INVENTING AMERICAN LITERATURE

T HE publication in 1941 of Harvard professor and scholar-critic F. O. Matthiessen's *American Renaissance: Art and Expression in the Age of Emerson and Whitman* was an epochal event in the history of American literary studies. It summarized and extended work on American writers that had been underway for several decades and laid out a rich array of themes about language, literature, and culture for scholars and teachers to develop and refine in the years ahead.

Matthiessen's book was compelling in literary terms: it dramatized connections between American writers of the 1830s, 1840s, and 1850s and seventeenth-century masters of English prose and illuminated the myths, symbols, and theories of language that organized *Walden*, *Leaves of Grass*, and *Moby-Dick*. It proved all the more inspiring because of the sense of mission that motivated it; as Matthiessen (1902–50) explained in his preface, he sought to "repossess" a "literature for our democracy" that would enable readers to feel "the challenge of our still undiminished resources." Matthiessen made the study of American literature an activity resonant with the patriotic spirit of reform. He led American scholars backward in time so that they could then return, enlightened and vitalized, for the labor of reimagining and reforming the present.

American Renaissance is such a constitutive fact that one can hardly conceive of American literary/critical life without it. But while *American Renaissance* now seems weighted with inevitability – its innovative terms became everyday terms that scholars relied upon, and later contested – it was a revelation, a moment of intellectual and spiritual awakening, for its first readers. Despite the efforts of V. L. Parrington (1871–1929), Van Wyck Brooks (1886–1963), Lewis Mumford (1895–1990), and Newton Arvin (1900–63), American literature in the 1920s and 1930s did not enjoy the aura and distinction attached then to English literature. Critics had begun to examine and think highly of the age of Emerson and Whitman, but these writers and others from the period we know as the "American Renaissance" had only recently secured their place in the literary canon. American literature was in the process of being formed and articulated.

During the first decades of the century, American literature was typically perceived as a branch of English literature. When critics and teachers paid attention to American writers, they asked how these writers contributed to *English* culture and letters. A specifically "American" literature, a body of texts different in a crucial way from English literature, was not a recognized category. New England provincialism and Protestant moral emphasis, combining with the Anglo-Saxon bias of philology, solidified the place of English literature in the academy and accented those American writers who seemed idealistic in their tone and morally beneficial in their values.

The turn-of-the-century canon of American literature included more poetry than prose, clung to New England worthies such as Whittier, Longfellow, and Lowell (who were valued for their nostalgic visions and didactic lessons), and simplified Emerson, Thoreau, and Hawthorne when it included them. As Van Wyck Brooks recalled in *Scenes and Portraits* (1954), when he was a student at Harvard at the turn of the century "English authors were always cited in preference to Americans," and "merely to have mentioned" this custom would have been viewed as a sign of American chauvinism.

Writing in 1932, the American critic Carl Van Doren (1885–1950) described the early twentieth-century canon:

Bearded and benevolent, the faces of Bryant, Longfellow, Whittier, Lowell, Holmes, and sometimes (rather oddly) Whitman, looked down unchallenged from the walls of schoolrooms. Emerson was the American philosopher, Irving the American essayist, Cooper the American romancer, Hawthorne the American explorer of the soul, Poe the American unhappy poet (unhappy on account of his bad habits), Thoreau the American hermit, Mark Twain the American humorist (barely a man of letters), Henry James the American expatriate, and Howells the American academy. Here were fifteen apostles set in a rigid eminence, braced by minor figures grouped more randomly about them.

Even to use the term "canon," however, is misleading, since it assigns to American literature a stature that it did not possess. In the early 1900s, American literature existed as a footnote to the study of English literature. This was particularly true in high schools, colleges, and universities. Recalling what the situation looked like in 1920, Van Wyck Brooks said that American literature then was "ignored in academic circles where Thackeray and Tennyson were treated as twin kings of our literature and all the American writers as poor relations." Most of the school textbooks in use during this period appended to the selections of American literature a short history of English literature, as though to remind students of the main stream of texts to which America was a tributary. During the 1920s, the members of the American Literature group pondered whether they should secede from the Modern Language Association and form their own organization, and, as late as 1930, American literary history still appeared under the heading of "English XI" or "English XII" at the annual MLA meetings. As one scholar said in 1935, American literature was "the orphan child of the curriculum."

There had been significant work on American literature during the late nineteenth and early twentieth centuries. The American historian Moses Coit Tyler (1835–1900), for example, in his impressive volumes *A History of American Literature, 1607–1765* (1878) and *The Literary History of the American Revolution* (1897), was a pioneer in the field, and his letters and diaries testify to his earnest conception of himself as "an American scholar and writer giving himself up, with pure heart, to the service of society" (*Diary*, 1869). An ordained minister and the pastor of a Congregationalist church in Poughkeepsie, New York before he turned to the teaching of rhetoric and English literature at the University of Michigan and, still later, to American history at Cornell, Tyler argued that the literature of America during the period from 1765 to 1815 expressed the revolutionary political currents of the period – "the effort for complete detachment of America from Europe." This literature, he maintained, included many different kinds of writers and writing: "ballads and other poetry; pamphlets; Doctor Franklin; the great political writers; diarists; letter writers, and historians; theological and religious; pure men of letters."

Along with Tyler's volumes, a number of textbooks, anthologies, and surveys had appeared as publishers responded to the marketing possibilities that schools and colleges offered – for instance, the poet-essayist (and Wall Street broker) E. C. Stedman's *Library of American Literature* (10 vols., 1880–90) and his *An American Anthology, 1787–1900* (1900), a collection of poems by US authors. Some cogent criticism existed as well. The Harvard scholar and professor of Romance languages Irving Babbitt (1865–1933) and the editor and critic Paul Elmer More (1864–1937) wrote a number of essays that drew attention to American literature. Babbitt examined the ethical implications of Emerson's philosophy, and More, showing greater sensitivity and tolerance, treated Hawthorne, Thoreau, Poe, Whitman, and other American writers in his *Shelburne Essays* (1904–36). The critic and elegant stylist W. C. Brownell (1851–1928), in *American Prose Masters* (1909), commented scrupulously on a range of nineteenth-century authors from Cooper to Henry James.

But the formal histories by Wellesley professor Katharine Lee Bates (1859–1929), Harvard scholar Barrett Wendell (1855–1921), and others were limited by racist assumptions and New England parochialism. Wendell's *Literary History of America* (1900), according to one of his contemporaries, should have been titled "A Literary History of Harvard University, with Incidental

Glimpses of the Minor Writers of America." The novelist William Dean Howells (1837–1920) thought a better title would have been "A Study of New England Authorship in Its Rise and Decline, with Some Glances at American Literature."

The New England literary scholars and historians included Irving and Cooper, but they could not see Poe, Melville, or Whitman as worthy of a place in the canon, and they underrated Thoreau, Emerson, and Hawthorne while overrating Whittier, Lowell, Longfellow, and Holmes. The New Englanders were writing not so much history as a version of pastoral; in 1893, Wendell reflected: "we are vanishing into provincial obscurity. America has swept from our grasp. The future is beyond us." These histories paid homage to a world that Wendell feared that he and his kinsmen, overtaken by urbanization, industrialism, and immigration, had lost.

Many scholars in the 1890s and 1900s and afterwards spoke of American literature in disappointed terms, calling attention to its thin achievement and failure to bear comparison with the work of foreign authors. In *America in Literature* (1903), the poet, critic, and Columbia professor George Woodberry (1855–1930) stated: "It is impossible to escape a sense of fragmentariness in the products [of American literature], of disproportion between the literary energy and the other vital powers of the people, and of the inadequacy of literature as a function of national expression . . . There has been no national author in the universal sense." The editor and Harvard professor Bliss Perry (1860–1954), in *The American Mind* (1912), emphasized that the "most characteristic American writing" was not the "self-conscious literary performance of a Poe or a Hawthorne," but was, instead, "civic writing" (the *Federalist Papers*, William Lloyd Garrison's abolitionist editorials, U. S. Grant's *Memoirs*) that was "without any stylistic consciousness whatever." "But in literature, as in other things," Perry added, "we must take what we can get."

Critics of sharply divergent sensibilities shared this dim appraisal. In "Patria Mia" (1913), Ezra Pound (1885–1972) predicted that "an American Renaissance" was imminent, but he conceded: "There is no man now living in America whose work is of the slightest interest to any serious artist." Paul Elmer More, even while writing about American literature, confessed to having little esteem for it. In 1900, he complained that critics and historians of American literature lacked a sense of proportion and "tried to make interesting (and so exaggerated its importance) a subject which we must sorrowfully admit is for the greater part of trivial magnitude. Eight or ten names, none of which reaches the very first rank, do not make a literature."

In 1903, More stated that Edwards, Emerson, Hawthorne, Poe, Whitman, and Parkman were important but not truly first-rate and, otherwise, "American literature is indeed a wilderness of mediocrity." It was this sense that American literature had not arrived that led so many writers and critics to offer prescriptions for American literary greatness, as when Hamlin Garland, in *A Son of the Middle Border* (1917), counseled: "American literature, in order to be great, must be national, and in order to be national, must deal with conditions peculiar to our own land and climate. Every genuinely American writer must deal with the life he knows best and for which he cares the most."

This pattern of complaint about American literature and lamentation about its prospects has its origins at least as far back as the mocking assessment that Sydney Smith, Scottish critic and editor of the *Edinburgh Review*, had issued in 1818: "Literature the Americans have none – no native literature, we mean. It is all imported." Many American statesmen and foreign observers in the late eighteenth and early nineteenth centuries made or implied the same judgment about the balked capacity of writers fated to dwell in a democratic land, with its hearty but, no doubt, undiscerning, or else overly conventional, readership. Alexander Hamilton, for example, in a June 18, 1787, speech at the Constitutional Convention, observed: "The voice of the people has been said to be the voice of God; and, however generally this maxim has been quoted and believed, it is not true to fact. The people are turbulent and changing; they seldom judge or determine right." John Adams, in a letter to John Taylor, April 15, 1814, remarked mordantly about America's future: "Democracy never lasts long. It soon wastes, exhausts, and murders itself. There never was a democracy yet that did not commit suicide." The French aristocrat Alexis de Tocqueville, reporting in *Democracy in America* on his travels to the new nation in 1831–32, stressed the impact of democracy, and of majority opinion, on the production of literature and wondered whether American authors would ever overcome it. "I know of no country," he stated, "in which there is so little independence of mind and real freedom of discussion as in America." Tocqueville saw "barriers around liberty of opinion" that were too formidable for original writers: "within these barriers an author may write what he pleases, but woe to him if he goes beyond them." "If America has not as yet had any great writers," he summed up, "the reason is given in these facts; there can be no literary genius without freedom of opinion, and freedom of opinion does not exist in America."

James Fenimore Cooper, in *The American Democrat* (1838), concluded, "the tendency of democracy is, in all things, to mediocrity." A notable visitor from England, Charles Dickens, writing to the English critic and historian John Forster, February 24, 1842, shared this view: "I believe there is no country, on the face of the earth, where there is less freedom of opinion on any subject in reference to which there is a broad difference of opinion, than in this." Emerson (1803–82), in "Nominalist and Realist" (*Essays, Second Series*, 1844), was at times not much different in his evaluation: "Democracy is morose, and runs to anarchy."

During the 1830s and 1840s, however, even as Tocqueville and others stressed that America had "no literature," Emerson and Hawthorne were articulating the tensions between liberty and conformity in America and transforming into rich material for literature the very dangers that the aristocratic Tocqueville had perceived. What threatened American writing, Tocqueville had said, was the pressure against the individual voice and conscience and the hostility directed toward original, unconventional persons and perspectives. This was in fact the situation that American writers took to writing about, and through the writing that they did they assailed and tried to transcend it. As Thomas Jefferson had noted much earlier, in a letter to Martha Jefferson, March 28, 1787: "It is part of the American character to consider nothing as desperate, to surmount every difficulty by resolution and contrivance." American literature developed from the restrictive set of conditions that Tocqueville suspected would forestall it, and it manifested an oppositional mode of address that critics and scholars in the twentieth century seized upon.

Tocqueville described another threat to a truly "American" literature, and that was the pervasive presence in America of the writings of English authors: "Not only do Americans constantly draw upon the treasures of English literature, but it may be said with truth that they find the literature of England growing on their own soil. The larger part of that small number of men in the United States who are engaged in the composition of literary works are English in substance and still more so in form." English literature had taken root in America, and it flowered even on the fringes of the frontier. To make his point, Tocqueville observed that he first read Shakespeare's *Henry V* in an American log cabin.

America's dependence on "the courtly muses" of Europe and England troubled Emerson during the decade of Tocqueville's visit, and he applied his literary prowess to cajole, inspire, and force American writers into being. In "The American Scholar" (1837), he called for creative reading that would break free from the "over-influence" exercised by the masterpieces of the past, and in "Self-Reliance" (1841) and "The Poet" (1844), he appealed for creative writing that would cast American materials into a proper artistic structure. In "Self-Reliance" he denounced imitation and summoned writers to find their inspiration at home: "If the American artist will study with hope and love the precise thing to be done by him, considering the climate, the soil, the length of the day, the wants of the people, the habit and form of the government, he will create a house in which all these will find themselves fitted, and taste and sentiment will be satisfied also."

In "The Poet," Emerson spoke even more explicitly about "the value of our incomparable materials" and vouched for their unsurpassed breadth and diversity:

Our log-rolling, our stumps and their politics, our fisheries, our Negroes and Indians, our boats and our repudiations [i.e., the "repudiation" of their debts by some states in the Union], the wrath of rogues and the pusillanimity of honest men, the northern trade, the Southern planting, the western clearing, Oregon and Texas, are yet unsung. Yet America is a poem in our eyes; its ample geography dazzles the imagination, and it will not wait long for meters.

In a sense Emerson was implying that an American literature already existed. Born late as a nation, the United States needed in a hurry to produce a national literature that could take some pride of place among the national literatures of England, France, and Germany. Emerson was saying that American literature had not happened yet, even as he emphasized that the country itself was a grand poem waiting to be vocalized.

Like Emerson, Margaret Fuller (1810–50) and Melville (1819–91) tied the promise of American literature (and its rivalry with English literature) to the expansiveness of the land. Fuller (1846) urged American writers to "develop a genius wide and full as our rivers, flowery, luxuriant, and impassioned as our vast prairies, rooted in strength as the rocks on which the Puritan fathers landed." Melville proclaimed in "Hawthorne and His Mosses" (1850): "Men not very much inferior to Shakespeare are this day being born on the banks of the Ohio." Americans, insisted Melville, needed to enact their ideals in literature as well as in daily living. These were the ideals that made America "modern" and that would enable its writers to soar beyond their English precursors and counterparts: "And the day will come when you shall say, who reads a book by an Englishman that is a modern?"

Thoreau (1817–62) and Whitman (1819–92) also explored these themes. "English literature," wrote Thoreau in a journal entry in 1851, "from the days of the minstrels to the Lake Poets, Chaucer and Spenser and Shakespeare and Milton included, breathes no quite fresh and, in this sense, wild strain. It is an essentially tame and civilized literature, reflecting Greece and Rome." Thoreau wanted American writing to display a wildness suited to the wilderness as it moved into unmapped territory. Whitman, too, highlighted the newness and the "largeness" of American nature and nation in his 1855 preface, where he gloried in the literary potential of America and, echoing Emerson, affirmed that "the United States themselves are essentially the greatest poem." He amplified this point in *Democratic Vistas* (1870), an essay that the critic Lewis Mumford in *The Brown Decades* (1931) described as "the most fundamental piece of literary and social criticism that has been written in America." Whitman spoke of the necessity for "a cluster of mighty poets, artists, teachers, fit for us, national expressers, comprehending and effusing for the men and women of the States, what is universal, native, common to all, inland and seaboard, northern and southern."

Francis Parkman, in the preface to *Pioneers of France in the New World* (1865), similarly affirmed:

The springs of American civilization, unlike those of the elder world, lie revealed in the clear light of history. In appearance they are feeble; in reality, copious and full of force. Acting at the sources of life, instruments otherwise weak become mighty for good and evil, and men, lost elsewhere in the crowd, stand forth as agents of Destiny.

Such charged language shows the flexing of the imaginative will that wrought the artistic achievements of the American Renaissance. Over and over again, American writers in the nineteenth century evoked the spirit of the people, the nation's glorious landscape, and its emerging commercial power in order to find strength for their contest with English literature. This language would be heard once more when the cultural critic Randolph Bourne inveighed in 1914 against America's "cultural humility" and beckoned for "creative pride" in the specialness of American literature, and when the critic Stuart Sherman in 1924 proposed that English literature should be dislodged from its preeminent position and viewed as "a part of American literature."

This rival literature had at first seemed a burden to be shed. As Emerson noted in *English Traits* (1856), "in all that is done or begun by the Americans towards right thinking and practice, we are met by a civilization already settled and overpowering ... See what books fill our libraries. Every book we read, every biography, play, romance, in whatever form, is still English history and manners." The clergyman, Civil War veteran, and editor Thomas Wentworth Higginson (1823–1911) stated, in "Americanism in Literature" (1871): "The highest aim of most of our literary journals has thus far been to appear English, except where some diverging experimentalist has said, 'O let us be German,' or 'Let us be French.' This was inevitable, as inevitable as a boy's first imitations of Byron or Tennyson. But it necessarily implied that our literature must, during this epoch, be second-rate. We need to become national."

But it was the sheer heft of English literature that provoked America's writers to be determined to cast it off. It both dismayed and empowered them: they drew upon English writers, saturating themselves in their texts, as they went about the business of crafting an American literature that would dramatize the modernity that the literature of England lacked. Americans drew deeply from English (and European) writers even as they complained about and defied their authority. There were, after all, productive stresses, empowering contradictions, in the views that Emerson held:

The American is only the continuation of the English genius into new conditions, more or less. (*English Traits*, 1856)

One day we will cast out the passion for Europe, by the passion for America. (*The Conduct of Life*, 1860)

Emerson himself harvested ideas from Samuel Taylor Coleridge and received inspiration from Thomas Carlyle. He was hardly defeated by the English and European literary traditions; as he wrote in "Power," in *The Conduct of Life* (1860), "there is no way to success in art but to take off your coat, grind paint, and work like a digger on the railroad, all day and every day." Thoreau discovered in the seventeenth-century physician/author Thomas Browne the correspondences between inner and outer worlds, microcosm and macrocosm, that informed the structure of *Walden*; Melville boosted the volume of the tortured, rebellious speech of his Ahab through the thunder of Shakespeare's and Milton's outcasts and rebels; and the young, enslaved African-American Frederick Douglass (1818–95) learned "the principles of liberty" from reading the "mighty speeches" of English reformers that were contained in the *Columbian Orator*. What the reformer Wendell Phillips (1811–84) pointed out in his lecture "The Lost Arts" was positive as well as negative, a solution perhaps even more than a problem: "Take the whole range of imaginative literature, and we are all wholesale borrowers. In every matter that relates to invention, to use, or beauty or form, we are borrowers."

English literature furnished American writers of the 1830s, 1840s, and 1850s with the artistic resources that would make American literature free and, as Emerson explained, that would eventually expose the worn-out condition of English literature. In *English Traits*, Emerson said that he was now beginning to suspect that English rather than American literature was inadequate. True, English literature was "wise and rich," but "it lives on its capital. It is retrospective. How can it discern and hail the new forms that are looming up on the horizon, new and gigantic thoughts which cannot dress themselves out of any old wardrobe of the past?"

The charge of being "retrospective," which Emerson had hurled against America in *Nature* (1836), thus became, for Emerson and others, the definitive feature of English culture and literature: England, not America, suffered from the burden of the past; English readers and critics could not apprehend bold and original literary forms. Yet Emerson developed his case by deploying the "clothing" and "wardrobe" metaphors that Carlyle had invoked and explored in *Sartor Resartus*, a book that Emerson himself helped to get published in the same year that his own book *Nature* appeared. Perhaps he took heart, too, from the judgment of English cultural achievement made by his friend Carlyle, who had said in *Past and Present* (1843) that "it is complained that [the English] have no artists; one Shakespeare indeed; but for Raphael only a Reynolds; for Mozart nothing but a Mr. Bishop: not a picture, not a song."

"Emerson has America in his mind's eye all the time," reflected the man-of-letters John Jay Chapman (1897), and it was part of Emerson's American crusade to cite, adopt, and transform England's literary traditions while devaluing English literature and petitioning for homemade texts. The existence of English literature, Emerson knew, did not really threaten to deny the creation of an American literature. The best American writers recognized that they would exploit English literature as they strove to supersede it. They turned to assets that English writers made available and integrated these with American materials.

The literature that Emerson, Whitman, Douglass, and Dickinson made was slow to gain recognition, which is why the complaints about America's literary insufficiency lingered so long. Writing in 1877, the poet-essayist Oliver Wendell Holmes (1809–94) concluded that "aesthetically speaking," America was "a penal colony." Nearly four decades later, in 1915, Van Wyck Brooks mourned that "something, in American literature, has always been wanting."

Related versions of this story – recalling complaints that Cooper and Hawthorne had voiced and that Henry James in his biography of Hawthorne (1879) reinforced – of absent traditions, intellectual and moral frailties, and indifferent audiences can also be found in Henry Adams's *The Life of George Cabot Lodge* (1911) and George Santayana's *The Last Puritan* (1936). "The society," said Adams, "no longer seemed sincerely to believe in itself or anything else; it resented nothing, not even praise." "Genteel American poetry," according to Santayana, "was a simple, sweet, humane, Protestant literature, grandmotherly in that sedate spectacled wonder with which it gazed at this terrible world and said how beautiful and how interesting it all was." As Henry Adams complained in his letters, "Everybody is fairly decent, respectable, domestic, bourgeois, middle-class, and tiresome. There is absolutely nothing to revile except that it's a bore" (December 17, 1908); "American society is a sort of flat, fresh-water pond which absorbs silently, without reaction, anything which is thrown into it" (September 20, 1911).

By the early years of the new century, with the publication of Brooks's *The Wine of the Puritans* in 1908, followed by the appearance of John Macy's

The Spirit of American Literature in 1913, there were signs of a counter-movement. These critics and others assaulted the New England canon (with its reliance on English models) and initiated a full-scale reassessment of American writing. Brooks, who worked in the genre of cultural polemic and critique, and Macy (1877–1932), who assembled a more familiar kind of appreciative overview, argued that critics should foreground native traditions. In addition, they affirmed that critics should unshackle American writers and readers from the genteel tradition and Puritan morality and enable them to write freely about the modern world.

America was now a huge, complex, dynamic society: How could it *not* be a vast and beckoning subject for writers? By the beginning of the twentieth century, there was an extraordinary range of "American" issues for American writers to examine and explore, and they did so in a variety of literary forms, including the essay, the novel, and autobiography.

This period witnessed the rise and consolidation of big business, monopolies, and trusts. By the 1880s, John D. Rockefeller's Standard Oil Company controlled 90 percent of the nation's oil. The U. S. Steel Corporation, the first billion-dollar corporation, formed in 1901 and based on the steel empire that Andrew Carnegie had built, employed nearly 170,000 workers and controlled 60 to 70 percent of the nation's steel business; its annual gross income was greater than that of the US Treasury. "The gospel left behind by [the railroad magnate] Jay Gould," said Mark Twain, "is doing giant work in our days. Its message is 'get money. Get it quickly. Get it in abundance. Get it dishonestly, if you can, honestly if you must.'" By 1900, 1 percent of the corporations exercised control over one-third of the nation's manufacturing. This was at a time when the average income of workers was somewhere between $400 and $500 per year; the minimum for a decent standard of living was $600.

In 1900, there were twenty million industrial workers; 1.7 million were children, double the number in 1870. By 1900 as well, accidents killed about 35,000 workers each year and injured half a million more. Critics, reformers, and progressive journalists turned their attention to these and related facts of modern American life in a host of significant books of reportage and analysis:

Henry Demarest Lloyd, *Wealth Against Commonwealth* (1894)
Jacob Riis, *How the Other Half Lives* (1890)
Frances Kellor, *Out of Work: A Study of Employment Agencies* (1904; rev. 1915)
John Moody, *The Truth About the Trusts* (1904)
Lincoln Steffens, *The Shame of the Cities* (1904)
Robert Hunter, *Poverty* (1904)

Ida Tarbell, *History of Standard Oil Company* (1904)
David Graham Phillips, *The Treason of the Senate* (1906)
Ray Stannard Baker, *Following the Color Line* (1908)

By the mid-1890s, the United States was the world's leader in industrial production, with an output greater than England, France, and Germany combined. In the mid-nineteenth century, in the era of Emerson and Thoreau, there had been few factories that employed more than 500 workers. By 1900 there were 1,500 factories that employed 500 or more workers; some were much larger, including the General Electric plants in Lynn, Massachusetts (11,000 workers) and Schenectady, New York (15,000), and the Cambria Steel factory in Johnstown, Pennsylvania, which employed 20,000 persons by 1910. The United States was now the leading industrial power in the world – an exhilarating, fearful reality that American writers would engage with.

The landscape, too, was being radically transformed. In 1900, the year that the Automobile Club of America held its first meeting and automobile show (in Madison Square Garden, New York City, November 3–10), there were only 4,000 registered automobiles in the entire country, with about ten miles of paved roads for them. By 1910, nearly 200,000 automobiles were built annually. In 1913, Henry Ford organized the first automobile assembly line, and soon 1,000 Model T cars were being produced each work-day. Before the assembly line came into operation, the manufacture of a car took Ford's workers nearly thirteen hours; the assembly line cut the time to an hour and a half. In the following year, the Ford Motor Company produced 250,000 cars. By 1915, there were 3.5 million cars in the nation, and by 1923, 15 million.

Ford alarmed many business owners by providing a high wage of $5 per day, but his revolutionary goal was to pay his workers well enough to enable them to buy the cars they made – and because of the assembly-line system, the price of a Model T was slashed from $950 in 1909 to $290 in 1924. As Ford explained in an entry for the *Encyclopaedia Britannica* (1926): "The experience of Ford Motor Co. has been that mass production precedes mass consumption and makes it possible, by reducing costs and thus permitting both greater use-convenience and price-convenience." (The success of assembly line and mass production techniques in automobile manufacturing led to the same process for the manufacture of farm equipment, typewriters, machine tools, sewing machines, and other items.) Many Americans, of course, still could not afford, or else did not want to own, a car; for them, there was public transportation, and beginning in 1915, the taxicab (a driver was called a "cabbie" in the Midwest, a "hacker" or "hackie" in the East). But installment-buying – another innovation – allowed many who could not afford the full price to purchase cars.

By 1929, the auto industry employed more than 375,000 workers, and hundreds of thousands of others held jobs related to it, for instance, making tires and building highways. The center of the industry, Detroit, grew in population from 285,000 in 1900 to 1.5 million in 1930. The romance and the horror of the automobile is best evoked in *The Great Gatsby*, with its sleek cars coming and going from Gatsby's estate, but it figures in much cultural criticism of the period, as when Paul Rosenfeld, writing about Van Wyck Brooks in *Port of New York* (1924), described the drift of America: "The spectacle of the youth of a land concentrating its mind entirely in the carburetors of motor cars; the vision of a population traveling about Sunday afternoons in automobiles, and swallowing the scenery through their open mouths, seemed to him a collapse of very life."

By the mid-1920s, 25,000 people each year were killed in traffic accidents, more than two-thirds of them pedestrians. But cars offered too many advantages for Americans to feel they could be given up. Robert and Helen Lynd, in *Middletown* (1929), concluded: "As, at the turn of the century, business-class people began to feel apologetic if they did not have a telephone, so ownership of an automobile has now reached the point of being an accepted essential of normal living." By 1930, more than forty-five million Americans, which was one-third of the total population, took "automobile vacations," traveling to tourist camps and cabins. As the Lynds noted, the automobile had "revolutionized leisure."

The automobile industry was powerful evidence of the transformation of the American scene, and of the changes taking place throughout the culture that would both equip American writers with dramatic material to write about and that would threaten them: Could a book compete with the thrilling practicality of a car and, as automobile-design became more dashing, with its colors and curves, its aesthetic appeal? For that matter, why write at all, when the allure of business was so great? As Andrew Carnegie observed in *The Empire of Business* (1902), becoming a financial success in twentieth-century America required visionary power and energy:

The young man who begins in a financial firm and deals with capital invested in a hundred different ways – in bonds upon our railway systems, in money lent to the merchant, and to the manufacturer to enable them to work their wonders – soon finds romance in business and unlimited room for the imagination.

For the worker without access to capital, the situation was less glamorous. In *My Philosophy of Industry* (1929), Henry Ford tried to claim that all was well:

It has been asserted that machine production kills the creative ability of the craftsman. This is not true. The machine demands that man be its master; it compels mastery more than the old methods did. The number of skilled craftsman in proportion to the working population has greatly increased under the conditions brought about by the machine. They get better wages and more leisure in which to exercise their creative faculties.

But as Frederick Winslow Taylor's words in *The Principles of Scientific Management* (1911) unintentionally revealed, the "science" of work, with its emphasis on machines and productivity, had made the situation of the laborer a grim one:

One of the very first requirements for a man who is fit to handle pig iron as a regular occupation is that he shall be so stupid and so phlegmatic that he more nearly resembles in his mental make-up the ox than any other type ... He is so stupid that the word "percentage" has no meaning to him, and he must consequently be trained by a man more intelligent than himself into the habit of working in accordance with the laws of this science before he can be successful.

Thorstein Veblen, in *The Theory of Business Enterprise* (1904), caught accurately this dehumanization of the American worker: "The machine ... compels the adaptation of the workman to his work, rather than the adaptation of the work to the workman. The machine technology rests on a knowledge of impersonal, material cause and effect, not on the dexterity, diligence, or personal force of the workman." Creativity crushed: Who would be the writers, and who would be the readers? Jurgis, the protagonist of Upton Sinclair's *The Jungle* (1906), saw how workers killed and carved cattle on the line: "They worked with furious intensity, literally upon the run – at a pace with which there is nothing to be compared except a football game. It was all highly specialized labor, each man having his task to do." A man's consciousness was that task.

At the time of Sinclair's novel, the United States Steel Works in Homestead, Pennsylvania was running two grueling shifts, one of ten and a half hours during the day, and the other of thirteen and a half hours through the night. According to one study, a steelworker on either of these shifts could not make enough money to support a family of five even if he worked every day of the year.

Corporations and monopolies meant power and control of wealth, resources, workers, and, eventually, authors. As the financier J. P. Morgan explained: "I like a little competition, but I like combination better." By 1910, 40 percent of the clerical workers and wage earners in the nation were living in poverty; and this figure did not take into account tenant farmers, sharecroppers, and others living in rural areas.

"Extremes of wealth and poverty are threatening the existence of the government," wrote the labor leader George McNeill in *The Labor Movement:*

The Problem of Today (1887): "In the light of these facts, we declare that there is an inevitable and irresistible conflict between the wage-system of labor and the republican system of government – the wage laborer attempting to save the government, and the capitalist class ignorantly attempting to subvert it." The social reformer and economist Henry George, campaigning in 1886 for mayor of New York, stated: "All men who work for a living, whether by hand or head, are underpaid. Labor nowhere has its full and fair reward. Everywhere the struggle for existence, the difficulty of making a living, is far greater than it ought to be." Speaking in Kansas in the 1890s, the Populist orator and agitator Mary K. Lease declared: "Wall Street owns the country. It is no longer a government of the people, and for the people, but a government of Wall Street, by Wall Street, and for Wall Street." "I am for Socialism," affirmed Eugene V. Debs, "because I am for humanity. We have been cursed with the reign of gold long enough. Money constitutes no proper basis of civilization."

Workers resisted and massed their forces in response to new industrial conditions, and their struggle was rendered in novels by writers as different as William Dean Howells (*Annie Kilburn*, 1889, *A Hazard of New Fortunes*, 1890), John Hay (*The Bread-Winners*, 1884), Mary Wilkins Freeman (*The Portion of Labor*, 1901), and Edith Wharton (*The Fruit of the Tree*, 1907). The National Labor Union (1866–72) and the Knights of Labor (1878–93) opposed the wage system and organized both skilled and unskilled workers. And the American Federation of Labor (AFL), formed in 1886 with 150,000 members, by 1897 had achieved a membership of 500,000 (60 percent of the union members in the nation).

By 1914, the AFL, led by Samuel Gompers, had 2 million members. It concentrated on skilled craftsmen, not unskilled and immigrant workers, and its goals were the improvement of working conditions and the increase of wages. The Industrial Workers of the World, formed in Chicago in 1905, welcomed all workers, including women, immigrants, minorities, and even the unemployed. From 1916 to 1920, more than 1 million workers went on strike every year. In 1919 alone, 4 million workers – 20 percent of the workforce – went on strike. In the two-year span from 1916 to 1918, membership in the AFL rose from 2 million to 2.7 million. By 1920, membership stood at almost 3.3 million.

Labor unrest during the first decades of the century was widespread. In early 1919, for example, tens of thousands of workers went on strike in Seattle, bringing the city to a halt. In the same year, 50,000 clothing workers went on strike in New York City; 120,000 textile workers struck in New Jersey and New England; and 400,000 coal miners and 350,000 striking steelworkers closed down the industry in ten states and sparked violent protests and brutal crackdowns by the company and police.

Women were working in increasing numbers too. By 1900, nearly 20 percent of the work-force was female; and in such industries as shoe- and garment-making, women numbered between 40 and 60 percent. By the first decade of the twentieth century, 60 percent of New York City's young immigrant women worked for wages. The women who toiled in the garment industry were between the ages of sixteen and twenty-five; they worked six days a week, about fifty-five to sixty hours per week, and were paid $6 weekly. Between 1920 and 1930, the number of employed women increased from 8 to 11 million and by 1915, women were responsible for 80 percent of consumer purchasing. More money in the hands of women led to a new measure of freedom for them, evident in, for instance, the change in the divorce rate, which increased from one in every twenty-one marriages in 1880 to one in every nine by 1915–16. For Edith Wharton, caught in an unhappy marriage, divorce was unthinkable at the turn of the century, but it became possible for her – something she could imagine doing without social shame – in 1913.

Many women remained at home, yet their lives were made easier because of developments in food processing and preparation, such as prepackaged flour, and soups and sauces in cans. Those in the upper class and upper-middle class, like Wharton, enjoyed the advantages, too, of indoor plumbing, central heating, and electricity. By the 1920s and into the 1930s, these changes improved the lives of even more women and their families; there were oil furnaces, electric stoves, vacuum cleaners, washing machines, and toasters – and radios to listen to while the work was being done.

And women finally received the right to vote. The suffrage movement was led by Carrie Chapman Catt and Anna Howard Shaw; its membership grew from 13,000 in the early 1890s to two million by the late 1910s. Congress passed the Nineteenth Amendment in June 1920, and it was ratified by the states in August 1920, enabling women to vote in the fall Presidential election. As Catt noted:

To get that word, male, out of the Constitution, cost the women of the country 52 years of pauseless campaign; 56 state referendum campaigns; 480 legislative campaigns to get state suffrage amendments submitted; 47 state constitutional convention campaigns; 277 state party convention campaigns; 30 national party convention campaigns to get suffrage planks in the party platforms; 19 campaigns with 19 successive Congresses to get the federal amendment submitted; and the final ratification campaign.

The impact of the movement on literature can be seen in all the genres, in, for example, such suffragist plays as Charlotte Perkins Gilman's *Something to Vote For* (1911) and Emily Sargent Lewis's *Election Day: A Suffrage Play* (1912), and in Gilman's speeches, stories, poems, and cultural criticism.

The latter decades of the nineteenth century and the early decades of the twentieth century also were periods of mass immigration to the United States, and the voices and idioms of these new Americans would enrich American literature – though some writers and critics at the time said that the immigrants' dissonant "alien" languages would imperil the nation's language and literature, as Henry James fretted in *The American Scene* (1907).

Between 1865 and 1915, 25 million immigrants arrived, 9 million of them in the single decade from 1900 to 1910. Some estimates have suggested that 80 percent of New York City's population, and nearly 90 percent of Chicago's, were immigrants or the children of immigrants. By 1905, the population density of some sections of New York City had reached 1,000 persons an acre, greater than that of Bombay. As the Christian sociologist Josiah Strong said, "We must face the inevitable. The new civilization is certain to be urban; and the problem of the twentieth century will be the city," where the majority of immigrants and workers congregated (*The Twentieth Century City*, 1898). Jane Addams made a related point in *The Spirit of Youth and the City Streets* (1909): "Let us know the modern city in its weakness and wickedness, and then seek to rectify and purify it until it shall be free at least from the grosser temptations which now beset the young people who are living in its tenement houses and working in its factories."

Addams and others criticized, and sought to improve, the conditions that immigrants faced in the cities, and that workers endured in factories and plants. But they proposed their reforms in the face of a general belief in the rightness of America's development as an industrial power and, by the turn of the century, as an imperialist power that Providence blessed and directed. In his second annual message to Congress, December 5, 1898, reviewing the United States' triumph in the war against Spain, which occurred from mid-April to mid-August, President McKinley declared: "In tracing these events we are constantly reminded of our obligations to the Divine Master for His watchful care over us and His safe guidance, for which the nation makes reverent acknowledgment and offers humble prayer for the continuance of His favor."

Senator Albert J. Beveridge, also in 1898, gave this claim an even more extravagant rendering, reaching back to the rhetoric of Puritan settlement:

Fellow-Americans, we are God's chosen people. Yonder at Bunker Hill and Yorktown His providence was above us. At New Orleans and on ensanguined seas His hand sustained us. Abraham Lincoln was His minister and His was the altar of freedom the boys in blue set up on a hundred smoking battlefields. His power directed Dewey in the east, and He delivered the Spanish fleet into our hands on Liberty's natal day as he delivered the elder Armada into the hands of our English sires two [*sic*] centuries ago.

A number of the country's foremost writers and intellectuals spoke and wrote fervently against imperial expansion, against this massing of power as it surged during and in the aftermath of the Spanish–American War. The critic and man of letters Charles Eliot Norton in April 1898 told his students at Harvard that they should not serve in "this wretched, needless and, consequently, iniquitous war." The war was, he later wrote, "a bitter disappointment to the lover of his country," a "turning-back from the path of civilization to that of barbarism." The philosopher William James, in "The Philippine Tangle," *Boston Evening Transcript*, March 1, 1899, stated: "We are destroying down to the root every germ of a healthy national life in these unfortunate people, and we are surely helping to destroy for one generation at least their faith in God and man. No life shall you have, we say, except as a gift from our philanthropy after your unconditional submission to our will." The African-American educator Kelly Miller made an even broader point in "The Effect of Imperialism Upon the Negro Race" (1900), linking imperialism and racism: "The whole trend of imperial aggression is antagonistic to the feebler races. It is a revival of racial arrogance . . . Will the Negro stultify himself and become a part of the movement which must end in his own humiliation?"

These moral, social, and cultural arguments were, however, made in the midst of America's relentless industrial development and ever-growing economic might worldwide and thus had little influence. As Frank Vanderlip, a top executive for the National City Bank of New York, explained in "The American 'Commercial Invasion' of Europe" (1902), America was acquiring "supremacy in the world's markets": "So many industries have been sending rapidly increasing contributions to swell the rising tide of our foreign commerce that it is difficult to tell any detailed story of American commercial expansion without making it read like a trade catalogue."

The United States thus was extending its power outward and attracting millions of workers and their families from abroad. To be sure, many immigrants came to America intending to stay only for a short time. In some years, 70 percent of the immigrants were men who came alone; and studies have suggested that during periods of slow or declining economic growth in the United States, more immigrants left the United States than entered it. Still, between 1890 and 1920, more than 18 million immigrants arrived in the United States, including nearly 4 million from Italy, 3.6 million from Austria-Hungary, and 3 million from Russia. Most of them settled in cities, and the city became even more of a source of horror and fascination for observers of the social and cultural scene. In 1860, there were nine cities with populations of 100,000 or higher; by 1910, that figure had grown to fifty.

By 1900, the nation's five largest cities – New York, Chicago, Philadelphia, St. Louis, and Boston – contained 10 percent of the population. New York City grew from 1.2 million in 1880 to 5.6 million in 1920. Chicago grew from 100,000 in 1860 to 2 million in 1910 to 2.7 million in 1920; and, as many black men and women left the South and headed North, its African-American population rose from 44,000 in 1910 to 234,000 in 1930. "Here," wrote the novelist Frank Norris about Chicago in *The Pit* (1903),

> of all her cities, throbbed the true life – the true power and spirit of America; gigantic, crude with the crudity of youth, disdaining rivalry; sane and healthy and vigorous; brutal in its ambition; arrogant in the new-found knowledge of its giant strength, prodigal of its wealth, infinite in its desires.

Many writers, cultural conservatives, and reformers were profoundly troubled by the high numbers of immigrants. In *How the Other Half Lives*, Jacob Riis reported of the Lower East Side in New York City: The native-born "are not here. In their place has come this queer conglomerate mass of heterogeneous elements, ever striving and working like whiskey and beer in one glass, and with the like result: final union and a prevailing taint of whiskey." In the city, said Riis, "One may find for the asking an Italian, a German, a French, African, Spanish, Bohemian, Russian, Scandinavian, Jewish, and Chinese colony . . . The one thing you shall vainly ask for in the chief city of America is a distinctly American community." To Josiah Strong, "the city is the nerve center of our civilization. It is also the storm center . . . The city has become a serious menace to our civilization." The editor and reformer Henry George observed: "This life of great cities is not the natural life of man. He must under such conditions deteriorate, physically, mentally, morally." Immigration was sharply cut back in the 1920s with the passage of the Immigration Restriction Act (1921; as part of this measure, Asian immigration was banned) and the National Origins Act (1924).

As American literature was being defined and debated, so on another level was the status of "American" itself. It was undergoing a canon-formation, with its inclusions and exclusions.

The population figures of the nation's largest cities suggest the ever-increasing market that existed for books, journals, and magazines. In this respect, conditions for American writers had improved because there were more, and more diverse kinds of, American readers, who were reading not only in English but also in a wide range of other languages. By 1900, 50 percent of African-Americans were literate, as were 85 percent of the immigrant population and 95 percent of the native-born white population. By 1930, more than 90 percent of the population was literate.

The rise in literacy was connected to the expansion of educational opportunities, which for American literature would lead to an expanding number of readers, courses, required and recommended texts. In 1860, there were only 100 public high schools; by 1914, there were 12,000. By 1910, the number of students attending public grammar and high schools had tripled from what it had been at the time of the Civil War, reaching a total of almost 18 million. Students spent more days in school, and funding had increased substantially – though unevenly (not in rural areas, not as much for African-Americans as for whites). In 1900, on average a child attended school for 100 days, an increase from 80 in 1880.

On the other hand, in 1900 only 50 percent of the white population, ages five to twenty, was enrolled in school, with the figure falling to 30 percent for nonwhites. The figures for subsequent decades were encouraging, but always showed much need for improvement. By 1930, 60 percent of high-school age children were in school – which meant that 40 percent were not; and one in seven college-age men and women was in college (a jump from one in thirty-three in 1900) – which meant that six out of seven were not. Between 1920 and 1930, college enrollment jumped from 600,000 to 1.1 million, though this still meant that only 5 percent of college-age Americans was enrolled.

Beginning in 1893 with the Committee of Ten, chaired by Harvard's president Charles Eliot, educators, scholars, and administrators reformed the curriculum for those attending college, deemphasizing classical languages and increasing the attention paid to science and foreign languages. In 1910, 5,000 students were enrolled at the University of Chicago, making it the largest in the country. The state universities of Minnesota and Michigan, and the private universities Harvard and Columbia, each enrolled about 4,000 students. But all of these were soon outpaced by the University of California, where the enrollment in 1920 reached 13,000.

For college-educated and non-college-educated readers alike, there were many newspapers, journals, and magazines, presenting articles on all sorts of subjects. In addition to the respected, well-established *Atlantic Monthly*, *Harper's*, *The Century*, and *Scribner's*, new general-audience periodicals appeared: *McCall's* (1870), *Popular Science* (1872), *Woman's Home Companion* (1873), *Ladies' Home Journal* (1883, reaching a circulation of 1 million by 1900), *Cosmopolitan* (1886), *Collier's* (1888), and *Vogue* (1892). By the early 1920s, ten magazines, including *Ladies' Home Journal* and the *Saturday Evening Post* (which had begun in 1821), had circulations of 2.5 million or more.

The author, editor, and classicist Harry Thurston Peck, who launched *The Bookman* in February 1895, included as one of his regular features a list of "Books in Demand" in the bookstores of a number of US cities; the heading was changed in 1903 to "The Six Best Sellers," the origin of the best-seller list. Such lists brought books to the attention of reader-consumers, making them feel under pressure to stay current by reading what others were reading. The Book of the Month Club, another means of promoting and selling books and turning them into best sellers, began in 1926.

Many popular American books showed little literary distinction, but they treated subjects and themes that readers found compelling. The rags-to-riches Horatio Alger books sold extremely well, as did the books by the industrialist and philanthropist Andrew Carnegie, such as *The Gospel of Wealth* (1900). The novelist Emily Post, at the request of her publisher, wrote *Etiquette* (1922), which promptly sold 500,000 copies. The Ohio-born Zane Grey published his first Western novel, *The Spirit of the Border*, in 1906; others soon followed, including *Riders of the Purple Sage* (1912), *Wanderer of the Wasteland* (1923), and *West of the Pecos* (1937), with sales totalling more than 13 million by the time of Grey's death in 1939. The New York clergyman Charles Monroe Sheldon's *In His Steps*, which told the story of a life lived as Jesus would have led it, sold more than 8 million copies in the decades after its publication in 1897.

Jesus was also enlisted in books, articles, and speeches in the cause of money-making and business, as in the Baptist preacher Russell H. Conwell's "Acres of Diamonds" lecture, which he delivered six thousand times; as Conwell stressed, "You ought to get rich, and it is your duty to get rich . . . To make money honestly is to preach the gospel" (1915). Bruce Barton, an advertising executive, achieved the greatest religious-literary success of all during the period, in *The Man Nobody Knows*, which portrayed Jesus as the first major businessman (1924); Jesus Christ "picked up twelve men from the bottom ranks of business and forged them into an organization that conquered the world."

Periodicals and books abounded for America's diverse religious and ethnic populations. By 1900, there were nearly 600,000 Jews in New York City, well over a million by 1910, and by 1930 the number exceeded 2 million. Jewish writers, editors, and publishers produced a thriving Yiddish literature that in its daily press reached hundreds of thousands of readers. In addition to the Yiddish newspapers in New York City, others were published in Chicago, Cleveland, and Philadelphia; these included everything from important national and local news to advice columns to serialized novels (for instance, by the Polish-born Yiddish writer Sholem Asch) to advertisements for Ivory Soap and Vaseline. (By 1940, New York City had nearly 250 foreign-language newspapers, magazines, and journals.) This is the context from which emerged the stories of assimilation told in Mary Antin's *The Promised Land* (1912) and Marcus Ravage's *An American in the Making* (1917), and also the fictional exploration of the necessity for and cost of assimilation and Americanization in Abraham Cahan's *The Rise of David Levinsky* (1917) and Anzia Yezierska's *Hungry Hearts and Other Stories* (1920) and *Bread Givers* (1925). "The very clothes I wore and the very food I ate had a fatal effect on my religious habits," Cahan's protagonist says; "If you attempt to bend your religion to the spirit of your surroundings, it breaks. It falls to pieces."

There were limits to how much Americans were reading or could read at the turn of the century. Many worked very long hours, with little time for reading, leisure, and recreation. In the 1890s, a steelworker on average worked sixty-six hours per six-day workweek, and a baker sixty-five. A housewife devoted six or more hours per day to the tasks of cleaning the home and preparing meals.

However, by 1920, housewives were spending less time on housework; and for working men, the hours of the workweek had declined to about fifty hours. Saturday work had either been reduced to a half-day or eliminated entirely, a reform pushed at first by Jewish workers in the clothing industry who wanted Saturday off from work in order to observe the Sabbath. In 1926 Henry Ford instituted the five-day week for workers in his automobile plant. To him, this was a good business move: working people needed leisure time to use the automobiles they bought with the wages that he paid them, so that they then would want to buy and enjoy another, better one.

Less time at work thus meant much more than an increase in time for reading, and the expansion of opportunities for leisure and entertainment complicated and challenged the efforts by American writers and critics to exercise the impact on the culture that they desired and give American literature a vivid presence. Americans had plenty of diversions, and more of them all the time. National mail-order houses, for example, were established by Montgomery, Ward and by Sears, Roebuck, enabling people across the country to enjoy access to the same goods. By 1900, each of these companies was selling well over 20,000 different items. There were also large department stores, such as that begun by John Wanamaker in Philadelphia (the first in the nation, 1875) and the Strauses in New York City. Americans could shop at home, or could travel to grandiose stores to shop for goods in person, as Theodore Dreiser described in *Sister Carrie* (1900).

And within cities, it was becoming much easier to get from place to place. The horse car was gradually replaced by the electric trolley car, which became the main means of public transportation in most cities by 1900. Major cities, in addition, built elevated railway lines and underground subway systems. In 1904, the subway in New York City made it possible to travel underground the entire length of Manhattan. Electricity illuminated the city at night, and the telephone enabled quick communication.

For their entertainment at home, Americans could listen to phonograph records (2 million phonographs were produced in 1919, and by 1921 sales of records reached 100 million), and outside the home, many began to attend classical concerts. A pressing concern among music critics, teachers, and patrons of the arts in fact was how to make it possible for more Americans to hear the music of the European masters. Carnegie Hall in New York City (1891), Symphony Hall in Boston (1900), and Orchestral Hall in Chicago (1904) were built so that audiences could attend performances of composi-tions by Beethoven, Brahms, and others. Musicians began to receive appoint-ments in classical music at colleges and universities to provide training in the European tradition for young American composers, and the teachers at conser-vatories – for example, the New England Conservatory in Boston – pursued similar aims to good effect. In 1915, there were 17 symphony orchestras in the United States; by 1939, there were 270. One of the great musical triumphs of the first decade of the century was the Austrian composer Gustav Mahler's performance in 1909 of Wagner's *Tristan und Isolde* at the Metropolitan Opera in New York City. Featuring Olive Fremstad in the role of Isolde – Fremstad was the model for the Wagner enthusiast Willa Cather's opera-singer protag-onist Thea Kronborg in *The Song of the Lark* (1915) – this production was an overpowering experience. Mahler said that he had "never known a performance of *Tristan* to equal this."

Classical music, compared to other forms of entertainment, was a minority taste. Vaudeville and minstrel shows were far more popular. In the 1880s the theater owner and vaudeville manager B. F. Keith began the practice of "continuous performances" running twelve hours at a time. In "The Vogue of Vaudeville" (*National Magazine*, November 1898), Keith said: "As to the sort of entertainment which seems to please most, light, frothy acts, with no particular plot, but abounding in songs, dances, bright dialogues and clean repartee, seem to appeal most." By 1915, Keith's company controlled 1,500 theaters, and there were as many as 20,000 acts competing for bookings. Vaudeville shows were outdrawing other forms of entertainment by ten to one.

There were spectator sports (especially boxing, baseball, and college foot-ball); and traveling shows, perhaps the most famous of which was Buffalo Bill's Wild West, begun by and starring William F. Cody (1846–1917), Indian fighter and scout, nicknamed "Buffalo Bill" for his buffalo-hunting exploits in the 1860s. In July 1869 he had been featured as the hero of a dime novel written by Ned Buntline, and this was the first of 1,700 books devoted to his adventures. Cody was soon the star of a hit play (hated by the critics) on Broadway in 1872, and after taking part in the Sioux Wars of 1875–76, he became an even more legendary figure. He capitalized on his renown in 1883 with the first of his Wild West shows, featuring expert marksmanship by "Little Sure Shot" Annie Oakley, reenactments of stagecoach robberies and Pony Express rides, and recreations of such historical events as Custer's Last

Stand. The Indian chief and warrior Sitting Bull was the star attraction in 1885.

Buffalo Bill's Wild West traveled the country every year until 1916 (Cody himself retired in 1912); in 1893, 6 million people saw the show. It was also popular in Europe, touring there in 1887, 1889, and 1891. In 1913, Cody started a film company, intending to produce films that would give accurate depictions (with as many of the original participants as possible) of episodes in his own life and in Western history. He made eight films (little of the footage from them survives), one of which took as its subject the massacre at Wounded Knee, South Dakota, where in 1890 the US Army killed 300 Sioux Indians. By the 1890s Indian tribes were scattered in reservations across the country, and were a minority population in territory undergoing settlement by whites; there were only 20,000 Sioux in South Dakota, in a total population of 400,000, in 1900; and 70,000 in Oklahoma, in a total population of 1 million, in 1907.

By the 1910s and 1920s, the film industry too was vigorously underway. The first movie with a plot had been *The Great Train Robbery* (1903); the first movie with sound was *The Jazz Singer* (1927); and the first movie in color was *Becky Sharp* (1935). By the mid-1920s, there were 20,000 movie theaters, and 50 million Americans each week were attending them. In New York City, as early as 1910, 300,000 persons (in a city with a total population of 4.8 million) attended the movies every day. In 1939, the major studios produced nearly 400 films, which brought in $673 million in revenue. Every week of this year, 50 million people attended at least one movie, seeing such films as *Gone with the Wind*, *The Wizard of Oz*, *Goodbye, Mr. Chips*, *Mr. Smith Goes to Washington*, *Stagecoach*, *Wuthering Heights*, *The Hunchback of Notre Dame*, *Ninotchka*, *Rules of the Game*, *The Roaring Twenties*, *Gunga Din*, and *Pinocchio*. By the mid-1940s, weekly attendance at movies was 90 million.

There was radio as well. The first professional broadcast occurred on November 2, 1920, when station KDKA in Pittsburgh presented the results of the 1920 presidential election. The first World Series game was broadcast from the Polo Grounds in New York City, in October 1922; the first broadcast of a political convention was that of the Democrats in New York City in July 1924; and the first radio broadcast of a presidential speech, December 1924, by President Coolidge. In September 1927, 50 million people listened to the heavyweight championship fight between Jack Dempsey and Gene Tunney, held in Chicago before a crowd of 104,000 people. This was also the year of the first national broadcast of the World Series, as Babe Ruth's New York Yankees swept the Pittsburgh Pirates in four straight games.

In 1930–31, the Columbia Broadcasting System began live Sunday broadcasts of performances by the New York Philharmonic Orchestra, conducted by

Arturo Toscanini. Listeners could also enjoy the jazz musicians Duke Ellington and Benny Goodman. By the late 1920s, there were 500 radio stations, and 6 million radios. By 1935, 70 percent of homes in the US had radios; according to surveys, it was America's favorite pastime, well ahead of, for example, "reading." By 1940, nearly every family owned a radio.

Television began in April 1939, with NBC's broadcast of President Roosevelt opening the New York World's Fair. The first televised sporting event also took place in 1939, as 400 TV sets tuned in to a baseball game between Columbia and Princeton at Baker Field in upper Manhattan. Only 0.4 percent of the population owned TV sets in 1948; by the end of the decade, the percentage was only a point or two higher. But by the late 1950s, the figure had soared to nearly 90 percent. By the 1990s, the average American was spending one-quarter of his or her life watching TV.

As the twentieth century approached, many writers, intellectuals, and cultural critics were already commenting on the astounding social, technological, and cultural transformations that had occurred in the United States and that would accelerate during the first decades of the new century. The historian Henry Adams observed: "My country in 1900 is something totally different from my own country in 1860. I am wholly a stranger in it. Neither I, nor anyone else, understands it." The novelist Jack London wrote: "Never in the history of the world was society in so terrific flux as it is right now . . . The swift changes in our industrial system are causing equally swift changes in our religious, political, and social structures. An unseen and fearful evolution is taking place in the fiber and structure of society. One can only dimly feel these things, but they are in the air, now, today." An English observer, James Bryce, author of *The American Commonwealth* (1888), stated in an essay in 1905:

That which most strikes the visitor to America today is its prodigious material development. Industrial growth, swift thirty or forty years ago, advances more swiftly now . . . With this extraordinary material development it is natural that in the United States, business, that is to say, industry, commerce, and finance, should have more and more come to overshadow and dwarf all other interests, all other occupations . . . Business is king.

At the same time, as America's newness as an industrial and commercial power was noted, the oldness, the datedness, of its literary ideas and cultural practices was targeted by progressive and liberal writers and intellectuals for change. The radical journalist John Reed, in a manifesto for *The Masses* (1912), announced: "The broad purpose of *The Masses* is a social one; to everlastingly attack old systems, old morals, old prejudices – the whole weight of outworn thought that dead men have settled upon us." The journalist and biographer Hutchins Hapgood, in the New York *Globe*, January 27, 1913, made a related point: "There seems a vague but real relationship between all the real workers of our day. Whether in literature, plastic art, the labor movement . . . we find an instinct to blow up the old forms and traditions, to dynamite the baked and hardened earth so that fresh flowers can grow." "Those who are young to-day," wrote Walter Lippmann, in *Drift and Mastery* (1914), "are born into a world in which the foundations of the older order survive only as habits or by default." "There isn't a human relation," he argued, "whether of parent and child, husband and wife, worker and employer, that doesn't move in a strange situation. There are no precedents to guide us, no wisdom that wasn't made for a simpler age."

This claim was voiced repeatedly. The economist, author, and writer for *The New Republic*, Walter E. Weyl, in *The New Democracy* (1912), maintained:

Every day new projects are launched for political, industrial, and social amelioration, and below the level of the present lies the greater project of the future. Reform is piecemeal and yet rapid. It is carried along divergent lines by people holding separate interests, and yet it moves toward a common end. It combines into a general movement toward a new democracy.

The Baptist clergyman and educator Walter Rauschenbusch, in *Christian-izing the Social Order* (1913), set the agenda for the coming years:

Our business is to make over an antiquated and immoral social system; to get rid of laws, customs, maxims, and philosophies inherited from an evil and despotic past; to create just and brotherly relations between great groups and classes of society; and thus to lay a social foundation on which modern men individually can live and work in a fashion that will not outrage all the better elements in them. Our inherited Christian faith dealt with individuals; our present task deals with society.

Looking back from the vantage-point of the mid-1930s, the critic and urban historian Lewis Mumford, in "The Metropolitan Milieu," included in a volume devoted to the photographer Alfred Stieglitz (1934), outlined the challenges that writers and artists faced at the turn of the century, when old ideas about art and culture reigned:

The problem for the creative mind in the 'nineties, whether he was a young writer like Stephen Crane or a young man with a passion for photography like Alfred Stieglitz, was to face this New York of boundless misdirected energy and to capture a portion of that wasteful flow for his own purposes, using its force without accepting its habitual channels and its habitual destinations. But there was still another problem: and that was to conquer, with equal resolution, the gentility, the tepid over refinement, the academic inertness and lack of passionate faith, masquerading as sound judgment, which were characteristic of the stale fugitive culture of the bourgeoisie. The genteel standards that prevailed were worse than no standards at all: dead objects, dead techniques, dead forms of worship, cast a morbid shadow on every enterprise of the mind, making mind itself a sham, causing vitality to seem somehow shameful.

In an interview published in *Arts and Decoration*, March 1913, the painter William Glackens also focused on the impact of inhibiting social conventions on artistic work: "Our own art is arid and bloodless. It is like nothing so much as dry bones. It shows that we are afraid to be impulsive, afraid to forget restraint, afraid above everything to appear ridiculous."

But for many, such as the poet E. A. Robinson (1869–1935), the obstacles to art and literature posed by a powerful society, highly developed in business and technology yet underdeveloped culturally, amounted to an exciting opportunity:

I am just beginning to fully realize that America is the hopper through which the whole civilization of the world is to be ground – consciously or otherwise. I am not much of an American, either – in a popular way but I am glad to feel an inkling as to what the western continent was made for.

The dynamism of American society seemed at first a terrible barrier to literature and art, and yet it presented to aspiring writers and artists something huge and energizing that they were inspired to take on, describe, work with, celebrate, denounce, and overcome.

The Cubist painter Max Weber, for example, born in Russia in 1881, wrote in late 1912 while living in New York: "This is a wonderful age we are living in now. Everyone has more creative liberty. The creative mind finds new ways and stops at no law laid down by, or piled upon us by lesser or non-creative minds... It is great to live now! It is harder, but what of that? The hunger we have now! The embrace!" Also in 1912, the painter John Butler Yeats exclaimed: "The fiddles are tuning as it were all over America." To Marcel Duchamp, in the *New York Tribune* (September 12, 1915), the problem if anything was that Americans themselves were slow in perceiving that the future was with them, not with the English and Europeans: "If only America would realize that the art of Europe is finished – dead – and that America is the country of the art of the future." During the first decades of the century, recalled the critic Malcolm Cowley (1898–1989): "Everywhere new institutions were being founded – magazines, clubs, little theaters, art or free-love or single-tax colonies, experimental schools, picture galleries . . . Everywhere was a sense of comradeship and immense possibilities for change."

The nationalism sparked by America's entry in April 1917 into World War I increased America's economic and industrial progress and kindled interest in the renewal of American culture. Though the United States was involved in the war for a relatively short time, by its end in November 1918 more than 4.7 million men and women had been mobilized, and well over 2 million had crossed the Atlantic Ocean to France. The powerful impact of English and European cultures reinforced the exploration of the "usable past" in mighty, massive, present-driven America that Van Wyck Brooks and other writers, critics, artists, and intellectuals were determined to discover.

In her *Tendencies of Modern American Poetry* (1917), the poet-critic Amy Lowell (1874–1925) commented on the impact of the war on American literature: the new "native school" in verse represented the "welding together of the whole country which the war has brought about, the mobilizing of our whole population into a single, strenuous endeavor." But really this tendency or movement was already launched. Carl Sandburg had published *Chicago Poems* (1916); Vachel Lindsay had published *The Tramp's Excuse and Other Poems* (1909), *Rhymes to be Traded for Bread* (1912), *General William Booth Enters into Heaven and Other Poems* (1913), and *The Congo and Other Poems* (1913); and three books by Robert Frost had appeared: *A Boy's Will* (1913), *North of Boston* (1914), and *Mountain Interval* (1916). American literature as a body of work and as a field of study thus was taking shape as part of a wide range of literary, artistic, and cultural activity, all in the midst of the expansion of the United States as an industrial, imperialist, and technologically innovative power and, in 1917, a nation involved in a world war. Literary critics and scholars shared in a process of cultural critique, discovery, and assertion that was occurring everywhere in the creative arts and in the contexts for them in the 1910s and 1920s.

Van Wyck Brooks continued to display the skeptical attitude toward American writers that had marked George Woodberry's judgment about the "fragmentariness" of American literature and would later show itself in Bliss Perry's remarks on its lack of "stylistic consciousness." Brooks, the son of a stockbroker, had grown up in Plainfield, New Jersey, attended public schools, traveled for a year in England and Europe with his mother and brother, and then did his undergraduate work at Harvard, where he wrote poetry and edited

The Harvard Advocate. He wrote *The Wine of the Puritans* during a two-year stay in England, having moved there because he could not find a job as a writer in the United States. He returned to New York, made some money from writing assignments, and then went west to Stanford University in California, where he taught literature and composition courses from 1911 to 1913.

Soon thereafter, Brooks, his wife, and their two children returned to England and France, where he worked on and completed three books that he published when he came back yet again to the United States at the start of World War I: biographies of the English scholar, poet, and travel writer John Addington Symonds (1914) and the writer-reformer H. G. Wells (1915), and *America's Coming-of-Age* (1915).

In his polemical books and essays of the 1910s and 1920s, and in studies of Mark Twain (1920) and Henry James (1925), Brooks showed little feeling for the literary complexity of such writers as Hawthorne or Melville, and he tended toward simplistic categories, as when he identified Emerson in 1921 as "the incarnation of optimism." But, a passionate writer, he gave American intellectuals a mission, which was "to quicken and exhilarate the life of one's own people." He was determined to reinspect the American literary past and through it to renew contemporary culture and prompt a finer kind of literary production.

Brooks's work sometimes drifted too close to the thumping rhetoric of Theodore Roosevelt's "new nationalism" and Woodrow Wilson's "new freedom." Yet the best literary voices of the period were not only progressive but also critical, and spurned the muscular pro-Americanism that Roosevelt touted and the program for extending American might worldwide that Wilson preached. Brooks's *America's Coming-of-Age* (1915) and H. L. Mencken's marvelous essays "Theodore Dreiser" (1917) and "The National Letters" (1920), as well as *The American Language* (1919), were potent forays into the reexamination of America's past. They spurred national debate about the condition of American culture, the literary heritage, and the power that an art liberated from religious and social constraints might exercise. The New Jersey-born novelist and critic Waldo Frank (1889–1967) declared in *Our America* (1919): "We go forth all to seek America. And in the seeking we create her. In the quality of our search shall be the nature of the America that we created."

From the late nineteenth century and driving forward during the 1900s, 1910s, and beyond, Americans made extraordinary, and revolutionary, contributions to all of the arts. In music, there were, among others, Charles Ives, Aaron Copland, Roger Sessions, Irving Berlin, Jerome Kern, Cole Porter, Louis Armstrong, and Duke Ellington; in architecture, Louis Sullivan and Frank Lloyd Wright; in photography, Alfred Stieglitz, Edward Steichen, Paul Strand,

Lewis Hine, Edward Weston, Dorothea Lange, Margaret Bourke-White, and Walker Evans; in painting, John Marin, Arthur Dove, Marsden Hartley, and Georgia O'Keeffe.

The writings by these artists bear witness to the high ideals – and the sheer excitement – with which they pursued their work. "The true function of the architect," Louis Sullivan (1856–1924) said, "is to initiate such buildings as shall correspond to the real needs of the people . . . to vitalize building materials, to animate them with a subjective significance and value, to make them a visible part of the social fabric, to infuse into them the true life of the people, to impart to them the best that is in the people." As Frank Lloyd Wright (1869–1959) explained: "Every great architect is – necessarily – a great poet. He must be a great original interpreter of his time, his day, his age."

The hostility that many of these men and women encountered, as their work surprised or stunned or horrified the public, rarely made them change what they were doing: such opposition validated the newness of the work, its daring, its originality. Consider Aaron Copland's Concerto for Piano and Orchestra, which premiered in Boston on January 28, 1927. Copland's symphonic exploration and development of blues and jazz in this piece were considered disgraceful. The reporter for the *Boston Globe* wrote:

The audience forgot its manners, exchanged scathing verbal comments, and giggled nervously while the piece was being played, creating so great a bustle that at times it was difficult to hear the music clearly . . . At the close of the piece there were a few scattered hisses, a few scattered handclaps, and a general appearance of stupefaction.

The reviewer in the *Boston Post* agreed: "If there exists anywhere in the world of music a stranger concatenation of meaninglessly ugly sounds and distorted rhythms, Boston has been spared it." According to the reviewer in the *Boston Herald*: "In this Concerto we found little to attract, little to admire, much to repel." These critics may have been successful in limiting the appeal of Copland's Concerto; it did not achieve much renown until Leonard Bernstein and the New York City Symphony performed it in 1946. But the critics had no effect on Copland's desire to draw upon jazz, elements of which can be heard in *Quiet City*, *Rodeo*, and *Music for a Great City*, nor did it diminish his interest in popular music – spirituals, folk songs, and cowboy songs.

Possibly the best example of this passionate American newness, as many writers noted at the time, was the work of the photographer Alfred Stieglitz (1864–1946) and his exhibitions of avant-garde art at his 291 Gallery in New York City. In 1903, Stieglitz published the first issue of the journal *Camera Work*, which for the next decade and a half included essays on criticism, art, and literature as well as photographs. He also arranged exhibitions of photography throughout the United States and Europe, and, in November 1905, with Edward Steichen's assistance, he opened the "Little Galleries of the Photo-Secession" – dedicated to the belief that photography was an art form – on the top floor of 291 Fifth Avenue in Manhattan. Stieglitz was the first in the country to exhibit Matisse (1908 and 1912), Cézanne (1911), Picasso (1911), and Brancusi (1914). He also was a supporter of Arthur Dove, Marsden Hartley, John Marin, Georgia O'Keeffe, and other artists living in the United States. As the literary and cultural critic Paul Rosenfeld affirmed, in *Port of New York* (1924): "If ever an institution in America came to bring the challenge of the truth of life to the land of the free, and to show the face of expressivity to a trading society living by middle-class conventions, it was the little gallery '291.' "

For the visual arts, and for the national and international cause of newness in the arts in general, the most significant cultural event of the period was the International Exhibition of Modern Art, numbering 1,300 works, which opened on February 17, 1913, at the 69th Regiment Armory, Lexington Avenue and 26th Street, New York City. The European sections of the show reached back to Goya, Ingres, and Delacroix, and moved forward to Cézanne, Gauguin, Van Gogh, and Matisse. A few of the later European artists – Duchamp and Brancusi in particular – were mocked by conservative critics, but their work forcefully reoriented and challenged artists in America by exposing them to post-impressionism and European modernism. As the theater designer Lee Simonson said of Duchamp's "Nude Descending a Staircase": "Before it, a painting truly modern was a rumor." Not only did the Armory Show display the work of older, more established American painters such as Childe Hassam, J. Alden Weir, and Albert Pinkham Ryder, but it also included younger, more progressive artists – among them, Arthur B. Carles, Stuart Davis, Hartley, Marin, Morgan Russell, and Lyonel Feininger.

Modern art had previously been difficult, if not impossible, for American artists and writers to see and learn from, unless they traveled to Paris, where Gertrude and Leo Stein showed works by Cézanne, Matisse, and Picasso. (It was at the Steins' apartment at 27 rue de Fleurus where the painters Hartley, Dove, Charles Demuth, Alfred Maurer, Max Weber, and others first were exposed to modern art.) The Armory Show, after its New York run, moved to the Art Institute of Chicago (March 24 – April 16) and Copley Hall, Boston (April 28 – May 19). Seventy thousand people attended the exhibition in New York, and many more in Chicago and Boston. The Mexican artist and writer (and associate of Stieglitz) Marius de Zayas described the Armory Show as "an avalanche of modern paintings and sculpture. It was overwhelming, colossal, stupendous, and best of all it was a tremendous success in all respects. It brought to New York all that could be known of modern art in

Europe, and it also brought New York to the minds of modern artists." The painter Guy Pène du Bois said that the exhibition was "a fact as great as the declaration of our political independence"; and Charles Sheeler, commenting on a painting by Matisse in the exhibition, observed: "We had never thought a picture could look like that – but there it was to prove it. Pictures like this offered evidence that a picture could be as arbitrarily conceived as an artist wished."

The invention of American literature as a serious, significant field of study took place within the context of American self-criticism and innovation in all of the arts. Surveying the field as it existed, literary scholars began by describing a bad situation: American literature had little status, and received only marginal respect. But this situation was the opposite of crippling or limiting to them: it gave scholars, critics, and creative writers a sense of important, thrilling work to be done, and when they met with opposition, this confirmed for them that they were moving in the right direction.

Norman Foerster (1887–1972), who taught at the universities of North Carolina and Iowa, made strong arguments for American literature in *The Reinterpretation of American Literature* and *American Criticism*, both of which were published in 1928. In the Introduction to the first book, containing nine essays by notable critics and historians as well as extensive bibliographies, Foerster said that "notwithstanding a few honorable names, American scholarship and education in the field of the national letters have till recently merited shame rather than pride." Foerster's contributors pushed the discussion of American literature dramatically forward and expanded the field. For the Pennsylvania State University professor (and the first in the nation to hold a chair in American literature) Fred Lewis Pattee (1863–1950), for example, in his "Call for a Literary Historian," American literature included popular fiction and magazines as well as poems and serious novels. The literary historian Harry Hayden Clark noted the neglect of *Moby-Dick* in prior decades and contended that Melville's novel is "a spiritual epic, of profound symbolism all compact." *The Reinterpretation of American Literature* had a major effect on scholars, critics, and teachers, including the young F. O. Matthiessen, who began a review of it by announcing that "it is time for the history of American literature to be rewritten."

The work of the critic and editor Stuart Sherman (1881–1926) has not aged well, but he, too, was influential in his commentaries on American literature during the 1910s and 1920s, as an essayist on Emerson, Hawthorne, James, and Twain, and as an editor of and contributor to the multi-volume *Cambridge History of American Literature* (1917–21).

The *Cambridge History* signaled the rise of American literature as an organized field, and some of the work in it is rewarding even now (e.g., Parrington's chapter on "The Puritan Divines, 1620–1720," and Paul Elmer More's flawed but provocative critiques of Edwards and Emerson). But perhaps the foremost contribution of the *History* was the set of comprehensive bibliographies that became the foundation for later, more astute, critical work. The volumes themselves were thin in ideas and insights, and – the product of very different degrees of knowledge and talent – suffered from the absence of a controlling sense of critical judgment.

John Macy, the author of *The Spirit of American Literature*, was a socialist as well as a literary critic and editor; his *Socialism in America* appeared in 1916. This points to the influence of American radicalism on the study of American literature during the first half of the century. Brooks, also a socialist, and, later, Granville Hicks (1901–82), V. F. Calverton (1900–40), and Bernard Smith (1909–), all of whom wrote Marxist histories of American literature and criticism in the 1930s, insisted on a literature intimately related to the contemporary scene. Their essays and books were characterized then (and are often dismissed now) as distortions of aesthetic truth, belonging more to the annals of the class struggle than to the history of literature. But these critics brought urgency to their criticism that made the fate of American literature momentous. Even their mistakes generated spirited responses and hence expanded debate about what American literature was and why it counted.

Socialist, Marxist, and Communist Party ideas about proletarian art did lead to skewed evaluations of texts. But membership in the Party and socialist/Marxist notions about the class struggle inspired many writers, particularly African-Americans, as the early work of Richard Wright and Ralph Ellison testifies and as Langston Hughes's career as poet, essayist, and storyteller reveals.

Especially by the time that the Popular Front period dawned in the mid-1930s, when Marxist, left, and liberal factions stood against fascism in common cause, the act of writing about (and contributing to) American literature had become a noble form of labor. As Malcolm Cowley stated in a 1935 speech, the revolutionary movement of the 1930s opened up "a whole new range of subject matter" for writers, offering them an enthusiastic audience and furnishing them with new perspectives that linked their work to that produced by writers in other lands who also were contending against the old order and the advance of fascism.

The radical left-wing movements stimulated new kinds of creative writing and provoked writers, journalists, and critics to rediscover and redescribe the American literary past. Calverton's *The Liberation of American Literature* appeared in 1932, and was shortly followed by Hicks's *The Great Tradition* (1933; 1935) and Smith's *Forces of American Criticism: A Study in the History of*

American Literary Thought (1939). For Joseph Freeman (1897–1965), a novelist and Marxist critic, "the most promising" development in American literature in the 1930s was a "taking over" of "the heritage of progressive and revolutionary thought." That heritage, as Hicks and others argued, honored an American literature that was critical, oppositional, resistant – a literature that traced the growth of industrial capitalism and exposed its ravaging of democracy and freedom, a literature that grew from injunctions like Whitman's in his 1855 preface to *Leaves of Grass*: "reexamine all you have been told at school or church or in any book, dismiss whatever insults your own soul."

American literature was taken to speak on behalf of the lowly, the unrepresented, the victimized; as Whitman said in "Song of Myself," he championed "the rights of them the others are down upon." American writing could become a source of enlightenment and inspiration for the masses, through which the ranks of the common people could name and attack the powers that exploited them.

Floyd Dell (1887–1969), an editor of the radical magazines *The Masses* and *The Liberator*, was a key contributor to this movement and supported its recovery of the critical tradition in American literature. In *Intellectual Vagabondage: An Apology for the Intelligentsia* (1926), Dell complained bitterly about the absence of dissenting voices from the roster of American authors most frequently taught and praised:

> In the literature of our own country, there was a mass of libertarian eloquence – the speeches of Wendell Phillips, the fiery abolitionist poems of Whittier, the dithyrambs of Walt Whitman in celebration of the individual, the burning advice of Emerson to be uncompromising, the invective of Thoreau upon the spirit of social conformity – a veritable arsenal of swordlike thoughts with which to fit youth for its first struggles with whatever tyrannies of traditional society it might meet . . . But the authorities did not want us to have weapons against social tyrannies, and none of these – literally, none – had been given to us in the schools.

For Dell, the main figures in his own intellectual growth were the British socialists H. G. Wells and Bernard Shaw, and he looked to them with gratitude because they provided the critique of conformity and the spirit of resistance missing from American literature as he had encountered it in school. He laid out an itinerary that Calverton, Hicks, and Smith followed; they resurrected the oppositional, dissenting texts of America's writers and equipped young people with strong tools, forged on native grounds, that they could deploy in their struggle against social custom and convention.

Hicks became a member of a John Reed Club in 1933 (these clubs, founded in New York in November 1929, and named after the radical journalist, were organized for literary education and agitation), the literary editor of *The New Masses* in 1934, and a member of the Communist Party in 1935. He made mistakes in his book-length Marxist study of the American "great tradition," misinterpreting and undervaluing Henry James, Willa Cather, and T. S. Eliot. But he tied American writing in the modern period to the figures of the nineteenth century and emphasized the presence in American literature of a strong "tradition" that readers needed to engage. Hicks portrayed Emerson, Thoreau, and Whitman as rebels who paved the way for Dreiser, Anderson, Lewis, Dos Passos, and their realist and naturalist comrades.

In the studies that Hicks and other radicals produced in the 1930s, American literature mattered enormously because it was for them, as Hicks suggested, both "critical" and "hopeful." "The great artist," the novelist Hamlin Garland had said in *Crumbling Idols* (1894), "never conforms," and it was this Emersonian note of resolute non-conformity in American writing to which radical critics hearkened and which gave them faith in the possibility of re-ordering American society and culture.

American literature also gained strength and legitimacy, and acquired greater seriousness as a subject, as contemporary American poets, short-story writers, and novelists did work that criticized the dominant culture and gave promise of a new one. This point appeared often in H. L. Mencken's writings about Dreiser and Sherwood Anderson. As he explained in 1921, "the whole history of the war period is a history of the subsidence of the van Dykes and the rise of the Cabells, Dreisers, Masterses, Andersons, and Sinclair Lewises – in brief, of the men who continued to question the national culture, despite the colossal effort to endow it with a mystical sort of perfection."

To Mencken (1880–1956), the books by these writers "were really a proof of the rise of nationalism – perhaps the first dawn of a genuine sense of nationality." Mencken's favorites were Dos Passos, O'Neill, Anderson, Lewis, Cabell, and Dreiser, all of whom he said were "wholly American" authors involved in a "first-hand examination of the national scene." Not all agreed with this list, but Mencken's claims shook up staid evaluations of America's literature and made responsiveness to American writers an index to a critical relationship to the culture as a whole.

American writing itself thus helped to establish American literature as a subject, tradition, and legitimate field. Take, for example, the single year 1925, when the following appeared:

Alain Locke (ed.), *The New Negro*
Theodore Dreiser, *An American Tragedy*
Ellen Glasgow, *Barren Ground*
Edith Wharton, *The Mother's Recompense*
Sherwood Anderson, *Dark Laughter*

F. Scott Fitzgerald, *The Great Gatsby*
Ernest Hemingway, *In Our Time*
John Dos Passos, *Manhattan Transfer*
Sinclair Lewis, *Arrowsmith*
William Carlos Williams, *In the American Grain*
T. S. Eliot, *Poems, 1909–25*
Robinson Jeffers, *Roan Stallion*
H. D., *Collected Poems*
Countee Cullen, *Color*
E. A. Robinson, *Dionysus in Doubt*
DuBose Heyward, *Porgy*
Willa Cather, *The Professor's House*
Eugene O'Neill, *Desire Under the Elms*
Anna Yezierska, *Bread Givers*
Gertrude Stein, *The Making of Americans*
Van Wyck Brooks, *The Pilgrimage of Henry James*
The New Yorker begins publication

The 1920s was the decade of the influential literary review *The Dial* (1920–29: a revival of the nineteenth-century journal of the same name), one of the many magazines and literary reviews that influenced the coming of age of American literature and criticism. These included *Poetry* (founded in 1912), *The Little Review* (1914–29, moving from New York to Paris in 1921), *The Seven Arts* (1916–17), *Others* (which ran from 1915 to 1919 and was intended as an "experimental" alternative to *Poetry*), and *Contact* (1920–23). "It is our faith and the faith of many," the first editorial in *The Seven Arts* stated, "that we are living in the first days of a renascent period . . . a time which means for America the coming of that national self-consciousness which is the beginning of greatness."

Still other publications were edited by, or actively involved, American expatriates in Paris, Rome, and London. Eliot, living in London, was the founding editor of *The Criterion* in 1922 and he held this post until 1939; and William Carlos Williams, Hart Crane, Malcolm Cowley, Allen Tate, Hemingway, and Stein contributed to the Paris-based *transition* (1927–38). Other notable little magazines abroad that were important for American readers and writers included *Broom* (1921–24), *Secession* (1922–24), and Pound's vehicle, *The Exile* (1927–28). There were many more such periodicals, some of them linked to radical or conservative political causes, and often they enjoyed only a very brief or irregular life.

The little magazines and literary reviews provided outlets for American writers of all kinds; and a number of them published Americans in the midst

of writers from other nations – which showed that the United States had
produced writers who were as noteworthy for modern times as those working
within richer literary and cultural traditions. *The Dial* published work by
Eliot, Sherwood Anderson, Edwin Arlington Robinson, E. E. Cummings, and
Gertrude Stein alongside such English and European masters as Thomas Mann,
Anatole France, Jules Romains, and William Butler Yeats.

In addition, these periodicals published high-quality literary criticism. *The
Dial* offered critical essays and reviews by Eliot, Pound, Cowley, Van Wyck
Brooks, Kenneth Burke, Conrad Aiken, and Paul Rosenfeld. Its concern for
intelligent standards of critical judgment and discrimination looked forward
to such important American literary reviews and quarterlies as *Hound and Horn*
(1927–34), *The Symposium* (1930–33), *The Southern Review* (1935–42; 1965–),
and *The Kenyon Review* (1939–).

Another notable publication begun in the 1920s was *The American Caravan*,
a "yearbook of American literature" that Rosenfeld, the poet-critic and literary historian Alfred Kreymborg (1883–1966), and Lewis Mumford started in
1927 and that continued until 1936. It was designed to serve "the interests
of a growing American literature" and was meant as a "medium able to accommodate a progressively broader expression of American life." This was a
period, said Sherwood Anderson in *A Story Teller's Story* (1924), when American writers and artists sought to "belong" to "an America alive, an America
that was no longer a despised foster child of Europe, with unpleasant questions
always being asked about its parentage." "The dominant note of the twenties,"
Mumford concluded in his autobiography (1982), was the "recognition of our
national identity and personal idiosyncrasy in the arts."

For Mumford in *The Golden Day* (1926), Emerson, Whitman, Melville, and
Thoreau were writers who "saw life whole, and sought a whole life." Born in
Flushing, New York, Mumford was the illegitimate son of a German Protestant
woman and a Jewish businessman, whose identity Mumford finally discovered
in 1942. His major interests as a teenager were science and technology. Like
other young men of his generation who lived in New York City, Mumford also
spent much time in libraries and museums. He continued his education at City
College, Columbia University, New York University, and the New School for
Social Research, though he did not complete enough courses to receive his
bachelor's degree.

Mumford wrote some journalism for hire, but in 1919 became a member of
the staff of *The Dial*, and, the following year, became the editor in London of the
Sociological Review, a position offered to him by the Scottish scientist and urban
planner Patrick Geddes. But Mumford soon returned to the United States,
and worked as a writer on a wide range of subjects throughout the 1920s and
1930s.

Though he sometimes referred to himself during the Red Decade of the 1930s as a communist (with a small "c"), Mumford was an American anti-capitalist critical of Marxism and the Communist Party; his true affinities were with Emerson and John Dewey, and with John Ruskin and William Morris, as his discussion of mechanical work and handicrafts ("the craftsman literally possesses his work, in the sense that the Bible says a body is possessed by a familiar spirit") in *Sticks and Stones* (1924) suggests.

Like Emerson, and Louis Sullivan and Frank Lloyd Wright, Mumford frequently used "organic" terms and metaphors to convey his belief in the need for a harmonious relationship between art and nature, country and city, individual and social group or unit. Architects must begin, Mumford affirmed in *Sticks and Stones*, "not with the building itself, but with the whole complex out of which architect, builder, and patron spring, and into which the finished building, whether it be a cottage or a skyscraper, is set. Once the conditions are ripe for a good architecture, the plan will flower by itself."

In his first book, *The Story of Utopias* (1922), Mumford attacked the utopian proposals of writers from Plato to the present as stultifying and unduly regimented. But as such later books as *Technics and Civilization* (1934) and *The Culture of Cities* (1938) show, and other books of the 1950s and 1960s about cities and regional planning attest, Mumford was not opposed to central planning or technological innovation. For him, the important values were harmony, balance, and openness. He recognized that new technologies – in building materials, for example – could help men and women to express and develop such values. "The best modern work," he wrote in *Sticks and Stones*, "does not merely respect the machine: it respects the people who use it."

Mumford was a major scholar-critic of architecture, both in his early books *Sticks and Stones* and *The Brown Decades* (1931) and in the "Sky Line" column he wrote for *The New Yorker* from 1931 to 1963. In this work Mumford made the case both for an American cultural awakening in the arts and for the recovery of the writers and artists of the nineteenth century, from Emerson and Thoreau, to Eakins and Ryder. As Mumford remarked in *The Brown Decades*: "Every generation revolts against its fathers and makes friends with its grandfathers."

In *The Golden Day*, Mumford acknowledged: "We cannot return to the America of the Golden Day, nor keep it fixed in the postures it once naturally assumed; and we should be far from the spirit of Emerson or Whitman if we attempted to do this." "But the principal writers of that time," he continued, "are essential links between our own lives and that earlier, that basic, America."

In their work we can see in pristine state the essential characteristics that still lie under the surface: and from their example, we can more readily find our own foundations, and make our own particular point of departure. In their imaginations, a new world began to form out of the distracting chaos: wealth was in its place, and science was in its place, and the deeper life of man began again to emerge, no longer stunted or frustrated by the instrumentalities it had conceived and set to work. For us who share their vision, a revival of the moribund, or a relapse into the pragmatic acquiescence is equally impossible; and we begin again to dream Thoreau's dream – of what it means to live a whole human life.

Mumford used impassioned, exorbitant language, as did Matthiessen, and the rise of the New Criticism during the late 1920s and 1930s supported their efforts to exalt American literature. Just a year before Matthiessen's *American Renaissance* was published, the New Critic Allen Tate (1899–1979) stressed that "literature is the complete knowledge of man's experience." Tate was primarily concerned with the restoration of "dissociated sensibility" and with the finely integrated mind that to him Henry James and T. S. Eliot represented. But his claim implied for Americanists that the most complete knowledge of this nation's experience was in the literature produced by American writers. Tate and others assigned great authority to texts and immense responsibility to the persons who studied and articulated literary meaning. For the New Critical generation, reading and criticizing literature was the most important work in the world.

Another important development in the making of American literature was the selection of Sinclair Lewis, in 1930, as the first American author to win the Nobel Prize. "When the Swedish academy gave its medal and its forty thousand dollars to a man from Minnesota," reflected Malcolm Cowley in 1937, "it was saying in effect that American literature had ceased to be a minor province of British literature and must now be recognized in its own right." In his acceptance speech, Lewis praised Dreiser, O'Neill, Cather, Mencken, Anderson, and Hemingway, and made clear that his own work belonged within the broader context of American literary achievement. Within two decades from the time of Lewis's award, American literature enjoyed international renown, honored in France, for example, by such formidable figures as Sartre, Gide, and Malraux. "Pour les jeunes en France," said Sartre to Cowley in 1945, "Faulkner c'est un dieu." The painter Willem de Kooning recalled watching Fernand Léger working on a mural a decade earlier: "We were so reverent, then all of a sudden he sticks a brush into some paint – just like we did – he makes a couple of strokes on the canvas that looked kind of dumb – like we did – and suddenly all that old mystery vanished. We thought, well, we can do that too, so maybe American artists aren't so bad after all."

Neither Pound nor Eliot, two of the major makers of modernism and sources for the New Criticism, found much value in an exclusively "American" literary tradition, or in the realism of Lewis, Dreiser, and Cather. Pound loathed

American provinciality and declared that "courses in 'American literature'" that slighted "foreign discoveries" made as much sense as "courses in 'American chemistry.'" But Pound's and Eliot's stress on "tradition" in their critical essays (e.g., on Henry James), impelled critics to investigate the nature of "tradition" in American art and culture. The prose and poetry of experimental modernist American writers such as Hart Crane (1899–1932) and William Carlos Williams (1883–1963) also played a role in this literary and cultural awakening. There were Crane's interactions with Melville and Whitman in *White Buildings* (1926), his "mythical synthesis of America" in *The Bridge* (1930), and Williams's pieces on Columbus, Cotton Mather, George Washington, and Poe in *In the American Grain* (1925).

The foremost text in this modernist recasting of American literary history, however, was the British novelist and critic D. H. Lawrence's *Studies in Classic American Literature* (1923). With exotic eloquence, Lawrence (1885–1930) emphasized the "double meaning," "symbolism," and "subterfuge" of American writing at its most supreme and argued that Americans had to rechart the literary landscape they thought they already knew. Lawrence made extraordinary judgments that named "the old people" – Poe, Melville, Hawthorne, Whitman – as not only the originators of American literature but also the most innovative and disquieting of modernists: "The furthest frenzies of French modernism or futurism have not yet reached the pitch of extreme consciousness that Poe, Melville, Hawthorne, Whitman reached. The European moderns are all trying to be extreme."

Lawrence furnished a language freighted with dark mythic overtones and symbolic majesty, and the New Criticism supplied the exacting analytical techniques. At least in part, American literature is a masterful modernist enterprise on a grand scale that was constructed by writers and critics inside and outside the university. This is the development to which Malcolm Cowley alluded when, from the vantage-point of the mid-1950s, he observed that "perhaps the principal creative work of the last three decades in this country has not been any novel or poem or drama of our time, not even Faulkner's Yoknapatawpha saga or Hemingway's *For Whom the Bell Tolls* or Hart Crane's *The Bridge*; perhaps it has been the critical rediscovery and reinterpretation of Melville's *Moby-Dick* and its promotion, step by step, to the position of national epic."

Cowley's judgment gets at an important literary historical fact about how American writers were *made*. In the literary histories published at the turn of the century, Melville's novels and stories were either absent or mentioned only in passing. George Woodberry, writing in the *Encyclopaedia Britannica* in 1910, concluded: "The sea novel was developed by Melville and his successors, but these tales, in spite of being highly commended by lovers of adventure, have taken no more hold than the work of [William Gilmore] Simms." When Melville was cited more favorably, it was usually in a perplexed tone, as when John Macy alluded to *Moby-Dick* as "a madly eloquent romance of the sea." (A further sign of the low level of interest in Melville's novel appears in a letter by D. H. Lawrence from February 1916: "I am reading *Moby-Dick*. It is a very odd, interesting book: to me interesting, the others can't bear it.")

By the early 1920s, galvanized by Raymond Weaver's biography (1921), the British publication of *The Works of Herman Melville* in sixteen volumes (1922–24), and the publication of *Billy Budd* (which had been found in a tin box among the Melville family's possessions), Melville's writing was rediscovered in the light of modernism and literary symbolism, and *Moby-Dick* was recreated as America's greatest book. It became a seminal text for many critics and scholars; Matthiessen's students declared that he "raised them" on *Moby-Dick* – the same novel that, as Matthiessen himself ruefully remarked, the library at Yale had listed under the "cetology" section of its card catalogue until 1930.

The elevation of Melville and *Moby-Dick* did puzzle a number of literary historians who were otherwise eager to participate in the reshaping of America's literary past. In *The New American Literature* (1930), Fred Lewis Pattee referred to "the case of Herman Melville" as the "strangest reversal of values," the "most amazing commandeering of leadership from the forgotten." When he turned to *Moby-Dick*, his words about it were both impassioned and puzzled: "It is a headlong, lawless hodgepodge, the most chaotic book that ever rose to the dignity of a classic. What a volume!" But the significant point is that Pattee felt obliged to honor *Moby-Dick* as a classic whatever his own doubts about it: its value had indeed been reversed.

Moby-Dick also dumbfounded Mencken; when he read the novel for the first time in 1941, he noted in his diary that its "badness" staggered him: "I found an overblown and windy piece of writing." But in the same year Mencken grumbled about *Moby-Dick*, Matthiessen identified it in *American Renaissance* as an American masterpiece that showed the "tragedy of extreme individualism, the disasters of the selfish will, the agony of a spirit so walled within itself that it seemed cut off from any possibility of salvation." For Matthiessen, *Moby-Dick* spoke to the demands and dangers of the culture – the ideology of American individualism – as did no other book.

The cause of American literature was also aided by the labors of the men and women involved in the Federal Writers Project, the New Deal program that began in July 1935. The Project ran until 1939, and employed thousands of researchers, writers, reporters, critics, and gatherers of folklore and interviews. It was a prodigious act of cultural history that inventoried the folkways of the American nation. Through its 50-volume "American Guide" series, and its 150-volume "Life in America" series, the Project gave America a "detailed portrait of itself." The material in these volumes was sometimes clumsily presented, but much of it (for instance, the thirty-five Southern "life histories" assembled in the 1939 book, *These Are Our Lives*) gave an expanded sense of the meaning of American tradition. The Project presented the idioms, images, legends, and myths through which common men and women defined their lives.

One of those involved in this mapping of American literary and cultural traditions was Constance Rourke (1885–1941). Educated at Vassar, where her English professors connected the response to and assessment of writing to its potential for "social service," Rourke was the author of six influential studies of folklore and popular culture that appeared between 1927 and 1941, as well as many reviews and essays (her first publication, in *The New Republic*, 1919, was on vaudeville); a seventh book, *The Roots of American Culture*, was published posthumously in 1942. During the 1930s, Rourke served as a director of the Works Progress Administration's Art Project, which dispatched hundreds of artists into the field to locate and make copies of American folk art. Her best-known book, *American Humor* (1931), was subtitled "a study of the national character," and it stressed the "folk" contexts of writers as different from one another as Poe, Whitman, Twain, and Henry James.

Rourke's appeal for sympathetic knowledge of American tradition awarded a central position to the critic and scholar:

Many artists have worked supremely well with little encouragement; few have worked without a rich traditional store from which consciously or unconsciously they have drawn. The difficult task of discovering and diffusing the materials of the American tradition – many of them still buried – belongs for the most part to criticism; the artist will steep himself in the gathered light. In the end he may use native sources as a point of radical departure; he may seldom be intent upon early materials; but he will discover a relationship with the many streams of native character and feeling. The single writer – the single production – will no longer stand solitary or aggressive but within a natural sequence.

Like Van Wyck Brooks, who influenced and encouraged her, Rourke was dedicated to making a "usable past" for American writers. This was the embassy of fact gathering, discrimination, critical analysis, and preparation for the art of the future that, she maintained, American scholars needed to perform so that social disunity and the split between high and low cultures could be healed.

There is an extraordinary breadth and curiosity in Rourke; she was interested in African-American spirituals, cowboy songs, tall tales, myths, the practical arts, and frontier humor as well as in Melville and James. Her *American Humor* was a landmark for Americanists such as F. O. Matthiessen during the 1930s and 1940s, and its conception of the country's "tradition" as "various, subtle, sinewy, scant at times but not poor" is open-minded and generous in what it reveals about the achievement and potential of America's cultures. Borrowing from and adapting the insights of the eighteenth-century Italian philosopher of history Giambattista Vico, the German philosopher and critic Johann Gottfried von Herder, the modern anthropologists Ruth Benedict and Jane Harrison, and the philosopher John Dewey, Rourke perceived a wealth of popular expression in America and examined its presence in the writings of America's major authors.

A somewhat comparable figure is the African-American novelist Zora Neale Hurston (1891–1960). After graduating from Barnard College in 1928, she studied with the eminent anthropologist and Columbia University professor Franz Boas, and soon became one of his students. In the South and in the Caribbean, she conducted research, and it formed the basis of her landmark collection of African-American folklore, *Mules and Men* (1935), which was followed by a second compilation, *Tell My Horse* (1938). Her essay "Characteristics of Negro Expression," published in *Negro: An Anthology*, edited by Nancy Cunard (1934), describes the resources of African-American dialect and folk expression, not only words and images, but also gestures, and forms of music and dance.

Neither Rourke nor Brooks was an academic, though Rourke did teach as an instructor of literature at Vassar from 1910 to 1915, when she resigned to devote more time to research. But the emergence of American literature was underway inside as well as outside the academy and its coming to prominence sometimes seems just a matter of time. As the profession of literary studies grew, so did the number of fields and specialties, and, for American academics teaching American students, American literature was an obvious subject. It is testimony to the prestige of English literature that it took so long for Melville and Whitman to appear serious enough to be frequently treated in courses. Members of history departments, after all, had always featured US history in their curricula and research; as the scholar John Higham observed in his study of the profession of history in America, "the earliest efforts of professional scholars were concentrated overwhelmingly in American history, for which original sources were most accessible and patriotic motives strong." By the late 1920s, professors of English were finally learning from the example of their colleagues in history even as the history professors themselves were, in turn, becoming increasingly alert to the undue "American" orientation of their discipline and shifting toward European topics.

American literature was becoming professionalized. *The New England Quarterly*, a journal devoted to literature, history, and culture, was launched in 1928, and *American Literature*, the main organ of the profession, started up in 1929. It was also receiving new attention from publishers, including the Viking Press, which issued in the 1940s a series of "portable" editions – originally designed for soldiers to carry in their pockets – of Hawthorne, Faulkner, and Hemingway. (Each of these three was edited by Malcolm Cowley.) By the 1940s, American literature was benefiting from American nationalism and wartime fervor, new trends in literary criticism, the prolific example of modern American writers, academic professionalism, and the spirit of American enterprise and discovery.

Throughout the 1930s, the literary scholars Jay B. Hubbell, Robert Spiller, and others were envisioning and step-by-step getting underway on preliminary discussion about a new American literary history that would surpass the *Cambridge History*. The monumental *Literary History of the United States* did not appear until 1948, and in its expansiveness, exhaustive detail, and, as the Preface states, faith in "democratic living," it is in part a product of consensus-building Cold War affirmations of American progress and power. But the preparation of this massive book spanned the Depression and World War II as well as the Cold War, and embodied its authors' commitment to American literature and the profession of American literary studies. It was propelled by a sustained desire to give American writers the acclaim they had been denied, and to provide students with a panoramic survey of the nation's achievements in philosophy and history – both of which the volume covered – as well as in literature.

An essay on the teaching of American literature, which appeared in the *American Mercury* in March 1928, summarizes what the situation looked like to Matthiessen, Spiller, and their fellow Americanists in the late 1920s – a date that represents a rough midway point between Van Wyck Brooks's advocacy of an American restoration in literature and the publication of the *Literary History of the United States*. The unknown author, using the pen name Ferner Nuhn, noted that while the number of dissertations on American literature and of scholars expert in the field had increased somewhat, colleges and universities persisted in failing to respect "the native culture of the Republic." Nearly all of the institutions that Nuhn examined offered only a single survey course on American literature; it was not a requirement, was often only a half-year in length, and was sometimes (as at Princeton) only available in alternate years.

On the undergraduate level, one of eleven courses in the typical English department concentrated on American literature; on the graduate level, the figure was even worse – one in thirteen. To judge from the various emphases in college and university courses, American literature stood:

About equal in importance to Scandinavian literature.
One-half as important as Italian literature.
One-third as important as Spanish literature.
One-third as important as German literature.
One-fourth as important as French literature.
One-fifth as important as Latin literature.
One-fifth as important as Greek literature.
One-tenth as important as English literature.

But Nuhn's observations matter less as a sign of what was wrong than as a final protest against a state of affairs that was already being corrected. The new canon of American literature had already emerged by the early 1930s, as the critic Carl Van Doren (1885–1950) remarked in 1932. The former classic names of American literature had lost their luster, and, Van Doren said, new names were replacing them:

> Emerson and Hawthorne and Thoreau, risen dramatically above Bryant, Longfellow, Whittier, Holmes, and Lowell, stand in the rarer company of Poe and Whitman. Irving and Howells have shrunk and faded. Cooper has scarcely held his own. Mark Twain seems a great man of letters as well as a great man. Henry James seems a brilliant artist whatever nation he belongs to. Herman Melville has thrust himself by main strength, and Emily Dickinson has gently slipped, into the canon.

Skeptics about the worth of American literature and proponents of the superiority of English literature remained vocal during the years between the wars. But during this same period were published Parrington's *Main Currents in American Thought* (1927–30), the first volumes of Brooks's *Makers and Finders* series on "the history of the writer in America" (1936, 1940), the Harvard scholar Perry Miller's *The New England Mind: The Seventeenth Century* (1939), Matthiessen's *American Renaissance* (1941), and Alfred Kazin's *On Native Grounds* (1942). Through these books, the status of American literature was raised within the academy and its importance amplified among the general public. American literature had acquired legitimacy as a subject for intensive reading and scholarly study. No one could ignore or dismiss it, or judge it as obviously inferior to the literatures of other lands.

The first two volumes of Parrington's *Main Currents* still stand as a lively Jeffersonian survey of American writing from its beginnings to the mid-nineteenth century, and they are the work of an intriguing, complex figure who taught and wrote far from the educational and cultural establishment of the East Coast. Parrington was born in Illinois in 1871, the son of a

Union officer who had commanded a regiment of African-American troops. He attended college for three years in Kansas, where the family had moved, but then transferred to Harvard, where he studied with Barrett Wendell and Lewis Gates in the English department. Upon graduation in 1893, Parrington chaired the English department first at the College of Emporia in Kansas and then at the University of Oklahoma. At both schools, Parrington also was the coach of the football team.

Parrington's early literary work focused almost entirely on the British tradition, even as he was drawn politically to the cause of American reform, the Populist movement, and in the mid-1890s, to the Democratic Party and its leader William Jennings Bryan. During a fourteen-month trip to England and France in 1903–04, Parrington became deeply interested in the writings of Ruskin and Morris. His belief in the connections among literature, culture, and politics was intensified when he and other faculty were fired in 1907 from their positions at the University of Oklahoma because of their liberal political and religious views. This led Parrington to reexamine all of American history and literature as a battle between reform and reaction, liberal and conservative forces.

Taking up a new position at the University of Washington, Parrington began to design undergraduate courses on American literature and graduate courses on American themes and topics. He also undertook research and writing on the book projects that, revised and expanded, became in the 1920s the *Main Currents* series.

At the time of their publication – on the recommendation of Van Wyck Brooks – Parrington's books were greeted with tremendous enthusiasm. "Readers in 1927 felt the same quality of excitement," the literary scholar Howard Mumford Jones has stated, "as [the editor Francis] Jeffrey experienced when in 1825 young Macaulay sent his dazzling essay on Milton to the *Edinburgh Review*." One of these readers was John Macy, who stated in a collection of essays published in 1931 that Parrington was not only a "scholar and teacher," but also "carried his learning easily and did not stay too long in the class-room; he dwelt in the open air of American life, explored the currents with a sense of adventure, and re-charted them by his own measurements." It was the range and independence of Parrington's work, as though its author were organically at one with the national spirit, that accounted for its appeal.

When historians were polled in 1950 to select the best book in "American history and biography" published between 1920 and 1935, Parrington's *Main Currents* was the easy winner. But the fact that it was a group of historians who saluted Parrington says something about his approach. Literary critics regarded *Main Currents* as economic and political rather than literary, and they concluded that an aesthetic criticism would have to remedy its defects. Parrington roused liberals and radicals in the turbulent political world of the 1930s. But he also dismayed many literary critics and teachers aligned with the aesthetic theory and practice of the fledgling New Criticism.

Parrington never claimed in his books to be conducting a literary analysis, so in a sense the cavils about the critical failures of *Main Currents* are unfair. As early as 1908, he said in a letter: "Officially I am a teacher of English literature, but in reality my business in life is to wage war on the crude and selfish materialism that is biting so deeply into our national life and character." True to this goal, Parrington observed in the Introduction to his first volume that he would "follow the broad path of our political, economic, and social development, rather than the narrower belletristic; and the main divisions of the study have been fixed by forces that are anterior to literary schools and movements, creating the body of ideas from which literary culture eventually springs." He reaffirmed this intention in the second volume: "With aesthetic judgments I have not been greatly concerned. I have not wished to evaluate reputations or weigh literary merits, but rather to understand what our fathers thought, and why they wrote as they did."

This, however, was not a good explanation for Parrington's lame chapters on Melville, Thoreau, and other writers. To Matthiessen and others who shared his views, it seemed that Parrington was engaging literary texts in a shallow and misguided way. One could not refer to *Moby-Dick* and *Walden* without addressing their aesthetic properties, argued Matthiessen. Nor should a critic commend a bad writer for his sincerity and "ideas," as Parrington did when he praised the naturalists in his third volume: "Their work might be bad art – as the critics love to reiterate – but it was the honest voice of a generation bewildered and adrift." A similar problem was exposed in a comment that Parrington made about Howells: "[he] came late to an interest in sociology, held back by the strong literary and aesthetic cast of his mind."

Matthiessen also found fault on aesthetic grounds with Van Wyck Brooks's *The Flowering of New England*, the opening volume in his *Makers and Finders* series, concluding that Brooks had failed to inspect carefully the ideas that drew the literary attention of his chosen writers and that he never explored texts themselves. Brooks appeared not only unresponsive to literary values, but, unable to provide "analysis of *The Week* or of *Walden* as works of art," he also lacked professional rigor: he was a good popularizer and synthesizer but not a serious literary critic or academic scholar.

Matthiessen's indictment was accurate, but *The Flowering of New England* was nevertheless a hugely popular book – it went through more than forty printings – and won Brooks the Pulitzer Prize. Brooks's impressionistic style, which braided his words with citations from the writers he considered, was precious and sentimental. Yet often he did manage successfully to evoke the Jeffersonian and Emersonian heritage that, in Brooks's estimation, characterized American experience and tradition.

Perry Miller (1905–63) did not identify himself as a literary critic – he preferred the term "literary historian." Born in Chicago in 1905, Miller attended private schools and then began his undergraduate studies in 1922 at the University of Chicago. He dropped out after a year, working as an actor, and then as a merchant sailor, and traveling in Mexico, Europe, and Africa. It was in Africa where he experienced, like a religious conversion, his sudden calling to become (as he put it) America's Edward Gibbon, "to have thrust upon me the mission of expounding what I took to be the innermost propulsion of the United States." He returned to the University of Chicago, completing his undergraduate degree and embarking on graduate training under the supervision of the critic Percy H. Boynton. He moved to Cambridge, Massachusetts, to do the research on his dissertation, which became his first book, *Orthodoxy in Massachusetts* (1933).

In *The New England Mind* and in later books and essays, Miller was concerned with the particulars of style, especially imagery, metaphor, and "plain speech" in texts, and with the psychological and emotional reverberations in literature of Puritanism and the English acts of settlement. Scholars have disputed Miller's findings, arguing that he erred in slighting typology, underemphasized the degree of difference among the early Puritans in his quest for a single dominant Puritan "intelligence," and ignored the majority of the people in his concern with the writings of theologians, ministers, and educators. Miller has also been attacked for his selection of sources, which some have judged less diverse than Miller claimed. And his approach, while rigorous, has seemed to some readers not only demanding but claustrophobic.

Still, *The New England Mind* was an astonishing achievement, and it was supplemented by other brilliant books and essays, including a penetrating biography of Jonathan Edwards (1949). Miller demonstrated the power and seriousness of the Puritans' errand into the wilderness, and their connections to the age of Emerson, and he effectively refuted the assertions about New England spirituality and culture that Parrington had presented in *The Colonial Mind*. In his scholarship, and in his teaching at Harvard, whose History and Literature program he had joined in 1931, Miller challenged, too, the simplifying satire that Mencken and others had tossed off about America's Puritan past, and he thus made Puritanism in America worthy of detailed study and historical reflection.

Like Miller's massive book, Matthiessen's *American Renaissance* has been battered by critics and theorists, above all for its focus on five white male authors and consequent exclusion of Margaret Fuller, Harriet Beecher Stowe,

Frederick Douglass, and other women and African-American writers of the pre-
Civil War years. In 1849, in an address on "the American scholar," Theodore
Parker (1810–60) had affirmed that "we have one series of literary productions that could be written by none but Americans, and only here; I mean
the Lives of Fugitive Slaves." When Wendell Phillips (1811–84) summarized the "philosophy of the abolition movement" in 1853, he contended that
the speeches and written texts that had resulted from the anti-slavery cause
answered the calls for a distinctive national literature: "This discussion has
been one of the noblest contributions to a literature really American." Two
years later, in his own review of the antislavery movement, Frederick Douglass
(1818–95) stated that the 1850s would "be looked to by after-coming generations, as the age of anti-slavery literature." Yet Matthiessen barely mentioned
slavery and abolition, and thereby perplexingly misrepresented the period that
he devoted so many pages to exploring.

This said, *American Renaissance* remains the most influential book in the
history of American literary studies. It redefined the terms for the study and
teaching of American literature, secured recognition for a new canon of texts,
and, in conjunction with Miller's work, led to the development of American
Studies in the United States and abroad.

Matthiessen was born in Pasadena, California, in 1902, the grandson of
the founder of the Western Clock Corporation, who left a $10 million estate
when he died in 1918. Matthiessen's father was a failure in business, and a
failure as a husband and father. Matthiessen and his three siblings were raised
by their mother in La Salle, Illinois, where his grandfather had been born.
After private schooling, Matthiessen matriculated at Yale, where he compiled
an outstanding record, and was influenced by the socialists Eugene Debs and
Norman Thomas, whose speeches he heard. He studied at Oxford as a Rhodes
scholar, and then did his graduate work at Harvard, receiving his Ph.D. in
1927 with a dissertation on Elizabethan translation. He taught at Yale from
1927 to 1929, and then moved to Harvard, where he remained until his death
by suicide in 1950. Matthiessen was a very complicated person – a tireless
scholar, a perceptive critic, an inspiring teacher, a Christian, a socialist, and
a homosexual (his companion for twenty years was a painter, Russell Cheney,
whom he met in 1924).

American Renaissance obtained its distinctive power not only because it highlighted the artistry of Emerson, Thoreau, Hawthorne, Melville, and Whitman
in convincing fashion and brought forward *Nature*, *Walden*, *The Scarlet Letter*,
Moby-Dick, and *Leaves of Grass* as (in Brooks's phrase from his *Scenes and
Portraits*) "the American scriptures." *American Renaissance* declared itself to be a
moral, social, and political act through which Matthiessen paid homage to the
capacity of American literature to renew the ideals of freedom and equality.

Matthiessen sharpened Parrington's and Brooks's (and before them, Barrett Wendell's) accounts of the "New England Renaissance." He linked his book to T. S. Eliot's return to English literature of the sixteenth and seventeenth centuries for that poet's own recasting of poetic tradition and understanding of the best context for modernist innovation. But the literary dimension of Matthiessen's project accrued its authority because it addressed a yearning for social and political change that had arisen in many readers of the 1930s and would continue in the 1940s – forms of change that would express in action the vision of American democracy that America's greatest writers had articulated.

Matthiessen connected his literary work to movements in radical politics of the 1930s, echoing in his title the language that appeared in the 1935 "Call for an American Writers' Congress," which stated that "a new renaissance is upon the world," a new opportunity for each writer to "proclaim both the new way of life and the revolutionary way to attain it." But *American Renaissance* also inspired many teachers and critics who were not politically radical, captivating and converting readers to American literature whatever their political loyalties and convictions. Matthiessen made reading and writing about American literature a disciplined, energizing endeavor that was essential for every American scholar and student.

In addition to *American Renaissance*, Matthiessen wrote monographs on Eliot (1935), James (1944), and Dreiser (posthumously published in 1951), and a tormented memoir of his postwar teaching abroad, *From the Heart of Europe* (1948). What emerges from all of his books are the contradictions that Matthiessen tried, with pain and difficulty, to manage and somehow resolve. He identified himself as a socialist, yet he revered the conservative Eliot and overlooked or sought to smooth out the intolerance that mars Eliot's social and political thought. He responded magnificently to Whitman's vision of solidarity, freedom, and comradeship even as he also perceived the accuracy of Melville's tragic diagnosis of human limitation and evil.

With an unnerving absoluteness, Matthiessen internalized the writers whom he read, researched, taught, and wrote about: they both exhilarated and wounded him. His career was very productive, but he died too soon, a suicide at the age of forty-eight, "exhausted and neutralized," as his fellow Americanist Richard Chase put it, "by the contradictions [he] contained."

A sense of urgency also motivated Alfred Kazin's *On Native Grounds*, termed by its author a "moral history, which is greater than literary history." Kazin (1915–98) was the son of Jewish immigrants (his father was a housepainter, and his mother a dressmaker) and a graduate of City College (B.A., 1935) and Columbia (M.A., 1938) who wanted to be a professional writer, a reviewer and an essayist. Beginning with his first pieces for *The New Republic* in the mid-1930s, Kazin quickly became a zealous man of letters, "crazy about America." He modeled himself as a critic on Edmund Wilson and Lewis Mumford, whom Kazin later described as "the American Ruskin, a furious social idealist who linked all the arts."

At the suggestion of the critic and Columbia professor Carl Van Doren, Kazin got underway on a big book about modern American literature. Reviewing *American Renaissance*, he praised Matthiessen for teaching readers to understand the American "democratic imagination" as it was displayed in the era of Emerson and Whitman. This same celebration of freedom and fellowship – spiked with a heightened, dramatic, sometimes hectic style – coursed through Kazin's own text. His explicit subject was realism and naturalism, but more fundamentally he quested for the soul and spirit of "America" and attempted to reconnect with the cultural renaissance of the years just before World War I and with the modernist literary and cultural discoveries of the 1920s.

In a passage that says much about the symbolic status that writing about American literature had acquired by the 1930s and 1940s, Kazin recalled in 1965 the era when he was working on his book:

Like so many writers who came of age in the Thirties, I took for granted the continuing spirit of the Twenties that I knew from *Winesburg, Ohio* and *Prejudices* and *The Sun Also Rises*. I was sure that we of the revolutionary Thirties would retain what was vital in the great books of the Twenties and direct it toward a more hopeful outlook, a fraternal society. We would improve on the nihilism of Hemingway, the callousness of Mencken, the frivolity of Sinclair Lewis. Like so many literary radicals who were becoming interested in American literature, I thought I could see across the wasteland of the Twenties to our real literary brethren in the utopians and Socialist bohemians of 1912. I felt connected to the socialist Van Wyck Brooks, the libertarian and revolutionary pacifist Randolph Bourne, the Edmund Wilson who in *Axel's Castle* has described the great twentieth-century writers as breaking down the wall of the present.

For Kazin, the "hunger" to absorb American literature was a desperate but ultimately hopeful effort to realize America's promise of opportunity and success. What could be more compelling for an American dreamer than an immersion in the literary work of the United States? Like others (for instance, Richard Wright) in the 1920s, 1930s, and afterwards, Kazin found a personal, professional, and political voice through the American writers that mattered most to him. In his criticism, in *On Native Grounds* and *An American Procession: The Major American Writers from 1830 to 1930 – The Crucial Century* (1984); in a series of memoirs, especially *A Walker in the City* (1951), *Starting Out in the Thirties* (1965), and *New York Jew* (1978); and in the teaching positions he held in the United States and abroad, Kazin inspired many to feel moved to take up their vocation as critics and teachers of the American democratic tradition in literature.

The books by Kazin, Parrington, Brooks, Miller, and Matthiessen differ in method and manner yet are all enlivened by an exploratory feeling for the truths of American literary and cultural history. Whatever their exclusions and excesses, and however much their radiance for some readers has faded, these books remain integral to the study of American literature. Each articulated and celebrated America's literary past, and gave to the activity of reading, teaching, and writing about American books a combination of critical seriousness, intensity, and prophecy.

By mid-century scholars and critics had established the field and tradition of American literature – its foundational authors, texts, and literary relationships. Perhaps the most famous of these relationships is that between Emerson and Whitman, and repeatedly it was chosen as a crucial point of departure or marker for college courses and books on the beginnings of American literature. Their letters and exchanges, and comments about one another to friends, which were keyed to the publication of *Leaves of Grass*, formed an intense dialogue about the meaning of an American literature, and these were cited by Matthiessen, Kazin, and others as setting an explicitly "American" agenda that these two and later writers triumphantly pursued.

Leaves of Grass, Emerson said to Whitman in 1855, was "a wonderful gift," the most "extraordinary piece of wit and wisdom that America has yet contributed." The poem, noted Emerson to Carlyle in the following year, was "a nondescript monster which yet had terrible eyes and buffalo strength, and was indisputably American." "American" – that was the term that Whitman himself repeatedly used when he hymned his own poem. He acknowledged the multiple English contexts that formed the ground for American writing, but, in his 1856 appendix to *Leaves of Grass*, he marked them as preparatory:

The lists of ready-made literature which America inherits by the mighty inheritance of the English language – all the rich repertoire of traditions, poems, histories, metaphysics, plays, classics, translations, have made, and still continue, magnificent preparations for that other plainly signified literature, to be our own, to be electric, fresh, lusty, to express the full-sized body, male and female – to give the modern meanings of things, to grow up beautiful, lasting, commensurate with America, with all the passions of home, with the inimitable sympathies of having been boys and girls together, and of parents who were with our parents.

For a literature to flourish that would be both American and modern, native authors would have to lay claim to and eclipse the cultural treasures of England.

This work would be sublime, yet also brutal and violent: "Authorities, poems, models, laws, names, imported into America, are useful to America today to destroy them, and so move disencumbered to great works, great days."

Yet Whitman's terms, paradoxically, show how difficult it is to define American literature as "American." Then, as later, the process of "destroying" rival or alternative traditions from England and Europe was registered in the American literary works themselves. American literature has always been more than merely "American," however much American writers have superbly declared their independence and produced their best work in the hope of breaking away from foreign influences. American literature as a field and its literary history become coherent when the nation's literature is perceived as richly multi-faceted and at odds with its own quest for national purity, and when it is seen to merge continually with the other literatures and their histories, especially, but not only, English literature.

The story of the rise of American literature, climaxing in the twentieth century as scholars and critics recounted it, thus is a story about America and a story about the literary and cultural engagement of America with the literatures and cultures of the world. The literature of the United States is a magnificent national literature, and an international literature as well. For every American writer who mocked or disputed the literatures of other lands, there were countless American writers who acknowledged their indebtedness – or else revealed it in the midst of disavowing the meaningfulness of all other literatures to them.

English authors bored the brashly, boisterously American Mark Twain (1835–1910) – his is a voice that strikes American notes all of the time; he wrote Howells in 1885 that he hated *Middlemarch*, "with its labored and tedious analyses of feelings and motives, its paltry and tiresome people, its unexciting and uninteresting story, and its frequent blinding flashes of single-sentence poetry, philosophy, wit, and what-not." But many American writers admired George Eliot and found her novels to be nurturing. "What do I think of *Middlemarch*?", observed Emily Dickinson (1830–86): "What do I think of glory?"

And whatever his hostility to George Eliot and loathing of Jane Austen, Twain was less provincial than he professed; he was fond of Ben Jonson's plays, loved Browning's poetry, and liberally quoted texts from "a vast number of tongues" in his first novel (co-authored with Charles Dudley Warner), *The Gilded Age* (1873). In his novels and stories, Twain parodied and paid tribute to English literature everywhere – his affectionate travesty of Hamlet's soliloquy in *Huckleberry Finn* is a notable instance – and his storehouse of allusions and references to English literature always formed a crucial part of his comic technique. (Twain's Colonel Sellers and Huck Finn are relatives of Dickens's Micawber and Pip.)

H. L. Mencken, a great admirer of Twain, judged this very quality of more-than-American bountifulness in Twain's imagination to be his greatest gift. Mencken criticized Twain for his "native Philistinism" but added that in *Huckleberry Finn*, Twain transcended the provinciality that he was so fond of professing. There was in Twain, argued Mencken (1917), "something of that prodigality of imagination, that aloof engrossment in the human comedy, that penetrating cynicism, which one associates with the great artists of the Renaissance." To Mencken, Twain did his best work as an American writer when he most resembled the Europeans who preceded him by three centuries.

Like Dickinson, Henry James and Edith Wharton esteemed George Eliot, and both studied Balzac, Turgenev, and Flaubert. Washington Irving drew from Addison and Goldsmith, William Cullen Bryant from Wordsworth, and James Fenimore Cooper from Walter Scott. In his books Melville drew upon Shakespeare, Milton, and the Bible; Catharine Maria Sedgwick and other popular women writers of the 1820s, 1830s, and 1840s were devotees of Maria Edgeworth; Susan Warner immersed herself in the British tradition and even compared herself to Charlotte Bronte's character Jane Eyre.

Howells looked appreciatively to Tolstoy; Kate Chopin to Guy de Maupassant; Frank Norris to Emile Zola; Dreiser to Hardy, Thomas Huxley, and Herbert Spencer; Pound to French, classical, and Oriental sources; T. S. Eliot to the French symbolists; Hemingway to Maupassant, Turgenev, Kipling, and many others; and Thomas Wolfe to James Joyce. Jack London jumbled bits of Nietzsche and Marx; and Ellen Glasgow came to understand her craft, she said, when she read *War and Peace*: "my first reading of Tolstoy affected me as a revelation from heaven, as the trumpet of the Judgment."

Gertrude Stein wrote *Three Lives* in 1905–06 under the stimulus of translating Flaubert's *Trois contes* (and while she was sitting near and looking at the portrait of her that Picasso had painted). Sherwood Anderson stated that he cared for Dostoyevsky more than any other writer, and he modeled his craft on the Victorian writer and traveler George Borrow, and, later, on D. H. Lawrence; and Lewis Mumford noted as his major influences Samuel Butler, Shaw, Wells, and the Scottish scientist Patrick Geddes. F. Scott Fitzgerald was a dedicated reader of Thackeray and connected his aims in *The Great Gatsby* to *Henry Esmond*, and in *Tender is the Night* to *Vanity Fair*. The poet Edgar Lee Masters filled his commonplace book with quotations from and comments on Shakespeare, Swinburne, Byron, Thackeray, Scott, Blackstone, Taine, Shelley, Milton, Chaucer, Spenser, Goethe, Montaigne, Addison, Bacon, and Macaulay. Countee Cullen based his verse on English romantic poetry; H. D. adapted

and borrowed from Greek mythology; the African-American poet and novelist
Claude McKay treasured D. H. Lawrence, saying that "what I loved was the
Lawrentian language, which to me is the ripest and most voluptuous expres-
sion of English since Shakespeare"; and Langston Hughes, though he loved
Whitman, Sandburg, and Du Bois, claimed that reading Maupassant's stories
made him "really want to be a writer and write stories about Negroes."

Hart Crane was committed to writing a modern American epic that would
fulfill the injunctions that Whitman had voiced in his prose treatises. But
while Crane read Whitman and Melville intensively, he took inspiration from
Blake, Rimbaud, Baudelaire, Dostoyevsky, Nietzsche, and Joyce, and, as T. S.
Eliot had advised aspiring poets, turned as well to Donne, Webster, and
Jonson. (Eliot said about his own practice: "I think that from Baudelaire I
learned first, a precedent for the poetical possibilities, never developed by any
poet writing in my own language, of the more sordid aspects of the modern
metropolis, the possibility of fusion between the sordidly realistic and the
phantasmagoric, the possibility of the juxtaposition of the matter-of-fact and
the fantastic.") In the first stages of learning to be an American poet, Crane,
like many of his American contemporaries, devoured the little magazines
and journals and became aware through them of the modernist experiments
underway overseas. Crane came across *The Little Review* in a bookstore in
Cleveland, his hometown, when he was a teenager, and he read Pound,
Wyndham Lewis, Eliot, and Yeats in the magazine's pages. The poet-critic
Yvor Winters, who was an adviser to, and, eventually, a harsh critic of, Crane,
followed a similar path; he began his subscription to *Poetry: A Magazine of
Verse* in 1916, when he was just sixteen years old, and could see there the
intersections between American and English and world literatures. As the
American novelist John Dos Passos (1896–1970) concluded, "once on
the library shelf Juvenal and Dreiser are equally 'usable.'"

American literature as a category, field, tradition, and social resource has always
strained against its boundaries; and sustained inquiry into American literary
history yields complicated conclusions about its status. To speak of and to call
for an "American" literature makes powerful and pragmatic sense, as the critics
and scholars of this century recognized: are not American writers themselves
continually pointing to the Americanness of their art and protesting that their
work could not have been produced anywhere else? Does not the long struggle
to win credibility for American literature bear witness to an identifiable body
of American texts? But Poe uttered an important truth when he stated in
1845 that American literature – a form of writing that adhered to "American
themes" and styles alone – was "rather a political than a literary idea."

To put the point another way: the work of American writers has rarely upheld their and their critical supporters' theories of national identity, and for every appeal to nationality, there is a warning against it or an acknowledgment of the need for any national American literature worth its name to learn about and incorporate the world's literary resources. The development of American literature, and its formation as an academic field, occurred while American writers were reframing and reworking the styles, strategies, and literary devices that writers from other lands devised. Breaking away from other literatures placed, and places, American writers in the midst of other literatures.

This literary inter-mixture holds true even for writers who sought vigorously to be die-hard and resolutely American. William Carlos Williams voiced an at times outrageous American exceptionalism, and, in his critical essays and creative work, he significantly contributed to the discourse that made American literature. In "A Point for American Criticism" (1929), he stated that "every time American strength goes into a mold modeled after the English, it is wholly wasted"; and in a piece on H. L. Mencken published a few years later (1936), he maintained that the language departments of universities should be reorganized "with American at the head and English and the other languages following." But Williams's praise of Henry Adams in a letter in 1928 indicates another dimension of his sensibility: "a fine old fellow, credit to his country and any country – or all countries, I should say, as any sensible person must be – being international."

William Faulkner (1897–1962), too, was robustly American and more than that. He remarked in an interview (*Paris Review*, 1956) that he "read Melville occasionally" but otherwise he cited only non-American writers and books as among his favorites: the Old Testament, Dickens, Conrad, Cervantes, Flaubert, Balzac, Dostoyevsky, Tolstoy, Shakespeare, and seventeenth-century and nineteenth-century English poets. When the critic and novelist Robert Penn Warren (1905–89) retraced the origins of *All the King's Men*, he said that it was informed by his reading of Machiavelli and the Elizabethan tragedians. It was through this literature that Warren became equipped to write an American novel, and his book's reliance on (and relation to) texts from other traditions makes *All the King's Men* exceed the category of "American" literature where from one point of view it manifestly belongs and where scholars, teachers, and critics have been proud to locate it, as they should.

As the letters of Robert Frost (1874–1963) reveal, he sought "to do something to the present state of literature in America" (August 1913). He termed his politics "wholly American" (July 1916), and spoke of the bonds between the language of his verse and America's identity as a nation: "I am as sure that the colloquial is the root of every good poem as I am that the national is the root of all thought and art" (January 1918). In a letter to Hamlin

Garland (February 1921), he even wondered, like a twentieth-century Emerson, whether American writers should muster "our resources a little against outside influences on our literature and particularly against those among us who would like nothing better than to help us lose our identity."

But Frost's poetry echoes Wordsworth almost as much as Emerson and is notable for the "outside influences," such as the poems included in F. T. Palgrave's *The Golden Treasury of the Best Songs and Lyrical Poems in the English Language* (1st edn., 1861), that Frost invokes, emulates, or wards off. Frost knew he owed much to English and European as well as American writers; as he playfully but revealingly remarked in a letter (July 1915), it was "some things in Turgenieff," along with several passages in *Walden*, that "must have had a good deal to do with the making of me."

As Mencken said in 1920, "the battle of ideas should be international." "I cannot imagine John Bunyan and Mark Twain as not thoroughly English and American," the poet-critic R. P. Blackmur (1904–65) stated, "but I cannot imagine either of them without the Greek and Hebrew testaments . . . Is not the past an institution like the Common Law?" "For better or worse," concluded the poet-critic Conrad Aiken in 1942, "American literature is henceforth a part of world literature."

American literature's status among other literatures was evident in small and large ways in popular culture too. In October 1941, for example, the Classic Comics series published the first comic-book retelling of a literary masterpiece, Dumas's *The Three Musketeers*. Other early titles included *Ivanhoe*, *Moby-Dick*, *Arabian Nights*, *Huckleberry Finn*, and *Gulliver's Travels*, each fitting into sixty-four pages. In 1947, the series was retitled Classics Illustrated. During the 1940s, the first twenty-eight titles sold more than 100 million copies. Melville, Twain, and other American writers were classics, as much as Dumas, Swift, or Scott.

Perhaps Norman Foerster, in his Introduction to the important 1929 book *The Reinterpretation of American Literature*, summed up the situation best when he observed that "the study of American literature is essentially a study of comparative literature, a study in the international history of ideas and their literary expression." No one worked harder than Foerster to legitimate American literature as a field, yet he intimated from the start the peculiarly mixed properties of the authors and texts he acclaimed. American literature was a national glory that was internationally produced. It merited separate study but could never and can never be studied alone. It demonstrably does, and does not, exist.

American literature is really a debate, an argument, and an effort to identify something that it is felt is there, or should be there, even though it is not and could not be. Foerster inside the academy, and Brooks, Bourne, and Mencken outside it, argued for American literature while citing Arnold, Carlyle, Shaw, Tolstoy, Dostoyevsky, Nietzsche, Strindberg, Bergson, Wells, Freud, and other English and European authorities.

T. S. Eliot, writing on the topic of American literature, expressed a version of this insight:

The justification for the history of American literature – instead of merely promoting the important Americans into a history of English literature – is that there is undoubtedly something American, and not English, about every American author. There is also something English about him, even when his ancestry is Swedish, German, or Italian. An American writer, to write a first-rate history of American literature, must know far more about England, and even more about the rest of Europe, than an Englishman needs to write a history of English literature, or a Frenchman to write a history of French literature. (*Times Literary Supplement*, January 10, 1929)

Through the great work of many writers, scholars, and critics, Americans came to appreciate that they had a literature of their own, and now that they possess it at last, they can perceive its dynamic interactions all along with the literatures of the world, and can begin to realize and value the complexities of American literary tradition and the multi-cultural and multi-ethnic makeup of its authors. The more that American literature is read and studied, the more difficult it is to see this literature – which is not and never was stably there for viewing anyway – as clearly or uniquely American. This complicated truth about what it is and is not gives American literature its complicatedness, its desperate energy, beauty, and grandeur.

INTELLECTUALS, CULTURAL CRITICS,
MEN AND WOMEN OF LETTERS

E MERSON and Whitman, and their contemporaries and successors in the early modern period, called for authors who would voice American democratic principles and give expression to the majesty of the land and the vigor of the nation's speech. But to a striking extent the makers of American literature invoked and pointed to European and, more often, British models, the Scottish essayist and historian Thomas Carlyle and the English poet and essayist Matthew Arnold above all.

Carlyle and Arnold were in a sense America's intellectual leaders and exemplars of critical conduct during much of the nineteenth century and into the first decades of the twentieth. This is not to discount Emerson, Whitman, and other leading American influences, but, rather, to identify the central figures from abroad, working in the English language, against whom American writers were defined and measured – the figures whom American writers would need to match in order for American literature to claim it had finally established itself.

Educated as a divinity student at the University of Edinburgh, restless and discontented as a teacher, Carlyle (1795–1881) was an incalculably important writer for Emerson and his contemporaries. His translations and selections of German authors, his exuberant and outrageous *Sartor Resartus* (1833–34), his epic *History of the French Revolution* (2 vols.,1837), and his provocative lectures *On Heroes, Hero-Worship, and the Heroic in History* (1841) seemed to American readers to be written to inspire and instruct transcendental poets and visionaries in America. Emerson praised Carlyle extravagantly in essays and letters, even recommending to him early in their friendship, in 1834, that he settle in America and "found a new academy that shall be church and school and parnassus, as a true poet's house should be." Emerson also shared the letters he received from Carlyle with friends and fellow Transcendentalists, as a type of scripture akin perhaps to Paul's epistles in the New Testament.

Others besides Emerson welcomed Carlyle's books and celebrated his verbal power – Thoreau remarked in an essay in 1847 that Carlyle possessed "the richest prose style we know of" and compared him to Milton and Cromwell; and they, too, urged Carlyle to come to America. Margaret Fuller summed up Carlyle's impact in a piece she published in *The Dial* in 1841: "Where shall we find another who appeals so forcibly, so variously to the common heart of contemporaries?"

Writing four decades later, at the time of Carlyle's death in 1881, Whitman made the same observation, honoring Carlyle's prophetic insight and commanding rhetoric:

As a representative author, a literary figure, no man else will bequeath to the future more significant hints of our stormy era, its fierce paradoxes, its din, and its struggling parturition periods, than Carlyle. He belongs to our own branch of the stock too; neither Latin nor Greek, but altogether Gothic. Rugged, mountainous, volcanic, he was himself more a French revolution than any of his volumes.

So formidable was Carlyle, added Whitman, that later generations of readers in America would be hard pressed even to begin to imagine his influence:

It will be difficult for the future – judging by his books, personal dissympathies, etc. – to account for the deep hold this author has taken on the present age, and the way he has colored its method and thought. I am certainly at a loss to account for it all as affecting myself. But there could be no view, or even partial picture, of the middle and latter part of our Nineteenth century, that did not markedly include Thomas Carlyle.

Neither Whitman nor Emerson could follow the anti-democratic path that Carlyle traveled in his later writings, particularly in sections of *Past and Present* (1843). During his second visit to England, in the late 1840s, Emerson noted that Carlyle "talks like a very unhappy man, profoundly solitary, displeased and hindered by all men and things about him." Carlyle's embittered irritability became even more prominent in *Latter-Day Pamphlets* (1850) and "Shooting Niagara: And After?" (1867), with its scathing indictment of "inexpressibly delirious" democratic reforms and its call for a "small Aristocratic nucleus" to set standards and campaign for the "Good Cause." Carlyle also portrayed blacks brutally in *Occasional Discourse on the Nigger Question* (1853), which he intended as a rebuttal to the "rampant *Uncletommery*" in England that in his view had been caused by the publication of Harriet Beecher Stowe's novel. And he scorned both sides during the Civil War. "There they are," Carlyle said, "cutting each other's throats, because one half of them prefer hiring their servants for life, and the other by the hour." This so enraged the abolitionist William Lloyd Garrison, editor of *The Liberator* (1831–65), that he could not bear any longer to look at Carlyle's portrait with its "hateful lineaments of that enemy of freedom."

These features of Carlyle's work, however, bothered Emerson, Whitman, and others less than one might have predicted. As Emerson told Carlyle in a letter in 1870, Carlyle's readers in America had already forgotten his "scarlet sins" during the war. They approved of Carlyle's attacks on moral and spiritual corruption, materialism, and the cash-nexus. His angry words, while targeted at England, appeared relevant to political and social tendencies that jeopardized America's future. Carlyle's intellectual honesty and uncompromising integrity, his dedication to the sacredness of "work" (which won the heart of Thoreau, who was given to enjoining himself to "work work – work!"), and his cultural criticism remained a source of enlightenment for Emerson and his contemporaries. He was a soul-shaking scold and an inspiration, saying, for example, in *Sartor Resartus*:

Be no longer a Chaos, but a World, or even Worldkin. Produce! Produce! Were it but the pitifullest infinitesimal fraction of a Produce, produce it, in God's name! 'Tis the utmost thou hast in thee: out with it, then. Up, up! Whatsoever thy hand findeth to do, do it with thy whole might. (II, 9)

The elemental force of Carlyle – the French critic Hippolyte Taine said in 1863 that "every thought with [Carlyle] is a shock" – survived the specific judgments he made about slavery and democracy from which his American admirers dissented.

When Emerson reviewed *Past and Present* for *The Dial* in July 1843, he established the terms by which Carlyle came to be known. He objected to a "certain disproportion" in Carlyle's account of the crisis that afflicted the English state, and regretted the lurid posturing and constant, if frequently spell-binding, exaggeration. But *Past and Present* nevertheless struck Emerson as a titanic book (an "*Iliad*" of English woes") that demonstrated the kind of "courage" that a "man of letters" must display when addressing practical and political issues. Carlyle showed himself a major "literary artist" who "has the dignity of a man of letters, who knows what belongs to him, and never deviates from his sphere; a continuer of the great line of scholars, he sustains their office in the highest credit and honor."

In an essay Emerson wrote after Carlyle's death – an essay that included passages from a letter of 1844 and the journals – he returned again to the preeminence in Carlyle's work of the magnificent "attitude of the writer." Emerson rehearsed the "liberal opinions" that Carlyle had violated (young men "praise republics and he likes the Russian Czar"), but he closed by brushing these aside and accenting Carlyle's independence: "he stood for scholars, asking no scholar what he should say." Carlyle, said Emerson, penetrated beneath the surface "to the heart of the thing."

Carlyle captivated Emerson and nearly all of his American contemporaries. Edgar Allan Poe (1809–49) was the exception. In an essay on William Ellery Channing, published in August 1843, Poe referred to Carlyle as "an ass," and he amplified this judgment in his marginalia for April 1846: "I have not the slightest faith in Carlyle. In ten years – possibly in five – he will be remembered only as a butt for sarcasm."

A more accurate, and more respectful, critique of Carlyle was recorded decades later by Henry James, Sr. (1811–82), for *The Atlantic Monthly* in May 1881. He acknowledged Carlyle's genius but detected a personal failure that for him tainted Carlyle's social criticism:

It always appeared to me that Carlyle valued truth and good as a painter does his pigments, – not for what they are in themselves, but for the effects they lend themselves to in the sphere of production. Indeed, he always exhibited a contempt, so characteristic as to be comical, for every one whose zeal for truth or good led him to question existing institutions with a view to any practical reform. He himself was wont to question established institutions and dogmas with the utmost license of scepticism, but he obviously meant nothing beyond the production of a certain literary surprise, or the enjoyment of his own aesthetic power. Nothing maddened him so much as to be mistaken for a reformer, really intent upon the interests of God's righteousness upon the earth, which are the interests of universal justice. This is what made him hate Americans, and call us a nation of bores, – that we took him at his word, and reckoned upon him as a sincere well-wisher to his species. He hated us, because a secret instinct told him that our exuberant faith in him would never be justified by closer knowledge; for no one loves the man who forces him upon a premature recognition of himself.

James fastened on a terrible, almost absurdly comical, contentment in Carlyle's fury. In James's estimation, this was the index to a self that was incapable of knowing and examining its motives; James probed and pricked Carlyle's stalwart self-representation, as Emerson, the Unitarian minister and reformer George Ripley (1802–80), the editor and essayist Orestes Brownson (1803–76), and other champions of Carlyle had not. Yet this judgment did not succeed in undermining the stature that Carlyle enjoyed, and that Emerson and so many others assigned to him.

Emerson's forceful language about his friend Carlyle suggests that the latter came as close as anyone to embodying the "American scholar" whom Emerson had beckoned for in 1837. This no doubt explains why Emerson was so eager that Carlyle travel to and perhaps reside permanently in America. Carlyle seemed to belong in America because he epitomized the forthright, visionary man of intellect and imagination that this country required but had not yet produced.

To Whitman, Carlyle was not only a stellar man of letters, but was instructive in his account of the limits of democracy. When Whitman first read "Shooting

Niagara," he thought it was preposterous ("such a comic-painful hullabaloo and vituperative cat-squalling"). Yet his own *Democratic Vistas* (1871), begun in part as a reply to Carlyle's essay, mimicked Carlyle's glowering prophecies and conclusions even as it rallied Americans to fulfill their nation's potential.

"I will not gloss over the appalling dangers of universal suffrage in the United States," Whitman declared, and he went on, with Carlyle-like vigor, to spotlight the decline in values and ideals that "business" and "money-making" had caused:

Confess that to severe eyes, using the moral microscope upon humanity, a sort of dry and flat Sahara appears, these cities, crowded with petty grotesques, malformations, phantoms, playing meaningless antics. Confess that everywhere, in shop, street, church, theatre, bar-room, official chair, are pervading flippancy and vulgarity, low cunning, infidelity – everywhere the youth puny, impudent, foppish, prematurely ripe – everywhere an abnormal libidinousness, unhealthy forms, male, female, painted, padded, dyed, chignon'd, muddy complexions, bad blood, the capacity for good motherhood deceasing or deceas'd, shallow notions of beauty, with a range of manners, or rather lack of manners, (considering the advantages enjoy'd,) probably the meanest to be seen in the world.

Whitman did not despair of the better future that America was empowered to attain, but he worried about social decadence and felt a kinship with Carlyle's criticism. The more that Whitman mulled over Carlyle's words, the truer these seemed to him, whatever their derivation (as he mentioned in a footnote) "from the highest feudal point of view." He deleted an explicit rejoinder to Carlyle from an early draft of *Democratic Vistas*, and, when his book was published, he mailed a copy to Carlyle, addressing it with his "true respects and love." Carlyle had written virulently about democracy, yet he stood for Whitman as the intellectual and "earnest soul" who merited the thanks of America's democratic men.

Whitman was far less patiently respectful toward Matthew Arnold (1822–88), who visited the United States on lecture tours in 1883 and 1886. Whitman once observed that Arnold was "the damndest of damned fools," a "total ignoramus" who "knew nothing at all about America"; he was "one of the dudes of literature." As Whitman explained to the editor and biographer Horace Traubel in 1888, Arnold simply "brings coals to Newcastle": he "brings to the world what the world already has a surfeit of: is rich, hefted, lousy, reeking with delicacy, refinement, elegance, prettiness, propriety, criticism, analysis: all of them things which threaten to overwhelm us."

Yet Whitman added: "We must be in no haste to dismiss Arnold." Whitman was not opposed to Arnold's conception of "culture," but, instead, sought to broaden it. He demanded "a programme of culture, drawn out, not for a single class alone, or for the parlors or lecture rooms, but with an eye to practical life, the west, the workingmen, the facts of farms and jackplanes and engineers, and of the broad range of the women also of the middle and working strata, and with reference to the perfect equality of women, and of a grand and powerful motherhood." Like Carlyle, Arnold uttered truths about American democracy and civilization that many Americans, including Whitman, felt forced to respond to, adapt, remedy. Even more than Carlyle, his ideas defined the crucial role of criticism and the importance of literature in an era of materialism, technology, industrialism, and conspicuous consumption. Carlyle was prophetic, but Arnold was modern.

Arnold delivered three lectures during his 1883 tour: "Numbers; or the Majority and the Remnant"; "Literature and Science"; and "Emerson." All are essential for appraising Arnold's influence upon American audiences and readers, especially cultured men in the universities and editors of journals and magazines. But "Literature and Science," which extended arguments that Arnold had presented in "The Function of Criticism at the Present Time" (1864), *Culture and Anarchy*, and "The Study of Poetry" (1880), is perhaps the most noteworthy, for it memorably told America of the prized place that literary study could secure in an industrial age.

Sounding like Whitman in *Democratic Vistas*, Arnold said that American society had no tradition and cohesion, suffered from bad manners, worshipped machines and money, feverishly quested after business success, and was too willing to taper its republican ideals and transform its optimism into an excuse for unreflective behavior. Literature, he affirmed, countered the momentum of materialism and both widened and enriched culture. Education, for Arnold, meant more than knowledge of science. It also involved responsiveness to classic texts that, when understood properly, fortified and elevated readers as nothing else could.

"The more that the results of science are frankly accepted," Arnold professed,

the more that poetry and eloquence come to be received and studied as what in truth they really are, – the criticism of life by gifted men, alive and active with extraordinary power at an unusual number of points; – so much the more will the value of humane letters, and of art also, which is an utterance having a like kind of power with theirs, be felt and acknowledged, and their place in education be secured.

The esteemed New England men of letters who presided over elite culture from the mid-nineteenth century to the 1890s, such as Oliver Wendell Holmes, James Russell Lowell, and Charles Eliot Norton, knew Arnold's poetry and prose well, counted him as a friend and correspondent, and looked to him as an intellectual authority. Sometimes they protested that he was not truly capable of understanding American civilization and its idioms. Lowell noted in a letter in 1883, for example, that Arnold failed to perceive the subtlety of Emerson's language and showed himself too often "in the habit of addressing a jury" in his prose. Others were dismayed by Arnold's evaluation of Emerson, which stressed that while Emerson stood as a "friend and aider of those who would live in the spirit," he was *not* "a great poet, a great writer, a great philosophy-maker." (Arnold proposed in this same essay that Carlyle, though more expressive than Emerson, was not a great writer, either.) Yet, whatever their doubts about Arnold's qualifications as a critic of American life and literature, the New England men of letters responded approvingly to his claims for culture and his commitment to standards in taste and judgment.

The New Englanders referred to Arnold's literary criticism with special admiration, and, in Holmes's case, treated his poetry favorably, too. Norton even valued the essay on Emerson; in a letter in 1884, he conceded that Arnold had aroused "the provincial ire" of Emerson's "pure disciples," but he concluded that the essay was "a piece of large, liberal, genuine criticism." In her book (1893) on the poet and editor John Greenleaf Whittier, Mrs. James T. Fields noted that Whittier recognized Arnold as "one of the foremost men of our time, a true poet, a wise critic, and a brave, upright man, to whom all English-speaking people owe a debt of gratitude." Another notable figure, the poet-critic and editor E. C. Stedman (1833–1908), writing at the time of Arnold's death, glanced at the shortcomings of Arnold's commentaries on America yet termed him a "preacher of taste and ethics" who inspired "the younger men in matters of taste, feeling, thought" and "broaden[ed] English criticism."

Arnold was both timely and timeless, a writer interested in current social problems and literary issues and mindful of norms that transcended the conflicts of the moment. It was this quality in Arnold that the young Henry James (1843–1916) singled out for praise when he reviewed the American edition of *Essays in Criticism* in 1865:

The great beauty of the critical movement advocated by Mr. Arnold is that in either direction its range of action is unlimited. It deals with plain facts as well as with the most exalted fancies; but it deals with them only for the sake of the truth which is in them, and not for *your* sake, reader, and that of your party. It takes *high ground*, which is the ground of theory. It does not busy itself with consequences, which are all in all to you . . . Its business is to make truth generally accessible, and not to apply it. It is only on condition of having its hands free, that it can make truth generally accessible. We have said just now that its duty was, among other things, to exalt, if possible, the importance of the ideal. We should perhaps have said the intellectual; that is, of the principle of understanding things. Its business is to urge the claims of all things to be understood.

James commended Arnold's focus on truth for its own sake and determination to remain free from using criticism to advance personal or party goals. This was the ideal that James wanted his American audiences to aspire toward, in order to turn back "votaries of the practical, of experimentalists, of empires." Such an ideal was particularly needed to preserve literature and culture, which, James insisted, dwell in a distinct domain and ought not to be evaluated according to practical or instrumental uses. James learned from many critics, particularly the nineteenth-century French literary historian Charles Augustin Sainte-Beuve ("I take him as the very genius of observation, discretion, and taste"), but Arnold's terms were crucial in his responses to both life and letters.

When James returned to Arnold in an essay in 1884 – which, conscious of the irony, he wrote as an American observer for an English magazine while Arnold was traveling in America – he again praised Arnold's leadership. James conceded his disappointment that Arnold had spent so much time in polemical campaigns when he might instead have given his "earnest hours" to "the interpretation of literature." But he praised Arnold's disinterestedness and emphasized that "all criticism is better, lighter, more sympathetic, more informed, in consequence of certain things he said." Once more he specified the lessons that Arnold, "the truly distinguished man of letters," had taught and should continue to teach to America:

It is Mr. Arnold, therefore, that we think of when we figure to ourselves the best knowledge of what is being done in the world, the best appreciation of literature and life. It is in America especially that he will have had the responsibility of appearing as the cultivated man – it is in this capacity that he will have been attentively listened to.

James's words about Arnold – whom James identified in *William Wetmore Story and His Friends* (1908) as "the idol" of his youth – forecast the language that Ezra Pound and T. S. Eliot would use about James himself. During the first decades of the twentieth century, James figured for readers as Arnold had for readers of the preceding era. He was for them what Arnold had been for him – the "cultivated man" devoted to the literary life and the passionate truths of art.

In his fiction and criticism, James displayed for the modernists the zealous pursuit of artistic form and demonstrated the moral meanings of the writer's craft. In "The Art of Fiction," which appeared in the same year as his second piece on Arnold, James not only described the nature of the novel, but also defined the nature of the persons who wrote the best novels. Such a person was equipped to "guess the unseen from the seen," could "trace the implication of things" and "judge the whole piece by the pattern," and could feel "life in general so completely" that no part of it would remain unknown.

One recalls the young James's praise of Arnold's devotion to truth and the claim of all things to be understood. This is a demanding ideal that James expressed, and it is paralleled by his grand statement of the expansiveness of the writer's, especially the novelist's, subject: "The advantage, the luxury, as well as the torment and responsibility of the novelist, is that there is no limit to what he may attempt as an executant – no limit to his possible experiments, efforts, discoveries, successes." James exemplified the dedicated artistic performance that Pound preached: "the mastery of any art is the work of a lifetime."

In theory, then, James embraced an Arnoldian ethic of disinterestedness. But the limitation, as well as the value, of his criticism is that it was supremely *interested* from the beginning and became even more so as James's career progressed. James criticized writers according to his own preoccupations; he was tactful and complimentary toward those whom he admired (Balzac, George Eliot, Flaubert, and Turgenev), but he found it taxing to be generous toward writers and texts that departed from his own norms. In his early days as a critic, he spoke narrow-mindedly about Dickens (and Whitman, too), and, in his final years, he was grudging toward Conrad and Lawrence. There were other blind spots (e.g., Baudelaire), and boundless condescension, especially toward Emerson and Hawthorne. Much of James's criticism is brilliantly executed and repays re-reading, but his judgments about what this or that writer should have done reflect James's certainty that he would have done the job better.

The best moments in James's criticism occur in his portraits of the personalities of writers, as when he brings together Balzac and Dickens in an essay on Balzac's correspondence (1877):

Each was a man of affairs, an active, practical man, with a temperament of almost phenomenal vigor and a prodigious quantity of life to expend. Each had a character and a will – what is nowadays called a personality – that imposed themselves irresistibly; each had a boundless self-confidence and a magnificent egotism. Each had always a hundred irons on the fire; each was resolutely determined to make money, and made it in large quantities. In intensity of imaginative power, the power of evoking visible objects and figures, seeing themselves with the force of hallucination and making others see them all but just as vividly, they were almost equal. Here there is little to choose between them; they have had no rivals but each other and Shakespeare. But they most of all resemble each other in the fact that they treated their extraordinary imaginative force as a matter of business; that they worked it as a gold-mine, violently and brutally; overworked and ravaged it.

To the modernist writers of the new century, James was a sensitive, sympathetic, finely intelligent person attuned to the whole of European culture. He was the serious critic who had composed *French Poets and Novelists* (1878), *Hawthorne* (1879), *Partial Portraits* (1888), *Notes on Novelists* (1914), and the prefaces to the New York edition (1907–09) of his novels and tales. Something of a high modernist himself, James was a passionate pilgrim and expatriate unable to practice his craft in America. Pound (1918) described James as "the greatest writer of our time and of our own particular language"; "in James," he added, "the maximum sensibility compatible with efficient writing was present."

Eliot (1918) named James "the most intelligent man of his generation," ascribing to him the quality – "intelligence" – that Eliot would later identify (1921) as the "method" of the true critic: "there is no method except to be very intelligent, but of intelligence itself swiftly operating the analysis of sensation to the point of principle and definition." Oddly, even as Eliot venerated James's intelligence and invoked intelligence as the primary virtue of the distinguished critic, he tagged James as "emphatically not a successful *literary* critic" and concluded that "his criticism of books and writers is feeble." By praising, yet diminishing, James, Eliot gave himself a significant role in the culture: he would be the figure whom James had envisioned but never became.

In a more favorable assessment (1934), the poet-critic R. P. Blackmur also fastened on Eliot's key word: for James, "the emphases were on intelligence – James was avowedly the novelist of the free spirit, the liberated intelligence – on feeling, and on form." Blackmur said about James's prefaces that "criticism has never been more ambitious, nor more useful." The African-American novelist Richard Wright (1908–60) studied Blackmur's edition of James's prefaces, and then advised his friend Ralph Ellison (1914–94), later the author of *Invisible Man* (1952), to do the same.

For Blackmur, Wright, and Ellison, and many others, James was the standard-setting critic and paragon of the man of letters. He even had an appeal for the Marxist journalist Floyd Dell (1887–1969), who interpreted James's labyrinthine style as a sign of his refusal to compromise with the superficial habits of a degraded culture: "We came to honor and love Henry James, irrespective of our ability to make head or tail of his sentences, simply because those sentences notoriously and haughtily ignored the demands of the ordinary reader for an ordinary meaning." The modernists cast James in the part that James had said Arnold was the first to perform, and that Eliot – called by Allen Tate in 1925 "the most intelligent man alive" – would fulfill triumphantly.

For the modernists, and for their followers and students, James gave substance to their ideas about art, morality, and truth, and by the 1940s he had acquired great symbolic power. In a review-article that appeared in 1945, John Berryman (1914–72) identified James as "the great novelist of our own time whose experience speaks most directly to us; the experience of others is nearer, but they have not his authority or size." In 1948, Lionel Trilling, who had earlier reexamined Arnold (1939) for the modern age, cited *The Princess Casamassima* as "an incomparable representation of the spiritual circumstances of our civilization." It was as though James knew in advance the kind of "moral realism" that men and women would require to temper the political extremism of the 1930s and confront the evils of Stalinism. Edmund Wilson, also in 1948, was skeptical about the "frantic enthusiasm" that had arisen about James. But he, too, certified James's emblematic status as novelist, critic, intellectual: "James stands out today as unique among our fiction writers of the nineteenth century in having devoted wholeheartedly to literature the full span of a long life and brought to it first-rate abilities."

William Dean Howells (1837–1920) did not receive the acclaim bestowed upon James, even though Howells also "devoted wholeheartedly to literature the full span of a long life." To the boisterous critic and editor H. L. Mencken, Howells was an Arnoldian in a badly dated sense, a "Victorian" with no robust lessons in style or content to offer to the present, a writer who "really had nothing to say." (Mencken dubbed James "a sort of super-Howells, with a long row of laborious but essentially hollow books behind him.") A Victorian: this, for most critics and intellectuals, was the large and irritating fact about Howells – his preference for solid nineteenth-century virtues of character formed within "the conditioned life" – which was in turn the phrase that, decades later, Trilling would use in a favorable essay on Howells (1951). A writer whose career had begun with a campaign biography of Lincoln (1860), Howells was viewed as irrelevant to the cultural critics and literary agitators of the early twentieth century.

Howells himself had honored Carlyle, terming him a man "in whom the truth was always alive," and like James, he respected Arnold, though Midwestern democrat that he was, he judged that Arnold had failed to realize the strength of America's commitment to equality when he had complained on his lecture tour about the absence of "distinction" here. Howells treated many of the same authors that James did, yet he was more curious (an Arnoldian virtue), supportive, magnanimous. He was more disinterested than James, and certainly less condescending.

Like James, Howells wrote about Turgenev, Zola, and the European realists and naturalists, yet he also wrote about the African-Americans Charles

Chesnutt, Booker T. Washington, and Paul Laurence Dunbar and the Jewish author and editor Abraham Cahan. He was the first major voice to declare the greatness of Dickinson's poetry (1891), and he encouraged and criticized writers as different from and as hostile to one another as James and Twain.

Not as penetrating as James, Howells nonetheless was an intelligent critic. What limited him for the modernists was his advice in 1886 that writers embrace the "more smiling aspects of life" and stand "true to our well-to-do actualities." This stamped Howells – a man of letters who decried the "civic murder" of the Haymarket anarchists in 1887, and a critic who championed Norris, Garland, Crane, and Dreiser – as a defender of America at its most buoyantly uncritical. It made him appear to be unwilling to take literature seriously as "a criticism of life" that tested prevailing social and cultural assumptions.

Howells "had the code of a pious old maid whose greatest delight was to have tea at the vicarage," said Sinclair Lewis in his Nobel Prize address (1930). Others acknowledged Howells's sincerity but tore into the rhythm and structure of his prose. "Howells was an honest novelist of manners," concluded Conrad Aiken (1924), "with an appallingly undistinguished style." "For more than one full generation," observed Ellen Glasgow in her autobiography *The Woman Within* (1954), "all the well-thought-of fiction in America was infected by the dull gentility of [Howells's] realism, and broke out in a rash of refinement." Howells knew by the early 1900s that his influence had waned, as he remarked to Henry James, "I am comparatively a dead cult with my statues cut down and the grass growing over me in the pale moonlight."

Howells was insignificant for many literary modernists not merely because of his prose style, however. He was not only a staunch democrat but, later, a socialist, and his political sympathies shaped his approach to literature. As he reflected in his essay on Arnold, "the arts must become democratic, and then we shall have the expression of America in art." From the point of view that most modernists adopted, Howells was lowering standards and accepting the everyday. But actually he was recommending a broad understanding of the meaning of America for writers and readers and for the selection of subjects for literature. The "distinctive" Americans whom he cited to refute Arnold included Lincoln, Longfellow, the Union army general and president U. S. Grant, Emerson, the abolitionist John Brown, Stowe, and Hawthorne – a mixed group that would not have pleased the highbrow intelligences of James and Eliot.

Howells responded intensely to the notion of the literary person's "criticism of life," and when, in his Arnold essay, he reviewed the society in which Americans lived in the late 1880s, he was disturbed by its political corruption, lack of economic opportunity for all, waste of public lands, tyrannical monopolies, and explosive relations between capital and labor. "There's something in the air," Howells said, "that won't allow you to live in the old way if you've got a grain of conscience or of humanity." His reading of Tolstoy informed his idea of his mission as a novelist, which was to "make men know each other better, that they may all be humbled and strengthened by a sense of their fraternity."

For Howells, the novelist was obliged to "teach" all persons and thereby dispute the boundaries of class. "Disdain[ing] the office of the teacher is one of the last refuges of the aristocratic spirit," he argued. Howells's view was ethical, not political, and in this respect he was not wholly equipped to understand the social crises erupting around him. But his commitments were authentic, and at odds with the social and literary exclusiveness that his gifted friend Henry James and, later, T. S. Eliot supported.

Throughout the late nineteenth and twentieth centuries, Howells, James, and other writers made use of Arnold's phrases, especially "criticism of life," to declare the responsibility of the intellectual and man of letters. Not everyone agreed with Arnold's social and cultural positions, nor was everyone convinced that all of his literary judgments were correct. But he stood for a fine ideal and represented stringent discrimination, emblematizing a sense of duty that many writers sought to fulfill, including writers who disapproved of one another.

Arnold was a significant influence on Eliot, who disagreed with Arnold but could not leave him behind, and upon the poet-critic Allen Tate, who referred to Arnold (1941) as "a great critic of ideas, of currents of ideas, of the situation of the writer in his time." He was also a revered figure for the literary and ethical critic W. C. Brownell, and for Stuart Sherman, who from 1907 to 1924 at the University of Illinois gave a famous course on Arnold as the "ideal literary man"; and he meant much to the novelist, Freudian critic, and recorder of Jewish experience in America, Ludwig Lewisohn (1882–1955), who described his response to Arnold's writings in his autobiography *Upstream* (1922) – "I read all of Arnold over and over again" – and remarked (also in 1922) that "we all talk Arnold, think Arnold, preach and propagate Arnold."

In the 1920s, recalled the intellectual and Marxist theorist and historian C. L. R. James (1901–89), he and friends in Trinidad were living "according to the tenets of Matthew Arnold"; as James remembered, he was trying then, like Arnold, to spread "sweetness and light and the best that has been thought and said in the world." Even earlier, the African-American teacher, clergyman, and missionary Alexander Crummell (1819–98), in *Africa and America* (1891), praised the "brilliant writer" Matthew Arnold's injunction, "force till right is ready," in order to justify Christian guardianship of Africa's "heathen tribes."

Arnold was an authority as well for William Morton Payne, best known in the history of criticism for having assembled reports in the 1890s on the state of "English" in American colleges and universities. Payne edited in 1904 one of the first collections of American literary criticism, and prefaced it with an epigraph from Arnold on the need "to get rid of provinciality." For Payne and others, Arnold validated the approach and goals of the new discipline of literary studies and helped scholars to see their work as offsetting the moneymaking and business fever of American life.

Given Arnold's own uneasiness about scientific method, it is a bit of shock to recall that in the 1870s Arnold considered seeking a professorship at the newly established Johns Hopkins University in Baltimore, Maryland. One wonders how Arnold would have reacted to the German model for graduate study that was adopted at Johns Hopkins and to its professional ethos. He was, at once, a figure responsible for and averse to the institutionalization of literary studies. William Dean Howells was invited to teach at Johns Hopkins in 1882, and he and Arnold would have made an odd and formidable pair alongside the philologists.

Arnold was an ideal critic and intellectual for conservatives, radicals, and those in between. When the cosmopolitan Edith Wharton (1862–1937) outlined her aims as a writer, she had recourse to Arnold, noting in a letter (December 5, 1905) that fiction was only valuable and interesting to her as "a criticism of life." In another letter (February 12, 1909), she complained that the dramatist and critic George Bernard Shaw was without the Arnoldian ability to "see things whole"; and in yet another (October 1912), she urged her fellow writer (and her lover) Morton Fullerton to recover "what Arnold called 'prose of the centre.'" In *The Autobiography of an Idea* (1924), Louis Sullivan (1856–1924), writing about himself in the third person, remembered his joy as a child when he watched men at work in the streets: "He had missed nothing; he had noted every detail. He had seen it whole and seen it steady."

These same phrases reappear in essays, books, and speeches by Marxists and socialists in the 1920s and 1930s for whose opinions (and company) Wharton and probably Sullivan would have had little sympathy. When the left-leaning Newton Arvin (1900–63) criticized distortions in Hawthorne's stories (1929), he did so in an Arnoldian manner by saying that Hawthorne failed to see "the thing as in itself it really is." In a still bolder argument, the novelist and social critic Waldo Frank (1889–1967), addressing the American Writers Congress in 1935, stated that the "American revolutionary writer, to act his part, which is to create the cultural medium for revolution, must see life whole." The Marxist Granville Hicks wrote positively about Arnold as late as 1939; Arnold had said "a number of shrewd and valuable things." And the Christian socialist and Harvard professor F. O. Matthiessen (1902–50) began a lecture in 1949,

"The Responsibilities of the Critic," by locating himself in "the tradition of Matthew Arnold," whom he named as his "first critical enthusiasm" when he was an undergraduate at Yale.

One of the central sources for liberal journalists and progressives was Herbert Croly's *The Promise of American Life* (1909), and this book, too, showed the presence of Arnold. Croly (1869–1930) criticized the "philistine public," esteemed the "disinterested intelligence," and called upon his readers to take up "the function of the critic in modern America." In words that stirred the critic Randolph Bourne, the journalist and cultural critic Walter Lippmann, the jurist Felix Frankfurter, and Edmund Wilson, Croly appealed for "moral and intellectual emancipation" and counseled critics and intellectuals to undertake and exemplify for others Arnold's work of intelligent judgment.

A few years after Croly's book appeared, the influential critic Van Wyck Brooks wrote a short study of the English novelist and social theorist H. G. Wells (1915) in which he affirmed the importance of socially conscious "intellectuals" and men of ideas, and spelled out the meaning of "the spirit of Wells" for a new American future. He linked Wells to Arnold, arguing that "the entire trend of Arnold's social criticism was anti-individualistic and in a straight line with socialism." This view would have surprised Croly, and it would have baffled Wharton, but it shows the range of causes that Arnold was taken to endorse.

As Lionel Trilling concluded in 1949,

[Arnold] provided us with the essential terms for our debate in matters of taste and judgment. He established criticism as an intellectual discipline among the people of two nations and set its best tone. Wherever English-speaking people discuss literature as it does its work in the world, literature in its relation to the fate of man and nations, the name of Matthew Arnold appears, not always for agreement but always for reference.

Arnold's commitment to literature as a "criticism of life" made him exemplary, and Wharton, H. L. Mencken, the novelist Thomas Wolfe, and many others cited this phrase. Yet this commitment authorized very disparate projects. Seeing literature and literary study as criticisms of life could imply either removal from life (distance, separation, detachment) or engagement with it – a direct grappling with life that was more immediate than anything Arnold himself had envisaged or would have wished to sponsor.

Arnold laid down a mandate to criticize literature and life, but the relationship between these terms proved controversial, and it was debated by critics, intellectuals, and men and women of letters. Some held that literature obeys its own laws, properties, and aesthetic rules, and hence criticizes life by being different from it. Others maintained that literature itself is a form of life; it educates people about life; it leads them better to comprehend and attack the problems of life. James and Wharton regarded Arnold as a major figure because he fought against confusing literature and life, whereas literary radicals saw him as powerful because he proposed that literature and life be brought into conjunction with one another.

It was the active, progressive potential of Arnold's definitions that made him especially important for Van Wyck Brooks. On the one hand, Brooks blasted the genteel tradition and its adoption of Arnold as its patron saint; for the genteel professors and humanists, he said, Arnold's values were merely an excuse for complacency, for what the Harvard philosopher George Santayana critically termed "a flutter of intelligence in the void." But Brooks identified an admirable Arnold even as he objected to the Arnold that many American professors and men of letters had embraced, and he thereby aimed to redeem Arnold as an engaged social critic.

In an April 1917 essay, "The Culture of Industrialism," Brooks set himself against "the ascendancy" of "the Arnoldian doctrine about 'knowing the best that has been thought and said in the world.'" Such an attitude led to lax acceptance of convention and to an evasion of social and political responsibility. The American Arnoldians, stated Brooks, enjoyed "the heritage of the civilization" without feeling obliged to examine the foundations upon which their elegantly cultured, leisured lives were based.

But in the following month, in an article titled "Our Critics," Brooks praised a different dimension of Arnold that the custodians of genteel culture had neglected:

In a famous essay, Matthew Arnold said that it is "the business of the critical power to see the object as in itself it really is." If any of our critics had been able to act upon this principle, if they had been able to put aside their prepossessions and merely open their minds to the facts of American life, even without attempting any of the more heroic measures our life notoriously demands, I think the predicament of the younger generation would be far less grave than it is. For, as Arnold goes on to say, by seeing the object as in itself it really is, criticism "tends to make the intellectual situation of which the creative power can profitably avail itself."

Brooks cited Arnold to argue that critics should "see" the American scene rather than – via a misapplied Arnold – flee from it to a haven of uncriticizable classics. In another Arnoldian note, Brooks also sought to foster a climate of closely inspected ideas that would nurture the creative arts. For Brooks, Arnold meant a dynamic relationship to the present and clear standards for judgment;

he inspired and gave credibility to the maintenance of a position between the lowbrow and highbrow extremes of American life, and he suggested that a creative and critical community might be organized around this new center.

Brooks himself performed a service for American culture during the first decade and a half of the new century (a time, Mencken later recalled, "of almost unbelievable complacency and conformity"). But the entry of America into the war interrupted Brooks's Arnoldian program. On April 2, 1917, Woodrow Wilson asked Congress to declare war on Germany, affirming that this crusade would make the world "safe for democracy." The vote was overwhelmingly in favor of war, and, in the next month, Congress passed the Selective Service Act that required the registration and draft of men between the ages of twenty-one and thirty – an act with dramatic consequences for the young men whom Brooks desired to awaken and assemble into communities.

Brooks's essays appeared in *The Seven Arts* magazine, a cosmopolitan monthly that had begun in 1916 under the editorship of James Oppenheim and Waldo Frank, and that published not only Brooks's criticism but also prose and poetry by Dreiser, Mencken, Frost, Bertrand Russell, and D. H. Lawrence. *The Seven Arts* was intended, as Frank explained in his *Memoirs* (1973), as "an expression of artists for the community." In its inaugural issue the editors announced "it is our faith and the faith of many, that we are living in the first days of a renascent period, a time which means for America the coming of that national self-consciousness which is the beginning of greatness." But, added Frank, *The Seven Arts* showed "the trend of the arts toward politics, a natural course when the society is menaced for causes exterior or internal." The pressure for ideological conformity smashed Brooks's hopes for independent thought and cultural rebirth. It also drove the authorities to destroy *The Seven Arts* for publishing the brilliant anti-war essays of Randolph Bourne. The magazine, quipped Robert Frost, died "a-Bourning."

Bourne (1886–1918) attacked Matthew Arnold and everything he stood for, but he recognized why Arnold enthralled American readers. In "Our Cultural Humility," Bourne noted both the clarity of the Arnoldian ideal of culture – it "dissolved the mists" in which culture "had been lost" – and its "democratic" resonance: "everyone who had the energy and perseverance could reasonably expect to acquire by taking thought that orientation of soul to which Arnold gave the magic name of culture." But Bourne disapproved of the manner in which Arnold's ideas had come to be understood and the "hypnotization of judgment" to which they had led.

Like Brooks, Bourne assailed the American Arnoldians' "cult of the best" and the view that students should reverently read the classics without quarrel or complaint. Bourne criticized the academy's over-investment in a literary canon that did not minister to the needs of American readers. As he explained in a letter (January 5, 1914), "Emerson, Thoreau, Whitman, William James, Henry James, Royce, Santayana, have delighted me infinitely more than all my official English reading. Why can't we get patriotic and recognize our great men?"

Facially deformed, tubercular, and hunch-backed, the young Bourne immersed himself in books, graduating from high school in 1903 as the senior-class president and valedictorian. He was an Emersonian eager for "spontaneity" and immediacy of personal judgment, "our native reactions to the freshness and sincerities of life." He felt that individual temperament and personality mattered more than the canonical standing of certain books, and he preferred the spirit of Emerson's "The American Scholar," with its appeal for creative, independent-minded reading, to Arnold's advocacy of touchstones before which readers must be humble. In an article titled "In a Schoolroom," which appeared in the first issue of *The New Republic* (November 7, 1914), Bourne emphasized that teachers and students should foster "personal expression" and independent ideas and thereby challenge the impersonality and imposition of authority that ruled in most schoolrooms.

Bourne's anti-war essays were effective because he saw the war as it really was. He described the reality of war as prosecuted by the modern state, and he criticized intellectuals who believed that war would enable them to reshape society according to the pattern of their instrumentalist theories.

During 1917, *The Seven Arts* printed a half-dozen pieces by Bourne on the war, the state, and the complicity of intellectuals in the horrors at home and abroad: "The War and the Intellectuals," "Below the Battle," "The Collapse of American Strategy," "Conspirators," "A War Diary," and "Twilight of the Idols." (Another important essay, "The State," which describes war as "essentially the health of the state," appeared in 1919, a year after Bourne's death.) There were other critics of the war, such as Senator George Norris, who in a speech in the Senate, April 4, 1917, argued that war served the interests of bankers and industrialists: "Their object in having war and in preparing for war is to make money. Human suffering and the sacrifice of human life are necessary, but Wall Street considers only the dollars and the cents." Bourne, however, stood pretty much alone among men of letters in his opposition to the war. Mencken urged him to keep silent and save his dissent until the war was over; and Brooks advised him to concentrate on literature, for any criticism of the war in the midst of America's patriotic frenzy was like "opposing an earthquake."

"The popular imagination," the philosopher William James had warned, "fairly fattens on the thought of wars," and the state of the nation in 1917 ratified this view. James himself was a staunch anti-imperialist, highly critical at the turn of the century of the United States' military and political actions in the Philippines. Speaking, for example, at the Fifth Annual Meeting of the New England Anti-Imperialist League (Boston, 1903), James had bitterly concluded:

All the anti-imperialistic prophecies were right. One by one we have seen them punctually fulfilled: – The material ruin of the Islands; the transformation of native friendliness to execration; the demoralization of our army, from the war office down – forgery decorated, torture whitewashed, massacre condoned; the creation of a chronic anarchy in the Islands, with ladronism [roguery and thievery] still smouldering, and the lives of American travelers and American sympathizers unsafe in the country out of sight of army posts; the deliberate reinflaming on our part of ancient tribal animosities, the arming of Igorrote [living in the northern part of Luzon] savages and Macabebe [also from Luzon] semi-savages, too low to have a national consciousness, to help us hunt the highest portions of the population down; the inoculation of Manila with a floating Yankee scum; these things, I say, or things like them, were things which everyone with any breadth of understanding clearly foretold; while the incapacity of our public for taking the slightest interest in anything so far away was from the outset a foregone conclusion.

It was an inspiration to Bourne that James, author of *Pragmatism* (1907) and *The Meaning of Truth* (1909), had spoken resolutely against injustice, and had done so as a member of a much-assailed minority. Some years later, Bourne similarly was determined to speak out – and to their credit, his editors at *The Seven Arts* published his work – because he saw the war as accelerating developments in American social, political, and intellectual life that alarmed him.

Intellectuals, including Bourne's former mentor, the pragmatist John Dewey (1859–1952), seemed to him to *desire* war, finding in it a congenial consensus and range of opportunities for movements for social reform and reconstruction. The war was a nightmare; to Bourne, America's leading intellectuals seemed not really to have absorbed this fact. Yet how could they miss feeling the impact of the war's devastation? When, for example, the British launched their attack on the first day (July 1, 1916) of the Battle of the Somme, they suffered 60,000 casualties; by mid-November British casualties had reached 400,000 for a gain of 8 miles. In his analysis of the war, and attention to facts like these, Bourne thus was also examining modern America's ever-increasing professionalism and specialization and its reliance upon the expertise of a pragmatic managerial class, a class, in his view, that had lost sight of the humane spirit of William James and that was ready and willing to use authoritarian controls against its subject-citizens.

Bourne's critique of Dewey was powerful but, it must be said, overwrought, and it still haunts Dewey's reputation, distorting it and leading attention away from the liberal democratic values that this philosopher and educator espoused through most of his career. As early as the late 1890s and early 1900s, when Dewey taught at the University of Chicago, he told his classes that the "democratic ideal" was expressed in the key words of the French Revolution – liberty, equality, and fraternity. In his writings on educational theory, which include such seminal texts as *The School and Society* (1900), *The Child and the Curriculum* (1902), and *Democracy and Education* (1916), and in the pedagogical reforms he fought for, Dewey strongly favored "cooperation" and "community." "Democracy," he stated in 1927, "must begin at home, and its home is the neighborly community," and he emphasized that "experience" must be the source of (and testing ground for) ideas.

Dewey was committed to freedom of speech and inquiry, to individual rights, and, particularly by the late 1920s and 1930s, to the democratic renewal of society. He called for a "socialization" of the economy, a plan that involved the redistribution of wealth, massive programs in public works and housing, and the nationalization of basic industries and resources. This was a plan that Dewey thought could unite farmers, workers, and members of the middle class in a radical third-party movement. He also continued to write important books during the post-war decades, including *Reconstruction in Philosophy* (1920), *Human Nature and Conduct* (1922), *Experience and Nature* (1929), and *Art as Experience* (1934), and he criticized Marxist philosophy, the Communist Party in America, and Stalinism.

Dewey's work as an anti-Stalinist – he chaired the commission of inquiry in 1937 that investigated the charges made against Leon Trotsky during the Moscow purge trials – and as a socialist democrat (which is how he understood himself) lay well in the future, however. In 1917, when America entered the war, Dewey seemed to Bourne to be a self-deluded agent for capitalism and militarism. Bourne's tone about Dewey and the other pro-war intellectuals resonates with a feeling of intellectual betrayal. He had valued and learned from Dewey's pragmatism and progressivism and his emphasis on philosophy as rooted in the community and actively engaged in the solving of problems. He appreciated the educational reforms that Dewey had undertaken and wrote about them in two books, *The Gary Schools* (1916) and *Education and Living* (1917). He believed that he knew the direction of Dewey's ideas – that they were in accord with William James's; he was shocked when this critical thinker and open-minded intellectual welcomed war (or so it seemed) and presumed he could direct it. Bourne concluded: "If the war is too strong for you to prevent, how is it going to be weak enough for you to control and mold to your liberal purposes?"

For Bourne, as he observed in "The War and the Intellectuals," government leaders, businessmen, and intellectuals had become allies:

The war sentiment, begun so gradually but so perseveringly by the preparedness advocates who came from the ranks of big business, caught hold of one after another of the intellectual groups ... The intellectuals, in other words, have identified themselves with the least democratic forces in American life ... Numbers of intelligent people who had never been stirred by the horrors of capitalistic peace at home were shaken out of their slumber by the horrors of the war in Belgium. Never having felt responsibility for labor wars and oppressed masses and excluded races at home, they had a large fund of idle emotional capital to invest in the oppressed nationalities and ravaged villages of Europe. Hearts that had felt only ugly contempt for democratic strivings at home beat in tune with the struggle for freedom abroad.

Bourne sometimes sounded like a Marxist, but he did not define himself as one, and his friends were unsure whether he had ever read Marx's and Engels's works. He was aware, of course, of the Russian Revolution (the Bolsheviks overthrew the Kerensky government in November 1917, and made peace with Germany in March 1918); and, beginning in late 1917, he referred to Lenin approvingly (and naively) on several occasions. (Cf. Max Eastman, in his editorial for the inaugural issue [March 1918] of *The Liberator*: "Never was the moment more auspicious to issue a great magazine of liberty. With the Russian people in the lead, the world is entering upon the experiment of industrial and real democracy ... America has extended her hand to the Russians. She will follow in their path. The world is in the rapids. The possibilities of change in this day are beyond imagination.") As a critic, however, Bourne's introduction to radical and progressive ideas originated with a reading of Henry George's call for social conscience and the single-tax in *Progress and Poverty* (1879). In this book and in *Social Problems* (1884), George had lashed the "unnatural inequality in the distribution of wealth which is fraught with so much evil and danger"; and he went on to mock the general praise for American "progress" when in truth the United States "differentiates our people into the monstrously rich and the frightfully poor." For Bourne, these words pointed to America's indifference to its suffering citizens, its lack of sympathy for the impoverished and victimized.

Bourne focused on the fearful destruction of persons – the deformations of minds and hearts – that industrialism had caused. He designed his own critical positions and alternatives – which combined personal and social liberation – through an always-in-process blend of the English essayist Goldsworthy Lowes Dickinson, Emerson, Whitman, Nietzsche, Dewey, William James, Henri Bergson, Josiah Royce, Tolstoy, and James Harvey Robinson, a reform-minded historian at Columbia. James, it bears repeating, was very important. Bourne noted in a letter (January 16, 1913) that James's books furnished "the most inspiring modern outlook on life and reality." James facilitated openness to experience and to pragmatic testing and exploration of ideas, and, said Bourne, he was everywhere opposed to dry, abstract "intellectualism" – which, in a letter (March 27, 1918) to Van Wyck Brooks, Bourne contrasted with the Jamesian "warm area of pragmatic life."

Both James and, until the war years, Dewey were exhilarating for Bourne, perhaps less in what they proposed than in what they dispensed with. As Dewey explained in "The Influence of Darwin on Philosophy" (1910):

Intellectual progress usually occurs through sheer abandonment of questions together with both of the alternatives they assume – an abandonment that results from their decreasing vitality and a change of urgent interest. We do not solve them: we get over them. Old questions are solved by disappearing, evaporating, while new questions corresponding to the changed attitude of endeavor and preference take their place.

Bourne referred to himself as a socialist, yet he indicted socialists as among the worst offenders in capitulating to the hysteria of the war. Waldo Frank remarked in 1919 that the war had driven most intellectuals "mad" but had driven Bourne "sane," and the art and music critic Paul Rosenfeld (1890–1946) a few years later praised him as "our bannerman of values in the general collapse."

Bourne was a progressive intellectual and a man of letters who preserved the practice of "irony," a term that for him connoted the second point of view, the dissection of majority opinion, the resistance to easy certitude, and the effort to avoid "premature crystallization" of thought. He ranged widely, writing sympathetically, for example, about the feminist movement, decrying "masculine domination" and its distorting effect on institutions. He caustically but productively treated education and, especially, the teaching of the humanities, and deftly assessed such literary figures as Mencken, the humanist scholar Paul Elmer More, Cather, Dostoyevsky, and Dreiser. (Dreiser judged Bourne's criticism of his novels to be superior to anything that Mencken had written about them.)

But even more significant than these pieces are two essays from 1916, "Trans-National America" and "The Jew and Trans-National America," which outlined Bourne's argument for cultural pluralism. These essays explored immigration and American identity, issues that the outbreak of the war had made all the more controversial.

Between 1880 and 1890, more than 5 million immigrants came to America. The number fell to under 4 million between 1890 and 1900, but then surged to nearly 9 million during the first decade of the new century. Many of those arriving in the early 1900s were Catholics, many more were Jews from Eastern Europe. By 1910, 36 percent of Chicago's population of 2 million was foreign-born. In New York City, the figure was 40 percent. It was a "devil's dream" of a city, remarked Michael Gold in *Jews Without Money* (1930), with its "crazy mingling of races and religions in its population of five million."

In the latter decades of the nineteenth century, and in the first decades of the twentieth, the vast numbers of immigrants disturbed political and intellectual leaders. The Democratic Party platform of 1892 stated: "We heartily approve of all legitimate efforts to prevent the United States from being used as the dumping ground for the known criminals and professional paupers of Europe." In the same year, *The Atlantic Monthly* published Thomas Bailey Aldrich's poem "The Unguarded Gates":

> Wide open and unguarded stand our gates,
> And through them presses a wild motley throng –
> Men from the Volga and the Tartar steppes,
> Featureless figures of the Hoang-Ho,
> Malayan, Scythian, Teuton, Kelt, and Slav,
> Flying the Old World's poverty and scorn;
> These bringing with them unknown gods and rites,
> Those, tiger passions, here to stretch their claws.
> In street and alley what strange tongues are loud,
> Accents of menace alien to our air,
> Voices that once the Tower of Babel knew!
> O Liberty, white Goddess! Is it well
> To leave the gates unguarded?

Even before the United States entered the war, politicians, educators, and journalists clamored for unswerving loyalty to the nation and warned against the unreliable, possibly treasonous attitudes of newly arrived foreigners who displayed a "hyphen" (e.g., Italian-American, Polish-American) in their name.

These immigrants frightened the Eastern establishment and genteel order: their customs were strange, and their language was not English. Writing in 1902, Woodrow Wilson stated that "the immigrant newcomers of recent years are men of the lowest class from the South of Italy, and men of the meaner sort out of Hungary and Poland, men out of the ranks where there was neither skill nor energy, nor any initiative or quick intelligence." This view was directly at odds with the hopes and ideals of the immigrants themselves. As Mary Antin – a Polish Jew who immigrated to Boston in 1894 when she was thirteen, and author of *The Promised Land* (1912) – observed in "They Who Knock at Our Gates": "Never was the bread of freedom more keenly relished than it is to-day, by the very people of whom it is said that they covet only the golden platter on which it is served up . . . Nobly built upon the dreams of the fathers, the house of our Republic is nobly tenanted by those who cherish similar dreams"

(March 1914). But by 1918, Wilson was intent upon mass obedience to his war aims and spoke even more crudely: "any man who carries a hyphen about him carries a dagger that he is ready to plunge into the vitals of this Republic."

The immigrant tide was dismaying as well to Henry James, who expressed his panic in *The American Scene* (1907) at the swarming masses he saw in New York City and lamented the manner in which their "babel of tongues" profaned the English language. And it troubled the liberals and progressives who edited, or were associated with, *The New Republic*, which had been launched in 1914. On the basis of a recommendation from Ellery Sedgwick, editor of *The Atlantic Monthly*, Bourne had been invited to join the staff of *The New Republic*, and he wrote a number of pieces for the journal in its first years. But Bourne was too radical for Croly, Lippmann, and others in their orbit. He judged that the liberal ideas favored by the editors wrongly stressed social control and efficiency and an ideology of "homogeneity" that sapped the strength that immigrant groups could bring to American culture. *The New Republic* warned of the dangers to social harmony that "unassimilable communities" posed and called for a national board to supervise and educate "aliens," a proposal that Bourne rejected.

The demands for a disciplining of immigrants grew more intense as the war slogged on in Europe and as America's soldiers joined the struggle. There was widespread suppression of dissent and vigorous efforts at propaganda. The Committee on Public Information, directed by George Creel, for instance, was a government effort to rally support behind war measures through posters, pamphlets, parades, "Loyalty Leagues" in immigrant neighborhoods, and 75,000 "Four-Minute Men" who gave four-minute pro-war speeches in schools and churches. As the US entered the war, President Wilson declared: "It is not an army we must shape and train for war. It is a nation." Creel's mission was to produce uniformity of opinion. He said he believed in "freedom of speech and press" but stressed that the country could not accept the divisions and disagreements that prevented unity in wartime: "These were conditions that could not be permitted to endure . . . What had to be driven home was that all business was the nation's business, and every task a common task for a single purpose" (*How We Advertised America*, 1920).

With the Espionage Act (June 1917), the Postmaster General banned the radical magazines *The Masses* and *American Socialist* from the mails. Other limitations on free speech were enforced by the Sabotage Act (April 1918); the Sedition Act (May 1918); and the *Schenck* v. *United States* case, in which the Supreme Court upheld the conviction of a socialist who had mailed pamphlets that advocated draft resistance. An editorial in the *Washington Post* maintained: "there is no time to waste on hair-splitting over infringement of liberty."

German books were removed from libraries. In Nebraska, "German names were frowned upon, the German language was tabooed in classrooms, and suspected pro-Germans were carefully watched for evidence of treason. Eight university professors were charged with 'lack of aggressive loyalty.' A hearing was conducted by the University Board of Regents and the resignation of three of the men requested." (WPA American Guide Series)

Posters declared that "German agents are everywhere," and notices were published in newspapers urging readers to report to the Justice Department "the man who spreads pessimistic stories, cries for peace, or belittles our effort to win the war." German music, opera, literature, and language fell from favor. Hamburgers were renamed "liberty sandwiches." This assault on everyone and everything German even contributed to the success of the long campaign to prohibit the drinking of alcohol. Passed by Congress in December 1917, ratified in 1919, and beginning on January 16, 1920, the Eighteenth Amendment, prohibiting the "manufacture, transport, and sale of intoxicating liquors," gained important momentum because brewers (for example, Busch and Pabst) and beer-drinking were associated with America's German enemies.

Speaking in 1918, in Canton, Ohio, in words that led to his arrest and a ten-year prison sentence, the socialist leader Eugene V. Debs declared: "They tell us that we live in a great free republic, that our institutions are democratic, that we are a free and self-governing people. This is too much, even for a joke . . . The master class has always declared the wars, the subject class has always fought the battles. The master class has had all to gain and nothing to lose, while the subject class has had nothing to gain and all to lose – especially their lives." Refusing to pardon Debs, Wilson said: "While the flower of American youth was pouring out its blood to vindicate the cause of civilization, Debs stood behind the lines sniping, attacking, and denouncing them." Debs, nonetheless, reaffirmed his views in his statement to the Court before he was taken to the federal penitentiary in Atlanta:

I am opposing a social order in which it is possible for one man who does absolutely nothing that is useful to amass a fortune of hundreds of millions of dollars, while millions of men and women who work all the days of their lives secure barely enough for a wretched existence.

A number of critics, journalists, and intellectuals were jingoistic and racist. Stuart Sherman, in "American and Allied Ideals – An Appeal to Those Who Are Neither Hot nor Cold" (1918), denounced immigrant groups who had failed to adopt "American" ways, and he decried "alien" desecration of the national genius. Writing some years after the war had ended (1923), the critic Ernest Boyd termed Sherman's literary, cultural, and political project an example of the rampant "Ku Klux Kriticism" that "would see to it that American literature be Nordic, Protestant, and blond" and that regarded the United States as "an Anglo-Saxon colony unfortunately afflicted by the influx of aliens." Such "Kriticism" was common during the war years, and it continued at a fever pitch afterwards.

In "Trans-National America," Bourne responded to this surging anti-immigrant sentiment. He criticized the idea of America as a "melting pot" that obliged immigrants to surrender their native cultures and mix into the mainstream. In Bourne's estimation, this was profoundly anti-democratic and jarred against America's commitment to the consent of the governed. He insisted that the immigrants themselves should "have a hand" in the making of the United States and should not be forced to accommodate to the wishes of the "ruling class" of "British stocks" who occupied the positions of power. These members of the dominant class and culture were simply the first immigrants, and, Bourne added, they had hardly shown any eagerness to "adopt the culture" of the Indians who were living on land upon which the British intended to settle.

World War I, Bourne went on to point out, was fomenting anti-immigrant feelings and leading to a new outpouring of assimilationist and pro-British attitudes. Endless assertions of the superiority of "English snobberies, English religion, English literary styles, English literary reverences and canons, English ethics, English superiorities, have been the cultural food that we have drunk in from our mother's breast." It was time to stop copying the Arnoldians, Bourne concluded, and time to begin capitalizing upon the potential for a dynamic America that was present in the traditions of the different immigrant groups.

Bourne hoped for "a new cosmopolitan ideal," a "federation of cultures":

America is a unique sociological fabric, and it bespeaks poverty of imagination not to be thrilled at the incalculable potentialities of so novel a union of men. To seek no other goal than the weary old nationalism, – belligerent, exclusive, inbreeding, the poison of which we are witnessing now in Europe, – is to make patriotism a hollow sham, and to declare that, in spite of our boastings, America must ever be a follower and not a leader of nations.

While Bourne aimed to displace the bigoted Eastern establishment (presided over by Matthew Arnold's spirit, Bourne believed), he was, in a sense, in the midst himself of an Arnoldian attempt to cut through provinciality. In "The Function of Criticism at the Present Time," Arnold had referred to the idea of Europe as, "for intellectual and spiritual purposes, one great confederation." He, too, fought against self-congratulatory nationalisms and the failure to widen cultural horizons. Bourne disliked Arnold's American followers, but, like Arnold, he was dedicated to flexibility and appreciation of multiple perspectives upon experience. An America populated by immigrants who retained their cultures would mean a better culture for all. Men and women could "breathe a larger air" and move toward an "international mind" and "new cosmopolitan outlook." They would be empowered to create an environment that Bourne, following the American philosopher Josiah Royce, named "the Beloved Community."

Like its companion-essay "The Jew and Trans-National America," which presented the Jew's "dual allegiance" to America and "the Jewish nation" as a form of "internationalism," "Trans-National America" articulated the benefits of cultural pluralism. Bourne urged America to crack through its shell of prejudice, and he named Jewish critics, jurists, philosophers, and journalists – Louis Brandeis, Felix Frankfurter, Harold Laski, Walter Lippmann, Horace Kallen, Morris R. Cohen – as representatives of the type of intellectual leadership he desired. One wonders how Bourne's critical work might have developed during the 1920s and beyond. He died, thirty-two years old, during the influenza epidemic of 1918–19 that killed 10 million people worldwide, 500,000 in the United States alone.

Sometimes an echo of Carlyle's voice in its less attractive tones skews Bourne's writing. His emphasis on fluidity and dynamism then is transformed into something restrictive and confining, as when he warns that without clear cultural values and loyalties, men and women arriving in America would pursue "license," not "liberty":

They become the flotsam and jetsam of American life, the downward undertow of our civilization with its leering cheapness and falseness of taste and spiritual outlook, the absence of mind and sincere feeling which we see in our slovenly towns, our vapid moving pictures, our popular novels, and in the vacuous faces of the crowds on the city street. This is the cultural wreckage of our time, and it is from the fringes of the Anglo-Saxon as well as the other stocks that it falls. America has as yet no impelling integrating force. It makes too easily for this detritus of cultures. In our loose, free country, no constraining national purpose, no tenacious folk-tradition and folk-style hold the people to a line.

For someone committed to cultural pluralism, Bourne also was limited in his understanding of popular culture and mass entertainment. In an article published in *The New Republic* in 1915, he assailed "lowbrow snobbery":

In a thousand ways it is as tyrannical and arrogant as the other culture of universities and millionaires and museums. I don't know which ought to be more offensive to a true democrat – this or the cheapness of the current life that so sadly lacks any raciness or characteristic savor. It looks as if we should have to resist the stale culture of the masses as we resist the stale culture of the aristocrat. It is very easy to be lenient and pseudo-human, and call it democracy.

Bourne's shortcomings should not detract from the courage and power shown by his work at its best. And it is one sign of the anti-immigrant fervor he was challenging that by the mid-1920s, the resurgent Ku Klux Klan, hostile not only to African-Americans but also to Jews and Catholics – had grown to more than 3 million members, including 500,000 women. On August 8, 1925, the Ku Klux Klan rallied in Washington, DC, and 40,000 Klan members paraded down Pennsylvania Avenue. In an essay published in 1926, Hiram Evans, Imperial Wizard of the Klan, declared:

The Klansman believes in the greatest possible diversity and individualism within the limits of the American spirit. But he believes also that few aliens can understand that spirit, that fewer try to, and that there must be resistance, intolerance even, toward anything that threatens it, or the fundamental national unity based upon it.

Others expressed similar views. Henry Pratt Fairchild, a Yale sociologist, comparing the nation to a tree in *The Melting-Pot Mistake* (1926), warned of the danger posed by "foreign forces which, among trees, are represented by minute hostile organisms that make their way into the very tissue of the tree itself and feed upon its life substances, and among nations to alien individuals who are accepted as immigrants and by a process of 'boring from within' . . . sap the very vitality of their host." Madison Grant, a lawyer, naturalist, and advocate of immigration restriction, stated in "Closing the Flood-Gates," in a collection titled *The Alien in Our Midst or, Selling Our Birthright for a Mess of Pottage* (1930): "Instead of a population homogeneous in race, religion, traditions and aspiration, as was the American nation down to 1840, we have – inserted into the body politic – an immense influx of foreigners, congregated for the most part in the large cities and in the industrial centers."

These were the anti-immigrant ideas and arguments that Bourne contested, and they had widespread support, reaching to the highest levels of the government. The words that the essayist John Jay Chapman wrote in a biography of the abolitionist William Lloyd Garrison (1913) could be applied to Bourne, and to the anger that greeted his anti-war and pluralist essays: "When a whole age is completely insane upon some subject, sane views upon that subject will seem like madness to the age."

Chapman (1862–1933) himself was, it seems, barely known to Bourne, Brooks, and other proponents of literary and cultural renaissance and political renewal. (An exception here is Herbert Croly, who admired Chapman and cited him

favorably in *The Promise of American Life.*) Chapman's marginality in the history
of American letters puzzled later admirers, such as Edmund Wilson, who
included a lively appreciation of Chapman in *The Triple Thinkers* (1938; rev.
1948). He should have counted in the life of the culture more than he did, and
have given progressive values a push forward. But, full of promise, his career
was a disappointment, and he was much the agent of his own downfall.

Chapman was a superb writer on political and literary subjects throughout
the 1890s and early 1900s. His biography of Garrison, along with a pungent
piece on Emerson, provided a shrewd examination of nineteenth-century individualism and reform; and Chapman elaborated the contemporary relevance
of the Garrisonian and Emersonian legacies in two political tracts, *Causes and
Consequences* (1898) and *Practical Agitation* (1900). He described with biting
accuracy the corruption of American politics, culture, and education by business and corporate power, and he stressed the importance of local (and often
lonely) forms of moral resistance against the pervasive rule of wealth. Chapman
wrote lively books and essays on religion and ethics, drama and poetry, and he
carried on an extensive correspondence.

But after his son Victor's tragic death at Verdun in June 1916 (he was the
first American pilot killed in the war), Chapman became a furious spokesman
for blood sacrifice and super-patriotism. He grew crazed about the influence
of the Catholic Church, feared the new immigrants, morbidly worried about
"the masses," vented wild notions about conspiratorial Jewish control of big
business, and cheered the Ku Klux Klan's "rational" program. Most of his
literary work in the final decades of his life was in an isolated way devoted to
Greek drama and philosophy, Dante, and Shakespeare. He had nothing valuable
to say about the outpouring of American, English, and European poetry, drama,
and criticism that began in the 1900s. Nor did he write about the development
of literary realism by Twain, Howells, James, Dreiser, Wharton, and others,
even though he knew and exchanged letters with a number of them. He either
was unaware of the central writers, texts, and tendencies of the modernist
movement or else was not interested enough to deal with them.

The main reason for Chapman's lack of influence was the limited range of
his sensibility, and his critical temperament hardened in the second half of
his career when he lapsed into moody, baffled resentment toward Americans
outside his social class. But the fault lay, too, with Bourne and Brooks, who
knew little about the liberal, progressive, and radical voices in America that
had preceded their own.

The most extraordinary moment in Chapman's career occurred in August
1911, when he traveled to Coatesville, Pennsylvania, to protest the lynching of
a black man. He rented a room in the hostile town and held a prayer meeting

there, at which time he read from the Bible and delivered a brief address. The only people who were present with him as he cried out against America's shame and compared this nation's "heart" to "the heart of the criminal – a cold thing, an awful thing" – were an elderly black woman and a spy for the town. Chapman's action and words had behind them his reverence for Garrison, Wendell Phillips, and his own abolitionist ancestors (one of whom was his grandmother Maria Weston Chapman, an activist in the anti-slavery agitation in Boston). The example of the abolitionists gave him strength and moral authority.

Yet their lessons did not lead Chapman toward a full concern for freedom, tolerance, and civil rights. During the war, he took issue with the principles of free speech, and he obsessively blasted Catholics, immigrants, and Jews. Chapman's career resembles Carlyle's, and it is striking that in 1923 the alienated Chapman wrote a lengthy essay (it was never published) on Carlyle. In it he noted Carlyle's internal conflicts, frustration, and pride, and the mismatch between this eloquent "genius" and the age in which he lived. Chapman etched a harsh, skeptical portrait of Carlyle that amounted to a confession of his own failure of democratic faith.

Another career that did not quite work out is Paul Rosenfeld's (1890–1946). Rosenfeld was born in New York City, the son of prosperous, cultured parents. But after his mother's death when the boy was eight, his father fell into decline and depression, dying in 1908. Raised by his maternal grandmother, Rosenfeld attended a military academy in Poughkeepsie, New York, and then went on to Yale and the Columbia School of Journalism. Keenly interested in the arts, and the beneficiary of a sizable inheritance, Rosenfeld spent a year in Europe and then returned to New York City where he became part of a group of innovative and progressive artists and writers, including Bourne, Brooks, and the photographer Alfred Stieglitz.

During the 1910s and 1920s, Rosenfeld wrote hundreds of articles on music, art, and literature, publishing them in *The New Republic*, *The Seven Arts*, *Vanity Fair*, *The Nation*, and other prominent journals, and throughout the 1920s his Gramercy Park apartment functioned as a salon for literary and artistic readings and presentations. His first book, one of his best, was *Musical Portraits* (1920), and it was followed by six other collections. *The Port of New York* (1924) is especially rich and coherently organized, featuring (in order) essays on "fourteen American moderns": Albert P. Ryder, Van Wyck Brooks, Carl Sandburg, Marsden Hartley, William Carlos Williams, the progressive educator Margaret Naumburg, the artist and teacher Kenneth Hayes Miller, Roger H. Sessions, John Marin, Arthur G. Dove, Sherwood Anderson, Georgia O'Keeffe, Randolph Bourne (who died in Rosenfeld's apartment in 1918), and Alfred Stieglitz. As Rosenfeld explained in the Foreword:

These creators, independently, through different mediums, and in different manners, had nevertheless all of them given me the sensation one has when, at the close of a prolonged journey by boat, the watergate comes by, and one steps forth and stands with solid under foot. For the first time, among these modern men and women, I found myself in an America where it was good to be.

Rosenfeld's prose can sometimes feel both perceptive and over-flush with his own exuberance, as in his opening paragraph from the essay on the painter Ryder:

The Ryders hang dark on the museum walls; pools of very dusk in gilt borders; cold glamorous patterns pitched so low that for a while they resist the eye, and open with extreme reluctancy their dreamy spells. The rigid, heavily enameled surfaces have the color of night when the moon is small and chill and hard; of ancient tapestries sewn with threads of tarnished metal; of sere leaves in November and the smoke-blue of winter woodlands. Disks of saddest silver burn icily amid profound and undulant blacks. Blacks glide smoothly, silently, like streams in the dark; pierced by bright-ness only in pinpricks, and limited by areas of citron or of gray nearly as low in key as they themselves. Dullest gold of night-cloud edge is subtly and mystically harmonized with sable, or with the aureate brown of embossed leathers. The utmost reaches in vibrance in the gorgeous, fissured rectangles are rose-violets of the ulti-mate agony of day in the west, and rims of light pale as the greening skies of the afterglow.

But to his contemporaries, these sentences were powerful and intense, show-ing what it meant to respond passionately, with conviction, to challenging works of art.

And many of Rosenfeld's sentences are sharp and vivid. In *Men Seen: Twenty-Four Modern Authors* (1925), he writes about D. H. Lawrence: "He holds the mirror up to men in their most secret trouble." He is provocative too about Wallace Stevens's playfully outlandish *Harmonium*: "Yet this fastidious, aris-tocratic nature possesses a blunt power of utterance, a concentrated violence, that is almost naturalistic . . . We discover him momentarily piling gristling images, fine roughnesses of color and acrid turns of language upon each other, hacking with lines of poetry and banging harsh rhyme upon rhyme."

Edmund Wilson recalled reading Rosenfeld's essays on Sibelius, Strauss, and other composers while he was in France in the late 1910s and then reading still more of Rosenfeld's work when he returned to New York City: "These essays amazed me. They had a kind of fullness of tone, a richness of vocabulary and imagery, and a freedom of the cultural world that were quite different from the schoolmasterish criticism that had become the norm in the United States." Rosenfeld, the critic Kenneth Burke later noted, made readers "feel the *urgency* of art" and possessed a rare "intensity of esthetic responsiveness."

Rosenfeld's career faltered in the 1930s, however. It was a different literary era – tough, grim, politicized – without the thrill of the new that had inspired him as a young man coming upon modernism in art, literature, and music. Rosenfeld suffered from poor health; his investments were nearly wiped out during the stock market crash of 1929; and he fell out of favor with the periodicals that had once welcomed him. He tried his hand at fiction and autobiography, but unsuccessfully, though his critical writing revived somewhat in the 1940s when he published in *The Kenyon Review* and literary quarterlies.

The reformer and settlement worker Jane Addams (1860–1935) was not a cultural critic like Rosenfeld, but a social critic, and another of the era's avid readers of Carlyle. She once remarked that she understood her religious and social mission "from the Bible and observation, from books and people and in no small degree from Carlyle." In particular Addams drew from Carlyle the belief that moral ideals should be translated into action. "But indeed Conviction," wrote Carlyle in *Sartor Resartus*, "were it never so excellent, is worthless till it converts itself into Conduct." Ruskin, William Morris, the French social theorist Auguste Comte, and Tolstoy (whom Addams met in 1896 and described as "one of the gentlest and kindest of human creatures I ever saw") also figured in the formation of this reformer's thought, and, even more, so did the pragmatism and experimentalism that William James and Dewey articulated.

Addams was renowned among intellectuals not only for the concrete achievement of Hull-House, the settlement that she helped to establish in 1889, but also for the manner in which her books and articles embodied her character and testified to her "oneness" with experience. "She simply *inhabits reality*," William James remarked, "and everything she says necessarily expresses its nature." Meeting Addams in 1898, the English reformer Beatrice Webb was struck by her "charming grey eyes and gentle voice and graphic power of expression."

Addams was born in the farming town of Cedarville, Illinois, the eighth child of wealthy parents. She attended local public schools, and then Rockford Female Seminary (later, Rockford College) from 1877 to 1881, where she was an outstanding student and campus leader. Having completed her B.A., she began studies at the Woman's Medical College in Philadelphia, but fell into a long period of poor health, which lasted two years, and she did not resume her medical education and training. In August 1883 Addams traveled to Europe, where for the next two years she devoted herself to literature, history, philosophy, foreign languages, art, and architecture. She returned to the United States in 1885 but then, still uncertain of her course in life, she made in December 1887 another trip to Europe, where she responded to the cause of social reform she witnessed in England, at the London settlement house Toynbee Hall. By January 1889, she was underway in her own mission of reform, seeking out a house in the poorest neighborhood of Chicago. Together with her companion Ellen Gates Starr, in September 1889 she rented and moved into the Hull mansion on South Halsted Street, and thus the Hull-House experiment began.

Cultural life at Hull-House included music and art studios and a book-bindery, and a theater company. But Addams went well beyond poetry readings and talks by visiting artists. She also started a day-care nursery, a boarding club for working girls, a boys' club and gymnasium, a woman's club, literacy classes to prepare those seeking to become US citizens, a community kitchen, and a labor museum. Expanding her work to the community at large, Addams and her colleagues embarked upon making changes in the court system, sanitation, playgrounds and schools, and drug and prostitution laws. One of her associates in reform was the philosopher John Dewey at the University of Chicago, and she was one of the leaders in establishing its School of Social Work. The influence of Dewey on Addams's thought is evident in *Twenty Years at Hull-House* (1910): "The one thing to be dreaded in the Settlement is that it lose its flexibility, its power of quick adaptation, its readiness to change its methods as its environment may demand."

Addams's interests and ventures in reform touched on education, city government, immigration, medicine, prostitution, factory conditions and trade unions, suffrage, and world peace, and she expressed her views in *Democracy and Social Ethics* (1902), *Newer Ideals of Peace* (1906), *The Spirit of Youth and the City Streets* (1909), *A New Conscience and an Ancient Evil* (1912), *Women at the Hague* (1915), and *Peace and Bread in Time of War* (1922). She also wrote two autobiographical volumes, *Twenty Years at Hull-House* and *The Second Twenty Years at Hull-House* (1930). All of these books demonstrated Addams's critical insight, and were enlivened by her commitment to social responsibility and community, especially forms of community that strong, courageous, independent women created.

Like Bourne, Addams was intent upon defining progressive solutions to the problems that immigration had created in America's major cities, and she implemented the changes in education, health, and culture in which she believed. Through *Twenty Years at Hull-House*, which soon became a handbook for social reform, the settlement movement, and working-class education, Addams inspired many women to take up her causes. The lawyer and labor reformer Florence Kelley (who lived at Hull-House for most of the 1890s), the physician and scientific researcher Alice Hamilton (who also lived for a decade at Hull-House), the social worker and welfare activist Julia Lathrop (who was at Hull-House from 1890 to 1909), and the social reformer and labor activist Frances Kellor (who also lived at Hull-House periodically) were among the reformers whose vocations took shape from Addams's life and writings.

Addams believed that "private beneficence is totally inadequate to deal with the vast numbers of the city's disinherited." "The common stock of intellectual enjoyment," she insisted, "should not be difficult of access because of the economic position of him who would approach it." She communicated these beliefs in her books and essays, summing up their purpose in the Introduction to *The Excellent Becomes the Permanent* (1932): "To marshal the moral forces capable of breaking what must be broken and of building what must be built; to reconstruct our social relationships through a regeneration of the human heart; to repair a world shattered by war and sodden with self-seeking; to establish moral control over a mass of mechanical achievements."

Again like Bourne, Addams stood among the small band of intellectuals and men and women of letters who opposed America's entry into World War I. She sent a letter to Bourne, thanking him for his critique of *The New Republic*'s endorsement of the war; and after the war was over, she observed in *Peace and Bread* that Bourne had accurately diagnosed Dewey's and the liberals' "pathetic belief in the regenerative results of war" and had exposed the "entire absence of critical spirit" with which intellectuals had supported the war effort. Before the war, one of the most admired persons in the nation, Addams was attacked in newspapers and magazines, and was expelled from the Daughters of the American Revolution. An article in the *Los Angeles Times*, March 1918, noted: "It was only when a great war raged in the world, tremendous international emotions were let loose, that this good woman essayed a task beyond her, and in excess of zeal and shocked horror, stood forth for peace when there was no peace, and made public utterances from a full heart that were better left unsaid."

Addams, however, was very tough-minded: she was hardly the genteel, spiritualized, unworldly lady that some mythmakers invented (though she sometimes encouraged this image of herself). It was her combination of political astuteness, business acumen, and skill at compromise and alliance-building that made Hull-House successful and marked Addams's break with earlier models of appropriate behavior for women.

Addams envisioned the process of reform as radiating outward from specific moral acts that individuals undertook in common cause. Addams began with a single house in an impoverished Chicago neighborhood and made it the foundation for a campaign for justice, tolerance, equality, brotherhood and sisterhood, and cooperation that spread throughout the city, the state, the nation (by 1900 there were more than 100 settlements), and the entire world. Addams recognized that events across the globe altered the most minor of day-to-day affairs at the settlement. And this "international" conception of her enterprise became even more apparent during World War I and afterwards; as she stated in *The Second Twenty Years at Hull-House*, "our own experiences are more and more influenced by the experiences of widely scattered people; the modern world is developing an almost mystic consciousness of the continuity and interdependence of mankind." The woman who in 1895 sought out and secured a post as a health inspector, rising at six in the morning to make certain that garbage was properly collected, was also the woman who in 1915 presided over an International Congress of Women, organized The Women's International League for Peace and Freedom, and received the Nobel Prize for Peace in 1931.

As a social critic, Addams shared the romantic optimism that animated the early essays of Bourne and Brooks. For her as for them, literary and philosophical texts functioned as instruments by which to respond to experience and furnished ideas and analogies that would elucidate politics and economics. Sometimes this tendency in Addams's own literary work seems quaint, as when she keyed a piece on the 1894 Pullman Strike to a comparison between the financier George Pullman and Shakespeare's King Lear. But this placement of labor struggle within a literary framework possessed polemical power and aroused heated opposition. One editor after another rejected this essay – Horace Scudder of *The Atlantic Monthly* complained that Addams implied that "Pullman was in the wrong" – and it did not appear in print until 1912.

In her many books and essays, Addams described the lives of the poor, even as she saw the difference between her status as a worker for the poor and the lot of the poor themselves. As she reflected in *Twenty Years at Hull-House*, she never lost "the harrowing consciousness of the difference in economic conditions between ourselves and our neighbors." She also conceded her frequent misperceptions of the people she wished to help, and delved into the ambiguities of her mission as a person carrying "culture" to men and women who were often too weary, ill, impoverished, and overburdened to enjoy it. Addams's work was informed by a sense of "human solidarity," yet as she embraced this ideal, she inquired into the self-interested purposes – social work made *her* feel better, she confessed – that it fulfilled.

Addams furthermore perceived, as many intellectuals and reformers did not, the segregation and bigotry that blighted the lives of black Americans. She called this, in *The Second Twenty Years at Hull-House*, "the gravest situation in our American life": "it means an enormous loss of capacity to the nation when great ranges of human life are hedged about with antagonism." Addams was alert to the antagonism – the hatred of "difference" – directed toward African-Americans and immigrants, and she condemned the repression and intolerance in the United States that World War I and the "Red Scare," the federal crackdown on Communists and radicals (1919–20), intensified.

Addams scrutinized her allegiance to literary and philosophical texts, remarking, for example, on the temptation to "lumber our minds with literature that only served to cloud the really vital situation spread before our eyes." She reassessed her fondness for Carlyle, too. In *Twenty Years at Hull-House*, she outlined her rapt interest in Carlyle's *Heroes and Hero-Worship* when she was a young woman, but added that Carlyle's exalted rendering of "the hero" eventually came to be replaced for her by Abraham Lincoln's invocations of the common people and passion for the distinctively American "democratic government."

Addams's life and work were limited by her lack of understanding of class conflict and industrialization. Like so many American intellectuals, she felt the divide between the rich and the poor yet could not perceive the clash of their interests and the intense economic opposition between them. She sensed the numbing impact of working conditions in the factories, but could refer only sketchily to how these might be structurally remedied. In her first book, *Democracy and Social Ethics*, she emphasized that the industrial worker "should get a sense of his individual relation to the system." Addams did not question the legitimacy of the system; she took it for granted.

"Feeding a machine," Addams stated,

with a material of which he has no knowledge, producing a product, totally unrelated to the rest of his life, without in the least knowing what becomes of it, or its connection with the community, is, of course, unquestionably deadening to [a man's] intellectual and moral life. To make the moral connection it would be necessary to give him a social consciousness of the value of his work, and at least a sense of participation and a certain joy in its ultimate use; to make the intellectual connection it would be essential to create in him some historic conception of the development of industry and the relation of his individual work to it.

Addams, like Bourne, lapsed into statements of what workers needed to have done *to* and *for* them, as though these people from the lower depths were unable to make the "connections" that intellectuals were smart enough to make. Addams was inclined to view the situation of the working poor as one of humane adjustment and accommodation to the system so that it could be more profitably experienced, with individuals at last morally and intellectually equipped to find an enriched cultural life within it.

On other occasions, Addams was more successful in imagining the capacities that workers already possessed, and, even more, she stressed the possibilities for social change that could proceed from the bottom up. In *Peace and Bread*, she

criticized Woodrow Wilson's self-approving quest for moral leadership during
the years of the war. She maintained that the entire modern period had shown
"the fallacy of such a point of view, a discrediting of the Carlyle contention
that the people must be led into the ways of righteousness by the experience,
acumen and virtues of the great man." In contesting the appeal of the Carlylean
hero and superior man, Addams was unusual among intellectuals and cultural
critics of her time. Most of her liberal and socialist contemporaries gravitated
toward this feature of Carlyle's social prophecy and incorporated it in their
definitions of the literary intellectual's role. The journalist Walter Lippmann
paid Addams this tribute: "She had compassion without condescension. She
had pity without retreat into vulgarity. She had infinite sympathy for common
things without forgetfulness of those that are uncommon . . . Those who have
known her say she was not only good, but great."

The liberals and radicals of the early twentieth century often had trouble
accepting in practice the democratic views they claimed to believe in and
value – a tension they shared with (and likely derived from) Carlyle and Arnold.
Van Wyck Brooks is a case in point. He was a self-professed socialist (Jane
Addams was not), but within limits; he identified himself as a supporter of
"aristocracy in thought, democracy in economics." He pleaded democratically
for a broad improvement of American culture and an end to its materialism,
isolation, and insularity. In *The Wine of the Puritans* (1908), he emphasized the
evils of "machinery," called attention to the accompanying "mechanization"
of the spirit, decried the cultural poverty of the United States, and chastised
writers and educators who were disconnected from the main currents of the
nation. These themes in Brooks's writing would seem to have required a mass
movement for the remaking of culture and consciousness. But to Brooks, the
revitalization of culture was the task of gifted men, Carlylean heroes.

Carlyle was one of Brooks's favorite writers, and his influence is pervasive
in Brooks's essays and books. America needed, Brooks stated on the final page
of *The Wine of the Puritans*, "great constructors, great positive forces, someone
to bind together the estranged fragments of society." His later book, *America's
Coming-of-Age*, reaffirmed this point, beckoning for that "one contagious personality" and "strong thinker" who might inspire working men in America as
Arnold, Morris, and Wells had done in England and as Heine and Nietzsche
had done in Germany.

American intellectuals and men and women of letters did not trust America's
people: they doubted the capacities of the "mass" to choose wisely in either
politics or culture. These sentiments can be located in literary and cultural
conservatives such as James and Wharton, and in the writings of many liberals,
radicals, progressives, and socialists who were anti-democratic democrats. They

denounced complacency, materialism, poverty, degradation, and exploitation, and they insisted on reform and reconstruction, even revolution. But they feared the people for whom they expressed sympathy, and sometimes scorned them as an ignorant herd.

Though Nietzsche was in the intellectual background of this view – as he said in *The Will to Power*, "a declaration of war on the masses by higher men is needed" – it came as much or more from Carlyle. Carlyle's energizing 1841 study, *On Heroes, Hero-Worship, and the Heroic in History*, was read by all of the leading American writers and thinkers; by 1928, there had already been twenty-five American editions. In part the attraction of the book lay in its grand account of captains of war, religion, and politics who fastened on "Truth" and willed their way past monumental difficulties, winning for themselves in the process the veneration of the masses. But for intellectuals intent upon defining their role amid the instabilities of the emerging modern era, Carlyle's book was forceful for another reason. Not only did Carlyle describe the ordering, organizing power of great men, but he also counseled that "men of letters" should be such men.

The "Man-of-Letters Hero," Carlyle reflected, "must be regarded as our most important modern person. He, such as he may be, is the soul of all. What he teaches, the whole world will do and make . . . Whoever can speak, speaking now to the whole nation, becomes a power, a branch of government, with inalienable weight in law-making, in all acts of authority." Carlyle depicted the man of letters as soon to become the acknowledged legislator of the world, and he offered soaring models of intellectual achievement himself. In *Letters and Leadership* (1918), Brooks took this cue and asserted that "poets and novelists and critics are the pathfinders of society; to them belongs the vision without which the people perish"; and later he cited Carlyle's multi-volume *History of Frederick the Great* as the kind of "monumental," visionary work that he aspired to emulate in his *Makers and Finders* series.

Carlyle gave meaning to, and prophetic cast for, the "Literary Life." Such a life would be affirmative and influential: it would be transformative in its impact upon disorderly masses of men and women. Neither the rightward-leaning Pound nor Eliot wrote about Carlyle (though Eliot knew Carlyle's work and taught it in the lecture courses that he gave in Southall beginning in 1916), but Carlyle's honoring of poets and men of letters would doubtless have drawn their assent. The Carlylean accent can be heard in Pound's claim that "artists are the antennae of the race," with its additional point that "the bullet-headed many will never learn to trust their great artists."

The Carlylean commitment to an elite remnant appeared among many literary and cultural opinion-makers. The poet, critic, and Columbia University professor George Woodberry (1855–1930), in "Man and the Race" (1905), affirmed his belief in "literature as an organ of the race-mind, and of education as the process by which the individual enters into the race-mind." For Woodberry, the responsibility for preserving literature rested in the hands of "the body of men" who comprise "the intellectual state," the "republic of letters." In an important early book on Nietzsche (1908), Mencken endorsed the German philosopher's judgment that society consists of "a vast, inert, religious moral slave class" standing beneath "a small, alert, iconoclastic, immoral, progressive master class." In another study of Nietzsche (1912), Paul Elmer More concluded that Nietzsche "saw, as few other men of our day have seen, the danger that threatens true progress in any system of education and government which makes the advantage of the average rather than the distinguished man its first object." The vogue for Nietzsche carried forward the themes that Carlyle had already articulated and embedded in American high-cultural discourse.

Carlyle even influenced the revolutionary anarchist and woman of letters, Emma Goldman (1869–1940). Born in Lithuania, the daughter of innkeepers, she immigrated with her sister to Rochester, New York, in 1885. She worked in a sweatshop, and soon was drawn to the causes of radical politics and women's rights. She moved to New York City (leaving her husband behind), and entered the anarchist circle of the German radical agitator Johann Most. Soon she became a controversial advocate of anarchism; as the editor and author Margaret Anderson (1886–1973) recalled, Goldman "was considered a monster, an exponent of free love and bombs."

In 1917, Goldman and her fellow anarchist Alexander Berkman were arrested for opposing the draft and sent to prison for two years, and in the midst of the Red Scare in 1919, she and Berkman were deported to Russia. There she grew disenchanted with the Bolsheviks, attacking them for betraying the people and persecuting dissenters. In December 1921, she and Berkman left Soviet Russia, and she continued her arguments against the Bolshevik regime while living and traveling widely in Europe and Canada.

Goldman wrote many provocative essays and books, including *The Social Significance of Modern Drama* (1914), *My Disillusionment with Russia* (1925), and her autobiography *Living My Life* (1931). She believed that revolution meant freeing the people from their enslavement to "authority, government, the State"; and when she wrote about the triumph of Communism in Russia, she denounced the Party's subjugation of the masses and its vicious insistence that "the end justifies all means." But her compassion for the masses and her anarchist's faith in popular organic communities had limits, as her best-known book, *Anarchism and Other Essays* (3rd edn., 1917), testifies.

Goldman echoed and alluded to Emerson, Thoreau, and Whitman and seconded their plea for the primacy of the individual. Like the short-story writer and essayist Charlotte Perkins Gilman (1860–1935) and the architect Louis Sullivan, among others, Goldman drew upon the Transcendentalists and their sense of "organic" form to describe the ideal social life. She demanded freedom for all persons, women in particular, describing marriage as a form of legalized prostitution. Like her contemporaries Bourne, Brooks, and Mencken, she also inveighed against the destructive pressure of "Puritanism," condemning it in fierce speeches and essays as a "poisonous germ." Like Bourne, she was opposed to Wilson's involvement of the United States in the war and his restrictions on free speech; as she recalled in *Living My Life*, "No American president had ever before succeeded in so humbugging the people as Woodrow Wilson, who wrote and talked democracy, acted despotically, privately and officially, and yet managed to keep up the myth that he was championing humanity and freedom."

Yet Goldman always stressed the stupidity of the masses of people whom she said she cared so deeply about. She could rant like Carlyle or Nietzsche, as when she announced "I repudiate the mass as a creative factor" and huffed about the "ignorance" of common people. Goldman contended that everybody would become better when authority no longer victimized them, but her repeated emphasis on their "mental indolence" made clear that she thought they were too dumb and docile to save themselves. They needed heroes – original, anti-conventional, inspirational thinkers and "artistic geniuses" such as herself.

"The mass bleeds," and is "being robbed and exploited," Goldman argued, "but the mass itself is responsible for this horrible state of affairs. It clings to its masters, loves the whip, and is the first to cry Crucify! the moment a protesting voice is raised against the sacredness of capitalistic authority or any other decayed institution . . . As a mass it will always be the annihilator of individuality, of free initiative, of individuality." Carlyle had praised German strongmen and judged that the masses should be drilled; Goldman said that the more drilling they received, the more they liked it. They would "always" remain this way.

Lincoln Steffens (1866–1936), unlike Goldman, supported the Russian Revolution, yet he, too, showed in his work an abiding disappointment in common people and favored the preeminent role of the Carlylean strongman or, as he put it, the "big" man who could solve social, political, and cultural problems that most regarded as intractable. Born in San Francisco, Steffens graduated from the University of California and continued his studies in Germany and France. He became a newspaper reporter in New York City, focusing on political corruption and urban reform. An excellent journalist, especially in his work

as managing editor of the mass-circulation magazine *McClure's* from 1901 to
1906, Steffens was frustrated by the slow pace and difficulty of reform, and
impatient toward the people whose lives he wanted to make better. This is
a theme throughout his muckraking journalism, including *The Shame of the
Cities* (1904) and many articles, and it accounts in large measure for his praise
of the Soviet experiment.

As Steffens observed in his autobiography (1931),

> Soviet Russia was a revolutionary government with an evolutionary plan. Their plan
> was, not by direct action to resist such evils as poverty and riches, graft, privilege,
> tyranny, and war, but to seek out and remove the causes of them. They were not
> practicing what we and they preached. They were not trying to establish political
> democracy, legal liberty, and negotiated peace – not now. They were at present only
> laying a basis for these good things. They had set up a dictatorship, supported by
> a small, trained minority, to make and maintain for a few generations a scientific
> rearrangement of economic forces which would result in economic democracy first
> and political democracy last.

Steffens did not believe that the masses, abroad or in America, knew how
to use democracy well, so he proposed the formation of an elite vanguard that
would dictate the conditions of life until the time was right for people to
receive political rights. Steffens admitted the dishonesty in his position, and
in Lenin's, too – the select minority champions rights for all and denies them
in practice – but he endorsed it nonetheless.

The political philosopher and editor Herbert Croly also relied on experts and
managers. As editor of *The New Republic* from 1914 to 1930, Croly supported
Wilson's war measures (though later he and his colleagues broke with Wilson
over the Treaty of Versailles) and argued for the expansion of the central government. By the end of his life, his views had become gloomily disappointed,
as can be seen in his unpublished manuscript *The Breach in Civilization* and in
the manuscript of his autobiography, which he described as "an obituary of a
past world of opinion and aspiration." Yet Croly at least assumed that common
men and women could learn democratic participation and rise to the level of
their social betters. As he said in the conclusion of *The Promise of American Life*,
"the common citizen can become something of a saint and something of a hero,
not by growing to heroic proportions in his own person, but by the sincere and
enthusiastic imitation of heroes and saints, and whether or not he will ever
come to such imitation will depend upon the ability of his exceptional fellow-
countrymen to offer him acceptable examples of heroism and saintliness."

Steffens's position was less benign; he was optimistic about strong leaders
because he was pessimistic about the people ever amounting to much on their
own. For Steffens, in the aftermath of World War I, the Treaty of Versailles,

the Great Crash of 1929, and the onset of the Depression, liberalism had obviously failed and piecemeal reform was inadequate to the immensity of the social reordering that was required. He respected and approved of the absolute authority that Lenin possessed (he spoke favorably about Stalin and Mussolini as well), for it enabled the powerful leader to cut through the maddening limits that were set when authority was dependent on popular vote. Walter Lippmann's books, *Public Opinion* (1922) and *The Phantom Public* (1925), made powerful versions of this same case, arguing that the citizenry was irrational and that the public sphere was so fragmented that it could never be looked to for leadership.

Steffens's autobiography was very influential during the 1930s; it converted many intellectuals and writers to Marxism and the defense of the Soviet Union. The left-wing editor Max Eastman (1883–1969) described it as "almost a textbook of revolution," and Newton Arvin and Granville Hicks commended it. The central reason for its success was that it spoke to the Carlylean desire among intellectuals and men and women of letters to see themselves as serving the masses without being obliged to allow the masses to govern.

Like Arnold, then, Carlyle was a complex, mobile figure, and his impact manifests itself in explicit as well as subterranean fashion. He was not a democrat in the slightest, but he was taken to be a teller of truths to democratic men, as Whitman had said. Democratic women, too: Dickinson and Louisa May Alcott (1832–88) read him intently, and Sarah Orne Jewett (1849–1909) not only admired him but also made him the subject of a short story (unpublished in her lifetime), "Carlyle in America." In a book published in 1915, Bliss Perry (1860–1954), editor of *The Atlantic Monthly* and professor of English at Harvard, portrayed Carlyle in terms that Emerson and his contemporaries would have approved of. Carlyle, said Perry, was a masterful "literary artist," a "seer and a prophet" who "perceived in an extraordinary way, the worth of the individual man."

Conservatives and New Humanists, such as W. C. Brownell and Paul Elmer More, praised Carlyle, and so did socialists like the literary historian John Macy. Mark Twain named Carlyle's *History of the French Revolution* as one of his favorite books, and he regularly re-read it. Henry Adams alluded to Carlyle and quoted from his writings in *The Education of Henry Adams* (privately printed, 1907) and Jack London depicted the protagonist of *Martin Eden* (1909) as one of "Carlyle's battle-scarred giants who will not be kept down."

Pound, evoking Carlyle in his preface to *The Spirit of Romance* (1910), declared that "the study of literature is hero-worship"; Mencken portrayed Carlyle (along with Arnold) as an "artist" in criticism; Sherwood Anderson (1876–1941) admired him and claimed to have read "every word" of Carlyle's works;

Willa Cather (1873–1947) studied Carlyle and published her first essay, in the *Nebraska State Journal* in 1891, on his writings; and Charlotte Perkins Gilman felt a special restorative power in Carlyle, saying that the reading of him was "a grand pleasure!"

The young John Crowe Ransom (1888–1974) began his personal library with Grote's *History of Greece*, a complete Shakespeare, Emerson's *Essays*, and the collected works of Carlyle; and the poet Marianne Moore (1887–1972), Bryn Mawr graduate and editor of *The Dial* from 1925 to 1929, recalled that she immersed herself in Carlyle's writings when she was a teenager. When Wallace Stevens (1879–1955) recorded his thoughts in his journal about the funeral of Stephen Crane, which he attended in June 1900, he commented on the foolishness of the service by saying that "there are few hero-worshippers . . . Therefore, few heroes." Carlyle's language for the hero seemed, to Stevens, ironically relevant to Crane, who had "lived a brave, aspiring, hard-working life" and yet who received at his death an "absolutely commonplace, bare, silly service."

The Jamaica-born poet, novelist, and short-story writer Claude McKay (1890–1948) and the African-American intellectual W. E. B. Du Bois (1868–1963) also valued Carlyle. Du Bois knew Carlyle's work especially well. He referred to Carlyle as early as 1888, in an editorial he wrote for his undergraduate newspaper, the *Fisk Herald*; and he alluded to *Sartor Resartus* in his last editorial for *The Crisis* (June 1934): "Surely, then, in this period of frustration and disappointment, we must turn from negation to affirmation, from the ever-lasting 'No' to the ever-lasting 'Yes.'"

During World War I, Carlyle's reputation suffered, for his "hero-worship" and exaltation of Prussian virtues appeared to some readers to make him a propagandist for Germany. Stuart Sherman, a staunch Arnoldian, in 1918 linked Carlyle to the Kaiser, and advised any reader who still desired "a reason for hating Prussianism with all his might" to read "in the light of the war Carlyle's shameless glorification of Prussianism's canonized forefathers."

Carlyle's reputation seemed to revive a bit, here and there, in the decades after the war. In 1939, for example, the African-American editor and literary historian J. Saunders Redding praised the "combination of scholarship and emotional power woven into bolts of symbolism" in W. E. B. Du Bois's writing, adding that "only Carlyle stands comparison." But with the steady rise of fascism and Nazism, Carlyle fell further from favor. In *A Century of Hero-Worship*, published in 1944, the editor and critic Eric Bentley viewed Carlyle as a fascinating but frightening figure who wept at the plight of the people yet horribly prefigured "the highbrow fascism of our time, the fascism of Knut Hamsun, Leon Daudet, Lawrence Dennis, and the professors of Hitler's Germany."

While Carlyle was disturbing and, to many, disreputable (he was a rabid anti-Semite), he still appealed greatly to American cultural critics. He had characterized the man of letters as a heroically active, charismatic shaper of society, and in forthright terms he indicted the failures of democracy. These elements of his work were powerfully received and present even in writers who would have admitted little or no affinity with Carlyle even while sounding very similar to him.

Carlyle also mattered because even as he spoke about the duty of the individual man of letters, he stressed that men of letters must form a specific community or class. He maintained in *On Heroes, Hero-Worship, and the Heroic in History* that "of all Priesthoods, Aristocracies, Governing Classes at present extant in the world, there is no class comparable for importance to that Priesthood of the Writers of Books," and he additionally described the "disorganic" nature of the "Literary Class" in England as perhaps the nation's worst "anomaly."

Carlyle made this point in the 1840s, and versions of it were repeated by American writers in the decades that followed. American intellectuals, critics, and men and women of letters repeatedly called for communities, academies, and organizations that would magnify and extend their efforts. Such appeals exposed Americans' nervousness about the literary profession in a nation that, in their view, business and commerce ruled. But the appeals also resulted from discontent about the disorderly, and yet at the same time overly specialized and highly rationalized, nature of American democratic society and commerce. America's democracy seemed neither organic nor integrated. It was inhospitable to unifying intellect and imagination, and it quarantined its important voices, as if to limit in advance the cultural and social reconstruction they could bring about.

When Oliver Wendell Holmes, for example, wrote about Emerson in a book-length study published in 1885, he praised Concord as an "intellectual center," contrasting it with the more fragmented American society that Holmes perceived in his own time. "To-day," he said, in "every profession, in every branch of human knowledge, special acquirements, special skills have greatly tended to limit the range of men's thoughts and working faculties." This reference to divided minds and the ebbing away of intellectual centers gains still greater force when linked to Henry James's observations about the American scene in his biography of Hawthorne, published in 1879. James was unable to find what Holmes did in Emerson's and Thoreau's community. Concord may have been a fertile place for a reformer, but not for the novelist and man of letters, James said. He admitted that American society in the 1870s was more receptive to writers than it had been in Hawthorne's day. But the improvement, he suggested, was minor, as his own decision in 1876 to settle in England, where he wrote and published the book about Hawthorne, demonstrated.

In the 1830s and 1840s, and continuing into the post-Civil War decades, American society, as James interpreted it, channeled men into "business" and "practical" occupations. The United States claimed to value literature yet failed to supply the economic support that the production of literature required. America lacked the distinctive class and community that a writer needed to fulfill his promise:

> The best things come, as a general thing, from the talents that are members of a group; every man works better when he has companions working in the same line, and yielding the stimulus of suggestion, comparison, emulation. Great things, of course, have been done by solitary workers; but they have usually been done with double the pains they would have cost if they had been produced in more genial circumstances.

These words are surprising coming from James, the dedicated, independent craftsman; he knew many writers well but, ultimately, he was an immense and eminent loner. At this stage of his career, however, James was less given to invocations of the supremacy of the artist and more inclined to evoke the conditions and communities that aspiring writers hungered to locate. James felt – and the feeling intensified through the years – that American democracy did not possess a cultural tone that obliged its citizens to show an abiding respect for artistic standards. People lived in very close proximity to one another in the booming cities, or else were widely dispersed across the continent, James remarked; in neither case was there sustained, challenging intellectual contact. No center existed that empowered and tested writers. Nor was there a community or class within which a writer could find himself or herself, and, in league with like-minded others, make an impact on the culture.

James sought the cultural context that numerous writers, critics, and intellectuals, including authors as different as Howells and Pound, said that they, too, desired – a "literary center" (Howells), an "artistic capital" (Pound) that would create and maintain standards, encourage innovation, stabilize the business of letters, and unite energies that would lose force if separated from one another. "The problem for the modern poet," the English poet-critic and, later, American citizen W. H. Auden concluded, "as for every one else today, is how to find or form a genuine community."

This concern was expressed by many. In, for example, a letter written in 1923 to his friend Waldo Frank, Hart Crane stated: "I am certain that a number of us at last have some kind of community of interest. And with this communion will come something better than a mere clique . . . It is a vision, and a vision alone that not only America needs, but the whole world." A very different

figure, the New Humanist critic Irving Babbitt, made a similar point in 1929 when he said that "there is probably even now a minority of shrewd observers who are ready to get together to resist successfully the stupid drift toward standardization." The desire was for a unit of main force, a saving remnant, a visionary phalanx that would either (in Crane's case) illuminate the future that the majority could not glimpse or (in Babbitt's) wed itself to principles that had held good in the past but that modernity had defiled.

The poet William Carlos Williams (1883–1963) performed variations on this theme. In a letter to Kenneth Burke (September 6, 1924), he emphasized that "we must all grow clearer, we must work in, together – not for comfort but for training and by bunching our candles to get more light. Join to gain head." Williams was not talking about a sect or party – this would stifle and oppress creativity, he said; but he did insist that writers could refurbish their craft and successfully speak to readers only if they formed relationships and worked as a group. In a letter to Marianne Moore (December 23, 1936), Williams again regretted the splitting up of America's writers, "exiled" and unable to "consort" together: "if only – I keep saying year in year out – it were possible for 'us' to have a place, a location, to which we could resort, singly or otherwise, and to which others could follow us as dogs follow each other – without formality but surely – where we could be known as poets and our work be seen – and we could see the work of others and buy it and have it!" "Literary men," Carlyle had observed, "are a perpetual priesthood," and such a chosen class of persons, inspired by a sense of their high vocation and mission, is what Williams and others wanted.

A similar yearning can be found in writers as different as Mencken, the Southern Agrarians, and the poets and novelists of the Harlem Renaissance. "I have been revolving a scheme," wrote Mencken to the editor and critic Louis Untermeyer in 1920, "for a small but effective organization of American authors. My proposal is that we start off with you, me, Dreiser, Cabell, Hergesheimer, Nathan, Cahan, and maybe one or two others, and then gradually build up an offensive and defensive alliance, letting in new ones most carefully." In a long letter to Donald Davidson, written in France in 1929, Allen Tate told of a proposal he had made to Robert Penn Warren that these three like-minded men establish "a society, or an academy of Southern *positive* reactionaries" through which they could express and defend "a complete social, philosophical, literary, economic, and religious system." In 1937, Claude McKay circulated a statement on behalf of a number of African-Americans united by "one clear and definite idea" – that "the time was ripe for Negro writers to draw closer together in mutual fellowship." He hoped "to establish through intellectual fellowship something like a living counterpart

of the unparalleled Schomburg collection of Negro books in the domain of scholarship."

Such organizations, alliances, groups, and movements proved difficult to begin and even more so to continue, though a number of them briefly flourished around clusters of editors and contributors to the little magazines. "Why can't such a thing come about?", Williams wondered. The question, however, was not only why such a thing had failed to come about, but also was why Williams and others so fervently desired it.

Here, Matthew Arnold's voice was again influential. When Arnold visited America in the 1880s, one of his overriding concerns was the absence of an intellectual class that would direct American civilization toward finer, more "interesting" activities and cultural pursuits. In Arnold's judgment, American life lacked "distinction," for its strength – equality – was accompanied by a perhaps fatal weakness – homogeneity. In his lecture "Numbers," he drew upon Plato and the Old Testament book of Isaiah to support his call for an independent "remnant" that would, in the United States as in England, identify the best that has been thought and said and practice the virtues of sweetness and light. These persons would be the lovers of goodness and wisdom and the enemies of sameness and standardization, and their effect on America would be "stronger" than in England because their numbers would be greater in the huge American nation.

In "Civilization in the United States" (1888), Arnold returned to this theme, lamenting the "void," the "want of what is elevated and beautiful, of what is interesting." Worst of all, Arnold indicated, was the refusal of the United States to enrich the souls of its populace: it was as though the mass of men and women had conspired to "deceive themselves" about the nation's success in solving "human" problems. There was no authentic cultural criticism in America, concluded Arnold; the nation's best writers were not only timid but were distant from one another and not fused in a critical and redemptive cause. "There are plenty of cultivated, judicious, delightful individuals there . . . They are our hope and America's hope; it is through their means that improvement must come. They know perfectly well how false and hollow the boastful stuff talked is; but they let the storm of self-laudation rage, and say nothing."

Arnold's judgments resemble those that Americans themselves made in the decades both before and after the turn of the century, and that were reinforced by reading Carlyle. (One of the major texts in this critical diagnosis took its title from Arnold's essay – Harold Stearns's 1922 collection, *Civilization in the United States*.) The United States, it was asserted, should develop an intellectual class whose power would "tell" over time on the shape of society

and culture. The members of such a class would benefit from the training that the newly modernized universities would supply, but they would not be specialized faculty.

As early as 1862, Henry Adams stated in a letter to his brother Charles Francis Adams, Jr., that America needed a "national set of young men like ourselves or better, to start new influences not only in politics, but in literature, in law, in society, and throughout the whole social organism of the country – a national school of our own generation." Adams lamented that the United States was unwilling to establish such a school. (It is odd that Adams would be making such a point with the Civil War underway.) The consequence was that "it's all random, insulated work, for special and temporary and personal purposes, and we have no means, power or hope of combined action for any unselfish end."

Adams's desire for a "concentrated power of influence" was echoed by another Harvard graduate and (like Adams) University of Berlin graduate student, W. E. B. Du Bois, in 1903. "The Negro race, like all races," wrote Du Bois in "The Talented Tenth," "is going to be saved by its exceptional men." The leaders of the race, its remnant, would be its highly educated critics, historians, sociologists, and educators – an "aristocracy of talent and character." Well before Du Bois, the African-American poet, lecturer, and intellectual Frances E. W. Harper (1825–1911) also affirmed the need for talented members of the race to "uplift" the masses; in her novel *Iola Leroy* (1892), the protagonist explains her esteem and affection for the mulatto Dr. Latimer by saying "I must have within me . . . a large amount of hero worship," and she dedicates herself to a "high, heroic" life with him in service to the people.

Four years after Du Bois's essay, in a speech at Radcliffe (the women's college affiliated with Harvard), titled "The Social Value of the College-Bred," William James, one of Du Bois's teachers, said that colleges should train young persons to acquire a "sense for human superiority" that would temper the drive for materialism and check the production of second-rate people and second-rate goods. James at moments sounded like Matthew Arnold and like his novelist brother in *The American Scene*, as he denounced "the cheap and trashy and impermanent" and counseled the cultivation of "the critical sense, the sense for ideal values."

Like Adams and Du Bois, James called for "class consciousness," for a group that might be named "Les Intellectuels":

A small force, if it never lets up, will accumulate effects more considerable than those of much greater force if these work inconsistently. The ceaseless whisper of the more permanent ideals, the steady tug of truth and justice, give them but time, *must* warp the world in their direction.

By the time James delivered his address, many of the professions, including law and medicine, had formed organizations to advance their interests, and a number of academic disciplines had done the same. But James and most others had in mind something different from professionalization, and frequently their proposals were directed against the new class of experts, bureaucrats, managers, and administrators who were beginning to populate colleges, universities, and other institutions. James argued for a genuinely liberal culture that would modify professionalism and influence the society and culture as a whole. Williams, Tate, and Du Bois understood literature, culture, and politics in contrary ways, yet they shared with one another, and with James, a determination to fight for kinds of artistic production and values that, they believed, the ethic of academic professionalism degraded.

James's address was published in *McClure's Magazine* in 1908, and this returns the story to Van Wyck Brooks, who in this same year graduated from Harvard and published his first book, *The Wine of the Puritans*, on America's failed critics, meager intellectual communities, impoverished traditions, and absence of Carlylean heroes. Brooks did not study with James, and later he chastised himself as a "puppy" for failing to make contact with such a renowned figure. But Brooks, like James, stressed energy, resolve, and forward-seeking power. He gave a Jamesian, and Emersonian, inflection to attitudes and ideals that had long been current in America, and that had been largely placed there through the agencies of Carlyle and Arnold. Brooks mastered an urgent critical tone and commandingly filled the office of cultural spokesman for the generation that came of age in the first two decades of the century. The early Brooks was, Edmund Wilson stated, "the principal source of ideas on the cultural life of the United States."

In his autobiography (1982), Lewis Mumford described even more fully than did Wilson the place that Brooks occupied in cultural life:

He once seemed, as no one else did, to be the central figure . . . of contemporary American literature. He was the embodiment of a promise that had hitherto not been visible in any single latter-day writer: the promise sounded in Longfellow's Bowdoin Commencement Address, in Emerson's "The American Scholar," in Whitman's Preface to "Leaves of Grass": the promise of an authentic American literature.

Brooks made arguments for cultural renewal that other American and English commentators had made before him, or were making at about the same time, but he stated them more effectively and did so during a period when literature, painting, dance, music, and other art-forms were in a phase of exciting experimentation and innovation. During the years before the war, the composer Charles Ives, the photographer Alfred Stieglitz, the architect

Frank Lloyd Wright, and countless others were engaged in major forms of distinctively modern work. As Mumford explained, "we all had a sense that we were on the verge of translation into a new world, a quite magical translation, in which the best hopes of the American revolution, the French Revolution, and the Industrial Revolution would all be simultaneously fulfilled." The war "battered and shattered those hopes," he added, but it did not entirely destroy them, and the flowering of creative work, and the accompanying recovery of the American past, developed throughout the 1920s under Brooks's guidance.

Other writers besides Brooks called for an American renaissance in the arts and declared their intention to lay hold of American idioms. "Most current verse is dead," noted William Carlos Williams in a letter in 1913 to the Chicago poet and editor Harriet Monroe; "life is above all things else at any moment subversive of life as it was the moment before – always new." "Verse to be alive," said Williams in a linkage of literary/cultural and ideological discourses typical of the time, "must have infused into it something of the same order, some tincture of disestablishment, something in the nature of an impalpable revolution, an ethereal reversal."

For Williams as for Brooks, newness in the arts was tied to American democracy. Democracy, they conceded, was a threat: it led to sameness and homogeneity, to everything that Arnold and, more ferociously, Carlyle deplored. Yet above all it meant freedom, the opportunity to take bold risks. America had failed to nourish and respond to the arts, but its founding myths and political system offered the potential for liberation that was unique and available for use.

More than anyone else, Brooks sounded the call for a renaissance in the arts, and he campaigned alongside Bourne, Mencken, Mumford, and Sherwood Anderson, who in their areas of expertise challenged the repressive norms of American society and won recognition for daring literary and critical enterprises. In *The Wine of the Puritans*, *America's Coming-of-Age*, and his essays for *The Seven Arts*, Brooks performed the work in the United States that Arnold and Carlyle had performed in England.

Perhaps the foremost challenge for critics, Brooks stated, was to promote in line with Arnold a "situation of which the creative power can profitably avail itself." A second, related challenge was to "discover, invent a usable past" like that which "Carlyle put together for England" and that would define the "tendencies in American civilization" that had thwarted writers in the past and that would need to be redressed for American art and literature at long last to prosper. "Carlyle's well-known appeal to Emerson still applies to the spirit of American culture," Brooks observed in 1915: "'Why won't you come and help us then? We have terrible need of one man like you down among us.'"

Brooks defined the mission that intellectuals would embark upon in modern America and merged the task of social reconstruction with literary and cultural renewal. As he affirmed in a later book, *Sketches in Criticism* (1932), no one is "more important to society than the artist and man of letters." One sign of Brooks's success is the tribute that Sherwood Anderson paid to him in a letter (May 31, 1918): "You are the first man I have seen stoutly at it trying to take the stones out of the field, to give the roots a chance." Another is that Malcolm Cowley's *After the Genteel Tradition* (1937), an anthology of critical essays on American literary modernism, was dedicated to him. Cowley's essayists proclaimed a "new literary tradition," and it was a tradition for which Brooks had established the terms.

H. L. Mencken, too, saw himself as a critical agitator, a reformer of American literature and culture. Though rarely studied in literature courses today, and figuring hardly at all in anthologies of literary criticism, Mencken was a tremendously powerful voice in the first decades of the twentieth century. In 1921 Edmund Wilson called Mencken "the civilized consciousness of modern America"; and, a few years later, Walter Lippmann named him "the most powerful personal influence on this whole generation of educated people." Mencken's magazine *American Mercury* was a force for literary and cultural change in the 1920s, and students carried copies around campus as a sign of their commitment to new ideas. This was the decade when, as Hemingway's Jake Barnes, in *The Sun Also Rises* (1926), says with some irritation, "so many young men" took "their likes and dislikes" from Mencken.

Mencken was highly prejudiced, and unapologetic about it. He trafficked in all sorts of racial and ethnic labeling, and he scorned democracy as a surrender to the whims of the mob. He hated Franklin Delano Roosevelt as a corrupt, dishonorable, war-mongering pro-English fanatic; and he scorned the New Deal's anti-poverty programs and public works policies as a crazed expansion of the federal bureaucracy and a raid on the earnings of hard-working, self-reliant Americans.

Mencken viewed himself as an extreme libertarian, a member of the sane minority, a Tory, and a reactionary. He appealed for a "civilized aristocracy" that would be "secure in its position, animated by an intelligent curiosity, skeptical of all facile generalizations, superior to the sentimentality of the mob, and delighting in the battle of ideas for its own sake." His central value, he insisted, was liberty (he declared that his "whole body of doctrine" rested upon it), and he proclaimed his allegiance to an absolutely "free" speech whereby all persons and parties, "from Communists to Methodists," would be allowed to utter and promote their ideas, however absurd or outrageous these might seem to the majority.

Mencken was impatient when his critics said that he merely mocked and caviled without recommending alternatives. In a dark mood he once noted that "the truth is that criticism, if it were thus confined to the proposing of alternative schemes, would quickly cease to have any force or utility at all, for in the overwhelming majority of instances no alternative scheme of any intelligibility is imaginable, and the whole object of the critical process is to demonstrate it." "I have little belief in human progress," Mencken stated in 1927. He reckoned that most men and women invariably crave security, are nervous about liberty, and are quick to indulge their envy of and hostility toward others different from themselves. Whenever someone boldly came forward with sensible "alternatives," he or she was hooted down, censored, or marched off to jail. "The human race is incurably idiotic," Mencken concluded. "It will never be happy."

Mencken's mordant views mask his own loyalties. Yet another reason for his dislike of programs for change is that he indicted the foibles of the American bourgeois from a sturdy bourgeois base of his own. Born in Baltimore, Maryland, he left school after the death of his father and went to work as a reporter for the *Baltimore Morning Herald*, and then as city editor, drama critic, and managing editor of the *Baltimore Evening Herald*. When the *Herald* failed in 1906, Mencken moved to the *Baltimore Sun*, his base of operations for most of his career. The son of a German cigar-maker who had immigrated to the United States in the mid-nineteenth century, Mencken made his way through hard work and self-discipline that his rollicking style disguised.

Mencken's loyalty to American ideals led him to show sympathy for the voices of persecuted minorities, as when he objected to the harassment and imprisonment of the socialist leader Eugene V. Debs and when he defended Scott Nearing, a socialist economist at the University of Pennsylvania whom the trustees there had fired in 1915 for his criticism of child labor. Nearing, declared Mencken, "was thrown out because his efforts to get at the truth disturbed the security and equanimity of the rich ignoranti who happened to control the university, and because the academic slaves and satellites of these shopmen were restive under his competition for the attention of the student-body." Nearing was an independent truth-seeker, and, to Mencken, that was what counted.

Mencken wrote significant books on George Bernard Shaw (1905) and Friedrich Nietzsche (1908). And in the periodical *Smart Set*, from 1908 to 1923, he published 182 articles on literature and criticism. He continued his day-to-day scrutiny and promotion (as well as publication) of fresh American talent in the *American Mercury*, which he launched with George Jean Nathan in 1924. Not only did Mencken call attention to, and critically assess, Dreiser,

Willa Cather, James Branch Cabell, Edgar Lee Masters, Ring Lardner, Sinclair Lewis, Eugene O'Neill, Sherwood Anderson, and other American writers; but he also praised Joseph Conrad ("a long series of extraordinary and almost incomparable works"), James Joyce (Mencken published "The Boarding House" and "A Little Cloud," later included in *Dubliners*, in the May 1915 issue of *Smart Set*), and a host of other British as well as continental authors. In *Prejudices, First Series* (1919), Mencken declared his goal as a critic: "The critic, to interpret his artist, even to understand his artist, must be able to get into the mind of his artist; he must feel and comprehend the vast pressure of the creative passion."

Though Mencken believed that "the battle of ideas should be international," he conceded that he was helplessly, "horribly American." Mencken wanted to learn about and foster ideas from abroad in order to enrich the quality of American writing and set high standards for authors here. In such notable essays as "The National Letters" (1920), Mencken campaigned against the repressive cultural norms that "Puritans," "professors," and "Comstocks" inflicted upon writers, critics, intellectuals, and freethinkers. ("Puritanism: The haunting fear that someone, somewhere, may be happy.") In other pieces he focused for debate and discussion the unorthodox ideas of Shaw, Nietzsche, H. G. Wells, Havelock Ellis, and Freud. He was particularly effective, during the 1920s, in his blistering satires on southern life and letters. Mencken's essays – above all "The Sahara of the Bozart" – and his journalistic forays and advisory labors as correspondent and editor were very important in sparking the Southern literary renaissance. Progressives, including Gerald W. Johnson, Howard W. Odum, and W. J. Cash, rallied behind Mencken; and the Nashville Agrarians, including Donald Davidson, John Crowe Ransom, and Allen Tate, developed a regional aesthetic to combat him and to defend their traditions.

Mencken's *Prejudices* and *A Book of Prefaces* (1917) proved a revelation to another Southerner, the African-American Richard Wright, when he read them in 1927. As he recalled in his autobiography: "I was jarred and shocked by the style, the clear, clean, sweeping sentences. Why did he write like that? And how did one write like that? I pictured the man as a raging demon, slashing with his pen, consumed with hate, denouncing everything American, extolling everything European or German, laughing at the weaknesses of people, mocking God, authority. What was this? I stood up, trying to realize what reality lay behind the meaning of the words. Yes, this man was fighting, fighting with words. He was using words as a weapon, using them as one would use a club."

Mencken undertook for American criticism exactly the task that Matthew Arnold (whom Mencken admired) had defined in "The Function of Criticism at the Present Time" (1864) – judgment and discrimination, circulation of "fresh thought, intelligent and alive," and the fostering of an "intellectual situation of which the creative power can profitably avail itself." As Mencken put it in 1923, "before the creative artist of genuine merit can function freely, the way must be cleared for him, and that clearly is best effected by realistic and unsentimental criticism." Dreiser, Lewis, Van Wyck Brooks, Edmund Wilson (whose reading of Mencken's *A Book of Prefaces* confirmed his vocation as a literary critic), Thomas Wolfe, and F. Scott Fitzgerald honored Mencken because he welcomed artistic innovation, applauded dissent and liberating self-examination, opposed censorship, loved the clash of ideas, and emboldened writers and critics who sought to expose American hypocrisy and cultural obtuseness.

Mencken's powers are displayed best in his many reviews of and essays on Dreiser's writings. Starting with *Jennie Gerhardt* in 1911, Mencken reviewed nearly all of Dreiser's books; and, drawing from these pieces, he assembled a number of long, detailed overviews – the best known of which is the Dreiser chapter in *A Book of Prefaces* – that describe and defend this writer's ungainly magnificence as an artist. Mencken also engaged in an elaborate correspondence with Dreiser, read his books in manuscript and in galleys, published him in *Smart Set*, and, in response to the suppression of *The Genius*, encouraged other writers to speak out on Dreiser's behalf.

Mencken prepared the way for Dreiser and aided his development as a novelist. This was not only a function that he sought to fulfill for Dreiser, but that he concluded American critics in general needed to undertake for creative writers. In writing to Ellery Sedgwick, editor of *The Atlantic Monthly* in November 1914, Mencken observed: "Dreiser sent me all of the notices of *The Titan*, perhaps 100. Not one of them gave any coherent account of what he had tried to do, nor did any of them offer any criticism that would help him. After he had read them he was frankly muddled. It seems to me that so honest and talented an artist has a right to expect something better of his country."

Mencken did not wait for opinion to consolidate itself before having his own say. In his letters, he stated his evaluation of Dreiser's books as they were being written, and he published his reviews the moment the books appeared in print. Mencken respected Dreiser enormously, esteemed his artistic integrity, and was inclined to be generous. But he was unsparingly objective in his criticism, and never refrained from declaring his disapproval of Dreiser's outpourings of verbiage and his slipshod literary structure. Yet he was nevertheless able to see even in *The Genius* that "Dreiser must do his work in his own manner," and that "his oafish clumsiness and crudeness are just as much a part of it as his amazing steadiness of vision, his easy management of gigantic operations, his superb sense of character." Mencken also recognized that whatever the faults of *An American Tragedy*, "as a human document," it is "searching and full of solemn dignity, and at times it rises to the level of genuine tragedy."

Mencken's frequent emphasis on Dreiser's "heroism" – echoing Carlyle's praise for the heroic man of letters – not only signals this novelist's distinction but also points to a more general concern in Mencken's writing for the demystifying, insurrectionary power that great literature – the work of doubters and inquirers and foes of the "prevailing platitudes" – possesses. The artist, Mencken wrote in 1921, "is never an apologist for his time; he is always in revolt against his time . . . His best work is always done when he is in active revolt against the culture that surrounds him, and in conscious conflict with the persons who regard it with satisfaction." Impatient toward orthodoxy and insistent on bucking the consensus, Mencken asserted in his "Footnote on Criticism" (1922), that "literature always thrives best" in "an atmosphere of hearty strife."

Both Mencken and Brooks were central figures for Alain Locke (1885–1954), the intellectual leader of the Harlem Renaissance, who closed his introductory essay to the landmark volume *The New Negro* (1925) by affirming that African-Americans could now "celebrate the attainment of a significant and satisfying new phase of group development, and with it a spiritual Coming of Age."

Locke was born in Philadelphia, the son of schoolteachers. After attending local schools, he went on to Harvard. He was an undergraduate there at the same time that Van Wyck Brooks was, and Locke was scheduled to graduate with Brooks in the class of 1908. But he did so well in his studies that he completed his four years of course-work in three years and finished in 1907.

While at Harvard, Locke enrolled in a course taught by Horace Kallen (1882–1974), a Zionist and philosopher whose mentor was William James. According to Kallen, "cultural pluralism," the idea that Kallen himself espoused and that Randolph Bourne described, emerged from conversations with his student and friend Locke. They continued their friendship at Oxford, where Kallen held a fellowship and where Locke was a Rhodes Scholar, the first African-American to be awarded that honor. As is evident from a syllabus for a course on "race contacts and inter-racial relations" that he gave in Washington, DC, in 1915 and 1916, and that was sponsored by the Howard University chapter of the National Association for the Advancement of Colored People (NAACP), Locke was intent upon the pluralistic "development of social solidarity out of heterogeneous elements." "Culture-citizenship," he believed, "is not acquired through assimilation merely, but in terms of a racial contribution to what becomes a joint civilization."

Like Kallen and Brooks, Locke was educated at elite institutions, and he knew and worked with prominent critics, philosophers, progressives, and pluralists. But when white writers surveyed the American scene, they rarely saw African-Americans as an inescapable fact that cultural criticism was obliged to take account of. Kallen in fact said that African-Americans posed a special problem, and he quartered them outside his own cultural program, where they awaited "separate analysis." Bourne similarly excluded them from "Trans-National America," though his letters contained angry judgments on Southern segregation as "the least defensible thing in the world." Bourne planned to "unburden" himself of his horror at America's treatment of its African-American population, but he died without having turned to that task.

Locke and his fellow Harvard student Du Bois were read by white intellectuals. But these two men were exceptions: they enjoyed educational experiences and contacts that were unavailable to the overwhelming majority of African-Americans. To whites, they were singular representatives of the race, examples of admirable achievement by members of an afflicted, unfortunate group. African-Americans were not seen as "within" American culture, and usually they did not figure in the white majority's ideas and visions for reforming it. Time after time, white men and women of letters employed organic metaphors to illustrate what America should strive to become, yet they almost never named African-Americans as part of this desired organic whole. In *The Wine of the Puritans*, Brooks touched briefly on "the Negro question" as one of the nation's major "problems," along with immigration, imperialism, and the hazards and corruptions of unchecked "financial prosperity." But he said nothing more on the subject in this book, in *America's Coming-of-Age*, or in his essays for *The Seven Arts*.

During the decades when Brooks was advocating cultural renaissance, and earlier, in the second half of the nineteenth century, many writers produced proposals for reform and wrote utopian fictions about the ideal future that America was empowered to attain through its technological ingenuity and industrial power. But "the Negro" was conspicuously absent from nearly all of them, Edward Bellamy's best-selling utopian novel, *Looking Backward* (1888), being the most obvious instance. Bellamy referred to "the solidarity of the race and the brotherhood of man" that his utopia affirmed: it was clear which "race" he had in mind.

Locke devoted his career to making African-Americans visible to whites, and he contributed to many areas of African-American culture. He taught philosophy at Howard University for four decades until his retirement in 1953; he helped a host of poets, novelists, short-story writers, playwrights, and essayists; he established the field of "comparative race studies"; he collected and celebrated African art; he assembled valuable anthologies of African-American art, music, and drama; he promoted African Studies programs; and he served as an intellectual model for several generations of African-Americans. Locke was an internationalist as well as a cultural pluralist, and he argued for the end of racism in America and in the colonies of Asia and Africa. He spoke for both "relativism" and "reciprocity," celebrating the specialness of each culture yet valuing, too, its interactions with other cultures.

Locke connected the future of his race to the future of the United States as a whole (1925): "The Negro today is inevitably moving forward under the control largely of his own objectives. What are these objectives? Those of his outer life are happily already well and finally formulated, for they are none other than the ideals of American institutions and democracy." But he insisted that modern life demanded a universal vision; as he stated in an essay published in 1942, "we must find common human denominations of liberty, equality, and fraternity for *humanity-at-large*."

Harlem was a powerful symbol for Locke, as he suggested in *The New Negro*, because it showed the possibility of fraternity among different peoples. Harlem, Locke explained,

attracted the African, the West Indian, the Negro American; has brought together the Negro of the North and the Negro of the South; the man from the city and the man from the town and village; the peasant, the student, the business man, the professional man, artist, poet, musician, adventurer and worker, preacher and criminal, exploiter and social outcast.

Locke affirmed the distinctive glories of "Negro American" and African cultures, their strands richly interwoven in Harlem, while at the same time he insisted that all cultures benefited from cross-cultural exchange. Locke was honest enough to concede his own ambivalent feeling about the losses that might accompany the gains of such cultural interaction. This was the thrust of one of his last essays, "The High Price of Integration" (1952). But ultimately his verdict was positive: "The Negro author is moving ever more and more into the field of general authorship, while at the same time, the white author is moving ever more boldly and competently into the delineation of Negro life. Each of these trends is in itself as desirable as it was inevitable."

Locke's greatest contribution was defining and advancing the "New Negro" or "Harlem" Renaissance of the 1920s, and he is best known for the collection of poems, plays, stories, essays, and music, *The New Negro*, that he edited and that was published in 1925. (Du Bois had used the phrase "the New Negro" in an article with that title in the November 1918 issue of *The Crisis*.) But Locke's interest in African-American art, literature, and culture extended well beyond the parameters of the Harlem Renaissance. In an essay published in 1953, "From *Native Son* to *Invisible Man*," he discussed his involvement in three major phases of African-American writing. The first occurred during the 1920s, and was best represented by Jean Toomer's *Cane* (1923); the second occurred during the Depression years – which were also the years of proletarian fiction and revolutionary art – and climaxed in Richard Wright's collection of stories *Uncle Tom's Children* (1938; 1940) and his novel *Native Son* (1940); and the third – underway as Locke wrote – blossomed after World War II and was distinguished by "a new height of literary achievement," as Ellison's *Invisible Man* (1952) revealed.

Locke's dateline could be moved backward so that it begins in 1903 with the publication of Du Bois's seminal text, *The Souls of Black Folk*, and it could be moved forward slightly to 1953, when James Baldwin's first novel, *Go Tell It on the Mountain*, appeared. (Always on the lookout for promising talent, Locke in 1949 singled out "a short story by an American newcomer, James Baldwin," and referred to him as "in all probability a significant young Negro writer.") The production of literature by African-Americans during this half-century was very impressive, and its list of authors includes Du Bois, Wright, James Weldon Johnson, Countee Cullen, Nella Larsen, Jessie Fauset, Claude McKay, Kelly Miller, Wallace Thurman, Rudolph Fisher, Sterling Brown, Zora Neale Hurston, Jean Toomer, Arna Bontemps, Gwendolyn Brooks, Chester Himes, Ellison, Baldwin, and Langston Hughes.

Locke read these writers carefully, and he criticized them when he found their work inadequate or flawed. He also followed developments in painting, sculpture, music, and the theater, and was attentive as well to books and essays in the social sciences. He covered African-American literary, critical, and scholarly production in a series of review-essays on "Negro literature" that he wrote from 1929 to 1942 for *Opportunity* and from 1946 to 1953 for *Phylon*. These pieces served as focal points for analysis and debate among African-American writers and critics.

When Locke began his career in earnest after completing his tenure as a Rhodes Scholar, he sounded similar to Brooks and Bourne in his arguments, as in a critique (1914) of America's overemphasis on business and material interests and its domination by "Puritanism." Like other progressive voices, Locke said that the United States was not committed to "culture"; he even wondered "whether American opinion [would] tolerate for any considerable time a leisure class devoted to this end, or a leisure class of any sort, so prepared is the America temperament to dispense with the reflective arts and all those posthumous satisfactions, dear to past civilizations, of leaving behind it adequate records and imposing traditions." For Locke, the triumphs of the "New Negro" movement proved African-American writers could break through racial stereotypes and show that they were taking part in the general "revolt against Puritanism," a "revolution of taste" that had opened literature to new subjects and forms.

Locke always emphasized "culture," and he was given to quoting Arnold's account of culture as "the best that has been known and thought in the world." Locke judged this definition to be incomplete, however, because it emphasized "the external rather than the internal factors of culture" (1923). "Rather," he claimed, culture is "the capacity for understanding the best and most representative forms of human expression, and of expressing oneself, if not in similar creativeness, at least in appreciative reactions and in progressively responsive refinement of tastes and interests." Locke linked culture to consciousness, and to the proud expression of African-American origins and identity. Arnold's own conception of culture failed to furnish terms, he said, for the artistic coming of consciousness of the "New Negro." And Arnold's American disciples, he added, never seemed inclined to incorporate the distinguished work that African-Americans produced.

While Locke objected to this aspect of Arnold's legacy, he nevertheless agreed with the Arnoldian and Carlylean notion of a "remnant," an intellectual vanguard for the protection and refinement of culture. "Culture," he stated, "must develop an elite, must maintain itself upon the basis of standards that can move forward but never backwards." As he explained in 1923, "by the evidence and promise of the cultured few, we are at last spiritually free, and offer through art an emancipating vision to America."

Locke stressed the role played by elite intellectuals: "Racial and national prestige is, after all, the product of the exceptional few" (1927). But he also foregrounded popular traditions, folklore, and folk-customs as essential material with which African-American writers and artists should create their work and which African-American intellectuals must know about and celebrate. In, for example, an essay (1934) on the poet Sterling Brown, author of *Southern Road* (1932), Locke accented "the ancient common wisdom of the folk" as "the real treasure trove of the Negro poet." Culture required "custodians," he suggested, but it derived from the people.

Even earlier, again writing about African-American poets, Locke emphasized the presence of a shared "folk temperament" and "race experience" in the best creative work:

Race is often a closer spiritual bond than nationality and group experience deeper than an individual's: here we have beauty that is born of long-suffering, truth that is derived from mass emotion and founded on collective vision. The spiritual search and discovery which is every artist's is in this case more than the personal; it is the epic reach and surge of a people seeking their group character through art.

African-American culture, for Locke, enabled the race to proclaim its achievements and gain entry to – as it also redirected – the mainstream culture of white America. In this sense, Locke differed from others on the intellectual scene (Paul Elmer More and T. S. Eliot, for example) who called for a group of intellectuals to preside over culture. Locke was concerned with equality and uplift, not, as was the case with Carlyle and Nietzsche, with an opposition between intellectuals and the masses.

In his literary and cultural criticism, Locke hewed to rigorous standards, and he argued against equating effective "propaganda" for the race's interests with "good" art. This explains why he so esteemed Toomer's book, which he saw as "artistically self-sufficient and innerly controlled" (1928). And it clarifies his judgments about writings that he respected on historical grounds but viewed as defective in artistic terms. "Art in the best sense," wrote Locke in 1928, "is rooted in self-expression and whether naive or sophisticated is self-contained. In our spiritual growth, genius and talent must more and more choose the role of group expression, or even at times the role of free individualistic expression, – in a word, must choose art and put aside propaganda."

This position would seem to place Locke at odds with Du Bois, who in *The Crisis* in 1920 had prophesied the arrival of "a renaissance of American Negro literature." Du Bois contended in "Criteria of Negro Art" (1926) that "all art is propaganda and ever must be, despite the wailing of the purists," and he was suspicious of appeals for art that neglected the race struggle. But while Locke, like Du Bois, was dedicated to the advancement of the race, he professed that art had its own rules and strictures, which writers, African-American or white, were bound to accept and reformulate. Through significant achievements in the realm of culture, African-Americans would make a major contribution of their own – thereby enabling white America better to understand them – and would affect the formation of American culture as a whole. Great art would doubtless have the impact of forceful propaganda for the race. "They'll see how beautiful I am / And be ashamed –," wrote Langston Hughes (1932), for "I too, am America." But serious art, said Locke, could never originate *as* propaganda.

A main feature of Locke's literary and cultural criticism was his emphasis on the interconnectedness of American and African-American cultures. "Negro art follows no peculiar path of its own," he professed (1939), "but is with slight differences of emphasis or pace, in step with the general aesthetic and social trends of contemporary American art and literature." Locke trusted that when white Americans perceived the cultural work that African-Americans had undertaken, and the affiliations between African-American and white writers, they would begin to accord the "New Negro" a new respect. As he stated in his introduction to *The New Negro*, it does not follow that if the Negro were better known, he would be better liked or better treated. But mutual understanding is basic for any subsequent cooperation and adjustment. The effort toward this will at least have the effect of remedying in large part what has been the most unsatisfactory feature of our present stage of race relationships in America, namely the fact that the more intelligent and representative elements of the two race groups have at so many points got quite out of vital touch with one another.

By the time that the literary scholar Morton Dauwen Zabel's major collection, *Literary Opinion in America*, was published in 1937, Locke had been presenting his case for more than two decades. Yet Zabel's book did not include a single piece by an African-American in its 600-plus pages. Nor did his extensive bibliography list even one book by an African-American author. In addition, in his roster of "American Magazines Publishing Criticism," which listed literary reviews as well as magazines and journals that combined literature and criticism with social and cultural commentary (e.g., Eliot's *The Criterion*), Zabel failed to refer to a single African-American publication. This meant that he omitted Du Bois's *The Crisis* (the NAACP periodical begun in 1910), A. Philip Randolph and Chandler Owen's *The Messenger* (1917–28), the Urban League's *Opportunity* (1923–49), and Marcus Garvey's newspaper, *Negro World* (1918–33). The revised version of Zabel's book – nearly 900 pages in length – appeared in 1951, and once again its contributors and bibliographical listings were entirely white.

Another indication of the failure of Locke's mission is apparent in Jay Hubbell's study, *Who Are the Major American Writers?* Hubbell's book was published in 1972, and it furnished a detailed account of changes in the American literary canon, with special emphasis on the dramatic developments in canon revision that had occurred during the first five decades of the modern period (i.e., roughly the span of Locke's career). At no point did Hubbell deal with African-American writers. This reflects not so much on him personally as on the innumerable white critics, literary historians, intellectuals, journalists, and pollsters whose writings formed the basis for his book. Not one of them treated African-Americans: it was as though Douglass, Du Bois, all of the writers of the Harlem Renaissance, and Richard Wright had never existed.

There were exceptions to the rule of non-contact between white and African-American intellectuals during Locke's lifetime. Locke's and Du Bois's own friendships with Kallen, William James, and others at Harvard are noteworthy, as are other examples from the ranks of the left and the cultural milieu of the Communist Party. The radicals and socialists organized around the short-lived journal *The Masses* (1911–17) were interested in the cultural and political situation of African-Americans; for example, in a piece written in 1913,

Max Eastman, one of the editors, even recommended that African-Americans in the South undertake "militant resistance against tyranny." The pro-Bolshevik *Liberator*'s editorial team included the Jamaica-born poet Claude McKay until his quarrel with fellow editor Michael Gold in 1922 over the journal's handling of the race question.

The New Masses, begun in 1926, also attended to African-American life and published Langston Hughes and Richard Wright. As the foremost African-American writer between the world wars, Hughes was able to place his poems and stories not only in radical magazines but also in *Esquire*, *Scribner's*, *The New Yorker*, and *Woman's Home Companion*; and he enjoyed the editorial support and patronage of such diverse white men and women as Carl Van Vechten, Harriet Monroe, Louis Untermeyer, and Whittaker Chambers.

A number of white playwrights, novelists, and short-story writers (Eugene O'Neill, Waldo Frank, Sherwood Anderson, Dreiser, Faulkner) wrote about African-American life and culture and portrayed African-American characters; white poets (Vachel Lindsay, Hart Crane, Robinson Jeffers) explored African-American themes; and white activists and patrons (for instance, Joel and Arthur Spingarn) supported African-American writers and scholars. In *Singing Strength*, his comprehensive "outline of American poetry" from 1620 to 1930, Alfred Kreymborg included a section on African-American writers, maintaining that the literary historian should not "segregate American Negro poetry."

V. F. Calverton included a number of African-American writers in his journal, *The Modern Quarterly*, and he edited an *Anthology of American Negro Literature* (1929), a book that identified the "contributions of the Negro" to American culture, art, and literature – spirituals, folklore, jazz – as "more striking and singular in substance and structure than any contributions that have been made by the white man to American culture." "In fact," Calverton continued, these "constitute America's chief claim to originality in its cultural history." (Calverton later stated, in 1938, that "being a Negro in the U.S. today is like being a prisoner in a jail which has several corridors and squares, in which it is possible occasionally to see the sun and walk amid the flowers and fields that belong to the unimprisoned elements of humanity.") In 1931, in a collection of essays on American literature, the socialist John Macy included a piece by Walter White (1893–1955) on "Negro literature" in which White, later the secretary of the NAACP, celebrated the entry of the African-American into American literature in the years after World War I "as a potent and not to be ignored figure."

H. L. Mencken, too, was in touch with African-American authors; he encouraged them and criticized their work, and during the decade he edited *The American Mercury* (1924–33), he published fifty-four articles by or about

African-Americans, including pieces by Du Bois and the sociologist E. Franklin
Frazier and stories by Langston Hughes. "One of the things that makes a Negro
unpleasant to white folks," Mencken observed, "is the fact that he suffers from
their injustice. He is thus a standing rebuke to them" (*Minority Report*, 1956).
African-American intellectuals such as Du Bois and James Weldon Johnson
praised Mencken for his satirical attacks on the South and his assault on American pretense and hypocrisy. Du Bois called him "calmly and judiciously fair"
in appraising work by African-Americans, and Johnson said that Mencken was
never "afraid to write the truth" about either African-Americans or whites.

Mencken exhorted his African-American contributors to *The American
Mercury* to be contentious, and even went so far as to propose that they affirm
"black superiority" and mock the antics of white people. Encouraging the black
newspaperman George S. Schuyler in 1927 to write an essay about "white folks"
as perceived by an "intelligent Negro," Mencken stated: "I'd be delighted to
see" the white man "dosed with the same kind of medicine that he has been
giving the Ethiop for so many years. Certainly he must be a ridiculous figure
seen from without." Mencken eagerly read and sought to publish Schuyler's
and others' work, and helped to get it published in other periodicals, and he
regularly corresponded with many African-American authors, offering advice
and suggestions for articles.

A number of white writers, intellectuals, and patrons of the arts emphasized the cultural gifts of African-Americans. The art patron and collector
Albert Barnes (1872–1951) observed in "Negro Art and America," in *Survey
Graphic* (March 1925): "The most outstanding characteristics [of the Negro]
are his tremendous emotional endowment, his luxuriant and free imagination
and a truly great power of individual expression . . . The Negro is a poet by
birth . . . The white man in the mass cannot compete with the Negro in spiritual endowment." Such claims had an obvious racist tinge to them, portraying
"the Negro" as a modern primitive. But more to the point is that Barnes
and others making similar statements were taking with full seriousness the
contributions that African-Americans had made, were making, and would be
making to American society and culture.

Perhaps the most noteworthy white patron and supporter of African-
Americans in the arts was Carl Van Vechten (1880–1964). Tall, blond-haired,
buck-toothed Van Vechten was a forceful, effective agent and publicist for
African-American culture from his college days to his death. He was a strange
and fascinating combination – an aesthete like Walter Pater, a dandy like
Oscar Wilde (it's said that Van Vechten was the first person to appear in public
wearing a watch on his wrist), and a tireless huckster and promoter like his
friend H. L. Mencken.

Van Vechten was an insightful music, dance, and literary critic who praised such diversely gifted figures as Erik Satie, Igor Stravinsky, Arnold Schoenberg, Isadora Duncan, the Russian ballet dancers Anna Pavlova and Vaslav Nijinsky, the blues singer Bessie Smith, Wallace Stevens, and Gertrude Stein (who named him her literary executor). As early as 1921, in the *New York Evening Post* (December 31), Van Vechten stated that Melville was "the most brilliant figure in the history of our letters" and that *Moby-Dick* – at that point known to few readers – was the greatest American novel, worthy to be ranked "with the great classics of all times, with the tragedies of the Greeks, with *Don Quixote*, with Dante's *Inferno*, and with Shakespeare's *Hamlet*."

Van Vechten convinced his publisher, Alfred Knopf, to publish Langston Hughes, beginning with *The Weary Blues* (1926), and also James Weldon Johnson, Nella Larsen, Countee Cullen, Rudolph Fisher, and Zora Neale Hurston (who later expressed the wish to write Van Vechten's biography). Interested in jazz and the blues as well as in Stravinsky and Rachmaninov, he gave support to, and wrote about, many black artists, writers, entertainers, and actors, such as Paul Robeson, Richmond Barthé, and Ethel Waters. He encouraged Hughes to move forward with his daring experimental use of the blues form and efforts to capture "the blues spirit" in poetry. Van Vechten supported Hughes throughout his career, speaking on his behalf to editors and publishers even when Hughes published pro-Communist poetry in the 1930s for which Van Vechten had no sympathy. Van Vechten also established wonderfully rich collections of letters, documents, books, manuscripts, musical scores, and photographs at Yale, the New York Public Library, and other institutions.

Born in Cedar Rapids, Iowa, Van Vechten was exposed by his parents at an early age to literature, art, and music. He was an avid reader (his mother was the founder of the local public library), and his father (a banker and insurance broker) kindled his son's interests in classical music and the theater. His father co-founded a school for African-American children in Mississippi, and he insisted that his son address African-American men and women with respect.

When Van Vechten was a student at the University of Chicago, he maintained an interest in classical music and art, but he also enjoyed the ragtime bars and clubs and brought African-American singers and entertainers (Bert Williams, Carita Day) to his fraternity house. In New York City, where he moved in 1909 and where he worked as a reporter and critic, he accompanied African-American guests to Mabel Dodge's literary and cultural salons. Through Dodge, Van Vechten met Alfred Stieglitz, Marsden Hartley, John Reed, and Emma Goldman. Between 1915 and 1920, he published seven collections of essays; and then from 1922 to 1930, he published seven novels. Except for personal essays and memoirs, he did little writing after this. Having

earned a good income from his books, and then receiving a $1 million in trust
from the estate of his brother, Van Vechten turned to his long-time hobby of
photography, taking more than 15,000 photographs (many of them portraits)
from the early 1930s until his death in 1964.

Van Vechten said with pride that whenever he lost his silver flask during a
late-night carouse at a bar or cabaret in Harlem, it was always returned to him
the next day. He recalled that by the early 1920s, he had become "violently
interested in Negroes," adding "I say violently because it was almost an addiction." Through Walter White and James Weldon Johnson, Van Vechten was
introduced to the people of Harlem. "I knew every educated person in Harlem,"
he said; "I knew them by the hundreds." He was always on the lookout for
the latest thing in art, music, and literature. Writing to Stein (November 15,
1924), Van Vechten noted: "There is always something in New York, and this
winter it is decidedly Negro poets and Jazz pianists." "Have you heard George
Gershwin's 'Rhapsody in Blue'?", he continued: "The best piece of music ever
done by an American."

Van Vechten was a tour guide for whites, taking them to Harlem clubs and
cabarets, jazz performances, and transvestite balls. His guest on one occasion
was William Faulkner, who embarrassed Van Vechten by drunkenly asking to
hear the "St. Louis Blues" in every club they visited. Later in life, he said: "That
was almost my fate, for ten years at least: taking people to Harlem." As the
English writer Osbert Sitwell remarked, Van Vechten was "the white master
of the colored revels." This role delighted him; he explained to Stein (March 4,
1926) that through his efforts, African-American performers were causing a
sensation all across New York City: "the race is getting more popular every day."

Van Vechten's apartment was on West Fifty-Fifth Street, and he was famous –
notorious – for his dinner parties, which included Somerset Maugham, Tallulah
Bankhead, Theodore Dreiser, F. Scott Fitzgerald, and Rudolph Valentino;
George Gershwin played the piano, Paul Robeson sang spirituals, and James
Weldon Johnson read poetry. The mix of white and black guests was considered
shocking – and so was Van Vechten's refusal to tell his white guests in advance
that they would be mingling with African-Americans. "I just invite them,"
he said; "I do not apologize for my friends." Harlem columnists reported in
detail on Van Vechten's dinner-parties, and it was said of him in tribute that
he was an honorary black himself; some even said that he was really a black
man passing as a white. Walter White referred to Van Vechten's apartment as
"the mid-town office of the NAACP."

Though married, Van Vechten (or "Carlo," as he preferred to be called)
was gay; he carried on affairs with young black men, and collected nude
photographs of them. His homosexuality explains much of the disapproval felt

for him by Du Bois, even as it may also have helped to secure Van Vechten's bonds to many African-American writers and artists whom the majority culture had mistreated or shunned outright.

The strangest episode in Van Vechten's career was the publication in 1926 of his scandalously titled novel *Nigger Heaven*. Van Vechten meant the title ironically to express (as one of his characters comments) the separate and second-class treatment that blacks faced in movie theaters and in the city of New York itself, where Harlem sits like a segregated balcony overhanging the downtown sections that the whites inhabited and where blacks were not welcome. He also hoped at least some readers would hear the implications of the second word as much as the first, connoting the pleasure-giving and soul-satisfying place that black people had labored to create for themselves.

But the first word in the title was the one that got the attention. Even Van Vechten's father, gravely ill and near death, tried to dissuade his son (late November 1925) to change the title: "I have myself never spoken of a colored man as a 'nigger.' If you are trying to help the race, as I am assured you are, I think every word you write should be a respectful one towards the blacks." A week later he repeated the point: "Whatever you may be compelled to say in the book, your present title will not be understood & I feel certain you should change it."

Van Vechten held firm, and many African-Americans in Harlem and elsewhere were angry with him. Langston Hughes supported his friend, but as he recalled, African-Americans "did not read [*Nigger Heaven*] to get mad. They got mad as soon as they heard of it. And after that, many of them never did read it at all. Or if they did, they put a paper cover over it and read it surreptitiously as though it were a dirty book – to keep their friends from knowing they were reading it" (*The Big Sea*, 1940). The novel was widely denounced, and Van Vechten was banned from some of his favorite night-clubs in Harlem; Du Bois – who termed the book "a blow in the face" and an "affront to the hospitality of black folk and the intelligence of white" – stated that it should be burned and that readers who hungered for scandal should instead turn to the *Police Gazette*. "I cannot for the life of me see in this work either sincerity or art, deep thought, or truthful industry," Du Bois concluded. "It seems to me that Mr. Van Vechten tried to do something bizarre and he certainly succeeded."

Van Vechten was supported by James Weldon Johnson, who told his friend: "it's all so fine, and so much in fulfillment of what my hopes and wishes were." Hughes came to his defense, as did other African-American writers who were themselves at odds with the more conservative cultural tastes of their fellow African-Americans. As Van Vechten noted to Stein (September 5, 1926), "all of my Negro *friends* like it but, naturally, not all Negroes."

Johnson said to Van Vechten: "Has anyone ever written it down – in black and white – that you have been one of the most vital forces in bringing about the artistic emergence of the Negro in America?" And he praised the novel in a review published in *Opportunity* (October 1926): "The book and not the title is the thing . . . If the book has a thesis, it is: Negroes are people; they have the same passions, the same shortcomings, the same aspirations, the same gradations of social strata as other people."

Van Vechten aimed to cause a sensation; he wanted *Nigger Heaven* to scandalize readers and draw attention to himself and, even more, to Harlem. The novel was clumsily written, and in a pot-boilerish way it veered from its educated and aspiring middle-class characters to revel in stereotypes of black primitivism and low-life sensuality. But it was a big success. Advertised through two sets of illustrations by the painter Aaron Douglas, one for white and the other for African-American periodicals, it quickly sold 100,000 copies and went through nine printings in four months. (The seventh printing included blues lyrics that Hughes wrote especially for the book.) Its faults to the side, *Nigger Heaven* was the first novel to portray African-American characters as highly cultured – bilingual, interested as much in Cocteau, Proust, Stevens, Stravinsky, and Stein as in Bessie Smith – even as it expressed too their bitter reflections on white racism.

Proud of his accomplishments in many fields, and highly cultured, W. E. B. Du Bois (1868–1963) was very impatient with whites – including, in his view, Van Vechten – who patronized African-Americans. Du Bois demanded always to be taken with the highest respect and utter seriousness. He did pioneering, influential work in history, sociology, education, economics, poetry and fiction, literary criticism and cultural theory, social commentary, and political journalism.

One of the most accomplished scholar-activists and public intellectuals in American history, Du Bois's extraordinary life spanned ninety-five years, from the presidency of Andrew Johnson and the period of Reconstruction that followed the Civil War to the presidency of John F. Kennedy and the political tensions of the Cold War. Raised and educated in the latter decades of the nineteenth century, Du Bois was a Romantic visionary and Victorian man of letters. The tradition he emerges from, and within, is that of Thomas Carlyle and Matthew Arnold. A triumphant combination of the two, Du Bois has the scale and range and social and cultural power of Carlyle and Arnold, of Ruskin and Mill. But he was also a twentieth-century African-American radical, Pan-African leader, and revolutionary, whose intellectual sources in the nineteenth century also included Karl Marx.

Du Bois was born in Great Barrington, western Massachusetts, a town of 5,000 residents that included an African-American community numbering about fifty. He was raised by his mother and her relatives after his father deserted the family when Du Bois was an infant. In his youth he became a lover of books; later in life, he proudly recalled his first purchase; it was the English historian Thomas Macaulay's five-volume *History of England* (1848–61), which he had eyed in a bookshop window in Great Barrington and managed to buy on an installment plan. From 1883 to 1885, Du Bois served as a correspondent for newspapers in Springfield, Massachusetts and New York City. He graduated with honors from the local high school in 1885, delivering an oration at commencement on the Boston abolitionist Wendell Phillips.

As he explains in his *Autobiography* (posthumously published in 1968), Du Bois then "went South," to "the South of slavery, rebellion, and black folk," spending four years (1885–88) at Fisk University, in Nashville, Tennessee. Both as a Fisk student and as a teacher in rural schools during the summers, he came into contact with many African-American families and communities, and, in his *Autobiography*, he celebrates the discovery that he made: "Into this world I leapt with enthusiasm. A new loyalty and allegiance replaced my Americanism: henceforward I was a Negro." It is a sign of Du Bois's complicated set of intellectual origins and influences, and of his sometimes strained theoretical and political commitments, that he chose the German chancellor Bismarck (who ruled as the "Iron Chancellor" of the German Empire, 1871–90) as the subject for his oration on commencement day at Fisk. Bismarck, he explained, was "my hero," for "he had made a nation out of a mass of bickering peoples."

Du Bois next attended Harvard University, where he received a second bachelor of arts degree, *cum laude*, in 1890. This time, his speech at commencement focused on Jefferson Davis, the pro-slavery US senator and president of the Confederate States of America; Du Bois pointed to Davis as representing a "type of civilization" that displayed "stalwart manhood and heroic character and at the same time moral obtuseness and refined brutality." Du Bois pursued graduate study at Harvard (M.A., 1891; Ph.D., 1895) and at the University of Berlin (1892–94), where he noted in his journal that his goal was "to make a name in science, to make a name in art, and thus to raise my race." During his period in Europe, Du Bois recalled, "I began to see the race problem in America, the problem of the peoples of Africa and Asia, and the political development of Europe as one."

In the 1890s there were few professional careers open to African-Americans. Du Bois taught English and classical and foreign languages at Wilberforce University (administered by the African Methodist Episcopal Church) in central Ohio (1894–96) and then undertook research (1896–97) in Philadelphia as an "assistant instructor" of sociology at the University of Pennsylvania. He joined the faculty of Atlanta University, which had been founded in 1865 to provide black youths with a "liberal and Christian education," where he taught economics, history, and sociology (1897–1910, 1933–44). He also organized the annual Atlanta University Conference for the study of African-American issues; these conferences led to sixteen important research monographs (1897–1914), written by Du Bois and others, on the church, landownership, urbanization, the family, and other topics in African-American life.

Du Bois's first book, based on his dissertation, was *The Suppression of the African Slave Trade to the United States of America, 1638–1870* (1896); it was the first volume in the Harvard Historical Studies series. His next was *The Philadelphia Negro* (1899), a study of African-Americans in Philadelphia, for which he conducted nearly 5,000 interviews in order to gather information about the people, their backgrounds, and the environment in which they lived.

Du Bois was a dedicated scholar, a well-trained professional who had studied at Harvard with William James and the historian Albert Bushnell Hart. He believed that once white Americans learned the truth about America's racial past and present, they would shed their prejudices and no longer try to perpetuate the folly of segregation. His years in Germany reinforced this conception of the transformative power of social science, and as an educator and researcher at Atlanta University he was devoted to the scientific study of race relations. But the turn of the century was a virulent period of racism in American history. Segregation laws increased, and anti-black terror and lynching intensified; between 1885 and 1910, 3,500 African-Americans were lynched. Du Bois finally was obliged to face the alarming contrast between his scholarly ideals and the unyielding racial myths and stereotypes that victimized African-Americans.

By 1900, Du Bois had already begun to project his vision of race relations outward from America's shores. He served in 1900 as secretary for the First Pan-African Conference, held in London; later, he played a leading role in the First Universal Races Congress, London, 1911, and he helped to organize congresses on Pan-Africanism in 1919, 1921, 1923, and 1927. In his major work *The Souls of Black Folk* (1903), he not only examined the history of slavery and segregation in the United States, but also emphasized, more generally, that "the problem of the Twentieth Century is the problem of the color line."

The Souls of Black Folk includes essays, sketches, and stories on African-American politics, history, education, music, and culture. Du Bois speaks in it of "the Veil" that separates blacks from whites, and he describes the "double consciousness" that defines the dual American and African identities of his people. In phrasing he had first used in an article, "Strivings of the Negro People" (*The Atlantic Monthly*, August 1897), Du Bois observes that the

African-American is "a sort of seventh son, born with a veil, and gifted with second-sight in this American world – a world which yields him no true self-consciousness, but only lets him see himself through the revelation of the other world. It is a peculiar sensation, this double consciousness . . . One ever feels his twoness – an American, a Negro; two souls, two thoughts, two unreconciled strivings; two warring ideals in one dark body, whose dogged strength alone keeps it from being torn asunder."

Du Bois was best known at this time for his opposition to Booker T. Washington (1856–1915), the founder of Tuskegee Institute in Alabama and the leading spokesman for African-Americans on the national scene. In a speech at the Atlanta Exposition in 1895, Washington had declared: "the wisest of my race understand that the agitation of questions of social equality is the extremest folly." In exchange for limited economic progress, he seemed willing to accept continued segregation, disenfranchisement, and restrictions on educational choice, funding, and advancement. In *The Souls of Black Folk* and elsewhere, Du Bois argued that white America had chosen Washington as the nation's leading African-American because he presented the accommodationist message that whites wanted to hear. Du Bois was far more militant, in the tradition of the abolitionist and anti-racist orator Frederick Douglass. He insisted on social and political rights, access to higher education, and the development of an elite African-American intellectual and professional class (the "talented tenth").

Du Bois's opposition to Booker T. Washington led him in 1905 to take a central role in the Niagara Movement for rights for African-Americans; at its meeting in Harpers Ferry, Virginia, August 15, 1906, he declared: "we claim for ourselves every single right that belongs to a free-born American, political, civil, and social; and until we get these rights we will never cease to protest and assail the ears of America." Du Bois became editor of *Horizon: A Journal of the Color Line* (1907–10); in 1909, he was one of the founders of the NAACP, for which he served as Director of Publications and Research. He expanded his role in the international Pan-African movement, and he was active, too, as a social critic and theorist, creative writer, and historian. His books of this period include *John Brown* (1909), a study of the white abolitionist executed in December 1859 for attempting to fire up a slave rebellion in Virginia; *The Quest of the Silver Fleece* (1911), a novel that depicts the struggles of African-American women and explores the appeal of political radicalism for blacks; and *The Negro* (1915) and *Darkwater* (1920), wide-ranging works of cultural critique and commentary on race and racism at home and abroad.

Beginning in 1910, Du Bois was the editor of the NAACP's monthly magazine, *The Crisis*, a position that he held until 1934, when he resigned in a

dispute over policy; by 1919, *The Crisis* reached an audience of 100,000 readers. His arguments and views were sharply stated and often controversial. He
was, for example, a bitter foe of Marcus Garvey (1887–1940), the popular
Jamaican-born American exponent of black nationalism and founder in 1914
of the Universal Negro Improvement Association. In 1926, Du Bois made his
first visit to the Soviet Union; in the November issue of *The Crisis*, he wrote: "if
what I have seen with my eyes and heard with my ears in Russia is Bolshevism,
I am a Bolshevik."

Du Bois was a crucial figure for the writers and artists of the Harlem Renaissance and the "New Negro" movement of the 1920s. In the pages of *The Crisis*,
he repeatedly urged readers to see "Beauty in Black," and it was this imperative
that the poets Claude McKay, Countee Cullen, and Langston Hughes, and the
novelists and short-story writers Jean Toomer, Nella Larsen, Jessie Fauset, and
Zora Neale Hurston, fulfilled. The performing arts flourished as well, in the
work of Duke Ellington and Louis Armstrong, the blues singers Bessie Smith
and Ma Rainey, and the singers and performance artists Florence Mills and
Josephine Baker.

These diversely gifted African-Americans were forming the cultural vanguard, the "talented tenth," for which Du Bois had called. But because their
emphasis was cultural rather than political, they received a mixed response
from him. He both agreed and disagreed with Alain Locke, who stated in
his essay "The New Negro" that African-Americans should "lay aside the
status of a beneficiary and ward for that of a collaborator and participant in
American civilization . . . The especially cultural recognition they win should
in turn prove the key to that revaluation of the Negro which must precede or
accompany any considerable further betterment of race relationships."

Like Locke, Du Bois welcomed innovative creative work by African-
American authors and artists, and he published writings by Hughes and Cullen
in *The Crisis*. But he regretted the dependence of African-American authors on
white patrons and audiences, such as Van Vechten, his friends, and the white
persons to whom he displayed the Harlem scene. And while Du Bois called
for greater openness and honesty about sexual subjects and themes, he was also
quick to criticize some African-American authors (for example, McKay) and
performers for reinforcing white stereotypes of black sexual behavior.

The Depression decade of the 1930s hit African-Americans hard, and provoked Du Bois to call for "voluntary segregation," which, he maintained,
would lead to economic self-sufficiency, solidarity, and self-advancement. As
he later noted in his *Autobiography*, he had concluded that the United States
was not seeking to reach the goal of racial integration, and that it was therefore
time for African-Americans to dedicate themselves in business and industry

to "new, deliberate, and purposeful segregation for economic defense." In "A Negro Nation within the Nation," *Current History*, June 1935, Du Bois enjoined African-Americans to organize "a cooperative state within their own group . . . Separate Negro sections [e.g., in schools] will increase race antagonism, but they will also increase economic cooperation, organized self-defense, and necessary self-confidence."

This nationalist argument troubled many of Du Bois's white and African-American allies. He claimed that he remained committed to the goal of complete integration, but few could understand how segregation, voluntary or not, would contribute to achieving it. Du Bois's separatist views caused tensions with the officers of the NAACP, and he was forced out of the organization in 1934. He returned to it in 1944, but left again, at age eighty, in 1948.

From the 1930s until his death in 1963, Du Bois was an activist and a prolific author. His books include the epic historical study *Black Reconstruction in America, 1860–1880* (1935); *Dusk of Dawn* (1940), which he described as "not so much my autobiography as the autobiography of a concept of race"; and *Color and Democracy: Colonies and Peace* (1945), one of many writings of the 1940s and 1950s that challenged imperialism and made the case for African independence. Du Bois's anti-colonialism and anti-imperialism arose from his commitment to Pan-Africanism, and on the international scene he was highly respected for his uncompromising work. But Du Bois's ever-deepening interest in Communism and favorable response to the Soviet Union marginalized him in the United States as the Civil Rights campaigns of the late 1940s and 1950s proceeded. In 1951, he was indicted and placed on trial with four others for being an "unregistered foreign agent" (that is, a Soviet sympathizer) in his activities for the Peace Information Center in New York City. He was acquitted in November 1951, but his passport was revoked from 1952 to 1958.

Embittered by his treatment at the hands of white America, Du Bois applied on October 1, 1961, for membership in the Communist Party of the USA. In a letter explaining his decision, he wrote: "Capitalism cannot reform itself . . . Communism – the effort to give all men what they need and to ask of each the best they can contribute – this is the only way of human life." He renounced his US citizenship and took up residence in Ghana, where, with the support of prime minister Kwame Nkrumah, he laid plans for his final project, a multi-volume Encyclopedia Africana, designed to gather information on the history and life of all Africans and persons of African descent world-wide. He died in Accra, Ghana, on August 27, 1963.

Du Bois's literary criticism and theory blended Victorian earnestness, literary realism and naturalism, and radical politics. In "Criteria of Negro Art"

(1926), perhaps his best-known piece, Du Bois stated that "all Art is propaganda and ever must be." He exhorted African-American writers and artists to strive for Truth and Beauty even as he called attention to the marketplace conditions and the institutional racism that, he argued, had limited African-American literary and cultural achievement. For Du Bois, art must function as agitation, protest, and racial propaganda.

In his literary and cultural criticism, Du Bois struggled to mediate between the freedom that art requires and the African-American fight for socio-political equality and progress. He valued literary innovation in style and content to a degree, which he realized enabled writers to shatter racial stereotypes and distortions. But frequently in his essays and reviews, he was made uneasy by literary and cultural works that, in his view, used such freedom unwisely, casting a bad or demeaning light on African-American life and threatening to confirm the low regard in which the white majority held them.

The flaw in Du Bois's position lies precisely in his extreme demand that art must be used for propaganda and for nothing else. His commitment to the cause of social justice and equality impelled this stark claim: he believed that the needs of his people mandated it. At the same time, however, in "Criteria of Negro Art" it clashed with his earlier evocation of the splendid beauty of Cologne cathedral and the Venus de Milo, which he valued for their own sake, rather than for any propagandistic service they performed for their first viewers or anyone in later periods. Du Bois's vision was always inclusive, and challengingly so: he linked the cathedral and the famous Greek statue to a village in West Africa and a Negro song and spiritual. But he did not recognize the reductive nature of his fiery dismissal: "I do not care a damn for any art that is not used for propaganda."

Among twentieth-century American men of letters, Du Bois's only rival is Edmund Wilson (1895–1972), who wrote about nearly everyone and everything except, it seems, for Du Bois, who is not mentioned in any of Wilson's books, essay, letters, or diary entries.

Intellectually curious and prolific, Wilson contributed to many journals and magazines and reached diverse audiences – writers, intellectuals, academics, and nonacademics – and functioned for them all as a source of informed taste and judgment. As Alfred Kazin said: "By the catholicity of his interests, the freshness and directness of his performance, he seemed more than any other critic in America the experimentalist who worked with the whole tradition of literature in his bones." By mid-century, Wilson was the leading critic, literary journalist, and man of letters in American culture. He was in the middle of literary modernism, while he carried forward into the twentieth century the breadth of interest and work ethic of a Victorian sage like Carlyle or Arnold.

Wilson experienced both privilege and pain during his childhood and adolescence. Born in Red Bank, New Jersey, in 1895, Wilson was the only child of prosperous but difficult, emotionally distant parents. His father, a successful lawyer, served as the state's attorney-general, but Edmund Sr. was afflicted by bouts of severe depression and melancholy. Possessing high standards for conduct and a direct, focused prose style (which his son would proudly claim as a model and as a sign of personal integrity), Wilson's father felt himself to be at odds with the loose business practices, unbridled individualism, and race for wealth in the Gilded Age of the 1880s and 1890s. Wilson's socially ambitious mother was angered by her husband's personal failings, and she disapproved of her son's bookish habits; she showed no interest in his literary work and aspirations.

Wilson was educated in the classics at the Hill School (1909–12) in Pottstown, Pennsylvania, where, he recalled, he was taught the virtues of "lucidity, force, and ease" in written expression. He then attended Princeton (1912–16), where his friends included F. Scott Fitzgerald (who came to identify Wilson as "my intellectual conscience") and the poet-critic John Peale Bishop.

After graduation, Wilson worked briefly as a reporter for the New York *Evening Sun*. Like his friends later in life, the novelists John Dos Passos and Ernest Hemingway, he served in a hospital unit during World War I; later, he was reassigned to the intelligence corps. When the war ended, Wilson freelanced as a writer and joined the staff of the magazine *Vanity Fair*, where he was managing editor (1920–21). He moved on to become associate editor of *The New Republic* (1926–31) and book reviewer for *The New Yorker* (1944–48).

Wilson's first important book was *Axel's Castle: A Study in the Imaginative Literature of 1870–1930* (1931), which examined the development of modernism in relation to French Symbolism, with chapters on William Butler Yeats, Marcel Proust, James Joyce, T. S. Eliot, Gertrude Stein, and Paul Valéry. There was no scholarship on these authors that Wilson could build upon; except for Proust, all of them were still active as writers, and Wilson did a superb job of critical foundation-laying as he described the sources for, and main themes of, their complicated, allusive texts. Yet even as he revealed his passionate interest in modernism, he voiced ambivalent feelings about it in *Axel's Castle* and in his correspondence. He told his editor, Maxwell Perkins, "I believe that any literary movement which tends so to paralyze the will, to discourage literature from entering into action, has a very serious weakness, and I think that the time has now come for a reaction against it."

Wilson concluded the 1930s with *To the Finland Station* (1940), a panoramic study of the origins of socialism, the careers and main ideas of Karl Marx and

Friedrich Engels, and the intellectual and historical contexts for the Russian Revolution. Linking political utopianism with literary work, Wilson portrayed Marx, Engels, and Lenin as "poets themselves in their political vision"; their "genius," he said, "lay in the intensity of their imaginations and in the skill with which through the written and spoken word they were able to arouse others to see human life and history as they did."

This keen feeling for persons as agents of grand historical change makes Wilson, at his best, thrilling to read; like Du Bois in *The Souls of Black Folk* and *Black Reconstruction*, Wilson tells captivating, dramatic stories. It also makes him hard to categorize as a critic. Wilson relished big projects: he knew what he needed in each case to learn. But he rarely explained what he was doing or paused to articulate how it differed from the work of other critics. In a broad sense Wilson has a distinctive approach to literature and history (and their interaction), but – here he differs from the New Critics – he does not present a specific method that readers and students in a college classroom might adapt for their own inquiries. That wasn't Wilson's aim, or his audience. He was not a literary critic as such; he was a superb writer, one of whose areas of skill was literary criticism.

Wilson was not much more of a close analytical reader of texts than Du Bois was; he sought instead to "spotlight" (one of his favorite terms) particular writers in the historical and literary contexts of their eras. He turned to biography, psychology, economics, politics, and history at roughly the same moment when John Crowe Ransom, Cleanth Brooks, and the other New Critics were calling for an "intrinsic" literary criticism based on detailed commentary on the words on the page. For them, with the classroom as a frequent reference point, the focus was on the work itself and the critical task was an explication of textual ironies, ambiguities, paradoxes, tensions. Wilson, however, was averse to the notion of specializing in a single field or subject and to the tedious (as he saw it) exercise of line-by-line close reading. He praised those critics of the past, such as the nineteenth-century French writers Charles Augustin Sainte-Beuve, Ernest Renan, and Hippolyte Taine, who had used criticism as "the vehicle of all sorts of ideas about the purpose and destiny of human life in general." "I never think of myself as a literary critic," he said in 1959: "I think of myself simply as a writer and as a journalist."

Wilson worked in a host of genres and on many subjects. His books include a novel, *I Thought of Daisy* (1929; rev. 1967); collections of literary essays, *The Triple Thinkers* (1938; rev. 1948) and *The Wound and the Bow* (1941); short stories, *Memoirs of Hecate County* (1946); an edited anthology of commentaries on American literature, *The Shock of Recognition* (1943); travel writings, in *Europe Without Baedeker* (1947; rev. 1966); *The Scrolls from the Dead Sea* (1955;

rev. 1969); *Apologies to the Iroquois* (1960); an 800-page study of the literature of the American Civil War, *Patriotic Gore* (1962); the polemical pamphlet
The Cold War and the Income Tax (1963); and *The Fruits of the MLA* (1969), in
which he criticized academic scholars in the Modern Language Association for
their pedantic editorial practices and failure to make the writings of American authors widely available in well-edited, inexpensive editions. Wilson also
assembled many collections of his essays and reviews – the best of which is
The Shores of Light: A Literary Chronicle of the Twenties and Thirties (1952). Still
other volumes of letters and journals were published after his death in 1972.

Wilson was one of the last American men of letters to produce such a wide
range of critical writing, for criticism after World War II became increasingly
specialized and centered in colleges and universities. But Wilson's impressive
range is not without its own limits. In *Patriotic Gore*, for example, he deals only
briefly with Whitman's and Melville's collections of Civil War verse, in part
because throughout his career he responded less attentively to poetry than to
fictional and nonfictional prose, and in part, too, because Wilson believed that
Whitman and Melville had already been studied by previous critics. This was
a reasonable view, but one that distorted the history of the period that Wilson
wrote about.

With the publication of *Axel's Castle* at one end and *To the Finland Station*
at the other, the 1930s was the most significant phase of Wilson's career. One
of the best essays from this period is "Marxism and Literature," included in
The Triple Thinkers (1938), and it revealed Wilson's indebtedness to Marxist
thought and his determination to correct mistaken ideas about it. But, even
more, it showed his regard for the act of literary creation, for the separateness
and specialness of the work of art, which, he maintained, should not be judged
on political grounds.

The relationship of literature and criticism to political change was a compelling issue for writers, critics, and intellectuals during the 1930s, as Du Bois's
books and essays also testified. For Wilson and others, Marxism explained what
had happened: capitalism was breaking apart because of its internal conflicts
and contradictions. And as a source of insight into the contemporary world-
scene, Marxism accrued further power from the example of the Soviet Union,
which, for many, confirmed the rightness of their faith in revolutionary transformation.

Wilson by 1930 was a radical. He explained in *The American Jitters: A Year
of the Slump* (1932; rev. 1958), a book of social reportage on his cross-country
travels in America during the early years of the Depression: "My present
feeling is that my satisfaction in seeing the whole world fairly and sensibly
run as Russia is now run, instead of by shabby politicians in the interests

of acquisitive manufacturers, business men and bankers, would more than compensate me for any losses that I might incur in the process." "So far as I can see," he stated, "Karl Marx's predictions are in process of coming true."

By the time *Axel's Castle* appeared, in March 1931, Wilson was already publishing the social and political articles that he would include in *American Jitters*. In this same year, too, Wilson wrote an "Appeal" to progressives to "take Communism away from the Communists" and plant its principles in authentically American soil. In later years Wilson said that the Depression decade, while a period of suffering and misery for many, for intellectuals like himself gave grounds for hope: "One couldn't help being exhilarated at the sudden unexpected collapse of that stupid gigantic fraud." Though never a member of the Communist Party, he supported its candidates for national office in the presidential election of 1932. He traveled to the Soviet Union in 1935 and reported on his experiences in *Travels in Two Democracies* (1936).

To Wilson and many other observers, capitalism was in crisis, and the signs were evident everywhere. Between 1930 and 1933, 9,000 banks closed their doors or went bankrupt; 9 million savings accounts were lost. National income was cut in half; manufacturing was down by half, and in some industries the situation was even worse (e.g., the steel industry operated at about 10 percent of its capacity). Between 1930 and 1933, investment had almost ceased; construction fell by three-quarters; manufacturing was cut in half. The Gross National Product fell from $104 billion in 1929 to $76.4 billion in 1932. Gross farm income fell from $12 billion to $5 billion from 1929 to 1932; one-third of American farmers lost their land. The terrible dust storms, "black blizzards," ruined huge areas from the Dakotas to Texas for farming and raising livestock. Three and a half million persons abandoned their farms and looked for work and homes elsewhere.

Work was nearly impossible to find. Between 1929 and 1932, a weekly average of 100,000 persons lost their jobs. In 1929, 2 million were unemployed; by 1930, 4 million; by 1931, 8 million; and by 1932, nearly 13 million. By 1933, 15 million Americans (one-third of the labor force) were unemployed. Throughout the 1930s, unemployment was always about 20 percent, never below 15 percent; and one-third of America's workers who were employed were underemployed.

The unemployment rate in cities was very high (e.g., 50 percent in Cleveland, Ohio). Unemployment was especially severe for African-Americans; by 1932, half of the African-American population in the South was without work. It was even worse than the official statistics suggest. Only one in two Americans who were employed held a full-time job. In New York City, for example, so many persons sold apples on street corners that they were counted as employed.

For many of America's families, life was a desolate struggle. The average family income by 1932 was $1,350, well below the minimum standard of $2,000 that was set in 1929 (even then, only 40 percent of the nation's families reached this level). For some segments of the population, the crisis was even more severe; the average income for African-American cotton farmers was less than $200 per year. Two million persons were homeless, including 25,000 families. The cost of living declined, but family income declined even more.

The hardships that Wilson witnessed in America propelled him toward a favorable view of the Soviet system. But he remained critical and independent, much more so than many others, including Du Bois. Wilson was suspicious of Stalin's cult of personality, distrusted the ever-expanding Soviet bureaucracy, balked at the Communists' tendency to evaluate literature and criticism only in narrowly political terms, and denounced the purge trials in the Soviet Union in the mid- to late 1930s, through which Stalin killed off or imprisoned his rivals and those he deemed disloyal. Wilson wrote in 1932 that the Communist Party candidate for president was "always talking about 'liquidating' things. 'Liquidating' something means getting rid of it. In Russia they liquidated the *kulaks* [i.e., prosperous landed peasants in czarist Russia], they liquidated the Church – and the Soviet prosecutor has recently demanded that the traitorous engineers be liquidated – in other words, shot."

To borrow a phrase he applied to the novelist Theodore Dreiser, Wilson was an "unrussianizable American." He was drawn toward Marxism, but he was a very undogmatic Marxist and not a Communist. In "Marxism and Literature," Wilson was both sympathetic and resistant to critics' attempts to connect Marxism and literature. These connections were being made vigorously in the United States in *The New Masses* and other radical magazines and journals, in collections of "proletarian" literature that depicted the struggles of the working class, and in books such as Granville Hicks's *The Great Tradition: An Interpretation of American Literature Since the Civil War* (1933).

Wilson covered much ground in "Marxism and Literature," as he mustered evidence to demonstrate that the views of Marx and Engels on literature had been misinterpreted, compared and contrasted their positions with Lenin's and Trotsky's, condemned the repressiveness of Stalin's dictatorship, and emphasized the folly of presuming that good literature could be made from ideological formulas. He also explored the prospects for literature and criticism in periods of political revolution, and sketched the differences between socio-cultural conditions in the United States and the Soviet Union. At the center of the essay was Wilson's depoliticizing of Marxism – he defines its value as "throw[ing] a great deal of light on the origins and social significance of works of art" – and his high regard for "literary appreciation."

So curious was Wilson about literature, culture, and politics that it is strange indeed that he had next to nothing to say about African-American literature; his discussions of modernism neglect the Harlem Renaissance entirely, and his work on the Civil War period fails to consider slave narratives and the speeches and writings of Frederick Douglass and other African-American abolitionists. If one were to judge the American literary situation from the 1920s to the 1960s on the basis of his "chronicles" – *The Shores of Light, Classics and Commercials* (1950), and *The Bit Between My Teeth* (1965) – one would have no sense that Locke or Du Bois or any African-American writers had lived. The same point applies to the gathering of Wilson's otherwise wide-ranging letters on literature and politics and his extensive journals.

It is precisely because Edmund Wilson was a brilliant, highly esteemed, and very accomplished critic that his omissions are so noticeable, and confirm so starkly Alain Locke's fear that African-American and white intellectuals and men of letters had lost "vital touch with one another." But while Locke may not have succeeded in realizing his great dream during his own lifetime, his arguments have proven valid in the long run and came to fruition in the 1980s and 1990s. "Culture" retains at least some of the aura that Arnold memorably assigned to it, and intellectuals inside and outside the academy enjoy much of the responsibility for maintaining it, just as Arnold and Carlyle had said they would. But it is now "inescapable" and "inevitable" (Locke's words) that the literary history of the United States incorporate the abundant contributions that African-Americans have made, and, in line with the pluralist vision that Randolph Bourne expressed, that it value the many cultures that this nation's racial and ethnic groups have created and will continue to develop and blend with one another.

Wilson dedicated his first book, *Axel's Castle*, to Christian Gauss, one of his undergraduate teachers at Princeton, noting that "it was principally from you that I acquired then my idea of what literary criticism ought to be – a history of man's ideas and imaginings in the setting of the conditions which have shaped them." Like other men and women of letters treated in this chapter, Wilson viewed literary criticism as a form of cultural criticism that explored and proffered judgments about writers, texts, and ideas within an understanding of history shaped by moral and political concerns. As Lionel Trilling, an admirer of Wilson, affirmed in 1939 in his study of Arnold, "literature is an agency, depending upon and supplementing other social agencies." For Trilling as well as Wilson, the responsibilities of the critic were great because his or her duties were multiple and the gamut of subjects so extensive.

Wilson and Trilling described the role of the critic broadly, and sometimes their recommendations seemed amateurish and unprofessional to skeptical readers. But the diversity of their writings is impressive, and this fact about them – and about Brooks, Bourne, Du Bois, and Locke – becomes all the more commendable when one surveys the history of criticism in the academy. Here, the New Critics led the way as they both revised and curtailed the critic's endeavors.

For Arnold and Carlyle, and for the non-academic intellectuals whom they awakened, literature mattered for its own sake *and* for the reflection upon society and culture that it prompted. "If our literary criticism," said Van Wyck Brooks, "is always impelled sooner or later to become social criticism, it is certainly because the future of our literature and art depends upon the wholesale reconstruction of a social life all the elements of which are as if united against the growth and freedom of the spirit." The New Critics made criticism more disciplined by showing how it illuminated the inner workings of texts. But in the process they forestalled the "social" analysis and commentary that Brooks had judged crucial, and they limited the role that literary studies might play in the reconstruction of culture.

3

SOUTHERNERS, AGRARIANS,
AND NEW CRITICS
THE INSTITUTIONS
OF MODERN CRITICISM

THE major Southern New Critics are John Crowe Ransom, Allen Tate, Robert Penn Warren, and Cleanth Brooks, but to refer to them as "critics" does them an injustice. It confines the scope of their achievements, just as the term "New Critic" itself names a movement that these writers launched but that their practice moved beyond. As Warren said, in an interview in 1957, the New Criticism is "a term without any referent, or with too many referents."

Even to identify Warren (1905–89) as a literary critic is misleading, for he excelled in a number of fields. His early publications included a biography of the abolitionist John Brown (1929), a collection of poems (1935), and a novel, *Night Rider* (1939). These writings established the pattern of disciplined engagement with a variety of genres that he maintained. Before his involvement with the New Criticism in the late 1930s and 1940s, Warren had already taken part in two other important groups in Southern culture and American literature: the Fugitive poets, based at Vanderbilt University in Nashville, Tennessee; and the Agrarian reformers and polemicists who spoke out against industrialism in the controversial volume *I'll Take My Stand* (1930).

Warren did much to define and institutionalize New Critical methods, above all through the influential textbook, *Understanding Poetry* (1938), that he and Brooks wrote. But the scope of Warren's literary achievement, in *All the King's Men* (1946) and ten other novels, poetry (fifteen volumes in all), short stories, and historical meditations – *Segregation: The Inner Conflict in the South* (1956), *The Legacy of the Civil War* (1961), and *Who Speaks for the Negro?* (1965) – shows that his New Critical commitments coexisted with (and were informed by) evolving attitudes toward history, politics, regionalism, nationhood, and race relations.

When Warren's career is seen as a whole, he cannot be judged as inattentive to history and unreflective about the social and political bearings of literature – which are the most frequent charges directed against him and the other New Critics. Like Ransom's and Tate's, and Brooks's to an extent, Warren's "New Criticism" formed only a portion of his substantial output.

In his critical writings, Warren was a dedicated teacher. There is fervor and fire in his verse and fiction, and these same features enlivened his literary criticism as well, especially when he wrote about Conrad and Faulkner, with whom his imagination is in sustained contact. Yet the criticism, in *Selected Essays* (1958) and *New and Selected Essays* (1989), is memorable for other sorts of teacherly virtues – tolerance, generosity, and alert, focused acts of discrimination.

This teacherly concern informed the writing of *Understanding Poetry*, which Warren and his friend Brooks originally prepared as a mimeographed pamphlet for students at Louisiana State University. They saw that students lacked basic skills in close reading and hence were cut off from classic texts and unable to respond to modern literature.

Warren had been very disappointed by the graduate school training he had received at the University of California, Berkeley, where he was enrolled in the late 1920s; it seemed to him, as he explained in a letter (1927) to Tate, that nearly all of the English faculty there were a "dull lot" and were "approximately half a century behind things." Later, when he went to Yale, he found, as he noted in a letter (February 12, 1928) to his Vanderbilt friend and fellow Fugitive-poet Andrew Lytle, that the graduate school "runs on the assumption that no one except a student who wants to learn scholarly method belongs here, and that all others are to be coerced into this regime or to be cast out and trodden under the foot of men."

Warren wanted to do better for students. He perceived his critical essays on Hawthorne, Melville, Coleridge, Dreiser, Hemingway, and others as "an extension of teaching – even of conversation." He believed in good literary instruction, and that it was a necessary part of his conception of himself as a writer and intellectual. Criticism ought to be precise yet informal, Warren proposed, and should bring together mutually respectful teachers, students, and friends.

A similar case could be made for Ransom (1888–1974), who was Warren's teacher at Vanderbilt. Ransom was a brilliant undergraduate at Vanderbilt (he entered at age fifteen and graduated first in his class); a trained classicist and reader of philosophy; a gifted poet of subtle, ironic lyrics; a central member of the Fugitive group and editorialist for, and contributor to, its magazine, *The Fugitive*, which was published from 1922 to 1925; a forthright foe of science and positivism and a defender of religion in *God Without Thunder: An Unorthodox Defense of Orthodoxy* (1930); the leading figure among the Agrarians; the founding editor in 1939 of a journal, *The Kenyon Review*; the author of two significant studies in aesthetics and literary theory, *The World's Body* (1938) and *The New Criticism* (1941); and an elegant essayist on literary subjects. Ransom was a wry, courteous teacher and colleague, first at Vanderbilt (1914–37) and later at Kenyon College (1937–58), in Gambier, Ohio. His students included Warren and Tate, and the poet-critics Robert Lowell and Randall Jarrell.

Tate (1899–1979) displayed formidable range in his work and resembles Warren in his achievements in biography, fiction, and verse. He was active in the Fugitive and Agrarian enterprises, and did more than any of his cohorts at Vanderbilt to kindle interest in Hart Crane and T. S. Eliot. He wrote biographies of the Confederate general Stonewall Jackson (1928) and the president of the Confederacy, Jefferson Davis (1929). He planned a third biography, on Robert E. Lee, but abandoned it in favor of fiction-writing, which led to his novel *The Fathers* (1938).

Tate wrote a long, forceful essay for *I'll Take My Stand* and edited another volume on politics and economics, *Who Owns America?* (1936), which included pieces by Ransom, Warren, and Brooks. Like Ransom and Warren, Tate was a significant poet, and he forged intense verse in the 1920s and 1930s. He served as editor of *The Sewanee Review* from 1944 to 1946, edited a number of books, and published hundreds of essays and reviews on literature, criticism, and literary theory, the best of which are gathered together in *Essays of Four Decades* (1968), *Memoirs and Opinions, 1926–1974* (1975), and *The Poetry Reviews of Allen Tate, 1924–1944* (1983).

Compared to the other three, Brooks (1906–94) may seem less imposing, but he was an accomplished figure in his own right. He was more of a formalist than Ransom, Tate, or Warren, and, in *The Well Wrought Urn* (1949) and many essays, he described and popularized the familiar New Critical method of "close reading" the text itself. But he was also a literary historian, whose early book, *Modern Poetry and the Tradition* (1939), like the British critic F. R. Leavis's *New Bearings in English Poetry* (1932), consolidated the traditions of English and American poetry along the lines that Eliot had suggested in "The Metaphysical Poets" (1921), "Andrew Marvell" (1921), and "Milton" (1936) – though Brooks later went on to examine Milton and the Romantics more sympathetically than had Eliot or Leavis.

Brooks also undertook old-fashioned, even "antiquarian" (as he called it) scholarly work, in his first book, *The Relation of the Alabama-Georgia Dialect to the Provincial Dialects of Great Britain* (1935), and in his multi-volume edition of the letters of the eighteenth-century poet, translator, and scholar Thomas Percy. In addition, Brooks, along with Warren, founded *The Southern Review*, editing it from 1935 to 1942. He wrote extensively about the relations between literature, history, and religion; edited important anthologies of poetry, fiction, and drama; and co-authored, with William K. Wimsatt, *Literary Criticism: A Short History* (1957).

In a number of books on Faulkner, including *William Faulkner: The Yoknapatawpha Country* (1963), *William Faulkner: Toward Yoknapatawpha and Beyond* (1978), and *William Faulkner: First Encounters* (1983), Brooks reinforced and enlarged upon studies by Malcolm Cowley and Warren. Cowley's contribution was his introductory essay for the Viking *Portable Faulkner* that was published in 1946, a volume that Warren reviewed in August of the same year in *The New Republic*. (A revised version of Warren's article was later published in both his *Selected Essays* and *New and Selected Essays*.) Brooks developed in particular Warren's emphasis on the themes of nature and class. His books secured Faulkner's reputation in the academy and made the intricate novels and stories more accessible to students.

Ransom, Tate, Warren, and Brooks, then, were New Critics but much more than that. They were also more than the designation "Southern" captures. Each of these men was rooted in the South, invested in its land and its customs and folkways. They were educated in its religious beliefs (Ransom and Brooks were the sons of ministers) and shared its tragic vision of historical defeat in the Civil War and Reconstruction. But all of them were severe critics of the South and defined themselves according to a complex set of cultural and geographical sites. Ransom, Warren, and Brooks were Rhodes Scholars at Oxford; the three of them, and Tate as well, were skilled in classical literature and foreign languages; and all four spent the greater part of their teaching careers at institutions in the North – Ransom at Kenyon College (1937–58); Warren (1950–73) and Brooks (1946–75) at Yale; and Tate at the University of Minnesota (1951–68).

The New Critics responded to the literary culture and new work underway not only in New York and Chicago, but also in London, Rome, and Paris. Tate made this point in an essay on Faulkner that he wrote in the late 1960s. Ransom, Faulkner, the poet and essayist John Peale Bishop, the Fugitive poet Donald Davidson, and "many others" from the South, said Tate, "had been in Europe" and had "become aware of the great European writers: Baudelaire, Rimbaud, Proust, Joyce." Tate lived in France on a Guggenheim Fellowship in 1929–30, and there he entered the Gertrude Stein/Ernest Hemingway circle even as, through long letters back home, he aided in generating the Southern defense of Agrarian principles in *I'll Take My Stand*. "The arts everywhere spring from a mysterious union of indigenous materials and foreign influences," Tate said in *On the Limits of Poetry* (1948); "there is no great art or literature that does not bear the marks of this fusion."

This holds for Warren too. He lived in Italy during the late 1930s, when he began *All the King's Men*, his novel about political corruption in the regime of the demagogic Southerner Willie Stark. Warren modeled Stark on the populist governor of Louisiana, Huey Long, and took inspiration from the tragic figures portrayed by Elizabethan and Jacobean dramatists. He also stated in interviews and lectures that he learned to understand Stark's seductive, dangerous character from watching and listening to the dictator Benito Mussolini.

But all four of the New Critics started in the South, and their critical program ultimately emerged from cultural studies and arguments on behalf of their region. A line can be drawn from Tate's, Warren's, and, above all, Ransom's extensive Agrarian writings in the late 1920s and early 1930s to their writings (along with Brooks's) as New Critics in the late 1930s and afterwards.

In their Agrarian work, Ransom and his colleagues sought an integrated critical enterprise that would be as much social and cultural (and explicitly so) as literary. In their New Critical phase, however, criticism no longer incorporated all that it once did. They limited the meaning of criticism to *literary* criticism, particularly as it should be taught in colleges and universities. In devising instruments for reading texts, the New Critics gave "English" a strong statement of purpose and self-definition. But they sacrificed something else – the general criticism they had envisioned in their Agrarian books and essays, a form of criticism that would include but not confine itself to the intensive study of texts.

Ransom and his co-authors in *I'll Take My Stand* combined bracing criticisms of American society and culture with reactionary proposals for change. (The title, chosen by Ransom and Davidson, echoed a line from the Confederate battle-hymn "Dixie's Land.") Their depiction of Southern farming during the ante-bellum period is unconvincing; their historical framework, based on regional distinctions between North and South, reason and sensibility, industrialism and agriculture, prose and poetry, is polarized and allegorical; and their attitudes toward slavery and race relations are detached from historical reality. As their contemporaries pointed out, the Agrarians misunderstood the drift of the South to which they preached: they did not perceive that their audience had already converted to industrialism and to the materialism of the New South creed.

Despite these shortcomings, the notion of criticism that *I'll Take My Stand* manifests is a compelling one. In its critique if not in its prescriptions, it was an important contribution to Southern literature and American conservative thought. Designed as a response to attacks upon the South by the Columbia scholar-journalist Joseph Wood Krutch and H. L. Mencken during the 1925 Scopes trial, in which a Tennessee biology instructor was found guilty of illegally teaching Darwin's theory of evolution, *I'll Take My Stand* was a provocative commentary on the culture and economy of the South.

By the late nineteenth century, the Southern economy had changed considerably from its agrarian past. Textile manufacturing (by 1900, 400 mills employed 100,000 workers), railway expansion, tobacco processing, iron and steel industries (much of this financed by Northern capital) had become features of the Southern landscape. From 1870 to 1910, industrial production and worker productivity in the South outpaced the national rates, and this trend was accelerated by the reforms of Franklin Roosevelt's New Deal (for example, the Tennessee Valley Authority, chartered by Congress in 1933, which brought electricity to rural areas in seven states).

I'll Take My Stand failed in its mission – the Agrarian campaign could not hold back the necessity of federal support for people in the midst of economic deprivation. Ransom conceded as much in later years, in an essay he contributed to a special issue of *The Sewanee Review* devoted to Tate (1959): "We were engaged upon a war that was already lost. Historically, we were behind the times."

The Agrarian critique of industrialism was evident in the first pages of the Introduction to *I'll Take My Stand*, which Ransom drafted, and which inveighed against the "Cult of Science" and modern degradation of labor:

The contribution that science can make to a labor is to render it easier by the help of a tool or a process, and to assure the laborer of his perfect economic security while he is engaged upon it. Then it can be performed with leisure and enjoyment. But the modern laborer has not exactly received this benefit under the industrial regime. His labor is hard, its tempo is fierce, and his employment is insecure. The first principle of a good labor is that it must be effective, but the second principle is that it must be enjoyed. Labor is one of the largest items in the human career; it is a modest demand to ask that it may partake of happiness.

The bad "tempo" of labor, Ransom contended, scourges thought and feeling. Men are forced by industrialism either to slave away at work or to consume things they do not need; they have no time for leisure and contemplation, and their religion and art suffer as a result. "Sensibility," concluded Ransom, falls into "general decay," worn down by the "industrial drive."

Ransom and his fellow essayists never reached the underpinnings of industrialism – class privilege, the division of labor, the worker's lack of control over (and inability to profit from) the product that he or she makes. But their insistence on the economic bedrock of culture was forcefully stated. "The trouble with the life-pattern," Ransom observed,

is to be located at its economic base, and we cannot rebuild it by pouring in soft materials from the top. The young men and women in colleges, for example, if they are already placed in a false way of life, cannot make more than an inconsequential acquaintance with the arts and humanities transmitted to them. Or else the under-standing of these arts and humanities will but make them the more wretched in their own destitution . . . We cannot recover our native humanism by adopting some stan-dard of taste that is critical enough to question the contemporary arts but not critical enough to question the social and economic life which is their ground.

Compare these words, however, to Ransom's preface to *The World's Body*, eight years later:

Where is the body and the solid substance of the world? It seems to have retired into the fulness of memory, but out of this we construct the fulness of poetry, which is counterpart to the world's fulness.

The true poetry has no great interest in improving or idealizing the world, which does well enough. It only wants to realize the world, to see it better . . . Men become poets, or at least they read poets, in order to atone for having been hard practical men and hard theoretical scientists.

By 1938 Ransom had turned his attention away from the "economic base" that was crucial to him in 1930; he focused instead on poetry, which in his view provides occasions for acts of atonement. Poetry, Ransom suggested, restores memories of a nature that men violate in their daily occupations.

By the time of *The World's Body*, Ransom judged society as beyond re-demption, at least in the Agrarian terms he had formerly endorsed. Society is degraded, but somehow persons must learn to live within it and adjust to its mechanized momentum. Poetry, he believed, is a sacramental tactic for accom-modation to a scarred world. It is the mission of literary men to be responsive to poetry and to teach young people to do the same in college and university classrooms.

As "Criticism, Inc.," the concluding essay in *The World's Body*, testifies, criticism for Ransom was now connected to, and equated with, an academic discipline. Located in the college and university, criticism should engage the verbal economy of poems and leave the "economic base" alone – even though, as the Agrarians had recognized, examining this "base" might clarify the poetry that men and women have written and their opportunities for contemplative reading.

Ransom and the others argued brilliantly for close, careful attention to lit-erary works: this was a very significant advance for both literary criticism and pedagogy. But as they made this case, they made it against other kinds of crit-ical study, work, and teaching. They enlivened and greatly improved literary criticism, and undercut it at the same time. Academics should "profession-alize" criticism, Ransom maintained, and certify that their "product" is the "close analysis" of literary texts:

Studies in the technique of the art belong to criticism certainly. They cannot belong anywhere else, because the technique is not peculiar to any prose materials discoverable in the work of art, nor to anything else but the unique form of that art. A very large volume of studies is indicated by this classification. They would be technical studies of poetry, for instance, the art I am specifically discussing, if they treated its metric; its inversions, solecisms, lapses from the prose norm of language, and from close prose logic; its tropes; its fictions, or inventions, by which it secures "aesthetic distance" and removes itself from history; or any other devices, on the general understanding that any systematic usage which does not hold good for prose is a poetic device.

All of the elements that Ransom named are essential to an investigation of a poem, but why is it imperative for poetic fictions to be perceived as "removed" from history?

This question takes on still more urgency when it is asked in the context of the late 1930s – a period of extreme economic depression at home and abroad, fascist and Nazi menace, and rancorous disputes about the cultural and political alternatives posed by the Communist Party and the Popular Front anti-fascist groups that Communists, fellow travelers, and their leftist and liberal allies supported. The late 1930s cried out for a criticism that could place literature and its study *in* history. But at this moment of crisis, perhaps because of it, Ransom emphasized poetic technique at the expense of historical reflection.

It is striking to observe Ransom's embrace in "Criticism, Inc." of the culture of professionalism and its business mentality. Here one recalls for contrast the stringent words spoken by the philosopher William James, about a colleague's proposal for a "Congress of Arts and Sciences" at the St. Louis Exposition in 1904. Such a proposal seemed to James to be

a kind of religious service in honor of the professional-philosophy shop, with its faculty, its departments and sections, its mutual etiquette, its appointments, its great mill of authorities and exclusions and suppressions, which the waters of truth are expected to feed to the great class-glory of all who are concerned. To me, truth, if there be any truth, would seem to exist for the express confusion of all this kind of thing.

Consider as well this judgment rendered by the American social philosopher and economist Thorstein Veblen in *The Higher Learning in America* (1919): "The intrusion of business principles in the universities goes to weaken and retard the pursuit of learning, and therefore to defeat the ends for which a university is maintained."

Ransom's earlier views were akin to those that James and Veblen expressed; they would appear to lead toward a general form of social-cultural criticism – a criticism that would weigh the consequences for literature of politics, economics, and history. For Ransom, though, critical inquiry now had to stay purely "technical." Criticism meant literary criticism only.

That this statement is not too strong becomes clear from a reading of Ransom's letters of the late 1930s, where he stressed that it was a strictly literary endeavor to which he was determined to adhere. To Edwin Mims, a professor at Vanderbilt, Ransom reported (June 8, 1937) that he had "contributed all I have" to regionalism and Agrarianism and had "of late gone almost entirely into pure literature . . . At my time of life it seems legitimate for me to work at literature a little more single-mindedly that I have been doing." A few months later (November 4, 1937), writing to Allen Tate, he related his desire, in the new "Review" he hoped to inaugurate at Kenyon College, "to stick to literature entirely. . . There's no consistent group writing politics . . . In the severe field of letters there is vocation enough for us: in criticism, in poetry, in fiction."

Once more writing to Tate, Ransom insisted (May 23, 1941) that he wanted to "repel any idea of a 'political' strategy" behind *The New Criticism*, his book published in 1941: "I wanted it to have *no politics at all*" (Ransom's emphasis). Given the important literary work that Ransom did and the issues of *The Kenyon Review* that he and his associates produced, it is difficult to quarrel much with the outcome of his appeal for a purely literary studies. But the achievements of the New Critics did exact a cost: something important was gained, much was lost.

A comparison: Margaret Anderson's magazine *The Little Review*, which began publication in Chicago in March 1914, in its early issues included poetry and fiction, political essays, articles on Emma Goldman and Friedrich Nietzsche, reviews of literature and music, manifestos by the Futurists, explorations of feminism, Cubism, and dadaism, and much else. One could argue that a literary journal could gain greatly from this kind of diverse cultural and political coverage. But for *The Kenyon Review*, Ransom wanted to stay within the "severe field" of literature as he defined it.

The "Postscript" to the 1950 edition of Brooks and Warren's *Understanding Poetry* – the book that Ransom had cited in *The Kenyon Review* in 1939 as a "monument" to "the Age of Criticism" – showed what the New Critics wrought. Committed to the principle that critics should fasten on "the poem in itself, if literature is to be studied as literature," Brooks and Warren were blocked from answering a question that they felt obligated to raise: "What Good is Poetry?" They are loyal to Ransom's injunction in *The World's Body* that poems be defined as integrated objects removed from history – which means that their theory only allows for speaking about the poem in a self-enclosed fashion, as though everything one needed to know and say were contained within it. Brooks and Warren could not deal with the question that they introduced because to do so they would have been obliged to move outside the self-contained poem and examine history, politics, philosophy, and ethics.

The New Critics were extremely intelligent and learned writers: they knew much more than their theoretical tenets allowed, and in their actual interpretations they used this knowledge effectively. But when they did, they cheated against the terms of their theory. The theory thus inadvertently licensed teachers and students to know less than they should and confounded efforts to represent the full value of literary studies.

It is precisely the positivist, utilitarian character of the industrial order, which the Agrarians had challenged, that ensures that the question, "what good is poetry?", will be raised. New Critical theory produced well-trained readers who were not equipped to explain the purpose of their activity.

There is no denying the New Critics' success, however. The New Critics remade the study of literature, and they triumphed while scholars and critics of rival schools faltered badly or else gained brief notice only to fade into obscurity. But the four key Southerners were part of a much broader movement toward a new style and strategy for criticism and pedagogy. Ransom, Tate, Warren, and Brooks significantly contributed to it, yet it accrued force from the work of many others.

At the beginning of the twentieth century, the field of English studies included much impressionistic "appreciation" of the classics. But it was chiefly governed by the search for "facts" and took its mandate from the lessons and models that German philology and positivist scholarship provided. Very little "criticism" existed in the academy. In graduate study, fact-centered research based on a grueling drill in classical and medieval languages was understood to be the objective of the profession and the foundation for the training that young scholar-teachers received. Though this research was burdensome, it was felt to be worthier of study and easier to assess than remarks about the great authors. It was rigorous and gave English the prestige of a science and a comparable sense of progress.

"Criticism" of a sort did surface, usually in the midst of celebratory comments about Shakespeare, the Romantic poets, and the Victorian sages. But critics were rare. This was so much the case that Tate said as late as 1940, in "Miss Emily and the Bibliographer," that if a young man "goes to graduate school, he comes out incapacitated for criticism": "he cannot discuss the literary object in terms of its specific form; all that he can do is to give you its history or tell you how he feels about it."

Critics were rare because criticism was at odds with the scholarly credentials needed to qualify for a place in a respectable department. They were also rare because it was assumed that students could read literature – as opposed to studying it scientifically – on their own.

At most colleges and universities during the first three decades of this century, there were no courses in American literature, modern literature, or criticism. This may seem strange, but it proceeded from the notion that reading literature could occur profitably anywhere, not just in the classroom. To those in English studies at the turn of the century, it was imaginable that literature could prosper outside English departments. What occurred in the best departments of that era was a disciplinary training that scholars viewed as different from the pleasurable reading that took place at home or in the library.

The philologists who dominated literary studies were concerned about the ethical and social effect of their work and its value for undergraduates. Albert Cook, a scholar at Yale, stated in an essay in 1897 that the pursuit of English added to the wisdom and humanity of the student and served "the State, – of man in society, in cooperation." Because literary studies preserved the State's good health, it should focus on texts that embody the spirit of "civilization." "There is no need to teach cynicism or frivolity, bestiality or despair," Cook emphasized: "Those productions which tend to sap or disintegrate society should be regarded as inimical to the human race and to every individual comprised within it."

In the same year, in his presidential address to the MLA, Cook described the work of the philologist in lofty terms:

The ideal philologist is at once antiquary, paleographer, grammarian, lexicologist, expounder, critic, historian of literature, and, above all, lover of humanity. He should have the accuracy of the scientist, the thirst for discovery of the Arctic explorer, the judgment of the man of affairs, the sensibility of the musician, the taste of the connoisseur, and the soul of the poet.

As Cook later wrote in *The Higher Study of English* (1906), he understood the mission of the English department to be equally compelling:

In America every one is called upon to be a shaper – to shape his own destiny, the destiny of his country, the destiny, in some sense, of the world. If he does not know the meanings and values of things, what shapes will he produce? And in all our education, what shall teach him these meanings and values, if not literature?

The two currents in English studies – scholarship and literary appreciation – flow through the volume titled *Anniversary Papers*, published in 1913 to honor George Lyman Kittredge (1860–1941) on his twenty-fifth year of teaching at Harvard. Kittredge was the author of books on Chaucer, the Gawain poet, Shakespeare, and witchcraft in England and America; and he taught at Harvard for nearly half a century, from 1888 to 1936. Most of the essays in the volume dedicated to him are scholarly with a vengeance, as a partial listing of the table of contents attests:

Caiaphas as a Palm-Sunday Prophet
Merlin and Ambrosius
Human Sacrifice Among the Irish Celts
The Twelfth-Century Tourney
Notes on Celtic Cauldrons of Plenty and the Land-Beneath-the-Waves
Medieval Lives of Judas Iscariot
The Breca Episode in *Beowulf*
From *Troilus* to *Euphues*

Written by members of English departments, these essays show the attention that the academy lavished on medieval literature. For Kittredge and his generation, literary scholarship meant delving into antique lore and accumulating facts.

Other, more appreciative essays in the volume touch on the modernity of major authors. Examples include "A Fantasy Concerning the Epitaph of Shakspere," "Johnson and His Friendships," and "The Modernness of Dante." At first sight this work may appear out of place in a volume slanted toward fact-gathering, but both the appreciative and the scholarly pieces signified a nostalgic attitude toward the past. Both implied a rejection by academic scholars and critics, in elite institutions, of the stranger, harsher social and cultural environment that such late nineteenth-century developments as mass immigration and industrialism had introduced.

Those who ruled the field of English studies were scrupulous historians, and up to a point they were very modern in their professionalized orientation toward their research. But their work often came layered in evocations of simpler, organically unified, pre-industrial eras, particularly the Middle Ages. The literary scholars in the academy were echoing the sentiments that such eminent men of letters as Henry Adams and Charles Eliot Norton expressed about a harmonious English and European past, and that Thomas Carlyle, John Ruskin, and William Morris had voiced more radically in England. For Adams, Norton, and academics following them, the cult of medievalism was a form of protest against the capitalist order and its hero, the uncultured financier fixated on "business" (the "all-devouring modern word," according to Walt Whitman).

Both the Columbia professor Joel Spingarn (1875–1939) and H. L. Mencken attacked Kittredge and "the professors" and proposed alternatives to pedantry and impressionism. In "The New Criticism" (1911) and "The American Critic" (1922), Spingarn, who taught comparative literature, replaced "impressionism" with an aesthetic theory of "expressionism" (derived from the Italian idealist philosopher Benedetto Croce); he recommended that a vital "humane scholarship" should dislodge deadening philology. Mencken sought to slay professorial impressionism, too, through a tough, vibrant, skeptical style based on George Bernard Shaw and Friedrich Nietzsche. In his "Footnote on Criticism" (1922), he said that the "motive of the critic who is really worth reading" is "the motive of the artist": "it is no more and no less than the simple desire to function freely and beautifully, to give outward and objective form to ideas that bubble inwardly and have a fascinating lure in them, to get rid of them dramatically and make an articulate noise in the world."

Neither Spingarn nor Mencken much affected criticism in the academy. Spingarn failed to supply practical examples that would buttress his abstract arguments, and Mencken was too idiosyncratic and irreverent to serve as a model for teachers and students in literature departments. No self-respecting academic could imagine writing sentences like these from Mencken's "On Being an American" (1922):

Here, more than anywhere else I know of or have heard of, the daily panorama of human existence, of private and communal folly – the unending procession of governmental extortions and chicaneries, of commercial brigandages and throat-slittings, of theological buffooneries, of aesthetic ribaldries, of legal swindles and harlotries, of miscellaneous rogueries, villainies, imbecilities, grotesqueries, and extravagances – is so inordinately gross and preposterous, so perfectly brought up to the highest conceivable amperage, so steadily enriched with an almost fabulous daring and originality, that only the man who was born with a petrified diaphragm can fail to laugh himself to sleep every night, and to awake every morning with all the eager, unflagging expectation of a Sunday-school superintendent touring the Paris peep-shows.

This was a terrific voice for newspapers and popular magazines, but it was not a voice that could be taught or that the academy could provide a home for.

The most truculent protest against *Anniversary Papers* was made by Stuart Sherman (1881–1926), a professor of English at the University of Illinois, who reviewed it for *The Nation* in 1913. Sherman conceded that Kittredge was a diligent researcher and friend of scholars but charged that this "professor" was unable, and unwilling, to instill the "love of literature." Kittredge has been a "potent force," Sherman alleged, "in bringing about the present sterilizing divorce of philology from general ideas." "If his school has not been very prolific in important books," Sherman added, "it should be remembered that one of his maxims is, 'Anyone can write a book; the difficult thing is to write an article.' This appears to be a veiled way of saying that the digestion of facts, however weighty, sinks into insignificance in comparison with the discovery of facts, however trifling."

Sherman's critique reaffirmed arguments he had advanced five years earlier in an essay titled "Graduate Schools and Literature." There, Sherman stated that "the very best men do not enter upon graduate study at all; the next best drop out after a year's experiment; the mediocre men at the end of two years; the most unfit survive and become doctors of philosophy, who go forth and reproduce their kind." The presiding scholars in English departments turned away "the student of real literary taste and power" and permitted the unfit and inept to prosper.

Many shared Sherman's judgment about the near-criminal tendencies of graduate study – the concentration on medieval literature, the lust for trivia, the overproduction of articles, the indifference shown by professors toward young men and women truly committed to a life of letters. Ezra Pound, for example, also in 1913, objected to a "system [that] aims at mediocrity, which is set to crush out all impulse and personality." Pound and others also attacked practices in undergraduate teaching, which to them appeared equally defective, consisting of a potpourri of facts and impressionistic remarks.

There is abundant evidence of the discontent felt by students as they set forth on the study of literature only to be beaten down and disappointed. The fate of Miro, the protagonist in Randolph Bourne's "History of a Literary Radical" (1919), reveals the misfortune faced by students whom the "professors" taught. When Miro began his first course in English literature, he was given

a huge anthology, a sort of press-clipping bureau of belles-lettres, from Chaucer to Arthur Symons . . . The great writers passed before his mind like figures in a crowded street. There was no time for preferences. Indeed, the professor strove diligently to give each writer his just due. How was one to appreciate the great thoughts and the great styles if one began to choose violently between them, or attempt any discrimination on grounds of their greater congeniality for one's own soul? Criticism had to spurn such subjectivity, scholarship could not be willful. The neatly arranged book of "readings," with its medicinal doses of inspiration, became the symbol of Miro's education.

Bourne once noted that he had considered becoming an English major but realized that nothing was "more deadening than the University study of literature for its own sake." In "The History of a Literary Radical," he protested against the attitudes and practices of literary study in the academy. For him, Matthew Arnold's touchstones of literary merit had taken on a parodic form, with renowned bits of literature everywhere and no time actually to enjoy and hone one's critical judgment.

Bourne lamented the lack of an education truly suited to the making of a distinguished, agile mind. For him as for Emerson in the 1830s and 1840s, the relentless pursuit of "facts" exposed an unwillingness to strive for an ideal beyond the data piled before one's eyes. Investing in facts alone meant that a person would never attain the capacity for generalization and judgment. ("Nothing in education," Henry Adams said in his autobiography, which became widely available in 1918, "is so astonishing as the amount of ignorance it accumulates in the form of inert facts.") It was a devout wish for true scholars, and anger at their miseducation, that motivated Bourne's satirical commentary on the rites of literary study.

Others made similar arguments. For example, in 1919, in his book *Comedians All*, the drama critic and editor George Jean Nathan (1882–1958) described the kind of theater study and criticism that the typical "college professor" produced; he said it was based on:

(1) an almost complete lack of knowledge of the actual theatre and the changes wrought therein in the last decade, (2) a stern disinclination, confounded with poise and dignity, to accept new things and new standards, and (3) a confusion of the stage with the tabernacle pulpit.

As the radical journalist John Reed (1887–1920) explained, in an attack on "the stupid education of our time": "We take young, soaring imaginations, consumed with curiosity about the life they see all around, and feed them with dead technique."

The anger and vexation that Bourne, Nathan, and Reed recorded are also expressed in Ludwig Lewisohn's *Upstream* (1922). Lewisohn (1882–1955), an immigrant Jew from Germany, fell in love with English literature when he was a teenager. By age thirteen, he was determined "to become not only a poet but a scholar and a man of letters," a "professor of English literature." But when he attended graduate school at Columbia, he did not find a stimulating atmosphere: "What I wanted was ideas, interpretative, critical, aesthetic, philosophical, with which to vivify, to organize, to deepen my knowledge, on which to nourish and develop my intellectual self. And my friends, the professors, ladled out information."

Lewisohn discovered an anti-Semitism more intense in English departments than anywhere else in the academy. The teaching of English in the early 1900s, Lewisohn wrote, was linked to the cultural authority of an Anglo-Saxon elite, and the professors of literature were unyielding in their "guardianship of the native tongue" against the challenge that to them Lewisohn represented: he was rejected by every English department to which he applied for a job.

To Bourne and others, the academic piling up of "facts" threatened to overwhelm the primary texts. To an extent this source of discontent derived from an abiding sense that criticism and scholarship in general were overtaking creative writing, and that the situation had worsened as the periodical press and the university attained greater size and power.

In "Criticism" (1891), Henry James had decried the impact of "contemporary journalism" on critical practice: "literary criticism flows through the periodical press like a river that has burst its dikes. The quantity of it is prodigious." James was troubled by the proportion of "the discourse uttered" to "the objects discoursed of" – an immense amount of criticism, but far too little "literary conduct" at its best. A critic should be the "helper of the artist, a torch-bearing outrider, the interpreter, the brother." But all too often, James said, critics interfered with the writer's labor and diverted attention away from literature.

James's verdict has a long history behind it – creative writers seem always to feel that there is too much criticism and that it is destructive. Montaigne had remarked centuries earlier that "there is more ado to interpret interpretations than to interpret things, and more books upon books than upon any other subject; we do nothing but comment on one another." But by the early 1900s, and decade by decade through the century, James's words were echoed by poets, novelists, and intellectuals; they scrutinized the state of criticism in the academy and concluded that the new horror was unprecedented. Those in the academy, it was said, who should have been helpers of artists had defaulted on their roles and had failed to capitalize upon the opportunities for important tasks offered to them.

Poet-critics from Ezra Pound to Randall Jarrell propounded this judgment from the 1900s through the 1950s, but it was given its most concise rendering by the poet William Carlos Williams in "The American Background" (1934):

Witness again the extraordinary dullness and sloth of the official preceptors as represented, let's say, by the heads of the cultural departments, the English departments in the lead, in the American universities. The tremendous opportunities under their nose have not attracted them. One would think that the Physics Department alone under the same roof might have given an inkling of the revolutions in theory and practice that had taken place during the last hundred years, the fundamental, immediate nature of the investigations necessary, on the ground, and that this would have started them thinking and into action. Instead, they have continued to mull over the old records, gallivanting back and forth upon the trodden-out tracks of past initiative, in a daze of subserviency and impotence.

The typical academic, Williams said, was opposed to innovation and hence averse to modern literature but was the dominant power in all of the influential journals and magazines. Risk-taking, boundary-testing writers had to make their way against rigid conventions that the academy mulishly clung to. In his series of essays on "The National Letters" (1920), Mencken had also bemoaned "the plain fact" that "the pedagogues have acquired almost a monopoly of what passes for the higher thinking in the land" and reproduce "the prevailing correctness of thought in all departments, north, east, south, and west." In "the American university," the literary critic Van Wyck Brooks charged, "ideals are cherished precisely because they are ineffectual."

Literary scholars and, for that matter, all academics in the humanities were viewed as effete and unworldly, distant from the demands and excitements of real life. As Oliver Wendell Holmes, Jr., a member of the faculty at Harvard Law School, complained in 1913 to Felix Frankfurter, the academy gave to a man "but half a life"; it was a "withdrawal from the fight in order to utter smart things," a "cloister."

When professors made forays into public commentary and criticism as Holmes recommended, they were rebuked for interfering in matters that were none of their concern. In his novel *Babbitt* (1922), Sinclair Lewis satirically evoked this irritation when his protagonist George Babbitt speaks about "The Ideal Citizen" before the Zenith Real Estate Board: "When it comes to these blab-mouth, fault-finding, pessimistic, cynical University teachers, let me tell you that during this golden coming year it's just as much our duty to bring influence to have those cusses fired as it is to sell all the real estate and gather in all the good shekels we can."

Sometimes the scholars moved to answer their critics. Kittredge tried to clarify the difference between "the scholar and the pedant" in a pamphlet published in 1916, and Edwin Greenlaw, editor of the journal *Studies in Philology*, defended "the province of literary history" in a book of that title that appeared in 1931. These scholars said that they had been abused and misunderstood, and that they were not collectors of useless information or self-serving professionals. They claimed that they were committed to ethics, morality, and art, as Albert Cook at the turn of the century had asserted. But in truth many scholars were displeased with the conditions of literary study. From within the academy, reformers emerged who spoke as sharply as did Pound, Bourne, Mencken, Williams, and other outsiders.

As early as 1906, G. R. Carpenter, in a survey of "the study of English" at Columbia University, criticized the emphasis in graduate training on "the minutiae of English linguistics and literary history, as well as the linguistics and literary history of cognate languages." This training had led, Carpenter stated, to "placing the college instruction of our country in the hands of young men of much erudition who have no especial interest in English literature and show no special aptitude for it."

Many academics denounced the work and ethos of professional literary studies. Spingarn (1922) maintained that "the scholar goes through all the proper motions, – collects facts, organizes research, delivers lectures, writes articles and sometimes books, – but under this outer seeming there is no inner reality"; Franklyn B. Snyder (1923) stressed that the teaching of literature was an exercise in irrelevance, for it showed no "contact with that world in which men live and love and struggle and die"; E. E. Stoll (1927) pointed to the crushing influence of philology on English departments, objected to the amount of scholarly publication, and mocked the "barren discussions" at professional meetings; Norman Foerster (1929) found that professionalism and specialization were driving "the literary scholar" away from his subject, as though the preparations for a journey mattered more than actually taking it; and John Livingston Lowes, in a Modern Language Association presidential address (1933), criticized the "torrent" of scholarly papers, the pointless accumulation of facts, and the endless quest for knowledge "about" literary texts rather than knowledge of the texts themselves.

To these scholars, writing in the first decades of the century, literary education seemed designed to prevent undergraduate and graduate students from reading literature. In a typical complaint, an eminent scholar of Italian literature, who attended graduate school in the 1930s, noted that he took a two-semester course on Boccaccio in which the first semester focused on "sources" and the second on "influences." Boccaccio's writings were not discussed.

George Woodberry, J. M. Manly, Bliss Perry, William Lyon Phelps, Irving Babbitt, and countless critics, scholars, and men-of-letters repeated the charges and offered their own testimonies. The bill of particulars was already familiar by the time that the Southern New Critics, and also R. S. Crane, Lionel Trilling, R. P. Blackmur, and Yvor Winters, presented their versions of the case against the pedantic historians and philologists in the mid- to late 1930s.

One can go back even earlier to William Morton Payne's *English in American Universities*, published in 1895, which consisted of reports on the state of the discipline written by faculty members at a number of institutions. The most consistent note in them was the desire that students begin to focus on literature as an art and that they be taught to examine the texts themselves.

Payne began by stating that "whatever the usefulness for discipline of such subjects [i.e., history, metrics, linguistics], the spirit of literature is not to be acquired by making chronological tables, or tracing the genealogies of words, or working out the law of decreasing predication." He and his fellow essayists then proceeded to outline the better, text-based alternative. One faculty member from the University of Chicago said that "the masterpieces of our literature" should be studied "as works of literary art"; another from the University of Indiana argued against the over-emphasis on biography, history, critical commentaries, and "petty details," and advised that the student be placed "face to face with the work itself"; still another at the University of Michigan recounted the effort there to "bring the student into direct contact with the literature";

last but not least, a professor at the University of Nebraska affirmed that his department believed in teaching students to "read literature as literature."

Few of these scholars would have appealed to an iconoclast like H. L. Mencken, but their emphasis on the text converged with his insistence, in "Puritanism as a Literary Force" (1917), that the critic respond to "a piece of writing as a piece of writing, a work of art as a work of art." Like the scholars, if for different reasons, Mencken wanted to free texts from the extraneous matter that kept them from direct view.

As a final example of the many internal critiques and calls for reform, here is the scholar Albert Feuillerat's summary (1924) of the problems that afflicted English studies:

There is no end of dissecting the literary works, submitting them to the lens of our microscopes, making statistics, cataloguing, indexing, tabulating, drawing diagrams, curves, angles (all the figures used in geometry), adding facts, still more facts, weighing data, accumulating an enormous mass of materialien. And so exciting has been this sort of labor that we have practically forgotten that the reason why literary works are written is that they may be enjoyed by all those who read them, critics included. In fact, we no longer suppose that they can be enjoyed or, at least, we refrain from enjoying them.

Buried under piles of information, "the books have ceased for us to have interest in themselves," Feuillerat concluded. "The books themselves": this phrase, for many reformers, expressed the true object and goal of literary studies, and it signified the need that the New Criticism fulfilled.

By the 1920s, many could see what had been missing and knew in general terms how to describe what they wanted. The opposition between the New Critics and the old-line scholars was heated, and advocates of New Critical procedures were often reviled. But the New Critics triumphed because they made essential (and practical) what many scholars desired as much as they did – the emergence at last of "the books themselves."

The New Criticism also resembled (and gained some support from) the "Great Books" movement and curriculum that the editor and essayist John Erskine (1879–1951) developed for the General Honors program at Columbia College. Lionel Trilling took part in this survey of the "classics of the western world" when he was a student at Columbia in the 1920s, and his reflections about this experience, recorded in "autobiographical notes" he jotted down in 1971, indicate the concentration on texts that Erskine fostered.

As Trilling explained, all of the texts – in philosophy and history as well as in literature – were examined in their own terms: "We were assigned nothing else but the great books themselves, confronting them as best we could without the mediation of ancillary works."

The type of reading favored by Erskine, however, blurred the boundaries between texts and did not privilege the particularity of *literary* texts – which is what mattered most to the New Critics. Trilling and his classmates were encouraged to explore the moral, ethical, and political issues that the Great Books addressed, and this was contrary to the purer aims of scholar-reformers and critics within English departments. But like so many others during the period, Erskine and his colleagues aimed to deal directly with texts, eliminating the distracting "mediation" that was preventing them from being read intensively. They reinforced the changes in critical approach that the New Critics advocated.

The rise of the New Criticism, then, occurred because of demands inside and outside the academy for an end to traditional forms of scholarship and literary appreciation; these were judged to be conservative, irrelevant, irresponsible, and at odds with creative writing and cultural needs. Almost always these calls were accompanied by a commitment to primary texts and by the appeal that the academy end its ivory-tower detachment. Few people during the 1920s and early 1930s were sure what examining the text itself might actually entail or how, specifically, it would supply English departments with a social mission. They knew what was needed but not how to do it.

This is where the New Critics came in: they managed persuasively to trace the contours of a text-centered approach, giving substance to the phrase "the text itself" and demonstrating in action the interpretive tools that the study of the text required.

An important source for the New Critical conception of close reading texts was the work of the English critic I. A. Richards, in *Principles of Literary Criticism* (1925) and *Practical Criticism* (1929). A writer and teacher of many interests – the poetry critic Helen Vendler described him as "a missionary of world intercultural literacy" – Richards was the author of books on literature, semantics, philosophy, classics, education, and other subjects. He was a revered teacher and lecturer in England, the United States, and China; he was one of the major figures, arguably the most important of all, in the development of literary studies in the university and in the effort to give it scientific rigor; and he inspired and shaped the work of such modern English critics as William Empson (who was Richards's student) and F. R. Leavis as well as many of the American New Critics, who adapted his terms and approach, even as they disputed his work on specific points.

As a student, Richards took few courses in English literature; he planned to pursue a career in medicine. But in 1919 Richards became a lecturer in

English at Cambridge, where the subject had just begun to receive institutional sanction. He used his knowledge of English literature to give presentations on the theory and practice of criticism, the contemporary novel, Samuel Taylor Coleridge, and other topics. Through these lectures Richards introduced "a new art of reading," according to the scholar M. C. Bradbrook, who attended them. This form of reading displaced the usual philological and historical preoccupation (even more prevalent in England than in the United States) with biographical and historical facts. Instead, Richards focused attention on the properties of the literary work itself.

During the 1920s, T. S. Eliot presented lectures at Cambridge on the metaphysical poets, and Richards in turn lectured on Eliot's work; for students at Cambridge, the central critics were Richards and Eliot and the basic reference points were their lectures, essays, and books. The method that Richards described thus seemed very contemporary, connected to the innovative, bold work of Eliot in poetry and criticism.

Richards's first books, *The Foundations of Aesthetics* (co-written with C. K. Ogden and J. Wood, 1922) and *The Meaning of Meaning* (co-written with Ogden, 1923), developed procedures from positivist philosophy to examine problems in art and language. Richards then turned directly to literature, criticism, and literary theory, in an effort to provide analytical techniques and terms for the discipline of English – and also to equip readers for the challenging task of responding to modern literature, especially to Eliot's verse and the seventeenth-century metaphysical poets and nineteenth-century French symbolists whom Eliot drew upon.

Richards's intention to put literary criticism on a firm foundation is clear from the first chapter of *Principles of Literary Criticism*, where he surveys the field:

A few conjectures, a supply of admonitions, many acute isolated observations, some brilliant guesses, much oratory and applied poetry, inexhaustible confusion, a sufficiency of dogma, no small stock of prejudices, whimsies and crotchets, a profusion of mysticism, a little genuine speculation, sundry stray inspirations, pregnant hints and random *aperçus*; of such as these, it may be said without exaggeration, is extant critical theory composed.

In *Principles*, and even more in *Practical Criticism*, Richards articulated a new theory and practice of literary analysis. He based *Practical Criticism* on university students' responses to a series of poems that he distributed. The evidence showed that students read poorly; they were insensitive to tone, unable to perceive irony, and in general applied to all texts the stock and sentimental expectations about what a poem should be and sound like. Richards's goal was to devise an approach that would prevent the mistakes that distorted the students' responses to literary works and that led to countless gaffes and wrong evaluations.

Richards's experiment was somewhat forced; here and there, he tinkered with the poems to make them more perplexing, and he held back from readers the knowledge of even a few basic facts – author, title, date, for instance – and thus to an extent gave the clues for the misinterpretations that he examined. Still, *Practical Criticism*, with its claim that "all respectable poetry invites close reading," was a noteworthy event for many poets, critics, and intellectuals; as Allen Tate said, "Nobody who read I. A. Richards's *Practical Criticism* when it appeared in 1929 could read any poem as he had read it before."

Like the Romantic poet-critics Coleridge and Percy Bysshe Shelley, both of whom he valued highly, Richards was a stalwart defender of poetry, a critic engaged in making the case for literature. As he explained in *Principles*:

The arts are our storehouse of recorded values. They spring from and perpetuate hours in the lives of exceptional people, when their control and command of experience is at its highest, hours when varying possibilities of existence are most clearly seen and the different activities which may arise are most exquisitely reconciled, hours when habitual narrowness of interests or confused bewilderment are replaced by an intricately wrought composure.

Poetry is intimately connected with how we live: it enables us to live *better*, with greater sympathy and sensitivity. But in another way poetry is disconnected from life, for it constitutes a different order or level of discourse, and hence it requires special instruments for analysis.

Poetry, concluded Richards in *Science and Poetry* (1926), presents pseudo-statements – statements that are not referential, that cannot be proven, and that are not cognitive but affective. It stimulates feelings, including those in conflict with one another, but organizes and harmonizes them. Coleridge, in *Biographia Literaria* (1817), had described the special power of the imagination in similar terms as the capacity to reconcile opposites; this, for Coleridge, is the creative work that the poet performs in his or her text. And to an extent Richards shifted the emphasis not so much from the poet to the text as from the poet to the reader; he was concerned with the poem's effects on the psychology of the reader. This is a dimension of his work that the American New Critics resisted, because of the subjectivism that it appeared to invite.

An utterance, Richards stated in *Principles*, "may be used for the sake of the reference, true or false, which it causes. This is the scientific use of language. But it may also be used for the sake of the effects in emotion and attitude produced by the reference it occasions. This is the emotive use of language." Science is *referential*: it asks, is a statement verifiable? Does it match with reality? Literature, on the other hand, is *emotive*; its impact lies within the reader and is involved with his or her attitudes, desires, and impulses, which the poem serves to bring into balance.

For Richards, the balancing power of poetry gives to the reader a feeling of equilibrium. It is – here he followed Matthew Arnold – a form of compensation for the loss of religious belief, a loss that he and other critics, intellectuals, and philosophers throughout the modern period described. As Paul Tillich noted in *The Courage To Be* (1952): "The decisive event which underlies the search for meaning and the despair of it in the 20th century is the loss of God in the 19th century." The poet Wallace Stevens, in his essay "Two or Three Ideas," in *Opus Posthumous* (1957), explained: "In an age of disbelief, or, what is the same thing, in a time that is largely humanistic, in one sense or another, it is for the poet to supply the satisfactions of belief, in his measure and in his style." In *Science and Poetry*, Richards likewise said that poetry "is capable of saving us, or since some have found a scandal in this word, of preserving us or rescuing us from confusion and frustration."

Poetry can only achieve this result, Richards maintained, if readers understand that the statements – the *pseudo-statements* – that it makes differ from those in scientific discourse. As he contended in *Science and Poetry*, we must "cut our pseudo-statements free from that kind of belief which is appropriate to verified statements." Poetry can do no good for a person who insists on reading it referentially, who expects it to be literally true in its statements. As he observed elsewhere in *Science and Poetry*, "It is never what a poem *says* which matters, but what it *is*." Thus Richards advised readers not to introduce beliefs into poetry.

On one level Richards was a New Critic, indeed the *first* New Critic, as John Crowe Ransom noted in his book *The New Criticism* (1941). He zeroed in on the complex, autonomous text at hand and was committed to the teaching of literature as a special form of language that produces distinctive effects. Richards's influence on the New Criticism can be seen in his emphasis on internal balance, poise, and equilibrium, on the complex unity of the poem, and in his definition of "irony" as "consist[ing] in the bringing in of the opposite, the complementary impulses." Richards told teachers and students to stay focused on the poem itself and not become distracted by biographical, historical, and other non-literary contexts. He demonstrated these lessons in courses he taught at Harvard, where he held an appointment from 1939 to 1963.

In some ways, however, Richards was more of a reader-based than a text-based critic, as he implied in *Principles*:

Whether we are discussing music, poetry, painting, sculpture, or architecture, we are forced to speak as though certain physical objects – vibrations of strings and of columns of air, marks printed on paper, canvases and pigments, masses of marble, fabrics of freestone, – are what we are talking about. And yet the remarks we make as critics do not apply to such objects but to states of mind, to experiences.

In an essay titled "The Interactions of Words," Richards similarly moved from the language of the text to the organizing mind of the reader:

There is a prodigious activity between the words as we read them. Following, exploring, realizing, *becoming* that activity is, I suggest, the essential thing in reading the poem. Understanding is not a preparation for reading the poem. It is itself the poem. And it is a constructive, hazardous, free creative process, a process of conception through which a new being is growing in the mind.

The experiences of readers – this, more than the meanings of the text itself – was perhaps Richards's main interest, and it preoccupied William Empson (1906–84) as well in *Seven Types of Ambiguity* (1930) and *Some Versions of Pastoral* (1934), where he showed how much particular texts by Shakespeare, Herbert, and Donne can be made to mean to the highly attentive, exploratory, question-asking reader. Empson drew on his work with Richards, and he also profited from the case-studies in explication that the poet-critics Laura Riding and Robert Graves had performed on poems by E. E. Cummings and Shakespeare in their *Survey of Modernist Poetry* (1927). Empson's readings of texts were always brilliant, and proved very influential, yet at times to the New Critics they seemed if anything too brilliant, overly ingenious, less about the work at hand than about the dizzyingly complex mind of Empson.

The larger problem with Richards's conception of poetry, from which Empson's criticism took shape, is that it threatened to marginalize what it attempted to defend. The more Richards tried in *Science and Poetry* and elsewhere to define the special nature of poetic discourse – it is non-referential, non-literal – the more he made some readers wonder why they should bother with poetry at all. What kind of knowledge does it actually give? Has a poem no connection to history, to the period when it was written, or to later periods when readers respond to and interpret it?

With clarity, wit, and precision, Richards presented the case for how readers should respond to poetry and why they should value it in their lives. But in a sense his work raised yet again the question he had hoped to answer: if *this* is what poetry is, then why *should* we value it? It is the same question that the New Critics struggled with and never managed to answer convincingly.

T. S. Eliot (1888–1965), more than Richards or Empson or anyone else, directly inspired the critical writings of the New Critics. Eliot rarely produced close readings himself, but in his critical prose he highlighted an understanding of literary language to which he gave complex form in his poetry. As E. E. Cummings remarked in 1920, Eliot's language possessed an astonishing "intensity": "a vocabulary almost brutally attuned to attain distinction; an extraordinarily tight orchestration of the shapes of sounds; the delicate and careful murderings – almost invariably interpreted, internally as well as terminally, through near-rhyme and rhyme – of established tempos by oral rhythm." Eliot's views on the function of the critic and on the nature of literary history were tremendously important, both because of their intrinsic interest and because they came from a poet of such power and originality. He was the author of the period's most influential poem, *The Waste Land* (1922), and its most authoritative literary essays and reviews.

In the history of modern literary theory and criticism, Eliot belongs among the important poet-critics – Samuel Johnson, Samuel Taylor Coleridge, and Matthew Arnold – who have defined the critical standards of an era, recast the literary tradition, and established terms for literary analysis and evaluation. So immense was Eliot's authority that the poet Dylan Thomas referred to him as "the Pope" and the critic Delmore Schwartz (1913–66) dubbed him a "literary dictator." Of Eliot, Wallace Stevens said in 1938, "I don't know what there is (any longer) to say about Eliot. His prodigious reputation is a great difficulty." "A Great Man Gone" was the title of the obituary for Eliot in the *Times Literary Supplement* (January 7, 1965); "for many readers," its author concluded, "Mr. Eliot's death will be like the death of a part of themselves."

Born in St. Louis, Missouri, the seventh and youngest child of Henry Ware Eliot, a businessman, and Charlotte Stearns Eliot, an amateur poet and volunteer social worker, Eliot attended private schools and then entered Harvard University in 1906, receiving his bachelor's degree in 1909, his master's in 1910–11, and completing all his doctoral work except for his dissertation, just before the outbreak of World War I. At Harvard, he became interested in philosophy and comparative literature – Dante's *Divine Comedy* was a sublime discovery for him. Central influences on his intellectual development included the Spanish-American philosopher, poet, and humanist George Santayana (1863–1952), from whom Eliot took a course on modern philosophy, and the literary scholar Irving Babbitt (1865–1933), with whom Eliot studied nineteenth-century French literary criticism. He also knew personally and studied the writings of the American philosopher Josiah Royce (1855–1916) and the British philosopher and mathematician Bertrand Russell, and, later, the French philosopher Henri Bergson. Bergson's theory of the dynamic flux and movement of consciousness in particular shaped Eliot's early verse.

For Eliot's poetry and criticism, however, the crucial experience of his Harvard years was his reading in December 1908 of the English poet-critic Arthur Symons's *The Symbolist Movement in Literature* (1899), which introduced French symbolist poetry to English and American readers. Eliot was already writing verse himself, publishing some of it in *The Harvard Advocate*; in the period from 1909 to 1911, he worked on two of his best poems, "Portrait of a Lady" and "The Love Song of J. Alfred Prufrock," making adept use of the style of irony and Symbolism he had encountered in the French poets – Charles Baudelaire, Arthur Rimbaud, and Jules Laforgue – whom Symons quoted and discussed.

"From Baudelaire," Eliot recalled, "I learned first, a precedent for the poetical possibilities, never developed by any poet writing in my own language, of the more sordid aspects of the modern metropolis, of the possibility of fusion between the sordidly realistic and the phantasmagoric, the possibility of the juxtaposition of the matter-of-fact and the fantastic." He also read Shakespeare and other Elizabethan dramatists, as well as the Victorian poets Robert Browning and Alfred, Lord Tennyson, whose poetry Eliot judged ill suited to the modern world, but whose verbal techniques (Browning's dramatic monologues, Tennyson's sound patterns) he borrowed, modified, and sometimes parodied.

Eliot was a self-made modernist; as his friend Ezra Pound later said, Eliot had "trained himself *and* modernized himself *on his own*." In his Introduction to Pound's *Selected Poems* (1928), Eliot made a version of this point himself: "The form in which I began to write, in 1908 or 1909, was directly drawn from the study of Laforgue together with the later Elizabethan drama; and I do not know anyone who started from exactly that point."

From October 1910 to September 1911, Eliot studied at the Sorbonne in Paris, and then, upon his return to Harvard, he pursued graduate work and served as a teaching assistant for two years. For his dissertation topic, he focused on the writings of the British idealist philosopher F. H. Bradley (1846–1924), author of *Appearance and Reality* (1893). His research led him to the University of Marburg in Germany in the summer of 1914, but then, as the threat of world war loomed, he relocated to Merton College, Oxford.

In London, in September 1914, Eliot met Pound, who quickly became his adviser, editor, and literary agent. "The Love Song of J. Alfred Prufrock" was published in *Poetry* magazine in June 1915, and, in the following month, Eliot married Vivien (sometimes Vivienne) Haigh-Wood, a relationship that soon unraveled and, as Vivien's mental and physical illnesses deepened in the 1920s and 1930s, proved harrowing for both of them. His despair at this personal disaster is reflected in the torment, bitterness, and isolation expressed in much of his poetry. It is intimated as well in the themes of impersonality, classical order, and discipline that he emphasized in his criticism, as if he were seeking as a critic and theorist of poetry to underscore the self-control that he struggled to maintain in the midst of his failed marriage.

"No artist produces great art," Eliot claimed, "by a deliberate attempt to express his personality. He expresses his personality indirectly through concentrating upon a task which is a task in the same sense as the making of an efficient engine or the turning of a jug or a table-leg" (*Selected Essays, 1917–1932*).

Eliot's work is itself impersonal and objective; it is filled – especially the poetry – with masks, role-playing, and multiple voices. Yet it is saturated everywhere with personal pain, regret, sexual desire, emotional and spiritual yearning. This is one of the potent paradoxes of Eliot's art, in his prose as in his poetry, and a main reason why it haunted and fascinated readers.

From 1915 to early 1917, Eliot taught in grammar schools and in London gave lectures on Elizabethan, Victorian, modern British, and modern French literature. He also wrote a dozen dense, technical articles and reviews on philosophy, largely, it has been suggested, to please his parents, who opposed his plan to become a poet – they had opposed his marriage too – and who wanted him to commit himself to an academic career. Because of the difficulty of traveling during the war, Eliot was unable to return to Harvard to defend his dissertation and he never was awarded his doctorate.

In March 1917, tired of makeshift teaching, Eliot took a job in the colonial and foreign department of Lloyds Bank. He held this position for the next eight years, while, at the same time, he labored on his poetry; his first volume, *Prufrock and Other Observations*, appeared in 1917. He also wrote literary criticism, publishing striking essays and book reviews in the *Times Literary Supplement* and other leading periodicals and including a number of them in *The Sacred Wood* (1920), a landmark collection of criticism and theory.

Worn down by the demands of caring for his wife, in October 1921 Eliot went to Margate, in southeast England, for rest and treatment of nervous disorder. A month later, he left for a sanatorium in Lausanne, Switzerland, where he was a patient for six weeks, and where he worked on the draft of a long poem he had started years earlier. In Paris, on his way back to London, he showed the draft to Ezra Pound, who edited it skillfully and turned it – in Eliot's words – from "a jumble of good and bad passages into a poem," the poem that became *The Waste Land*.

Allusive, collage-like, experimental and technically daring, idiomatic, hallucinatory, showily learned and archly witty, ominous to the point of being apocalyptic, *The Waste Land* was a primary text of literary modernism, rivaled in importance only by James Joyce's *Ulysses*. The poem was published in *The Criterion* – a new literary and cultural quarterly edited by Eliot – in October 1922, reprinted in *The Dial* in November, and then was included in Eliot's *Poems 1900–1925*. *The Waste Land* was, Pound declared, "the justification of the 'movement,' of our modern experiment, since 1900."

For many writers, critics, intellectuals, and general readers, *The Waste Land* evoked the waste and sterility of a western world ravaged by World War I, which had ended in November 1918. More than 8.5 million soldiers died during the war; and civilian deaths totaled 13 million. The scale of death was unlike anything history had ever witnessed, and *The Waste Land* reflects the trauma that the war caused: Eliot's sense of revulsion and horror informed his poem from beginning to end.

Eliot was a literary and cultural force throughout the 1920s and 1930s. After serving as assistant editor of *The Egoist* from 1917 to 1919, he became in 1922 the editor of the quarterly *The Criterion*, a commitment that lasted until the journal's demise in 1939. In its pages he published E. M. Forster, Virginia Woolf, James Joyce, and D. H. Lawrence. He was also the first editor of an English journal to publish such significant European writers as Jean Cocteau, Paul Valéry, Marcel Proust, and the literary historian E. R. Curtius. In 1925, Eliot accepted a position in the publishing firm of Faber and Gwyer (later, Faber and Faber), and in subsequent years he published Pound's *Selected Poems* and *Cantos* as well as work by Marianne Moore, Wallace Stevens, W. H. Auden, Ted Hughes, and Sylvia Plath.

From 1932 to 1933, Eliot held the Charles Eliot Norton professorship of poetry at Harvard, where he delivered the lectures that became *The Use of Poetry and the Use of Criticism* (1933). During this same period, Eliot delivered the Page Barbour Lectures at the University of Virginia, later published as *After Strange Gods: A Primer of Modern Heresy* (1933), a book that displayed a censorious attitude toward modern literature and that was marred by anti-Semitism. *The Idea of a Christian Society* (1939) and *Notes Towards the Definition of Culture* (1948) presented gloomily resentful social and cultural criticism and theory, and they seem to have had little impact even at their time of their first publication.

Once he became an eminent figure, Eliot took pleasure in depreciating his earlier writings, which the New Critics and others had so earnestly read and responded to. In a lecture in 1956, he stated:

The best of my *literary* criticism – apart from a few notorious phrases which have had a truly embarrassing success in the world – consists of essays on poets and poetic dramatists who had influenced me. It is a by-product of my private poetry-workshop;

or a prolongation of the thinking that went into the formation of my own verse... My criticism has this in common with that of Ezra Pound, that its merits and limitations can be fully appreciated only when it is considered in relation to the poetry I have written myself.

While noteworthy for linking his criticism to the development of his poetry, Eliot's self-assessment here and elsewhere should not be taken at face value. In part its apparent modesty was a dig at professional critics and academics who had written about literary art without practicing it themselves. Pound made the same point that Eliot did, writing in *The Criterion* (January 1923): "I consider criticism merely a preliminary excitement, a statement of things a writer has to clear up in his own head sometime or other, probably antecedent to writing; of no value unless it come to fruit in the created work later." (Perhaps in the background is Aristotle's dictum [*Politics* 8.6] that "they who are to be judges must also be performers," and Flaubert's remark in a letter [October 1856] to Louise Colet that "a man is a critic when he cannot be an artist, in the same way that a man becomes an informer when he cannot be a soldier.")

Nothing that Eliot said could lessen the impact and ongoing influence of his critical work. As early as 1929, Edmund Wilson identified Eliot as "the most important literary critic in the English-speaking world... Eliot's opinions, so cool and even casual in appearance, yet sped with the force of so intense a seriousness and weighted with so wide a learning, have stuck oftener and sunk deeper in the minds of the post-war generation of both England and the United States than those of any other critic."

Through "Tradition and the Individual Talent" (1919), Eliot made "tradition" a central topic for poets, critics, intellectuals, and teachers of literature in the academy. Two of the canonical texts of modern Anglo-American literary criticism, F. R. Leavis's *Revaluation: Tradition and Development in English Poetry* (1936) and Cleanth Brooks's *Modern Poetry and the Tradition* (1939), were expansions of Eliot's ideas about tradition, and many other New Critical books and essays, and countless syllabi year after year, were similarly based on the terms that Eliot articulated.

For Eliot, each poem exists within the terms of the tradition from which it emerges and which it, in turn, redefines. One might wonder: is tradition something that the poet acquires, and to which he or she must be "faithful," or is tradition something that the poet actively makes? The answer for Eliot was that both are true. Poets, he believed, operate within the tradition that precedes and surrounds them, but poets themselves must work to group, absorb, and apply the tradition's main elements. Originality is a result of being steeped in tradition.

Ralph Ellison, in *Shadow and Act* (1967), described his response to Eliot, whose poetry he discovered when he was a second-year student at Tuskegee Institute in Alabama in the 1930s:

The Waste Land seized my mind. I was intrigued by its power to move me while eluding my understanding. Somehow its rhythms were often closer to those of jazz than were those of the Negro poets, and even though I could not understand then, its range of allusion was as mixed and as varied as that of Louis Armstrong. And there were its discontinuities, its changes of pace and its hidden system of organization which escaped me. There was nothing to do but look up the references in the footnotes to the poem, and thus began my conscious education in literature.

Reacting against the Romantics, Shelley and Wordsworth especially, Eliot maintained that the poet's craft should be impersonal. He was not saying that personal feelings should never enter into the sensibility that a poet develops, but, rather, that poets should avoid displaying their *personality* in their work.

Later critics sometimes characterized Eliot as a "weak" poet-critic because of the priority that he assigned to tradition and impersonality. But there was another dimension of Eliot's argument. "What happens when a new work of art is created," he stressed, "is something that happens simultaneously to all the works of art that preceded it." The poet defers to tradition yet, ultimately, challenges and revises it. As Eliot contended in "The Frontiers of Criticism" (1956): "When the poem has been made, something new has happened, something that cannot be wholly explained by *anything that went before*."

"The Metaphysical Poets" (1921) was another essay that crucially influenced the New Critics. Almost as soon as it appeared, the situation that Eliot described, in which John Donne, Andrew Marvell, and their contemporaries were "more often named than read, and more often read than profitably studied," was dramatically reversed. The difficult metaphysical poets became models of good poetry.

Eliot's essay was condensed in its argument, highly suggestive, and extraordinarily ambitious. In it he seized on the evaluative terms that in the eighteenth-century Samuel Johnson had used against the metaphysical poets ("the most heterogeneous ideas are yoked by violence together"); and he deployed them to elevate the very poets whom his eminent precursor had assailed, insisting that modern poetry *must* be difficult. He packed "The Metaphysical Poets" with unelaborated argument and assertion, illustrating in the process how much "tradition" is made, is *forced*, into the form that later generations of writers like Eliot require.

Eliot liked being a troublemaker, saying outrageous things from on high and often not quite clarifying whether he meant them seriously, as was the case with harsh comments he made, for instance, about Milton, both the man and the poet. He was willing to take on Shakespeare, too. In "Hamlet and His Problems," included in *The Sacred Wood*, Eliot presented his theory of the "objective correlative": "The only way of expressing emotion in the form of art is by finding an 'objective correlative'; in other words, a set of objects, a situation, a chain of events which shall be the formula for that particular emotion; such that, when the external facts, which must terminate in sensory experience, are given, the emotion is immediately evoked."

Developing this theory further, Eliot considered *Hamlet*, which he labeled an "artistic failure" precisely because in it the "emotions" that Shakespeare evokes are purportedly "in excess" of the facts of the story, the dramatic action. "Far from being Shakespeare's masterpiece," Eliot concluded, "the play is most certainly an artistic failure" – an absurd judgment that Eliot may not have believed, but that he uttered with such assurance that it is still cited and debated, as if it were embedded now in the text of the play itself.

Eliot was skillful at pithily summing up the nature and function of literary criticism, and the New Critics Ransom and Brooks invoked his critical practice as exemplary. Eliot described criticism as "the disinterested exercise of intelligence . . . the elucidation of works of art and the correction of taste . . . the common pursuit of true judgment." He insisted that critics should center their arguments in the analysis of specific passages and poems, and it was this injunction that the New Critics followed.

"Comparison and analysis," Eliot said, "are the chief tools of the critic"; through these tools, the literary critic can gain the skill that he or she needs most of all – "a very highly developed sense of fact" ("The Function of Criticism," 1923), by which Eliot means a precise perception of literary effects, relationships, and values. The New Critics and others took inspiration from Eliot, praising him in terms akin to those he used about Aristotle in *The Sacred Wood*: "In whatever sphere of interest, [Aristotle] looked solely and steadfastly at the object; in his short and broken treatise he provides an eternal example – not of laws, or even of method, for there is no method except to be very intelligent, but of intelligence itself swiftly operating the analysis of sensation to the point of principle and definition."

By the 1950s, Eliot was lamenting copiously detailed interpretation of texts, calling it "lemon-squeezing." (Cf. Emerson in his *Journals* [1858]: "Taking to pieces is the trade of those who cannot construct.") Yet, more than any other critic, he had presided over the New Critical movement. The critic must "stick to his job," Eliot said in a lecture in the 1930s, and this means being concerned with "the question whether the poet has used the right word in the right place, the rightness depending upon both the explicit intention and an indefinite irradiation of sound and sense." "Honest criticism and sensitive appreciation are directed not upon the poet but upon the poetry," Eliot concluded in section II of "Tradition and the Individual Talent."

Ransom, Tate, Warren, and Brooks learned what it might mean to read closely by responding to Eliot's language in action, and by reading the critical essays and books that Eliot, and Richards and Empson, produced. It was not merely that the New Critics invented techniques for reading Eliot and his fellow modern poets. Eliot's poetry, supported by his criticism, encouraged readers to behave in ways that altered their general response to texts.

(A word should be inserted here for the English critic F. R. Leavis, who was very "English" in his orientation, but whose essays sometimes appeared in journals edited by the Southern New Critics, and who did much through his books and essays and journal *Scrutiny* [1932–53] to advance the cause of close reading in the context of Eliot's ideas about literary tradition.)

Modern poetry and modern criticism reinforced one another, as the response to Eliot attested. As Tate said in 1956 in a survey of modern verse from 1900 to 1950, "never have poetry and criticism in English been so close together, so mutually sensitive, the one so knowing about the other." For decades, Eliot was the foremost authority in both areas. Warren said that his "discovery" of Eliot in the early 1920s, when Warren was just seventeen, "was the guiding influence of my whole career": "he broke up the conventional world I had known and presented a literature from which one could assemble a whole new fluctuating world." So daunting was Eliot's authority that, according to Malcolm Cowley, the poet-critic John Peale Bishop took to studying Italian "so that he could get the full force of the quotations from Dante" identified in Eliot's notes to *The Waste Land*.

As late as the 1970s, as Alfred Kazin noted, Eliot remained extremely influential: he "has continued to dominate the thought of two generations without ever being fundamentally challenged for his reactionary social-religious doctrine." Only in subsequent decades did Eliot's problematic views on race, ethnicity, and class come in for stringent critique, and his influence begin to wane.

Eliot's poetry and criticism advanced the general modernist emphasis on the direct, unsparing renewal of language. From the English poet-essayist T. E. Hulme (killed in action in 1917), with his demand for "accurate, precise, and definite description," to the American expatriates in London and Paris, the major modernists time and again emphasized the exacting use of language. This prompted the New Critics to take the language of poetry as their preserve and to endow it with special significance.

Eliot declared that "the poetry of a people takes its life from the people's speech and in turn gives life to it; it represents its highest point of consciousness, its greatest power, and its most delicate sensibility." Gertrude Stein, Hemingway, and Pound similarly upheld the primacy of language as an index to social and cultural well-being. "As language becomes the most power-ful instrument of perfidy," Pound counseled, "so language alone can riddle and cut through the meshes." "Used to conceal meaning, used to blur meaning," he added, language at its worst could be overcome only through language at its best. Only "a care for language, for accurate registration by language avails." The poet William Carlos Williams said about Stein that she was "smashing every connotation that words have ever had, in order to get them back clean."

Such descriptions and injunctions appeared often during and after World War I, an event that writers judged literally to have twisted and deformed the language. As Henry James stated in 1915, in a claim that Pound and Hemingway reiterated, "the war has used up words; they have weakened, they have deteriorated like motor car tires ... We are now confronted with a depreciation of all our terms, or, otherwise speaking, with a loss of expression through an increase of limpness, that may well make us wonder what ghosts will be left to walk." In an August 1917 letter, written while he was serving in France in an ambulance unit, John Dos Passos (1896–1970, later the author of *Three Soldiers*, *Manhattan Transfer*, and the *U. S. A.* trilogy) declared: "The war is utter damn nonsense – a vast cancer fed by lies and self-seeking malignity on the part of those who don't do the fighting ... Everything said & written & thought in America about the war is lies – God! They choke one like poison gas." The dramatist and critic George Bernard Shaw (1922) agreed about the war's corruption of language: "Men with empty phrases in their mouths and foolish fables in their heads have seen each other, not as fellow-creatures, but as dragons and devils, and have slaughtered each other accordingly."

Eliot and Pound wrote approvingly about James, and their valuation of his work played a role in the ascendancy of the New Criticism. James's evocations of the integrity of the work of art – the organic wholeness of the story or novel – were presented not only in many essays and reviews but also in the Prefaces to the New York Edition of his writings published in 1907–09. Form, style, and structure: James complicatedly examined these terms and others in his criticism, and he thereby gave a technical vocabulary to the New Critics for their treatment of fiction.

When, for example, in "The Art of Fiction" (1884) James referred to the novel as a "living thing, all one and continuous, like any other organism," he employed a metaphor for formal unity that I. A. Richards, Cleanth Brooks, and others would later flesh out in their analyses of the "organic" structure of literary texts, both poetry and prose. James's disciple, the critic Percy Lubbock (1879–1965), also disseminated this concern for coherent inter-relationships among the "parts" that constitute the artistic "whole." "In fiction," Lubbock observed in *The Craft of Fiction* (1921), "there can be no appeal to any authority outside the book itself." "In the fictitious picture of life," he went on to say, "the effect of validity is all in all and there can be no appeal to an external authority."

Such an understanding of, and critical approach to, the text was, Lubbock insisted, the only one that had credibility: for critical "discourse" about writers to proceed constructively, "we have really and clearly and accurately" to see and understand the books themselves. This anticipated Tate's words in his essay "Narcissus as Narcissus" (1938): "The only real evidence that any critic may bring before his gaze is the finished poem." And Richards's words, in "How Does a Poem Know When It Is Finished?" (1963): Poems are "living, feeling, knowing *beings* in their own right; the so-called metaphor that treats a poem as organic is not a metaphor, but a literal description. A poem is an activity, seeking to become itself."

The ability of the New Critics to respond passionately to James's writings, and to Eliot's and his fellow modernists' newly charged imagery, complex metaphors, wordplay, and allusion, derives from yet another source. Ransom, Brooks, and the other Southerners were trained in classical languages and, some of them, in the philological discipline – a training that reinforced the biblical exegesis in Sunday sermons that they had heard. They were ready to deal analytically with language because they had been in the midst of this activity all along in school and in church.

Brooks stated in an interview with Warren (1976) that it was his "prep school discipline in reading Greek and Latin" that readied him for the "new discipline of literary exploration." He and the New Critics departed from what had been done before, but perhaps they managed their reorientation all the more effectively because both classical literary study and philology had furnished them with something positive. Philology itself was more than a bad practice waiting to be corrected: it helped equip a critic to examine the texts themselves.

Smart and determined as they were, the New Critics thus were not saying something unique when they called for attention to the words on the page. They were saying it in a more compelling and rigorous fashion. The Southern New Critics' achievement was to annex terms already present in literary criticism and teaching, apply the innovative theories of modernist poets and intellectuals, and underscore "the text" as the central term for and controlling feature of critical work. By highlighting the text and refining techniques for its analysis, they defeated the scholars and the appreciators of the masterpieces.

Sympathetic to complaints like those that Bourne, Spingarn, and Sherman uttered, they furnished students with immediate training in the skills of "close reading" and discrimination.

While the New Critics did contest the scientific cast of the older fact-based scholarship, they made clear that their own methods remained "scientific" – a term whose prestige Ransom invoked in "Criticism, Inc.," his 1938 charter of rights for the New Criticism. They displayed and benefited from a love-hate relationship with science, opposing the positivist research undertaken by the scholars yet preserving the aura of science in order to lay claim to professional rigor. Science gave dignity and authority to criticism, even as criticism defined itself against the unchecked tyranny of scientific methods, values, and habits of mind.

The concern for precision in critical instruments led the New Critics to develop a set of key terms, a discourse, for describing the action and structure of poetic language. Some of these terms the New Critics adapted from the work of Richards and Empson. When the New Critics referred to "ambiguity," for example, they were borrowing the term that Empson had explored in his discussion of the complex, even contrary, feelings and implications of imagery and word choice that poems contained. Similarly, when the New Critics focused on "tone" and "attitude," as did Brooks and Warren in one of their chapters in *Understanding Poetry*, they were drawing upon the detailed consideration of these terms that Richards had supplied.

"The tone of a poem," said Brooks and Warren, "indicates the poet's attitude toward his subject and toward his audience." The crucial element of "tone" in poetry results from the fact that "all poems" are "fundamentally dramatic." The best poems "present their themes" concretely, "not abstractly," through the tone of voice of a speaker whose language conveys his attitude, his stance of judgment, toward both his subject and his readers.

The "speaking tone of voice" was also a central concern for the Amherst and, later, Harvard professor Reuben A. Brower (1908–75), a widely admired teacher and critic who drew upon the sounds and rhythms and patterns of Robert Frost's poetry, and from Frost's prose and letters about "tone" and "sentence sounds." As Frost said about tone, in the kind of remark that Brower found so stimulating, "it's one thing to hear the notes in the mind's ear. Another to give them accuracy at the mouth. Still another to implicate them in sentences and fasten them to the page. The second is the actor's gift. The third is the writer's." Brower's books (which fall outside the period covered here) included: *The Fields of Light: An Experiment in Critical Reading* (1951); *The Poetry of Robert Frost: Constellations of Intention* (1963); and, as coeditor with Richard Poirier, *In Defense of Reading: A Reader's Approach to Literary Criticism* (1962).

Brower's and his colleagues' and students' books and essays derive more directly from Frost, Empson, Leavis, and the teaching of instructors of composition whom Brower knew and worked with at Amherst than they do from Ransom, Tate, and the other Southerners. But Brower always featured the analysis of texts, and in this respect he fostered an approach that resembled closely the work done by the New Critics and their followers.

For Brooks and Warren, as well as for Ransom and Tate, it was important that critics and readers at last possess a clear, coherent language for speaking accurately about poems. The philologists had provided information about the sources for and influences upon poems, and the impressionists and appreciators had borne witness to the emotions they felt when poems lifted them up. But neither group had succeeded in describing the actual organization of texts and the nature of a truly *literary* response. For the New Critics, the most successful poems, as perceived by trained readers, were "organic" wholes, with each part related to the other parts and all forming a vital structure, like living tissue. "Organic form," Coleridge had affirmed in his *Biographia Literaria*, "is innate; it shapes as it develops itself from within, and the fullness of its development is one and the same with the perfection of its outward form."

Coleridge's point was highly significant for the New Critics, and it had a number of consequences:

1. The "form" and the "meaning" of a poem cannot be separated.
2. Its form and meaning bonded to one another, the poem is complete in itself. It need not be viewed as dependent upon such extrinsic matters as the biography of the poet or the historical circumstances within which it was produced.
3. Again because form and meaning are one, the analysis of a poem should not be equated to a prose statement of its content. In *The Well Wrought Urn*, Brooks dubbed this mistake "the heresy of paraphrase."
4. However complex and ambiguous a poem might be, it is (or should be) an organically unified "whole" in which all of the elements are integrated.

Each of the New Critics contributed to this general conception of poetry and criticism even as he sometimes performed his own variations on it, calling notice to this or that aspect of the text as especially meaningful, bringing forward a new element of interpretive technique, or disputing a precept of critical procedure that another New Critic had outlined. The New Criticism was a common enterprise that was spacious enough to absorb disagreement.

Brooks, for instance, commented often on "irony" in poems, observing in his essay "Irony as a Principle of Structure" (1949) that poets as different as Donne and Wordsworth made use of a "pattern of thrust and counterthrust," deftly shifting rhythm and tone and balancing, adjusting, and contrasting the implications of lines of imagery: "In the work of both men, the relation between part and part is organic, which means that each part modifies and is modified by the whole."

What Brooks said here about irony is akin to his account of "paradox" (another key New Critical term) in *The Well Wrought Urn*. This signified the witty fusion of contraries and opposites that poems accomplish. For Brooks, "the language of poetry *is* the language of paradox," and this doubleness, this managed multi-meaningfulness, of language distinguishes literature from science – a discipline that "requires," declared Brooks with astonishing confidence, "a language purged of every trace of paradox" and "freezes" words "into strict denotations."

Brooks's credo of "the language of paradox" can be glimpsed in his interpretation of the concluding stanza of Donne's "The Canonization."

> And thus invoke us; You whom reverend love
>   Made one anothers hermitage;
> You, to whom love was peace, that now is rage;
>   Who did the whole worlds soul contract, and drove
>   Into the glasses of your eyes
>   (So made such mirrors, and such spies,
> That they did all to you epitomize,)
>   Countries, Townes, Courtes: Beg from above
>   A patterne of your love!

"In this last stanza," Brooks explains,

the theme receives a final complication. The lovers in rejecting life actually win to the most intense life. This paradox has been hinted at earlier in the phoenix metaphor [in the third stanza]. Here it receives a powerful dramatization. The lovers in becoming hermits, find that they have not lost the world, but have gained the world in each other, now a more intense, more meaningful world. Donne is not content to treat the lovers' discovery as something which comes to them passively, but rather as something which they actively achieve. They are like the saint, God's athlete:

Who did the whole worlds soul *contract*, and drove
  Into the glasses of your eyes . . .

The image is that of a violent squeezing as of a powerful hand. And what do the lovers "drive" into each other's eyes? The "Countries, Townes," and "Courtes," which they renounced in the first stanza of the poem. The unworldly lovers thus become the most "worldly" of all.

This analysis perhaps suggests why foes of New Criticism said that it tended to simplify or reduce poems into the expression of a single theme or element, and that it made all good poems the same, each one a specimen of an ironic or a paradoxical structure. But Brooks's and his New Critical colleagues' style of working with texts marked an advance in both criticism and pedagogy – an analysis like this was very helpful to critics and to students in particular – and it should not be underrated.

The New Critics were in contact with the words on the page, and with the consecutive development of the language in the poem as a whole. They gave readers a rigorous sense of the strategies and practices that poets use and that readers of poetry must be able to recognize. The New Critics were showing what close reading was, that much-sought-after thing for which so many had been beckoning for decades.

Ransom and Tate mostly concurred with Brooks's formulations, but each expressed a preference for coinages of their own. Ransom, in "Criticism as Pure Speculation" (1941), defined a poem as a "logical structure having a local texture," with "texture" embracing all – imagery, meter, rhythm, verbal surprises and inventions – that differentiates poetry from prose. It is the texture that the critic of literature should dwell upon; the critic should not slight the logical structure, Ransom maintained, but "if he has nothing to say about its texture he has nothing to say about it specifically as a poem." Ransom's vocabulary did not match Brooks's, yet Ransom, too, emphasized the integrity of the text, its autonomous status as a work of art.

Tate made a similar point in his essay "Tension in Poetry" (1938), where he argued that the meaning of good poetry lies in "its 'tension,' the full organized body of all the extension and intension that we can find in it." Through this term Tate professed that poems weld the general and the particular, the abstract and the concrete, the idea and the image, the literal and the figurative, the denotative and connotative powers of language. For Tate as for the others, the primary goal was to learn to see poems as complex, organized structures, and to register the necessity for responding to and cross-questioning them with a quality of care and sensitive deliberation that was modern, professional, "new."

The New Critics' terms and tenets have become so embedded in critical analysis that it's often forgotten that there were once alternatives to them. None of them got very far in college and university teaching, however. The insistent desire within the academy for a method that privileged the inspection of "literary texts themselves" made critics and scholars unreceptive to proposals that called for something else.

In 1931, the following books appeared: Max Eastman's *The Literary Mind: Its Place in an Age of Science*, Edmund Wilson's *Axel's Castle: A Study in the Imaginative Literature of 1870–1930*, and Kenneth Burke's *Counter-Statement*. Each was widely reviewed and discussed, but not one in any significant way affected academic criticism and scholarship. Eastman urged that literary criticism be viewed as one of the human sciences and that its methods gain depth and precision from discoveries and research in sociology and psychology. Wilson emphasized that he viewed literary criticism as the study of writers and texts in "the setting of the conditions which have shaped them." And Burke postulated that criticism should be connected to rhetoric, history, and psychology, even saying at one point that literary "form," rightly understood, means not the form of the text but, rather, "the creation of an appetite in the mind of the auditor, and the adequate satisfying of that appetite."

Eastman, Wilson, and Burke were not supplying what academics felt that the discipline of English demanded. Critics and scholars in English studies could acknowledge that they had learned from the books that non-academics like Eastman, Wilson, and Burke had written, but they could not implement the strategies and techniques of such books. These seemed interesting and adventurous but too far from the specific task that a legitimate academic enterprise should undertake. The books by Eastman, Wilson, and Burke displayed, for the academy, unusable kinds of innovation.

There were at least two other, more general contenders for critical authority during the 1920s and 1930s – New Humanism and Marxism. Both received considerable attention and stirred up debate outside and, to an extent, inside the academy, and the New Criticism measured and defined itself against them.

The New Humanism came to prominence in the early 1900s. It was morally and philosophically serious, but it was doomed to fail, despite the assiduous labors of Irving Babbitt, Paul Elmer More (1864–1937), and Norman Foerster (1887–1972). This movement included men in key positions at major universities – Babbitt taught at Harvard, More at Princeton, and Foerster at North Carolina and, later, at Iowa. It attracted a few students and established small bases of institutional support from those unsympathetic to the experimental styles and subjects favored by Eliot, Joyce, and Hemingway. But the support was never deep or widespread, and in retrospect, the New Humanists appear as earnest but lonely voices speaking in an outdated language. They privileged a narrow canon, were hostile to modernism, and declared their disgust with nearly all of contemporary literature.

In *The Demon of the Absolute* (1928), More attacked Sinclair Lewis, Theodore Dreiser, Sherwood Anderson, and John Dos Passos for their immorality. He labeled *Manhattan Transfer* "an explosion in a cesspool" and urged that American writers adhere to the "discipline of classical humanism." According to H. L. Mencken (1920), More, like Babbitt, found contemporary literature "too near to be quite nice. To More or Babbitt only death can atone for the primary offense of the artist."

"Standards" was the presiding principle for the New Humanists. In literature, according to Babbitt in *Literature and the American College* (1908), these standards could only be secured from the reading of masterpieces:

Some of the ancients and a few of the greatest of the moderns, may be regarded as the fixed stars of literature. We may safely take our bearings with reference to them and be guided by them in deciding what is essence and what is accident in human nature. They are a sort of concrete *idea hominis*. There is something definitive in their rendering of life – something that is purged of all localism and deserves to be received as typical.

In his essay "Natural Aristocracy" (1915), More indicted trends in education that turned young men away from the themes that he and Babbitt endorsed:

The enormous preponderance of studies that deal with the immediate questions of economics and government inevitably results in isolating the student from the great inheritance of the past; the frequent habit of dragging him through the slums of sociology, instead of making him at home in the society of the noble dead, debauches his mind with a flabby, or inflames it with a fanatic, humanitarianism.

As Babbitt later observed (1918), the critic's standards "must rest on an immediate perception of what is normal and human," and "the best type of critic may therefore be said to be creative in the sense that he creates standards." "Our whole modern experiment," he added, "not only in art and literature, but in life, is threatened with breakdown, because of our failure to work out new standards."

Babbitt believed that standards were missing from American politics and education as well as from literature and criticism. *Manhattan Transfer* bothered Babbitt, too – he termed it a "literary nightmare" – because it exemplified the depraved art and immorality that were corroding modern America. He also assailed Dreiser's *American Tragedy* as a "genuinely harrowing work" where "one is harrowed to no purpose."

A reactionary enterprise, the New Humanism climaxed in 1930 with the publication of *Humanism and America*, a collection of essays by various authors. It then expired, demolished by the rival volume, *The Critique of Humanism*, edited by C. Hartley Grattan and with essays by Tate, Kenneth Burke, Lewis Mumford, R. P. Blackmur, Yvor Winters, and others, published in the same year. In *Humanism in America*, the New Humanists' disdain for modern literature reached a level of unintended self-parody. For Gorham B. Munson, one of the essayists in the book, "modern" literature meant almost everything: "objectively considered, literature may be found to have been in decline, not just for a century and a half or just six hundred years, but almost from its classical sources and from the Scriptures of ancient lands." The New Humanist method had reached such an exquisite height that no texts were worthy of it.

During the Depression years, as New Humanism faded fast, Marxism in one form or another had a broader appeal. Marxism offered an alternative to the skepticism and despair preached in the great modernist texts; it proclaimed that literature and literary criticism could serve the cause of revolution. The allure of Marxism may seem hard to fathom, with Communism now discredited, but many intellectuals judged in the 1930s that capitalism had failed, and the evidence appeared to them plain for all to see.

In his speech accepting the Republican Party presidential nomination, August 11, 1928, Herbert Hoover declared:

We in America today are nearer to the final triumph over poverty than ever before in the history of any land. The poorhouse is vanishing from among us. We have not yet reached the goal, but given a chance to go forward with the policies of the last eight years, and we shall soon, with the help of God, be within sight of the day when poverty shall be banished from this nation.

During the 1920s, much in American life had indeed gotten better. Education, diet, and life expectancy had improved; the Gross National Product had increased by 39 percent; corporate profits had doubled; and workers' net earnings had increased. In 1921, unemployment had stood at 12 percent but by 1923 it had fallen to 4 percent. Between 1922 and 1927, the economy grew by 7 percent each year – the largest peacetime rate in the nation's history. Manufacturing output, new construction, worker productivity – all showed significant increases.

With these facts and figures in mind, President Hoover had reason to be optimistic in mid-1928, and he reaffirmed his upbeat claims in his inaugural address in March 1929: "Ours is a land rich in resources; stimulating in its glorious beauty; filled with millions of happy homes; blessed with comfort and opportunity. In no nation are the institutions of progress more advanced. In no nation are the fruits of accomplishment more secure."

The heartening statistics masked serious problems. In the 1920s the minimum standard of living for a family of four was set at $2,000 per year; but in 1929, 60 percent of American families had incomes below $2,000, and the average wage for an industrial worker was $1,300. For the bottom 40 percent of the population, the average family income was $725; $290 went for food, $190 for housing, and $110 for clothing, which meant that the remaining $135 had to cover medical care and emergencies and anything else.

Even as productivity rose during the 1920s by 43 percent, the income gap widened substantially. By 1929, the top 1 percent owned between 30 and 40 percent of all personal wealth; and the 200 largest corporations held

50 percent of the nation's corporate wealth and received more than 40 percent of all corporate profits.

One-third of all income was held by the top 5 percent of the population, while, lower down the scale, farmers in particular – hurt by overproduction at home and abroad and by falling prices – had seen their share of the national income decline from 16 percent in 1919 to 9 percent in 1929. The value of farmland fell nearly 40 percent during the decade. In addition, though the nation was benefiting from advances in industry and manufacturing, the new technologies were leading to unemployment for hundred of thousands of persons each year whose work was taken over by machines.

The nation's prosperity was limited and fragile. In order to purchase much-desired items (cars, radios, refrigerators, phonographs, sewing machines, washing machines), consumers had become accustomed to installment-buying; by 1929, consumer lending was the tenth largest business in the nation, and American consumers were borrowing $7 billion annually. (It was hard to resist these products; advertising for them was everywhere and amounted to 3 percent of the country's Gross National Product.)

By August 1929, 300 million shares of stock were being carried on margin, as the buying of stocks moved at a hectic pace. When prices of stocks peaked and started to fall in the following weeks, holders of stocks not only lost their investments but many suffered the loss of their entire savings and property.

With the crash of the stock market in October 1929, companies and shareholders suffered huge losses. General Motors stock, for example, fell from $212 in September 1929 to $8 in 1932; and the market as a whole declined from $452 to $52 during the same period. Countless businesses, farms, and banks failed (5,000 in the first three years of the Depression) – and because there was no insurance of bank deposits, a bank failure meant that a depositor's money was gone for good. By 1932, the price of wheat had fallen 50 percent, and the price of cotton by 66 percent. In the words of F. Scott Fitzgerald, in "Echoes of the Jazz Age" (1931): "The most expensive orgy in history was over . . . the utter confidence which was its essential prop received an enormous jolt, and it didn't take long for the flimsy structure to settle earthward."

Recalling the impact of the crash of 1929 and the panic that ensued, the critic and journalist Malcolm Cowley wrote in *Exile's Return* (1934):

When the Bank of United States went under, on December 11 [1930], it was described by the *New York Times* as "the largest bank in the United States ever to suspend payments"; it had fifty-nine branches and more than four hundred thousand depositors. People began to fear that the whole structure of American finance would crash to the ground.

Construction fell by nearly 80 percent, and private investment by nearly 90 percent. Somewhere between 25 and 50 percent of the workforce was unemployed; the number of jobless shot from 3 million to 17 million; and personal income was cut in half, from a total of $82 million in 1929 to $40 million in 1932. *Fortune* magazine reported in its September 1932 issue that in New York, "About 1,000,000 out of the city's 3,200,000 working population are unemployed. Last April 410,000 were estimated to be in dire want." By 1932, the US economy was functioning at half of its 1929 capacity.

Education was badly hit as well. By the fall of 1933, thousands of schools and colleges were closed; 200,000 teachers were unemployed; and well over 2 million children were not able to attend school. During the 1930s, discouraged and demoralized, more than 250,000 young men and women left home to live as hoboes and tramps on the road. During the 1930s, about 1.2 million eighteen- to twenty-two-year-olds attended college, which was fewer than one of every ten in the country who were eligible.

As the Depression worsened, exports and imports plummeted, and America's financial institutions and markets received further shocks from abroad, including the failure of Austria's largest bank in May 1931. President Hoover's efforts to address the crisis were futile: it seemed systemic, beyond the capacity of mere reforms and relief measures to resolve. In an essay published in the New York *Evening Journal* in 1932, the critic Gilbert Seldes wondered: "If these bad times continue, what is to become of culture?" "Are we faced with a world without beauty," he asked, "without books or pictures, without arts of any form, with no escape from actual drab existence to the realms of imagination, of forgetfulness?" Frances Perkins, Secretary of Labor from 1933 to 1944, said in *People at Work* (1934): "With the slow menace of a glacier, depression came on. No one had any measure of its progress; no one had any plan for stopping it. Everyone tried to get out of its way."

Marxism to many appeared to offer a compelling response to the economic and cultural crisis. For writers and critics, Marxist theory and practice explained the function of literature in a society in disarray: literature and criticism could engage the afflicted society and help lead it toward a revolutionary transformation.

Marxist criticism also gained prestige from the Soviet Union, which, for many intellectuals and working people, confirmed their faith in revolutionary change. The Soviet Union, it seemed, demonstrated that social protest and activism could succeed against colossal odds in opening a path to a wondrous new world.

The radical journalist John Reed (1887–1920) set the tone in *Ten Days That Shook the World* (1919), writing of the Bolshevik revolution that "adventure it was, and one of the most marvelous mankind ever embarked upon, sweeping into history at the head of the toiling masses, and staking everything on their vast and simple desires." For the editor and writer Michael Gold (1893–1967), the Soviet state in the mid-1920s was "as fresh, as new and beautiful as first love." "I have been over into the future," announced Lincoln Steffens in 1931 after his visit to the Soviet Union, "and it works... Russia is the land of conscious, willful hope."

There had been a radical political movement in the United States before the Depression decade. In the presidential election of 1912, Eugene V. Debs, the Socialist Party candidate, received 6 percent of the popular vote, running on a platform that urged voters to make "the working class the ruling class." By 1912, there were many Socialists in public office, including nearly eighty mayors; and Victor Berger (Wisconsin) and Meyer London (New York) were elected to Congress. The *Appeal to Reason*, the major socialist periodical, published in Girard, Kansas, soared in circulation from 30,000 in 1900 to 300,000 in 1906, and by 1912–13, to 760,000, with some issues exceeding four million copies. In 1919, Socialist Party membership was about 110,000, and in the presidential election of 1920, Debs received more than 900,000 votes.

Even as many American radicals had embraced the Russian Revolution in 1917, President Wilson had assailed it, eventually dispatching 15,000 troops to Russia as part of the Allied forces' resistance to the new Bolshevik government that Lenin had organized. The Soviet Union and the United States did not have diplomatic relations until 1933.

By 1921, with Debs in prison (1919–21), and with left-wing activity still suffering from wartime repression, Socialist Party membership fell to 13,000; by 1928, it was less than 8,000. The Communist Labor Party, formed in summer 1919, and the Communist Party of the USA, formed in fall 1919, had a combined membership of 70,000. Communist Party membership grew somewhat in the 1920s; there were 6,500 members in 1929; 20,000 members in 1932 (presidential candidate William Z. Foster received 100,000 votes in the 1932 election); and somewhere in the 80,000 to 100,000 range by the mid-1930s.

These were not high figures, but the Communist Party and its non-party-member supporters nonetheless had an impact. During the 1930s, the Party organized many large demonstrations, such as those that occurred on March 6, 1930, which was declared "International Unemployment Day," with more than 50,000 persons in Boston and the same number in Chicago taking part in the protests.

The Party also organized black sharecroppers, and held meetings and marches to protest hunger, poverty, and unemployment. It played a crucial role in such important organizations as the National Negro Congress (founded in February 1936 and led by A. Philip Randolph), the American Writers Congress, and the League of American Writers. From the mid- to late 1930s, through its Popular Front strategy – a democratic alliance of all anti-fascist groups and organizations ("Communism is twentieth-century Americanism"), the Communist Party also influenced the production of literature, film, and theater.

But politically, by far the dominant fact of the 1930s was the presidency of Franklin Delano Roosevelt and his efforts to implement the policies of the New Deal. By 1934, the Democrats had increased their majority in the House of Representatives to 319, and in the Senate to 69. By 1936, the Democrats were receiving 90 percent of the African-American vote; and by the presidential election of 1940, the figure neared 100 percent. In the presidential election of 1936, Roosevelt won all of the electoral votes except for those of Maine and Vermont, and 63.5 percent of the popular vote, and the Democratic Party achieved huge majorities in both the House of Representatives and the Senate.

Many persons were still unemployed, but 6 million new jobs had been created, and both industrial production and personal income had risen substantially from their levels in 1932–33. In 1938, organized labor gained the passage of a maximum-hour and minimum-wage bill, and also a bill that prohibited child labor in interstate industries.

Marxism, as advanced through the Socialists, Communists, and other sects, never anchored itself in college and university life, though it did win the support of some faculty and students through the forums and political stands and cultural productions of the Popular Front. Administrators on campus and politicians chafed at Marxism and made clear that the academic Marxist would find his or her job in jeopardy.

Outside the academy, Marxist literary and cultural critics, including Granville Hicks, Michael Gold, and Joseph Freeman, fought for Marxism as a critical position at conferences and congresses and in books and journals. For them, it explained the strife-torn 1930s; as Hicks (1901–82) recalled in 1969, "to me and others like me in the early thirties the teachings of Marx offered both a program for action and a key to the understanding of history."

Leon Trotsky, an enemy to staunch Communists but a heroic figure to others among the anti-Stalinists, in *Literature and Art* (1925) expressed the dream that so many radicals found inspiring:

In a society which will have thrown off the pinching and stultifying worry about one's daily bread, in which community restaurants will prepare good, wholesome and tasteful food for all to choose, in which communal laundries will wash clean everyone's good linen, in which children, all the children, will be well fed and strong and gay, and in which they will absorb the fundamental elements of science and art as they absorb albumen and air and the warmth of the sun, in a society in which electricity and the radio will not be the crafts they are today, but will come from inexhaustible sources of superpower at the call of a central button, in which there will be no "useless mouths," in which the liberated egotism of man – a mighty force! – will be directed wholly towards the understanding, the transformation and the betterment of the universe – in such a society the dynamic development of culture will be incomparable with anything that went on in the past.

In part the appeal of such language lay in its connection to the strong traditions of English and American cultural criticism as practiced in the nineteenth and early twentieth centuries. William Morris, for example, had spoken in "Art Under Plutocracy" (1883) of the evils of "the present system of society" and their consequences for art and the sense of beauty: "All art, even the highest, is influenced by the conditions of labour of the mass of mankind, and that any pretensions which may be made for even the highest intellectual art to be independent of these general conditions are futile and vain; that is to say, that any art which professes to be founded on the special education or refinement of a limited body or class must of necessity be unreal and short-lived."

For Americans marginalized because of their race, ethnicity, or social class, the Communist Party proved to be a great source of hope, as Richard Wright explained in *American Hunger* (published in 1977):

Here at least in the realm of revolutionary expression was where Negro experience could find a home, a functioning value and role. Out of the magazines I read came a passionate call for the experiences of the disinherited, and there were none of the same lispings of the missionary in it. It did not say: "Be like us and we will like you, maybe." It said: "If you possess enough courage to speak out what you are, you will find that you are not alone." It urged life to believe in life.

But through the National Industrial Recovery Act (1933), the Wagner Labor Bill (1935, which guaranteed to labor the right to organize and bargain collectively), the Social Security Act (1935), and other legislation, the Roosevelt administration was able to turn many liberal and left-leaning men and women away from Marxism, as well as away from membership in the Communist Party, and toward the New Deal.

Roosevelt was working for everyday Americans, and they responded to his leadership. A writer for the *New York Times*, May 1933, referred to "that curious community" that exists "between the mind of the President and the mind of the people. 'Let's try something else!' is the almost unanimous sentiment of America at this moment." Joe Marcus, an economist working on New Deal relief programs, remembered: "The climate was exciting. You were part of a society that was on the move. You were involved in something that could make a difference. Laws could be changed. So could the conditions of people."

In his second inaugural address, January 1937, Roosevelt acknowledged that millions of Americans were suffering: "I see one-third of a nation ill-housed, ill-clad, ill-nourished." But he immediately added: "It is not in despair that I paint you that picture. I paint it for you in hope – because the Nation, seeing and understanding the injustice in it, proposes to paint it out." (This was the first time a president was inaugurated in January rather than in March, the result of the twentieth amendment, passed in February 1933.) The literary critic Alfred Kazin was in Washington on inauguration day, and in *Starting Out in the Thirties* (1965) he remembered cheering for the President as he rode in his car "out of the White House drive": "Like all my friends, I distrusted Roosevelt as a wily politician and a professional charmer . . . But I could almost believe in him now, there was so much need of him to do the right thing."

During the 1930s and into the 1940s, the Southern economy – the focus of the Agrarian movement – improved dramatically. Through New Deal programs, billions of dollars were spent in the South on housing, education, and other forms of direct relief and work-relief programs. In 1933, only one in ten Southern farms had electricity; as a result of the Rural Electrification Administration, begun in 1935, this figure jumped to eight in every ten farms, which meant a major change for the better in living standards (hot water heaters and refrigerators, for example). During the 1940s, the South received billions of dollars in war contracts; its shipbuilding and textile industries boomed; so did agriculture, mining, and the coal and petroleum industries. From 1941 to 1945, industrial capacity in the South grew by 40 percent. Both large and small urban areas experienced sizable increases in population. How far away Ransom's and the Agrarians' arguments now seemed.

The case of F. O. Matthiessen, Harvard professor and author of *American Renaissance* (1941), reveals Roosevelt's impact on radical and left-leaning writers, critics, intellectuals. Matthiessen regarded the Bolshevik Revolution as the most significant event of the twentieth century, and he identified himself as a socialist. In 1932, when the Depression was at its worst, he joined the Socialist Party in the belief that it was poised to recover the fairly broad base that it had enjoyed during the presidential campaigns of Eugene V. Debs. As a Socialist Party member and supporter of Norman Thomas, leader of the Party in the late 1920s and 1930s, Matthiessen felt little fondness for Roosevelt, the Democratic candidate in 1932. But, he later said, "Roosevelt in office was something quite other than I had foreseen, and after he began to effect even some of the things for which Thomas had stood, I voted for him enthusiastically, though always from the left, until his death."

Roosevelt declared, "I have no expectation of making a hit every time I come to bat. What I seek is the highest possible batting average . . . The country needs, and unless I mistake its temper, the country demands, bold, persistent experimentation." There were programs in Federal Emergency Relief, Civil Works, Public Works, Farm Security, Rural Electrification, Farm Credit, Federal Housing, National Youth, and also the Social Security Act (1935), which provided an insurance system for the elderly.

The Works Progress (later, Projects) Administration (1935), which undertook many building and improvement projects, was also important. One branch of it was the Federal Writers Project, which produced nearly 1,000 publications in its six years of operation, and which included such aspiring writers as John Cheever, Richard Wright, Ralph Ellison, and Saul Bellow. Among the FWP's publications were state, city, and regional guides; a 150-volume "Life in America" series; collections of folklore; and a series of interviews with 2,000 former slaves.

The Arts and Music Projects were other major WPA initiatives. The Arts Project employed nearly 6,000 artists (among them Jackson Pollock and Willem de Kooning), and their work included hundreds of murals for government buildings. From 1933 to 1937, a government-sponsored program in "public art" led to 15,000 paintings, murals on public buildings, prints, and watercolors that focused on America at work. The Music Project employed 18,000 musicians and sponsored thousands of free concerts.

In "Art Becomes Public Works," *Survey Graphic*, June 1934, Florence Loeb Kellogg described "the rewards to the artist in times of depression":

The letters received by the administrative office show once more how little the artist measures his career by the money he makes. Though he chooses dire need no more than any other man, he asks mainly for a chance to do his work. Letters refer gratefully to the actual relief the weeks of employment offered (typical is: "I had not been on the commissary but I have been almost there many times"), but all of them dwell on another benefit of this nation-wide encouragement of art. They speak of the restoration of morale, of renewed self-confidence, of the sense of being at last acknowledged as an important member of the social family, with a place in the economic system . . . "Never in my career," to quote from one letter, "have I experienced such a sense of lift as I feel now in my work for the government. No newspaper criticism, however kind, no exhibition of my work, no scholarship, no patronage, has fired me as does this project."

The Federal Theater Project was productive as well, if also controversial, coming under Congressional scrutiny for its left-leaning activities and its ties to the Roosevelt administration. Directed by Hallie Flanagan, former head of Vassar College's Experimental Theater, its members included the director and actor Orson Welles, the playwright Arthur Miller, and the director John

Huston. The FTP produced Shakespeare plays, Sinclair Lewis's *It Can't Happen Here*, T. S. Eliot's *Murder in the Cathedral*, and many other works throughout the country. Sixteen Negro theater units were formed, one of which, in Harlem, staged an African-American *Macbeth* that was set in Haiti. Though the FTP lasted only four years, ending in 1939, it brought serious drama, puppet shows, circuses, and children's plays to a total of 30 million people.

The Farm Security Administration also made significant cultural contributions. It dispatched photographers, including Walker Evans, Dorothea Lange, and Arthur Rothstein, to record the lives of American workers and families suffering from the Depression, and they took 250,000 photographs, many of extraordinary quality and insight.

Not only these New Deal programs, and the millions affected by them, but also factional squabbles and endless polemical battles within and near the Communist Party in the US limited the impact of Marxism. Developments on the international scene damaged the cause further. In a memorandum written in August 1932, George Kennan, an expert on Russian history and a member of the Foreign Service, noted that "almost every detail in the life of every individual in Russia is regulated by a centralized political power which is unparalleled in modern history . . . This power is not at present being exercised in the interests of the welfare and happiness of the present generation."

Some chose to ignore or overlook this fact. Surely, it seemed, the ideals of the Soviet Union – a nation on a new path – promised something better. But once the truth of the Soviet purge trials of 1936–38 came to light, and once Stalin signed his pact with Hitler in 1939 and tightened his alliance with Nazism and fascism, it was nearly impossible to remain a Marxist or a Soviet sympathizer with a clean conscience.

"One of the worst drawbacks of being a Stalinist," said Edmund Wilson in 1937, "is that you have to defend so many falsehoods." To retain Marxism as a motivating idea, one somehow had to do so free from the taint of the Soviet example and Communist Party affiliation – which was an arduous conceptual and emotional task. In George Orwell's words, in *The Road to Wigan Pier* (1937): "As with the Christian religion, the worst advertisement for Socialism is its adherents." "*Why* did the Russian revolution get into its present situation?," asked Malcolm Cowley of Edmund Wilson in an anguished letter written in February 1940. "Is it Stalinism or Leninism or Marxism that is essentially at fault?"

Marxism struck many intellectuals and critics as accurate about capitalism – E. B. White (1899–1985), essayist and humorist, remarked that "the trouble with the profit system has always been that it was highly unprofitable to most people" (*One Man's Meat*, 1942). But few Americans could conceive of it actually working in practice. To American writers, including some who portrayed themselves as Marxists, there was a disjunction between Marxism and the United States. It was not only that this nation lacked a feudal past and allowed at its rags-to-riches best for movement between classes. It was also that America's spirit as a nation and the folkways of its people jarred against the anti-individual rigidities of Marxist policies and terms for utopian change.

In 1917, John Dos Passos identified himself as "red, radical, and revolutionary," but in the mid-1920s he said, "I don't think there should be any more phrases, badges, opinions, banners, imported from Russia or anywhere else . . . Why not develop our own brand?" Ten years later, William Carlos Williams made the same point more emphatically: "The American tradition is completely opposed to Marxism." Marxism, he said, was based on "regimentation" and "force" and could never replace the "democratic principles" of Americans. Though more sympathetic to the Soviet Union, the novelist Theodore Dreiser doubted Marxism's chances in the United States. Writing in 1936, he observed that for "Marxian ideology" to take hold in America, it would first need to adapt itself to the native "revolutionary tradition – even if it has to lose its own identity."

To the cultural critic Lewis Mumford, Marxism was outdated. In a letter to Van Wyck Brooks (April 10, 1932), he judged that the Marxism of the Communist Party could not furnish the "moral and spiritual regeneration" that America required, for the Communists were afflicted with "silly animosities and materialist superstitions." Mumford described himself in a later letter to Brooks (September 14, 1932) as "post-Marxian," announcing that "if I didn't think that I had a more adequate and applicable philosophy than Marx, even in the economic realm, I would dig six feet of earth for myself and get buried."

Dos Passos, Williams, Dreiser, and Mumford concluded that most Marxist critics were too Marxist, too doctrinaire. But in fact most of the Marxist interpretations of literature from the 1930s were very loosely conducted. As the literary historian René Wellek (1903–95) concluded, "Marxism usually did not mean an actual grasp of the Marxist doctrine but merely a generalized anti-capitalism, sympathy for the working classes, and admiration for the Russian Revolution."

When Malcolm Cowley noted his allegiance to "Marxian criticism" in a letter to his friend Kenneth Burke (October 20, 1931), he professed that he viewed "art as organically related with its social background, and functionally affecting it." This was hardly subversive. In his essay "Marxism and Literature" (1937), Edmund Wilson similarly stated that the strength of Marxism was its capacity for "throwing a great deal of light on the origins and social significance of works of art."

For Cowley and Wilson, Marxism spurred the literary critic to be attentive to social and historical forces. Such a lesson was not specifically Marxist; it was not a lesson that a non-Marxist would feel obliged to contest, and it could endure even after any Marxist program or Communist Party affiliation had been given up.

It was less a belief in Marxism than a general disenchantment with the United States that led many critics and writers to drift toward the Communist Party in the early 1930s. Politics in America appeared futile, at a dead end. According to Wilson, in his "Appeal to Progressives" (1931):

The Buicks and Cadillacs, the bad gin and Scotch, the radio concerts interrupted by advertising talks, the golf and bridge of the suburban household, which the bond salesman can get for his money, can hardly compensate him for daily work of a kind in which it is utterly impossible to imagine a normal human being taking satisfaction or pride . . . Who today, in fact, in the United States can really love our meaningless life?

Wilson was too skeptical to become imprisoned by Stalinist dogma, but it was the anti-capitalist thrust of the Communist Party's policies that made it compelling for a brief period for him and for a longer period for Cowley and others.

Surprisingly enough, for all their occasional "vulgar" application of Marxism to texts, the Marxist-influenced critics on the Left and even some Communist Party members were eager to stress the distinctive nature of literary art and the importance of the aesthetic properties of the work itself. They, too, were responsive to the tendency upon which the Southern New Critics capitalized during the 1930s and 1940s.

The literary critic and socialist Newton Arvin, who signed a pledge in 1932 committing himself to vote for Communist candidates, stated that "the duty of the critic is certainly not to file an order for a particular sort of fiction or poetry before the event; his duty is to clarify, as best he can, the circumstances in which fiction and poetry must take shape, and to rationalize their manifestations when they arrive." In a speech before the American Writers' Congress in 1935, Granville Hicks warned against the dangers of formalism ("the art-for-art's sake dogma"), yet he also commented on the "weakness" that afflicted Marxist criticism: "it too frequently ignores those qualities of the artist that distinguish him, as an individual and especially as an artist, from other men." In the same year the editor, critic, and biographer Matthew Josephson (1899–1978), author of *The Robber Barons* (1934), rebuked Marxist critics for behaving like prosecuting attorneys, and reminded them of their duty to heed "style" and "craftsmanship." In theory if not always in practice, Marxist critics and literary radicals sought (and were expected) to examine "the text itself" even as they engaged in political commentary and critique.

A closer look at Hicks, a member of the Communist Party until the Nazi–Soviet pact, helps to indicate how Marxist critics struggled to stress politics and ideology while keeping a sense of the separateness of the literary work. Hicks declared in 1933 that his goal as a critic was to show the relationship of literature to "the economic organization of society," but he noted that "aesthetic categories" should not be equated with "economic categories." Literature did not disappear into economics, but, for Hicks, was valued for its distinctive textual power, for its capacity to express truths about the structure of the society in which it was produced.

The Marxist and Communist critics of the 1930s, writing in a time of crisis, were convinced that their work was powerful and innovative, broad and flexible. Hicks, for example, in a review in 1936 of Matthiessen's study of T. S. Eliot, said that critics should consider literary "form," but not form alone. This was Matthiessen's error in his book on Eliot, Hicks argued. He countered that Eliot's poetry raises questions about politics and philosophy, and that Matthiessen's approach was too simple, allowing the critic to "dismiss a difficult question by talking about the poet's quality as an artist or his mastery of form." Hicks stressed that the critic must delve into the "integration of content and form"; without giving up attention to the properties of the text, he was trying to do something that Matthiessen, in his view, had failed to achieve.

Others were more dogmatic, though even in their dogmatism calling attention to the real shortcomings of literary education during the period. In his autobiography, *An American Testament* (1938), the editor and critic Joseph Freeman (1897–1965) asserted: "The Party has a rich and varied literature on every aspect of life." Describing his journey toward Communism, Freeman told of the miseducation he received when he was an undergraduate at Columbia from 1916 to 1919. These were years of radical upheaval and dissent at home and abroad; the war was raging in Europe; the Bolshevik revolution erupted and the Soviet state was launched. Yet neither radical politics nor radical experiments in art entered literature classrooms, Freeman recalled. He and his friends discussed and argued at lunch and between classes about Frost, Edgar Lee Masters, Amy Lowell, Pound, and Eliot, as well as about the leftist verse published in the radical journal *The Masses*; and they talked animatedly about the war, socialism, and Woodrow Wilson's proposals and policies. But in academic literary study, said Freeman, "we confined ourselves to the classics and wrote papers on Castiglione's *Il Cortigiano*, Sir Philip Sidney's sonnets, and the chivalrous characteristics of men. From a twentieth century college we absorbed uncritically the ideas of the Renaissance."

Freeman said that the curriculum at Columbia placed literature in the eternal realm of "beauty" and lacked any concern about (or even awareness of)

the crises of the modern world and new forms of literary production. But the
next claim that he made was more dubious. Having traveled to the Soviet
Union, he praised the spirit of community that, Freeman was sure, ordered all
of life there in positive ways:

It was as though these factories and fields and schools and theatres and clubs belonged
not to the Soviet workers and peasants alone, but to all of us the world over who
were engaged in the same struggle for the classless society. The sense of isolation
which haunted the declassed intellectual in the Western world, the exploitation which
darkened the worker's days, the persecution which hounded the militant proletarian
and the revolutionary, were like a frightful chimera dissolving in the dawn.

Marxism for many, and the Communist Party for some, gave literary criticism an immediacy that it had been missing, and made criticism into an
activity immersed in social and political change. Freeman and Hicks did not
see themselves to be imposing crude categories on literature; in their estimation, they had glimpsed at last how literature was related to everything
else. (The Italian Marxist theorist and political activist Antonio Gramsci, put
on trial and sent to prison by the fascists in 1926, wrote in his *Prison Note-
books*: "The mode of being of the new intellectual can no longer consist in
eloquence, which is an exterior and momentary mover of passions and feelings, but in active participation in practical life, as constructor, organizer,
'permanent persuader' and not just simple orator.")

The Marxists William Phillips and Philip Rahv of the journal *The Partisan
Review* also maintained that critics should not "distort the function of criticism
by isolating the political equivalents of books from their total contexts, and
by judging these equivalents chiefly on the basis of immediate tactics" (1935).
After 1937, this tenet became even more pronounced in their writings, because
by then they had decided that the Communist Party was ruining the moral
and humanistic tenets of Marxism. For Phillips and Rahv, the fault of the Party
was not that it was Marxist but that it was Stalinist – and hence cordoned off
from the socialism and democracy that Marx and Engels had championed, and
from the liberating poems and novels of major modernist writers.

Judging from their speeches, lectures, and writings, it appears that many on
the Left truly believed that the future belonged to the Communists. The critic
Waldo Frank, for example, in "Values of the Revolutionary Writer," an April
1935 speech at the American Writers Congress in New York City, declared:
"My premise and the premise of the majority of writers here assembled is that
Communism must come, and must be fought for."

Not everyone agreed. The Protestant theologian Reinhold Niebuhr – whose
work influenced Matthiessen, among others – observed in *An Interpretation of
Christian Ethics* (1935): "The belief that communistic oligarchs have an almost

mystical identity of interest with the common man, may seem to justify itself for a brief period in which a radical leadership is kept pure by the traditions of its heroic revolutionary past. But there have been oligarchies with as heroic and sacrificial a tradition in the past. The potency of the tradition hardly outlasts the second generation." Alfred Kazin, who was teaching at City College in the late 1930s, later recalled that the Party "faithful" in his classes "resisted every example of free thought, of literary originality . . . The arrogant stupidity of Communist instructors at this time passed beyond anything I had ever known before."

As the painter Lee Krasner said in an interview (1967):

My experiences with Leftist movements in the late 1930s made me move as far away from them as possible because they were emphasizing the most banal, provincial art. They weren't interested in an independent and experimental art, but rather linked it to their economic and political programs . . . To me, and to the painters I was associated with, the more important thing was French painting and not the social realism and the picture of the Depression that they were interested in, even if it was going on right under our noses. Painting is not to be confused with illustration.

For their part, the Southern New Critics, during their Agrarian phase, wrote with a Marxist-sounding bitterness about capitalism and its effect on literature, culture, and society, and they mounted social and cultural protests against the dominant industrial order. As the introduction to *I'll Take My Stand* affirmed, the Agrarians "all tend to support a Southern way of life against what may be called the American or prevailing way; and all as much as agree that the best terms in which to represent the distinction are contained in the phrase, Agrarian *versus* Industrial."

The Agrarians insisted on the connections between politics and the arts, and between literary and social criticism. "We cannot recover our native humanism," the Introduction stated, "by adopting some standard of taste that is critical enough to question the contemporary arts but not critical enough to question the social and economic life which is their ground." "Criticism," said the poet Donald Davidson (1893–1968) in the same volume, "for which Arnold and others have hoped so much, is futile for the emergency if it remains wholly aloof from the central problem, which is the remaking of life itself. We are drawn irresistibly toward social criticism."

Allen Tate made similar arguments throughout the 1930s; as late as 1940, he prophesied the coming of "totalitarianism" to America within "the next few years," and concluded: "the tradition of free ideas is as dead in the United States as it is in Germany." But the conservative and, in some cases, reactionary New Critics, once they left their explicitly Agrarian platform behind, never

integrated literary criticism and cultural and political criticism. Such a project
was set aside. Instead, they proposed a method for the reform of English studies
and promoted it as a pedagogical tool.

For academics and most writers and intellectuals, this made the New Criticism far more appealing than Marxism – or, for that matter, than Agrarianism.
Marxism was criticized for making literature into a target for "Marxmanship,"
according to the novelist James T. Farrell in *A Note on Literary Criticism* (1936).
For Farrell, criticism "should become the agent that makes for the understanding and evaluation of works of literature," and "this understanding cannot be
merely in terms of formal ideology; it must also relate to the internal structure
of events in the book."

Farrell, author of the Studs Lonigan trilogy (1932–35), was a socialist by
the late 1920s; he sympathized with the Communist Party and contributed to
the Party's *New Masses* and the *Daily Worker* in the 1930s. Yet here he sounded
like a New Critic, like Ransom or Tate.

Allen Tate's essays in the 1930s indicated the direction that the New Critical
study of literature would take in subsequent decades. Tate objected, first, to
"historical, fact-based scholarship":

In our time the historical approach to criticism, in so far as it has attempted to be a
scientific method, has undermined the significance of the material which it proposes
to investigate ... The historical scholars, once the carriers of the humane tradition,
have now merely the genteel tradition; the independence of judgment, the belief in
intelligence, the confidence in literature, that informed the humane tradition, have
disappeared; under the genteel tradition the scholars exhibit timidity of judgment,
disbelief in intelligence, and suspicion of the value of literature.

This sounds like Randolph Bourne, and very much like the Harvard professor and philosopher George Santayana, who in 1911 had described the starved,
abstract, and mediocre qualities of the genteel tradition in American philosophy, and who expanded and updated this same argument in his 1931 critique
of the New Humanism, *The Genteel Tradition at Bay*. In Tate's view, scholars
were timid and unmanly in their pale retreat from the challenge of making
independent judgments. Misapplied "scientific method" had fostered uncritical habits of mind and encouraged teachers and students to allow "research"
to exempt them from literary and critical risk.

Tate advised those in literary studies to focus on the text as the true literary
"object." "The question in the end comes down to this," he concluded: "What
as literary critics are we to judge? ... The formal qualities of a poem are the
focus of a specifically critical judgment because they partake of an objectivity
that the subject matter, abstracted from the form, wholly lacks." For criticism

to exist as a discipline, it required an objectivity that would provide a center for interpretive dialogue and a standard for judgment. Scholarship gave some useful information, Tate conceded, but also much that was useless. It neither cohered around a particular object nor led to a body of critical discriminations; as Tate said in an essay on Emily Dickinson, scholarship "is no substitute for a critical tradition." By concentrating on the text itself and engaging in formal analysis, it would be possible to objectify criticism, transforming it into an intensive discipline.

Tate's accent on "form" showed his opposition to efforts to merge criticism and teaching with politics and morality. Tate was eager to prevent political propagandists from appropriating the literary text and deploying it as a weapon in ideological battles. And he wanted to defend modernism against the dogmatic responses of the standard-setting New Humanists. He therefore emphasized that poetry "does not explain our experience. If we begin by thinking that it ought to 'explain' the human predicament, we shall quickly see that it does not, and we shall end up thinking that therefore it has no meaning at all."

The consequences of Tate's arguments proved unfortunate in later decades when the New Criticism became institutionalized and lost the sensitivity and suppleness that the first generation of Southern New Critics in their practice possessed. For by defending the poem against claims that it "explains" experience, Tate sanctioned the belief that poetry is disconnected from other forms of experience and that worldly concerns sully and disfigure criticism.

But amid the critical debates of the 1930s, Tate's point made tactical sense. Tate opposed the scholars who ruled literature in the academy; he protected literature from the New Humanists and moralists who enlisted texts in ethical crusades; and he fought against Marxist-influenced and Communist Party intellectuals who enrolled literature in the class struggle. Tate cherished the special quality of literary experience, and he aimed to make it the center of English studies.

The pedagogical thrust of the New Criticism, as well as the limitations that it encouraged, can be seen clearly in Leo Spitzer's important essay "History of Ideas versus Reading of Poetry" (1940). The Austrian émigré Spitzer (1887–1960) did not portray himself as a New Critic, but his essay supplemented points made in Tate's essays and demonstrated the extent to which "close reading," "formal analysis," and "the texts themselves" were becoming the dominant terms for literary study. Brooks and Warren accepted "History of Ideas versus Reading of Poetry" for publication in *The Southern Review*, the journal that they co-edited, because they regarded it as authoritative testimony on behalf of a new kind of critical undertaking.

Like others before him, Spitzer was critical of source-hunting, biographical research, and background information. Teachers, he contended, should acknowledge the needs of their students and should return to the "particular work of art":

Most of our textbooks cram the students with the sources of a work while failing to describe the work itself – as if to imply that to "teach" the work of art itself would be an encroachment upon the personal reaction of the reader. Thus, on the pretext that any description of a poem must be emotional, personal, subjective (a pretense that perpetuates the escapist attitude), they fail to train their pupils to avoid subjectivity and emotionalism by learning to form and to express objective observations, to fix in their minds the exact contents, the relationships between the part and the whole, the structure and the formal qualities of a poem – all of which may be formulated with clarity and objectivity.

Spitzer stressed that his method was as disciplined as any procedure that scholars had devised and did not surrender to impressionism. Like the New Critics, he insisted on rigor and objectivity, so that no one would confuse his method with vacuous appreciation of great authors. As the poet-critic Conrad Aiken (1889–1973) had neatly explained in 1923, *that* mode of criticism meant a "deplorable vagueness," an "almost total lack of system or any scale of values, with its inevitably solipsistic outcome."

Teachers and critics must concentrate on the "form" of the work and the "exact contents" of what they observed, said Spitzer. In contrast to the New Humanists, he maintained that students should forgo using moral or didactic principles to appraise the text. Rather, students should learn to interpret the particular work that they examine and elucidate its status as "art."

This attention to the text also functioned for Spitzer to separate literary study from politics. Unlike a Marxist filtering texts through ideology, Spitzer's teacher-critic analyzes what is concretely "there" in what he or she reads. Such a person possesses "objective observations" that are the product of training and experience, and is equipped with a technique to convey in the classroom. This objectivity means that there is a norm, a standard, by which to discriminate between good and bad readings (bad readings are "subjective"), and thus the critic can truly gauge when politics have been imposed on the experience of art.

"It should be impressed upon the minds of students of literature," Spitzer argued, "that art and outward reality should, at least while the work of art is being studied, be kept separate . . . Art is not life, but a new architecture, built of fancy and the poetic will, apart from life and beyond life."

Spitzer's words attest to what was becoming policy for literary study by 1940, a policy that defined the object that critics and teachers should take as their province. "The work of art" must be distinguished from "life" and accorded a pure examination. This was the essence of the New Criticism, and it established the agenda that the New Critics and their followers articulated in their many books and essays. These critics had what Ransom described as "a strategy for English studies."

"It is really atrocious policy," Ransom concluded in 1938, in *The World's Body*,

for a department to abdicate its own self-respecting identity. The department of English is charged with the understanding and the communication of literature, an art, yet it has usually forgotten to inquire into the peculiar constitution and structure of its product. English might almost as well announce that it does not regard itself as entirely autonomous, but as a branch of the department of history, with the option of declaring itself occasionally a branch of the department of ethics.

Ransom and his colleagues revamped the discipline of English and secured its boundaries. The study of literature occurred within "departments" of English at colleges and universities; literary analysis meant focusing on "artistic objects"; and critics and teachers were to investigate how the specifically "literary" terms of their work dramatized the difference between this work and that underway in other departments. By the early 1950s, these were the principles of English studies, and even its detractors grew wedded to them: they could only dispute the New Criticism within the discourse of the texts themselves that the New Critics had established.

The New Criticism had the advantage of skilled theorists and polemicists who expounded its distinctive properties. William K. Wimsatt (1907–75) argued that "the verbal object and its analysis constitute the domain of literary criticism"; as he and Monroe Beardsley said in "The Intentional Fallacy" (1946), the critic must seek "to find out what the poet tried to do. If the poet succeeded in doing it, then the poem itself shows what he was trying to do." René Wellek and Austin Warren (1899–1986) insisted too that "the object of literary study" is "the concrete work of art," giving forceful expression to this principle in their handbook *Theory of Literature* (1949).

It may be true, as the New Critics claimed, that the New Criticism was not anti-historical and did in fact assume that ancillary disciplines would enrich the study of literature. But in their position papers the New Critics zeroed in on the priority of the text itself and labored to make English studies equivalent to the analysis and explication of texts. According to the critic Kenneth Burke, writing in 1947, the New Critics had taken charge of the profession and set up an "explication-de-texte racket."

During the late 1940s and 1950s, the Chicago neo-Aristotelians and the myth critics contested the New Critics' authority. The Chicago School was headed by

R. S. Crane (1886–1967), and the myth critics were led by Northrop Frye (1912–91) in his study of William Blake (1947) and in the essays that culminated in *Anatomy of Criticism* (1957), as well as by Richard Chase (1914–63) in *Quest for Myth* (1949). But what was being challenged were ways of interpreting literary texts, not the assumption that interpreting texts and English studies were identical.

As Frye explained in "The Function of Criticism at the Present Time" (1954): "Critical principles cannot be taken over ready-made from theology, philosophy, politics, science, or any combination of these . . . If criticism exists, it must be . . . an examination of literature in terms of a conceptual framework derivable from an inductive survey of the literary field." By this time the New Criticism had ingrained its ideas about literature and criticism into the procedures of criticism in general. By the early 1950s, the New Criticism was the Establishment.

The New Critics had from the beginning combined their advocacy of a "new" criticism with the reform of pedagogy – which gave their ideas great currency. As Brooks explained in 1976, four decades after the publication of *Understanding Poetry*, he had been "appalled" during his own schooldays by the prevailing historical, biographical, and philological methods that "seemed to have nothing to do with the interior life of the poem," and he and Warren and the others worked to design better methods for their own students.

The New Critics' methods were indeed teachable, and they remain more so than any method yet developed. Neither the teacher nor his or her students require special background or preparation to begin their literary work in the classroom. From the first day, teacher and students can read and respond to poems, exchange views about tone, paradox, ambiguity, and imagery, and comment on degrees of complex thought and feeling in texts. Teacher and students gather round a common object and join to give a detailed, sensitive reading of it.

Brooks was not at all a narrow technician. As he said of his work with Warren in the 1930s on their textbooks:

There is no discrepancy between teaching people to read poetry, to appreciate life by enlarging the imagination, to develop character and responsibility – all of this on the one hand – and what is sometimes called the technical detail, e.g., the way in which rhythm is expressed. Ultimately, we have here a seamless garment.

The New Critical method enabled, and still enables, a student to feel accomplished as a reader. He or she can learn to locate subtle meanings in texts and experience the satisfaction of a new type of expertise. This pleasure is particularly gratifying when it occurs in response to modernist writings that flaunt their difficulty and grant meanings to novice readers grudgingly.

"Poets in our civilization," Eliot had said, "must be *difficult*." Some modern poetry grew so difficult that the poets themselves ended up explicating their work, as did Hart Crane when he analyzed "At Melville's Tomb" and as did Allen Tate when he explained the organization of "Ode to the Confederate Dead." It was Eliot's poetry in particular that the Southern New Critics – three of whom were poets – wished to interpret for students and, Brooks noted, for "common readers" outside the classroom to whom modern poetry seemed "illogical and puzzling."

Brooks started his work on *Modern Poetry and the Tradition* while he was a Rhodes Scholar at Oxford in the early 1930s, and he had in mind as his audience his students and friends who were *not* fulltime in literature, but, rather, were in anthropology, mathematics, law, and other fields. As Brooks observed in "What Does Poetry Communicate?" (1947), "the modern poet has, for better or worse, thrown the weight of responsibility upon the reader," but, he added, "the difficulties are not insuperable." He might have quoted Wallace Stevens: "Poetry must resist the intelligence almost successfully." *Almost*, not entirely.

The New Critics achieved their pedagogical goal with a success that Brooks and Warren might not have anticipated or even welcomed. As Lionel Trilling reported, "if we are on the hunt for *the* modern element in literature, we might want to find it in the susceptibility of modern literature to being made into an academic subject." Others shared Trilling's ambivalence. In his essays, letters, and autobiography, William Carlos Williams, for example, spoke about T. S. Eliot in contemptuous terms because Eliot seemed to him to have countenanced the New Critical takeover of poetry and criticism. "Eliot returned us to the classroom," said Williams about *The Waste Land*, "just at the moment when I felt that we were on the point of an escape to matters much closer to the essence of a new art form itself – rooted in the locality which should give it fruit" (1951). Williams's motives in attacking Eliot were complicated (envy was part of his complaint), but he was right to say that there were affinities between Eliot's criticism and poetry and New Critical close reading.

As early as the 1940s, a sizable number of poets and critics, Williams among them, were making known their dismay about the New Criticism and were attacking its "exclusiveness." This was the term that Conrad Aiken used in 1940 to assail Ransom, Tate, and Brooks – "these earnest theoreticians of poetry – these scholiasts – subtle eyebrow-combers of style, calligraphic textcombers." To Aiken, poetry was "badly in need of liberation," a "wholehearted Romantic revival" that would disrupt the narrow New Criticism with its "schoolmaster's vision" of verse that had always to be subjected to the arid precision of classroom study.

The New Critics devoted far more attention to Eliot and Yeats, and Donne and Marvell, than to Williams and Whitman – Williams wasn't mistaken in feeling slighted. In part the New Critics simply followed Eliot's lead in seeing the best modern poetry by Yeats, Eliot himself, and W. H. Auden as hearkening back to the imagery, wit, irony, and ambiguities of the metaphysical poets.

The New Critics did show a certain range in the canon of poets, dramatists, short-story writers, and novelists they admired or at least took seriously enough to write analytically about. In *The Well Wrought Urn*, Brooks included chapters on Donne's "The Canonization," *Macbeth*, Milton's "L'Allegro" and "Il Penseroso," Herrick's "Corinna's going a-Maying," Pope's *The Rape of the Lock*, Gray's "Elegy Written in a Country Churchyard," Wordsworth's "Ode: Intimations of Immortality," Keats's "Ode on a Grecian Urn," Tennyson's "Tears, Idle Tears," and Yeats's "Among School Children." Warren's *Selected Essays* included discussions of Conrad, Faulkner, Hemingway, Frost, Katherine Anne Porter, Eudora Welty, Thomas Wolfe, Melville, and Coleridge. But the writers whom the New Critics treated most sympathetically were the metaphysical poets, the major modernists, and the poets and novelists of the Southern literary renaissance, as well as a few special cases, such as Melville, who were ranked highly because they could be located within the interpretive frameworks of seventeenth-century poetry and high modernism.

The New Critics' interests and techniques kept them close to lyric poetry. They also directed the New Critics to novels like those by Conrad and Faulkner, and like those that Tate and Warren wrote themselves. Such novels possessed an intricate verbal texture – as packed and as suggestive as a lyric poem – and a heightened symbolism.

A poet such as Whitman, on the other hand, posed a problem – Brooks objected in *Modern Poetry and the Tradition* to Whitman's "too frequent, vague, and windy generality about democracy and progress." The New Critics underrated not only Whitman but also Williams and other poets who followed in his and Whitman's lines. While the New Critics made modern verse and its precursor texts approachable, and described a number of novelists well, they also defined the literary tradition in a manner that omitted much.

Many African-American poets, critics, and writers of fiction were, like Williams, extremely unsympathetic toward Eliot and his Southern kinsmen, the New Critics. "The whole T. S. Eliot coterie," said the poet and novelist Arna Bontemps (1902–73) in a letter (June 1949) to his friend and fellow poet Langston Hughes, "including Ezra Pound and those who gave him that big award [the Bollingen Prize] this year, is a sick lot." (In a controversial decision announced in 1949, the pro-fascist and anti-Semitic Pound had been awarded the first annual Library of Congress Bollingen Award for American Poetry for his book *The Pisan Cantos*.) As Bontemps explained in a later letter (June 1953) to Hughes, the New Critics traced their genealogy "to the Fugitives of Nashville, the group which produced *I'll Take My Stand*, a very anti-Negro book. Not all have been reconstructed. Naturally they have their own reasons for opposing protest in fiction writing. They are ready enough to protest the things they don't like. They simply object to protesting the disabilities of the Negro in America."

Not a single African-American appeared in Brooks and Warren's *Understanding Poetry*. Nor were any included in Matthiessen's *Oxford Book of American Verse* (1950); Matthiessen omitted Paul Laurence Dunbar, the only African-American poet whom Bliss Carman had included in his edition of the Oxford book in 1927.

To the New Critics, African-American writing, when visible at all, was social and political rather than literary. Its texts were not self-contained, were not verbal icons. Matthiessen was a Christian socialist, and was involved in many radical activities, including (as an NAACP member) the fight to end racism. But when he studied literature, he did so as a New Critic, however much he aimed to treat social and democratic themes. Surely there must have been some poems by African-Americans that qualified for inclusion in Matthiessen's anthology according to his and the New Critics' own criteria. But he was unable to see them.

During the first decades of the century, a wide range of African-American writers did provocative work in fiction, poetry, drama, and criticism, and a number of new periodicals featured them. The NAACP's monthly *The Crisis* (1910–), launched under the editorship of W. E. B. Du Bois, included poems, stories, translations, and reviews; Chesnutt, James Weldon Johnson, Countee Cullen, and Jean Toomer published work in its pages; Hughes's first poem, "The Negro Speaks of Rivers," was published in *The Crisis* in 1921. Circulation fluctuated, but by 1918 it stood at an impressive 100,000.

There was also the National Urban League's *Opportunity: Journal of Negro Life* (1923–49), edited by the social scientist and educator Charles S. Johnson; McKay, Cullen, Hughes, Hurston, Bontemps, Gwendolyn Bennett, and Georgia Douglas Johnson appeared in its pages, and the journal sponsored literary contests and held awards dinners. And there was the labor leader A. Philip Randolph and Chandler Owen's *Messenger* (1917–28); it published poetry by McKay, Hughes, and Cullen, and in the late 1920s, Hughes's first short stories and Zora Neale Hurston's "Eatonville Anthology." The social activist Marcus Garvey's weekly newspaper *Negro World* published not only Hurston, the historian Carter G. Woodson, and the historian, curator, and bibliographer Arthur

A. Schomburg, but also writers from Africa, the Caribbean, and Central and South America.

With one or two exceptions, African-American writers were invisible to the New Critics. "The old Southern life," said Ransom in *I'll Take My Stand*, was a "kindly society," yet a "realistic one" where "people were for the most part in their right places"; "slavery was a feature monstrous enough in theory, but, more often than not, humane in practice." This claim was a staple of ante-bellum pro-slavery ideology. What seemed "humane enough" to Ransom doubtless struck the enslaved African-Americans differently. "The darkey is one of the bonds that make a South out of all the Southern regions," he observed in "The Esthetic of Regionalism" (1934), a defense of Southern tradition that failed to consider the kind of treatment that these "darkeys" experienced in a segregated society.

The first decades of the twentieth century were horrible for many African-Americans, and it is impossible to ignore this fact when considering the Agrarian campaign that Ransom, Tate, and the others undertook and the New Critical program, with its white-only canon, that they established. The 1890s saw the disenfranchisement of African-Americans through poll taxes, property qualifications, literacy tests, and the grandfather clause (which was a means of denying the right to vote to the descendants of slaves). The new state-constitution of Mississippi, in 1890, included a poll tax and literacy test, and the result was that the eligible electorate fell from 250,000 in 1890 to 77,000 in 1895 (many poor whites, as well as blacks, became ineligible to vote). In Louisiana, the number of registered black voters fell from 130,000 in 1896 to 1,000 in 1904. During the 1890s, there were hundreds of lynchings, and more than 1,000 between 1900 and 1910.

The majority opinion in the Supreme Court case of *Plessy* v. *Ferguson* (1896) stated: "We consider the underlying fallacy of the plaintiff's argument to consist in the assumption that the enforced separation of the two races stamps the colored race with a badge of inferiority. If this be so, it is not by reason of anything found in the act [i. e., the Louisiana law requiring railroad facilities to be segregated by race], but solely because the colored race chooses to put that construction upon it." Two years later, an editorial in the Charleston, South Carolina *News and Courier* stated: "If there must be Jim Crow cars on the railroads, there should be Jim Crow cars on the street railways. Also on all passenger boats . . . If there are to be Jim Crow cars, moreover, there should be Jim Crow waiting saloons at all stations, and Jim Crow eating houses . . . There should be Jim Crow sections of the jury box, and a separate Jim Crow dock and witness stand in every court – and a Jim Crow Bible for colored witnesses to kiss."

By the 1890s, 90 percent of the African-American population lived in the South, and, mistreated in all sectors of life, they constituted about 40 percent of the South's population. As late as 1915, five Southern states had still not established a public school system for African-American children. Conditions in the South led 825,000 African-Americans to move north during the 1920s, tripling the black population of Detroit and doubling that of Cleveland, Chicago, and New York City.

In 1932, Allen Tate refused to meet Langston Hughes and James Weldon Johnson when these two African-American writers visited Nashville, Tennessee. Tate forced one of his younger colleagues in the English department at Vanderbilt to cancel a party that was scheduled in honor of Hughes and Johnson, saying that while both men were "interesting" authors, they could not be allowed to mingle with whites on equal terms in the South. Meeting with them at a party, said Tate in an open letter to the community, would be equivalent to meeting socially with his African-American cook.

Tate described the relation between whites and African-Americans in the South in his contribution to *I'll Take My Stand*: "the white race seems determined to rule the Negro in its midst; I belong to the white race; therefore I intend to support white rule." Three years later, in a letter to Lincoln Kirstein, Tate stated: "the negro race is an inferior race." (Also in 1933, after meeting with Seward Collins, the reactionary editor of the *American Review*, Tate said: "Collins has the same idea we have on the Jewish nature of liberalism and on the Old Testament . . . [He] has worked himself into a great froth over the Jews. Let us not discourage him.") Robert Penn Warren, more liberal than his friends, descended into crude imagery and attitudinizing about African-Americans in his poetry and prose, as in his poem "Pondy Woods" (included in *Selected Poems, 1923–1943*), with its portrait of the "slick black buck" Big Jim Todd and the "one lean bird" that declares to him, "Nigger, your breed ain't metaphysical."

Many landmarks of the New Criticism appeared during the late 1930s and early 1940s: *Understanding Poetry* (1938), Ransom's *The World's Body* (1938) and *The New Criticism* (1941), Brooks's *Modern Poetry and the Tradition* (1939), Tate's *Reactionary Essays on Poetry and Ideas* (1936) and *Reason in Madness: Critical Essays* (1941). This same period also marked the publication of seminal scholarly and critical works on American and, especially, African-American literature by African-American critics, scholars, editors, and intellectuals, and these were works that the New Critics in their books and their followers in the academy ignored.

Notable among these books on African-American literature and criticism were Sterling Brown's *Negro Poetry and Drama* and *The Negro in American Fiction* (both in 1937); Brown, Arthur P. Davis, and Ulysses Lee's 1,000-page collection of "writings by American Negroes," *The Negro Caravan* (1941); and Richard Wright's *12 Million Black Voices: A Folk History of the Negro in the United States* (1941). All three, along with many essays and reviews by other African-Americans, extended and developed the literary criticism and scholarship that Kelly Miller, W. E. B. Du Bois, Alain Locke, Benjamin Brawley, William Stanley Braithwaite, and James Weldon Johnson had produced. And they reinforced and fixed a measure of attention upon the creative writing done by African-Americans during the 1930s, when Wright, Ralph Ellison, Zora Neale Hurston, Melvin Tolson, Robert Hayden, Langston Hughes, Claude McKay, Jessie Fauset, Wallace Thurman, Frank Marshall Davis, Countee Cullen, Sterling Brown, William Attaway, and Arna Bontemps were generating a formidable body of poetry and prose.

However, this attention was primarily paid within the African-American intellectual and cultural community, not within the white one. The central literary critical text for African-Americans at this time was J. Saunders Redding's *To Make a Poet Black* (1939), and it went unrecognized by white scholars and teachers who were very aware of the latest New Critical offerings. Like Brown and Locke, Redding (1906–88) was responsive to the African-American vernacular and the popular roots of the literature that his people crafted and composed, and he presented his analysis of the history of "American Negro literature" in an African-American as well as an American and English context. Redding alluded to Hawthorne, Hardy, Donne, Wordsworth, and other white American and English authors, yet he keyed his discussion of the "tradition" – from Jupiter Hammon and Phillis Wheatley in the eighteenth century to Toomer, Hughes, and others active in the 1920s through the mid-1930s – to the internal relationships, structures, and themes of African-American texts and the social conditions within which they emerged.

Redding must have been familiar with the New Critics' writings. He attended Brown University as an undergraduate (B.A., 1928) and as a graduate student (M.A., 1932), and he did additional work at Columbia from 1932 to 1934. One of the positions he held was that of chairman of the English department at Southern University from 1934 to 1936, an institution located in Baton Rouge, Louisiana, the same city in which Brooks and Warren were teaching as members of the English department at Louisiana State University.

To Make A Poet Black (the title refers to a phrase in a poem by Countee Cullen) was a powerful counterstatement to the New Critics, particularly in its concern for the connections between literature and history and in its valuation of the popular sources for literature and art. Redding nowhere named or cited Ransom, Tate, Brooks, Warren, or anyone else associated with the emerging New Critical movement: they were silent about African-American literature, and perhaps for this reason he did not invoke them. His book defined "literature" in a social, political, and cultural context that the New Critics would not have favored and frequently spoke out against.

"Almost from the very beginning," Redding argued, "the literature of the Negro has been literature either of purpose or necessity, and it is because of this that it appeals as much to the cognitive as to the conative and affective side of man's being. The study of the literature of these dark Americans becomes, therefore, a practical, as opposed to a purely speculative, exercise." For Redding, "American Negro literature" is a form of art that gives knowledge about the struggles of a people. It arose because it *needed* to be written to express and accomplish social, political, and cultural purposes. This literature was nurtured by the customs and traditions, the spirituals and folklore of the people, and hence it derived from the hopes and aspirations – and the materials – of the masses.

Redding made cutting judgments about writers who he believed had failed in their art or were unable fully to take advantage of the resources that African-American life made available to them. Yet his words often took a generous turn, as Redding strove to redeem and honor the writers of the past so that readers and writers in the present could profit from their texts.

The African-American writers of the mid-nineteenth century, Redding said,

often sacrificed beauty of thought and of truth – the specific goals of art – to the exigencies of their particular purposes. But a great and good work was done. They created in the Negro a core of racial pride without which no great endeavor is possible. Though they were not artists enough to see and recognize with love and pride the beauty of their own unaffected spirituals, tales, and work songs, they nevertheless acknowledged the possibilities for artistic treatment in Negro peasant life, the southern scene, and the enigmatic soul of the simple Negro.

Redding set high standards for art even as he affirmed the importance of perceiving and valuing the popular and socio-political bases for it. He was concerned to demonstrate that the best literary texts spring from the vital activity of a people, and he advised contemporary African-American writers to remain proudly in contact with and build upon the idioms and images and rhythms of African-American speech and music.

In his closing chapter, Redding praised James Weldon Johnson's "return to these things" and described Johnson's influence upon "the gratifying new work of Sterling Brown in poetry and Zora Neale Hurston in prose." This organizing theme in *To Make A Poet Black* not only illuminated a creative path that later African-Americans would pursue in their poems, novels, and stories, but also taught a lesson about critical theory and practice that Redding embodied in his own work. Like the New Critics Brooks and Warren, he aimed to write, as he stated in his Preface, "with a mind for the problems of students," yet he preserved a personal tone that he hoped would enable his scholarship to "appeal to popular taste . . . For ultimately literature, if it is to live at all, must be in the strictest sense popular."

Women writers, especially poets, fared poorly at the hands of the New Critics. T. S. Eliot, in a letter of October 31, 1917, about his editing of *The Egoist*, acknowledged, "I struggle to keep the writing as much as possible in male hands, as I distrust the Feminine in literature." In "The Poet as Woman," an essay included in *The World's Body*, Ransom observed that "less pliant, safer as a biological organism, [a woman] remains fixed in her famous attitudes, and is indifferent to intellectuality." Sensibility, tenderness, and love, rather than intellectual precision and power, defined "woman," and differentiated the verse that women penned from that written by John Donne – "the poet of intellectualized persons" – and by the male modernists equipped to emulate him. Commenting on Marianne Moore in a chapter on modern poetry written for *The Literary History of the United States* (1948), Matthiessen remarked that she "is feminine in a very rewarding sense, in that she makes no effort to be major." In the words of Louise Bogan, writing in her journal in the 1930s: "I am a woman, and 'fundamental brainwork,' the building of logical structures, the abstractions, the condensations, the comparisons, the reasonings, *are not expected of me.*"

Eliot, Pound, and the New Critics approved of, but underrated, the origin-ality of such modernists as Gertrude Stein, H. D., and Marianne Moore; and they neglected or simplified Millay, Louise Bogan, Elinor Wylie, and Sara Teasdale. If there was a "modern" woman poet they did admire, it was Emily Dickinson, whose greatness for the New Critics lay in her close connection to the seventeenth-century and twentieth-century male poets and novelists whom they celebrated. In an essay published in 1928, Allen Tate linked Dickinson to Donne and explored her interest in the "moral" themes taken up by Hawthorne and Henry James. Her "intellectual toughness" distinguished her as a poet and, for Tate, marked her difference from the literary behavior in which women typically indulged.

In *Modern Poetry and the Tradition*, Brooks focused on Yeats, Eliot, Ransom, Tate, Frost, MacLeish, and Auden. He understood the terms of his title as bearing upon the verse of a select group of male poets, and he provided no discussion of women writers. (He also excluded Marxist and left-leaning au-thors of "proletarian" verse.) In 1950, Brooks and Warren issued a revised and greatly enlarged edition of their classic textbook, *Understanding Poetry*, noting in it that their "personal tastes had changed a little"; they welcomed "enrichments of perception and expansions of critical sympathy." But their selection of texts remained overwhelmingly male and white, and their stress upon the dangers of "sentimentality" and "message-hunting" in poetry and critical commentary continued to implant in literary studies a definition of verbal value that prevented many women authors from being favorably heard.

A further sign of the unnatural form that literary history and criticism assumed under the New Criticism is the exclusion or marginalization of women from the ranks of critics who mattered. During the 1930s and afterwards, the New Critics, as well as literary historians who heeded them, named Eliot, Pound, Wilson, Burke, Winters, Ransom, Tate, Brooks, Warren, Trilling, and Blackmur in America, and Leavis, Richards, and Empson (with Eliot and Pound appearing once again) in England. Marianne Moore (1887–1972) wrote hundreds of essays, reviews, and letters on modern poetry during the major phase of modernism, yet she never appeared on a list of important, influential critics. Her critical prose was unusual – sharply edged, daring, witty, and playful, generous in the slant of its commentary and in its ample quotations. She was intimately involved in the formation of modern literature, and she showed a focus and enlightening exuberance in her phrasing that few of her contemporaries matched.

In Eliot's "Marina," Moore saw a "machinery of satisfaction that is powerfully affecting, intrinsically and by association. The method is a main part of the pleasure: lean cartography; reiteration with compactness; emphasis by word pattern rather than by punctuation; the conjoining of opposites to produce irony; a counterfeiting verbally of the systole, diastole of sensation – of what the eye sees and the mind feels; the movement within the movement of differentiated kindred sounds" (1931). Moore possessed a vivid, alert intelligence, and she framed her insights with energy and intensity. "Struggle is a main force in William Carlos Williams," she stated in one of her pieces about his verse (1934): "And the breathless budding of thought from thought is one of the results and charms of the pressure configured."

Moore's contemporaries valued the services to poetry she performed in her criticism and in her editorial labors for *The Dial* from 1925 to 1929. Her many letters to them, or to others about them, contain shrewd and finely turned assessments, as when she writes (January 7, 1943) to a young author named John Putnam about her response to Wallace Stevens: "Wallace Stevens is a philosopher and so concentrated in his reasoning, that often it seems to me, the person interpreting him, takes too strongly to heart, some facet of his thought. Always he is defining, – saying – By 'sentiment' I mean so and so.

And often I find I had inferred some opposite meaning, from the one implied. So if I may say so, let the 'enjoyment' be your guide." Of Eliot's *Four Quartets*, Moore said (July 20, 1943) to her friend Elizabeth Bishop, "The quartets seem to me very sad; so unegoistic a precipitate, there is something alarming about them. Technically, I am too inexperienced to know how prose-like, transitions between lyrics should be; and tend to think that every word of every poem should be as melodious as a Handel allegro – but the intensified honesty of this writing of T. S. Eliot's is resolute and helpful – I can't seem to dwell over-much on the form. (Not that I would imply that some of the writing wasn't honest.) It is just that I feel self-consciousness is in abeyance." But when male poets and critics dealt with the state of criticism, or named literary critics who counted, they left Moore out.

The New Critics knew but said next to nothing about the women poets, critics, editors, and patrons of arts and letters who were active in the modernist movements. A number of them led unconventional, indeed anti-conventional, lives – which may also account for their inability to be seen: they perceived their bisexuality, lesbian partnering, and sexual experimentation as related, even as essential, to the kinds of artistic identities that they sought to define and explore.

Some of these women (for example, Amy Lowell) were condescended to, if not outright dismissed, in the critical record; others (above all, Gertrude Stein) were labeled gifted eccentrics; others, such as H. D., were credited with a degree of excellence in their craft but were always located well below their male counterparts; and still others, including Harriet Monroe, the editor of *Poetry* from 1912 to 1936, Margaret Anderson, editor of *The Little Review* (Chicago, New York, Paris, 1914–29), and Sylvia Beach, proprietor of the bookshop and library "Shakespeare and Company" in Paris and publisher of the first edition of *Ulysses*, were judged mere handmaidens to their betters.

Some women writers even came to accept their own devaluation at the hands of modernist men, promulgating the work of Eliot, Yeats, and Pound that the New Critics exalted and bypassing or marginalizing women poets. The poet, critic, editor, and novelist Babette Deutsch (1895–1982) is an example. She grew up in New York City, and attended Barnard College, where she studied under the progressive historian Charles Beard and, later, assisted Thorstein Veblen at the New School for Social Research. She drew inspiration from Randolph Bourne's call to young Americans to lead a cultural renaissance, and she became radicalized in response to the Russian Revolution. Her own best verse from the 1920s and 1930s is brooding, intense, socially and politically charged; and in her novel, *A Brittle Heaven*, she showed her sensitivity to gender issues, sexual stereotyping, male privilege, and women's communities.

Yet when Deutsch surveyed modern poetry in *Poetry in Our Time* (1952), she relied on the interpretive approach and the canon that the New Critics had advanced; she accorded only scanty treatment to the women poets who had been her own cohorts, colleagues, and soulmates. Eliot and Yeats are great writers: Deutsch was right about that. But they and their fellow male poets were not the only great or significant writers. Nor did they exhaust the forms that literature might take. Such omissions not only disserved the work of the women poets, novelists, and critics themselves, but also restricted the understanding of literature.

A revealing later report on the limits of the New Critical canon, as it was institutionalized in the 1950s and 1960s, was given by Florence Howe, a feminist critic, president and publisher of the Feminist Press, and former president of the Modern Language Association. In *Myths of Coeducation* (1984), Howe described the beginning of her teaching career in the early 1960s at Goucher College in Baltimore, Maryland, where she took as one of her goals the reform of a required course for sophomore majors. The course she helped to design focused exclusively on male authors, and it failed even to include "a single admirable woman as central character" in any of the chosen texts.

Howe was imbued with standard notions about the "universal" greatness of male-authored texts interpreted in New Critical fashion; she was unaware that women authors and characters had been excluded from her own education, and that she was perpetuating the same limited canon and pedagogy herself. When Howe worked in a Freedom School in Mississippi in 1964, she developed an expanded curriculum that included texts by Langston Hughes, James Baldwin, and Richard Wright even as it continued to omit women. Her particular mission at this school impelled her to include the work of African-American writers, yet, as she explained, she "naturally" focused on male authors and was oblivious to women.

Not only did the New Critical canon need to be revised so that it included such women writers as Zora Neale Hurston, Nella Larsen, Margaret Fuller, Harriet Beecher Stowe, Rebecca Harding Davis, Charlotte Perkins Gilman, Agnes Smedley, Kate Chopin, and Mary Wilkins Freeman. As Howe made clear, the critical approach to them was inadequate as well. Critics and students trained in New Critical analysis had learned to explicate the style, structure, and rhythm of a text without dwelling upon or exploring the writer's beliefs, particularly as these might be connected to women's lives and experiences. In Howe's case, this meant that she prepared a lengthy study of Swift's poetry, delving into his rhyme and wit, without ever considering or evaluating what his language was actually saying about women.

The triumph of the New Criticism, and the fact that the New Critics and their supporters wrote the history of modern literature and criticism, meant that the voices of past and present women critics in the academy (the few of them that there were) generally were not taken seriously or even listened to.

There was, for example, the critic, scholar, editor, and essayist Vida Scudder (1861–1954), who taught at Wellesley College from 1887 to 1928. Scudder was born in India, the daughter of a Congregationalist minister and missionary. After her father's death in 1862, she and her mother returned to Boston, where both her mother's and father's families lived. She did undergraduate work at Smith College, and pursued graduate study at Oxford, where she attended John Ruskin's lectures and moved toward the Christian socialism that empowered her literary criticism and life as a settlement worker and activist. While at Wellesley, she aided immigrant groups and supported labor unions. In 1912, she addressed a meeting of workers on strike at a textile mill in Lawrence, Massachusetts, and local newspapers demanded that Wellesley fire her from her teaching post – which the administration refused to do. Scudder never married; she loved and lived with women.

Nearly all of Scudder's many books were concerned with freedom, democracy, community, Christianity, and socialism. When she wrote about and taught literature, she was especially drawn to discuss the relevance of writers and texts for human progress and solidarity. The first sentence of *Social Ideals in English Letters* (1898) announced: "this book is to consider English literature in its social aspect." This study, as well as *The Life of the Spirit in the Modern English Poets* (1895) and *Socialism and Character* (1912), emphasized social conscience and responsibility and the prophetic majesty of the English literary tradition.

Scudder noted the limitations of Carlyle, Ruskin, Arnold, and Morris as spokesmen for her socialist views, but she nevertheless praised these Victorian sages highly. She adapted from their writings, and from the ideals of Christianity and socialism, her passionate affirmations of the organic wholeness of society – which implied, for her, a bond between the college and the community, the classroom where literary masterpieces were studied and the neighborhoods of workers and poor people whom she felt obliged to know and serve. Scudder undertook courageous work, but because she was a socialist woman who taught and wrote at a women's college, contemporary men of letters and male critics ignored her. Scudder's vision of the role and mission of teaching, criticism, and scholarship was far removed from what the Agrarians and New Critics would ever have accepted.

Another interesting, if less accomplished, figure is Gertrude Buck (1871–1922), who taught at Vassar College from 1907 until her death. Buck's only book was the pamphlet-length study *The Social Criticism of Literature* (1916). As the Preface indicates, Buck sought to outline a "theory of social criticism" and the "conception of literature underlying it." This, she explained, formed the basis of all of the course-work in the English department at Vassar (one of Buck's own prize students was the Americanist and folklorist Constance Rourke), and it derived from John Dewey's "philosophy of society" and progressive ideas.

Buck criticized the static positions held by philologists, aesthetes, New Humanists, and impressionists. For her, following Dewey and William James, "reading" was "a process rather than a product, something that takes place rather than something which has been made." She articulated a new conception of literature and criticism that was "vitalized" and "democratic." What mattered was not a canon of classic texts but, instead, the personal and social transformations that many kinds of texts could bring about for readers at different stages of their lives:

Good literature, as judged by the social standard, is that which efficiently performs the function of literature for any individual or for any group of individuals, namely the function of making common in society all peculiar advantages of mental endowment or experience . . . Such a standard of literature will, it is apparent, yield us no immutable five-foot shelf of "the best books" . . . A book that is "good literature" in the social sense for one reader or for one community may not be good for another. But it is good for each reader and for each community in the degree in which it furthers the development of each as part of the social whole.

Buck over-emphasized "sincerity" in literature, a virtue that she took to be central to all texts that function for the social good but that she failed to justify and probe. Yet her book was a cogent statement of the progressive notion of criticism and pedagogy that the faculty at Vassar practiced. It charted a critical method that could have been supplemented and strengthened if readers in college and university settings had been given the opportunity to examine it and the curriculum based on it.

The women faculty at Vassar conducted their teaching along the lines that Van Wyck Brooks and Randolph Bourne – two others whom James and Dewey influenced – advocated in their calls for a "renaissance" in literature, criticism, and the arts. Two years after the publication of Buck's book, Brooks and Bourne co-authored a piece for *Poetry* magazine in which they objected to Harriet Monroe's limited sense of what criticism entailed:

By criticism we mean discussion of a larger scope. You can discuss poetry and a poetry movement solely as poetry – as a fine art, shut up in its own world, subject to its own rules and values; or you can examine it in relation to the larger movement of ideas and social movements and the peculiar intellectual and spiritual color of the time. To treat poetry entirely in terms of itself is the surest way to drive it into futility and empty verbalism.

Buck and her colleagues were practicing the "social criticism" that Brooks and Bourne endorsed. But the future lay with the insistence on treating poetry "entirely in terms of itself," the approach that the New Critics represented. The kind of work that Brooks and Bourne called for, and that in their different ways Scudder and Buck performed, was not attended to in the academy.

This is true enough, but the New Criticism was nonetheless right to insist that teachers and students should first focus on, and seek to understand and enjoy, the literary work itself. In an essay on Coleridge's "Rime of the Ancient Mariner" (1946), Robert Penn Warren made the point well: "The first piece of evidence is the poem itself... The criterion is that of internal consistency. If the elements of a poem operate together toward one end, we are entitled to interpret the poem according to that end. Even if the poet himself should rise to contradict us, we could reply that his words do speak louder than his actions." Cleanth Brooks, in "Criticism and Literary History" (*Sewanee Review* 55, Spring 1947), reaffirmed this view: "There is surely a sense in which any one must agree that a poem has a life of its own, and a sense in which it provides in itself the only criterion by which what it says can be judged." The text is available for study, and the readings that can be derived from it provide a center for serious literary teaching.

The development of New Critical explications suggests, however, the weakness of the New Criticism as it played itself out in pedagogy in the post-World War II decades. It led to close readings without apparent limit, covering the text with so much interpretation that "the text itself" tended to disappear.

Before the era of the New Criticism, many people said that literature was being lost amid piles of scholarly information, or else was being tarnished by unconstrained impressionism, insipid moralizing, and political huckstering. The New Critics brought forward a new brand of scientific rigor and recovered the text, showing everyone how to examine formal patterns and structures and basing the discipline of "English" upon this activity. But they never were able to explain when the production of readings should cease or why it should continue indefinitely. Nor could they convince growing numbers of skeptics why some readings were right and others wrong – a distinction that a true discipline would seem compelled to maintain.

No sooner were the texts restored to view and the New Critical revolution won than a fresh chorus of complaints sounded that once again literature was being mistreated and mismanaged, driven into the dim background by incessant interpretation and the ballooning status of "criticism." According to R. P. Blackmur, in "A Burden for Critics" (1948),

In an unstable society like ours, precisely because the burden put upon the arts is so unfamiliar and extensive (it is always the maximum burden in intensity), a multiple burden is put upon criticism to bring the art to full performance. We have to compare and judge as well as analyze and elucidate. We have to make plain not only what people are reading, but also – as Augustine and the other fathers had to do with the scriptures – what they are reading about.

Critics – so the charge went – were not doing the best or right type of work, yet they had become too important, more so than creative writers themselves. The poet Robert Lowell inadvertently made this clear in an interview in 1961 when he noted that the members of his generation anticipated New Critical essays by Blackmur and Tate "the way we would wait for a new imaginative work." It was just this upside-down state of affairs that the New York intellectual Irving Howe (1920–93) lamented when he said in the 1950s that "learned young critics who have never troubled to open a novel by Turgenev can rattle off reams of Kenneth Burke."

Even as the New Critics said that their method was disciplined and precise, other critics and scholars objected that New Critical procedures were not disciplined at all but showed ignorance about literature itself, triggered an undue emphasis upon critical production, and invited impressionism and subjectivity. The New Criticism was intended to stop meandering personal commentary on the masterpieces yet it seemed to authorize each person to be a sensitive reader whose response was significant and somehow in touch with the meaning, or a meaning, of the text. The most curious aspect of the New Criticism is that it preserved the grounds for complaints about criticism at the same time that it addressed and answered them.

By the 1960s, the New Criticism faced ever-increasing opposition. The French structuralist Roland Barthes and other theorists from abroad were winning support in the United States for a criticism of texts that drew upon the linguistic and anthropological models of Ferdinand de Saussure and Claude Lévi-Strauss. Structuralism promised a systematic study of the core relationships that organize literary works, and, like other vanguard disciplines in the human sciences, it demonstrated a methodological intensity that a thinned-out New Criticism lacked.

From a different direction, the American theorist E. D. Hirsch, in *Validity in Interpretation* (1967), also criticized the New Critics and called for disciplinary rejuvenation and coherence. Dismayed by the relativism that he took to be rampant in literary studies, Hirsch stated that a text means what the author intended it to mean. This verbal meaning remains always the same – it does not alter or waver through time – and critics, teachers, and students can identify and know it. Equipped with a defensible principle for judging inter-pretations, they can, Hirsch concluded, thereby make distinctions among the contradictory readings of texts that have been presented.

The fiercest opposition to the New Criticism resulted from the social protest movements of the 1960s and early 1970s. Many critics, faculty, and students during this period denounced colleges and universities as institutions that backed an unjust war in Vietnam and reinforced racism. They declared that pious talk about aesthetic values and reverence for close reading of litera-ture cloaked anti-human institutional realities and prevented students from striving to end the evils of the world outside the academy.

The literary radicals claimed that by focusing on the text alone, the New Critics had tried to ensure that students would accept the status quo. In 1972, the Marxist critic Richard Ohmann referred to the "flight from politics" that the New Criticism encouraged; and, in the same year, H. Bruce Franklin described it as a "crude and frankly reactionary formalism," adding that the "essence" of such a critical approach is that "the ostrich sticks his head in the sand and admires the structural relationships among the grains."

While the New Criticism appeared to the 1960s radicals as irrelevant to politics and society in one sense, it seemed to them disturbingly relevant in another. Because it was not "oppositional," it allowed the "governing culture," said Louis Kampf and Paul Lauter, to continue on its exploitative course. New Critical analysis, in Kampf and Lauter's view, not only removed "the experi-ence of literature from the here and now to some world of fantasy, or to the realm of an autonomous, disinterested aesthetic." It also taught the skills and attitudes that capitalism required, training students for positions in corpo-rate middle-management and accommodating them, said the radical feminist Ellen Cantarow, to "bureaucratic thinking." The New Critical method, she concluded, mirrored "the sterility of life under capitalism."

The paradox here is that many of the New Critics in their Agrarian writings of the late 1920s and early to mid-1930s described the sterility of life under capitalism in a jaded voice that few radicals of the 1960s could match. But it is true that radicals in the 1960s were reacting in large measure to the separation of literary criticism from politics and history that Ransom and his colleagues had established after the Agrarian program of *I'll Take My Stand* failed. As a means to consolidate literary studies in the college and university, the New Critics' arguments for fastening on "the text itself" worked well. But these finally proved inadequate during a period of social and political upheaval when historical events shattered kinds of work in the classroom that once appeared eminently humane and defensible.

Still another paradox is that the New Critics themselves knew as early as the 1940s and early 1950s that something had gone wrong. For them, the problem was less the failure of critics to deal with politics and history than it was the emptiness and routinization of criticism. The New Critics had appealed for a disciplined method of formal analysis that wide reading and knowledge would support; they did not envision – though their writings reinforced – the formulaic kind of "close reading" that eventually prevailed in the academy.

In 1949, Cleanth Brooks stated that a "close reading of the text" should involve "careful attention to the language" and its human and symbolic meanings; it should not be mere "verbal piddling," nor a mechanical application of codified procedures. Ransom, in 1952, reflected that while the New Critics had accomplished much estimable work, they had allowed their approach to grow "tiresome": "the critics of poetry have tended to rest in the amorphous experience which they make of the poem without finding there, or seeking, anything to bind it all together or to engage with some notable human concern in the reader." In "Modern Poetry" published three years later, Tate emphasized that "our critics, since Mr. Richards started them off with *The Principles of Literary Criticism* in 1924, have been perfecting an apparatus for 'explicating' poems (not a bad thing to do), innocent of the permanently larger ends of criticism."

It was a mechanical thing that many critics and teachers believed that the New Criticism had become. Ransom hoped to build "Criticism, Inc.," but, to the 1960s radicals, he had ushered in an impersonal, programmatic business that displayed many of the anti-human features he himself had denounced in his Agrarian days. The radicals were really expressing just a fiercer version of the judgment of the New Critics' work that Ransom, Tate, and the others had already made. "There would seem to be needed," Ransom said in 1952, "some acknowledgment of the actual warmth and feel, and the powerful psychic focus, with which poetry comes into our experience." This was the quality of literary experience that Ransom missed in the criticism he encountered inside and outside the academy, the criticism he had done so much to devise and promote.

Others made the same case, again as early as in the 1940s and 1950s, and often did so in words that satirized or mocked the corporate identity for literary studies that Ransom had argued for in the late 1930s. Alfred Kazin, in *On Native Grounds* (1942), attacked the New Critics: "The passion of these critics for form made a fetish of form and had become entirely disproportionate to the significance of form in the artistic synthesis. Form had, in a word, become a sentimental symbol of order in a world that had no order; it had become the last orthodoxy in the absence of all other orthodoxies." Philip Rahv, in "Art and the Historical Imagination" (1952), also objected to the restricted nature of the New Critical approach: "Their attachment to the text is what is appealing about the 'new critics'; what is unappealing is their neglect of context." Rahv indicted the New Critics for "the impoverishment of the critical faculty and a devitalized sense of literary art," and for "a narrow textual-formalistic approach which cannot account for change and movement in literature and which systematically eliminates ideas from criticism."

In *Poetry and the Age* (1953), Randall Jarrell (who had studied and worked with Ransom at Vanderbilt and Kenyon College) complained that "a great deal" of contemporary criticism might just as well have been written "by a syndicate of encyclopedias for an audience of International Business Machines." In *The Democratic Vista* (1958), Richard Chase lamented the fact that "so many literary professors have become indistinguishable from clerks, statisticians, and positive thinkers." To Chase, the safe, timid, bureaucratic style of modern criticism was yet another sign of the mediocrity, standardization, and conformity that had overtaken the culture as a whole.

Those who were sympathetic to the New Criticism made some of the most forceful protests against it. In "The Sense of the Past" (1942; rpt. *The Liberal Imagination*, 1950), Lionel Trilling stated that the New Criticism had moved too far away from "historical method" and had forgotten that "the literary work is ineluctably an historical fact." In 1949, in "The Responsibilities of the Critic," F. O. Matthiessen went even further, maintaining that "we have come to the unnatural point where textual analysis seems to be an end in itself." The New Criticism, he concluded, had become a "new scholasticism"; its journals were "not always distinguishable from the philological journals."

Launched in reaction to philology, the New Criticism now was attacked for its resemblance to the self-enclosed activity that it had sought to displace. It might seem hard to intensify the indictment beyond this, but Van Wyck Brooks did so in *The Writer in America* (1953) when he stressed that the triumph of "close reading" signaled the death of reading: "the age of the new criticism has been, in point of fact, the age in which general reading seems almost to have vanished." Trilling, writing in 1967, observed that to many literature seemed to exist "chiefly to provide occasions for its being explicated, and expounded and judged" (*The Experience of Literature*).

Still, it is important to make a distinction between the work of the best New Critics and the broader New Critical movement. The reputation of Cleanth Brooks in particular suffered during the 1970s and 1980s when his books and essays were cited repeatedly to illustrate the flaws of the American New Criticism. Brooks, it was said, isolated literary criticism within the boundaries of intensive analysis of the text itself, ignored history, discounted readers, failed to consider writings by women and minorities, and disabled any and all attempts to relate literary study to political, social, and cultural issues and debates. But while there are shortcomings to Brooks's criticism, he is far more interesting and complex than the standard accounts suggest. He was a subtle, incisive interpreter of literary texts, and an adept theorist whose turns and twists of argument anticipated the theories later deployed against him.

Brooks was born in Murray, Kentucky, one of six children of a Methodist minister. He attended McTyeire School, a private classical academy in Tennessee, and then Vanderbilt (1924–28) and Tulane (M.A., 1929). He next studied at Exeter College, Oxford University, as a Rhodes Scholar, returning to the United States in 1932 to begin his teaching career at Louisiana State University in Baton Rouge.

While at Oxford, Brooks became good friends with Robert Penn Warren, another Vanderbilt graduate and Rhodes Scholar, and when Warren joined LSU's English department in 1934, the two of them started to work together on criticism and pedagogy. It was this need to improve literary study in the classroom that led to Brooks and Warren's influential, best-selling textbooks *An Approach to Literature* (1936), *Understanding Poetry* (1938), *Understanding Fiction* (1943), *Modern Rhetoric* (1949) and, with Robert Heilman, *Understanding Drama* (1945). Brooks, looking back in 1979, said:

> Our dominant motive was not to implant new-fangled ideas in the innocent Louisiana sophomores we faced three times a week. Our motive was to try to solve a serious practical problem. Our students, many of them bright enough and certainly amiable and charming enough, had no notion of how to read a literary text.

From 1935 to 1942, Brooks and Warren coedited *The Southern Review*, making it one of the foremost journals of its era. They published not only critical essays but also creative writing by Eudora Welty, Katherine Anne Porter, and others. In the first year alone, the authors appearing in *The Southern Review* included John Crowe Ransom, Allen Tate, Wallace Stevens, Kenneth Burke, R. P. Blackmur, Randall Jarrell, Ford Madox Ford, and Yvor Winters. In 1947 Brooks left LSU for a professorship at Yale University (Warren later joined him), and he taught there until his retirement in 1975. He researched, wrote, and published many essays and books on modern fiction and literary criticism, as well as editing textbooks.

Brooks's two most important critical books, *Modern Poetry and the Tradition* (1939) and *The Well Wrought Urn: Studies in the Structure of Poetry* (1947), focused on poetry, and he extended and reinforced their arguments in essays, reviews, and lectures. For example, with J. E. Hardy, he edited and wrote detailed commentary for *Poems of Mr. John Milton* (1951), showing that Milton's verse, which T. S. Eliot had attacked as numbing and monolithic, could be appreciated in all of its subtlety and complexity when examined closely.

In an essay (*American Scholar*, Spring 1989) on his teacher and friend John Crowe Ransom, Brooks stated that as a Vanderbilt student he had read the Southern Agrarian manifesto *I'll Take My Stand* "over and over": "I tried my best to assimilate the whole position, philosophical and political. I learned a great deal from my intensive study." But in his own work he never argued on behalf of Southern traditions, values, and beliefs as specifically and as forcefully as did Ransom, Warren, and Tate. For him the lesson put forward by the Agrarians was a general one: "They asked that we consider what the good life is or ought to be." Few could object to this; the conservative Southern tenets of the Agrarians' ideology are wholly absent from it.

Brooks was above all a literary critic and theorist, and he did more than anyone to articulate and codify the principles of Anglo-American New Criticism and demonstrate how it could be applied to a wide range of texts. He was a student of the Greek and Roman classics, and he was also affected by the approach to literature and criticism taken by his teachers and friends at Vanderbilt, especially the poets, "who were talking about the making of poems." At Oxford, he read I. A. Richards's books *The Principles of Literary Criticism* and *Practical Criticism*; these helped to equip him with terms, such as tone, irony, and attitude, that he carried over to his own work.

Like many young literary critics in the 1930s, Brooks rebelled against the emphasis in graduate studies on "historical and biographical" information and protested against the lack of attention to "the interior life of the poem." Brooks did not accept everything he found in Richards's work – he disapproved of its "psychological terminology" and "confident positivism"; but he read and reread *Principles* ("perhaps a dozen times" the first year he encountered it) and *Practical Criticism*, and developed Richards's guidelines for examining the poem itself into an approach of his own, an intrinsic (or formalist) criticism.

For Brooks, criticism meant scrutinizing technical elements, textual patterns, and incongruities in texts; as he indicated at the outset of *The Well Wrought Urn*, the critic should always begin "by making the closest examination of what the poem says as a poem." Genuine literary criticism, he argued, is neither biographical nor historical; it is not a matter of sources-and-influences and background information. Nor is it subjective, the record of a reader's impressions as he or she reacts to a literary work.

In "The Heresy of Paraphrase," included in *The Well Wrought Urn*, Brooks emphasized that the purpose of a poem is not to produce a statement, a proposition, a didactic lesson or message. A poem, he explained, is not equivalent to a paraphrase of its content, as though the content somehow might be detachable from the formal structure. Through irony, paradox, ambiguity, and other rhetorical and poetic devices of his or her art, the poet works constantly to resist any reduction of the poem to a paraphrasable core, favoring the presentation of conflicting facets of theme and patterns of resolved stresses. For Brooks, all poetry exhibits "irony," by which he means pervasive incongruity.

Brooks reiterated this point in "The Formalist Critics" (1951): "In a successful work, form and content cannot be separated." Echoing the conclusions that Wimsatt and Beardsley had presented in "The Intentional Fallacy" and "The Affective Fallacy," Brooks maintained that literary study deals not with the author's intention or the reader's responses or the historical context, but, instead, with the specific text at hand: "the formalist critic is concerned primarily with the work itself."

Throughout his career, Brooks insisted that the charge that he shunned the study of contexts was inaccurate and unfair. He claimed that he was not ignoring biography and history, but that as a *literary* critic he was intent on exploring the attitudes toward history that an author expressed in the language of the text itself. As René Wellek, in defense of the New Critics, pointed out in a discussion of Brooks's analysis of Andrew Marvell's "Horatian Ode": "Brooks constantly appeals to the historical situation for his interpretation, though he is rightly very careful to distinguish between the exact meaning of the poem and the presumed attitude of Marvell towards Cromwell and Charles I" ("Literary Theory, Criticism, and History," *Sewanee Review* [1960]). For Brooks, the text possesses organic unity; a poem by Donne or Marvell does not depend for its success on knowledge that readers import into it from the outside; it is richly ambiguous, yet harmoniously orchestrated, coherent in its own special aesthetic terms.

Brooks's close readings, while illuminating, ran the risk of always coming more or less to the same conclusion. Each poem that he examined, from whatever period, received the same kind of inspection of its images, metaphors, tones of voice, and was valued or reproved for its handling of irony and paradox in the labor of controlling incongruities. The scholar-theorist R. S. Crane (1886–1967), in "The Critical Monism of Cleanth Brooks" (*Modern Philology*, May 1948), criticized Brooks on this score when he remarked that all of the texts from the Renaissance through the modern period treated in *The Well Wrought Urn* end up seeming like seventeenth-century lyrics. As Crane noted in *The Languages of Criticism and the Structure of Poetry* (1953), "the corruption of the literary critic in the modes of literary criticism we are chiefly familiar with at the present time is most commonly perhaps a cult of the paradoxical."

But Brooks from the outset pretty much conceded this point; as he said in "The Heresy of Paraphrase," he was undertaking in his book an analytical experiment – reading eighteenth- and nineteenth-century poems "as one has learned to read Donne and the moderns." Brooks acknowledged the historical differences among the poems and then moved on to show that there are common elements in their uses and organizations of language.

A striking, and somewhat curious, feature of Brooks's work is the uneasy mix of terms and emphases that shaped his argument about how poetry operates. Often, he referred to the warping, resisting, and violating of meaning (e.g., "the resistance which any good poem sets up against all attempts to paraphrase it"). Yet, taking his cue from Coleridge and I. A. Richards, he spoke too of harmony, balance, order, unity. Perhaps there is no necessary contradiction; a poem could contain a "tension" among its paradoxical meanings while maintaining its coherence. But there was an opening here in Brooks's position that later theorists saw and exploited. If a warping or resisting of meaning exists, how intense and deep is it? Does it create the essential structure of the text or, rather, prevent readers from identifying such a structure? Does irony empower the poem to achieve unity, or is irony the dimension of literary language that undermines and forestalls unity? In the work of poststructuralist theorists such as Jacques Derrida and Paul de Man, it was precisely the competing, conflicting, indeed warring relationship among the words in the text that in their view keep it from the self-contained equilibrium that Brooks celebrated. But the significant point is less their revision of Brooks's argument than the fact that Brooks's stress on analytical reading made such revisionary work possible. No Brooks, no de Man.

The most distinguished American literary critic of the mid-twentieth century was R. P. Blackmur (1904–65), the New Critic whose studies of texts were even more penetrating than Brooks's and whose criticism met the ideal that the New Critics professed. Blackmur was an adept reader of poems, but he was remarkable as a close reader because he both performed and transcended that role. He exemplified and exceeded the category of New Critic.

John Crowe Ransom pointed to Blackmur as the typical "new critic" in his preface to *The New Criticism*, the 1941 book that assigned a label to the movement as a whole. But unlike later followers of the New Criticism, Blackmur rarely produced lengthy explications. His analyses concentrated only on parts of texts as he strategically advanced general arguments about a poet's techniques. Blackmur's commentary generally was keyed to larger literary issues: "authority" in Hardy's poetry, the relationship between literature and belief in

Eliot's writing, the nature of artistic "consciousness" and dramatic "form" in Melville's novels. Blackmur "elucidated" (his term) rather than "explicated," in order to discover how words sound and feel as well as how they mean.

Blackmur differs very much in background from the Southern New Critics. He was born in Springfield, Massachusetts, and for the most part he was self-educated. His parents' marriage was an unhappy one; his father failed at a number of jobs, and the family depended on the modest income from a boardinghouse in Cambridge where they lived. Blackmur left high school after two years, working from his teens to his mid-twenties in Cambridge bookstores and reading in the library at Harvard. His first stroke of good fortune came when he met the writer and Harvard graduate Lincoln Kirstein (later, the co-founder with the choreographer George Balanchine of the School of American Ballet, which led to the New York City Ballet). With Kirstein, he helped to launch and edit the important literary journal *Hound and Horn*.

Scraping along as a job-to-job critic and reviewer, Blackmur and his wife lived in poverty throughout the 1930s, until he received in 1940 an appointment in the Creative Arts Program at Princeton University. This gave him some security, but he was not awarded the position of associate professor until 1948 and even then a number of his colleagues felt that no one of his irregular education belonged in their midst.

As a critic, Blackmur quested for depth and difficulty, and his arguments can seem dauntingly intricate when set alongside those by more teacherly kinds of close readers. (The poet-critic Louise Bogan was not the only person who admired Blackmur but balked at "the coils and tangles of his subtlety.") Blackmur did not gear his criticism toward pedagogy, which most of the original New Critics saw as the testing ground for their interpretations, and his own goals cost him clarity. He once noted that "whenever any of my own work is attacked I am attacked as a New Critic. Usually when people wish to make more pleasant remarks about me they say how it is that I have departed from the New Criticism."

As "the outsider" (his favorite name for himself), Blackmur was uneasy about being portrayed as a member of a movement and did not wish to be designated as an executive in the enterprise "Criticism, Inc." In two essays in *The Lion and the Honeycomb* (1955), Blackmur treated the institutionalized New Criticism skeptically, condemning its narrow canon, its adherence to methods that are "useless" when applied to Chaucer, Goethe, Racine, and Dante, and its bad effect on creative writing. Though an adroit New Critical reader, he was not a spokesman for or a defender of New Critical doctrines.

Blackmur's major books are *The Double Agent: Essays in Craft and Elucidation* (1935) and *The Expense of Greatness* (1940), and they are among the best works of modern criticism. In these collections of essays, which include luminous analyses of Cummings, Pound, Stevens, Lawrence, Crane, Moore, Eliot, Hardy, Dickinson, and Yeats, Blackmur engaged in a tactfully managed probing of the rational organization of words. Blackmur responded to words with reverential deliberation, and he loved to unfold the manner in which writers connect and interanimate them. As he said in *The Double Agent*, he was intent on studying the structure and texture of poetic form:

The sense of continuous relationship, of sustained contact, with the works nominally in hand is rare and when found uncommonly exhilarating; it is the fine object of criticism: as it seems to put us into direct possession of the principles whereby the works move without injuring or disintegrating the body of the works themselves.

He made a similar point in "The Enabling Act of Criticism" (1941):

[Criticism] consists, first, in being willing to concentrate your maximum attention upon the work which the words and motions of the words – and by motions, I mean all the technical devices of literature – perform upon each other. Secondly, it consists in submitting, at least provisionally, to whatever authority your attention brings to light in the words.

Blackmur did not seek to interpret texts as much as to place himself and his reader in contact with the central principles and patterns that fortify a particular writer's art. Blackmur wanted above all to inform and prepare the mind of the reader – to show for the reader the internal motivation for a body of poems, and to convert him or her, at least for the moment, to the attitudes that these poems invite readers to bring to them.

In *The Double Agent*, for example, Blackmur offered a negative judgment on the poetic practice of Hart Crane, first quoting a passage from "Lachrymae Christi" – "Let sphinxes from the ripe / Borage of death have cleared my tongue / Once and again . . . " – and then sorting out the meanings of Crane's language so as to express how this language shuns rational organization and evades understanding:

It is syntax rather than grammar that is obscure. I take it that "let" is here a somewhat homemade adjective and that Crane is making a direct statement, so that the problem is to construe the right meanings of the right words in the right references; which will be an admirable exercise in exegesis, but an exercise only. The applicable senses of "let" are these: neglected or weary, permitted or prevented, hired, and let in the sense that blood is let. Sphinxes are inscrutable, have secrets, propound riddles to travellers and strangle those who cannot answer. "Borage" has at least three senses: something rough (sonally suggestive of barrage and barrier), a blue-flowered, hairy-leaved plant, and a cordial made from the plant. The *Shorter Oxford Dictionary* quotes this jingle from Hooker: "I Borage always bring courage".

Blackmur's reliance upon the dictionary as a treasure and resource is akin to William Empson's tactic in *Seven Types of Ambiguity*, but Blackmur has a persuasive power of summary and judgment that his English contemporary in that book lacked: his verbal inspections are more controlled and directed toward larger statements and evaluations. Continuing his analysis of Crane, Blackmur stated that "Crane had a profound feeling for the hearts of words, and how they beat and cohabited, but here they overtopped him; the meanings in the words themselves are superior to the use to which he put them. The operation of selective cross-pollination not only failed but was not even rightly attempted."

This analytical concern for rational control and order was crucial to Blackmur, and it is evident throughout the essays in *The Double Agent* and *The Expense of Greatness*, above all in his critiques of the private musings of the poet in "Notes on E. E. Cummings' Language" and in his account of flawed craftsmanship in "Masks of Ezra Pound." "What I want to evangelize in the arts," Blackmur insisted in a later essay, "A Burden for Critics," "is rational intent, rational statement, and rational technique; and I want to do it through technical judgment, clarifying judgment, and the judgment of discovery, which together I call rational judgment."

Blackmur believed that the writer should be devoted to words without capitulating to them. This requires an appreciation for words (and a measure of poise), and it is different from a "surrender" to words, which suggests abandonment, "intoxication," and disorder. This distinction implies the detachment that Blackmur sought in both literature and criticism even as he appealed for an "inner contact" with texts.

Such an approach has limits, as is evident in Blackmur's commentary on Crane, which is just on the verge of seeming fussy rather than exact. Blackmur was right to say that "Crane had a profound feeling for the hearts of words," and that is why Blackmur's "rational" perusal of them is illuminating yet feels a little narrow-minded. Blackmur opened up the language helpfully, but he was not receptive enough to the kind of writer that Crane is, not astute or sensitive enough to accept how Crane's poetry operates.

If sustained "inner contact" gets at one aspect of Blackmur's performance as a critic, then "irony" intimates another that was even more privileged in his vocabulary. In "The Dangers of Authorship," he said that the writer is "an independent mirror of the processes of life which happen to absorb him; he creates by showing, by representing; and his only weapons for change are the irony of the intelligence that can be brought to bear on the contemptible and the stupid, and the second irony of a second point of view, implicit in his work, alien to that of his subject-matter." And in "A Critic's Job of Work,"

Blackmur described the "imaginative skepticism and dramatic irony" that are invigorating in Plato and Montaigne: "Is it not that the early Plato always holds conflicting ideas in shifting balance, presenting them in contest and evolution, with victory only the last shift? Is it not that Montaigne is always making room for another idea, and implying always a third for provisional, adjudicating irony?"

When Blackmur wrote "A Critic's Job of Work," he was defining his position against critical doctrines that he judged to be disfiguring art by aligning it with political causes. But the values that Blackmur advocated have political implications, or at least possibilities, in that they can enable an incisive critique of orthodoxy and misused language. A concern for the rational ordering of words, an interest in clarifying judgments, an attentiveness to the duplicities of thought, a desire always to cultivate the second and third points of view – these were Blackmur's primary goals and interests and they give his criticism a powerful distinctiveness.

In a limited sense Blackmur's status as the New Critic who wasn't one connects him to Yvor Winters (1900–68) and Kenneth Burke (1897–1993). Neither should be classified as a New Critic, but both were often linked to the New Critical revolt against academic scholarship and to the modern reform of literary studies. Blackmur wrote pointedly about both Winters and Burke, and he learned lessons about critical style and literary value from Winters's reviews of contemporary poetry in the 1920s and 1930s.

Winters and Burke are hard to assess, however, largely because of the extreme idiosyncrasy that they manifest. Winters handed down notoriously severe evaluations of poets and periods, scorning nearly all of the poetry from the nineteenth century and most from the twentieth in English and American literature – poetry that he perceived as yielding to associationism, sentimentalism, and romanticism. Burke, in turn, was far more wide-ranging and open to nearly everything, but as a consequence he appeared to many readers to lack the literary discrimination that a good critic should possess.

Blackmur was correct about Burke when he said, in "A Critic's Job of Work," that Burke's "method could be applied with equal fruitfulness either to Shakespeare, Dashiell Hammett, or Marie Corelli." There is an arbitrariness and artificiality that confined Burke's criticism for all of its exploratory verve. Burke wrote a great deal; his major books include *Attitudes Toward History* (1937), *The Philosophy of Literary Form* (1941), *A Grammar of Motives* (1945), and *A Rhetoric of Motives* (1950). But while he won a few disciples and was saluted for his ingenuity and inventiveness, and for his own writerly performances, he did not exercise a lasting impact on literary criticism. Periodic attempts to recuperate him have never gotten far.

Burke's ideas have always sounded attractive, for he described exciting new interdisciplinary directions beyond the New Criticism. In *The Philosophy of Literary Form*, he made stimulating suggestions, and did so in provocative prose. Critics in their inquiries, he maintained, should ask "leading questions" and structure the field that they investigate: "every question selects a field of battle, and in this selection it forms the nature of the answers." Literary texts, Burke added, reveal the same kinds of concerns that "motivate" other texts: all texts can be treated in terms of their "strategies" and designs on audiences. "The analysis of aesthetic phenomena can be extended or projected into the analysis of social and political phenomena in general," and, hence, "the question of the relationship between art and society is momentous."

Burke favored an approach that would give "definite insight into the organization of literary works" (a goal he shared with the New Critics) but that would also "break down the barriers erected about literature as a specialized pursuit." As he explained in "Literature as Equipment for Living" (1937): "Sociological criticism, as here understood, would seek to assemble and codify . . . It might occasionally lead us to outrage good taste, as we sometimes found exemplified in some great sermon or tragedy or abstruse work of philosophy the same strategy as we found exemplified in a dirty joke. At this point, we'd put the sermon and the dirty joke together, thus 'grouping by situation' and showing the range of possible particularizations."

In theory, then, Burke restored connections between literary and non-literary texts, literature and society, criticism and culture and politics, that the New Critics had renounced when they left Agrarianism behind. But except for several essays on Shakespeare, Burke's actual commentaries on literary works are clumsy. He was always more in touch with the organization of his own rhetorical machines and apparatus than with the "internal organization" of texts. His cultivation of interpretive models, figures of speech, charts, and schemes subverted the potential richness of his goals.

Such a skeptical judgment on Burke may seem more appropriate to Winters, and there is little question about the willfulness and perversity that distorted his last book, *Forms of Discovery* (1967), and that such earlier volumes as *Primitivism and Decadence* (1937), *Maule's Curse* (1938), *The Anatomy of Nonsense* (1943), and *The Function of Criticism* (1957) reflected as well. Winters dismissed far too much – Milton, Wordsworth, Whitman, Browning, Eliot, Yeats. The list is a long one that includes most of the names that modern critics have prized.

Winters labored earnestly, yet with a grim humor and an ironic sense of futility, to displace the familiar canon and upgrade Charles Churchill, Frederick Godard Tuckerman, T. Sturge Moore, Adelaide Crapsey, and a half-dozen or so of his own students. But he succeeded only in exasperating readers and discrediting his principles, which seemed to license an absurd intolerance.

Here again, though, Blackmur offers a key insight, noting in 1940, in *The Expense of Greatness*, the strange fact that Winters's outlandish evaluations did not really "touch the work he has actually performed." Winters made clear how he defined poetry: a poem is a rational statement of human experience, in which this experience is judged by the quality of feeling that the poet both expresses and controls. This definition furnished him with a powerful, if egregiously selective, means to rewrite the history of English, American, and, to an extent, French poetry; as developed and extended in *Maule's Curse*, it also provided an enlightening perspective on the American novel and romance.

Winters brought forward wonderful discoveries, particularly in his analyses of Gascoigne, Fulke Greville, Jonson, and the "plain style" writers of sixteenth- and seventeenth-century lyrics. His rigorous discussions of Puritanism, Calvinism, and allegory in Hawthorne and Melville preceded the major, and more renowned, studies by F. O. Matthiessen and the Harvard literary historian Perry Miller. And in this work from the 1920s and 1930s, perhaps the most surprising aspect of Winters's manner was his generous praise – not only for many of his contemporaries (including Stevens and Crane), but also for Dickinson, Edwin Arlington Robinson, Wharton, James, and others whom critics had overlooked or had not quite learned to describe justly and coherently. Like F. R. Leavis in England, Winters descended into alarming forms of self-caricature as his career unfolded (and as his bitterness and alienation increased), but he showed a strenuous clarity in his critical procedures and stayed impressively distant from the conventional views that would have won him a more favorable hearing.

While Burke and Winters were important, neither was truly part of the mainstream that included the Southern New Critics and their supporters. Nor, really, was Blackmur. It was the New Criticism of Brooks, Tate, Warren, and Ransom that defined the field, epitomized the establishment, and became the object of vilification by radicals during the 1960s. But the radicals of the 1960s were able to see why the New Criticism was skewed because they had been trained as New Critics and had absorbed the humanistic values and skills that Ransom and his friends had introduced and fought for.

As Richard Ohmann was candid enough to concede in his appraisal of the legacy of the New Criticism (1976), "the very humanism we learned and

taught was capable, finally, of turning its moral and critical powers on itself."
The New Criticism not only enabled several generations of students to read
literary texts closely, but also equipped them to read the New Criticism itself –
and, even more, to interpret the world from which the New Critics and their
successors had apparently turned away.

Nearly all of the literary-critical and theoretical challenges to the New
Criticism were also dependent – one is tempted to say, parasitical – upon it.
In *The Anxiety of Influence* (1973), Harold Bloom argued: "Let us give up the
failed enterprise of seeking to 'understand' any single poem as an entity in
itself. Let us pursue instead the quest of learning to read any poem as its poet's
deliberate misinterpretation, *as a poet*, of a precursor poem or of poetry in
general." Jonathan Culler, in "Beyond Interpretation," in *The Pursuit of Signs*
(1981), made a different proposal, but, like Bloom, defined it in opposition
to the New Criticism: "To engage in the study of literature is not to produce
yet another interpretation of *King Lear* but to advance one's understanding
of the conventions and operations of an institution, a mode of discourse." At
the time these struck many as bold new positions, but in the long view they
amount to footnotes to the New Criticism, dramatic-sounding efforts to move
past the interpretive goal that the New Critics had reached and made central
to so many critics, teachers, and students.

The same holds true for deconstruction, which in the 1970s and 1980s
seemed so daringly and dangerously avant-garde. Deconstructionists frequently stated that their emphasis on intertextuality and indeterminacy broke
with all prior methods, and that they found meaning dazzlingly unfathomable
whereas the New Critics tried to simplify and bottom it out. But deconstruction gained many converts because it took the New Criticism as its point of
departure. The New Critics had called for and had practiced close reading; so
did the deconstructionists, who made much of the relatively minor point that
the New Critics had failed to read closely or deeply enough.

Deconstructionists took up and adapted the New Critical attentiveness to
the text even as they professed to be doing something radically different.
J. Hillis Miller, in "Stevens' Rock and Criticism as Cure, II" (*Georgia Review*,
Summer 1976), claimed: "Deconstruction as a mode of interpretation works
by a careful and circumspect entering of each textual labyrinth . . . The decon-
structive critic seeks to find, by this process of retracing, the element in the
system studied which is alogical, the thread in the text in question which will
unravel it all, or the loose stone which will pull down the whole building."
Paul de Man, in "Semiology and Rhetoric" (1979), stressed that deconstruction enabled critics to observe how "rhetoric radically suspends logic and opens

up vertiginous possibilities of referential aberration." And Jacques Derrida, in "Plato's Pharmacy," in *Dissemination* (1981), touted the brilliance of his reading strategies: "Within the same tissue, within the same texts, we will draw on other filial filaments, pull the same strings once more, and witness the weaving or unraveling of other designs." Deconstruction made its impact as a new form of interpretation primarily because it extended the New Critics' procedures. It was not as innovative as its proponents claimed, or as distressing as its foes feared.

Deconstructionists focused on the unstable, incoherent nature of textual meaning and the presence of conflicting, contradictory elements in texts, and in this sense they appeared to move beyond the New Criticism and its belief (via Coleridge, in the *Biographia Literaria*) in the reconciliation of opposites. But the New Critics were acutely aware of, and they regularly examined, tensely complementary, contradictory, or destabilizing features of texts. This New Critical context for deconstruction in America can be located in many pieces by the Southern New Critics from the late 1930s and 1940s. For example:

However the critic may spell them, the two terms are in his mind: the prose core to which he can violently reduce the total object, and the differentia, residue, or tissue, which keeps the object poetical or entire. (John Crowe Ransom, "Criticism, Inc.," 1938)

Poetry wants to be pure, but poems do not. At least, most of them do not want to be too pure. The poems want to give us poetry, which is pure, and the elements of a poem, in so far as it is a good poem, will work together toward that end, but many of the elements, taken in themselves, may actually seem to contradict that end, or be neutral toward the achieving of that end. (Robert Penn Warren, "Pure and Impure Poetry," 1942)

The poem . . . comes to the same thing as I. A. Richards's "poetry of synthesis" – that is, a poetry which does not leave out what is apparently hostile to its dominant tone, and which, because it is able to fuse the irrelevant and discordant, has come to terms with itself and is invulnerable to irony. Irony, then, in this further sense, is not only an acknowledgement of the pressures of a context. Invulnerability to irony is the stability of a context in which the internal pressures balance and mutually support each other. (Cleanth Brooks, "Irony as a Principle of Structure," 1949)

The Platonist . . . might decide that Marvell's "To His Coy Mistress" recommends immoral behavior to young men, in whose behalf he would try to suppress the poem. That, of course, would be one "true" meaning of "To His Coy Mistress," but it is a meaning that the full tension of the poem will not allow us to entertain exclusively. (Allen Tate, "Tension in Poetry," 1938)

When Ransom drew notice to the poet's desperate struggle to integrate logical structure and poetic texture, when Warren focused on impurities in texts, when Brooks limned the poem's hostility to its own meaning, and when Tate referred to the tension of contrary meanings, they contributed to a program of their own and anticipated the terms through which later critics and theorists would challenge them.

The New Critics thus supplied their followers with techniques for literary criticism and pedagogy and, at the same time, passed on to future antagonists almost everything that was required to challenge the New Criticism's reign. They led one revolution, and then faced a second that their own arguments and insights made possible.

CHRONOLOGY 1910–1950

Jonathan Fortescue

	American Poetry and Criticism	American Events, Texts, and Arts	Other Events, Texts, and Arts
1910	Addams, Jane (1860–1935), *Twenty Years at Hull-House* (social criticism)	Mann–Elkins Act gives Interstate Commerce Commission control of telephone, telegraph, cable, and wireless companies.	Mexican Revolution begins against the autocratic rule of Porfirio Diaz.
	Pound, Ezra (1885–1972), *The Spirit of Romance* (criticism)	Victor Berger is first socialist to be elected to the US Congress.	China abolishes slavery.
	Robinson, Edwin Arlington (1869–1935), *The Town Down the River* (poetry)	US Population is 92,228,496.	Japan annexes Korea.
		President Taft dismisses Gifford Pinchot, US Forest Service Chief, when he alleges that the administration is undermining conservation efforts.	Halley's Comet passes near the Earth.
		William Boyce charters the Boy Scouts of America.	Henri Matisse finishes *Music* (painting).
		W. E. B. Du Bois begins to publish *Crisis* under auspices of newly founded NAACP.	Igor Stravinsky composes *The Firebird* (ballet).
		Child Hassam finishes *Against the Light* (painting).	Betrand Russell publishes *Principia Mathematica* (logic and mathematics).
		George Herriman publishes first "Krazy Kat" (cartoon).	
1911	Pound, Ezra (1885–1972), *Canzoni* (poetry)	US Supreme Court orders break-up of the Trusts – Standard Oil, American Tobacco, Du Pont Co.	US, Great Britain, and Japan sign treaty to abolish seal hunting in the north Pacific for 15 years.
		Triangle Shirtwaist fire kills 146 workers, mostly women, who were locked inside the factory by the management.	Roald Amundsen becomes the first person to reach the South Pole.
		Charles Kettering perfects the electric starter for the automobile.	Ernest Rutherford formulates theory of the structure of the atom.

1912

Boas, Franz (1858–1942), *The Mind of Primitive Man* (anthropology)

Taylor, Frederick (1856–1915), *Principles of Scientific Management* (economics)

The Masses publishes its first issue. "Memphis Blues" (popular song)

Woodrow Wilson defeats Theodore Roosevelt and William Taft in the election for President of the United States.

New Mexico and Arizona admitted to the Union as 47th and 48th states.

US Supreme Court dissolves the merger of Union Pacific and Southern Pacific railroads.

Harriet Monroe founds *Poetry* magazine.

Jim Thorpe wins the decathlon and pentathlon at the 5th World Olympics.

The presence of electrons and protons is detected in a cloud-chamber photograph.

Georges Braque finishes *Man With a Guitar* (painting).

Paul Klee finishes *Self-Portrait* (painting).

Richard Strauss composes *Der Rosenkavalier* (opera).

The HMS *Titanic* sinks on her maiden voyage across the Atlantic. 1,513 people drown.

US marines invade Nicaragua.

Jung, C. G. (1875–1961), *The Theory of Psychoanalysis* (psychology)

Pablo Picasso finishes *The Violin* (painting).

Claude Debussy composes *Images* (orchestral music).

McKay, Claude (1890–1948), *Songs of Jamaica* (poetry)

Pound, Ezra (1885–1972), *Ripostes* (poetry)

Scudder, Vida (1861–1954), *Socialism and Character* (criticism)

1913

16th Amendment to the US Constitution authorizes the federal income tax.

17th Amendment to the US Constitution permits the direct election of Senators to the US Congress.

Garment workers strike over the length of the workday.

Niels Bohr formulates his theory of the structure of the atom.

London Peace Treaty divides European Turkey among the victors of the first Balkan War.

Apollinaire, Guillaume (1880–1918), *Peintres Cubistes* (essay)

Frost, Robert (1874–1963), *A Boy's Will* (poetry)

Pound, Ezra (1885–1972), "Patria Mia" in *New Age* (essay)

Williams, William Carlos (1883–1963), *The Tempers* (poetry)

	American Poetry and Criticism	American Events, Texts, and Arts	Other Events, Texts, and Arts
1914	Frost, Robert (1874–1963), *North of Boston* (poetry)	Ford Motor Co. installs the first assembly line in its factories.	Claude Debussy composes *Préludes*, Book II (piano music).
	Goldman, Emma (1869–1940), *The Social Significance of Modern Drama* (criticism)	Armory Show of modern art in New York City.	Igor Stravinsky composes *The Rite of Spring* (ballet).
	James, Henry (1843–1916), *Notes on Novelists* (criticism)	The Great Migration of blacks from rural South into northern industrial cities accelerates.	World War I begins after the assassination of Archduke Ferdinand.
		Merrill, Lynch brokerage house opens for business.	Mexican Revolution unsettles Latin America.
		Federal Trade Commission Act passes.	Mahatma Gandhi returns to India to support national sovereignty movement.
	Lindsay, Vachel (1879–1931), *The Congo and Other Poems* (poetry)	*The New Republic* and *The Little Review* publish their first issues.	Panama Canal opens to shipping.
	Stein, Gertrude (1874–1946), *Tender Buttons* (poetry)	Brandeis, Louis (1856–1941) *Other People's Money* (essay)	Oscar Barnack develops the 35mm still camera in Germany.
		John Sloan finishes *Backyards, Greenwich Village* (painting).	Hardy, Thomas (1840–1928), *Satires of Circumstance, Lyrics and Reveries* (poetry)
		W. C. Handy composes "St. Louis Blues" (popular song)	Yeats, William Butler (1865–1939), *Responsibilities* (poetry)
			Adolf de Meyer takes *Sur le Prélude à L'Après-midi d'un faune* (photographs).
1915	Brooks, Van Wyck (1886–1963), *American's Coming-of-Age* (criticism)	J. P. Morgan & Co. agree to loan $500 million to Britain and France to help finance war.	*Lusitania* torpedoed by German submarine. 1,198 people drown.

Du Bois, W[illiam] E[dward] B[urghardt] (1868–1963), *The Negro* (cultural criticism)	1st transcontinental phone call made from New York to San Francisco.	Tetanus epidemic breaks out across World War I battlefields.
Macy, John (1877–1932), *The Spirit of American Literature* (criticism)	Taxicabs arise as new form of local transit in the major cities.	Latin American nations convene with the US to seek end to Mexican Revolution.
Masters, Edgar Lee (1868–1950), *Spoon River Anthology* (free-verse epitaphs)	State of Georgia grants the Ku Klux Klan a new charter.	**Albert Einstein** proposes the General Theory of Relativity.
	Birth of a Nation (film) directed by **D. W. Griffith**	**Claude Debussy** composes *Etudes* (piano music).
	Max Weber finishes *Chinese Restaurant* (painting).	**Fernando Pessoa** founds *Orpheu* (magazine).
	Provincetown Players, a dramatic group, is formed.	
1916 Buck, Gertrude (1871–1922), *The Social Criticism of Literature* (criticism)	US Senate orders the build-up of the armed forces.	Theory of shell shock emerges from treatment of WWI veterans.
Doolittle, Hilda [H. D.] (1886–1961), *Sea Garden* (poetry)	Federal Farm Loan Act made money available for farmers in need.	Dadaists converge on Zurich.
Frost, Robert (1874–1963), *Mountain Interval* (poetry)	Congress averts a railroad workers strike by passing 8-hour workday legislation.	British troops suppress the Easter Rebellion in Ireland.
Macy, John (1877–1932), *Socialism in America* (social commentary)	Federal Child Labor Law passes.	Pancho Villa invades US at New Mexico border. US sends troops to Mexico.
Pound, Ezra (1885–1972), *Lustra* (poetry)	Woodrow Wilson appoints first Jew, Louis Brandeis, to the US Supreme Court.	Ballet Russe tours the United States.
Robinson, Edwin Arlington (1869–1935), *The Man Against the Sky* (poetry)	**Dewey, John** (1859–1952), *Democracy and Education* (philosophy)	
Sandburg, Carl (1878–1967), *Chicago Poems* (poetry)	*Seven Arts* magazine publishes its first issue.	

	American Poetry and Criticism	American Events, Texts, and Arts	Other Events, Texts, and Arts
1917	Eliot, T[homas] S[tearns], (1888–1965), *Prufrock and Other Observations* (poetry)	US enters World War I. 2,000,000 land in France. 49,000 killed. 230,000 wounded.	Germans begin unrestricted submarine warfare.
	Lindsay, Vachel (1879–1931), *The Chinese Nightingale and Other Poems* (poetry)	Woodrow Wilson delivers ten points speech in favor of a World Federation.	The Red Army deposes the Czar as the Communists rise to power in Russia.
	Lowell, Amy (1874–1925), *Tendencies of Modern American Poetry* (criticism)	The Jones Act makes Puerto Rico a territory of the US.	The Third Battle of the Ypres is fought.
	Mencken, H[enry] L[ouis] (1880–1956), *A Book of Prefaces* (criticism)	Congress overrides Wilson's veto of literacy test for immigrants and exclusion of Asians.	Eluard, Paul (1895–1952), *Le devoir et l'inquiétude* (poetry)
	Millay, Edna St. Vincent (1892–1950), *Renascence And Other Poems* (poetry)	Empey, Arthur (1883–1963), *Over the Top* (war narrative)	Hardy, Thomas (1840–1928), *Moments of Vision and Miscellaneous Verses* (poetry)
	Sherman, Stuart [editor] (1881–1926), *Cambridge History of American Literature* (criticism)	Goldman, Emma (1869–1940), *Anarchism and Other Essays* (social criticism)	Sassoon, Siegfried (1886–1967), *The Old Huntsman* (poetry)
	Van Doren, Carl [editor] (1885–1950), *Cambridge History of American Literature* (criticism)	The Original Dixieland Jazz Band debuts in New York City.	Maurice Ravel composes *Le Tombeau de Couperin* (piano music).
	Williams, William Carlos (1883–1963), *Al Que Quiere!* (poetry)	A. Philip Randolph and Chandler Owen launch *The Messenger*.	Erik Satie composes *Parade* (ballet).
1918	Brooks, Van Wyck (1886–1963), *Letters and Leadership* (criticism)	Woodrow Wilson presents his *Fourteen Points* for fighting the War to Congress. Sedition Act passed.	US and Allies score big victories in Aisne-Marne and Meuse-Argonne. World War I ends on November 11.

| 1919 | Aiken, Conrad (1889–1973), *Scepticisms* (criticism) | Eugene Debs sentenced to ten years in prison for "wartime sedition." | Virulent strain of influenza sweeps the world and kills over 20 million. |

Streeter, Edward (1891–1976), *Dere Mable: Love Letters of a Rookie* (humor)

Sassoon, Siegfried (1886–1967), *Counter-Attack* (poetry)

Strachey, Lytton (1880–1932), *Eminent Victorians* (biographical history)

Frank, Waldo (1889–1967), *Our America* (social commentary)

Debut of Giacomo Puccini trio of one-act operas: *Il tabarro, Suor Angelica, Gianni Schicchi.*

Versailles Peace Conference begins.

Mencken, H[enry] L[ouis] (1880–1956), *The American Language* (philology)

The 18th Amendment to the US Constitution prohibits the making, selling, or transportation of alcohol in the United States.

Red Army scores major victory in the Russian Revolution.

Mencken, H[enry] L[ouis] (1880–1956), *Prejudices, First Series* (social criticism)

Woodrow Wilson presents League of Nations covenant to Peace Conference.

Afghanis massacred by British Army at Amritsar.

Nathan, George Jean (1882–1958), *Comedians All* (criticism)

US Senate rejects Treaty of Versailles.

Walter Gropius founds the Bauhaus in Weimar.

Post-war recession leads to labor unrest that paralyzes many major cities.

Yeats, William Butler (1865–1939), *The Wild Swans at Coole* (poetry)

Racial strife around the country peaks in Chicago where a weeklong riot kills 15 whites, 23 blacks, and leaves 1,000 people homeless.

Pound, Ezra (1885–1972), *Quia Pauper Amavi* (poetry)

Communist Labor Party of America is founded, adopts platform of the 3rd International.

The Cabinet of Dr. Caligari (film) directed by Robert Wiene

Pound, Ezra (1885–1972), *Pavannes and Divisions* (criticism)

Jack Dempsey becomes the Heavyweight Champion of the World.

Nosferatu (film) directed by F. W. Murnau

	American Poetry and Criticism	American Events, Texts, and Arts	Other Events, Texts, and Arts
1920	Untermeyer, Louis [editor] (1885–1977), *Modern American Poetry* (poetry anthology)	*New York Daily News*, the first tabloid newspaper, publishes its first issue.	Treaty of Sèvres dissolves the Ottoman Empire.
	Brooks, Van Wyck (1886–1963), *The Ordeal of Mark Twain* (criticism)	US population is 105,710,620. First time in history that more than 50% live in urban areas.	Freud, Sigmund (1856–1939), *Beyond the Pleasure Principle* (psychology)
	Du Bois, W[illiam] E[dward] B[urghardt] (1868–1963), *Darkwater* (cultural criticism)	Warren Harding wins the election for President of the US over James Cox and Eugene Debs.	Owen, Wilfred (1893–1918), *Poems* (poetry)
	Eliot, T[homas] S[tearns] (1888–1965), *Poems* (poetry)	The 19th Amendment to the US Constitution gives women the right to vote.	Man Ray creates *Rayographs* (photograph).
	Eliot, T[homas] S[tearns] (1888–1965), *The Sacred Wood* (criticism)	US Attorney General Palmer persecutes supposed Bolsheviks in the "Red Scare."	
	Lindsay, Vachel (1879–1931), *The Golden Whales of California* (poetry)	Woodrow Wilson wins Nobel Peace Prize.	
	Mencken, H[enry] L[ouis] (1880–1956), *Prejudices, Second Series* (social criticism)	Radio Station KDKA in Pittsburgh, Pennsylvania begins first regular broadcasting.	
	Pound, Ezra (1885–1972), *Hugh Selwyn Mauberley* (poetry)	Illiteracy in the US declines to a new low of 6%.	
	Rosenfeld, Paul (1890–1946), *Musical Portraits* (criticism)	Life expectancy in the US rises to 54.09 years.	
	Williams, William Carlos (1883–1963), *Kora in Hell* (prose poetry)	Dewey, John (1859–1952), *Reconstruction in Philosophy* (philosophy)	

1921

Doolittle, Hilda [H. D.] (1886–1961), Hymen (poetry)
Lubbock, Percy (1879–1965), The Craft of Fiction (criticism)

Millay, Edna St. Vincent (1892–1950), Second April (poetry)
Moore, Marianne (1887–1972), Poems (poetry)
Van Doren, Carl (1885–1950), The American Novel (criticism)

Williams, William Carlos (1883–1963), Sour Grapes (poetry)

1922

Eliot, T[homas] S[tearns] (1888–1965), The Waste Land (poetry)
Johnson, James Weldon [editor] (1871–1938), The Book of American Negro Poetry (poetry)
McKay, Claude (1890–1948), Harlem Shadows (poetry)

Mencken, H[enry] L[ouis] (1880–1956), Prejudices, Third Series (social criticism)
Mumford, Lewis (1895–1990), The Story of Utopias (criticism)

Congress sets limit of 357,000 new immigrants per year.
US Supreme Court rules that labor unions can be prosecuted for restraining interstate trade.

Ku Klux Klan rampages in the South and attracts widespread media attention.
Industries around the US make broad wage cuts.

Albert Einstein arrives in New York and lectures on relativity; introduces the concept of time as the 4th dimension.
Cable Act makes it legal for an American woman to marry a foreigner.
The US Supreme Court upholds the constitutionality of the 19th Amendment (woman's suffrage).
WEAF, New York, broadcasts first program with a commercial sponsor.

Bell Telephone installs in New York City the first mechanical switchboard: the "Pennsylvania" exchange.
Dr. Alexis Carrel discovers the existence and purpose of white blood cells in the human body.
Louis Armstrong moves from New Orleans to Chicago to join King Oliver's Creole Jazz Band.

The US, Britain, France, Italy, and Japan sign the Naval Limitation Treaty.
The BBC (British Broadcasting Corporation) is founded.

Rapid inflation in Germany destabilizes its economy.
Faisal I becomes King of Iraq.

Wittgenstein, Ludwig (1889–1951), Tractatus Logico-Philosophicus (philosophy)
Yeats, William Butler (1865–1939), Michael Robartes and the Dancer (poetry)
The Soviet Union forms under the rule of Lenin.

Mussolini rises to power in charge of a fascist state.

Britain recognizes the sovereignty of the Kingdom of Egypt.

Insulin proves to be an effective treatment for diabetic patients.

Valéry, Paul (1871–1945), Charmes ou poèmes (poetry)

	American Poetry and Criticism	American Events, Texts, and Arts	Other Events, Texts, and Arts
1923	Bogan, Louise (1897–1970), *Body of This Death* (poetry) Frost, Robert (1874–1963), *New Hampshire* (poetry) Millay, Edna St. Vincent (1892–1950), *The Harp-Weaver and Other Poems* (poetry) Moore, Marianne (1887–1972), *Marriage* (poetry) Stevens, Wallace (1879–1955), *Harmonium* (poetry) Williams, William Carlos (1883–1963), *Spring and All* (poetry)	Post, Emily (1873–1960), *Etiquette* (manual) *Nanook of the North* (film) directed by Robert Flaherty President Harding dies in office. Vice President Calvin Coolidge becomes President. Senate begins to investigate oil leases in Wyoming leading to the Teapot Dome Scandal. Colonel Jacob Shick patents the first electric razor. Bessie Smith records "Down Hearted Blues." 1 million copies sell within year of release. "Barney Google" (popular song)	Hitler fails to seize power in Germany in the Beer Hall Putsch. French armed forces occupy the Ruhr valley in Germany to exact war reparations. Edwin Hubble calculates the astronomical distance to the Star Nebula. Freud, Sigmund (1856–1939), *The Ego and the Id* (psychology) Lawrence, D. H. (1885–1930), *Studies in Classic American Literature* (criticism) Rilke, Rainer Maria (1875–1926), *Duino Elegies & The Sonnets of Orpheus* (poetry)
1924	Doolittle, Hilda [H. D.] (1886–1961), *Heliodora* (poetry) Jeffers, Robinson (1887–1962), *Tamar and Other Poems* (poetry)	Calvin Coolidge wins election for President of the US. Number of radios in the US tops 2,500,000. Ford Motor Co. makes its 10 millionth car.	Greece becomes a national republic. The Socialist Giacomo Matteotti is killed in Italy.

Mencken, H[enry] L[ouis] (1880–1956), *Prejudices, Fourth Series* (social criticism)
Moore, Marianne (1887–1972), *Observations* (poetry)
Mumford, Lewis (1895–1990), *Sticks and Stones* (criticism)
Rosenfeld, Paul (1890–1946), *Port of New York* (criticism)

1925 Brooks, Van Wyck (1886–1963), *The Pilgrimage of Henry James* (criticism)
Cullen, Countee (1903–46), *Color* (poetry)
Cummings, E. E. (1894–1962), *&* (poetry)

National Origins Act passes.

Radio Corporation of America transmits first photograph to London via wireless telegraph.

Nathan Leopold and Richard Loeb are found guilty of the thrill killing of a child.

Proposed amendment to the Constitution against child labor does not pass.

H. L. Mencken and George Nathan found *The American Mercury*.

George Gershwin, *Rhapsody in Blue* (orchestral music)
"Sweet Georgia Brown" (popular song)

At Scopes Trial, Clarence Darrow humiliates William Jennings Bryan when questioning him about his disbelief of the theory of evolution.

Army courtmartials Col. Billy Mitchell because he insists that air power is key to war strategy.

Mrs. William Ross, Wyoming, becomes first woman Governor in US history.

The German dirigible Z-R-3 crosses the Atlantic Ocean.

Insecticides are sprayed for the first time.

Breton, André (1896–1966), *Manifesto of Surrealism* (art theory)

Hitler, Adolf (1889–1945), *Mein Kampf* (autobiography)
Richards, Ivor A[rmstrong] (1893–1979) *Principles of Literary Criticism*

Dmitri Shostakovich composes First Symphony (orchestral music).
The Last Laugh (film) directed by F. W. Murnau

Physicist Wolfgang Pauli proposes "Exclusion Theory," which spurs the development of Quantum Theory.

Hindenburg becomes the President of Germany.

Abd el-Krim revolt in Morocco against Spanish rule.

American Poetry and Criticism	American Events, Texts, and Arts	Other Events, Texts, and Arts
Doolitle, Hilda [H. D.] (1886–1961), Collected Poems (poetry)	Dillon, Read & Co. buy Dodge Bros. Automobile Co. for then record $146 million.	Border disputes in Western Europe settled in Locarno Conference.
Locke, Alain (1885–1954), The New Negro (social criticism)	Drs. George Frederick and Gladys Dick formulate antitoxin for scarlet fever.	Hardy, Thomas (1840–1928), Human Shows, Far Phantasies, Songs and Trifles (poetry)
Pound, Ezra (1885–1972), A Draft of XVI Cantos (poetry)	Frank Lloyd Wright builds Taliesin in Spring Green, Wisconsin.	Yeats, William Butler (1865–1939), A Vision (poetry theory)
Rosenfeld, Paul (1890–1946), Men Seen: Twenty Four Modern Authors (criticism)	New Yorker magazine founded.	Whitehead, Alfred publishes Science and the Modern World (non-fiction)
Stein, Gertrude (1874–1946), The Making of Americans (experimental narrative)	The "Charleston" becomes a popular dance step.	Potemkin (film) directed by Sergei Eisenstein
Williams, William Carlos (1883–1963), In the American Grain (essays)	Aaron Copland, Symphony for Organ and Orchestra (orchestral music)	
	The Gold Rush (film) directed by Charlie Chaplin	
1926 Crane, Hart (1899–1932), White Buildings (poetry)	President Coolidge signs the Revenue Act in his continued effort to repeal taxes.	Germany is admitted to the League of Nations.
Dell, Floyd (1887–1969), Intellectual Vagabondage: An Apology for the Intelligentsia (social commentary)	Henry Ford shocks industrial leaders when he orders 8-hour day, 5-day work week.	Hirohito succeeds as Emperor of Japan.
Hughes, Langston (1902–67), The Weary Blues (poetry)	Drs. George Minoz and William Murphy devise a cure for pernicious anemia.	Ibn Saud becomes King of Saudi Arabia.

| 1927 | Mencken, H[enry] L[ouis] (1880–1956), *Prejudices, Fifth Series* (social criticism) | "Jelly Roll" Morton and his Red Hot Peppers make a series of seminal jazz recordings: "Black Bottom Stomp," "Jelly Roll Blues." | Eluard, Paul (1895–1952), *Capital of Sorrow* (poetry) |

Mumford, Lewis (1895–1990), *The Golden Day* (criticism)

Parrington, Vernon (1871–1929), *The Connecticut Wits* (criticism)

Brooks, Van Wyck (1886–1963), *Emerson and Others* (criticism)

Hughes, Langston (1902–67), *Fine Clothes to the Jew* (poetry)

Jeffers, Robinson (1887–1962), *The Women at Point Sur* (poetry)

Mencken, H[enry] L[ouis] (1880–1956), *Prejudices, Sixth Series* (social criticism)

Parrington, Vernon (1871–1929), *Main Currents in American Thought* [3 vols., 1927–1930] (criticism)

Parrington, Vernon (1871–1929), *Sinclair Lewis, Our Own Diogenes* (criticism)

Robinson, Edwin Arlington (1869–1935), *Tristram* (poetry)

Sandburg, Carl [editor], *The American Songbag* (folk music)

Fire!! ed. Wallace Thurman publishes its only issue.

The General (film) directed by Buster Keaton

Nicola Sacco and Bartolomeo Vanzetti are executed.

US Supreme Court declares unconstitutional a Texas law forbidding black vote in primaries.

Charles Lindbergh makes first solo non-stop transatlantic flight.

Commercial transatlantic telephone service begins.

Radio Act allows for public ownership of the airwaves.

Drs. Phillip Drinker and Louis A. Shaw devise the first "iron lung" respirator.

The Jazz Singer (film) with Al Jolson is first major film with sound.

Aaron Copland, Concerto for Piano and Orchestra (orchestral music)

Max Ernst finishes *Mary Spanking the Christ Child* (painting)

Metropolis (film) directed by Fritz Lang

Chang Kai-shek oppresses communists in China.

German economy collapses.

Heidegger, Martin (1889–1976), *Being and Time* (philosophy)

Heisenberg, Werner (1901–76) writes 14-page letter to Wolfgang Pauli in which he outlines the "Uncertainty Principle."

	American Poetry and Criticism	American Events, Texts, and Arts	Other Events, Texts, and Arts
1928	Foerster, Norman (1887–1972), *American Criticism* (criticism anthology) Foerster, Norman (1887–1972), *The Reinterpretation of American Literature* (criticism anthology) Frost, Robert (1874–1963), *West-Running Brook* (poetry) Millay, Edna St. Vincent (1892–1950), *The Buck In the Snow* (poetry) More, Paul Elmer (1864–1937), *The Demon of the Absolute* (criticism) Pound, Ezra (1885–1972), *A Draft of Cantos XVII to XXVII* (poetry)	Congress passes Alien Property Act to compensate Germans for property seized in the US during World War I. Herbert Hoover defeats Al Smith in the election for President of the United States. George Eastman shows first color motion pictures in his lab in Rochester, New York Boas, Franz (1858–1942), *Anthropology and Modern Life* (anthropology) Mead, Margaret (1901–71), *Coming of Age in Samoa* (anthropology) *Plane Crazy* (cartoon) by Walt Disney marks first appearance of Mickey Mouse.	Alexander Fleming cultures penicillin, the first antibiotic. First Five-year plan begins in the Soviet Union. Auden, W. H. (1907–73), *Poems* (poetry) Lawrence, D. H. (1885–1930), *Collected Poems* (poetry) Yeats, William Butler (1865–1939), *The Tower* (poetry) Maurice Ravel composes *Bolero* (ballet).
1929	Bogan, Louise (1897–1970), *Dark Summer* (poetry) Cullen, Countee (1903–46), *The Black Christ* (poetry) Matthiessen, F[rancis] O[tto] (1902–50), *Sarah Orne Jewett* (criticism) Mumford, Lewis (1895–1990), *Herman Melville* (criticism)	The US Senate agrees to the Brand–Kellogg Pact banning war as an instrument of national policy. Agricultural Marketing Act fails to hold prices when farmers refuse to reduce acreage under cultivation. The Great Depression begins. *American Literature* (scholarly journal) publishes its first issue.	The world economy slumps into the Great Depression. Astronomer Edwin Hubble proves that the Universe is expanding. Leads to development of the Big Bang Theory. The Lateran Treaty establishes Vatican City as an independent region in Italy. Jews and Arabs clash at the Wailing Wall.

1930

Crane, Hart (1899–1932), *The Bridge* (poetry)

Eliot, T[homas] S[tearns], (1888–1965), *Ash-Wednesday* (poetry)

Frost, Robert (1874–1963), *Collected Poems* (poetry)

Ransom, John Crowe [editor] (1888–1974), *I'll Take My Stand* (criticism)

Stein, Gertrude (1874–1946), *Dix portraits* (poetry)

Georgia O'Keeffe finishes *Black Flower and Blue Larkspur* (painting).

Cole Porter has first hit show with *Fifty Million Frenchman*.

President Hoover signs the Smoot–Hawley Tariff Act in failed attempt to boost farm economy.

Hoover asks Congress for $100 million for public works projects designed to stimulate the economy.

The population in the US is 122,775,046.

1 of every 5 Americans owns an automobile.

Edward Hopper finishes *Early Sunday Morning* (painting).

Grant Wood finishes *American Gothic* (painting).

Richards, Ivor A[rmstrong] (1893–1979) *Practical Criticism* (criticism)

Woolf, Virginia (1882–1941), *A Room of One's Own* (feminist criticism)

The Blue Angel (film) directed by **Josef von Sternberg**

France constructs the Maginot Line.

Haile Selassie becomes Emperor of Ethiopia.

The Turkish rename Constantinople as Istanbul.

Yellow fever vaccine is developed.

Gas turbine is invented.

Auden, W. H. (1907–73), *Poems* (poetry)

Empson, William (1906–84), *Seven Types of Ambiguity* (criticism)

Japan invades Manchuria.

1931

Burke, Kenneth (1897–1993), *Counter-Statement* (criticism)

Congress sets aside funds to run Muscle Shoals power plant on Tennessee River. Forerunner of the Tennessee Valley Authority.

	American Poetry and Criticism	American Events, Texts, and Arts	Other Events, Texts, and Arts
	Doolittle, Hilda [H. D.] (1886–1961), Red Roses for Bronze (poetry)	Congress overrides Hoover veto of Veterans Compensation Act.	Alfonso XIII is overthrown in Spain. Spanish Republic is formed.
	Eastman, Max (1883–1969), Enjoyment of Poetry (criticism)	More than 3,800 banks fail as financial bank spreads across and debtors default on loans.	The planned capital of India, New Delhi, opens.
	Hughes, Langston (1902–67), Dear Lovely Death (poetry)	Commission reports on bootlegging and declares Prohibition unenforceable.	Gödel, Kurt (1906–78), "Incompleteness Theorem" (mathematics)
	Hughes, Langston (1902–67), The Negro Mother (poetry)	Chicago mob boss, Al Capone, is sentenced to 11 years in prison for tax evasion.	M (film) directed by Fritz Lang
	Mumford, Lewis (1895–1990), The Brown Decades (criticism)	Empire State Building and George Washington Bridge are completed in New York City.	
	Rourke, Constance (1885–1941), American Humor (criticism)	Dreiser, Theodore (1871–1945), Tragic America (social commentary)	
	Stevens, Wallace (1879–1955), Harmonium (2nd edition, poetry)	Santayana, George (1863–1952), The Genteel Tradition at Bay (social commentary)	
	Wilson, Edmund (1895–1972), Axel's Castle: A Study in the Imaginative Literature of 1870–1930 (criticism)	City Lights (film) directed by Charlie Chaplin	
1932	Brooks, Van Wyck (1886–1963), Sketches in Criticism (criticism)	President Hoover calls for friends, charities, and local governments to help those in need.	Worldwide economic depression leaves many millions unemployed.

Calverton, V. F. (1900–40), *The Liberation of American Literature* (criticism)

Eliot, T[homas] S[tearns] (1888–1965), *Selected Essays* (criticism)

Hughes, Langston (1902–67), *The Dream Keeper* (poetry)

Hughes, Langston (1902–67), *Scottsboro Limited* (poetry)

Wilson, Edmund (1895–1972), *American Jitters: A Year of the Slump* (social documentary)

1933   Crane, Hart (1899–1932), *Collected Poems* (poetry)

Eliot, T[homas] S[tearns] (1888–1965), *The Use of Poetry and the Use of Criticism* (criticism)

Hicks, Granville (1901–82), *The Great Tradition* (criticism)

The Glass–Steagall Act separates brokerage and banking businesses.

Norris–LaGuardia Act forbids employers from discriminating against workers in unions.

Farmers refuse to accede to bank foreclosures.

Unemployment in some cities reaches 40%.

Douglas MacArthur uses force to remove protesting servicemen from Washington.

Franklin Roosevelt defeats Herbert Hoover in election for President of the United States.

Charles Burchfield finishes *November Evening* (painting).

"Brother Can You Spare a Dime" (popular song)

President Roosevelt announces new federal banking policy in first radio "fireside chat."

Harry Hopkins heads the new Federal Emergency Relief Administration.

Federal Securities Act mandates public information accompany new stock issues.

James Chadwick discovers the neutron.

English physicists split the atom for the first time.

German industrialists back Hitler.

British government declares Congress of India illegal. Arrests Gandhi.

Japan attacks Shanghai.

Auden, W. H. (1907–73), *The Orators* (poetry)

Leavis, F[rank] R[aymond] (1895–1978) *New Bearings in English Poetry* (criticism)

Hitler becomes Chancellor of Germany. Japan leaves League of Nations.

Severe famine in the Soviet Union.

Milosz, Czeslaw (1911–), *Poemat O Czasie Zastylglym* (poetry)

	American Poetry and Criticism	American Events, Texts, and Arts	Other Events, Texts, and Arts
	Miller, Perry (1905–63), *Jonathan Edwards* (criticism)	Congress passes National Industrial Recovery Act, including Public Works Administration.	Neruda, Pablo (1904–73), *Residence on Earth* (poetry)
	Pound, Ezra (1885–1972), *A Draft of XXX Cantos* (poetry)	Prohibition is repealed.	Paz, Octavio (1914–98), *Luna silvestre* (poetry)
	Stein, Gertrude (1874–1946), *The Autobiography of Alice B. Toklas* (autobiography)	Confidence in banking system in the US gradually returns.	Pessoa, Fernando (1888–1935), *Mensagem* (poetry)
		Judge John M. Woolsey lifts the ban on James Joyce's *Ulysses*.	Yeats, William Butler (1865–1939), *The Winding Stair* (poetry)
		Aaron Copland composes *Short Symphony*.	Brassaï produces *Paris du nuit* (photography).
1934	Cowley, Malcolm (1898–1989), *Exile's Return* (criticism)	Massive drought plagues the Great Plains. The Dust Bowl.	Hitler orders the assassination of his rivals in Germany.
	Dewey, John (1859–1952), *Art as Experience* (philosophy)	Congress creates the Federal Communications Commission to regulate radio and telegraph.	The Soviet Union is admitted to the League of Nations.
	Mumford, Lewis (1895–1990), *Technics and Civilization* (criticism)	Du Pont patents the formula for nylon.	Mao's army begins the "Long March" to northern China.
	Pound, Ezra (1885–1972), *Eleven New Cantos, XXXI–XLI* (poetry)	Julianna Force organizes the American pavilion at the Venice Biennale.	Kirov is assassinated in the Soviet Union.
	Pound, Ezra (1885–1972), *ABC of Reading* (criticism)	Cole Porter composes *Anything Goes* (musical).	Thomas, Dylan (1914–1953), *18 Poems* (poetry)
	Williams, William Carlos (1883–1963), *Collected Poems, 1921–1931* (poetry)	Reginald Marsh finishes *Negroes on Rockaway Beach* (painting).	Henri Cartier-Bresson takes *Enfants jouant dans les ruines* (photograph).
		It Happened One Night (film) directed by Frank Capra	

	Literature	North American events	World events
1935	Blackmur, R[ichard] P. (1904–65), *The Double Agent* (criticism) Hurston, Zora Neale (1891–1960), *Mules and Men* (criticism) Johnson, James Weldon (1871–1938), *Selected Poems* (poetry) Matthiessen, F[rancis] O[tto] (1902–50), *The Achievement of T. S. Eliot* (criticism) Moore, Marianne (1887–1972), *Selected Poems* (poetry) Stevens, Wallace (1879–1955), *Ideas of Order* (poetry)	Roosevelt creates Works Progress Administration. Harry Hopkins, WPA head, employs artists, writers, actors to document state of nation. Congress passes the Social Security Act. Revenue Act of 1935 sharply increases the taxation of the rich in the US Congress of Industrial Organizations (CIO) forms as a labor union. Cleanth Brooks and Robert Penn Warren found the *Southern Review*. George Gershwin composes *Porgy and Bess* (opera). *Top Hat* (film) starring Fred Astaire and Ginger Rogers *The Informer* (film) directed by John Ford	Italy invades Abyssinia. Germany incorporates the Saarland. The Nuremberg Laws against Jews go into effect in Germany. Persia changes its name to Iran. British Parliament separates Burma and Aden from India. Empson, William (1906–84), *Some Versions of Pastoral* (criticism) Yeats, William Butler (1865–1939), *Parnell's Funeral and Other Poems* (poetry)
1936	Brooks, Van Wyck (1886–1963), *The Flowering of New England* (criticism) Frost, Robert (1874–1963), *A Further Range* (poetry) Moore, Marianne (1887–1972), *The Pangolin and Other Verse* (poetry) Sandburg, Carl (1878–1967), *The People, Yes* (poetry)	Congress passes Soil Conservation Act to boost efforts to end erosion of Great Plains. Robinson–Putnam Act forbids national chains from underselling businesses in small towns. Hoover Dam is completed near Las Vegas, Nevada. Sitdown strikes and industrial unrest sweep the nation.	Spanish Civil War begins between fascist forces and republican government. Germany, Italy, and Japan form Axis Alliance. Japanese invade China and capture Beijing. The British Broadcasting Corporation begins television broadcasts.

	American Poetry and Criticism	American Events, Texts, and Arts	Other Events, Texts, and Arts
	Stein, Gertrude (1874–1946), *The Geographical History of America* (experimental writing) Stevens, Wallace (1879–1955), *Owl's Clover* (poetry) Tate, Allen (1899–1979), *Reactionary Essays* (criticism) Toomer, Jean (1894–1967), "The Blue Meridian" (poem)	Radar system developed by the US Signal Corps. Frank Lloyd Wright designs *Fallingwater* in Bear Run, Pennsylvania. Samuel Barber's First Symphony premieres in Rome, Italy. *The Plow that Broke the Plains* (documentary film) directed by Pare Lorentz *Life* magazine publishes its first issue. Jesse Owens wins four gold medals at the Berlin Olympics, upsetting Hitler's theories of racial superiority. US Steel recognizes the United Mine Workers as a legitimate labor union. Roosevelt appoints Hugo Black to the US Supreme Court thereby solidifying a pro-New Deal Court. National Cancer Institute founded.	Oil is found is Saudi Arabia. Auden, W. H. (1907–73), *Look Stranger!* (poetry) Leavis, F[rank] R[aymond] (1895–1978) *Revaluation* (criticism) Thomas, Dylan (1914–53), *Twenty-Five Poems* (poetry) Keynes, John Maynard (1883–1946), *A General Theory of Employment, Interest, and Money* (economics) Sergei Rachmaninov composes Symphony No. 3 (orchestral music). Leon Trotsky exiled from the Soviet Union. Spanish forces under Francisco Franco bomb Guernica. Sino-Japanese war resumes near Beijing.
1937	Brown, Sterling (1901–89), *The Negro in American Fiction* (criticism) Brown, Sterling (1901–89), *Negro Poetry and Drama* (criticism) Cowley, Malcolm [editor] (1898–1989), *After the Genteel Tradition* (anthology of criticism) Pound, Ezra (1885–1972), *The Fifth Decad of Cantos* (poetry)	The news account of the Hindenburg explosion is first nation-wide radio broadcast.	Pablo Picasso finishes *Guernica* (painting).

	Literature	Science, Society, and Politics	Arts
1938	Stevens, Wallace (1879–1955), *The Man with the Blue Guitar* (poetry) Winters, Yvor (1900–68), *Primitivism and Decadence* (criticism)	Lippmann, Walter (1889–1974), *The Good Society* (social commentary)	*La Grande Illusion* (film) directed by **Jean Renoir**
	Frost, Robert (1874–1963), *Collected Poems* (poetry) Hughes, Langston (1902–67), *A New Song* (poetry) Hurston, Zora Neale (1891–1960), *Tell My Horse* (criticism) Mumford, Lewis (1895–1990), *The Culture of Cities* (criticism)	President Roosevelt asks Congress for funds to begin military build-up. Civil Aeronautics Act ushers in era of passenger airplanes. MacLeish, Archibald (1892–1982), *Land of the Free* (social documentary) Stearns, Harold E. (1891–1943), *America Now: An Inquiry into Civilization in the United States* (symposium)	Neville Chamberlain signs Munich Accord with Adolf Hitler. Stalin purges the Communist Party of USSR after several Show Trials. Anti-Jewish pogrom, Kristallnacht, in Germany. Otto Hahn experiments successfully with nuclear fission.
	Ransom, John Crowe (1888–1974), *The World's Body* (criticism) Wilson, Edmund (1895–1972), *The Triple Thinkers* (criticism)	Walker Evans produces *American Photographs* (photography). *The War of the Worlds* (radio play) by **Orson Welles** scares public who take it literally. *Snow White and the Seven Dwarves* (feature cartoon) by **Walt Disney**	**Yeats, William Butler** (1865–1939), *New Poems* (poetry)
1939	Brooks, Cleanth (1906–94), *Modern Poetry and the Tradition* (criticism) Miller, Perry (1905–63), *The New England Mind: The Seventeenth Century* (criticism)	Drs. Philip Levine and Rufus Stetson discover the presence of Rh factors in human blood. Sears, Roebuck catalog carries fashion dresses for the first time.	Germany invades Czechoslovakia and Poland; World War II begins. Germany and Soviet Union sign non-aggression pact.

American Poetry and Criticism	American Events, Texts, and Arts	Other Events, Texts, and Arts
Redding, J. Saunders (1906–88), To Make a Poet Black (criticism)	Lange, Dorothea (1895–1965) and Taylor, Paul (1917–), An American Exodus: A Record of Human Erosion in the Thirties (documentary)	Russia invades Finland.
Smith, Bernard (1909–), Forces of American Criticism: A Study in the History of American Literary Thought (criticism)	McKenney, Ruth (1911–72), Industrial Valley (social documentary)	Italy invades Albania.
Winters, Yvor (1900–68), Maule's Curse (criticism)	Frank Lloyd Wright builds Taliesin West and the Johnson Wax Co. building. First performance of the Second Piano Sonata by Charles Ives Stagecoach (film) directed by John Ford	Swiss scientist, Paul Müller, synthesizes dichlorodiphenyltrichloroethane (DDT). Yeats, William Butler (1865–1939), Last Poems and Two Plays (poetry) The Rules of the Game (film) directed by Jean Renoir
1940 Blackmur, R[ichard] P. (1904–65), The Expense of Greatness (criticism)	President Franklin Roosevelt reelected for third term.	Radar invented in Scotland.
Brooks, Van Wyck (1886–1963), New England: Indian Summer (criticism)	Congress passes law requiring alien residents to register with the US government.	Germany invades Norway, Denmark, Belgium, and Paris.
Doolittle, Hilda [H. D.] (1886–1961), Collected Poems (poetry)	29.5 million households in the US own a radio. US population is 131,669,275.	Leon Trotsky is assassinated in Mexico.
Pound, Ezra (1885–1972), Cantos LII–LXXI (poetry)	Life expectancy in the US reaches 64, 15 years higher than at the turn of the century.	Germany, Italy, and Japan sign an alliance for mutual protection.

	Literature	Arts and Events	World Events
	Wilson, Edmund (1895–1972), *To the Finland Station* (social criticism) **Winters, Yvor** (1900–68), *Poems* (poetry)	First compulsory peacetime draft in the US begins. **Woody Guthrie** writes "This Land is My Land" (folk song). *Philadelphia Story* (film) directed by **George Cukor** *The Great Dictator* (film) directed by **Charlie Chaplin**	Japan invades Indochina. Winston Churchill becomes Prime Minister of Britain.
1941	**Burke, Kenneth** (1897–1986), *The Philosophy of Literary Forms* (criticism) **Hughes, Langston** (1902–67), *Shakespeare in Harlem* (poetry) **Matthiessen, F[rancis] O[tto]** (1902–50), *The American Renaissance* (criticism) **Moore, Marianne** (1887–1972), *What Are Years* (poetry) **Ransom, John Crowe** (1888–1974), *The New Criticism* (criticism) **Tate, Allen** (1899–1979), *Reason in Madness* (criticism) **Williams, William Carlos** (1883–1963), *The Broken Span* (poetry)	Lend-Lease Act signed with Britain. Advent of common use of penicillin. Coal and steel workers lead protracted strikes. Japan bombs Pearl Harbor. US declares war on Axis powers. **Shirer, William** (1904–93), *Berlin Diary* (non-fiction) **Snow, Edgar** (1905–72), *The Battle for Asia* (non-fiction) **Edward Hopper** finishes *Nighthawks* (painting).	Germany and Italy combine to invade the Balkans. Germany bombs London and invades Russia. Soviet Union and Japan sign non-aggression treaty. Edwin McMillan and Glenn Seaborg discover plutonium. **Auden, W. H.** (1907–73), *New Year Letter* (poetry) **Dmitri Shostakovich** composes Symphony No. 7 in Leningrad siege.
1942	**Wilson, Edmund** (1895–1972), *The Wound and the Bow* (criticism) **Frost, Robert** (1874–1963), *A Witness Tree* (poetry)	*Citizen Kane* (film) directed by **Orson Welles** Executive Order 9066 sends Japanese Americans to internment camps.	Battle of the Coral Sea: first naval flight conducted only by airplane.

	American Poetry and Criticism	American Events, Texts, and Arts	Other Events, Texts, and Arts
1943	Kazin, Alfred (1915–98), On Native Grounds (criticism) Rourke, Constance (1885–1941), The Roots of American Culture (criticism) Stevens, Wallace (1879–1955), Notes toward a Supreme Fiction (poetry) Wilson, Edmund [editor] (1895–1972), The Shock of Recognition (anthology of criticism)	US Supreme Court finds Georgia labor laws violate the Thirteenth Amendment. First nuclear chain reaction produced in the labs of Enrico Fermi (University of Chicago). First electronic computer developed. "White Christmas" (popular song) US government forbids racial discrimination by war contractors. US government begins to collect paycheck withholding tax. Widespread rationing of food and clothes in the United States. Pollock, Jackson (1912–56), Mural Painting (painting) Oklahoma! premieres on Broadway. Casablanca (film) directed by Michael Curtiz	Battle of Midway: first major defeat of Japanese navy. Battle of El Alamein forces German retreat out of North Africa. Germans begin to use gas chambers to murder Jews in mass numbers. Camus, Albert (1913–60), The Myth of Sisyphus (essay) Russians push back German invasion at Battle of Stalingrad. American and British forces invade Sicily. Mussolini deposed. Thomas, Dylan (1914–53), New Poems (poetry) Sartre, Jean-Paul (1905–80), Being and Nothingness (existential philosophy)
1944	Brooks, Van Wyck (1886–1963), The World of Washington Irving (criticism)	Franklin Roosevelt reelected to a fourth term as President.	D-Day: Allied forces invade Normandy on June 6.

Doolittle, Hilda [H. D.] (1886–1961), *The Walls Do Not Fall* (poetry)

Matthiessen, F[rancis] O[tto] (1902–50), *Henry James: The Major Phase* (criticism)

Moore, Marianne (1887–1972), *Nevertheless* (poetry)

Mumford, Lewis (1895–1990), *The Condition of Man* (criticism)

Williams, William Carlos (1883–1963), *The Wedge* (poetry)

1945   Burke, Kenneth (1897–1986), *A Grammar of Motives* (criticism)

Cowley, Malcolm [editor] (1898–1989), *The Portable Faulkner* (anthology)

Doolittle, Hilda [H. D.] (1886–1961), *Tribute to the Angels* (poetry)

Congress passes the GI Bill of Rights.

Communist party of the US reconfigures itself into Communist Political Association

Government freezes prices on rationed domestic goods to prevent inflation.

Lemkin, Raphaël (1900–59), *Axis Rule in Occupied Europe* (non-fiction)

Myrdal, Gunnar (1898–1987), *An American Dilemma* (non-fiction)

US Senate ratifies United Nations charter.

Franklin Roosevelt dies. Harry Truman becomes President.

Tupperware is invented.

The Lost Weekend (film) directed by Billy Wilder

Dizzy Gillespie (1917–93) and Charlie Parker (1920–55) record *Groovin' High, Ko Ko* (jazz).

Allied forces march toward Berlin and score several victories in the Pacific.

Germans launch V-2 rockets toward London.

Auden, W. H. (1907–73). *For the Time Being: A Christmas Oratorio* (poetry)

Sartre, Jean-Paul (1905–80), *No Exit* (drama)

Francis Bacon finishes "Three Studies for Figures at the Base of a Crucifixion" (painting).

Winston Churchill, Joseph Stalin, and Franklin Roosevelt meet in Yalta.

Victory in Europe: May 8, V-E Day.

US drops atomic bombs on Hiroshima and Nagasaki.

The United Nations is established.

Larkin, Philip (1922–85), *The North Ship* (poetry)

Milosz, Czeslaw (1911–), *Ocalenia* (poetry)

Ivan the Terrible (film) directed by Sergei Eisenstein

	American Poetry and Criticism	American Events, Texts, and Arts	Other Events, Texts, and Arts
1946	**Bishop, Elizabeth** (1911–79), *North & South* (poetry) **Doolittle, Hilda [H. D.]** (1886–1961), *The Flowering of the Rod* (poetry) **Williams, William Carlos** (1883–1963), *Paterson* (Book I, poetry)	Atomic Energy Commission created. In a speech in Fulton, Missouri, Winston Churchill declares that an "Iron Curtain" divides eastern and western Europe. Hobbs Bill passed, preventing unions from interfering with interstate commerce. US Marines put down an inmate riot at Alcatraz prison. First houses are built in Levittown, New York, as suburban housing tracts rise on periphery of US cities. *The Big Sleep* (film) directed by **Howard Hawks** *The Best Years of Our Lives* (film) directed by **William Wyler**	Joseph Stalin warns of anti-communist threat to Russia. Communists in Indochina resist the reassertion of French rule. British and French forces pull out of Lebanon. British Labour Party nationalizes health care. Nuremberg tribunal convicts 13 Nazis for crimes against humanity. **Thomas, Dylan** (1914–53), *Deaths and Entrances* (poetry) *Beauty and the Beast* (film) directed by **Jean Cocteau** *Open City* (film) directed by **Roberto Rossellini**
1947	**Brooks, Van Wyck** (1886–1963), *The Times of Melville and Whitman* (criticism) **Frost, Robert** (1874–1963), *Steeple Bush* (poetry) **Frye, Northrop** (1912–91), *Fearful Symmetry* (criticism)	George Marshall proposes a plan to rebuild the war-ravaged nations of the world. Congress passes Taft–Hartley Labor Act in an effort to limit power of organized labor. An Act of Congress founds the Central Intelligence Agency.	India and Pakistan gain independence from United Kingdom. Civil War in Greece and Soviet actions against Turkey cause US to send aid. The US becomes trustee of Pacific islands once claimed by Japan.

Hughes, Langston (1902–67), *Fields of Wonder* (poetry)

Matthiessen, F[rancis] O[tto] (1902–50), *The James Family* (criticism)

Stevens, Wallace (1879–1955), *Transport to Summer* (poetry)

Winters, Yvor (1900–68), *In Defense of Reason* (criticism)

1948 Matthiessen, F[rancis] O[tto] (1902–50), *From the Heart of Europe* (criticism)

Pound, Ezra (1885–1972), *The Pisan Cantos* (poetry)

Spiller, Robert [editor] (1896–1988), *Literary History of the United States* (criticism)

Tate, Allen (1899–1979), *On the Limits of Poetry* (criticism)

Williams, William Carlos (1883–1963), *Paterson* (Book II, poetry)

Williams, William Carlos (1883–1963), "The Poem as a Field of Action" (essay)

President Truman consolidates armed forces into Department of Defense and commits to fight communism in foreign nations.

The long-playing, or LP, record is invented.

The transistor is invented.

Chuck Yeager breaks the sound barrier in a rocket plane.

Charlie Parker (1920–55) records *Quasimodo* (jazz).

Harry Truman reelected President.

Television becomes a national phenomenon (number of stations grows from 11 to 65).

Alger Hiss is indicated for espionage.

President Truman desegregates the armed forces.

US Supreme Court declares religious instruction in public schools unconstitutional.

Kinsey, Alfred (1894–1956), *Sexual Behavior in the Human Male* (sociology)

Thor Heyerdahl and colleagues sail reed boat across Pacific: Kon-Tiki Voyage.

The Dead Sea Scrolls are discovered.

Auden, W. H. (1907–73), *The Age of Anxiety: A Baroque Eclogue* (poetry)

Mahatma Gandhi assassinated in India.

State of Israel created.

World Health Organization founded.

Communists seize power in Czechoslovakia and blockade Berlin.

Holograph invented in Britain.

Leavis, F[rank] R[aymond] (1895–1978), *The Great Tradition* (criticism)

	American Poetry and Criticism	American Events, Texts, and Arts	Other Events, Texts, and Arts
1949	Zukovsky, Louis (1904–78), *A Test of Poetry* (criticism) Brooks, Cleanth (1906–94), *The Well Wrought Urn* (criticism) Chase, Richard (1914–63), *Quest for Myth* (criticism) Doolittle, Hilda [H. D.] (1886–1961), *By Avon River* (poetry) Hughes, Langston (1902–67), *One-Way Ticket* (poetry)	**de Kooning, Willem** (1904–97), *Asheville* Housing Act supports low-income housing development. US Courts convict eleven member of the US Communist party for plot to overthrow the government. US Justice Department files anti-trust suit against American Telegraph and Telephone. **Barber, Samuel** (1910–81), *Knoxville: Summer of 1915* (orchestral music) **Johnson, Philip** (1906–), *Glass House* (architecture) **Miles Davis and Gil Evans** release *The Rebirth of Cool* (cool jazz).	*The Bicycle Thief* (film) directed by **Vittorio de Sica** NATO founded. Mao Tse-Tung establishes Communist rule in China. Soviets explode their first atomic bomb. Apartheid established in South Africa. J. F. J. Cade introduces lithium for treatment of manic depression. **de Beauvoir, Simone** (1908–86), *The Second Sex* (feminist theory)
1950	Warren, Austin (1899–1986) and René Wellek (1903–89), *Theory of Literature* (criticism) Williams, William Carlos (1883–1963), *Paterson* (Book III, poetry) Burke, Kenneth (1897–1986), *A Rhetoric of Motives* (criticism) Smith, Henry Nash (1906–86), *Virgin Land: The American West as Symbol and Myth* (criticism) Stevens, Wallace (1879–1955), *The Auroras of Autumn* (poetry)	*The Third Man* (film) directed by **Carol Reed** US Army takes over railroads to prevent a labor strike. House Committee on Un-American Activities accuses broad spectrum of citizens of subversive activity. 45 million households own a radio. Sales of televisions reach 1 million.	**Paz, Octavio** (1914–98), *Libertad bajo palabra* (poetry) North Korea invades South Korea. Korean War begins. Klaus Fuchs arrested for espionage. American military advisers arrive in South Vietnam.

Trilling, Lionel (1905–75), *The Liberal Imagination* (criticism)

Riesman, David (1909–2002), *The Lonely Crowd* (sociology)
All About Eve (film) directed by Joseph K. Mankiewicz
The Men (film) directed by Fred Zinneman
"Your Show of Shows" debuts on television.
Charlie Brown (cartoon) by Charles Schulz first appears in syndication.

China invades Tibet.
Albert Einstein proposes the General Field Theory.
Neruda, Pablo (1904–73), *Canto General* (poetry)
Rashomon (film) directed by Akira Kurosawa

BIBLIOGRAPHY

This selected bibliography is drawn from lists provided by the contributors to this volume. It represents works that they have found to be especially influential or significant. The bibliography does not include dissertations, articles, or studies of individual authors. We have also excluded primary sources, with the exception of certain collections that present materials that have been generally unknown or inaccessible to students and scholars.

Aaron, Daniel. *Writers on the Left: Episodes in American Literary Communism*. New York: Columbia University Press, 1992 [1961].

Alexander, Charles C. *Here the Country Lies: Nationalism and the Arts in Twentieth Century America*. Bloomington: Indiana University Press, 1980.

Baker, Jr., Houston A. *Blues, Ideology, and Afro-American Literature: A Vernacular Theory*. Chicago: University of Chicago Press, 1984.

Modernism and the Harlem Renaissance. Chicago: University of Chicago Press, 1987.

Barrish, Phillip. *American Literary Realism, Critical Theory, and Intellectual Prestige, 1880–1995*. Cambridge and New York: Cambridge University Press, 2001.

Barthes, Roland. *The Pleasure of the Text*. New York: Hill and Wang, 1975.

Bassett, John E. *Harlem in Review: Critical Reactions to Black American Writers, 1917–1939*. Selingsgrove, Pa.: Susquehanna University Press, 1992.

Beck, Charlotte. *The Fugitive Legacy: A Critical History*. Baton Rouge: Louisiana State University Press.

Benstock, Shari. *Women of the Left Bank: Paris, 1999–1940*. Austin: University of Texas Press, 1986.

Bercovitch, Sacvan. *The American Jeremiad*. Madison: University of Wisconsin Press, 1978.

The Puritan Origins of the American Self. New Haven: Yale University Press, 1975.

The Rites of Assent: Transformations in the Symbolic Construction of America. New York: Routledge, 1992.

Bercovitch, Sacvan, ed. *Reconstructing American Literary History*. Cambridge, Mass.: Harvard University Press, 1986.

Berthoff, Warner. *The Ferment of Realism: American Literature, 1884–1919*. Cambridge and New York: Cambridge University Press, 1981 [1965].

Biel, Steven. *Independent Intellectuals in the United States, 1910–1945.* New York: New York University Press, 1992.

Blackmur, R. P. *Language as Gesture.* Westport, Conn.: Greenwood Press, 1997 [1952].

Blake, Casey Nelson. *Beloved Community: The Cultural Criticism of Randolph Bourne, Van Wyck Brooks, Waldo Frank, and Lewis Mumford.* Chapel Hill: University of North Carolina Press, 1990.

Bloom, Alexander. *Prodigal Sons: The New York Intellectuals and Their World.* New York: Oxford University Press, 1986.

Bloom, Harold. *The Anxiety of Influence: A Theory of Poetry.* New York: Oxford University Press, 1973.

  Figures of Capable Imagination. New York: Seabury Press, 1976.

Bloom, James D. *Left Letters: The Culture Wars of Mike Gold and Joseph Freeman.* New York: Columbia University Press, 1992.

Borroff, Marie. *Language and the Poet: Verbal Artistry in Frost, Stevens, and Moore.* Chicago: University of Chicago Press, 1979.

Bradbury, John M. *The Fugitives: A Critical Account.* Chapel Hill: University of North Carolina Press, 1958.

Bradbury, Malcolm and James McFarlane, eds. *Modernism: 1890–1930.* Harmondsworth; New York: Penguin, 1976.

Brockman, John. *Einstein, Gertrude Stein, Wittgenstein and Frankenstein: Reinventing the Universe.* New York: Viking, 1986.

Broe, Mary Lynn and Angela Ingram, eds. *Women's Writing in Exile.* Chapel Hill: University of North Carolina Press, 1989.

Brooks, Cleanth. *Modern Poetry and the Tradition.* Chapel Hill: University of North Carolina Press, 1939.

Browder, Laura. *Rousing the Nation: Radical Culture in Depression America.* Amherst: University of Massachusetts Press, 1998.

Chielens, Edward, ed. *American Literary Magazines: The Twentieth Century.* New York: Greenwood Press, 1992.

Conkin, Paul. *The Southern Agrarians.* Knoxville: University of Tennessee Press, 1988.

Conn, Peter J. *The Divided Mind: Ideology and Imagination in America, 1898–1917.* Cambridge and New York: Cambridge University Press, 1983.

Cott, Nancy F. *The Grounding of Modern Feminism.* New Haven, Conn.: Yale University Press, 1987.

Cowan, Louise. *The Fugitive Group: A Literary History.* Baton Rouge: Louisiana State University Press, 1959.

Crunden, Robert M. *Body and Soul: The Making of American Modernism.* New York: Basic Books, 2000.

Cutrer, Thomas W. *Parnassus on the Mississippi: The Southern Review and the Baton Rouge Literary Community, 1935–1942.* Baton Rouge: Louisiana State University Press, 1984.

de Jongh, James. *Vicious Modernism: Black Harlem and the Literary Imagination.* Cambridge and New York: Cambridge University Press, 1990.

Dekoven, Marianne. *Rich and Strange: Gender, History and Modernism.* Princeton, NJ: Princeton University Press, 1991.

de Man, Paul. *Blindness and Insight.* New York: Oxford University Press, 1971.

Dembo, L. S. *Conceptions of Reality in Modern American Poetry.* Berkeley: University of California Press, 1996.

Denning, Michael. *The Cultural Front: The Laboring of American Culture in the Twentieth Century.* New York: Verso, 1996.

Diggins, John P. *The Promise of Pragmatism: Modernism and the Crisis of Knowledge and Authority.* Chicago: University of Chicago Press, 1994.

Douglas, Ann. *Terrible Honesty: Mongrel Manhattan in the 1920s.* New York: Farrar, Straus, and Giroux, 1995.

Duffey, Bernard. *Poetry in America in the Times of Bryant, Whitman, and Pound.* Durham, NC: Duke University Press, 1978.

DuPlessis, Rachel Blau. *The Pink Guitar: Writing as Feminist Practice.* New York: Routledge, 1990.

Eagleton, Terry, Frederic Jameson, and Edward Said, *Nationalism, Colonialism, and Literature.* Minneapolis, University of Minnesota Press, 1990.

Eksteins, Modris. *Rites of Spring: The Great War and the Birth of the Modern Age.* Boston: Houghton Mifflin, 1989.

Eysteinsson, Astradur. *The Concept of Modernism.* Ithaca, NY: Cornell University Press, 1990.

Felski, Rita. *The Gender of Modernity.* Cambridge, Mass.: Harvard University Press, 1995.

Fiedler, Leslie A. *What Was Literature?: Class Culture and Mass Society.* New York: Simon and Schuster, 1982.

Foley, Barbara. *Radical Representations: Politics and Form in U.S. Proletarian Fiction. 1929–1941.* Durham, NC: Duke University Press, 1993.

Friedman, Susan Stanford. *Mappings: Feminism and the Cultural Geographies of Encounter.* Princeton, NJ: Princeton University Press, 1998.

Gass, William. *The World within the Word.* New York: Knopf, 1978 [1976].

Gates, Jr., Henry Louis. *The Signifying Monkey: A Theory of Afro-American Literary Criticism.* New York: Oxford University Press, 1988.

Loose Canons: Notes on the Culture Wars. New York: Oxford University Press, 1992.

Gates Jr., Henry Louis and Cornel West. *The African-American Century: How Black Americans Have Shaped our Country.* New York: Free Press, 2000.

Gilbert, Sandra M. and Susan Gubar. *No Man's Land: The Place of the Woman Writer in the Twentieth Century.* 3 vols. New Haven, Conn.: Yale University Press, 1988–1994.

Golding, Alan. *From Outlaw to Classic: Canons in American Poetry.* Madison: University of Wisconsin Press, 1995.

Gorman, Paul R. *Left Intellectuals and Popular Culture in Twentieth-Century America.* Chapel Hill: University of North Carolina Press, 1996.

Graff, Gerald. *Professing Literature: An Institutional History*. Chicago: University of Chicago Press, 1987.

Gray, Richard J. *Southern Aberrations: Writers of the American South and the Problem of Regionalism*. Baton Rouge: Louisiana State University Press, 2000.

Green, Martin. *New York 1913: The Armory Show and the Paterson Strike Pageant*. New York: Scribners, 1988.

Guillory, John. *Cultural Capital: The Problem of Literary Canon Formation*. Chicago: University of Chicago Press, 1993.

Hanscombe, Gillian E., and Virginia L. Smyers. *Writing for Their Lives: The Modernist Women 1910–1940*. Boston: Northeastern University Press, 1988.

Hegeman, Susan. *Patterns for America: Modernism and the Concept of Culture*. Princeton, NJ: Princeton University Press, 1999.

Higham, John. *Strangers in the Land. Patterns of American Nativism, 1860–1925*. New Brunswick, NJ: Rutgers University Press, 1994 [1955].

Hollinger, David A. *In the American Province: Studies in the History and Historiography of Ideas*. Bloomington: Indiana University Press, 1985.

Homberger, Eric. *American Writers and Radical Politics, 1900–39: Equivocal Commitments*. New York: St. Martin's Press, 1986.

Hosek, Chaviva and Patricia Parker, eds. *Lyric Poetry: Beyond the New Criticism*. Ithaca, NY: Cornell University Press, 1985.

Huggins, Nathan Irvin. *Harlem Renaissance*. New York: Oxford University Press, 1971.

Hutchinson, George. *The Harlem Renaissance in Black and White*. Cambridge, Mass.: Belknap Press of Harvard University Press, 1995.

Huyssen, Andreas. *After the Great Divide: Modernism, Mass Culture, Postmodernism*. Bloomington: Indiana University Press, 1986.

Jameson, Fredric. *Postmodernism, or, The Cultural Logic of Late Capitalism*. Durham, NC: Duke University Press, 1991.

Jancovich, Mark. *The Cultural Politics of the New Criticism*. Cambridge and New York: Cambridge University Press, 1993.

Janssen, Marian. *The Kenyon Review, 1939–1970: A Critical History*. Baton Rouge: Louisiana State University Press, 1990.

Johnson, Abby Arthur, with Ronald Maberry. *Propaganda and Aesthetics: The Literary Politics of African-American Magazines in the Twentieth Century*. Amherst: University of Massachusetts Press, 1991.

Kadlec, David. *Mosaic Modernism: Anarchism, Pragmatism, Culture*. Baltimore, Md. Johns Hopkins University Press, 2000.

Kalaidjian, Walter. *American Culture between the Wars: Revisionary Modernism and Postmodern Critique*. New York: Columbia University Press, 1993.

Karl, Frederick. *Modern and Modernism: The Sovereignty of the Artist, 1885–1925*. New York: Atheneum, 1985.

Kellner, Bruce, ed. *The Harlem Renaissance. A Historical Dictionary for the Era*. Westport, Conn.: Greenwood Press, 1984.

Kenner, Hugh. *A Homemade World: The American Modernist Writers*. New York: Knopf, 1974.

   The Pound Era. Berkeley and Los Angeles: University of California Press, 1971. London: Faber & Faber, 1972.

Klein, Marcus. *Foreigners: The Making of American Literature, 1900–1940*. Chicago: University of Chicago Press, 1981.

Kutulas, Judy. *The Long War: The Intellectual People's Front and Anti-Stalinism, 1930–1940*. Durham, NC: Duke University Press, 1995.

Lauter, Paul. *Canons and Contexts*. New York: Oxford University Press, 1991.

Leach, William. *Land of Desire: Merchants, Power, and the Rise of a New American Culture*. New York: Pantheon Books, 1993.

Lears, T. J. Jackson. *Fables of Abundance. A Cultural History of Advertising in America*. New York: Basic Books, 1994.

   No Place of Grace: Antimodernism and the Transformation of American Culture, 1880–1920. New York: Pantheon Books, 1981.

Leitch, Vincent B. *American Literary Criticism from the Thirties to the Eighties*. New York: Columbia University Press, 1988.

Lentricchia, Frank. *Ariel and the Police: Michel Foucault, William James, Wallace Stevens*. Madison: University of Wisconsin Press, 1988.

   Modernist Quartet. Cambridge and New York: Cambridge University Press, 1994.

Levenson, Michael H. *A Genealogy of Modernism: A Study of English Literary Doctrine, 1908–1922*. Cambridge and New York: Cambridge University Press, 1984.

Levin, Jonathan. *The Poetics of Transition: Emerson, Pragmatism, & American Literary Modernism*. Durham, NC: Duke University Press, 1999.

Lewis, David L. *When Harlem Was in Vogue*. New York: Knopf, 1981.

Lewis, Wyndham. *Time and Western Man*. Santa Rosa, Ca.: Blacksparrow Press, 1993 [1928].

Livingston, James. *Pragmatism and the Political Economy of Cultural Revolution, 1850–1940*. Chapel Hill: University of North Carolina Press, 1994.

Malvasi, Mark G. *The Unregenerate South: The Agrarian Thought of John Crowe Ransom, Allen Tate, and Donald Davidson*. Baton Rouge: Louisiana State University Press, 1997.

Marek, Jayne E. *Women Editing Modernism: "Little" Magazines & Literary History*. Lexington: University Press of Kentucky, 1995.

Martin, Robert K. *The Homosexual Tradition in American Poetry*. Austin: University of Texas Press, 1979.

Martz, Louis. *The Poem of the Mind: Essays on Poetry, English and American*. New York: Oxford University Press, 1966.

Maxwell, William J. *New Negro, Old Left: African-American Writing and Communism Between the Wars*. New York: Columbia University Press, 1999.

Menard, Louis. *The Metaphysical Club*. New York: Farrar, Straus, and Giroux, 2001.

Miller, J. Hillis. *Poets of Reality: Six Twentieth-Century Writers*. Cambridge, Mass.: Belknap Press of Harvard University Press, 1965.

Miller, Nina. *Making Love Modern: The Intimate Public Worlds of New York's Literary Women*. New York: Oxford University Press, 1999.

Mitchell, Charles E. *Individualism and its Discontents: Appropriations of Emerson, 1880–1950*. Amherst: University of Massachusetts Press, 1997.

Mitchell, W. J. Thomas. *Picture Theory: Essays on Verbal and Visual Representation*. Chicago: University of Chicago Press, 1994.

Moretti, Franco. *Modern Epic*. London: Verso, 1996.

Morrisson, Mark S. *The Public Face of Modernism: Little Magazines, Audiences, and Reception, 1905–1920*. Madison: University of Wisconsin Press, 2001.

Mullen, Bill. *Popular Fronts: Chicago and African-American Cultural Politics, 1935–46*. Urbana: University of Illinois Press, 1999.

Murphy, James F. *The Proletarian Moment: The Controversy over Leftism in Literature*. Urbana: University of Illinois Press, 1991.

Murphy, Paul V. *The Rebuke of History: The Southern Agrarians and American Conservative Thought*. Chapel Hill: University of North Carolina Press, 2001.

Nelson, Cary. *Repression and Recovery: Modern American Poetry and the Politics of Cultural Memory, 1910–1945*. Madison: University of Wisconsin Press, 1989.

Nicholls, Peter. *Modernisms: A Literary Guide*. Berkeley: University of California Press, 1995.

Nielsen, Aldon Lynn. *Reading Race: White American Poets and the Racial Discourse in the Twentieth Century*. Athens: University of Georgia Press, 1988.

North, Michael. *The Dialect of Modernism. Race, Language, and Twentieth-Century Literature*. New York: Oxford University Press, 1994.

Ohmann, Richard M. *English in America: A Radical View of the Profession*. Hanover, NH: University Press of New England, 1996 [1976].

Orvell, Miles. *The Real Thing: Imitation and Authenticity in American Culture, 1880–1940*. Chapel Hill: University of North Carolina Press, 1989.

Parrinder, Patrick. *Authors and Authority: English and American Criticism, 1750–1990*. New York: Columbia University Press, 1991.

Pearce, Roy Harvey. *The Continuity of American Poetry*. Princeton, NJ: Princeton University Press, 1961.

Pells, Richard H. *Radical Visions and American Dreams: Culture and Social Thought in the Depression Years*. Middletown, Conn.: Wesleyan University Press, 1984.

Perkins, David. *A History of Modern Poetry*. 2 vols. Cambridge, Mass.: Harvard University Press, 1976, 1987.

Perloff, Marjorie. *The Dance of the Intellect: Studies in the Poetry of the Pound Tradition*. Cambridge and New York: Cambridge University Press, 1985.

The Futurist Moment: Avant-Garde, Avant Guerre, and the Language of Rupture. Chicago: University of Chicago Press, 1986.

Radical Artifice: Writing Poetry in the Age of Media. Chicago: University of Chicago Press, 1991.

Poirier, Richard. *The Renewal of Literature: Emersonian Reflections*. New York: Random House, 1987.

Posnock, Ross. *Color and Culture: Black Writers and the Making of the Modern Intellectual*. Cambridge, Mass.: Harvard University Press, 1998.

   The Trial of Curiosity: Henry James, William James, and the Challenge of Modernity. New York: Oxford University Press, 1991.

Pritchard, William H. *Lives of the Modern Poets*. New York: Oxford University Press, 1980.

Rado, Lisa, ed. *Rereading Modernism: New Directions in Feminist Criticism*. New York: Garland, 1994.

Rainey, Lawrence. *The Institutions of Modernism*. New Haven: Yale University Press, 1998.

Reising, Russell J. *The Unusable Past: Theory and the Study of American Literature*. New York: Methuen, 1986.

Ross, Andrew. *The Failure of Modernism. Symptoms of American Poetry*. New York: Columbia University Press, 1986.

Schleifer, Ronald. *Modernism and Time: The Logic of Abundance in Literature, Science, and Culture, 1880–1930*. New York: Cambridge University Press, 2000.

Schudson, Michael. *Advertising, the Uneasy Persuasion: Its Dubious Impact on American Society*. New York: Basic Books, 1984.

Scott, Bonni Kime, ed. *The Gender of Modernism. A Critical Anthology*. Bloomington: Indiana University Press, 1990.

Seigfried, Charlene Haddock. *Pragmatism and Feminism: Reweaving the Social Fabric*. Chicago: University of Chicago Press, 1996.

Shi, David E. *Facing Facts: Realism in American Thought and Culture, 1850–1920*. New York: Oxford University Press, 1995.

Shulman, Robert. *The Power of Political Art: The 1930s Literary Left Reconsidered*. Chapel Hill: University of North Carolina Press, 2000.

Shumway, David R. *Creating American Civilization: A Genealogy of American Literature as an Academic Discipline*. Minneapolis: University of Minnesota Press, 1994.

Singal, Daniel Joseph. *The War Within: From Victorian to Modernist Thought in the South, 1919–1945*. Chapel Hill: University of North Carolina Press, 1982.

Singh, Amritjit et al., eds. *The Harlem Renaissance: Revaluations*. New York: Garland, 1989.

Smethurst, James Edward. *The New Red Negro: The Literary Left and African-American Poetry, 1930–1946*. New York: Oxford University Press, 1999.

Sollors, Werner. *Beyond Ethnicity: Consent and Descent in American Culture*. New York: Oxford University Press, 1986.

   Neither Black nor White Yet Both: Thematic Explorations of Interracial Literature. New York: Oxford University Press, 1997.

Spengemann, William C. *A Mirror for Americanists: Reflections on the Idea of American Literature*. Hanover, NH: University Press of New England, 1989.

Stansell, Christine. *American Moderns: Bohemian New York and the Creation of a New Century*. New York: Metropolitan Books, 2000.

Stead, C. K. *Pound, Yeats, Eliot, and the Modernist Movement*. New Brunswick, NJ: Rutgers University Press, 1986.

Steinman, Lisa M. *Made in America. Science, Technology, and American Modernist Poets*. New Haven, Conn.: Yale University Press, 1987.

Stewart, John Lincoln. *The Burden of Time: The Fugitives and Agrarians; the Nashville Groups of the 1920's and 1930's, and the Writing of John Crowe Ransom, Allen Tate, and Robert Penn Warren*. Princeton, NJ: Princeton University Press, 1965.

Sundquist, Eric J. *To Wake the Nations: Race in the Making of American Literature*. Cambridge, Mass.: Belknap Press of Harvard University Press, 1993.

Susman, Warren. *Culture as History: The Transformation of American Society in the Twentieth Century*. New York: Pantheon Books, 1984.

Szalay, Michael. *New Deal Modernism: American Literature and the Invention of the Welfare State*. Durham, NC: Duke University Press, 2000.

Tashjian, Dickran. *Skyscraper Primitives: Dada and the American Avant-Garde, 1910–1925*. Middletown, Conn.: Wesleyan University Press, 1975.

Tichi, Cecelia. *Shifting Gears: Technology, Literature, Culture in Modernist America*. Chapel Hill: University of North Carolina Press, 1987.

Trachtenberg, Alan. *Brooklyn Bridge: Fact and Symbol*. 2nd edn. 1965. Chicago: University of Chicago Press, 1979.

    The Incorporation of America: Culture and Society in the Gilded Age. New York: Hill and Wang, 1982.

Vanderbilt, Kermit. *American Literature and the Academy: The Roots, Growth, and Maturity of a Profession*. Philadelphia: University of Pennsylvania Press, 1986.

Vargish, Thomas and Delo E. Mook. *Inside Modernism. Relativity Theory, Cubism, Narrative*. New Haven, Conn.: Yale University Press, 1999.

Vendler, Helen. *Part of Nature, Part of Us*. Cambridge, Mass.: Harvard University Press, 1980.

Waggoner, Hyatt H. *American Poets: From the Puritans to the Present*. Boston: Houghton-Mifflin, 1968.

Wagner, Jean. *Black Poets of the United States: From Paul Laurence Dunbar to Langston Hughes*. Translated by Kenneth Douglas. Urbana: University of Illinois Press, 1973 [1963].

Wald, Alan M. *The New York Intellectuals: The Rise and Decline of the Anti-Stalinist Left from the 1930s to the 1980s*. Chapel Hill: University of North Carolina Press, 1987.

Watson, Steven. *Strange Bedfellows: The First American Avant-Garde*. New York: Abbeville Press, 1991.

Webster, Grant. *The Republic of Letters: A History of Postwar American Literary Opinion*. Baltimore, Md. Johns Hopkins University Press, 1979.

Wellek, René. *A History of Modern Criticism: 1750–1950*. 8 vols. New Haven, Conn.:
     Yale University Press, 1955–92.
Williams, Raymond. *The Politics of Modernism*. London: Verso, 1989.
Wilson, Edmund. *Axel's Castle: A Study in the Imaginative Literature of 1870–1930*.
     New York: Charles Scribner's Sons, 1959 [1931].
Winters, Yvor. *In Defense of Reason*. Denver: Alan Swallow, 1937. London: Routledge &
     Kegan Paul, 1960.

INDEX

Note: works are listed under author's name; individual poems are indexed if discussed. In titles of works the definite and indefinite articles are ignored for alphabetization.